COMMUNICATION
AND THE
LAW

Communication Law Writers Group

COMMUNICATION
AND THE
LAW
1999 Edition

W. Wat Hopkins, Editor

VISION PRESS

Communication and the Law

1999 Edition
Communication Law Writers Group
W. Wat Hopkins, editor

ISBN 1-885219-12-1

Vision Press
3230 Mystic Lake Way
P.O. Box 1106
Northport, Alabama 35476

Printed in the United States of America

Preface

The first forty-five words of the Bill of Rights may establish the essence of a democracy more than any other single part of the Constitution. They provide a unique guarantee: the right of individuals to express themselves, even when the expression is offensive or critical of the government. The guarantee is simply stated, but during the first 108 years of the First Amendment, jurists, attorneys and free speech advocates have come to learn just how complex those simple forty-five words can be.

Communication law has grown to draw upon virtually every type and source of the law — from the First Amendment, to regulations, to statutes; from contract law to constitutional law. And the law is constantly changing. Each year Congress, regulatory agencies and the Supreme Court provide a wealth of information that those who follow communication law must locate, digest and come to understand. Because of the mass of material that makes up communication law, and because of the changeable nature of the law, it is not rare for a communication law textbook to be out of date by the time it reaches the hands of its readers.

That's why this book is important. *Communication and the Law* is designed to keep up with the changes in the law in a timely and comprehensive way. Its authors are leading communication law scholars from around the country who follow, write about and teach the law. They are committed to producing a new edition of this book each year. In that way, *Communication and the Law* is the first book of its kind. That is, it is the first book to draw upon the knowledge and skill of a wide variety of scholars, each committed to comprehensively review the law in a specific area and to report changes annually. Some years there will be major changes; other years, there will be minor changes, but *Communication and the Law* will always be the most up-to-date work of its kind.

This second edition, for example, contains new information on Internet copyright, trademark dilution and the v-chip. Authors also discuss unfolding legislative developments regarding access to campus crime information, possible restrictions on the university press and the possible erosion of reporters' privileges. And, in addition to discussion of U.S. Supreme Court cases handed down within the last year — *Arkansas Educational Television Commission v. Forbes* and *Reno v. ACLU*, for example — there are expanded discussions of some older landmark cases.

We need the help of our readers, however, to make *Communication and the Law* even better. This edition of the book will barely be in the mail to the publisher before we begin planning the 2000 edition. If you have comments or if there are changes you would like to see, don't wait — let us know now. Our goal is to provide a comprehensive, readable text.

A number of people played a big part in making *Communication and the Law* possible. I would like to thank longtime friend and colleague David Sloan of the University of Alabama and Joanne Sloan of Vision Press for suggesting the project to me, for encouraging its completion and for careful reading of the manuscript. The fifteen people who, with me, make up the Communication Law Writers Group have been a pleasure to work with. I thank them for their willingness to engage in this venture and for their willingness to work hard to see it through. I also thank Bob Hughes and Bob Trager, who were original members of the Communication Law Writers Group, but who have moved on to other things. As always, I am thankful for my colleagues in the Department of Communication Studies at Virginia Tech, a wonderfully supportive group that makes it a pleasure to come to work each day. Finally, I owe special thanks to the members of my family, especially to my wife, Roselynn, for continued love and support. They make it a pleasure to come home each day.

W. Wat Hopkins
December 1998
Blacksburg, Virginia

i

Table of Contents

Expanded Table of Contents

Contents

Contents

COMMUNICATION
AND THE
LAW

The Law in Modern Society

By Louise W. Hermanson

The American legal system is a complex structure of ever-changing checks and balances designed to protect the rights of individuals, punish those who take advantage of others and serve as a referee between disputants. The law establishes a minimal standard of behavior in areas deemed appropriate by the founding fathers, state and federal legislatures, governmental officials and courts in fifty-two different, but interdependent, legal systems.

Communication law textbooks usually focus on First Amendment decisions by the U.S. Supreme Court and specialized areas of the law, such as advertising and broadcast regulation. Although these legal areas are extremely important, professional communicators also need to understand the structure of the law.

Actions of state and federal legislatures, town councils, zoning boards, police departments and other enforcement agencies are frequently overlooked in the study of communication law. It is necessary for those who plan to work in print or broadcast journalism, advertising, public relations or other mass communication fields to understand the legal system for several important reasons.

First, most professional communicators deal with matters directly affected by the law.

Journalists report on legal issues as interpreted by officials in court and non-court settings, and they must be able to determine goals of laws and how they should be applied to an orderly society. While a journalist's work has no legal weight, the influence journalists have on public policy frequently drives changes. Journalists who understand legal structure and the events that surround it provide better stories for readers and viewers.

Print and broadcast reporters are asked to understand, analyze and write stories on arrests, court decisions, contracts between a variety of parties and rulings by various governmental policy-making and administrative agencies. They must cover crime; report accurately on local, state and federal trials; outline important information about changes in rules and regulations; and monitor political contests, elections and referenda. A foundational function of the press is to report actions taken at meetings of policy-making bodies such as town councils, legislatures, zoning boards and school boards.

Advertisers must deal with federal and state laws governing commercial speech, defamation and financial disclosure. In many states, advertising salespeople are responsible for informing clients about the law, and many of these laws are obscure and complex. Examples include Georgia's laws concerning the running of flag pictures in advertising and federal laws about using pictures of paper money. Financial reporting requirements must be followed in a number of areas, and disclosure laws must be applied and explained to business people who purchase advertising.

Public relations professionals must be able to explain the implications of legal issues to CEOs and others governing and covering their organizations. They must understand what permits are needed to conduct promotional events and how to get those permits. They must understand how contracts work when they secure works-for-hire and how to protect their own company's products and messages as well as how to avoid infringing on the intellectual property rights of others. And, if they are working in publicly traded organizations, they must understand securities law.

Second, professional communicators need to understand how to stay out of court or how to win if sued.

In today's litigious society, being involved in a lawsuit is complex, time consuming, stressful and expensive. Successfully defending a libel or invasion of privacy suit can cost hundreds of thousands of dollars and take reporters, editors, news directors and other media workers away from their jobs through depositions, emotional preoccupation and time in court. In most cases, no outlet is available for recouping attorneys' fees or costs of lost time and energy, even if the media organization wins. Just defending a lawsuit can bankrupt a small news organization, and losing in court can mean awards in the millions of dollars.

Even good journalists, who take steps to avoid trespassing on the legal rights of others, sometimes are sued. But an awareness of how the law works can minimize the chances of litigation and help news people take appropriate steps when readers and viewers become angry about the contents of media messages.

In the mid-1980s, researchers in Iowa found that those who sued the media for libel usually contacted offending news organizations soon after stories appeared.[1] Many reported asking for explanations, corrections or apologies before seeking legal advice. Respondents said they found news people arrogant and defensive, and those attitudes fueled the move to litigation. Mass communicators who understand how courts interpret legal issues realize an apology or a few minutes to listen to someone who is obviously upset is better than lengthy and expensive litigation.

Third, professional communicators need to learn about laws that free them to do their jobs aggressively.

First Amendment protections in America are significant. The Constitution provides the oldest and strongest protection for freedom of speech in the world. The protection afforded to American journalists allows them to pursue stories aggressively, knowing that actions government can take in retribution are extremely limited. This leaves journalists free to responsibly criticize governmental officials and critique performance of policy-making bodies without fear.

The preferred position doctrine provides that constitutionally enumerated rights, such as the free speech and press rights found in the First Amendment, receive more protection than other rights. This means that when expressive rights are balanced against other rights not specifically mentioned in the Constitution, expressive rights should win.

This chapter is designed to provide an overview of
- purposes of the law,
- sources of American law,
- relationships between federal and state law,
- differences and similarities between civil and criminal law,
- how a trial progresses,
- how to find official legal doctrine, rules and regulations, and
- alternatives to resolving disputes through the courts.

The chapter also provides a foundation for understanding the importance of statutes, administrative law rulings and court decisions. And it provides a brief overview of differences between common-sense logic and precise legal reasoning in resolving disputes or punishing wrongdoers. All who study the law should learn to be precise when dealing with legal terms because legal definitions frequently differ considerably from dictionary definitions. While many legal terms are defined in this text, *Black's Law Dictionary* is a good investment for any professional communicator who will deal with legal issues.

PURPOSES OF LAW

The law is a body of rules designed to allow government to regulate behavior. It describes what is allowed, how rule breakers will be dealt with and what procedures are to be followed in enforcing the rules. The goal is to provide ways to resolve or avoid disputes peacefully, predictably and with limited confusion. Laws define relationships among individuals and groups and serve as guides for people in planning and carrying out their individual and collective affairs.

Laws can be broad and far-reaching, such as the First Amendment which prohibits government from punishing people for the content of their speech. Or they can be specific and confined to a small geographic area, such as the ordinance specifying maximum size for signs on Dauphin Island, Alabama, an island community of less than sixteen square miles and fewer than 1,000 residents.

In a democratic society, each law stems from public attitudes and values at the time it is crafted. Changes in the law follow changes in values and reflect the slow evolution of civilization.

---

[1] Randall Bezanson, Gilbert Cranbert and John Soloski, *Libel Law and the Press: Myth and Reality* (New York: Free Press, 1987).

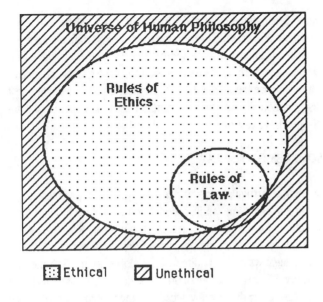

Illustration 1

The whole of human activity includes ethical and unethical behavior. Laws usually strive to set limits on unethical behavior, thereby encouraging individuals to treat others ethically. However, laws passed by unethical individuals, with unethical intent or without a complete understanding of the implications can encourage unethical behavior.

Laws relating to African-Americans from the days of slavery to affirmative action are examples of shifting attitudes and values.

When humans lived in isolated caves, rules and regulations on behavior were not important. Natural laws allowed for survival of those who adhered to them and extermination of those who did not. As humans created more sophisticated living conditions by cooperating with other humans, it became necessary to have some structure for resolving disputes.

The natural progression was for wise individuals in society to hear both sides of a dispute and make binding rulings that balanced the rights of the individuals involved. These rulings provided guidance for future similar disputes, creating what is called "common-law precedent." When society was faced with a problem similar to one already resolved, judges looked to previous cases for guidance. Differences were noted and taken into account, providing precedent for other cases with different factual twists. Use of the body of law that resulted was dependent on whether judges had dealt with related issues in the past and whether those decisions were known or available to the judge hearing the case at hand. That system of establishing and using precedent still drives much decision-making.

As societies became more complex, governments took over the role of codifying appropriate behavior before disputes developed. In a democracy, legislators are expected to provide protection from those who wish to take advantage of others through physical, financial or personal harms. These codified or statutory laws are written in code books and provide forewarning to society about actions legislatures and other governing bodies find inadvisable or inappropriate for the orderly function of society.

Statutes in the United States can be changed in a number of ways, creating a constantly fluid body of law. Federal and state laws are created, modified or repealed through legislative debate. To become a law, a bill — or proposed law — must be passed by a house of representatives and senate and then signed by the president or a governor. This process of debate and approval sets up a series of checks and balances that culminates when the courts are asked to interpret the laws in light of constitutional documents or legal precedents. Individuals contribute to the process by informing their elected representatives about their values either at election time or while debate is taking place in legislatures. Through this open discussion of what laws should be passed and how existing laws should be changed, citizens have an opportunity to participate and, frequently through the diligence of mass media, are forewarned about pending legislation that affects their lives.

Laws are generally of two types, those that ensure freedom to do certain things and those that prohibit certain behavior. The First Amendment is a positive law that allows all citizens freedom to speak without government interference. This freedom to speak without fear of punishment is frequently used by journalists to expose wrongs in society and becomes very important when those involved in wrongdoing are in political power. The First Amendment prevents those in power from silencing media through criminal laws that punish speech. By allowing this criticism of government, the First Amendment has helped establish what has come to be known as the "fourth estate;" the media function as a watchdog on the three branches of government.

Negative laws apply limits and provide punishment guidelines for behavior that harms other members of society. Murder laws that provide jail sentences, and in some states the death penalty, are examples of negative laws. So are laws against speeding, stealing and assault. A variety of other laws provide written guidelines for individuals so they can know what they can and cannot do without penalty. Actions that are not codified as inappropriate cannot carry criminal penalties, because citizens have not received appropriate warning the behavior is legally forbidden.

If a criminal action is brought, a statute has been violated. One party in the action is the government — represented by a district attorney — whose job it is to prosecute persons charged with violating the law.

Civil suits, on the other hand, are actions brought by individuals who believe they have been victims of hurtful behavior or other wrongs. In a civil action, an individual or group asks the government to help resolve a dispute with another individual or group. Many laws give individuals ways to seek redress for harmful or irresponsible activities, faulty products, mean-spirited actions or misunderstandings in agreements between individuals. These laws balance rights and offer compensation, vindication or verification for those who have been harmed by the actions of others.

In a perfect world, laws would serve as deterrents, but more often they provide a means for victims to seek justice. People become involved in the court system for many reasons. The most obvious are to seek punishment when crimes have been committed and to seek compensation for some wrong. But on a practical level, many litigants want more philosophical rewards, such as vindication of reputation, verification of the position an individual strongly believes is correct, or harassment of a hated individual, group or organization. The law allows actions with these less-than-noble goals to go forth because, without some degree of flexibility, the law would not be able to accommodate the infinite variety of legitimate conflicts courts are asked to referee.

While laws are designed to serve as guides for behavior, they should not be mistaken for codes of ethics. Many people think if something is legal, it must be ethical, but that is not necessarily so. What people morally and emotionally believe to be right and how the law applies to specific sets of facts are sometimes quite different and difficult to accept.

Laws set limits and can be ethical or unethical depending on the desires and motives of those who craft and interpret them. Ethics is a broader concept of how individuals should treat each other and is based on philosophical thought across cultures and time. Laws punish behavior below a certain standard; ethics encourage voluntary compliance with good behavior. Law is reactive and created in response to a recognized problem within a society. It serves as notice to citizens about what will be tolerated, forbidden or encouraged in dealings with others. Law is imposed on behavior retroactively when people in a society deal with each other in ways the society has determined should be prohibited.

It is important to understand, however, that even if all people acted ethically at all times, courts would still be needed to serve as referees in honest disputes. Because of the complexity of human interaction, it is not always clear who is right or wrong in a dispute. Usually, if it is clear who should win, a case will be settled before it reaches court. Litigation is expensive and difficult; so there must be a chance of winning for the process to be worth the effort. Only cases where both sides believe they have a viable chance of winning arrive before a judge. These cases usually involve honest disagreement about how one or more rules of law apply to a complicated fact situation.

SOURCES OF THE LAW

As a group struggles to set up a new system of government, its members seek some familiar model upon which to base the new structure. For the American settlers, the most familiar legal structure involved the courts and laws from their homelands. The British legal system was quite well developed by the Seventeenth Century. The large number of British settlers and British rule in the colonies during the first few decades made incorporation of those legal rules natural when the framers of the republic drafted early rules for the new nation. But because those very rules sparked the dissatisfaction that prompted emigration, resettlement and eventual revolution, framers also looked elsewhere for models. Ideas were gleaned from the most thoughtful writers of the time, including those who promoted individual liberties, autonomy of thought, encouragement of individual freedom and intelligence, and a need for checks and balances on power.

The religious heritage of the settlers was also an influential source of rules. Because religion plays a major role in defining what is acceptable and unacceptable in society and because many settlers were deeply religious, that tradition infiltrated the society's laws. Laws dealing with murder, theft, assault and the dignity of individual rights reveal the distinctly Judeo-Christian roots of the colonists. Although early ecclesiastical — church — rulings did not serve as precedent for secular courts, the beliefs of those individuals who framed the laws were reflected in the documents they produced.

As the society developed into a democracy with lawmakers elected to represent constituencies, experience from other cultures and beliefs permeated the legal system to provide a complex reflection of multi-cultural values. The diversity of cultures involved in creating and maintaining laws in the United States has resulted in vastly different laws defining acceptable behavior in different states.

In the United States, almost all laws have roots in one of four sources: common law, constitutional law, statutory law and administrative law.[2]

Each source of law can be found in all levels of all jurisdictions. Umbrella laws, which apply to all citizens within a broad geographic area, serve as guides for the more specific laws coming under them. Laws for smaller geographic areas must be compatible with laws of the larger area; that is, the lower jurisdiction's laws must not contradict umbrella laws. The lower governmental bodies, however, are free to pass laws dealing with areas ignored by higher level governmental bodies as long as the laws are compatible with those of the higher governing body.

More than one source of law can be applied to a single fact situation, but it is important to understand the different sources and levels of law individually to fully understand the process. Intellectual property rights are a good example. Multiple sources of the law are applied to new mouse traps, unique identification symbols for athletic shoes, music compact disks, novels, plays, textbooks and other original works. Article I, Section 8 of the Constitution empowers Congress "to promote the Progress of Science and useful Arts, by securing for limited Times to Authors and Inventors the exclusive Right to their respective Writings and Discoveries," so constitutional law applies. But the Constitution was designed to grant broad powers; the details of protecting intellectual property were left for Congress to provide through statutes.

Because evaluation of new inventions and creative ideas usually requires specialized knowledge or expertise, Congress set up a special federal agency to oversee patents, trademarks and copyright. The statute creating the agency provides a general philosophy of how works should be protected. Leaders of the agency are appointed by the president. Those leaders then hire staff to work out specific rules regarding how individuals' works should be protected and to pass judgment on issues that come before the agency. Courts resolve disputes resulting from violations of those rules.

This example is one where a significant number of sources and types of laws — constitutional, statutory and administrative — are incorporated into one area of governmental authority. Other areas of the law deal with different sources and types of law. For example, libel law, which allows individuals to sue in civil courts to protect reputations, is basically state law. States have statutes with varying provisions that allow citizens to seek monetary damages when false stories have been published or broadcast causing them to lose face or income opportunities. But because all libel cases involve speech, libel law has evolved into a very complex combination of federal and state constitutional, statutory and common law.

Common Law

Common law is the oldest form of law in the U.S. legal system. It derives authority solely from uses and customs within the courts throughout history, relying exclusively on precedent or balancing of rights for its definitions.

The common law developed in England in the Eleventh Century and was considered "discovered law." As members of society sought the wisdom of judges in resolving disputes and punishing wrongs, the judges listened to countervailing arguments and arrived at solutions to problems. In this process, judges would look to previous cases to see if similar facts had been presented and decided. If so, the judge would seek precedent from the earlier cases to guide the dispute at hand. Although courts are not absolutely bound by precedent, earlier cases are considered very important in deciding future cases, and judges usually seek significant differences in facts of the cases, errors in logic or changes in society to justify ignoring or altering what has been determined appropriate in earlier cases dealing with the same points of law.

When a judge uses precedent to decide a case, the judge applies what is called *stare decisis*, which means "let the decision stand." For example, when courts have decided a point of law as it relates to a set of facts, that principle should be applied to future cases where facts are substantially the same, even though the parties involved in the new cases are different and the specific details of the case may vary.

In addition, each court can look beyond its own rulings for guidance from other courts but is not bound by precedent from lower courts or courts from other areas. An ad hoc balancing of rights is used in cases where there is no precedent. An example of such a case would be the first time a court was asked to decide a custody dispute between a surrogate mother and the couple who had contracted with her to carry a child. No fact situation remotely similar had been decided by the courts; so the judges had to pull legal issues from a variety of areas related to parts of the facts and

---

[2] The U.S. Constitution also charges the president with seeing that laws are carried out properly. The president has considerable impact on laws through presidential proclamations, executive orders, line-item vetoes, recommendations to Congress and classification of documents. Congress can also give the president powers within statutes. Because these actions are seldom direct law-making events, however, they are not considered primary sources of law in this chapter. In addition, tribal law is a separate body of law that exists for Indian tribes under treaty with the United States. It is applicable only on the tribes' individual reservations and is not included here.

balance rights of parenthood and contracts in new ways.

Common law is slow in evolving. It can take as much as half a century to establish effective precedent in an area of law. In addition, the law can be cumbersome to apply and difficult to understand.

The law of equity is a type of common law. The two have merged in jurisdiction, and, frequently, remedies sought in a single case include traditional monetary remedies from common law and more creative remedies from the law of equity. The law of equity allows judges more freedom to establish practical solutions to disputes where money is not appropriate. Possession of property, custody of children, reinstatement to a job and injunctions against certain actions are examples of such remedies. The law of equity also has its roots in Great Britain and grew from the frustration with common law that provided only monetary relief. Originally, chancery courts were parallel courts that decided equity cases. Today almost all state and federal courts deal with both common and equity law remedies.

Constitutional Law

Constitutional law is designed to be broad, long-lasting and fundamental. A constitution is a charter document that establishes the character of a government and outlines how the government is to be structured. It should be difficult to modify so it can serve the society through changes in mores, economic welfare, lifestyles and leadership.

The U.S. Constitution, signed September 17, 1787, and ratified by the necessary majority of the states in June 1788, is the oldest continuously active written document of its kind. It spells out powers, responsibilities and restrictions among the three branches of government, outlines rights of individuals and defines the federal government's relationship with voters and state governments.

The document establishes a brilliant system of checks and balances designed to prohibit any one group from obtaining too much power. It specifies areas where government has no control over individuals and provides for a hierarchy of laws that, except for specific fundamental rights, leaves most legal questions to the states. The Tenth Amendment to the Constitution reflects this intent: "The powers not delegated to the United States by the Constitution, nor prohibited by it to the States, are reserved to the states respectively, or to the people."

Constitutional law is the supreme law in any jurisdiction operating under a constitutional-style government. This supremacy was clearly established for the United States in an 1803 Supreme Court decision, *Marbury v. Madison*,[3] in which the Supreme Court established the right of the judicial branch of government to determine the constitutionality of federal statutes. The powers of the Supreme Court in balancing the branches of government had previously been unclear. The Constitution, which clearly spells out the powers of the executive and legislative branches of government, is vague on the role the judiciary is to play.

The Constitution's diversity of language — specific in some places, vague in others — allows for interpretation to meet the needs of society at different times in history but establishes a consistent framework within which government must operate over time. In his First Inaugural Address in 1933, Franklin D. Roosevelt said, "[O]ur Constitution is so simple and practical that it is possible always to meet extraordinary needs by changes in emphasis and arrangement without loss of essential form."[4] Throughout the history of the country, the Supreme Court has reinterpreted the Constitution many times, especially in areas of free speech, due process and religious freedoms. This reinterpretation does not change the original document, but it does affect practical application of its provisions.

As with all U.S. law, the Constitution was written through a process of debate and compromise where strong beliefs were discussed, analyzed, accepted, discarded or modified as decisions were made and wording refined. Delegates to the constitutional convention, each representing a specific constituency, had widely differing views about how the government should be structured. It is amazing that they were able to create a document acceptable to so many for so long.

Amendments to the Constitution can be proposed in one of three ways: (1) two-thirds vote of each house of Congress; (2) a request from the legislatures of two-thirds of the states; or (3) conventions in three-fourths of the states. Then ratification must be proposed by Congress, and an amendment must be ratified by three-fourths of the states. Once an amendment has been ratified, the actual constitutional document is changed. This formidable process has resulted in only twenty-seven amendments, ten of which were ratified as the Bill of Rights in 1791. That means only seventeen amendments have become part of the Constitution in 205 years. A number of other amendments have been proposed over the years and failed to receive the necessary approval. One of

---

[3] 5 U.S. (1 Cranch) 137 (1803).

[4] "The Constitution of the United States," *The Annals of America*, vol. 3, 1784-1796 (Chicago: Encyclopaedia Britannica, Inc., 1968), p. 122.

the most recent was an amendment that would have made illegal an open display of disrespect for the American flag.

The Constitution gives the president considerable influence in the legal process by requiring the president to assure the laws are faithfully executed. This role is carried out through appointments, nominations, executive orders, proclamations and political maneuvering. A particularly powerful tool the executive branch controls is classification of documents that should be withheld from public scrutiny.

Within our system of government, each state has a constitution that serves as the supreme law of that state as long as it is consistent with the federal Constitution. Each state constitution provides for an executive (governor), legislative (general assembly) and judicial branch with checks and balances similar to the federal structure. However, language, provisions and structure of state constitutions vary widely. Some state constitutions provide citizens with more freedoms than does the federal Constitution.

The process for amending state constitutions is also unique to each document. Most states allow amendment by a direct vote of the people, and most state constitutions have been amended numerous times. Alabama, for example, has had six constitutions since its first in 1819, and its current constitution, adopted in 1901, has been amended 556 times. In contrast, Indiana has had only two constitutions since 1816, and the most recent, adopted in 1851, has been amended thirty-eight times.

City charters and other foundational documents establishing the structure of smaller governmental bodies also carry the weight of constitutional law for the jurisdictions they control. The result is a hierarchy of constitutions, with state constitutions having supreme power over local and city structural documents, and the federal Constitution serving as the last word where federal rights are concerned. (See Illustration 2.)

Two Supreme Court opinions are important in understanding the relationship of the federal constitution to other laws. In 1925, the Court ruled in *Gitlow v. New York*[5] that the due process clause of the Fourteenth Amendment prohibits states from infringing on the First Amendment rights of citizens. Before that time, the prohibitions against governmental interference in basic rights listed in the Constitution applied only to the federal government; state governments could apply different standards to their citizens. The second important case had nothing to do with freedom of speech. A footnote in a milk regulation case established rights spelled out in the federal Constitution as having a "preferred posi-

tion" over other rights not specifically mentioned in the Constitution.[6] The footnote has become established doctrine that tips the scales toward free speech and other fundamental rights when they compete with rights not mentioned in the constitution.

Each of these decisions amounted to a reinterpretation of constitutional law that took years to filter into decisions specifically related to mass communication. And the doctrine cannot apply when two constitutionally enumerated rights, such as First Amendment speech and Sixth Amendment fair trial rights, compete.

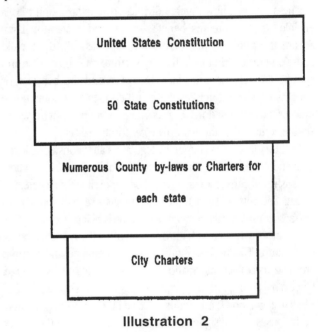

Illustration 2

Each level of constitutional or similar law must be compatible with all constitutions or similar documents above it. For example, city charters may not violate the laws of county governments, state governments or the federal constitution. Each level may address issues and rights not included in the higher-level documents in any way it chooses. It then becomes the guide for all documents below it on that issue. Also statutory and common law cannot violate the constitutional provisions that apply to the jurisdictions the statutory law covers. For example, statutory law at the state level must be compatible with state and federal constitutions where federal constitutional provisions apply to the specific rights of the individual, but they must be compatible only with the state constitution where the state constitution provides protections the federal constitution does not.

---

[5] 268 U.S. 652 (1925).

[6] *United States v. Carolene Products Co.*, 304 U.S. 144 (1938).

Statutory Law

Statutory law is written law passed by federal, state or local governments. This codified law spells out acceptable behavior and penalties for violating that behavior. Statutes set limits on specific activities, prohibit violations of certain rights, provide benefits or establish procedures for accomplishing certain goals of society.

Statutes govern most situations in everyday life. Procedures for becoming a registered voter, what vaccinations a pet must have, how fast drivers may go on the highways, what is necessary for business licenses, how much individuals owe in taxes and who is eligible for what veterans' benefits are covered by statutory laws. So are the punishments for murder, rape, assault, theft, child abuse and other criminal behavior. A statute must be precise and specific enough for individuals to understand the behavior or benefits to which it applies but broad enough to accommodate unforeseen fact situations. Courts interpret but may not disregard statutes unless the statutes violate constitutional law.

Statutory law is voted upon by legislators after considerable debate and compromise. Although statutes are supposed to reflect the wishes of constituents, it would be impossible for all voters to be satisfied with all laws. But elected officials seem responsive to citizens' comments when major legislation is being discussed.

The process begins with introduction of a bill in one chamber of a legislature. That bill frequently goes to a committee, and hearings are held to collect information on issues related to its passage. Once a bill comes out of committee, it is voted on by members of the legislative body. A bill must receive independent approval in both houses and be signed by the executive officer — president or governor — before it becomes law. If two houses approve similar bills with slightly different provisions, the bill will be sent to a joint committee for the differences to be resolved, and a new vote will be taken.

At any time during the process, a bill can fail because it is voted down or abandoned by one house. It can also fail because the executive does not sign it or vetoes it. If a president vetoes a bill, Congress can override the veto if two-thirds of members of both houses agree to do so. Transcripts of the debate on statutes are available in the *Congressional Record* or state records, allowing citizens to review the legislative history of a statute to determine legislative intent long after the bill becomes law.

Once a statute becomes law, it is more difficult to change than common law, but not as difficult to change as constitutional law. A statute remains valid until it is found unconstitutional by the courts, is repealed or changed by the legislature, or expires due to a stated time limit. Many old, forgotten statutes remain on the books but are not enforced by officials or brought to contemporary courts for interpretation. However, they remain valid for creative lawyers to use after years of dormancy.

Statutes must be compatible with constitutional law and are subject to review by the courts. State supreme courts have final say over the constitutionality of state statutes that do not contain federal constitutional issues, and the Supreme Court is the final arbiter of the constitutionality of federal and state statutes involving federal constitutional issues.

Statutes may be permanent or may contain expiration dates that require action by the legislature for their continuance. Responsibility for assuring statutes are effectively enforced rests on the creating legislature, but it may give other agencies or groups authority to define parameters or establish administrative processes to carry out the laws. Frequently the makeup and political philosophy of an agency that establishes the rules used to carry out statutes is controlled by the executive branch through the right to appoint administrators.

City and county ordinances are variations of statutory law. Each governing body establishes rules of law for a specific geographic area based on provisions of the document setting up the governing body. Notice to the public, percentage of the representatives required for passage, number of times votes must be taken and details of final steps vary. But even governing bodies of small towns, local school boards and city or county zoning boards must provide notice to the public and follow specific procedures in passing laws that affect citizens.

Administrative Law

Administrative law is created through a two-step process: (1) Legislatures create specialized agencies and appointed bodies, and (2) those bodies determine what specific rules should apply to their assigned areas. Administrative law is the most recent source of law and became necessary as society and technology became increasingly complex. Legislators recognized the need for rule makers with education and understanding about highly technical areas. Jurisdiction for administrative law is established by subject matter rather than geographic boundaries.

The statute that establishes an administrative agency outlines the basic philosophy of regulation for highly specialized organizations, equipment or materials. The executive branch appoints appropriate rule makers to the created posts, and those rule makers establish the structure of the agency and the rules under which it will oversee the highly technical operations.

Federal agencies provide oversight for activities taking place across state lines. Examples of such agencies are the Federal Communications Commission, which regulates broadcasting; the Food and Drug Administration, which controls prescription medications and food processing; the Social Security Administration, which keeps track of and provides benefits to millions of Americans; and the Federal Trade Commission, which regulates trade and advertising. States also establish administrative agencies to oversee regulation within their borders.

Administrative law makes up a significant portion of the laws affecting individuals today. Administrative agencies set standards for consumer products, establish guidelines for operating various businesses and provide protection for important functions in society. Within each agency, appointed administrative leaders establish the equivalent of common law through reference to earlier agency decisions and statutory law through the establishment of administrative rules. Legislation that establishes the agency functions as equivalent of a constitution.

In addition to establishing rules, which have the force of law, administrative agencies have their own internal courts to hear appeals from the agency's decisions. This system allows administrative law judges — adjudicators with specialized knowledge in highly technical areas — to determine the fairness of contested decisions. Administrative agency rules can be appealed through regular federal or state courts, especially on constitutional grounds, but judges without special expertise in a given area are reluctant to change an administrative ruling unless the administrative agency exceeds its authority or violates its own rules.

Although the process of establishing administrative agencies removes them an additional step from voters' control and inserts an additional step in the court process, having knowledgeable individuals making decisions concerning specialized areas prevents many serious mistakes that might be made by regular legislators and courts.

The executive branch of the government plays an important role in rules made by administrative agencies. Because the president or governor has the power to appoint leaders to these agencies, individuals can be selected for political philosophies compatible with those of the executive. In many administrative agencies, appointees serve for terms limited by the fortunes of those who appoint them. A new president or governor, then, can change the direction of an agency by carefully appointing those he believes carry his philosophies. Checks and balances result from the continually revolving appointments.

Treaties and Other Laws

As a practical matter, most laws are country-specific. They are developed by individual governments and apply only to those under jurisdictions of the governments. As mass media become global, concern has increased about who will regulate misbehavior and how differing views about freedom of speech and protection of intellectual property will be handled. For example, because U.S. copyright laws have no validity in China and the Chinese government was unwilling to adopt protections, millions of U.S.-produced music CDs were sold in China without compensation going to the creators or performers. U.S. law provides protection for creators of artistic works; so similar actions in the United States would have landed the pirates in jail.

Because there is no world governmental organization having authority over international activities, copyright and similar protections must be worked out through treaties signed by the heads of each government. Treaties constitute a small body of law but are becoming more important as technology makes it convenient and economical for people throughout the world to interact. Under the Constitution, power to enter into treaties is vested in the president with the consent of two-thirds of the Senate. States may not enter into treaties. Other countries have different rules for entering into treaties. The United Nations and other international groups deal with international rights but have authority of enforcement only if given to them through agreements signed by individual governments.

While the basic structure of laws is similar in a variety of countries throughout the world, there are numerous variations. Some countries have no constitutions, and others have constitutions with different provisions. Australia, for example, has a constitution but no equivalent of the First Amendment protection of speech.

Individuals traveling in other countries come under their laws; so it is important for a traveler to respect the customs and laws of host countries. An Ohio teen discovered this the hard way in 1994 when he was punished for vandalism in Singapore. Citizens of the United States were horrified that, for spray painting private property, a youngster could receive six lashes with a brine-soaked rattan cane, which can leave permanent scars. But the act was committed in Singapore and the case duly processed under Singapore law. Although the defendant was a U.S. citizen and U.S. law prohibits such punishment, U.S. officials were unable to prevent the punishment in Singapore.

CIVIL AND CRIMINAL LAW

Among the most important distinctions in the U.S. judicial system are those between civil and criminal law. Sources of law, procedures for enforcement, application of the law and players differ. So do society's goals.

Civil Law

Civil law usually involves a dispute between two private parties, with the government merely providing a neutral forum for resolving the dispute by balancing rights. Parties may be individuals, organizations, community groups, classes of people, businesses or governmental entities in infinite variation, but primarily an individual brings suit against another individual or group. Civil law includes wrongs to an individual's person, property or rights. Examples are disputes involving contracts, property and reputational rights, employment agreements, divorces, civil rights and product liability. The plaintiff — the party who brings the suit — and the defendant — the party against whom the suit is brought — usually enter court with equal status. The plaintiff claims specific damages and requests relief in the form of money, custody or control of property.

A variety of damages may be sought: compensatory, consequential, incidental, special and punitive. Damages are awarded to a plaintiff to compensate for actual injury or to punish a defendant for particularly reprehensible conduct. Punitive damages are the most unpredictable because, unlike other types of damages, no proof of loss is required. Punitive damages are designed to be large enough to deter similar behavior in the future and frequently result in windfalls for plaintiffs while serving a broader social good in discouraging future harms to others. Recent multi-million dollar punitive damage awards have caused legislators to reevaluate the use of punitive damages for controlling harms in society. Businesses have argued that excessive punitive damages have a chilling effect on the orderly production of quality goods and thereby do not serve the best interest of the society. Legislative efforts to place limits on punitive damages continue to be discussed on federal and state levels.

In civil law, either party may appeal a decision on grounds that the law was misapplied. Appeals are generally based on arguments that there have been violations of the rules of civil procedure. Common arguments are that evidence was admitted improperly, officers of the court were biased or improper instructions were given to a jury.

Civil lawsuits theoretically have no limits. Because they may stem from common, statutory or constitutional law, creative attorneys sometimes bring and win lawsuits in situations many people think are ridiculous. Product liability cases are among the best examples. Misinformation in such cases frequently results from time and space limitations on media, but can also be due to a journalist's lack of understanding of the law or imprecision in reporting the details.

The civil suit in which a woman won a large damage award after she was badly burned when she spilled a cup of coffee in her lap is a classic example of public reaction based on limited information. Most people reading news reports considered a multi-million dollar verdict against McDonald's excessive, but few read about the jury's reasoning in the case, published primarily in specialized legal news outlets. The jury heard evidence that McDonald's had repeatedly ignored complaints that the temperature of its coffee was dangerous, even after others had been injured. The jury's award of punitive damages, which made up most of the award, was apparently to send a clear message to the restaurant chain that such concerns should not be taken lightly.

In civil cases it is possible to shop around for state law that is favorable to the plaintiff. For example, a major magazine can be sued for libel in any jurisdiction where the publication circulates. This allows individual plaintiffs to study varying state laws to identify trends in jury verdicts, longer statutes of limitations or other advantages before deciding where to bring suit.

Criminal Law

Criminal law encourages behavior in the best interest of society. It is exclusively statutory, and crimes may be punished only by laws in the geographic area where the crimes occurred. Criminal law includes acts as diverse as murder, theft, assault, speeding, fraud and deception. The goal of criminal law is to promote an orderly society where people can feel secure. The government punishes violators to promote the common good, not to provide retribution for victims.

In criminal law, the government brings an action, through a district attorney or other prosecutor, against an individual — the defendant — for action prohibited by statute. The defendant is considered innocent until proven guilty, and the burden is on the government to prove guilt beyond a reasonable doubt. Even a guilty individual must be set free if the state fails to prove that guilt in court, using established rules of criminal procedure and evidence designed to protect individual rights. The foundational philosophy favors letting occasional guilty individuals go free rather than punishing innocent individuals.

A common misconception is that the victim of a crime brings charges in a criminal case. The state must prove the case in court but frequently will not bring charges against a suspect without the cooperation of the victim, because the victim's testimony is often necessary for a conviction. The government will ask the victim to sign a complaint against the individual charged with the crime to assure the victim's willingness to cooperate in the prosecution. The victim's cooperation is not necessary if the state can gather enough other information to prove the case.

This need for the state to prove the charges in court also means the government cannot bring charges unless it has solid evidence indicating a specific individual committed a specific crime. For example, it is common knowledge that most individuals have broken speeding laws. But only those against whom solid evidence is collected are charged, and a number who are guilty may not be punished because of the condition of radar equipment, quality of testimony or procedure used in gathering evidence.

By the same token, the state may negotiate a plea bargain with a defendant without the consent of the victim of the crime. The victim may be justifiably upset and want the defendant to answer to criminal charges in court. The victim may want to testify, but the prosecutor may believe the case is not strong enough to win. The victim's identification of the suspect may have been shaky due to poor lighting at the crime scene or other circumstances. The prosecutor may believe that the victim's testimony, although true, will not be believed by a jury, especially after cross examination by the defendant's attorney. The defendant may have an alibi that, even though untrue, will cast enough doubt on the defendant's guilt to mandate a not-guilty verdict.

In criminal cases, the state punishes violators — usually with fines or jail sentences — according to guidelines spelled out in statutes. Judges have some latitude in punishment, but usually the options are stated in statutes. Criminal law is complex, however, and various degrees of behavior alter potential charges and sentences. A person who causes a fatal traffic accident while driving under the influence of drugs or alcohol may be charged with reckless driving, vehicular homicide, first-degree murder or second-degree murder, depending on the details of the case. Each classification reflects degrees of seriousness and carries a different penalty, allowing prosecutors to charge a defendant with several levels of crime related to a single incident hoping to be able to prove at least one of the crimes and get the law breaker off the streets for at least some time.

One Event, Two Types of Law

The distinctions between civil and criminal law become important when both types of cases arise from a single incident, such as a traffic accident. The driver of an automobile who runs a red light while under the influence of alcohol or drugs is guilty of breaking several criminal laws, even if there was no traffic accident. If a law enforcement official saw him do it and has adequate proof that the driver was under the influence, the state, represented by the officer writing the ticket, officially charges the driver with a crime.

The driver may decide the case against him is so strong it is wise to pay the fine without going to court. Or he may decide to go before a judge to prove his innocence, demonstrate that the evidence against him is faulty or get the punishment reduced. If the driver is found guilty in court, a judge may waive fines or jail if the driver agrees to attend driving school. If the driver caused an accident because of these actions and someone was killed or injured, the driver may face serious criminal charges, up to and including murder. All charges are brought against the driver by the state in which the crime was committed.

In addition, in the event of a traffic accident, civil suits may be brought. A civil suit can be brought by anyone who suffered loss due to the driver's actions. Plaintiffs may include passengers in the car with the driver, pedestrians, passengers in any other vehicle involved in the accident, owners of property damaged when cars left the road and insurance companies. Plaintiffs may seek reimbursement for car repairs, medical bills, lost wages due to disability, or the deaths of loved ones.

In major accidents, such as the Amtrak train wreck that killed forty-seven people in 1994 or a major airline crash resulting in the deaths of hundreds, criminal charges against multiple parties and hundreds of civil suits by people from many geographic areas may be brought. Civil actions are not brought by the state nor are they mandated by law. Individuals and groups merely use laws to help resolve disagreements between private parties.

Criminal charges are limited by the laws that apply to the particular activity in the geographic area of the accident. Even when someone is obviously guilty of serious mistreatment of another person, criminal charges cannot be brought against the individual unless there is a specific statute prohibiting the activity.

THE COURTS

The U.S. legal system consists of thousands of courts on a variety of levels. And each court has specific subject-matter and geographic areas within its jurisdiction or responsibility. Fifty-two separate court systems operate in the United States: the federal system, fifty state systems and a separate system for the District of Columbia.[7]

Authority for establishing courts comes from federal and state constitutions. The federal Constitution provides for only one court, the Supreme Court of the United States, and gives Congress authority to establish other federal courts as needed. Each state constitution also provides for the establishment of courts. The courts serve as a third prong in the checks-and-balances system of government. Courts interpret the laws made by other governmental bodies and have the last word on how those laws should be applied.

There is no overlap in authority from state to federal courts unless a federal constitutional question is at issue or citizens of different states are involved in a lawsuit. Even the Supreme Court is prohibited from interpreting state constitutions, unless the state constitution violates a provision in the federal constitution. (See Illustration 3.)

The power to appoint federal judges is vested in the president, with confirmation by the Senate. Appointment of judges gives the president considerable influence on how laws are interpreted for extended periods of time.

Federal judges are appointed for life and can be removed from the bench only by impeachment and conviction by the Senate. Impeachment requires that charges be brought for serious wrongdoing, usually misconduct on the bench that involves gross injustice. Once a judge has been impeached, the Senate holds hearings and passes judgment on guilt or innocence. This is the same process used to remove the president from office. Because the crimes must be very serious and the process is difficult, impeachment is seldom used; fewer than a dozen federal judges have been impeached, and only four have been found guilty and removed from the bench.

The lifetime protection for federal judges is designed to free them to operate in court without fear of being removed from office for unpopular decisions. Most states, however, elect at least some of their judges, making them directly responsible to the voters. Creative variations of this system can be found in states that have identified problems with making judges directly accountable to the emotional whims of the electorate. The most popular state

variation allows the executive or a special judicial committee to appoint qualified judges for set terms, with the voters electing or rejecting reappointment when the terms expire. This system attempts to assure qualified candidates rather than having voters select from anyone who wishes to run for office, regardless of qualifications.

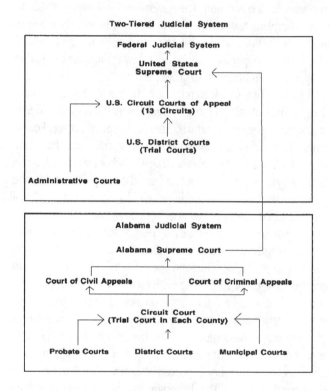

Illustration 3

Trial and Appellate Courts

All court systems in the United States have trial courts and appellate courts. Trial courts determine the facts of a case and decide how the law should apply to those facts. Once a verdict is reached at the trial court level, the loser may appeal the case if errors in the application of the law can be specified. Appellate courts review facts in a case from the trial court record, but they do not receive new testimony or collect new facts. They deal exclusively with whether the law was correctly applied.

Those who lose at the trial court level cannot appeal just because they do not agree with the decision. Attorneys must identify specific instances where the law was misapplied. This may include such things as a judge's refusal to allow a particular witness to testify, admission of evidence that should have been excluded or in-

---

[7] U.S. territories also have legal systems that can differ from those in the fifty states, but are excluded from this chapter. Cases from U.S. territories, however, fall within the jurisdiction of the U.S. Supreme Court.

First Circuit	Maine, Massachusetts, New Hampshire, Rhode Island and Puerto Rico
Second Circuit	Connecticut, New York and Vermont
Third Circuit	Delaware, New Jersey, Pennsylvania and Virgin Islands
Fourth Circuit	Maryland, North Carolina, South Carolina, Virginia and West Virginia
Fifth Circuit	Texas, Mississippi and Louisiana
Sixth Circuit	Kentucky, Michigan, Ohio and Tennessee
Seventh Circuit	Illinois, Indiana and Wisconsin
Eighth Circuit	Arkansas, Iowa, Minnesota, Missouri, Nebraska, North Dakota and South Dakota
Ninth Circuit	Alaska, Arizona, California, Hawaii, Idaho, Montana, Nevada, Oregon, Washington (state), Guam and Northern Mariana Islands
Tenth Circuit	Colorado, Kansas, New Mexico, Oklahoma, Utah and Wyoming
Eleventh Circuit	Alabama, Florida, Georgia and the Canal Zone
D.C. Circuit	District of Columbia
Federal Circuit	Specialized courts

Illustration 4

accurate instructions to a jury. Appellate courts are bound by law to consider some types of appeals, such as those of persons who have been sentenced to death, but most appeals are accepted or rejected at the discretion of the appellate court.

Appellate courts can affirm, reverse or remand a decision. Affirming a decision allows the original court's opinion to stand. Reversing overthrows the decision, and remanding invites the lower court to hold a new trial avoiding the problems that caused the case to be remanded.

A case may go through several levels of appellate courts and take years to resolve. A case dealing with a constitutional question, such as free speech, can be brought to a state trial court, appealed to the intermediate appellate court of that state, then to the state supreme court and on to the U.S. Supreme Court. After the Supreme Court, however — or a state supreme court in matters exclusive to state law — there is no other place to appeal. Decisions disliked by a majority of the citizens can be changed only by constitutional amendment.

The decision to drop or pursue a remanded case after an appeal is in the hands of the parties involved. Prosecutors in remanded criminal cases sometimes decide not to retry a case because evidence has been lost, witnesses have disappeared or died, or other reasons. A remanded civil case may be dropped because the plaintiff is tired of the fight or can't afford to continue. In such cases, it may appear that the appellate court freed an individual or overturned a ruling when it merely ruled on the correct application of the law. At any time during the process of a legal case, the parties may decide on a mutually acceptable settlement, and that, too,

means a case may not be retried.

Jurisdiction

Each court's jurisdiction is determined by the constitutional or statutory provisions creating it, and no court can decide cases outside its jurisdiction. Jurisdiction can be modified, but to do so is a long, involved process. The most frequent modification of jurisdiction comes when a court docket becomes overcrowded. When this happens, new courts can be created to spread out the workload and provide speedier justice.

Each state's court structure is unique, as might be expected since each state has its own legal history and philosophy. Some states — Alaska is one — have a relatively simple structure, similar to the federal structure of trial court, intermediate appellate court and supreme court. Others, like New York, have numerous specialized courts dealing with limited subjects and damage awards. The complexity of a state's court structure frequently reflects the population and amount of litigation within the state.

The federal system can be used as an example. Because the Constitution establishes only one federal court — the Supreme Court — that court could theoretically function as a trial court that hears facts and decides the law. But it would be impossible for the Supreme Court to handle the volume of cases that goes through all federal trial courts.

The Supreme Court, then, though it can decide facts in some cases, serves mainly as the highest appellate court in the land. It receives requests to hear thousands of cases each year but ac-

PROCESS FOR CIVIL CASE

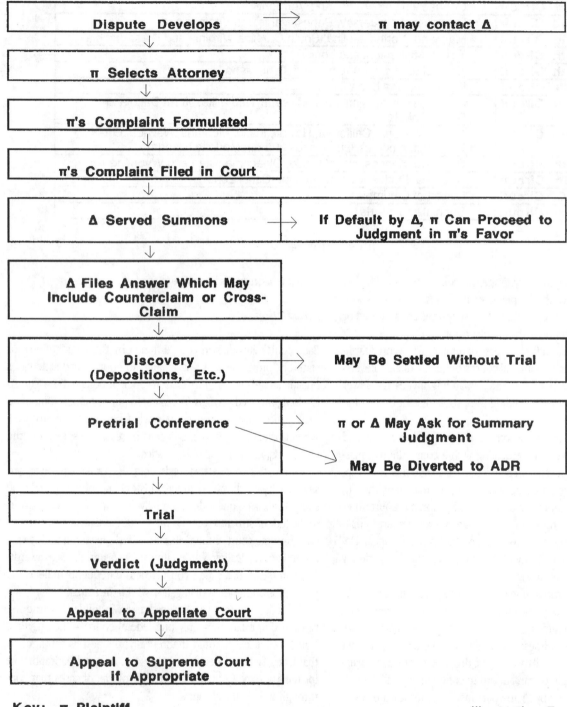

Key: π Plaintiff
      Δ Defendant

Illustration 5

cepts only a few hundred for review. The Supreme Court may reject a case — deny *certiorari (cert* for short) — without reason, or agree to give it a full hearing — grant *cert.*

Congress has created a number of lower federal courts to assist the Supreme Court. More than 100 federal district courts exist in thirteen federal circuits. (See Illustration 4.) Within each circuit, courts and judges are assigned based on case loads, with the intent of providing an efficient flow. Approximately 600 federal judges sit on federal court benches throughout the country. Each circuit is made up of trial courts and intermediate appellate courts.

Jurisdiction for federal courts is spelled out in the Constitution. Federal courts hear cases involving:
- the Constitution, U.S. law and U.S. treaties;
- ambassadors and ministers of foreign countries;
- maritime or admiralty law;
- the United States as party to a suit;
- two or more states or citizens of different states.

That is, federal courts usually hear cases that go beyond state lines.[8]

In the federal system, cases originate in district courts. These courts hear the facts of a case, have juries and hand down decisions about how the law applies to the facts. Witnesses testify, evidence is presented, arguments about how the law should apply are first made, and truth or falsehood of information presented to the court is determined. This stage of the legal process is the most emotionally consuming because it means those involved must provide detailed information to the court about exactly what happened to cause the dispute or charges.

The process for a case at the trial court level is quite complex and involves interviews, analysis of what laws apply to the facts, depositions, collection of documents, filing of briefs and strategic planning. (See Illustration "Process for Civil Case.") It is also where the parties are most directly and emotionally involved. They must watch their attorneys present the case to the court in ways that often do not make sense to those not trained in the law.

The court process is often slow and frustrating. From the time a dispute develops until a verdict is handed down by the trial court, several years may elapse. If the case goes on to the highest appellate court, the time for final resolution of a case can be more than ten years.

FINDING THE LAW

Beginning students are often intimidated by the complexity and volume of law. With fifty-two major legal systems involving thousands of rule-making bodies producing laws interpreted by thousands of courts, trying to find and understand law can seem overwhelming. Each system is different because each is the product of a unique history and legal background, but basic similarities exist. The intimidation fades once the efficient cataloging of U.S. law is understood.

In many states, law librarians or legal experts have written guide books explaining the history and legal structure of those states. A professional communicator who will be dealing with legal issues on a regular basis will find these guides particularly helpful.

Citations for all areas of U.S. law follow the format spelled out in *A Uniform System of Citation*, established by the Harvard Law Review Association and published by a group of law review associations. The stylebook is known in legal circles as the "Bluebook" and specifies the way all legal materials will be cited in legal scholarship. The system makes it possible to find decisions from any of the appellate courts in the country, statutes from all fifty states and the federal government, references to the *Congressional Record* and histories of legislative debates for more than 150 years.

Appellate court decisions are published for each of the fifty-two systems. These decisions are more useful for precedent than trial court decisions, since appellate courts deal with how the law was applied. Court decisions are cited by the names of the plaintiff and defendant, the particular court reporter or book series in which the decision is contained, the volume in which the decision is published, and the page number where the decision begins. (See Illustration 6.)

The first volume of state appellate court reporters was published in 1789, and the publication of U.S. Supreme Court decisions began officially in 1817. More than four million judicial cases had been published as of 1994, and that body is added to at the rate of approximately 130,000 cases each year from more than 600 courts throughout the United States.

The first name listed in a case citation usually reflects the party bringing the issue to the court. Some confusion exists when the first name in a case citation shifts as the case goes through the appeals process. For example, a case that starts out as *Smith v. Jones*, where Smith is the plaintiff who brings suit against Jones,[9]

---

[8] Federal trial courts hear only cases in which the damages sought exceed $75,000. Cases involving smaller damages go to courts in one of the states.

[9] Note that the case name tells you it must be a civil suit. If it were a criminal suit, a governmental body must be listed as one of the parties.

Plaintiff, Prosecutor or Appellant		Defendant	Volume	Case Reporter	First Page	Date
New York Times	v.	Sullivan	376	U.S.	254	1964

New York Times v. Sullivan, 376 U.S. 254 (1964).
Hodges v. Oklahoma Journal Publishing Co., 671 P.2d 191 (Okla. 1980)
McNair v. Hearst Copr., 494 F.2d 1309 (9th Cir. 1974)

Illustration 6

In the citations above, the first name represents the plaintiff, prosecutor or appellee. "v." is short for "versus." The second name represents the defendant. The number following the case name represents the volume of the case book, the abbreviation of which follows the number. The number immediately following the case book abbreviation represents the first page of the decision. Information in parenthesis indicates the state or circuit and the date the decision was handed down. The first citation is from the United States Supreme Court appellate decision. The appeal was brought to the high court by the *New York Times* against a lower court ruling in favor of Sullivan. The decision begins on page 254 of volume 376 of United States Reports. The decision was handed down in 1964.

may become *Jones v. Smith* on appeal if Jones is appealing the lower court ruling. An appeal of the appellate court ruling could shift the parties again if Smith is the party appealing the appellate court ruling; the case would again become *Smith v. Jones*. Each step represents the same set of facts and the same case.

Constitutional, statutory and administrative laws are also coded systematically, using the legal jurisdiction, the code book, the article and the date. (See Illustrations 7 and 8.) Once this system is understood, a researcher can find the specific legal material and can use the legal history of statutes published in the code books to determine whether the law or decision has been modified by the legislature or court decisions. A researcher can also consult a series of books called *Shepherd's Citations* to determine when and how a case has been cited in other court decisions.

A number of printed and computerized sources are available to help individuals find and understand the law. Legal encyclopedia, such as *American Jurisprudence* and *Corpus Juris Secundum*, provide broad overviews of general areas of law. They are most helpful in referring researchers to other sources and in providing a history of the law dealing with the major issues. In addition, a number of text and subject-specific books can be found in law and public libraries that help with a solid understanding of a specific type of law. These sources, however, are of limited value in a particular discussion of current law, because the law is constantly changing, and books take time to create. Often there is a year or more between the time an author finishes a book and the time it is published.

Law reviews and journals are published by law schools and provide more current discussions of legal topics. They also provide valuable references in footnotes. Frequently law review footnotes, which may number in the hundreds, provide more useful information than the actual texts of the articles.

Task forces and special study groups are established periodically by governmental agencies or private interest groups to study a particular area of the law. Examples of governmental task forces include the president's 1995 task force to study how the Internet should be regulated and two earlier task forces, one in the 1970s and the other in the 1980s, to study pornography. Examples of privately supported task forces include the famous Hutchins Commission that looked at the future of free speech in America in the 1940s and the Annenberg study of libel law in the 1980s. These task forces produce reports, which sometimes are published with limited circulations, but more and more frequently can be found on the Internet. Sometimes these reports are quite long and detailed, such as the 1986 Meese Commission report on pornography.

Legal research has changed dramatically since the on-line services WESTLAW and Lexis were created. These full-text databases of laws from throughout the country allow researchers to use traditional word searches to identify sources related to particular topics. A computer search will locate all material related to a properly strung request and makes updating information quite easy. However, these services are very expensive to use, especially for the inefficient researcher. Lexis-Nexis has put out a special handbook to assist journalists in using that system. Information in *The*

Source	Article	Section	Clause
U.S. Const.	art. 1	§ 9	cl. 2

Illustration 7

The citation above refers to Article 1, Section 9, Clause 2 of the United States Constitution.

Source	Book	Section	Date
Okla. Stat.	Tit. 14A	§ 6-203	(Supp. 1984)

Illustration 8

The citation above refers to an Oklahoma statute found in Code Title 14A, sections 6-203 of the 1984 Supplement to the code book. It is important to update all legal references by referring to the supplements found in the back of the printed code books. These supplements, called "pocket parts," are published annually and reflect changes in statutes made by legislative bodies since the publication of the entire work. Due to the expense and complexity of publishing complete multiple-volume sets of code books, years may pass before a complete set is updated. The supplements contain information about new laws, laws that have been modified or appealed and references to recent important court interpretations of laws.

Journalists' Handbook for Using LEXIS-NEXIS is transferable to most full-text databases, including WESTLAW. The handbook requires time and practice to understand because it provides research strategies with little explanation in narrative form.

In addition, a number of unofficial publications exist for specific areas of the law. *Media Law Reporter* is the most valuable for professional communicators. It reports most decisions that affect freedom of speech. Frequently it is the only place texts of lower court rulings can be found without going to individual courts.

ALTERNATIVES TO THE COURTS

Within the past twenty-five years, additional remedies have become popular in the U.S. legal system. Termed "alternative dispute resolution" in the early 1970s, the movement sought to find better, more efficient ways to handle disputes than taking them to court. Since the 1990 Civil Justice Reform Act requiring federal districts to devise plans for reducing costs and delays, many federal districts have implemented programs for alternative dispute resolution, and judges have been granted broad discretion in using ADR. In addition, more than forty states either require or offer third-party mediators to help parties settle civil appeals before arguments are heard by appellate courts. In the Sixth Circuit alone, the ADR pro-

gram reportedly provides the work equivalent to one full-time judge. In 1993, more than 100,000 civil cases were resolved through ADR, and more than 1,200 programs throughout the country received referrals from state courts.

Alternative dispute resolution has specific meaning in the legal system, but the elements of ADR vary, since a number of paths may be taken to solve disputes without going to court. Although alternatives to litigation have existed in America since before the American Revolution, the current wave of alternative dispute resolution devices started in the early 1970s. In 1979, Congress passed, but did not fund, the Minor Dispute Resolution Act to support local development of alternatives to court. In 1983, the Federal Rules of Civil Procedure were amended to encourage consideration of "extrajudicial procedures" to resolve legal disputes, and since 1987 the Federal Rules of Civil Procedure allow use of advisory juries in a number of circumstances.

A variety of alternative dispute resolution systems have been tried. They include:

- *Court-Annexed Arbitration.* A judge diverts cases to an arbitration panel which makes a binding or nonbinding decision. Under certain circumstances this alternative may become more expensive than other adjudication techniques since it requires two presentations of evidence in cases not settled after the arbitration panel issues its recommendation. This is also not seen as a way of making adjudication more accessible to the public since it is merely the diversion of cases already within the court system to a different form of resolution.

- *Voluntary Arbitration.* Parties in a dispute contract or agree to let a third-party make a binding decision in the dispute.
- *Mediation.* A third party meets with those involved in the dispute and tries to help them reach a settlement through non-coercive means.
- *Summary Jury or Mini-Trials.* Each side in a dispute is given a limited time (usually one hour) to present its case before a six-member jury selected from the regular jury pool. The jurors then issue a non-binding verdict, which the parties use to evaluate their chances of prevailing at trial. The procedure is used to encourage settlement.
- *Rent-A-Judge Programs.* Retired judges hear the issues in a dispute and give an advisory ruling.
- *Neighborhood Justice Centers.* Two or three mediators meet with parties in a dispute and encourage agreement.

Each of the models provides more flexibility and less formality than litigation and encourages a greater emphasis on accommodation between the parties than on rights and liabilities.

An example of a voluntary alternative to the courts is the Minnesota News Council, begun in 1971. Although Minnesota's is the only surviving adjudicating American news council, more than fifty other countries have similar bodies. The Minnesota council decides disputes between members of the public and Minnesota media. The council requires complainants to waive rights to sue in exchange for a less formal, speedier resolution of the issues. Some complainants do not participate when they discover that they must give up their right to sue, but others welcome the opportunity to be heard without having to involve attorneys.

The council hears disputes about breaches of ethics as well as those that may become lawsuits, and the only sanction is publicity concerning errors media make. Although the council has received more than 2,000 complaints about Minnesota media, it has handed down decisions in fewer than 150 cases in twenty-six years. A handful involved defamation cases that may have made it to court had the council not been available. Complainants in these cases report they mainly wanted vindication and, therefore, were willing to have the less formal body decide the issues.

ADRs have particular appeal to businesses and corporations because they encourage settlement quickly at low costs. Participants often appreciate the more relaxed procedures that allow them to tell their stories in their own ways. Throughout the ADR

movement, however, voluntary programs have failed to attract a large number of cases, and such programs seldom have funds for massive publicity campaigns. Many have suffered from refusal to participate. Minimal research has reported a high level of user satisfaction with the fairness of the processes, the quality of decisions handed down, the more humane and relaxed procedures, and the elimination of high costs associated with litigation.

Attorney opposition was originally a concern, since it was assumed attorneys would be unlikely to advise their clients to give up rights assured to them in courts of law. As the movement evolved, however, attorneys have encompassed ADR as another valuable means of resolving disputes. Numerous business and employment contracts now include agreements to use arbitration or mediation in disputes arising from the terms therein.

An obvious concern is the secrecy under which many alternatives to the courts dispense justice and the lack of any system for recording the activities. But those who practice in the communications field should also realize such mechanisms can be used to resolve disputes between the public and media more quickly and less expensively than going to court.

FOR ADDITIONAL READING

Abramson, Jeffrey. *We, the Jury: The Jury System and the Ideal of Democracy.* New York: Basic Books, 1994.

Bezanson, Randall, Gilbert Cranberg and John Soloski. *Libel Law and the Press: Myth and Reality.* New York: Free Press, 1987.

Campbell, Douglas S. *The Supreme Court and the Mass Media: Selected Cases, Summaries and Analyses.* New York: Praeger, 1990.

Dershowitz, Alan M. *Reasonable Doubts.* New York: Simon & Schuster, 1997.

Fletcher, George P. *With Justice for Some: Victims' Rights and Criminal Trials.* New York: Addison-Wesley Publishing Co., 1995.

Franklin, Mark A. *The Biography of a Legal Dispute.* Mineola, N.Y.: Foundation Press, 1968.

Jacobstein, J. Myron, Roy M. Mersky and Donald J. Dunn. *Legal Research Illustrated.* Westbury, N.Y.: The Foundation Press, Inc., 1996.

Kaplar, Richard T. *Beyond the Courtroom: Alternatives for Resolving Press Disputes.* Washington, D.C.: Media Institute, 1991.

Lewis, Anthony. *Make No Law.* New York: Random House, 1991.

Thaler, Paul. *The Watchful Eye: American Justice in the Age of the Television Trial.* Westport, Conn.: Praeger Publishers, 1994.

2

The First Amendment in Theory and Practice

By Paul E. Kostyu

Tonight Show host Jay Leno once broadcast a person-on-the-street interview in which he tested people's knowledge of the Bible. When asked to name any of the Ten Commandments, one woman responded, "Freedom of expression." Our country's heritage of free and open debate goes back a long way, but usually it's not tied to Moses' trip up Mount Sinai.

Free expression is essential to a free government and to U.S. society. The First Amendment gives us the right to express ourselves without fear of punishment. It also gives us access to information and protection from prior restraint. But, just as some people can't identify the Ten Commandments, many don't know that free expression has constitutional protection. Only fifteen percent of the respondents to a recent survey by the Newseum, the Freedom Forum's museum dedicated to the news industry, could name freedom of the press as one of the five rights guaranteed by the First Amendment.[1]

Maybe this shouldn't be surprising, given the public's view of freedom of expression. A 1990 survey commissioned by the American Society of Newspaper Editors demonstrated that most Americans:[2]

- believe there should be governmental control over the publishing of partisan editorials, government classified information, names of rape victims, photographs of violent events, criticism of political leaders and news about the sexual habits of public figures;
- favor restrictions on television programming and musical recordings regarding nudity, sex and violence;
- approve of limits or bans on speech dealing with sex, homosexuality, religious cults, undemocratic forms of government and other potentially controversial subjects the public may not like;
- have censored themselves out of fear of retaliation and social ostracism.

A 1997 survey by the Center for Media and Public Affairs found that most people want journalists to be licensed, like doctors and lawyers. The same survey found that the public wants to make it easier for plaintiffs to win lawsuits against the press, to empower judges to impose fines for bias and inaccurate reporting, to allow government to monitor journalists for fairness and to compel the press to give equal coverage to various sides controversial issues.[3]

"Free speech in the land of the free is not as free as you might think," Associated Press writer Nancy Benac recently wrote. "In a

---

[1] Stacy Jones, "Survey: First Amendment Is In Trouble," *Editor & Publisher,* 29 March 1997, p. 9.

[2] Richard Harwood, "Public Likes Theory of Free Press, Not Practice," *The American Editor,* April 1998, p. 12.

[3] *Id.*

debate as old as the republic, Americans are weighing once again when it is proper to place limits on the First Amendment's protections of unbridled speech." Benac quoted free speech lawyer and scholar Floyd Abrams as saying, "First Amendment issues are always unpopular. That's why we need a First Amendment."[4]

Abrams is right.

THE HERITAGE OF FREE EXPRESSION

Freedom of expression is not exclusive to the United States, and it has no identifiable "father" or "mother." It dates probably to the ancient Greeks, notably Plato and Socrates and their philosophical writings during the establishment of western civilization. But there is a more recent history.

In the mid-Fifteenth Century Johann Gutenberg developed movable type, and, shortly thereafter, William Caxton introduced the printing press to England. The concept of printing was new, so Caxton faced little, if any, restriction. But that quickly changed. The British government recognized the power of the printed word and sought to control it.

The Sixteenth and Seventeenth centuries in England also saw battles that mixed politics and religion. Dissent was a capital offense. The monarchy and the Church of England wanted opposition silenced. Religious and political fighting were linked to economic differences between the aristocracy, a rising middle class and the poor. All sides in these battles came to understand the importance of the printing press.

Government became involved early, implementing a system of licensing in 1520. The licensing allowed officials to preview material, thus controlling both content and distribution. A license became a coveted commodity, so much so that licensed printers often protected their own self-interests by uncovering those who published without government approval. Often the government engaged in heavy-handed means to censor ideas it considered dangerous. People were jailed, tortured and executed for expressing ideas contrary to those espoused by government officials. Presses were wrecked, publications destroyed and buildings burned.

But the period was not without support for free expression. One of the most notable arguments came from poet John Milton, whose now-famous *Areopagitica* criticized government censorship in 1644. In the essay, subtitled *For the Liberty of Unlicensed Printing*, Milton protested a 1643 order by Parliament requiring the registration of all publications by the Stationer's Company,

which was founded in 1557. Milton viewed the order as a means of establishing a system of censorship and wrote:

> Though all the winds of doctrine were let loose to play upon the earth, so Truth be in the field, we do injuriously by licensing and prohibiting to misdoubt her strength. Let her and Falsehood grapple; who ever knew Truth put to the worse in a free and open encounter?[5]

Milton's argument was that censorship, in whatever form, is unnecessary because truth will always win in a battle with falsity. Open debate, the argument goes, is the only way for people to discern the truth and reject falsehood. Milton was advocating what has come to be known as the "marketplace of ideas" theory, even though the metaphor, in its purest form, refers to an exchange or competition of ideas rather than a battle of ideas.

Milton made a lasting contribution to freedom of expression, but freedom had its limits, even to Milton. He opposed freedom of expression for Catholics and others who advocated ideas Milton considered dangerous, subversive, impious or evil. Seven years after writing *Areopagitica*, Milton joined Oliver Cromwell's government as a censor, helping impose a strict Puritanical doctrine on England. The beliefs of other religious groups were granted little tolerance by the government, despite Milton's earlier argument.

Though the most famous advocate of freedom of expression in the mid-Seventeenth Century, Milton was not alone. Roger Williams, a former Puritan minister who had visited the North American colonies, wrote in the same year as Milton's *Areopagitica* that freedom of expression should be allowed even for Catholics, Jews and Muslims. The Levellers, a radical Puritan group of the same period, also had consistently condemned censorship and licensing in their tracts. Suppressing the truth kept people ignorant, they argued, allowing tyrants to use that ignorance for unjust ends.

In the late Seventeenth Century, other philosophers advocating freedom of expression emerged. A notable among them was John Locke, who argued that government should answer to the people, instead of the people to the government. People have natural rights, Locke wrote, including life, liberty and property ownership; government, through its grant by the people, should safeguard those rights, to which freedom of expression is central.

Free expression, of course, is linked to a free press. The ability to write one's thoughts and then pass them on to others is a

---

[4] Nancy Benac, "Free Speech Not Always As Free As You Think," *The Delaware Gazette,* 23 June 1997, p. 4.

[5] John Milton, *Areopagitica and Of Education,* ed. George H. Sabine (Northbrook, Ill.: AHM Publishing, 1951), p. 50.

foundation of free speech theory. The development of the theory continued into the Eighteenth Century. Perhaps the most quoted representative of that period is English jurist William Blackstone, who, in 1769, wrote:

> The liberty of the press is indeed essential to the nature of a free state: but this consists in laying no previous restraints upon publications, and not in freedom from censure for criminal matter when published. Every freeman has an undoubted right to lay what sentiments he pleases before the public; to forbid this, is to destroy the freedom of the press: but if he publishes what is improper, mischievous, or illegal, he must take the consequence of his own temerity. To subject the press to the restrictive power of a licenser ... is to subject all freedom of sentiment to the prejudices of one man, and make him the arbitrary and infallible judge of all controverted points in learning, religion, and government.[6]

Blackstone suggested that there must be a means for distributing ideas, that is, that there must be publication, but that writers must be held accountable for their words. Protection does not extend to false or other "mischievous" material.

Blackstone's view is important, not only because it advances the concept of a free press, but because Blackstone was a jurist rather than a philosopher; he had the power to do more than theorize — he could interpret the law. Blackstone's impact resonated long after his death. As late as 1907, Supreme Court Justice Oliver Wendell Holmes consulted his work when looking for guidance on expression issues.[7]

At the time of Blackstone, other forces advancing freedom of expression were at work:

- Parliament gained a major victory over the monarchy in 1688, leading to strictly limited powers of the throne.
- A two-party system, which encouraged spirited debate, emerged. Both parties — the Whigs and Tories — relied on the printing press to espouse and circulate their views.

While licensing pressures lessened, punishment for seditious libel — criticism of the government — grew as the prevailing form of censorship. A prosecution for seditious libel did not allow truth as a defense. In fact, truth exacerbated the crime. Since true criticism would make people more suspicious of government, thus providing the impetus for disorder or revolt, a key theory in a prosecution for sedition was, the greater the truth, the greater the libel. Despite reforms, criticism of government was viewed as criminal throughout the Eighteenth Century. It wasn't until passage of the Fox Libel Act in 1792, which allowed juries instead of judges to decide what was libelous, that prosecutions began to diminish.

These same influences had significant impact on the current view of prior restraint, which is discussed in detail in Chapter 4.

THE CONSTITUTION AND THE BILL OF RIGHTS

While the Mother Country was dealing with freedom of expression, parallel issues faced the American colonists. They had a strong desire to ensure that the censorship experiences of England didn't find a home in the new country. Censorship was part of the colonial way of life before the break with England, because colonial governors loyal to the crown exerted the same kinds of control in the New World. The assumption was, if restrictions could be imposed in England, they could be imposed in the colonies.

The First Amendment grew from those experiences. Colonists came to the new country to escape religious and political oppression, but found similar restrictions. Licensing became commonplace, and papers carried on their nameplates the words "published by authority," even after English papers had been freed from such a requirement.

A variety of laws — from those prohibiting seditious libel to those, like the Stamp Act of 1765, requiring governmental stamps on published material — were used to control publishing. Colonists saw the laws as unfair, and their strict enforcement was one of the causes of the American Revolution.

One of the most famous seditious libel cases of the period was that of John Peter Zenger, a German immigrant who printed the *New York Weekly Journal*. Lewis Morris and James Alexander, who backed the paper, were political opponents of New York's colonial governor William Cosby. Zenger published harsh attacks on the governor — attacks probably written by Morris, Alexander or others — and was jailed for seditious libel in 1734. There was little doubt that Zenger was guilty of publishing the libel. Indeed, his attorney, Andrew Hamilton, admitted as much at trial. Hamilton, however, convinced the jury that no one should be jailed for publishing truthful information, even if it was critical of government or officials. Jurors ignored the law that obligated them to find Zenger guilty and acquitted the printer.

---

6 William Blackstone, *Commentaries on the Laws of England, 1765-1769*, vol. 4, ed. William Carey Jones (San Francisco: Bancroft-Whitney, 1916), p. 152.

7 *Patterson v. Colorado*, 205 U.S. 454 (1907). See also the discussion of Blackstone in William W. Van Alstyne, *First Amendment Cases and Materials* (Westbury, N.Y.: Foundation, 1991), pp. 6-21.

Some scholars interpret the Zenger case as a historic blow for freedom of the press, while others see it as a victory for free speech rights. The difference lies in the interpretation of Hamilton's action. Legal historians argue that Hamilton appealed to the wisdom of local juries and the right of a free people, rather than a free press, to criticize government.

As the country moved toward independence, revolutionary leaders realized that they did not want to repeat the mistakes of the past. Before the end of the Revolutionary War, the Articles of Confederation, the nation's first constitution, provided the guidelines for the formation of a loose-knit federation of thirteen states with a weak federal government. The document contained no bill of rights, because the drafters thought the government didn't have the power to infringe upon the rights that would be enumerated in such a bill. Many of the rights, including freedom of expression, were found in most state constitutions. Freedom of the press, for example, was guaranteed by the Virginia constitution five years before the adoption of the Articles of Confederation.

But the government formed by the Articles began to falter, requiring fundamental changes in its structure. In 1787, the states — all but Rhode Island, that is — sent delegates to Philadelphia to rewrite the Articles. Instead, the delegates created a new charter — the Constitution — giving increased powers to a central government while keeping state law supreme in some matters.

Historians have little to go on regarding the discussions that took place at the Constitutional Convention, because no official record was kept, and the public was not admitted. But it seems clear that a bill of rights was not a high priority.

At least partly because the absence of provisions protecting fundamental, individual rights, supporters of the Constitution had a difficult time winning ratification by three-quarters of the states. Some delegates wanted the protections listed first; others wanted them included somewhere in the document, and still others didn't want them included at all. Thomas Jefferson, writing to James Madison in 1787, found the absence of protection for fundamental rights one of the shortcomings of the Constitution: "I will now tell you what I do not like. First, the omission of a bill of rights, providing clearly ... for freedom of religion, freedom of the press...."[8]

The Constitution was ratified without a bill of rights, but legislators in some states — Virginia was one — supported the document only upon promises that attempts would be made in the first Congress to approve such a bill. James Madison, who made some of those promises in Virginia, introduced a bill of rights during the first session of the First Congress. His original amendment dealing with free expression read: "The people shall not be deprived or abridged of their right to speak, to write or to publish their sentiments and freedom of the press, as one of the great bulwarks of liberty, shall be inviolable."[9]

That wording did not survive congressional committees, however. Though it is impossible to tell how the courts over time would have interpreted Madison's original amendment, its wording seems to provide more broad-based protection for both speech and the press than the version eventually adopted:

Congress shall make no law respecting an establishment of religion, or prohibiting the free exercise thereof; or abridging the freedom of speech, or of the press; or the right of the people peaceably to assemble, and to petition the Government for a redress of grievances.

It's tempting to assign more importance to the protections of speech and press because they come first in the Bill of Rights, but, in fact, the First Amendment wasn't always first. When Madison's proposed bill of rights came out of a joint conference committee, there were twelve amendments. What would eventually become the First Amendment was third, behind an amendment providing for a fixed schedule for apportioning seats in the House of Representatives and one restricting the way representatives and senators could give themselves raises. Those two amendments were not ratified, so the third amendment came to be first. Even had the amendment been listed first originally, however, there is no indication that courts would or should consider it more important than other rights. As Justice Harry A. Blackmum once wrote, "The First Amendment, after all, is only one part of an entire Constitution."[10]

It took two years for the required ten states — three-fourths of the thirteen original states — to ratify the Bill of Rights. Connecticut, Georgia and Massachusetts did not ratify the first ten amendments to the Constitution until 1941.

The First Amendment, unlike Madison's original proposal, applies only to Congress. The wording clearly represents the founders' fear that the new federal government might overpower the states. They wanted to ensure that states' rights came first by preventing Congress from interfering with the protection of speech or press found in state constitutions. Consequently, if newspaper

---

8 "Thomas Jefferson to James Madison, 1787," *Thomas Jefferson on Democracy,* ed. Saul K. Padover (New York: Hawthorn Books, Inc., 1939), p. 47.

9 Annals of Congress (House), June 8, 1789, I:434.

10 *New York Times Co. v. U.S.,* 403 U.S. 713, 761 (1971)(Blackmum, J., dissenting).

publishers wanted to seek recourse from attempts to muzzle them by state governments, they would have to do so through state constitutions; there was no help in the federal Constitution. It would take nearly 140 years for that interpretation to change.

THE FIRST AMENDMENT APPLIED TO THE STATES

In 1925, the Supreme Court extended the prohibition on Congress's interference with free speech and press rights to the states. The ruling came in a case involving a Communist named Benjamin Gitlow, who had been charged with and convicted of criminal anarchy in New York. Gitlow was convicted of advocating the violent overthrow of the government through his writings in *The Left Wing Manifesto* and *The Revolutionary Age*. The First Amendment does not explicitly prohibit the states from infringing upon speech and press rights, but Gitlow's attorney contended that Gitlow's conviction under state law still violated his First Amendment free press rights.

In 1868, some fifty-seven years prior to Gitlow's case arriving at the Supreme Court, the Fourteenth Amendment to the Constitution was adopted to endow newly emancipated slaves with the same constitutional rights as everyone else in the country. The amendment has several provisions, including the Constitution's only statement of citizenship. Its best-known language, however, is that no state shall "deprive any person of life, liberty, or property, without due process of law; nor deny to any person within its jurisdiction the equal protection of the laws."

The language is almost identical to language in the Fifth Amendment. The Fifth Amendment is directed toward Congress, however, while the Fourteenth is directed at the states.

Justice Edward Sanford, writing for the majority in *Gitlow v. New York,* applied the First Amendment to the states through the Fourteenth, but did so in a somewhat casual reference: "We may and do assume that freedom of speech and of the press — which are protected by the First Amendment from abridgment by Congress — are among the fundamental personal rights and 'liberties' protected by the due process clause of the Fourteenth Amendment from impairment by the States."[11]

Sanford's *dicta* was a precursor to changes in the way of thinking about the Constitution that would have an enormous impact on expressive rights. In effect, Sanford said state governments, just like the federal government, are bound by the Constitution. While judges and scholars recognized that state constitutions could provide more expansive rights than those provided in the federal Constitution — indeed, some do — the concept that state laws and constitutions could not grant fewer rights was relatively new. This is called the "concept of incorporation." It didn't help Gitlow — the Court affirmed his conviction — but it provided a touchstone that has protected expressive rights ever since.

While the Court in *Gitlow* assumed the Fourteenth Amendment protected fundamental rights, it wasn't until 1931 that the Court actually struck down a state statute that it said violated the press clause of the First Amendment, doing so in *Near v. Minnesota,*[12] a prior restraint case.

Incorporation also gives federal courts authority to review the constitutionality of state laws, allowing them to be the final interpreters of freedom of expression. The courts would prefer not to rule on issues from states involving fundamental rights. If legislation does not affect these fundamental rights, the Court assumes the legislation is constitutional. But if legislation — state or federal — is seen to infringe on First Amendment rights, the Court will not defer to the legislature. In First Amendment cases, the Court examines the whole record of a lower court decision to determine whether the decision handicaps freedom of expression.

The government usually cannot regulate expression based on its content. "If there is a bedrock principle underlying the First Amendment," wrote Justice William Brennan in 1989, "it is that the government may not prohibit the expression of an idea simply because society finds the idea offensive itself or disagreeable."[13] That is, a regulation must be content neutral — the regulation must be based on factors not related to the content of the message that will be hampered by the regulation. This is true unless the regulated speech falls into one of the categories of expression that is not protected by the First Amendment — obscenity, fighting words or information that would harm national security, for example.

In addition, the time, place and manner in which messages are expressed *can* be regulated. Time, place and manner regulations allow a local, state or federal government, for example, to require permits for parades, specifying the route the parade will follow and the time of day the parade can take place. The government can ban the parade because it would go down main street during rush hour, but cannot ban the parade because of the nature of the message being espoused by the marchers. Time, place and manner

---

[11] *Gitlow v. New York*, 268 U.S. 652, 666 (1925).

[12] 283 U.S. 697 (1931). After *Near,* the Court, on a case-by-case basis, brought other clauses of the Bill of Rights under Fourteenth Amendment protection.

[13] *Texas v. Johnson*, 491 U.S. 397, 414 (1989).

restrictions are constitutional as long as they are not arbitrary — for example, it might be unconstitutional to ban all messages without a valid reason — and as long as they are neutral — that is, they treat all messages the same way. A Cincinnati ordinance, for example, was ruled unconstitutional when city officials tried to ban both a Jewish menorah and a Ku Klux Klan cross from display on public property. The city said allowing the menorah was a violation of the separation of church and state, while permitting the cross constituted fighting words. A federal judge said the First Amendment protected a Jewish organization's right to display the menorah, and an appellate court said the city also had to allow the cross, even though many people are offended by the KKK.[14]

The Supreme Court requires that there be what it calls "strict scrutiny" of any action that infringes on First Amendment freedoms. When a court uses strict scrutiny to determine whether a regulation is constitutional, it must find (1) that there is a compelling government interest for the regulation, and (2) that the regulation is necessary and narrowly tailored to meet that government interest. That is, the government must take the least drastic measures to accomplish a necessary goal. Regulations that are not specific enough or are not sufficiently narrow are generally ruled to be vague, overbroad or both.

An unconstitutionally vague law is so unclear that persons of common intelligence must guess at its meaning and will differ in their methods of application. A vague law makes speakers unnecessarily cautious. An example of such a law was one preventing the desecration of the U.S. flag. The law prohibited contemptuous treatment of the flag in public. "Contemptuous" was not defined. Burning the flag may be "contemptuous," but so may be wearing a scarf or tie that appears to be a flag. Wearing a small flag on the seat of the pants or using a flag as a rug in an art gallery might also be contemptuous. A statute that leaves authorities broad discretion to curb expression and does not define the line between protected and unprotected expression is unconstitutionally vague.

An overbroad law, on the other hand, can be very clear about what it prohibits, but it prohibits too much. That is, it prohibits protected as well as unprotected speech. The Georgia Supreme Court struck down as overbroad a state statute regulating lewdness, because under the statute a bumper sticker reading "shit happens" would have been illegal.

Suppressing speech is not an easy task. The courts require that a specific legal procedure be followed that allows them to decide what expression is protected. The procedure, called "First Amendment due process," requires certain legal safeguards so that individual rights are protected. Those safeguards include requiring the government to notify an individual when action is being taken against the individual and providing an opportunity to be heard in court.

The process is left to the courts, which are seen as unbiased interpreters of government legislation and individual rights. This is part of the system of checks and balances of power. By following due process, the courts require the government to bear the burden of proving that legislation does not violate individual rights. That is, the courts assume that expression is protected unless the government proves otherwise.

First Amendment due process is intended to prevent self-censorship, which occurs when individuals are unable to distinguish between protected and unprotected expression. In order to protect themselves, store owners may not stock certain books, magazines or videos, for example, to avoid being prosecuted, even though that material may be protected. Another way to interpret due process is to view expression as innocent (protected by the First Amendment) until proven guilty (not protected).

The courts in their examination of First Amendment cases apply rules and principles that have been developed over time, primarily from legal precedent established in earlier cases. When First Amendment due process is involved, courts usually expedite the decision-making process, because the impact is much broader than in other types of cases.

THE DISTINCTION BETWEEN "SPEECH" AND "PRESS"

The First Amendment requires that both speech and the press be protected. Almost from the time of its drafting, there has been debate over what the terms "speech" and "press" mean. And, even though the First Amendment says nothing about either expression or conduct, the Supreme Court has held that some conduct is protected as a form of expression. Chapter 3 covers conduct and speech in greater detail.

In a 1989 case, Justice Brennan, an ardent supporter of the First Amendment who retired a year later, wrote that "the First Amendment literally forbids the abridgement only of 'speech,' but we have long recognized that its protection does not end at the spoken or written word."[15] Government restriction, he wrote, "is not dependent on the particular mode in which one chooses to ex-

---

[14] Associated Press, "Cincinnati Renews Fight over Klan Cross," *Columbia Dispatch*, 26 October 1994, p. 2B; *Knight Riders of the Ku Klux Klan v. Cincinnati*, 72 F.3d 43 (6th Cir. 1995).

[15] *Texas v. Johnson*, 491 U.S. at 404.

press an idea."[16]

In the colonial period, speech manifested itself in meetings, on street corners, from pulpits and through traveling balladeers. The press produced bills of sale, advertisements, poetry, promotions, books, essays and newspapers. Colonists found value in their freedom to listen to the speech makers and to read the products of the printers.

When the First Amendment was drafted, was there a clear sense of what "speech" and "press" meant? Scholars disagree. It may seem clear that "speech" is the spoken word and "press" is the written word, but as technology developed, the distinctions between these two terms have increasingly blurred. The blurring continues to challenge the courts to develop new interpretations of "speech" and "press." Computer technology has made it cheaper to provide information to a broad audience. We can publish *and* speak *via* the Internet. We can use computers to produce small special-interest publications cheaply and quickly. There has been an explosion of specialty magazines and newsletters addressing a variety of interests and needs.

The word "press" no longer applies to traditional newspapers and magazines, but also must be applied to shows like *Hard Copy, Inside Edition* and *Extra;* tabloids like the *National Enquirer,* the *Star* and the *Globe;* documentaries and docudramas, and to the products of every special interest group or individual with a computer, printer and modem.

The courts have found themselves wrestling with how to apply the freedoms the First Amendment provides. Are the speech rights less for some categories of people than others? Do freelance writers have the same rights as journalists who work for mainstream publications? What are the other expressive activities that may fall under the broad categories of oral and printed words? Do they include pictures, gestures, dances, the Internet?

The Supreme Court has had to interpret the words "speech" and "press" in a variety of ways. The Court has been required to go beyond the verbal and written communication of ideas based on what the framers were thinking — or what we think they were thinking — to issues involving the development of modern technology. Jefferson said as much in 1816 when he wrote, "I know also that laws and institutions must go hand in hand with the progress of the human mind.... As new discoveries are made, new truths disclosed, and manners and opinions change with the change of circumstances, institutions must advance also, and keep pace with the times."[17] The founders had no concept of film, videotape or computers when they wrote the First Amendment.

In a broad sense, the courts have provided First Amendment protection to expression, a term that incorporates speech, press and some conduct. Expression also incorporates many forms of entertainment like theater performances, movies and dancing.

Still unanswered is the question of whether the protection of expression includes the right to gather information. The Court has said that newsgathering deserves some protection but has never backed up that *dicta* by providing protection.[18] The Court has also limited access to some public places and information.

THE THEORIES OF PROTECTING EXPRESSION

First Amendment issues manifest themselves in a variety of ways:

- A history department faculty member sued the University of Minnesota at Duluth for violating his First Amendment rights. The school's administration removed from a display case a picture of the professor striking a pose with a cardboard laurel wreath and a dull sword. The photo was taken by students for a history club project.

- The Food and Drug Administration regulates the promotion of drugs and medical devices on the Internet. Critics fear the free flow of information may be blocked.

- In Berkeley, California, the trial of two women arrested for violating the city's anti-nudity ordinance ended with a hung jury. The women, who perform in parks as the "X-plicit Players," claimed they had a First Amendment right to perform without clothes.

- A 13-year-old eighth grader was told by school administrators in Delaware, Ohio, that she could not wear T-shirts with religious messages. The school took the action after also banning shirts with satanic overtones.

- In a highly publicized case, the Supreme Court turned down a challenge to the Clinton administration's so-called "don't ask, don't tell" policy on gays in the military. A former Navy officer claimed the policy violated homosexual service members' free speech rights.

The list goes on and on. Can indecency be banned from the Internet? How do we balance free speech and sexual or racial harassment? When can a college administration tell a professor what not to say in the classroom? Can a college prevent political campaigning on its computer network? Can a private company fire an employee because of a shirt the employee wears to work?

---

16 *Id.* at 414.
17 "Thomas Jefferson to Dr. Priestley, 1802," *Thomas Jefferson on*

Democracy, p. 67.
18 *Branzburg v. Hayes,* 408 U.S. 665 (1972).

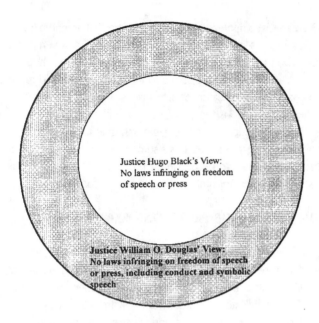

Justice Hugo Black's View:
No laws infringing on freedom
of speech or press

Justice William O. Douglas' View:
No laws infringing on freedom of speech
or press, including conduct and symbolic
speech

Figure 1

Absolutist View of the First Amendment

The First Amendment says that "Congress shall make no law...." The words seem clear enough. They don't say Congress can make some laws, or it can make a few, reasonable laws. It says Congress can make *no law* that abridges the freedom of speech or the press. Yet, courts have often decided that, in some circumstances, speech and press rights must yield to other rights.

Some First Amendment scholars and jurists, because of the clear language of the First Amendment, argue for absolute protection for all speech — regardless of content, motive of the speaker or consequences of the speech. Others argue that speech contributing to a self-governing society should receive absolute protection. Philosopher Alexander Meiklejohn, who promoted this theory, based it upon an analysis of the Constitution and Bill of Rights. He concluded that the document was intended only to protect speech of self-governing importance: "No one who reads with care the text of the First Amendment can fail to be startled by its absoluteness. The phrase 'Congress shall make no law ... abridging freedom of speech,' is unqualified. It admits of no exceptions."[19]

Former Supreme Court Justice Hugo Black also had what some might call an "absolutist" view of the First Amendment. He argued

that, because freedom of speech and press are explicitly mentioned, those forms of expression are protected. He believed that no expressive conduct was protected, however, because speech, not conduct, is explicitly mentioned in the First Amendment. In Justice Black's view, freedom of speech and press are contained within a circle of freedom; conduct lies outside that circle.

Another justice who was nearly absolutist was William O. Douglas, who took a broader view than his colleague. Douglas believed symbolic speech — wearing armbands, burning draft cards — fell within the circle of protection. He was opposed to weighing the First Amendment against other values because, he said, doing so ran counter to the intent of the framers and the express language of the First Amendment:

> The First Amendment provides that "Congress shall make no law ... abridging the freedom of speech." The Constitution provides no exception. This does not mean, however, that the Nation need hold its hand until it is in such weakened condition that there is not time to protect itself from incitement to revolution. Seditious conduct can always be punished. But the command of the First Amendment is so clear that we should not allow Congress to call a halt to free speech.... The First Amendment makes confidence in the common sense of our people and in their maturity of judgment the great postulate of our democracy.... Unless and until extreme and necessitous circumstances are shown, our aim should be to keep speech unfettered and to allow the processes of law to be invoked only when the provocateurs among us move from speech to action.[20]

But, despite the views of Justices Douglas and Black, nothing close to an absolute interpretation of the First Amendment has ever commanded a majority of the Supreme Court. As a result, a number of exceptions and limitations have been whittled into First Amendment law. The United States, then, can be seen as falling on a spectrum. At one end of the spectrum is totalitarian government that controls all expression; at the other end is a pure libertarian government, which allows complete freedom — anarchy. The United States is somewhere between those two poles.

One of the most notable conditions under which the government can bar expression is when speech threatens national security or public safety. But there are other reasons for barring expression. Exceptions to freedom of expression depend on what is

[19] Alexander Meiklejohn, *Free Speech and Its Relation to Government* (New York: Harper & Brothers, 1948), p. 17.

[20] *Dennis v. United States*, 341 U.S. 494, 590 (1951) (Douglas, J., dissenting).

said, who is speaking and the harm that may be caused by the expression. As you read this book, you will discover some of the exceptions. Pornography, for example, is protected while obscenity is not; some forms of commercial speech are protected, some are not. Libel and reporting on trials push First Amendment protections to the edges of the circle. In the end, the only absolute — found dead center in the circle — is that political speech is protected all the time. The trouble, as with any issue, is in the definition. What constitutes political speech?

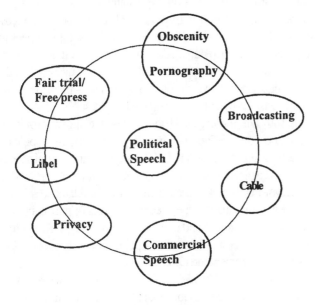

Figure 2

The First Amendment through Supreme Court Interpretation

THE VALUE OF FREE SPEECH

We value free speech because it advances some important social goals:

- The discovery of truth: If people have no access to the truth or to information, then they have no way of judging error and, thus, cannot make reasonable decisions.
- The continuance of self-government: People cannot govern themselves without understanding the issues.
- A check on government power: The media become a means through which the public can keep track of the three branches of government. It is through this role that the media came to be referred to as "the fourth estate," that is, as a fourth branch in the system of self-government.

- A promotion of stable change: Free speech allows those who disagree with policy to work for change without seeking a violent overthrow of government.
- Individual fulfillment: Free speech encourages us to express ourselves and, thereby, enriches and enhances our lives.

Each of these benefits of free speech deserves some explication.

Discovery of the Truth

Freedom of expression is widely believed to be an effective method of searching for truth. The model for this search is called "the marketplace of ideas." The theory is that, just as consumers search for the best products in a market, individuals are able, because free expression ensures a wide variety of ideas in circulation, to determine the most useful or original information, that is, the truth. The theory is that good ideas, like good products, will prevail in a free market. Under this theory, censorship is not only obnoxious, it is impractical.

A different, but similar, philosophy was espoused by John Stuart Mill in the Nineteenth Century. Mill valued free speech because, he argued, without it truth would have no chance to prevail in the marketplace. If people have no access to the truth, then they have no way of judging error and no way of substituting truth for error. Mill's classic work *On Liberty,* published in 1859, established the boundaries for authority and freedom in the modern state. Mill said the press plays a valuable role by providing security against a "corrupt or tyrannical government."

Mill argued that even one voice against a majority should not be silenced because "if the opinion is right, [the people] are deprived of the opportunity of exchanging error for truth: if wrong, they lose, what is almost as great a benefit, the clearer perception and livelier impression of truth, produced by its collision with error." In one of his most-quoted phrases, Mill wrote, "If all mankind minus one were of one opinion, and only one person were of the contrary opinion mankind would be no more justified in silencing that one person, than he, if he had the power, would be justified in silencing mankind."[21]

Mill offered four defenses for the diversity of opinion that is at the heart of freedom of expression:

1. Some opinion may be false; thus other opinion may be true.

2. Conflict between opinion leads to a clearer comprehension of truth.

3. Conflicting opinions share truth between them.

---

21 John Stuart Mill, *On Liberty,* ed. David Spitz (New York: W.W. Norton & Company, 1975), p. 18.

4. Non-conforming opinion is needed to supply truth.[22]

In order to maintain viability and vitality, truth needs to be challenged. If there are fewer avenues of challenge, Mill would argue, then truth is injured. Thus, the marketplace suffers when more media outlets are concentrated under fewer owners. Such concentration could be as restrictive as government censorship. In addition, the marketplace means little to minorities, dissidents and fringe groups who do not have access to the media. First Amendment scholar Jerome Barron discounts the marketplace concept, saying that if it ever existed, it has long ceased to do so because "there is an inequality in the power to communicate ideas just as there is inequality in economic bargaining power."[23]

The marketplace of ideas may still be viable, but it is changing as media conglomerates grow, as new media are offered to consumers and as computers become cheaper and more versatile. The marketplace theory also suffers because of technology overload: 500 cable television channels, an untold number of home pages on the Internet, literally thousands of sources of information. With countless messages, how can truth rise to the top? Instead, the truth could become more obscured by the overwhelming number of false messages. While the discovery of truth is an ongoing process, in the short term a false message can cause harm. Thus, the government could argue, there is a need for intervention to protect the public.

Governance

Thomas Jefferson, himself often maliciously criticized in the press, wrote in 1787 that people should have full information about public affairs through the press:

> The basis of our government being the opinion of the people, the very first object should be to keep that right; and were it left to me to decide whether we should have a government without newspapers, or newspapers without government, I should not hesitate a moment to prefer the latter.[24]

Alexander Meiklejohn is the best known modern proponent of freedom of expression as a value for the governance of a people. Discovery of the truth, he said in the 1940s, is needed for a demo-cratic society to exist because citizens need to understand the issues before they can be expected to act. Free speech "is not, primarily, a device for the winning of new truth, though that is very important," Meiklejohn wrote. "It is a device for the sharing of whatever truth has been won. Its purpose is to give to every voting member of the body politic the fullest possible participation in the understanding of those problems with which the citizens of a self-governing society must deal."[25] Voting is the key act of self-governance, and Meiklejohn argued that the free flow of information, by protecting discussion, beliefs and associations, was part of the voting process. The theory is applied to education, philosophy, science, literature, the arts and public issues; it applies to any speech relating to public affairs. The First Amendment guarantee is "assured only to speech which bears, directly or indirectly, upon the issues with which voters have to deal — only, therefore, to the consideration of matters of public interest."[26]

As with any theory, Meiklejohn's has definitional problems. How does one define "matters of public interest," "political speech" or similar terms? Meiklejohn argued that political speech should be defined broadly, including the sciences, the arts and issues involving morality, because they can all be related to self-government. Consequently, they become matters of public interest. In order to have robust and uninhibited debate on public matters, Meiklejohn advocated immunizing political speech unconditionally from government interference.

Clearly influenced by Meiklejohn, former Justice William Brennan developed his own theory about the First Amendment and its value. As one scholar wrote, Brennan adhered to the theory that "the First Amendment's primary purpose is to guarantee protection when speech touches on areas of self-government ... no individual or institution has greater or lesser free-speech protection than any other individual or institution. Therefore, when First Amendment rights come into conflict, those rights must be balanced."[27] Brennan's balancing scale was vested in the First Amendment's role in society, which the justice found paramount. For Brennan, free expression was guaranteed for its societal benefit, not its benefit to individuals.

Justice Brennan argued that public debate must not only be "uninhibited, robust and wide open" but also informed.[28] In a

---

[22] *Id.* at 44.

[23] Jerome Barron, "Access to the Press — A New First Amendment Right," *Harvard Law Review* 80 (1967): 1647.

[24] "Thomas Jefferson to Edward Carrington, 1787," *Thomas Jefferson on Democracy,* p. 93.

[25] Meiklejohn, *Free Speech and Its Relation to Self-Government,* pp. 88-89.

[26] *Id.* at 79.

[27] W. Wat Hopkins, *Mr. Justice Brennan and Freedom of Expression* (New York: Praeger, 1991), p. 83.

[28] Karen Green, "'Uninhibited, Robust and Wide-Open' — But In-

democratic society, Brennan argued, "the government, the press, and the people all have roles to play. Self-government of a society requires a communications process, and it is that process the First Amendment is designed to protect."[29]

Some critics argue that the promotion of democracy will only be realized if the mass media do a thorough and responsible job of covering public affairs. They say the media are a long way from that kind of coverage and won't do it without government encouragement. A recent movement, called "public journalism" or "civic journalism," is an attempt by some media outlets to respond to this criticism.

Professor Zechariah Chafee Jr. was one of the earliest of these critics. He argued that it would prove difficult to separate political and private speech. He also questioned the role of the courts in defying legislatures. When the nation faces a crisis or an emergency, particularly one involving a threat from outside its borders, then the mood of society will reflect less toleration for certain types of expression. If speech is viewed as putting the country at risk, then society, in general, won't have a problem with legislation controlling speech, because protection of society becomes more important than individual rights.[30] Such thinking follows the underlying philosophy of the clear and present danger test, which was first espoused by Justice Oliver Wendell Holmes in 1919:

> We admit that in many places and in ordinary times the defendants in saying all that was said in the circular would have been within their constitutional rights. But the character of every act depends upon the circumstances in which it is done. The most stringent protection of free speech would not protect a man in falsely shouting fire in a theatre and causing a panic. It does not even protect a man from an injunction against uttering words that may have all the effect of force. The question in every case is whether the words used are used in such circumstances and are of such a nature as to create a clear and present danger that they will bring about the substantive evils that Congress has a right to prevent.[31]

Holmes developed his test as a way to prevent, or at least limit, legislatures from getting too repressive in times of crisis. In Holmes' view, determining what is a clear and present danger still falls to the courts, not the legislatures. Holmes' effort to protect speech backfired. The test did not provide a broad spectrum of protection for expression. Six months after enunciating the test, Holmes repudiated it as unworkable. However, the damage was already done. For more than fifty years courts used the test, in one form or another, to limit expression.

And while Meiklejohn's alternative to the clear and present danger test is absolute protection for all public or political expression, Chafee argued that such a view is unrealistic. Not all speech deserves protection, Chafee wrote. A form of the clear and present danger test can be applied to language that has no social interest — profanity, indecency or defamatory speech — because in those cases the speech is not essential to the development of ideas. Using language similar to Chafee's, the Court ruled that fighting words are not constitutionally protected speech.[32]

Justice Brennan's apparent acceptance of Meiklejohn's philosophy was manifested in the landmark case *New York Times Co. v. Sullivan*. Brennan, in his unanimous opinion, wrote that a libel suit against a newspaper must be considered "against the background of a profound national commitment to the principle that debate on public issues should be uninhibited, robust, and wide-open."[33] Five years later, Justice Byron R. White, also for a unanimous Court, wrote in *Red Lion Broadcasting Co. v. FCC*: "It is the right of the public to receive suitable access to social, political, esthetic, moral, and other ideas and experiences which is crucial here." This right of the public, he wrote, is paramount: "It is the purpose of the First Amendment to preserve an uninhibited marketplace of ideas in which truth will ultimately prevail, rather than to countenance monopolization of the market whether it be by the Government itself or a private licensee."[34]

Check on Government Power

The ability to express ideas freely and, with them, to critique government is an important check against abuse of power. The Constitution provided three branches of government, with a division of power, so the judiciary, legislature and executive could be checks on one another. Implicit in the Constitution, however, was the concept that government was of the people. Therefore, social

---

formed: Justice Brennan's Structural Model of the First Amendment," paper presented at the AEJMC Southeast Colloquium, New Orleans, La., March 1988, p. 2.

[29] *Id.*

[30] Zechariah Chafee Jr., *Free Speech in the United States* (Cambridge, Mass.: Harvard University Press, 1941), and Zechariah Chafee Jr., *The Blessings of Liberty* (Philadelphia: Lippincott, 1956).

[31] *Schenck v. U.S.*, 249 U.S. 47, 52 (1919).

---

[32] *Chaplinsky v. New Hampshire*, 315 U.S. 568 (1949).

[33] 376 U.S. 254, 270 (1964).

[34] 395 U.S. 367, 390 (1969).

critics argue, for people to be their own governors, they must know what the government is doing. In such a model, citizen critics are vital to the process, and the primary way most of us know what is transpiring is through the media.

A free press, therefore, is essential in bringing to light abuses of power. From Tammany Hall to Watergate, the media have been bringing down unscrupulous governments. Watergate was surely the most sensational example. The *Washington Post* was instrumental in uncovering political dirty tricks, wire tapping, money laundering and obstruction of justice by the Nixon Administration in the 1970s. When a Congressional committee made it clear that it would be recommending that President Nixon be impeached, he resigned.

Without the freedom to aggressively become a watchdog of government at all levels, the press would not be able to uncover these governmental abuses.

Stable Change

Freedom of expression allows those who disagree with governmental or social policy to work for change within the system and without violence. Those in power often see public criticism as obstructionist, but the structure of government and protection for government criticism demonstrate that the framers believed flexibility and stability work together; tradition and change coexist. Stable change occurs because problems can be dealt with incrementally, reducing the need for drastic change, which could be disruptive.

Without freedom of the press and freedom of speech, real problems of society may remain hidden and will fester; fear, hatred and resentment breed; no safety valve exists to allow the ventilation of problems. Compromise becomes more difficult under such circumstances and makes problem solving nearly impossible. Consequently, what erupts from this mix is social unrest and the potential for violent action against authority.

Individual Fulfillment

Many of the arguments for free speech presented thus far are tied to the practical or functional aspects of expression, that is, free expression promotes self-government. In late Seventeenth Century England, however, philosopher John Locke argued that free speech is a good unto itself, even if it does not add to the functioning of government. It is good, Locke argued, because it is self-fulfilling.

Locke's argument is based on the belief that expressing opinion is part of human nature. We want to express ourselves; indeed, we need to express ourselves. This helps each of us discover what it means to be human. If we feel good about ourselves, we can help society feel good.

In the early United States, Thomas Jefferson and James Madison were believers of the self-fulfilling role of free expression. "A right of free correspondence between citizen and citizen, on their joint interest, whether public or private,.. is a natural right," Jefferson wrote to James Monroe in 1797. "It is not a gift of any municipal law."[35]

FIRST AMENDMENT TESTS

Despite the apparently absolute language of the Constitution, there is no absolute protection for speech or press. The right of expression is often balanced against other personal rights or social interests. In addition, as will be demonstrated later in this book, some types of speech receive more protection than others. Under this hierarchy, speech critical of the government and speech broadcast over the airwaves that fulfills equal time requirements mandated by federal communications law receive almost absolute protection.

Because most speech is not absolutely protected, the courts have used a variety of tests by which to balance freedom of expression against other rights to determine which must give way. When a test is applied in a case, the outcome of the case depends on the competing interests and the application of the test.

Some of the most common tests — past and present — are discussed here.

Bad Tendency Test

The bad tendency test was espoused in the early 1900s and provided virtually no protection for speech. Thomas L. Tedford described the test as the "nip-it-in-the-bud," the "killing the serpent in its egg" or the "putting out the spark before the conflagration" approach.[36] Under the test, if expression was expected to cause even the slightest tendency toward harm, the speech could be prevented.

The classic use of the test came in 1925 when Justice Edward T.

---

35 "Thomas Jefferson to James Monroe, 1787," *Thomas Jefferson on Democracy,* p. 15.

36 Thomas L. Tedford, *Freedom of Speech in the United States* (New York: Random House, 1985), p. 450.

Sanford, in upholding the conviction of Benjamin Gitlow, wrote:

> A single revolutionary spark may kindle a fire that, smouldering [sic] for a time, may burst into a sweeping and destructive conflagration. It cannot be said that the State is acting arbitrarily or unreasonably when in the exercise of its judgment as to the measures necessary to protect the public peace and safety, it seeks to extinguish the spark without waiting until it has enkindled the flame or blazed into the conflagration.[37]

Fortunately, the test was discontinued because speakers and writers had no way of knowing if they could be punished for their expression. There was no warning because the test was so vague that it could be applied multiple ways. Gitlow's actions, the Court said, were "inimical to the public welfare" and could "corrupt public morals," which was enough to stop him.[38]

Clear and Present Danger Test

As previously indicated, the clear and present danger test was first enunciated by Justice Oliver Wendell Holmes in 1919. It allows expression to be controlled when there is a clear and present danger that the expression will bring about substantive evils. The test was a significant improvement over the bad tendency test because it provided a judge with a narrower window for restricting expression. In theory, speech would have to pose a serious and immediate danger in order for the government to restrict it. The test was not rigorously applied, however, and Holmes later backed off its use. The Court held that the government need not wait until the very moment damage was imminent to restrict speech. If all the ingredients for trouble are present, the Court reasoned, the government has a right to halt the offensive speech. That interpretation gave the government flexibility Holmes had not intended.

The clear and present danger test was intended to punish threatening speech rather than the mere advocacy of illegal acts at some future time. If the advocacy is directed to incite or produce imminent lawlessness, however, it may be halted or, if the action is carried out, it may be punished. Holmes would allow speech to be regulated only if the danger was both clear and imminent, like a man in falsely shouting fire in a theater and causing a panic.

In a 1969 Ohio case, the Court held that the mere advocacy of illegal activity is protected by the First Amendment.[39] In what some scholars interpret as a variation of the clear and present danger test, the Court said only when there is an imminent danger of incitement of illegal activity can authorities step in to stop speech. In a *per curiam* decision, the Court ruled unconstitutional the 1919 Ohio Criminal Syndicalism Statute, which was used to convict a Ku Klux Klan leader. In doing so, the Court established a two-part test to evaluate the likelihood that speech will lead to illegal activity:

- Who is the speaker? Does the person have a history of illegal activity or affiliation with an organization that does so? Do people take the speaker seriously.?
- Is there a likelihood that the espoused actions will be carried out?

The standard was upheld in a 1973 case involving an anti-Vietnam War street protester.[40]

Brandenburg v. Ohio, which is still the precedent for such issues, essentially put an end to the use of sedition as a threat against anti-government speech, though the government has filed sedition charges against white supremacists, neo-Nazis and others involved in bombings, racketeering and robberies.

The clear and present danger test continues to survive, despite judicial urgings that it be abandoned.[41] The test, however, is used almost exclusively in areas related to the administration of government or the judiciary. In *Nebraska Press Association v. Stuart,* for example, the Court invalidated a gag order that was intended to restrict the reporting of a murder trial. Quoting appellate Judge Learned Hand, Chief Justice Warren Burger wrote that the Court had to determine whether "the gravity of the 'evil,' discounted by its improbability, justifies such invasion of free speech as is necessary to avoid the danger."[42]

In addition, Virginia tried to protect the reputations of members of its judiciary by using the clear and present danger test to prevent the publication of confidential information about the proceedings of the state's judicial disciplinary commission. The state argued that publication of the information represented a clear and present danger to the administration of justice. The Court did not accept the argument,[43] but the case illustrates how broadly the test may be stretched and how it can put expression — even political speech — at risk.

---

[37] *Gitlow,* 268 U.S. at 669.

[38] *Id.* at 667.

[39] *Brandenburg v. Ohio,* 395 U.S. 444 (1969).

[40] *Hess v. Indiana,* 414 U.S. 105 (1973).

[41] See, for example, *Branzburg,* 395 U.S. at 452 (Douglas, J., concurring).

[42] 427 U.S. 539, 562 (1976).

[43] *Landmark Communications, Inc. v. Virginia,* 435 U.S. 829 (1978).

Balancing Test

A balancing test is implicit in all the methods used by courts to gauge the interests of speech to society. But when courts deliberately weigh the values of speech against conflicting values or interests, they are "balancing" those interests. Courts decide which value in a particular instance deserves greater protection. Balancing provides more flexibility than the clear and present danger test because the judge can assign weights to different facts as they appear in the case. The outcome, however, is often unpredictable.

Strict Scrutiny

Courts employ strict scrutiny when confronted with governmental actions specifically aimed at restricting expression. Under the strict scrutiny test, the government must show a compelling reason for instituting a regulation that abridges speech. The reason, in fact, must be so compelling that it requires free expression to take a subordinate role. In addition, the government must demonstrate that the regulation is narrowly tailored to meet the specific goal without restricting speech that is not related to the goal. The courts will often examine the circumstances of a case to see if the government could have taken action that was less destructive of First Amendment rights. If such a method exists, the courts will rule in favor of the First Amendment and strike down the regulation. In many cases, the burden is so great the government cannot meet it.

Strict scrutiny is also discussed in Chapter 3.

THE LEVELS OF PROTECTED SPEECH AND SPEAKERS

A constant theme throughout this chapter — indeed, throughout this book — has been that the First Amendment is not absolute. There are instances in which speech — and speakers — can be restricted, and restrictions vary based on the type of speech employed and the speaker.

The Hierarchy of Protected Expression

The Supreme Court has indicated that there are three levels of protection for speech:
- Political expression receives the highest level of protection. Speech that is of governing importance is strictly protected. The definition of "governing importance" can be broad. Indeed, some First Amendment advocates expand the definition beyond speech about government and politics to include education, health, agriculture, and culture, among others.
- Commercial speech receives less protection. The Court has recognized that advertising and other forms of commercial speech are protected. Because commercial speech is a particularly sturdy form of speech, that is, because it has a tendency to survive despite restrictions, and because the speaker has a vested interest, the Court has recognized that the government can impose stricter regulations on commercial speech.
- Obscene material, false advertising and fighting words are not protected.

Commercial speech and false advertising are discussed in Chapter 9; obscenity is discussed in Chapter 5, and fighting words are discussed in Chapter 3.

Who Is Protected?

The rights of all people to speak and publish are basic. So are the rights to engage in symbolic speech and to associate with others. And, the Court has said, because of the right to speak and disseminate ideas, there may be an implied right to receive some kinds of information. The First Amendment also guarantees the right to contribute money and to solicit funds.

Freedom of expression also guarantees some right to remain silent. A person cannot be compelled to salute the flag, to affirm a belief in God or to associate with a political party or particular ideology.[44] New Hampshire, for example, lost its bid to require all car owners in the state to bear license plates with the slogan "Live Free or Die." The Court upheld the right of a Jehovah's Witness saw to block out the slogan because the Witness said it violated his religious beliefs.

Levels of protection attach to classes of people, just as they do to classes of speech. No person or class of people has absolute protection, and all classes of people have some free speech rights.

Adults. There is no language in the Bill of Rights that distinguishes categories of people and their levels of protection. Yet, over the years the courts have realized that there are distinctions, often based on age. The courts also have classified people by their employment — in the public versus the private sector — as well as whether they are in prison. Adult, private citizens enjoy the most rights. And, while many of those same rights apply to students, children and government employees, the level of protection is not

---

[44] *West Virginia Board of Education v. Barnette*, 319 U.S. 624 (1943); *Torcasso v. Watkins*, 367 U.S. 488 (1961); *Elrod v. Burns*, 427 U.S. 347 (1966); *Wooley v. Maynard*, 430 U.S. 705 (1977).

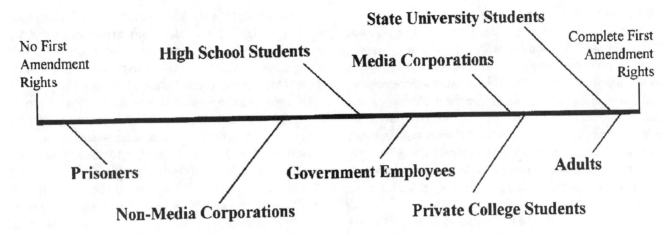

Figure 3: First Amendment Protection Spectrum

the same. The ambiguity of protection is demonstrated in a recent ruling by the Washington Supreme Court. The court weighed the First Amendment rights of a newspaper to maintain its editorial integrity against the free speech rights of one of its reporters who was involved in political activism outside the workplace. The court ruled in favor of the newspaper.[45]

University Students. For the most part, the Court has said the First Amendment has the same force on public college campuses as in the community at large: "Mere dissemination of ideas — no matter how offensive to good taste — on a state university campus may not be shut off in the name alone of 'conventions of decency.'"[46] College students cannot be held to a higher standard of expressive conduct just because they're on state university campuses. There is no "dual standard in the academic community with respect to the content of speech," the Court has said.[47] But that hasn't stopped the lower courts from threatening campus expression rights. A Kentucky federal district court, for example, has ruled that the same restrictions applied to high schools could be used with the college and university press.[48]

Students at private colleges and universities may have even fewer expressive rights because the First Amendment is aimed at the government. It has no bearing on private entities. At public colleges and universities, the administration is tantamount to the government. Private colleges and universities, however, are not

supported by state funds, so their administrations are not considered "governments" under the law, and the First Amendment does not apply. State laws, specifically state constitutions, may provide greater protection on both public and private campuses. Most states have affirmative speech provisions in their constitutions.

High School Students. High school students, like adults, have some fundamental expressive rights. But while students are at school, those rights may be more easily restricted by administrators and teachers. A school district cannot prevent students from symbolically protesting a war — by wearing black armbands, for example — so long as the symbolic expression does not disrupt school activities. The Supreme Court has recognized, however, that schools have specific functions, and the Court has said that function may be protected. Speech can be curbed if it disrupts class or invades the rights of others. And school-sponsored publications may be restricted if they don't promote the pedagogical mission of the school.

Student expressive rights are discussed in greater detail in Chapter 12.

Government Employees. Government employees have the right to speak and publish but with limitations. They may speak as private persons on public issues, just as they may vote for whomever they want. They cannot be fired, for example, for remarks hostile to the government or even to their own governmental agency, unless those remarks are likely to impede the agency's operations. Federal government employees, however, may not participate in political campaigns. In addition, in 1991 the Court said employees of federally financed family planning clinics can be

---

[45] *Nelson v. McClatchy Newspapers,* 936 P.2d 1123 (Wash. 1997), *cert. denied* 118 S.Ct. 175 (1997).

[46] *Papish v. Board of Curators,* 410 U.S. 667, 670 (1973).

[47] *Id.* at 671

[48] *Kincaid v. Gibson,* Civ. No. 95-98 (E.D. Ky., Nov. 14, 1997). See the discussion of this case in Chapter 12.

barred from providing information about abortions.[49]

For more than fifty years, federal government employees could not participate in political campaigns. That changed, however, when Congress passed, and President Clinton signed, the Hatch Act Reform Amendments of 1993.[50] Most government employees still cannot solicit campaign funds from the public and may not run for partisan office, but they can, if they choose, take active roles in campaigns.[51] The same law also states that employees cannot be forced to participate in a campaign, and it allows conditions to be set involving participation in municipal elections in Maryland, Virginia and the immediate vicinity of the District of Columbia.

Prisoners. Prisoners have fewer rights to speak, publish and receive information than free adults. Prison officials can enact reasonable restrictions to control their access to people and information. Officials can regulate, for example, a prison newspaper.

CONCLUSIONS

The First Amendment is essential to a free government and to U.S. society. Without it, there is no protection from frivolous libel or invasion of privacy suits; there is no right of access to government proceedings; there is no protection from prior restraint; there is no right to investigate or criticize government. Without the First Amendment, newspapers, magazines, broadcast stations and other media would not exist as we know them.

The First Amendment's guarantees of free speech and press are not absolute. Courts throughout the country continue to interpret its language as new issues arise. Arguments and justifications for free expression are found in our English heritage in the words of John Milton, William Blackstone and others, who challenged the authority of government under threat of sometimes brutal punishment.

The First Amendment was the result of debate and political ma-

---

[49] *Rust v. Sullivan,* 500 U.S. 173 (1991).

[50] Pub. L. 103-94, Sec. 2(a), Oct. 6, 1993, 107 Stat. 1001 (1993).

[51] Employees of the following federal agencies may not participate in political campaigns: Federal Election Commission; FBI; Secret Service; CIA; National Security Council; National Security Agency; Defense Intelligence Agency; Merit Systems Protection Board; Office of Special Counsel; Office of Criminal Investigation of the Internal Revenue Service; Office of Investigative Programs of the U.S. Customs Service; Office of Law Enforcement of the Bureau of Alcohol, Tobacco, and Firearms; the Central Imagery Office, and the Criminal Division of the Department of Justice. In addition, FEC employees cannot contribute financially to a political campaign.

neuvering among colonists. It was not always first. Thus, an argument can be made that it has no more weight than any of the other nine amendments that make up the Bill of Rights. Though it was initially interpreted to apply only to the federal government, the First Amendment became applicable to the states in 1925.

The rights found in the First Amendment manifest themselves in a variety of ways. People often claim a right of expression — a right to speak or publish — without understanding the limits on those rights. Those limits have been placed by the Supreme Court as it balances conflicting rights. However, the Court has made it clear that any regulation of expression must be content neutral. The Court has also said that any government regulation that affects First Amendment rights must pass strict scrutiny. The government — whether it be federal, state or local — must be able to justify its action to control expression by demonstrating that it used the means least damaging to the First Amendment.

There is value in the First Amendment because it allows us to discover the truth, continue to govern ourselves, provide a check on government power, promote stable change and enrich ourselves. While not everyone enjoys the same protection offered by the First Amendment, everyone has some protection.

FOR ADDITIONAL READING

Demac, Donna A. *Liberty Denied, The Current Rise of Censorship in America.* New Brunswick, N.J.: Rutgers University Press, 1990.

Frohnmayer, John. *Out of Tune, Listening to the First Amendment.* Nashville, Tenn.: Freedom Forum First Amendment Center, 1994.

Hentoff, Nat. *Free Speech for Me — But Not for Thee.* New York: HarperCollins, 1992.

Hopkins, W. Wat. *Mr. Justice Brennan and Freedom of Expression.* New York: Praeger, 1991.

Quill. September 1976.

Siebert, Frederick. *Freedom of the Press in England 1476-1776.* Urbana: University of Illinois Press, 1952.

Terry, Carolyn. "First Under Fire, Are Americans Having Second Thoughts About the First Amendment?" *Presstime,* September 1995, pp. 36-42.

Wriston, Walter B. *Mistress of the World, The Marketplace and Public Opinion in the Information Age.* New York: Freedom Forum Media Studies Center, 1993.

3

Conduct and Speech

By W. Wat Hopkins

As readers of this book will no doubt learn, much First Amendment jurisprudence depends upon interpretation and, beyond that, degrees of interpretation. One man's art is another's obscenity; one woman's opinion is another's libel; one author's fair use is another's copyright infringement.

One of the best examples of the divergence of attitudes toward free speech might be the battle waged in the 1960s and '70s between Justice Hugo Black and some of his brethren on the Supreme Court. Justice Black took the position that the government cannot restrict the distribution of material because that material is obscene, defamatory, indecent, or even because it might harm the national security. "I read 'no law ... abridging'" freedom of speech and press, Justice Black wrote, "to mean *no law* abridging."[1] Speech, he maintained, was absolutely protected.

The great free-speech advocate, however, had a very narrow definition of "speech." Just as "no law" meant "no law," in Justice Black's view, "speech" meant "speech" and nothing else. He disagreed, therefore, when the Court ruled that students could not be punished for wearing black arm bands to school, or that a protester could not be punished for wearing a jacket bearing the words "Fuck the draft." These cases, Justice Black contended, involved conduct and did not implicate the First Amendment; no "speech" was involved.

Fortunately for picketers, flag-burners and dozens of others who have chosen over the years to express their views by doing rather than saying, a majority of the Supreme Court has never agreed with Justice Black's definition of "speech." Indeed, a majority of the Court has always recognized that "speech" is more than talking. Justice Abe Fortas, for example, wrote that those students who wore armbands to school to protest the Vietnam war were participating in activity that was "closely akin to 'pure speech.'"[2] Justice Fortas's was a momentous characterization. If something that was so clearly an action could be considered "pure speech," many other types of conduct could be recognized as speech as well and, therefore, eligible for First Amendment protection. Under such a construction, expression, which is not mentioned in the First Amendment, is protected alongside "speech" and "press."

That has long been the case in First Amendment jurisprudence. Indeed, the Court has recognized a variety of activities as being speech: carrying or displaying a flag; marching or picketing; burning a flag, cross or draft card. The Court has also said that a sit-in is a form of expression, as is the "silent, reproachful presence" of a group of African Americans who refused to leave an all-white library.[3] In fact, in some circumstances, even sleeping could be described as "speech."[4]

[1] *Smith v. California*, 361 U.S. 147, 157 (1959)(Black, J., concurring).

[2] *Tinker v. Des Moines Independent School District*, 393 U.S. 503, 505-06 (1969).

[3] *Brown v. Louisiana*, 383 U.S. 131, 141-42 (1966).

[4] *Clark v. Community for Creative Non-Violence*, 468 U.S. 288 (1984).

This is not to say, however, that the First Amendment protects all expressive or symbolic conduct. Conduct, after all, may intrude on individual rights more than other forms of speech. It may literally do what an advertisement for a long-distance telephone service suggests consumers figuratively do: It may reach out and touch someone. The Court has said, therefore, that there must be some balance between the rights of the actor and the rights of others present when conduct is used as a means of expression. This tension between rights has been at the heart of expressive conduct cases since the 1960s, when the Court's first substantive analysis in this area of the law began.

CONDUCT AS SPEECH

In general, there are three kinds of conduct: (1) conduct that has no communicative value, (2) conduct that is purely communicative and (3) conduct that has a mix of communicative and non-communicative elements.

Sometimes it's easy to tell the difference. One spring, for example, a home owner noticed that his U.S. flag had become frayed and moth-eaten. The home owner decided to replace the flag and learned from the U.S. Code that one proper way of disposing of a damaged flag is by burning. The home owner took the flag into the back yard, dropped it into the grill, doused it with lighter fluid and set it ablaze. No one saw the action, and the flag burner later disposed of the cold ashes by spreading them in the flower bed. The act had no communicative value; its purpose was solely to dispose of a damaged U.S. flag as instructed by the U.S. Code.

Come summer, the home owner replaced the damaged flag and, on July 4, put it on a flag-pole attached to the garage. The act is purely communicative; the home owner displayed the flag to demonstrate patriotism on Independence Day.

But when fall arrived, the home owner became dismayed. An incumbent president had taken actions with which the home owner violently disagreed. The home owner had a series of arguments with a neighbor, who happened to be the local chairman of the president's political party. The home owner's irritation was inflamed even more because the president was using hundreds of flags in his re-election campaign, even using the flag as a background on campaign posters, bumper stickers and other paraphernalia. To demonstrate his distaste, the home owner doused his recently purchased flag with lighter fluid, set it ablaze and tossed it on the neighbor's front porch. The burning flag destroyed a "Welcome" mat and left a large, sooty spot, requiring the porch to be repainted.

This action by the home owner contains both communicative and non-communicative elements. The home owner communicated displeasure with presidential politics, but also caused property damage.

Under the rulings of the Supreme Court, purely communicative conduct may be regulated by the government only in extremely rare circumstances. Conduct that has both speech and non-speech elements, however, may be regulated more readily. Courts must balance the rights of an individual to express viewpoints through action against the rights of individuals who may be impacted by the action. The balancing is complex and often controversial.

Over the years, the Court has developed a series of tests it applies in adjudicating cases in which individuals or groups claim constitutional protection for symbolic speech. First, the Court asks, is the conduct expressive? If not, the First Amendment is not implicated, the inquiry ends, and the government may regulate the conduct. If the conduct *is* expressive, however, the Court then asks the more difficult question: Is the expressive conduct protected by the First Amendment?

Is the Conduct Expressive?

If conduct is expressive, that conduct is "speech." The expressive nature of the conduct is the element that moves action from simply doing to communicating. The home owner is no longer burning a damaged flag in his grill; the home owner is burning it in public for the express purpose of communicating a message.

To determine whether conduct is purely utilitarian or has some communicative elements, the Court asks two questions: (1) Is there an intent to express a message? (2) Is there a likelihood the message will be understood by a witness? If there is no intent to express a message, or if it is not likely that a witness will understand the intended message, the conduct is not expressive, and the First Amendment does not apply. Figure 1 demonstrates the flow of this inquiry.

The Court does not require that a viewer of expressive conduct understand the exact message the actor intends; only a general understanding of the message is necessary. For example, when spectators watched in 1984 as Gregory Lee Johnson burned an American flag outside the meeting-place of the Republican National Convention in Dallas, it was unnecessary that they knew Johnson was demonstrating his distaste for President Ronald Reagan, who was seeking re-nomination. It was sufficient that the spectators understood that Johnson was dissatisfied with some aspect of the

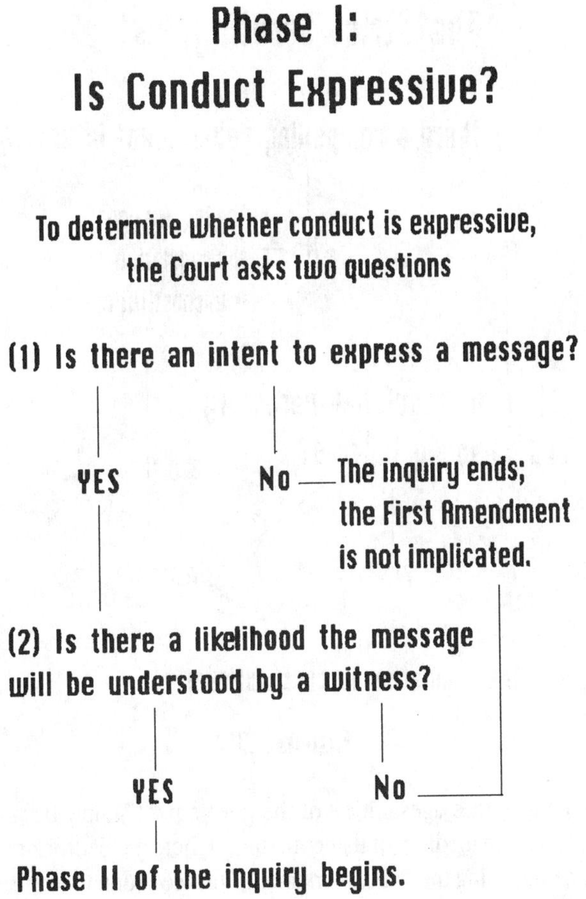

Phase I:
Is Conduct Expressive?

To determine whether conduct is expressive, the Court asks two questions

(1) Is there an intent to express a message?

YES — No — The inquiry ends; the First Amendment is not implicated.

(2) Is there a likelihood the message will be understood by a witness?

YES — No

Phase II of the inquiry begins.

Figure 1

United States or of the U.S. government — those entities symbolized by the flag.

Even though Johnson's action could be interpreted as a demonstration of disgust with Reagan, the Republican Party, the U.S. government *or* the United States itself, Justice William Brennan, upholding Johnson's right to burn the flag, wrote, "The expressive, overtly political nature of this conduct was both intentional and overwhelmingly apparent."[5]

Members of the Court have recognized a wide array of conduct to be expressive: displaying a flag, burning a draft card, burning a cross, saluting a flag, displaying a license plate and nude dancing.[6]

Not all these activities, however, are constitutionally protected. Once an action has been determined to be expressive, the Court must determine whether the expressive conduct is protected by the First Amendment. Cases involving expressive conduct date to the early Twentieth Century, but the Court's first substantive treatment of expressive conduct was in 1968. In *U.S. v. O'Brien,* the Court recognized that burning a draft card as a means of protesting the Selective Service system and U.S. involvement in Vietnam was expressive conduct, but ruled that other concerns outweighed David Paul O'Brien's right to burn the card.[7] In *O'Brien,* the Court, for the first time, delineated the test for determining whether expressive conduct is protected by the First Amendment.

Is the Expressive Conduct Protected?

At first glance, O'Brien's burning of his draft card is remarkably similar to Johnson's burning of a U.S. flag. Both men had audiences, both were expressing distaste with political agendas and both were using an age-old method of destruction to demonstrate that distaste. In both cases, there was an intent to express a message and there was a likelihood that the message would be understood by witnesses.

But the Court found significant differences in the two acts. Ironically, the differences were based primarily upon the intent of the government rather than upon the intent of the actors.

After the Court finds conduct to be expressive, the Court determines whether the conduct may be regulated by examining the rationale behind the government regulation being applied. The Court must determine whether the regulation is directed at the suppression of speech or at some other goal. If the purpose of the regulation is to restrict speech, the Court applies what it calls a "strict scrutiny test" to determine whether the regulation is constitutional; if the regulation is not directed at the suppression of speech, but at some other goal, the Court applies a test of intermediate scrutiny. Figure 2 demonstrates the flow of this inquiry.

Strict Scrutiny. Attorneys for Texas argued to the Texas and U.S. supreme courts that the state's purpose in adopting its flag desecration act was to protect the U.S. flag as a symbol of patriotism and unity. And, the attorneys argued, the state had the right to do so. The Court agreed that protecting the flag is a noble cause. The method used to protect the flag, however, was directed at the suppression of free speech; the statute would allow expression supporting the state's goals, but would not allow expression

---

[5] *Texas v. Johnson,* 491 U.S. 397, 406 (1989).

[6] *Stromberg v. California,* 283 U.S. 359 (1931); *U.S. v. O'Brien,* 391 U.S. 367 (1968); *R.A.V. v. St. Paul,* 505 U.S. 377 (1992); *West Virginia Board of Education v. Barnette,* 319 U.S. 624 (1943); *Wooley v. May-*

nard, 430 U.S. 705 (1977); *Barnes v. Glen Theatre,* 501 U.S. 560 (1991).

[7] 391 U.S. 367 (1968)

Phase II:
Is The Expressive Conduct Protected By The First Amendment?

Is the government regulation aimed directly at the suppression of free expression?

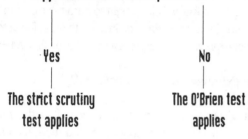

Yes — The strict scrutiny test applies

No — The O'Brien test applies

Figure 2

The Strict Scrutiny Test

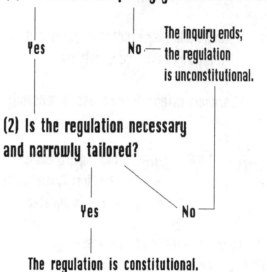

(1) Is there a compelling government interest?

Yes

No — The inquiry ends; the regulation is unconstitutional.

(2) Is the regulation necessary and narrowly tailored?

Yes

No

The regulation is constitutional.

Figure 3

contrary to those goals. Because the statute was directly related to the suppression of speech, therefore, strict scrutiny was required to determine whether the statute was constitutional. Figure 3 demonstrates the flow of the strict scrutiny test, which consists of two parts:

(1) Is there a compelling government interest for the regulation? The government interest advocated by the regulation must be more than a passing interest; it must be vitally important to governmental operations. In *Texas v. Johnson,* Justice Brennan recognized that there may be a compelling government interest in protecting the flag as a symbol of national unity. National unity is important, Justice Brennan wrote, and the flag may be the single best symbol of the United States and that unity.

(2) Is the regulation necessary and narrowly tailored to advance the government interest? A necessary regulation is one that is essential, rather than optional, for the advancement of the government's interest. To survive strict scrutiny, a regulation must be necessary, but it must also be narrowly tailored. Being narrowly tailored means that the regulation goes as far as necessary to advance the government interest, but does not overstep its bounds. In the area of speech, a narrowly tailored regulation is one that does not encompass protected speech in its prohibitions. Justice Brennan said the Texas act was not narrowly tailored. Even though protecting the flag is a compelling government interest, an individual's right to criticize the government is powerful. The government may promote the flag, Justice Brennan wrote, but may

not control messages critical of the government simply because the flag is the medium of that criticism. "If there is a bedrock principle underlying the First Amendment," Justice Brennan wrote, "it is that the government may not prohibit the expression of an idea simply because society finds the idea itself offensive or disagreeable."[8]

Intermediate Scrutiny: The O'Brien Test. The Court came to a different conclusion in *U.S. v. O'Brien.*

When David Paul O'Brien burned his draft card, he was, like Johnson, voicing his discontent with governmental policy, specifically, with Selective Service. At the time, all men in the United States who were eighteen or older were required by federal law to carry draft cards until they surrendered them to Selective Service officials upon induction into the armed forces or until they were no longer eligible for the draft.

O'Brien did not deny burning his draft card but contended that the law prohibiting the destruction or mutilation of the card was unconstitutional because it inhibited free speech and served no legitimate legislative purpose. He was found guilty in federal district court in Massachusetts of violating the law. The First U.S. Cir-

---

[8] *Texas v. Johnson,* 491 U.S. at 414.

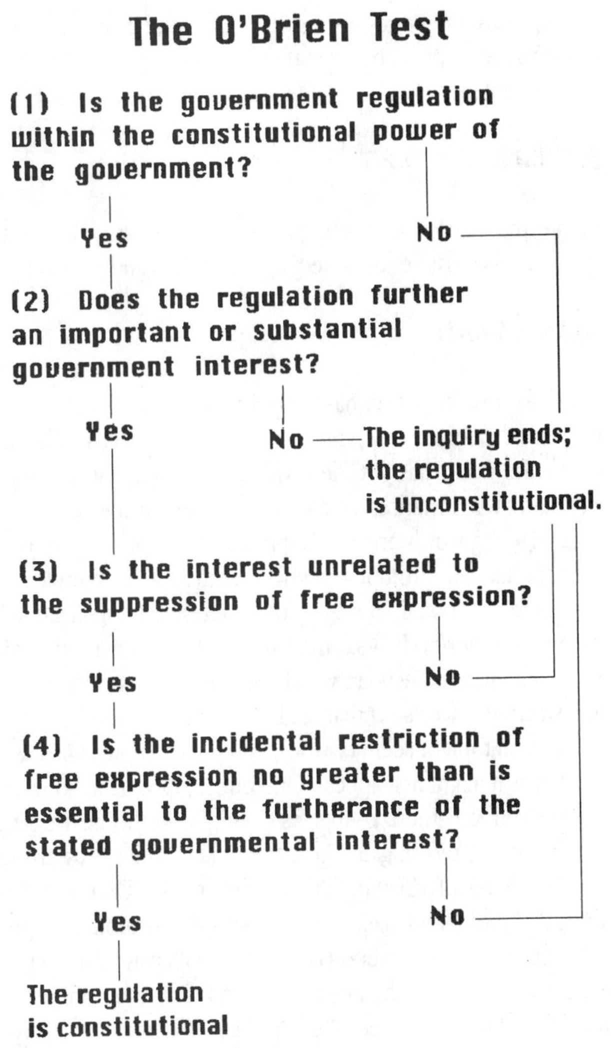

The O'Brien Test

(1) Is the government regulation within the constitutional power of the government?

Yes — No

(2) Does the regulation further an important or substantial government interest?

Yes — No — **The inquiry ends; the regulation is unconstitutional.**

(3) Is the interest unrelated to the suppression of free expression?

Yes — No

(4) Is the incidental restriction of free expression no greater than is essential to the furtherance of the stated governmental interest?

Yes — No

The regulation is constitutional

Figure 4

cuit Court of Appeals found the statute unconstitutional but affirmed the conviction on grounds that O'Brien should have been convicted of the less serious offense of not having possession of the draft card. Both the government and O'Brien appealed to the Supreme Court.

Chief Justice Earl Warren, writing for a seven-member majority, did not dispute O'Brien's contention that the burning of a draft card was expressive conduct. Instead, based upon the assumption that the conduct was sufficient to implicate the First Amendment, he took issue with O'Brien's argument that freedom of expression includes all modes of "communication of ideas by conduct." Wrote Warren: "We cannot accept the view that an apparently limitless variety of conduct can be labeled 'speech' whenever

the person engaging in the conduct intends thereby to express an idea." When speech and nonspeech elements combine in some form of expression, Warren wrote, a sufficiently important governmental interest in regulating the nonspeech element of the communication can justify incidental limitations of First Amendment freedoms.[9] Warren delineated a four-part test for determining when the government regulation is justified:[10]

(1) Is the regulation within the constitutional power of the government? The government has a right to raise and support armies, the Court noted, and to make all necessary and proper laws to that end; therefore, the Selective Service Act was within the power of the government.

(2) Does the regulation further an important or substantial government interest? Because the draft card and other Selective Service documents further the smooth and proper functioning of the system, Congress has a legitimate and substantial interest in preventing their wanton and unrestrained destruction and assuring their continuing availability by punishing people who knowingly and willfully destroy them.

(3) Is the governmental interest unrelated to the suppression of free expression? The non-destruction requirements of the law were aimed at the continued smooth operation of the Selective Service System, the Court held. That is, they were aimed at the non-communicative aspects of O'Brien's conduct and nothing else.

(4) Is the incidental restriction of free expression no greater than is essential to the furtherance of the stated governmental interest? The Court noted that the restriction O'Brien violated was narrowly drawn.

O'Brien's conviction was upheld, therefore. More importantly, however, the Court established a test to be applied in cases involving expressive conduct. The flow of the O'Brien Test is demonstrated in Figure 4.

Summary

Based on *U.S. v. O'Brien*, *Texas v. Johnson* and other Supreme Court cases, the Court follows a carefully delineated course in dealing with expressive conduct. That course is described in Figure 5. In traveling that course, the Court must answer some specific questions.

I. Is the conduct expressive? The conduct is expressive if there is an intent to express a message and if there is a likelihood

[9] *O'Brien*, 391 U.S. at 376-77.
[10] *Id.* at 377-82.

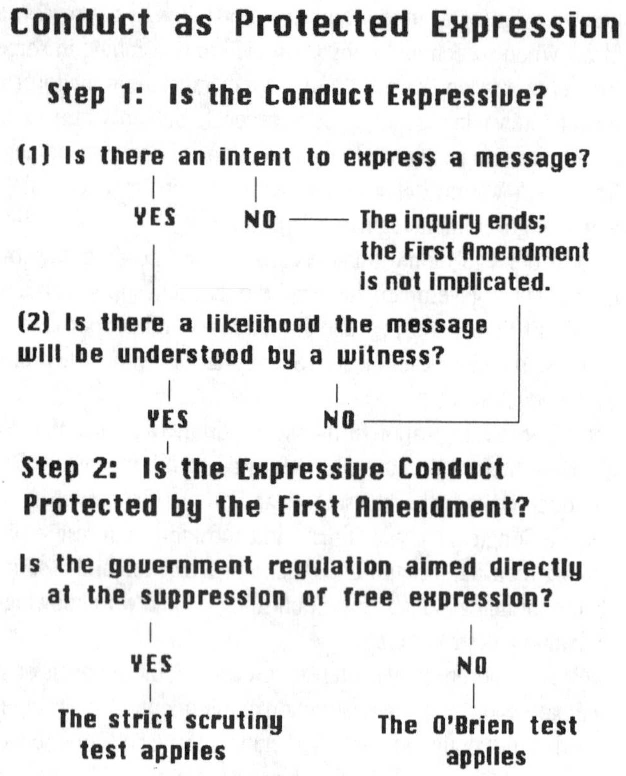

Conduct as Protected Expression

Step 1: Is the Conduct Expressive?

(1) Is there an intent to express a message?

     YES   NO —— The inquiry ends; the First Amendment is not implicated.

(2) Is there a likelihood the message will be understood by a witness?

     YES   NO ——

Step 2: Is the Expressive Conduct Protected by the First Amendment?

Is the government regulation aimed directly at the suppression of free expression?

     YES   NO

The strict scrutiny test applies   The O'Brien test applies

Figure 5

the message will be understood. If there is either no intent or no likelihood of understanding, the conduct is not expressive, the First Amendment is not implicated, and the inquiry is over. If the conduct is expressive, however, the inquiry continues.

II. Is the expressive conduct protected? The path to determining whether expressive conduct is protected begins with the rationale behind the government regulation. The Court first determines whether the regulation is aimed directly at speech? If it is, the Court applies a strict scrutiny test by asking two questions: (1) Does the regulation advance a compelling government interest; (2) is the regulation necessary and narrowly tailored? If the answer to either question is no, the regulation is unconstitutional. If the answer to both questions is yes, the regulation is constitutional.

If the Court finds that the regulation is not aimed specifically at speech, it applies a test of intermediate scrutiny, called the O'Brien Test, to determine whether the regulation is constitutional. Under the test, a regulation is required to meet four points: (1) The activity regulated must be within the constitutional power of the government; (2) the regulation must advance an important government interest; (3) the government interest must be unrelated to

the suppression of free expression; and (4) the incidental restriction on speech must be no greater than necessary to advance the government interest.

SPEECH AS CONDUCT

Before the discussion of conduct and speech is complete, two special cases must be addressed: fighting words and picketing.

Fighting Words

Thus far, this discussion has centered on conduct that takes on the role of speech, that is, conduct that is expressive. Another area of law the Court has wrestled with is the regulation of fighting words, that is, instances when speech takes on the role of conduct. Fighting words are words that are so vile or obnoxious that they are likely to prompt a physical reaction. For example, what might the result be if, during a hotly contested football game between two bitter rivals — say the University of Virginia and Virginia Tech — a Virginia Tech fan wandered into the U.Va. student section wearing a sweatshirt that read "Fuck the Cavaliers?"

The result might seem obvious, and the example is not as far-fetched as it might first appear. On April 26, 1968, Paul Robert Cohen walked into the Los Angeles County Courthouse wearing a jacket bearing the slogan "Fuck the draft." Cohen was arrested and convicted of violating that portion of the California Penal Code that prohibited maliciously and willfully disturbing the peace or quiet of any neighborhood or person by offensive conduct.

The Supreme Court, however, found that the conduct was speech and was protected. Three justices disagreed. Harry Blackmun, Warren Burger and Hugo Black argued, in a dissent drafted by Blackmun, that "Cohen's absurd and immature antic ... was mainly conduct and little speech."[11] They said Cohen should have found another way of expressing his opinion on the draft.

In the majority opinion, however, Justice John Marshall Harlan pointed out the importance of the emotive as well as the cognitive force of speech:

We cannot overlook the fact, because it is well illustrated by the episode involved here, that much linguistic expression serves a dual communicative function: it conveys not only ideas capable of relatively precise, detached explication, but otherwise inexpressible emotions as well. In fact, words are often chosen as

---

11 *Cohen v. California*, 403 U.S. 15, 27 (1971)(Blackmun, J., dissenting).

much for their emotive as their cognitive force. We cannot sanction the view that the Constitution, while solicitous of the cognitive content of individual speech, has little or no regard for the emotive function which, practically speaking, may often be the more important element of the overall message sought to be communicated.[12]

Even though the Court found Cohen's "absurd and immature antic" to be protected speech, the antic demonstrates the type of speech that can take on the role of conduct: The words become like actions. Either Cohen or the reckless Virginia Tech football fan could have been confronted by a person willing to respond to the words with physical violence.

The Court first recognized the so-called "fighting words" doctrine in 1942 in the case of *Chaplinsky v. New Hampshire*. A Jehovah's Witness was arrested for calling a police officer a "damned fascist" and a "God damned racketeer." The Court upheld the conviction, calling the verbal assault an attack of fighting words, that is, words "which by their very utterance inflict injury or tend to incite an immediate breach of the peace." Such utterances, the Court said, "are no essential part of any expression of ideas, and are of such slight social value as a step to truth that any benefit that may be deprived from them is clearly out-weighed by the social interests in order and morality."[13]

Not only must the words be particularly violent or obnoxious, they must be aimed directly at an individual for the fighting-words doctrine to apply, as the Court demonstrated seven years later in *Terminiello v. Chicago*.[14] A well-publicized speech by a right-wing anti-Semite was met by a crowd of protesters, some of whom were able to break into the meeting hall where the speech was held. The speaker, Arthur Terminiello, repeatedly referred to the protesters as "scum" or "slimy scum." The speech so stirred members of the crowd that police indicated they feared unrest. Like Chaplinsky, Terminiello was convicted of breaching the peace by using language that would stir the public to anger. In Terminiello's case, however, the Court reversed. Justice William O. Douglas, in one of his few free-speech majority opinions, wrote that free speech is designed to invoke dispute:

It may indeed best serve its high purpose when it induces a condition of unrest, creates dissatisfaction with conditions as they are, or even stirs people to anger. Speech is often provocative and challenging. It may strike at prejudices and preconceptions and have profound unsettling effects as it presses for acceptance of an idea. That is why freedom of speech, though not absolute ... is nevertheless protected against censorship or punishment, unless shown likely to produce a clear and present danger of a serious substantive evil that rises far above public inconvenience, annoyance, or unrest. There is no room under our Constitution for a more restrictive view.[15]

What's the difference in the two cases? *Terminiello* did not involve a face-to-face confrontation. In an important lower court case, the Illinois Supreme Court upheld the rights of neo-Nazis to march in Skokie, Illinois, displaying the swastika, which an appellate court ordered removed because of the fighting-words doctrine.[16] The state supreme court recognized, however, that the march removed the speech from that one-on-one dialogue to a more abstract insult. Ironically, after winning the right to march in Skokie, the neo-Nazis never did.

The confrontational nature of language has been important to the Supreme Court as well. The Court has consistently struck down as vague and overbroad state laws prohibiting the use of abusive, menacing, insulting or profane language, if those statutes had not been narrowed by state courts to focus on fighting words.[17] Though the Court has upheld convictions for the use of abusive language when there was a threat of a riot, the threat must be relatively direct. A speaker's shout that "We'll take the fucking streets," for example, was not ruled to be fighting words, nor did it tend to incite a riot, because the speaker was obviously not referring to an imminent action, but, rather, to an action some time in the future.[18]

The Court has faced few fighting words cases, but did so in 1993. In *R.A.V. v. St. Paul*,[19] it held that a conviction for burning a cross in the yard of a black couple who had moved into a predominantly white neighborhood could not stand under the fighting-words doctrine. The cross that the juvenile burned didn't cause much of a fire — it was made from broken chair legs — but the Min-

---

[12] *Id.* at 25.

[13] 315 U.S. 568, 571 (1942).

[14] 337 U.S. 1 (1949)

---

[15] *Id.* at 4.

[16] *Village of Skokie v. National Socialist Party of America,* 69 Ill. 2d 605, 373 N.E.2d 21 (1978).

[17] See, e.g., *Gooding v. Wilson,* 405 U.S. 518 (1972); *Plummer v. City of Columbus, Ohio,* 414 U.S. 2 (1973); *Lewis v. New Orleans,* 415 U.S. 130 (1974).

[18] *Hess v. Indiana,* 414 U.S. 105 (1973). See also, *Feiner v. New York,* 340 U.S. 315 (1951).

[19] 505 U.S. 377 (1992).

nesota Supreme Court said the act amounted to fighting words. It upheld the conviction for violating a city ordinance prohibiting the burning of a cross, the placing of a Nazi swastika, or other similar action for the purpose of arousing anger, alarm or resentment "on the basis of race, color, creed, religion or gender." The Supreme Court reversed.

The Court said St. Paul could prohibit fighting words but that the ordinance allowed fighting words unless those words were aimed at a member of one of the classes specified. It would be acceptable under the ordinance, the Court said, to use fighting words against someone based on political affiliation, union or non-union membership or sexual preference: "The First Amendment does not permit St. Paul to impose special prohibitions on those speakers who express views on disfavored subjects."[20] The Court recognized that the conduct was reprehensible but ruled that the subject was being unconstitutionally punished under an ordinance that advanced what amounted to viewpoint discrimination.

Picketing

The Court has recognized that picketing is a time-honored method of expressing a message. It is often used by people who cannot afford to publish their complaints, and it is generally aimed at a narrow problem. Therefore, the Court has granted picketers broad protection, still balancing their rights against those of other individuals and against public peace and safety. It has held that peaceful picketing cannot be licensed, that restrictions on picketing must be content-neutral and that picketing cannot be banned from public property.

One of the Court's most important rulings on picketing came near the middle of the century. In striking down Alabama's statute prohibiting picketing a place of business, the Court noted that freedom of speech and press "are among the fundamental personal rights and liberties which are secured to all persons" by the Constitution, and that picketing was one of the activities that "may enlighten the public on the nature and causes" of public debate.[21]

The rights of individuals to picket or distribute information often depend upon where the picketing occurs and the rationale behind government regulations restricting the picketing. Picketing in an area designated a public forum — like a park or sidewalk — is almost always protected, if the picketing is peaceful and if it does not interfere with other valid uses of the public forum.[22] Even in the absence of a public forum, the Court has held that absolute bans on First Amendment activity — including picketing — may be unconstitutional because the government cannot justify such bans.[23]

Picketing on private property is more problematic. Often, however, even the private property rights of individuals and corporations must give way when individuals choose to express themselves by picketing. While the Court has recognized that owners have certain rights over their property, when the property is used for a public purpose and when it's obvious that the picketers are expressing their own viewpoints and are not speaking for the property owners, the Court has allowed picketing on private property.[24]

The Court, however, has also allowed some picketing to be restricted, including in shopping malls and at private residences. It also allowed the military to restrict picketing and the distribution of literature on military bases — even those portions of the bases open to the public.[25]

Finally, the Court has allowed restrictions on persons who picket abortion clinics and attempt to prevent women from obtaining abortions. The Court held that restrictions on picketing were not aimed at the anti-abortion message of the activists, but were aimed at conduct, that is, at efforts by the activists to interfere with people entering or leaving the clinics. The Court also upheld the use of zones in which picketing could be banned but held that 300-foot buffer zones were unreasonable and burdened more speech than necessary to serve the government's interest in guaranteeing the free flow of traffic.[26] The Court also held that a so-called "floating buffer zone" requiring picketers to stay at least fifteen feet from people or vehicles entering or leaving the clinics violated the First Amendment because it overburdened speech.[27]

---

[20] *Id.* at 391.

[21] *Thornhill v. Alabama*, 310 U.S. 88, 95 & 104 (1940).

[22] See, e.g., *Gregory v. Chicago*, 394 U.S. 111 (1969); *Henry v. Rock Hill*, 376 U.S. 776 (1964); *Cox v. Louisiana*, 379 U.S. 536 & 559 (1965); *Bachellor v. Maryland*, 397 U.S. 564 (1970)

[23] *Board of Airport Com's v. Jews for Jesus*, 482 U.S. 569 (1987).

[24] See, e.g., *Amalgamated Food Employees Union v. Logan Valley Plaza, Inc.*, 391 U.S. 308 (1968); *Lloyd Corp., Ltd. v. Tanner*, 407 U.S. 551 (1972); *Pruneyard Shopping Center v. Robins*, 447 U.S. 74 (1974).

[25] See, e.g., *Greer v. Spock*, 424 U.S. 828 (1976). But see also, *Flower v. U.S.*, 407 U.S. 197 (1972), and *U.S. v. Albertini*, 472 U.S. 675 (1985)

[26] *Madsen v. Women's Health Clinic, Inc.*, 512 U.S. 753 (1994).

[27] *Schenck v. Pro-Choice Network of Western New York*, 117 S.Ct. 855 (1997).

Summary

Just as conduct can take on the role of speech, speech can some-times become like conduct. Words can be so vile or obnoxious that they prompt a physical response. Courts allow such words to be regulated but take care to ensure that governments don't trammel free expression in their efforts to protect other individual rights. Statutes prohibiting offensive or abusive language, for ex-ample, have routinely been held to be unconstitutional unless they have been narrowed so they only prohibit fighting words.

In addition, courts have recognized the value of picketing and have allowed individuals to picket on both private and public property. Picketing in areas traditionally held to be public fora is almost always allowed. Picketing on private property is more prob-lematic, but the Supreme Court has often allowed such picketing.

FOR ADDITIONAL READING

Baker, C. Edwin. *Human Liberty and Freedom of Speech.* New York: Oxford University Press, 1989.

Emerson, Thomas I. *The System of Freedom of Expression.* New York: Vintage, 1970.

Haiman, Franklyn S. *Speech and Law in a Free Society.* Chicago: University of Chicago Press, 1981.

Hopkins, W. Wat. *Mr. Justice Brennan and Freedom of Expres-sion.* New York: Praeger, 1991.

Katsh, M. Ethan, ed. *Taking Sides — Clashing Views of Contro-versial Legal Issues.* Guilford, Conn.: Dushkin, 1995.

Smolla, Rodney A. *Free Speech in an Open Society.* New York: Vintage, 1993.

4

Prior Restraint

By Steven Helle

"Censorship" is a word casually used in editorials or angry speeches to denounce everything from postal rate increases, to obscenity prosecutions, to theft of campus newspapers. But the term meant something specific in historical usage, and it is rarely what writers or speakers mean today. Those who denounce contemporary attempts to control speech, however, are taking advantage of the considerable distaste that became associated with the historical form of censorship.

Therein lies the dilemma that runs throughout this chapter. The battles against the historical form of censorship have been won, and an extensive body of law seems to have extinguished the prospect of future censorship as long as the First Amendment retains any vitality. But is it advisable to expand the notion of censorship and the extent of protection available under the First Amendment in order to combat innovative forms of regulation that accomplish much the same thing as historical censorship? Or would stretching the First Amendment to offer the same degree of protection against more types of control ultimately dilute and weaken the protection provided, just as a balloon that expands becomes thinner — and more susceptible to breaking?

HISTORICAL BACKGROUND

Much of U.S. law has its roots in English law. England, of course, imposed its law on its American colonies. But even after the American Revolution, twelve of the thirteen newly established states expressly adopted the common law of England as their own. Lawyers on this side of the Atlantic educated themselves primarily by reading Sir William Blackstone's *Commentaries on the Law of England*. "In the first century of American independence, the *Commentaries* were not merely an approach to the study of law; for most lawyers they constituted all there was of the law," wrote Daniel J. Boorstin, Librarian of Congress emeritus.[1] Because English law influenced not only U.S. law, but the framers of the U.S. Constitution as well, it is important to trace the English experience with censorship to better understand how and why U.S. law on the subject evolved the way it did.

Printing on a press was introduced to England in 1476, and not long afterward the Crown attempted to impose controls. The Roman Catholic Church was interested in suppressing what it considered heretical opinions. In 1501, Pope Alexander VI attempted to require printing to be licensed. In 1517, Martin Luther posted his *95 Theses* on the door of the Castle Church in Wittenberg, Germany, questioning the practice of contributing to the church as a means of buying forgiveness for sins. The Church burned the writings of Luther and others who questioned its authority or practices, dismissed them from the Church, prohibited the faithful from reading the works and issued rebuttals. But the demand — and profit for publishing the works — only grew.

---

[1] Daniel J. Boorstin, *The Mysterious Science of the Law* (Boston: Beacon Press, 1941), p. 3.

King Henry VIII

King Henry VIII of England, at the request of the Church, used this religious debate as the impetus for asserting the Crown's control over printing. Henry, in fact, secretly encouraged the reformers while publicly condemning them, even publishing his own response to Luther. By appearing to lead the effort to denounce and control the heretics, he hoped to win the favor of Rome and the Pope's blessing for his divorce from Queen Catherine.

When the clergy was unable to control the speech of the heretics, Henry issued his first list of prohibited books in 1529, and several booksellers and others who possessed the banned books were executed. In 1530, Henry issued a proclamation establishing the first non-religious licensing system. He decreed that no person could print any religious book until it was examined and approved by the clergy, and every printer would obey or "answere to the kinges highnes, at his uttermost peryll." Executions, fines and imprisonments followed. When Henry did not get the dispensation he desired from Rome, he switched sides and began executing the Catholic faithful.

As historian Fredrick Siebert noted, Henry was fully aware of the influence of the printing press in easing his break with Rome. He was an early and excellent master of manipulating public opinion by controlling the press, and he certainly had the tools and will to exercise that control to its fullest. "His policy henceforth was not only to eliminate undesirable reading matter but to stimulate the circulation of that which would strengthen his cause," Siebert wrote.[2]

Thus, the Proclamation of 1538 extended the king's censorship to all printing, not just religious writings, including "errors and seditiouse opinions." Sedition, or criticism of government, had no ecclesiastical foundation. The matter is muddled because Henry had made himself the head of the Church of England. Therefore, an attack on the Church could be considered an attack on the state, or vice versa. But for the first time, speech that was expressly political was subject to censorship through a licensing system, and Henry's political appointees, not the Church, would decide what violated the regulations and deserved the King's displeasure. As Siebert noted: "The shift in the administration of the licensing regulations from the clergy to state officers was one of Henry's contributions to the regulation of the press. The method was subsequently adopted on the continent, even in Catholic countries."[3]

---

[2] Fredrick S. Siebert, *Freedom of the Press in England, 1476-1776* (Urbana: University of Illinois Press, 1965), p. 47.

[3] *Id.* at 49.

Henry also instituted the practice of requiring printers to post bonds, which would be forfeited if their publications offended him. He offered printers "privileges" or copyrights in certain works, which protected them from piracy. And the Tudor sovereigns who followed him engaged in a brilliant maneuver by recognizing a Stationer's Company, or organization of officially sanctioned printers. Just as broadcasters in this country did in the 1920s, these early printers actually sought government regulation. In the same way that the broadcasters favored by the U.S. government gained monopolies on the use of certain radio frequencies, the favored English printers obtained monopolies on the printing of certain works, such as the Bible, which were very profitable.

But the monopolies served the interests of the government, as well, because the economic interests of the printers ensured that they would do nothing to alienate the government and risk losing their monopolies. Furthermore, the government gained an ally in controlling unlicensed printing. The members of the Stationer's Company were given broad powers of search and seizure to protect their monopolies from renegade printers. Their zealousness in exercising these powers led directly to the enactment of the Fourth Amendment to the U.S. Constitution, prohibiting unreasonable searches and seizures and requiring warrants based on probable cause.

Henry's licensing system endured until the close of the Seventeenth Century, and it was more or less successful, depending on how aggressively it was enforced or evaded at any given time. It took a brave printer to risk forfeiture of property, fines, imprisonment, torture, amputation and execution for flouting the system. The Stationer's Company sniffed out the trail of a press that had been secretly moved all over England to avoid capture in 1589. John Hodgkins was finally arrested and charged with printing unlicensed Puritan tracts critical of the Church of England. He refused to confess, was tortured, jailed for a year and then put on the rack. There is no record of his fate after that.

Ingenious printers and authors attempted to circumvent the regulations, forging the signatures of censors, changing portions of manuscripts after they had been approved or by writing ostensibly fictional dramas whose characters everybody understood to represent real-life figures. But the stakes, depending on the political temper of the times and one's choice of political patrons, could be high.

Parliament eventually took control of the licensing system from the Crown in 1643, but the structure of censorship remained essentially what it had been in 1538. Publication came to be subject to other forms of governmental regulation, primarily prosecutions for seditious libel and taxation, and the penalties associated with those forms of regulation could be just as severe. But the licensing system was distinctive not only because it was first, but because it applied to every publication, it gave the government complete discretion regarding the content of each publication, and it occurred in advance of publication. This latter feature indicates why this censorship was called "prior restraint."

Understandably, the members of the Stationer's Company did not object to the licensing (unless, as sometimes happened, certain members obtained licenses that others did not). Objections came from those without licenses — and the philosophy and value of freedom of the press began to take shape. Two Puritans who wrote an unlicensed religious pamphlet in 1572 argued that they had presented the tract to Parliament and, in doing so, they should have the privilege of "writing and speaking freely." This, according to Siebert, was the first time that the ancient right of Englishmen to petition Parliament was translated into an argument for a free press.[4] The pair was sentenced to a year in prison, however.

Milton and Areopagitica

In 1644 John Milton presented in *Areopagitica,* which was itself unlicensed, what law professor Vincent Blasi has labeled the classic attack on prior restraint. Ironically, the impetus for this great treatise arose from Milton having been cited for an earlier unlicensed tract on divorce, which was no easier for him to obtain than it had been for King Henry VIII. Milton framed his argument broadly:

> And though all the windes of doctrin were let loose to play upon the earth, so Truth be in the field, we do injuriously by licencing and prohibiting to misdoubt her strenth. Let her and Falshood grapple; who ever knew Truth put to the wors, in a free and open encounter.... [I]t is not possible for man to sever the wheat from the tares, the good fish from the other frie; that must be the Angels Ministery at the end of all mortall things. Yet if all cannot be of one mind, as who looks they should be? This doubtles is more wholsome, more prudent, and more Christian that many be tolerated, rather than all compell'd.[5]

Although it is an eloquent tribute to diverse expression without government suppression or endorsement of any one opinion, there is the view that Milton really was more interested in his divorce than in freedom of expression because he became a government censor just seven years after *Areopagitica.* In his defense, however, Professor Jeffery Smith noted that Milton's role as censor primarily involved overseeing publication of the government's own newsletter — and, as censor, he had to recall his arguments from *Areopagitica* when he was questioned for approving a catechism that Parliament afterward condemned. Smith noted that, although Milton's arguments showed up in a few other tracts in his time, he probably had more impact in later centuries as philosophers, statesmen and jurists crafted libertarian theory.[6]

An abridged version of *Areopagitica* was published in 1693, but when the Licensing Act came up for renewal in 1694, the treatise apparently had no influence on the decision by the House of Commons to let the act lapse. A list of eighteen reasons for not renewing the Act was presented in the House of Commons. The reasons, thought to be written by John Locke, had to do with the vagueness of the licensing standards, the impediments to free trade, the ineffectiveness of the system, and other objections unrelated to the philosophy of freedom of the press.

Under the two-party political system that had evolved, censors risked offending somebody important whether they licensed a publication or not. Important people did not want to undertake the task of censoring, and they did not trust unimportant people to do it. As Thomas Macaulay wrote in his *History of England* nearly two centuries later, "On the great question of principle, on the question whether the liberty of unlicensed printing be, on the whole, a blessing or a curse to society, not a word is said."[7] After more than a century and a half, licensing was dead in England.

---

[4] *Id.* at 96.

[5] John Milton, *Areopagitica* (Eng. Rep. 1972)(1st ed. n.p. 1644), pp. 74-76.

---

[6] Jeffrey A. Smith, *Printers and Press Freedom — The Ideology of Early American Journalism* (New York: Oxford University Press, 1988), pp. 33-35, 40.

[7] Thomas B. Macaulay, *The History of England from the Accession of James II,* vol. 5 (Chicago: Belford, Clarke & Co., 1889), pp. 16-17. Macaulay observed that the event produced no excitement and was little noted, probably because Parliament was preoccupied with the funeral for Queen Mary. But the vote by the House of Commons not to renew the Licensing Act did "more for liberty and for civilisation than the Great Charter or the Bill of Rights," at 15-16. The House of Lords did not object, probably because it assumed a different bill for regulating the press would be introduced — and, indeed, one was, but it did not clear committee before the session ended. Macaulay noted that "petty grievances did what Milton's *Areopagitica* failed to do."

The American Experience

Licensing continued in the American colonies until the 1720s. In 1723, the Massachusetts legislature, stung by constant criticism from James Franklin, publisher of the *New England Courant,* ordered Franklin never to publish the *Courant* or any other publication, "Except it be first Supervised, by the Secretary of this Province." Franklin published a new, unlicensed edition and went into hiding, making his brother Benjamin publisher. The legislature had not prohibited his soon-to-be-famous brother from publishing without a license.

James was eventually arrested, and the legislature sought an indictment from the grand jury, which historian Leonard Levy described as the government's mistake. The grand jury refused to indict, "probably motivated by a detestation of the licensing system which had ended a generation earlier in England.... Thus, Franklin went luckily free, and prior restraint of the press was at an end in Massachusetts," Levy wrote.[8]

Blackstone accurately summarized the law on both sides of the Atlantic when, in the late 1760s, he wrote in his *Commentaries* perhaps the most famous lines regarding the prior restraint doctrine:

> The *liberty of the press* is indeed essential to the nature of a free state; but this consists in laying no *previous* restraints upon publications, and not in freedom from censure for criminal matter when published. Every freeman has an undoubted right to lay what sentiments he pleases before the public: to forbid this is to destroy the freedom of the press: but if he publishes what is improper, mischievous, or illegal, he must take the consequences of his own temerity.[9]

Freedom from prior restraint looked like quite a lot when measured against the lack of any freedom whatsoever just a few generations before. If subsequent punishment remained an option, that may only seem to be meager progress when viewed from the vantage point of more than two centuries later. But there were voices, even as Blackstone wrote, who argued that freedom *did* mean more, that subsequent punishments such as seditious libel prosecutions were also inconsistent with the notion of freedom of the press.

---

[8] Leonard W. Levy, *Emergence of a Free Press* (New York: Oxford University Press, 1985), p. 32.

[9] William Blackstone, *Commentaries on the Laws of England,* vol. 4 (London: 1769), pp. 151-52.

The Framers' Intent

What did the framers intend in 1791 — a little more than two decades after Blackstone's pronouncement — with the drafting of the First Amendment? Did they intend just to prohibit prior restraint, or did they mean to ban subsequent punishment as well? Professors Smith and Levy lead the opposing camps on this question. The arguments of Levy and the narrow constructionists, those who think the framers were only thinking of prior restraint, can be summarized this way:

• Blackstone's definition of the law was the notion of free speech and press commonly accepted at the time; so it must be what the framers were contemplating.

• If the framers thought they were banning subsequent punishment such as seditious libel prosecutions, then how could many of those same members of Congress, just seven years later, enact the Alien and Sedition Act of 1798 with the express intent of punishing people who criticized government?

• Prosecutions for seditious libel may have ended with the John Peter Zenger trial in 1735, but state legislatures brought citizens up on contempt charges for criticizing government at least twenty times after that date and before passage of the First Amendment, thus indicating endorsement of subsequent punishment as an alternative to prior restraint.

The broad constructionists, who think the First Amendment went beyond banning prior restraint, counter:

• Blackstone may have summarized the English common law that had been practiced up to his time, but he was not summarizing U.S. law, and, indeed, why have a First Amendment at all if it was only intended to commemorate the common law supposedly already in place?

• The American experience with free press far exceeded the English common law. Not only were there no judicial prosecutions for seditious libel since 1735 and no examples of legislative contempt charges after independence in 1776, but politicians, printers and others exercised considerable freedom and espoused a distinctly libertarian theory of a free press in the century before the First Amendment. In short, how could there be so much freedom in practice if the law was so repressive?

• James Madison, author of the First Amendment, passionately proclaimed that the Sedition Act violated the First Amendment and criticized the Federalist party members of Congress for returning America to "ancient ignorance and barbarism." The act expired by its own terms three years later, which was also the time that Republican Thomas Jefferson became president and pardoned the twenty-five or so Republican printers and journalists convicted under the Act. Thus, it can be argued that Congress, as it has demonstrated many times since, was not invoking Constitutional principles in enacting the Sedition Act, but petty party politics.

- Why was a Sedition Act necessary if the common law already contemplated prosecution for seditious libel?

- Finally, the theme of the entire Constitution, not just the Bill of Rights, is the limiting of the power of government — in the words of Madison, "fortify[ing] the rights of the people against the encroachments of the government." A broad conception of freedom of speech and press is fundamental to limiting government and placing power in the people, and a narrow conception of the First Amendment would be inconsistent with the rest of the document. A freedom to criticize government without fear of prosecution is implicit in self-governing; so the First Amendment must have encompassed more than mere freedom from prior restraint.

It is impossible to provide a definitive answer to the question of whether the framers intended the First Amendment to go beyond freedom from prior restraint. Not only was there little debate on the question at the time, but the very issue of "framers' intent" is chimerical because there is no single way to gauge that intent. Whose intent? Do you look to Madison because he wrote the First Amendment, or to a poll of the legislators who voted on the measure, or to the sentiment in the states that ratified it? At what moment is the intent assessed? When proposed, when voted on, or when the framers first spoke on the meaning, which may be many years later? Does it matter if their understanding may be a bit different, more refined, or even contrary a few years later?

It may even be that there actually was no "intent" in the minds of the legislators at the time of passage. They may have deliberately left the First Amendment, and the rest of the Bill of Rights, vague to reduce controversy and facilitate passage. Who can be opposed to freedom of speech and press at that level of abstraction? The legislators may even have been forward-thinking enough to want to leave the interpretation to later generations, which would face problems the framers could not anticipate.

The answer is relevant because current interpretation of the Constitution often begins with an inquiry into the intent of the framers, and several Supreme Court justices seemingly would also end the inquiry there as well. But most jurists and scholars believe that the framers' intent is only one factor and that the Constitution is an evolving document that must take into account chang-

ing circumstances. So, even if we could determine what the framers intended regarding the First Amendment, and even if they only meant it to prohibit prior restraint, that would not necessarily bind current interpretation. Of course, once you break free from the historical intent, current interpretation could yield less as well as more freedom than the framers had in mind.

The strength of the doctrine against prior restraint, dating as it does to well before the First Amendment, is that it carries a certain cachet, a reminder of the baseline of individual freedom. The historical record of suppression and manipulation of the press by governments eager to promote their self-interests serves as evidence of what can happen in the absence of a prior restraint doctrine. The doctrine was created to serve two needs: individual freedom and limited government. At a minimum, the First Amendment was created to serve the same needs, with the same doctrine.

Historical Prior Restraint Defined

A number of other conclusions can be drawn regarding the historical record. The nature of prior restraint that Blackstone, Milton and King Henry VIII had in mind involved a licensing system. Prior restraint, historically understood, involved (1) submitting all proposed publications (2) to government censors (3) who exercised considerable discretion regarding the content to be approved for publication, and it was (4) imposed specifically on publication (5) in advance of the publication.

Prior restraint did not refer to isolated efforts by government officials to suppress, say, a judge's order not to print a libelous tract. Historically, the all-inclusiveness of the regulatory system, the fact that *every* proposed publication must be reviewed and approved, defined prior restraint. Therefore, even the works ultimately approved would still have been subject to prior restraint. "Prior review" is a phrase synonymous with "prior restraint."

Prior restraint meant suppression only by the government, although employers, parents and others obviously suppress speech regularly. Indeed, the historical system of prior restraint did not apply to speech at all, because licensing was a reaction to the introduction of the printing press, although speech in the form of parades or plays, for example, could conceivably be subjected to licensing or a permit system. But any interference with publication, even if it entirely precluded publication, did not constitute prior restraint if undertaken by individuals or institutions not associated with government.

If the standards for what could be published could ever be delineated clearly enough, then a censor's discretion would have been unnecessary, because the violations could be handled easily enough through subsequent punishment of individual violators. The considerable discretion exercised by censors is a critical objection to a system of prior restraint.

Of course, the aspects of prior restraint most commonly associated with it had to do with its narrow focus on controlling the actual publication, in advance of publication. Other government restrictions that might have the effect of inhibiting or entirely foreclosing publication would still not be included within the scope of prior restraint, even if they occurred in advance of publication. Restrictions on news-gathering, for example, or punishment for not revealing a journalist's confidential source would not qualify as prior restraint because they were not directed specifically at stopping publication.

Consider the 1664 case of printer John Twyn. He was caught with proofs for a book claiming the government was accountable to the people and the people were entitled to revolt. Setting the standard for current journalists, Twyn refused to name the author. For his temerity he was hanged, drawn and quartered in 1664 — a vicious and ultimate penalty that certainly precluded his publication. Technically, however, it was not prior restraint because the government did not specifically target publication.

A recent U.S. Supreme Court case is less brutal in its outcome but just as illustrative in its narrow conception of what constitutes as prior restraint. In *Alexander v. United States,*[10] the government had prosecuted the owner of more than a dozen stores and theaters dealing in sexually explicit magazines and videotapes. Four magazines and three videotapes in the inventory were found to be obscene. Under a statute that allows the state to seize any property connected to a pattern of criminal behavior, the court ordered Alexander to forfeit his adult entertainment businesses and their inventories. The government then burned all of the magazines and videotapes.

Alexander maintained that the seizure and destruction of all his magazines and videotapes — which had *not* been found to be obscene and were therefore protected speech — constituted prior restraint. How could a ban on speech be more total than by destroying the speech, he argued? But the Court noted that the term "prior restraint" applied only to orders that forbid certain communications in advance of the communications; this, on the other hand, was only punishment for his obscenity convictions. Prior restraints, by their nature, stop the speech completely and perpetually, Chief Justice William Rehnquist wrote for the Court.

Alexander could theoretically open another adult entertainment store the next day, restock with new inventory, and sell videotapes and magazines, all without obtaining prior approval from any court, Rehnquist wrote. The statute that allowed the government to seize property connected with criminal activity did not differentiate between expressive and non-expressive property, he noted, and to do so would encourage criminals to invest their ill-gotten gains in expressive property to protect them from forfeiture. He added:

> By lumping the forfeiture imposed in this case after a full criminal trial with an injunction enjoining future speech, petitioner stretches the term "prior restraint" well beyond the limits established by our cases. To accept [Alexander's] argument would virtually obliterate the distinction, solidly grounded in our cases, between prior restraints and subsequent punishments.[11]

RATIONALES FOR PRIOR RESTRAINT

The doctrine against prior restraint can be considered merely a stepping-stone in the evolution of free speech and press; having served its purpose, it can now be relegated to the dustbin of history. But there are reasons why distinguishing prior restraint from subsequent punishment still makes sense. The extent to which subsequent punishment is prohibited by the First Amendment is a different question, however, than whether prior restraint should be prohibited. The doctrine against prior restraint accords so wholly with the premises of limited government that disregarding the doctrine can be considered antithetical to the very form of government prescribed by the Constitution.

Why Distinguish Subsequent Punishment?

Distinguishing prior restraint from subsequent punishment is a matter of some significance. The Supreme Court has said the First Amendment offers some protection from subsequent punishment. But the Court has also maintained that prior restraint is the most odious and least tolerable infringement of free speech. It would help to have some justification for the differential treatment beyond the venerable age of the prior restraint doctrine. After all, the point of subsequent punishment is to restrain speech in advance, too. Legislatures enact laws not to fill some prison quota,

---

[10] 509 U.S. 544 (1993).

[11] *Id.* at 549-50.

but to deter conduct, and laws punishing speech are no different. So how does the fact that the governmental force is applied prior to publication make it worse?

Professor Thomas Emerson attempted to answer that question more than forty years ago in an important essay.[12] First, he noted the *breadth* of prior restraint. Because all publications are subject to prior restraint, necessarily more communication is affected than when individual publications are targeted for subsequent punishment.

Second, Emerson emphasized the temporal aspect implicit in the two forms of regulation. With prior restraint, *timing and delay* are in the hands of government. At least with subsequent punishment, the publication reaches the marketplace of ideas and the timing is at the discretion of the publisher. But the requirement of prior review imposes an obvious hitch in the editorial process, and sometimes mere delay can undermine the impact of a story, of which the government is all too aware.

Third, a system of prior restraint has a *propensity toward an adverse decision.* To obtain a judgment after publication, no matter how stacked the trial may be, is still more bother than a system of censorship, which entails, as Emerson wrote, "a simple stroke of the pen." The publisher has practical advantages after publication that are missing beforehand, when the advantages favor government. Thus, Emerson concluded, a system of prior restraint by its very nature makes it easier and more likely that the result will be adverse to the expression.

Similarly, matters of *procedure* favor the government in prior restraint. Prior restraint is an administrative procedure rather than a criminal procedure. In the latter, there are presumptions of innocence, burdens of proof, stricter rules of evidence — all of the trappings that are intended to make courts more deliberative and fairer forums than administrative agencies. Juries are available in criminal proceedings, but in an administrative proceeding the case is heard only by a minor bureaucrat.

Fifth, subsequent punishment provides an opportunity for *public appraisal and criticism.* Administrative proceedings can avoid the glare of publicity, but court hearings have a rich history of openness, which can be said to be more consistent with democracy and the goal of informing public opinion.

Sixth, the *dynamics of prior restraint* are such that absurd and unintelligent administration is foreordained. Emerson noted that the personality of a person willing to be a censor tends toward overzealousness. Not only that, but quite bluntly, "The func-

tion of the censor is to censor," Emerson wrote. The job title does not include promotion of expression: When in doubt, excise. There is far greater risk if the censor approves something that later meets with disapproval than if the censor censors. "The long history of prior restraint reveals over and over again that the personal and institutional forces inherent in the system nearly always end in a stupid, unnecessary, and extreme suppression," Emerson wrote.

Seventh, a system of prior restraint favors *certainty over risk.* Scholars and publishers sometimes note that the advantage of a licensing system is that there is a seal of approval if the work passes review, and the work is presumably immune from further sanction. But in a system of subsequent punishment, a publisher could be punished even if the publisher intended to remain within the law; the publisher may have made an error in interpretation and faced punishment for that error. Prior restraint reduces risk, Emerson agreed, but he added that favoring such a system implies a "philosophy of willingness to conform to official opinion and a ... timidity in asserting rights that bodes ill for a spirited and healthy expression of unorthodox and unaccepted opinion."

Finally, prior restraint systems have greater *effectiveness* going for them. When it comes to enforcement, the question is only whether the publication received prior approval. Everybody understands the rules of prior restraint. Indeed, the virtue of the system is its simplicity, at least from government's perspective. Cases are open and shut. Publishers either obey or they don't, and most do. Thus, prior restraint can be distinguished from subsequent punishment, not only definitionally, but rationally. "These ... considerations which underlie the doctrine of prior restraint ... are the reasons why the doctrine is not simply an arbitrary historical accident, but a rational principle of fundamental weight in the application of the First Amendment," Emerson concluded.

Premises of Prior Restraint

Apart from the definition, differentiation or appropriate treatment of subsequent punishment, prior restraint would be contrary to the First Amendment simply because it is inconsistent with a constitutional system of limited government. Professor Vincent Blasi, with a nod to Milton's *Areopagitica,* identified three premises underlying any system that endorses prior restraint, all of which are inconsistent with limited government and the libertarian theory that spawned the First Amendment: [13]

12 Thomas I. Emerson, "The Doctrine of Prior Restraint," *Law and Contemporary Problems* 20 (1955): 648.

13 Vincent Blasi, "Toward a Theory of Prior Restraint: The Central Linkage," *Minnesota Law Review* 66 (1981): 11, 69-82, 85.

1. Prior restraint implies trust in the state rather than in the individual and public.

2. Speech is too risky in a democracy.

3. Individuals should have no autonomy from the state.

Blasi believes censorship to be an indignity to both writers and readers because the inherent paternalism of the state associated with censorship implies a general distrust of speakers and audiences. The state is a "suspicious, omnipresent tutor" if it must oversee and approve everything that is disseminated. "No system of political authority premised on the consent of the governed can admit the state to that role, whatever the behavioral consequences," Blasi wrote.

Preoccupation with government power is a trademark of the prior restraint doctrine and libertarian theory generally. Some contemporary free speech theorists are less skeptical of government and more concerned with what they see as the exercise of power by speakers, particularly the media and other corporations engaging in expression. They also are suspicious of the rational capacities of the public and propose a need for a "particularly active and absolute form of intervention by the state" that Blasi noted would be consistent with prior restraint.

Blasi responded that we may distrust the rationality of citizens, but the lesson of the First Amendment is that we distrust the state more. "To trust the censor more than the audience is to alter the relationship between the state and citizen that is central to the philosophy of limited government," Blasi wrote.

The second "troublesome premise" implicit in prior restraint is that speech is no different than other hazardous activities that are licensed or enjoinable. But licensing, Blasi explained, is a method of enforcing social norms. Free speech, by its nature, does not observe such norms; social conformity distorts public discourse. Speech — like democracy — is risky, but that is its virtue. "Only when the public views controversial speakers as normal people, with a legitimate role to play in the social system, can the fragile state-individual balance be maintained," Blasi noted.

The third and perhaps most obvious premise of prior restraint is its subordination of individual autonomy. Blasi contended that prior restraints such as

licensing systems and injunctions coerce or induce speakers to relinquish full control over the details and timing of their communications. These regulatory systems must be premised, therefore, on the notion that either such control is not an essential attribute of the autonomy of speakers, or that such autonomy need not be respected. Either premise is objectionable.[14]

Thus, prior restraints cannot be consistent with the implementation of limited government. Those cases in which the Court has condemned the regulation as a prior restraint aptly illustrate the libertarian principles providing the intellectual foundation for the doctrine against prior restraint: distrust of government, acceptance of the risk inherent in speech, and individual autonomy from government.

CASE LAW AND PREMISES

A review of the major cases embracing the prior restraint doctrine yields a treasure trove of commentary and rulings adopting the premises of the doctrine.

Distrust of Government

In 1931, the Supreme Court in *Near v. Minnesota*[15] for the first time explicitly adopted the doctrine against prior restraint as constitutional law. In *Near,* the Court referred time and again to the danger of government regulation as a means of deterring criticism of government. The Court expressed concern about governmental abuse of its authority, with regard to both official misconduct and the exercise of the discretion necessary to implement the statute, which was intended to quell seditious libel. In striking the statute, the Court served notice that prior restraint doctrine had broken free from its historical moorings.

The case involved a governmental ban on speech in advance of publication, based on content, but it was in the form of a nuisance statute enforced by judicial injunction. Jay M. Near had published in his *Saturday Press* malicious and scandalous libels adjudged to be nuisances. As partial punishment, he was ordered not to publish any more under threat of contempt of court.

Some Supreme Court justices argued that the case did not involve previous restraint but a remedy for past transgressions. The majority disagreed, however, arguing on three separate occasions in the opinion that the scheme "must be tested by its operation and effect." Writing for the Court, Chief Justice Charles E. Hughes interpreted the statute as directed, not just at libels of private citizens, but "at the continued publication by newspapers and periodicals of charges against public officers of corruption, malfeasance in office, or serious neglect of duty." Thus constituted, the

---

[14] *Id.* at 85.

[15] 383 U.S. 697 (1931).

Minnesota law was the "essence of censorship." Liberty of the press, Hughes wrote, is "especially cherished for the immunity it afforded from previous restraint of the publication" in such matters.

This was a somewhat remarkable conclusion, given that the Court cited no specific language in the statute or in Minnesota Supreme Court opinions to support its conclusion that the statute concerned primarily libels of public officers. The Minneapolis mayor, a chief of police and a county attorney had been libeled by the defendant, but so had grand jurors, two newspapers and the "Jewish race." The Court, however, seemed to emphasize the "operation and effect" of the law when it noted that the newspaper had been targeted because its principal content was criticism of government. Seventeen times in the opinion, the Court expressed concern for protecting expression about official misconduct. Skepticism of government's capacity to oversee publications critical of government was hardly ameliorated by allowing a judge to determine if future issues of the *Saturday Press* were consistent with the "public welfare," the Court noted. If the statute operated to suppress expression critical of official misconduct, the doctrine against prior restraint was designed to thwart its operation as well as its effect.

The majority's expansion of the notion of prior restraint to include judicial injunctions, as well as administrative licensing systems, initiated an academic debate that continues to this day. It is significant, however, that in the Court's first pronouncement on prior restraint, it signaled its intention not to be bound by classical conceptions. Not coincidentally, it is also significant that this first opinion stands as tribute to the checking function, which the framers held dear and which presupposes governmental abuse of its authority.

The Court continued its concern for governmental exercise of discretion in matters relating to speech in a line of prior restraint cases, many of which were closer in kind to the licensing system contemplated by Blackstone. But a prior restraint case five years after *Near* illustrated that the Court considered taxation of the press as well as systems to suppress seditious libel as within the scope of prior restraint. The characteristic that was constant was a concern for government's abuse of its authority.

Grosjean v. American Press Co., Inc. [16] involved a Louisiana tax on selected newspapers that on its face did not even seem to qualify as a subsequent punishment. The tax was imposed, not on content, but on the basis of circulation, with all newspapers that circulated more than 20,000 copies weekly to pay a tax of two percent on gross receipts. The tax was imposed by statute, and the penalty for failure to pay the tax was a possible fine of up to $500 as well as imprisonment not exceeding six months.

The Court traced the history of "taxes on knowledge" to the English experience, taking judicial notice of the framers' familiarity with that legacy. Writing for the unanimous Court, Justice George Sutherland observed that stamp taxes and taxes on advertising historically had not been intended to gain revenue, but to control the flow of information regarding government. They shared that characteristic with prior restraint, but of course, the same might have been said of seditious libel laws, which constituted subsequent punishments and which operated concurrently with the English system of taxes on the press. Justice Sutherland concluded his survey of English repression of the press with a quote from Eighteenth Century scholar and attorney Thomas Erskine: "The liberty of opinion keeps governments themselves in due subjection to their duties." The quote, although it is not clear from Sutherland's opinion, dates from the year after the First Amendment was enacted — and was made in defense of freedom from seditious libel.

The *Grosjean* case articulates quite nicely the checking function of the press and the threat that governmental abuse of its authority poses to that essential value of freedom of the press. Using the British government as its example, the Court assailed the "persistent effort" to curtail any criticism, true or false. The "predominant purpose" of the First Amendment was "to preserve an untrammeled press as a vital source of public information." The Court described public opinion as "the most potent of all restraints upon misgovernment." The key to informed public opinion is a free press performing the vital function of the Fourth Estate. "To allow it to be fettered is to fetter ourselves," the Court wrote.

From this emphasis on government's sensitivity to criticism and the importance of insulation for critics, the Court concluded that the First Amendment was meant to preclude "any form of previous restraint upon printed publications, or their circulation, including that which had theretofore been effected by these two well-known and odious methods," referring to a stamp tax and a tax on advertising.

---

[16] 297 U.S. 233 (1936). Professor Emerson was particularly critical of the Court's application of the prior restraint doctrine in the tax cases. The doctrine could only be relevant to tax cases, he wrote, if it applied to any regulation that inhibited First Amendment freedom. "When employed in this way the concept becomes so broad as to be worthless as a legal rule," Emerson wrote. Thomas I. Emerson, *The System of Freedom of Expression* (New York: Random House, 1970), p. 511.

A virtue of the prior restraint doctrine as it has come to be construed is that it puts a heavy burden, indeed an insurmountable burden if case outcomes are any indication, on government. While tests and even balancing have been advocated in the same breath as the doctrine against prior restraint, a great strength of the doctrine is that it brings historical weight to bear in asserting outright skepticism of government. Prior restraints are presumed unconstitutional, and it is up to government to bear the heavy burden of attempting to overcome that presumption. The doctrine has a pedigree that no test of compelling or overriding interests can match. The lessons embodied in the doctrine against prior restraint should not be forgotten, but they can easily be lost through mere balancing.

Acceptance of Risk

Worst-case scenarios are integral to the second premise implicit in a system of prior restraint identified by Blasi: risk aversion. In imposing prior restraint, government is attempting to avert the consequences of speech that has yet to be uttered. This necessarily involves the government, including the courts that are passing on the constitutionality of the prior restraint, in gazing into crystal balls. Rationalizing the need for prior restraint thus lends itself to posing the worst possible consequence of the speech if it were to occur.

The only antidote to threats of worst-case scenarios is straightforward acknowledgment that speech does involve risk and that freedom includes freedom for the potent as well as the impotent. "That at any rate is the theory of our Constitution," Justice Oliver Wendell Holmes wrote. We "wager our salvation," he added, "upon imperfect knowledge." He addressed the penchant for concocting worst-case scenarios head-on when he then observed that we must be "eternally vigilant against attempts to check the expression of opinions that we loathe and believe to be fraught with death."[17] Freedom is not for the faint of heart.

Holmes's caveat against caution was tested in the *Pentagon Papers* case. There, if documents the government had classified as secret were published in the newspapers, then the alleged resultant danger would be "the death of soldiers, the destruction of alliances, the greatly increased difficulty of negotiation with our enemies, the inability of our diplomats to negotiate," as well as prolonging the Vietnam war and extended delay in freeing U.S. prison-

ers.[18] Dangers do not get any worse.

One might have wondered at this characterization of the danger, however, given that the Pentagon Papers were historical documents relating to U.S. involvement in the Vietnam war. They not only did not give away any planned troop movements or strategic objectives, but they contained nothing the North Vietnamese did not already know about. Indeed, the people most ignorant of their content was the constituency of the government that was attempting to conceal them.

The papers, for example, revealed that the U.S. government had deliberately engaged in a manipulative public relations campaign aimed at U.S. citizens and foreign allies with little relation to the actual war effort or negotiations, of which the North Vietnamese were, of course, intimately aware. Justice Hugo Black, voting with the majority to allow the *New York Times* and other newspapers to continue publication of a series based on the documents, identified what might have been the real danger that the U.S. government perceived: its own embarrassment.

In the last opinion he was to write before he died, Justice Black zeroed in on the government's use of "national security" as its cover for censorship in the case. The phrase demonstrates a felicitous choice of words by the government. Advocating "security" is meant to be comforting, an appeal to our natural tendency to avoid risk. It also put the newspapers that would disclose these papers in the unappealing role of exposing us to hazards. But Justice Black cautioned that the word was "a broad, vague generality." He seemed to be suggesting that a government whose capacity for deception in conducting war was revealed in the papers would not hesitate to deceive in promising security to its citizens. Free speech does involve risks, but the framers of the First Amendment, who fully appreciated what it took to defend a nation, nevertheless understood that free speech provided the only real security, Black wrote.[19]

This paradox of security through risk is only one of many associated with the First Amendment: a freedom to espouse no freedom, freedom for the speech we hate, a right to be wrong. All, however, share an implicit acknowledgment of the risk of free speech. Such paradoxes perhaps explain why Professor Emerson wrote that the theory of freedom of expression "does not come naturally to the ordinary citizen, but needs to be learned."[20] One does not ordinarily choose the more hazardous course, much less

---

[17] *Abrams v. United States*, 250 U.S. 616, 630 (1919)(Holmes, J., dissenting.)

[18] *New York Times v. United States*, 403 U.S. 713, 763 (1971) (Blackmun, J., dissenting).

[19] *Id.* at 719 (Black, J., concurring).

[20] Emerson, *supra* note 12, at 12.

associate risk with security. Prior restraint appeals to that impulse favoring the safer path. But the doctrine against prior restraint teaches not only that the government's worst-case scenarios seem not to come true when information is ultimately published, but that attempts to achieve security through suppression pose the greater risk. The risk is not in speech being published, but in it *not* being published. That, as Holmes said, at any rate is the theory of our Constitution.

Regard for Individual Autonomy

The final premise of prior restraint that is also at odds with a constitutional system of limited government is a depreciation of individual autonomy. The Court in *Schneider v. State*,[21] for example, took note more than once of the police power to promote the public interest in regulating the public streets. But when municipal ordinances sought to license the dissemination of leaflets on those thoroughfares, the Court found that they infringed not only on individual speech, but a system of government:

> This court has characterized the freedom of speech and that of the press as fundamental personal rights and liberties. The phrase is not an empty one and was not lightly used. It reflects the belief of the framers of the Constitution that exercise of the rights lies at the foundation of free government by free men. It stresses, as do many opinions of this court, the importance of preventing the restriction of enjoyment of these liberties.
>
> ...Mere legislative preferences or beliefs respecting matters of public convenience may well support regulation directed at other personal activities, but be insufficient to justify such as diminishes the exercise of rights so vital to the maintenance of democratic institutions.[22]

If speaking in a public forum imposes burdens or inefficiencies on the state, such is the price of maintaining individual autonomy. The ordinance in *Schneider* was particularly odious to the Court in that it allowed a police officer, acting "as a censor," to determine what literature could be distributed and who would distribute it, and required pamphleteers to submit to an inquisition, photographing and fingerprinting. Such censorship struck at the heart of free expression because it placed discretion in the officer rather than the speaker. Moreover, the Court made clear that individual autonomy extended not only to the message but to the site of the

speech: "[O]ne is not to have the exercise of his liberty of expression in appropriate places abridged on the plea that it may be exercised in some other place."

The concept of individual autonomy answers the fundamental question in each prior restraint case of "Who is to decide?" The choice of what, when and where to speak is either left to the discretion of the speaker or overruled by the state. Autonomous speech is the condition precedent to the autonomous citizenship contemplated in the democratic model.

First Amendment doctrine, with its focus on individual autonomy, may be quaint in the eyes of those who advocate that individuals must yield to the public interest, whether the issue involves mandatory motorcycle helmets, zoning or bans on racist speech. But the First Amendment, as exemplified by the prior restraint doctrine in particular, is one of the last areas of constitutional law to uphold the democratic tradition as it was historically understood. If autonomy in speech is rejected, Robert Post observed, the implications go to the core of our belief in self-government, and "beguiling visions of progressive reform" should not obscure that democratic legitimacy, and not just autonomous speech, is at issue.[23]

RECENT CASES

The doctrine against prior restraint shows amazing vitality despite having roots stretching back more than three centuries. Perhaps even more amazing is that cases involving prior restraint persist and questions still emerge. Drawing on those three centuries of history seems to facilitate answering the questions, however.

Origin of a Test

The case in which the Supreme Court most recently employed the prior restraint doctrine shows evidence of distrusting government, embracing risk and prizing individual autonomy, and it contains the Court's most thorough analysis, which ironically was borrowed from some of its earliest First Amendment cases. Those early cases did not even involve prior restraint, and the analysis was taken not from the majority opinions, but from a dissent and a concurring opinion.

The first early case, *Abrams v. United States*,[24] involved a pros-

---

[21] 308 U.S. 147 (1939).
[22] *Id.* at 161.

[23] Robert Post, "Meiklejohn's Mistake: Individual Autonomy and the Reform of Public Discourse," *University of Colorado Law Review* 64 (1993): 1137.
[24] 250 U.S. 616 (1919).

ecution for publishing two leaflets in 1918 containing objections to U.S. military intervention against the Bolsheviks, who would ultimately form what came to be known as the Soviet Union. Justice Holmes had written an earlier opinion for the Court, in which he had framed the issue as "whether the words used are used in such circumstances and are of such a nature as to create a clear and present danger that they will bring about the substantive evils that Congress has a right to prevent."[25] He had endorsed the conviction of speakers in that case, but Harvard Law Professor Zechariah Chafee Jr. prevailed upon Holmes to impart more meaning to the clear and present danger test,[26] which he did in *Abrams*.

When he circulated his dissent to the majority opinion in *Abrams* and defended it at the justices' Saturday conference, Chief Justice Edward White, his long-standing friend and daily companion on the long walk home, asked him not to issue it. When he persisted, three justices took the highly unusual step of calling on him at his home, where they were joined by his wife in attempting to persuade him not to publish the dissent. Holmes did not relent, and the effect was electric. "A great noise of vilification and praise went up all over the country," wrote biographer Sheldon M. Novick.[27]

In his famous dissent, which has eclipsed the majority opinion and become the law of the land, Holmes stiffened the meaning of a "present danger." He wrote that "nobody can suppose that the surreptitious publishing of a silly leaflet by an unknown man, without more, would present any immediate danger." Opinions should be allowed "unless they so imminently threaten immediate interference with the lawful and pressing purposes of the law that an immediate check is required to save the country," he wrote. Holmes's stress on the immediacy of the danger before speech would be unprotected presents a nearly impossible hurdle to regulation, but, curiously, it also seems to protect only speech that is unimportant or ineffective or both. Still, it was a major milestone in the evolution of the First Amendment.

Justice Holmes and Justice Louis Brandeis had a forty-year-old friendship before Brandeis was appointed to the Court, and they collaborated on some of the great opinions of their era. Brandeis

joined in Holmes's dissent in *Abrams*, and Holmes joined Brandeis's concurrence in *Whitney v. California*,[28] a case in which a woman was convicted of criminal syndicalism for joining the Communist Labor Party. Brandeis's opinion concurring in the majority decision seems to favor her acquittal, but because she did not raise at trial the argument that Brandeis presents, she could not do so on appeal, Brandeis wrote.

This judicial restraint probably left Ms. Whitney unimpressed, but the plain fact is that Brandeis did not have the votes on the Court to overturn her acquittal. So whether Brandeis labeled his lesson on First Amendment law a concurrence or a dissent seems less important than the fact that it fleshed out the clear and present danger test in a way that lower courts could apply it.

Brandeis pointed out that the Court had not yet determined "when a danger shall be deemed clear; how remote the danger may be and yet be deemed present; and what degree of evil shall be deemed sufficiently substantial to justify resort to abridgement of free speech." First, he turned the question around and suggested that the real danger lay in repression of speech and "that the path of safety lies in the opportunity to discuss freely supposed grievances and proposed remedies."

Brandeis believed that, without more, fear of serious injury did not justify suppression of speech. "Those who won our independence were not cowards.... They did not exalt order at the cost of liberty," he wrote. In the same libertarian vein, Brandeis indicated that the limited role of the State was to make individuals free to develop their faculties and to avoid "silence coerced by law — the argument of force in its worst form." He continued:

> To justify suppression of free speech there must be reasonable ground to fear that serious evil will result *if free speech is practiced*. There must be reasonable ground to believe that the danger apprehended is *imminent*. There must be reasonable ground to believe that the evil to be prevented is a *serious* one.[29]

To summarize, the speech must cause the alleged danger, the danger must be immediate, and it must be grave.

Nebraska Press Association

Nearly a half century later, the Court expanded on these themes in

---

[25] *Schenck v. United States,* 249 U.S. 47, 52 (1919)

[26] See Donald L. Smith, Zechariah Chafee, Jr., *Defender of Liberty and Law* (Cambridge: Harvard University Press, 1986), p. 30; Fred D. Ragan, "Justice Oliver Wendell Holmes, Jr., Zechariah Chafee, Jr., and the Clear and Present Danger Test for Free Speech: The First Year, 1919," *Journal of American History* 58 (1971): 42-43.

[27] Sheldon M. Novick, *Honorable Justice — The Life of Oliver Wendell Holmes* (Boston: Little, Brown and Co., 1989), p. 332.

---

[28] 274 U.S. 357 (1927).

[29] *Id*. at 375-76. Emphasis added.

Nebraska Press Association v. Stuart.[30] Erwin Simants had been arrested for the murder of six people in a small Nebraska town. Three days later, Judge Hugh Stuart issued an order prohibiting the public dissemination of any testimony or evidence. The Nebraska Press Association appealed the prior restraint.

The Supreme Court granted *certiorari* and used the case to review its decisions involving the "heavy presumption" against the constitutional validity of prior restraint, including *Near v. Minnesota* and the *Pentagon Papers* case. That heavy presumption translated into a near-impossible burden on government to justify the exercise of such authority and such implicit trust in the state rather than speakers. "The thread running through all these cases is that prior restraints on speech and publication are the most serious and the least tolerable infringement on First Amendment rights," wrote Chief Justice Warren Burger for a unanimous Court.

He distinguished prior restraints from subsequent punishments, noting that penalties for violating a criminal statute or libel judgments do not become effective until after trial and all appeals are ended. "A prior restraint, by contrast and by definition, has an immediate and irreversible sanction," Burger wrote. "If it can be said that a threat of criminal or civil sanctions after publication 'chills' speech, prior restraint 'freezes' it at least for the time."

Burger noted the possible risk that pre-trial publicity posed for a defendant's Sixth Amendment right to a fair trial by unbiased jurors. But he also quoted from an earlier case praising the press as the "handmaiden" of justice, because it "guards against the miscarriage of justice."[31] As Brandeis might have put it, the risk of free speech is real, but the risk of enforced silence is greater. In particular, an effective check on governmental abuse would be missing.

In the *Pentagon Papers* case, Burger had voted with the three dissenters in favor of prior restraint. He seemed particularly bothered by the fact that the *New York Times* had three to four months to review and edit the classified documents, but the Court had a very few days to digest the case. Why, he asked, after months of deferral, must the right to publish be vindicated so precipitously? He answered his own question fifteen years later in *Nebraska Press Association*, noting it was a matter of the speaker's autonomy:

> Of course, the order at issue ... does not prohibit but only postpones publication. Some news can be delayed and most commentary can even more readily be delayed without serious injury, and there often is a self-imposed delay when responsible editors call for verification of information. But such delays are normally slight and they are self-imposed. Delays imposed by governmental authority are a different matter.[32]

As Brandeis had observed — and Milton before him — thinking and speaking are private, individual matters sensitive to governmental interference. If speakers are to maintain their autonomy, the choice not only of what to say, but when to say it, must be left to individual discretion.

To uphold the prior restraint, Burger wrote,

> we must examine the evidence before the trial judge when the order was entered to determine (a) the nature and extent of pre-trial news coverage; (b) whether other measures would be likely to mitigate the effects of unrestrained pre-trial publicity; and (c) how effectively a restraining order would operate to prevent the threatened danger. The precise terms of the restraining order are also important. We must then consider whether the record supports the entry of a prior restraint on publication, one of the most extraordinary remedies known to our jurisprudence.[33]

First, Burger wrote, the trial judge had reasonably concluded that there would be intensive local and national press coverage. Judge Stuart had found "a clear and present danger that pre-trial publicity *could* impinge upon the defendant's right to a fair trial," the Court observed (emphasis added by the Court). But he was wrong. As Holmes and Brandeis had postulated, a clear and present danger requires immediacy; mere conjecture is insufficient.

Burger wrote that the trial judge's "conclusion as to the impact of such publicity on prospective jurors was of necessity speculative, dealing as he was with factors unknown and unknowable." Nobody could tell what would be disseminated, who would read or view it, what impact it would have, who would be picked as jurors, or whether they would be able to decide the case based solely on the evidence introduced in court. One cannot even be certain there will be a trial. Simants could plead guilty — or have a heart attack. When the Court referred to factors unknown and unknowable, the case was over. Once the burden of proof is assigned, that party loses, because it is impossible to prove factors unknown and unknowable. Because the government has a heavy burden to overcome the presumption of unconstitutionality, it loses.

[30] 427 U.S. 539 (1976).
[31] *Id.* at 560, quoting *Sheppard v. Maxwell*, 384 U.S. 333, 350 (1966).
[32] 427 U.S. at 559.
[33] *Id.* at 562.

Likewise, in the second step of the analysis, Burger noted that the government has the burden of proving no other measures would mitigate the effects of publicity. That, too, is unknown and unknowable, without actually implementing the measures. Multiple options exist: change of venue to a jurisdiction with less publicity, postponement of the trial to allow the effects of publicity to subside, intensive questioning of prospective jurors to determine possible bias, instructions to jurors on avoiding publicity and considering only evidence presented in court, sequestration of jurors, restraints on leaks by trial participants, and, of course, a new trial. The obligation to provide a fair trial is on the state, not the press, and if the state holds an unfair trial, it must hold another, fair trial or not try the defendant. The press cannot deny defendants their Sixth Amendment rights.

Third, the Court questioned the effectiveness of the prior restraint. That is, as Brandeis put it, would the danger result if the free speech in question were allowed? If the speech were stopped, would the danger stop, too? In *Nebraska Press Association,* the Court said the danger remained. The trial court might have had difficulty implementing its order regarding media outside the court's jurisdiction.

More telling, though, was the impossibility of stopping a whole community of 850 people from discussing the case and quite likely generating rumors that would be more damaging to the defendant than publicity. Although everybody was restrained from disseminating information about the case, only the media would leave behind evidence of disobeying the order. The townspeople — who constituted the pool of prospective jurors — would gossip no matter what the court decreed. If the restraint would be ineffective, that by itself is a reason for invalidating it.

Finally, the Court noted that the order was defective because it was vague and overbroad. Vague speech regulations inhibit speakers who cannot be sure if they will violate the regulation. An overbroad regulation might be constitutional if more narrowly crafted, but a regulation that proscribes protected speech as well as unprotected speech is constitutionally suspect. This court order, as modified by the Nebraska appellate court, banned "information strongly implicative of the accused." Would saying Simants had been arrested for six murders be "strongly implicative"? Too vague. If the order would cover such an allegation, then it would cover speech that would not prejudice the outcome because the jury would learn that as soon as the trial began anyway. Therefore, the order was overbroad as well.

Applying the Test

So the case left a blueprint for how the Court would likely approach prior restraint cases in the future, whether the restraint involves fair trials or not. The Court is not willing, apparently, to merely determine if the government regulation qualifies as a prior restraint and declare it unconstitutional on those grounds alone, as it did in *Near v. Minnesota.*

First, the regulation must fit the definition of prior restraint, which has relaxed since the days of King Henry VIII, but is not so elastic to include every restraint on publishing, as the Court illustrated in *Alexander v. United States.*[34] Today, a licensing system would still qualify as prior restraint, unless it was imposed by the government on its own employees (as with CIA agents), a condition of accepting a government subsidy (although this area is still developing and the case law is somewhat inconsistent), or involved the high school or elementary press. As well, though, (1) a government prohibition (2) of a specific publication (3) based on its content (4) after the exercise of discretion and (5) in advance of publication would still constitute prior restraint.

When a regulation is defined as prior restraint, it is presumed unconstitutional, and the government bears a heavy burden to overcome that presumption. This aspect cannot be emphasized too strongly, because the tendency is to give the government the benefit of the doubt and avoid the risk of speech. It is easy to concoct worst-case scenarios and hard to favor an abstract concept such as free speech, but the presumption weights the balance solidly in favor of the latter at the outset.

To overcome the presumption of unconstitutionality, the government must prove that the danger is serious; that it is imminent; that the speech is the cause of the danger and that stopping the speech will stop the danger; that no alternatives to prior restraint will work; and that the terms of the prior restraint are neither vague nor overbroad. The prior restraint can fail at any of these steps and need fail only one to remain unconstitutional.

A danger can be serious without being imminent, as in the *Nebraska Press Association* case. Likewise, as Brandeis noted, a danger can be imminent without being serious. Advocacy of trespassing could be so persuasive that the speaker's audience immediately sought out backyards to traverse, but even so, it would not rise to the level of a serious danger justifying prior restraint. Seriousness is usually the easiest element of the test to meet, because the government's asserted danger is taken at face value, and

---

[34] See text accompanying *supra* footnote 10.

the government is always able to posit a danger of some magnitude.

Imminence, on the other hand, is generally the element least likely to be demonstrated. Proving something will immediately and inevitably occur is generally impossible. Nobody can know what will happen in the future. The *Nebraska Press Association* Court echoed Brandeis's observation that fear of serious injury alone will not justify suppression when it wrote that the trial judge's conclusions regarding the impact of publicity were necessarily speculative. Conjecture is *always* possible; evidence of imminence rarely so.

But even if the danger is imminent, it need not be caused by the speech. If the danger occurs whether the speech is practiced or not, then the rationale for the restraint fails. This element of the test often comes into play when the proscribed speech is already in the public domain, as it was in the *Pentagon Papers* case where historical data was being suppressed. If the content of the speech is already available elsewhere, even if it poses an imminent danger, then there is no reason to stop the speech in a given case. The question is whether *the speech at issue in the case* causes the danger.

Alternatives to the prior restraint are almost always available to deal with the danger. The question here is not whether an alternative, narrower form of prior restraint would be preferable. That is an overbreadth question. Alternatives to regulating speech altogether are at issue in this context. Even if alternatives would impose substantial costs on government, as in moving the entire trial, regulating speech must be the last resort, not the first.

In any event, to preserve individual autonomy from government, the burden is on government to prove no means other than infringing on the speaker would adequately address the problem. Publishing something different or at a later time is not an alternative because it shifts the burden to the speaker, when government must do everything possible to defer to the speaker's discretion. The question is not why the speaker wishes to speak, but why the government wants to censor, and the burden is heavy.

Legacy of Nebraska Press Association: CNN

Although the Supreme Court has not considered a prior restraint against the press in recent years, it did have the opportunity in 1990 and declined to do so. The case began when prison officials made tape recordings of conversations between Manuel Noriega and his attorney. Cable News Network obtained copies, but Noriega asked a judge to impose a prior restraint on the dissemina-

tion of the tapes to preserve his right to a fair trial.

The judge asked CNN to turn over the tapes so he could listen to them and decide whether they imperiled Noriega's fair trial right, but CNN refused. The judge imposed the ban, and CNN appealed. The case is muddied because the refusal to turn over the tapes became the issue that seemed to become more important in the court's mind than the constitutionality of the prior restraint. The case illustrates the legacy of *Nebraska Press Association* in the sense that the judge believed he had to have access to the tapes before he could apply the test. If the *Near v. Minnesota* approach had been in place, it would only have been necessary to define the regulation as a prior restraint and find it unconstitutional, without applying any test. Even though the burden seems impossible to meet after *Nebraska Press Association,* the fact that there is a test suggests that some prior restraints will pass the test; otherwise, why have a test?

As Professors Sigman Splichal and Matthew Bunker have noted, however, even if the trial judge had assumed the dissemination of the conversations on the tape posed a threat to Noriega's fair trial, without actually obtaining the tapes or hearing them, he could still have applied the test and the prior restraint would have been unconstitutional. Indeed, the prior restraint would have failed at every step of the test because of the questionable imminence, ineffectiveness of the restraint and availability of alternatives.[35]

In any event, the Supreme Court met and discussed the case on a Sunday morning, which it had not done in forty years, before deciding not to hear it. The denial of *certiorari* provoked a passionate dissent from Justice Thurgood Marshall, joined by Justice Sandra Day O'Connor. He considered the case to be "of extraordinary consequence for freedom of the press." Marshall noted the presumed unconstitutionality of prior restraint and that the proponent of "this drastic remedy" carries a heavy burden to justify it. He continued:

> I do not see how the prior restraint imposed in this case can be reconciled with these teachings. Even more fundamentally, if the lower courts in this case are correct in their remarkable conclusion that publication can be automatically restrained pending application of the demanding test established by *Nebraska Press,* then I think it is imperative that we re-examine the premises and operation of *Nebraska Press* itself. I would grant

---

35 Sigman L. Splichal and Matthew D. Bunker, "The Supreme Court and Prior Restraint Doctrine: An Ominous Shift?" *Media Law & Policy* 3 (Spring 1994): 11.

the stay application and the petition for certiorari. [36]

Justice Marshall is no longer on the Court, and the fact that the Supreme Court declined to hear the case means the Court still has never actually decided in favor of a prior restraint against the press. Perhaps the best that can be said about this case is that it has not served as precedent for any other cases. Yet.

Business Week

In 1996, the U.S. Court of Appeals for the Sixth Circuit offered a ringing endorsement of the prior restraint doctrine.[37] Procter & Gamble had sued Bankers Trust, alleging fraud in a business deal. The trial judge authorized the parties before trial to interview each other and collect evidence that would be kept secret, although on file with the court. The secrecy order was intended to protect trade secrets and other confidential information.

The parties later notified the judge that *Business Week* magazine had obtained a copy of documents that the parties wanted to keep secret and asked the judge to order *Business Week* not to publish them. He sent a facsimile to McGraw-Hill, publisher of *Business Week,* imposing a prior restraint three hours before the presses would have rolled and without any chance for McGraw-Hill to contest the order.

The next day, McGraw-Hill's lawyers asked the judge to withdraw his order and also filed a request for an expedited appeal with the Sixth Circuit. The Sixth Circuit turned McGraw-Hill down on procedural grounds, as did Supreme Court Justice John Paul Stevens when McGraw-Hill asked him for an emergency stay of the order. McGraw-Hill was effectively at the mercy of the trial court.

The trial judge conducted hearings off and on for three weeks, during which he was most interested in learning how *Business Week* had obtained the documents in violation of the secrecy order. It turned out that someone in the Procter & Gamble public relations office had notified a *Business Week* reporter that some fascinating documents had been filed in the case, and another *Business Week* reporter had obtained them from an acquaintance at a New York law firm representing Bankers Trust. Apparently neither the reporter who obtained the documents nor the New York lawyer who provided them knew anything about the secrecy order.

Upset that his order had been violated, the trial judge issued a permanent prior restraint ordering *Business Week* not to publish any of the documents it had obtained. But, at the same time, he held that the parties to the case had not given any good reason why these particular documents should be secret, and he made copies of them public — enabling *Business Week* and everybody else to obtain copies from the courthouse that could be published!

The Sixth Circuit panel concluded that the trial judge was trying to keep his prior restraint order from being appealed when he put the documents on the public record and allowed everybody, including *Business Week,* to publish them. But the Sixth Circuit was not fooled. Chief Judge Merritt wrote that "appellate courts cannot allow themselves to be done out of their jurisdiction so cleverly.... So long as the permanent injunction remains technically in effect, we will review it as an injunction just as technically."

Merritt then turned to the First Amendment analysis, observing that the order was a "classic prior restraint" and therefore presumed unconstitutional. He applied textbook post-*Nebraska Press Association* analysis, beginning with a heavy burden on the proponent of prior restraint. The interests of Procter & Gamble and Bankers Trust fell vastly short of the "exceptional circumstances" required to justify prior restraint. According to the Sixth Circuit,

> Far from falling into that "single, extremely narrow class of cases" where publication would be so dangerous to fundamental government interests as to justify a prior restraint, ... the documents in question are standard litigation filings that have now been widely publicized. The private litigants' interest in protecting their vanity or their commercial self-interest simply does not qualify as grounds for imposing a prior restraint. It is not even grounds for keeping the information under seal, as the District Court ultimately and correctly decided.... The permanent injunction, therefore, was patently invalid and should never have been entered.

The court addressed three other bothersome aspects of the case. First, it criticized the trial judge for his extensive investigation into how *Business Week* obtained the documents. Not only did the trial court fail to conduct any First Amendment inquiry before sending the facsimile to *Business Week,* "but it compounded the harm by holding hearings on issues that bore no relation to the right of *Business Week* to disseminate the information in its possession," wrote the appeals court.

Preoccupation with the motive or knowledge of the speaker

---

[36] *Cable News Network, Inc. v. Noriega,* 498 U.S. 976 (1990) (Marshall, J., dissenting from *denial of certiorari.*)

[37] *Procter & Gamble Co. v. Bankers Trust Co., BT Securities Corp.,* 78 F.3d 219 (6th Cir. 1996).

seems to cast the speaker in the role of suspect, when it is government whose motives are presumed suspect in prior restraint. Inquiring into how *Business Week* obtained the documents shifts the burden from the government to the magazine. In the *Pentagon Papers* case, the newspaper stories were based on documents that were not only classified, but stolen! Yet the origin of the stories was irrelevant to the outcome.

Second, the appeals court chided the trial court for relying on the Supreme Court opinion in *Seattle Times Co. v. Rhinehart* [38] as authority for its prior restraint. In that case, the Court ruled that if one litigant could be required to disclose confidential information, the other party could be required not to disseminate the information, at least until it was revealed in open court. The Sixth Circuit said *Rhinehart* only applied to the actual parties to a case. *Business Week* was not involved in this case and was not using a court to obtain information from another party; quite the opposite.

Third, the Sixth Circuit disapproved of the temporary prior restraint that stopped the *Business Week* presses and continued while the judge held hearings until the permanent prior restraint was issued. Temporary restraining orders, known in the legal trade as TROs, are common as a means of maintaining the status quo while a court gathers evidence and reaches a decision. Chief Judge Merritt quoted from a First Circuit case involving the *Providence Journal:* "This approach is proper in most instances, and indeed to follow any other course of action would often be irresponsible. But, absent the most compelling circumstances, when that approach results in a prior restraint on pure speech by the press it is not allowed." [39]

A temporary prior restraint is still a prior restraint. As the Sixth Circuit noted in considering if the situation was capable of recurring, there is no three-week exception to the prior restraint rule. Indeed, the court quoted from an opinion by Supreme Court Justice Harry Blackmun that "each passing day may constitute a separate and cognizable infringement of the First Amendment."[40]

The *Providence Journal* case should not be taken too far as authority, however. The First Circuit held that the newspaper could disobey a prior restraint order that was "transparently invalid" as long as it made a "good faith" effort to appeal it. That was

contrary to earlier authority holding that the press should ordinarily abide by an order and work within the judicial system to overturn it, which is what McGraw-Hill did. The Supreme Court soon granted certiorari to hear the *Providence Journal* case.

"I have read the oral argument before Supreme Court and there is no doubt in my mind that the Supreme Court granted cert to reverse *Providence Journal,*" noted Ken Vittor, Senior Vice President and General Counsel for McGraw-Hill.[41] Perhaps fortunately for the press, media lawyer Floyd Abrams (who also argued the *Nebraska Press Association* case before the Supreme Court) was able to convince the Supreme Court to dismiss the *Providence Journal* case because of a procedural problem with the prosecutor who had been assigned to the case.

SUMMARY

Questions remain in this age-old area of the law. If even temporary restraints are so disdained and obviously unconstitutional, should the speaker be able to maintain autonomy and speak at will? Can the judiciary effectively censor the press through TROs in a way that it would not allow the executive branch to do? Are speakers better off to sacrifice principles for pragmatism and obey the prior restraint so they can appear before the appellate court with "clean hands"? It probably helped *Business Week* that it could point out that the only party who had violated the court order was one of the litigants, and it obviously hurt CNN when it refused to turn over the tapes so the judge could review them.

The prior restraint doctrine will not survive simply because it has a venerable pedigree. The government will continue to attempt to control and manipulate expression, and the doctrine may have to adapt to remain viable. That's what happened in *Near v. Minnesota* when the Court expanded the doctrine to include judicial orders as well as administrative licensing. But the test that the Court used in *Nebraska Press Association* to test the constitutionality of a judicial prior restraint might be considered a step back, because the *Near* Court, and even Blackstone, contemplated a clear rule rather than a balancing test, albeit one heavily weighted in favor of speech. A test seems to open the door to temporary prior restraints at a minimum, and it may significantly diminish the strength of the doctrine in the long run.

Ultimately, the future of the doctrine depends on those who understand its roots and its rationale and can explain both, whether in editorials, court papers or coffee shops.

---

[38] 467 U.S. 20 (1984).

[39] *In re Providence Journal,* 820 F.2d 1342, 1351 (1st Cir. 1986), *modified on rehearing,* 820 F.2d 1354 (1987), *cert. granted and dismissed on other grounds.*

[40] *Nebraska Press Association,* 423 U.S. 1327, 1329 (Blackmun, J., in chambers).

---

[41] Speech during panel discussion at Practising Law Institute Seminar on Communication Law in New York City (8 Nov. 1996).

FOR ADDITIONAL READING

Abrams, Floyd. "Recent Developments in Prior Restraints Law," in *Communications Law 1996,* vol. 2. (New York: Practising Law Institute, 1996): 539.

Anderson, David A. "The Origins of the Press Clause," *UCLA Law Review* 30 (1983): 455.

Barnett, Stephen R. "The Puzzle of Prior Restraint," *Stanford Law Review* 29 (1977): 539.

Blanchard, Margaret A. "Filling in the Void: Speech and Press in State Courts Prior to Gitlow," in *The First Amendment Reconsidered — New Perspectives on the Meaning of Speech and Press,* Bill Chamberlin and Charlene Brown, eds. New York: Longman, 1982.

Bickel, Alexander. *The Morality of Consent.* New Haven: Yale University Press, 1975.

Friendly, Fred W. *Minnesota Rag: The Dramatic Story of the Landmark Supreme Court Case That Gave New Meaning to Freedom of the Press.* New York: Vintage Books, 1981.

Helle, Steven. "Prior Restraint by the Backdoor," *Villanova Law Review* 39 (1994): 817.

Jeffries, John C. "Rethinking Prior Restraint," *Yale Law Journal* 92 (1983)409.

Kalven, Jr., Harry. "The Supreme Court, 1970 Term — Forward: Even When a Nation is at War," *Harvard Law Review* (1971): 3.

Knoll, Erwin. "National Security: The Ultimate Threat to the First Amendment," *Minnesota Law Review* 66 (1981): 161.

Litwack, Thomas R. "The Doctrine of Prior Restraint," *Harvard Civil Rights-Civil Liberties Law Review* 12 (1977): 519.

Mayton, William T. "Toward a Theory of First Amendment Process: Injunctions of Speech, Subsequent Punishment, and the Costs of the Prior Restraint Doctrine," *Cornell Law Review* 67 (1982): 245.

Meiklejohn, Alexander. *Free Speech and its Relation to Self-Government.* New York: Harper & Brothers, 1948.

Morland, Howard. "The H-Bomb Secret — How We Got It, Why We're Telling It," *The Progressive* (Nov. 1979): 14.

Redish, Martin H. "The Proper Role of the Prior Restraint Doctrine," *Virginia Law Review* 70 (1984): 53.

Rudenstine, David. *The Day the Presses Stopped: A History of the Pentagon Papers Case.* Berkeley: University of California Press, 1996.

Scordato, Martin. "Distinction Without a Difference: A Reappraisal of the Doctrine of Prior Restraint," *North Carolina Law Review* 68 (1989): 1.

Strong, Frank R. "Fifty Years of 'Clear and Present Danger': From Schenck to Brandenburg — and Beyond," *The Supreme Court Review* (1969): 41.

Ungar, Sanford J. *The Papers & the Papers: An Account of the Legal and Political Battle Over the Pentagon Papers.* New York: Dutton, 1972.

5

Regulating Pornography

By F. Dennis Hale

Paul Cohen and Robert Mapplethorpe illustrate how judges, artists and jurors can disagree about what is obscene or indecent. In 1968 Cohen was sentenced to thirty days in jail for disturbing the peace by wearing a jacket in the Los Angeles County Courthouse bearing the inscription, "Fuck the Draft." When the U.S. Supreme Court reversed the conviction, Justice John Marshall Harlan conceded that the message was distasteful to many people but noted that "it is nevertheless often true that one man's vulgarity is another's lyric."[1]

Two decades later, residents of Cincinnati debated issues of decency and taste when a grand jury indicted an art museum director for exhibiting photographs by Robert Mapplethorpe, some of which portrayed homoerotic subject matter. The photographer was accustomed to defending his controversial photographs. "I don't think there's that much difference between a photograph of a fist up someone's ass and a photograph of carnations in a bowl," he had said years earlier. At the conclusion of the criminal trial for obscenity, a Cincinnati jury sided with Mapplethorpe and exonerated the museum director.

Despite the outcomes of the two cases, many believe that both Cohen's jacket and Mapplethorpe's photographs are, if not obscene, indecent. The cases, then, demonstrate the subjectivity and disagreement that surround pornography and obscenity. A discussion of these controversial issues must necessarily begin with an understanding of terms, particularly "obscenity," "pornography," "erotica" and "indecency."

Indecency, the broadest of the four terms, refers to material — both sexual and nonsexual — that is offensive to manners or morals. Indecency is as much a question of taste and ethics as it is of legality. Broadcast stations, newspapers and magazines generally avoid disseminating messages that would be judged indecent by most of their consumers — the repeated use of harsh profanities, for example. Since 1897 the *New York Times* has boasted on its front page that it is devoted to "All the News That's Fit to Print," implying that some news is unfit — indecent — and, therefore, undeserving of public exposure.

Obscenity, as that term is commonly used, is similar to indecency because it is defined as including both sexual and nonsexual meanings. It is material that is disgusting to the senses or abhorrent to morality or virtue. On a ladder of offensiveness, obscenity is up a few rungs from indecency. The adjective "obscene" has been used to deride a variety of nonsexual targets including petroleum company profits, movie violence and television toy ads targeted at children. Most often, however, "obscenity" refers to graphic portrayals of sex acts intended to arouse lustful thoughts.

The terms "pornography" and "erotica" also refer to graphic portrayals of sex for a lustful purpose. Some such portrayals, such as classic photographs or paintings of nude models, are less graphic and explicit. But even the milder portrayals of sexuality may be illegal if broadcast when children are likely to be watching television, or if sold directly to children. "Erotica" is generally a more neutral term, while "pornography" usually is directed at material that is

---

[1] *Cohen v. California,* 403 U.S. 15, 25 (1971).

demeaning.

In this chapter the terms "pornography" and "obscenity" are used in the legal sense. "Pornography" refers to material that explicitly portrays sex acts for the purpose of sexual arousal. Such material is protected unless it is determined to be "obscene." The term "indecency" is used in this chapter to refer to media portrayals of sexual behavior that are milder and less explicit than obscenity and that are protected by the First Amendment for adults. The terms "hard-core" and "soft-core" porn have similarly been used to distinguish between more explicit and less explicit sexual content.

Erotic expression and obscenity are important because they exist at the outer limits of protected speech. Obscenity, fighting words and defamation are narrow categories of speech that are unprotected by the First Amendment. The expansion and contraction of these categories mirror the vigor of free speech and thought in the United States.

Obscenity is a legal issue that never dies. A constant tension exists between free speech liberals and conservatives over the control of sexually explicit speech. The controversy predates the Greek philosopher Aristotle, who advocated that legislators should banish from the state, as they would any other evil, all unseemly talk and indecent remarks. The Supreme Court, state appellate courts, Congress, state legislatures, city councils and local police and prosecutors are continually involved in the drafting and enforcement of obscenity and indecency laws. The issues and how to handle them can arise from unusual circumstances:

- When members of the rap group 2 Live Crew were charged with obscenity for performing songs from their album "As Nasty As They Wanna Be," the *Fort Lauderdale News-Press* faced a challenge. How do you communicate the sexually explicit lyrics so that readers may judge the offensiveness of the songs without offending too many subscribers? The newspaper's executive editor, Ev Landers, made copies of the lyrics available to persons over eighteen who came to the newspaper office.

- Boston television stations encountered taste questions when the Robert Mapplethorpe photo exhibit opened there. Seven of the 175 photos had been judged obscene by a grand jury sitting in Cincinnati. The most controversial of the photos, which were characterized as homoerotic, were broadcast by public television station WGBH. More than 120 viewers phoned the station, most to praise the broadcast. But complaining phone calls to the FCC prompted an investigation into the explicit broadcast. One of the commercial stations in Boston, WLVI, opted to televise only the less objectionable of the homoerotic photos.

- *Toledo Blade* reporter Sam Roe visited local sex clubs, C.E.X. and Adventures, to discover what went on there and to determine whether safe sex was practiced. The story related the occurrence of group and couple sex, various sex practices and the availability and use of condoms.

- When the Sunday newspaper supplement, *Parade*, distributed twenty-seven million copies of a fall 1984 issue with a sex-in-America cover story, three of 133 newspapers refused to distribute it. And two newspapers later published apologies to readers for the sexual content.

Such tests of taste and decency constantly confront the news media and the public. The supply of such news stories is as endless as the allure of sex and the desire of some citizens to close down sexually oriented businesses. And that's where the sides collide.

OBSCENITY AND THE LAW

The pornography issue is entertaining, controversial, stimulating, informative and even humorous. Many a cartoon in the 1960s made light of robed appellate court justices, representing the nation's keenest minds on constitutional law, watching hours of porn movies to determine whether they were obscene.

But there is a serious side as well. Obscenity laws make it a crime to sell some erotic materials, even to willing adults. A felony conviction for disseminating obscenity may result in years of imprisonment, hefty fines or attorneys' fees and the forfeiture of property. Such a conviction amounts to a socially sanctioned punishment for the dissemination of ideas. Some may find the ideas offensive, crude and meritless, but they are ideas nonetheless.

In addition, a person convicted more than once for disseminating obscene material may be classified a racketeer and punished even more severely under RICO laws — the abbreviation stands for *racketeer influenced and corrupt organizations*. An obscenity RICO conviction in Indiana means a maximum of ten years in prison, $20,000 in fines and forfeiture of business property.[2] When Ferris Alexander was convicted by federal authorities of disseminating obscenity, he was sentenced to six years in federal prison, fined $100,000 and ordered to forfeit $9 million in business assets. The action was upheld by the Supreme Court in 1993.[3] Similarly, in 1994 the Court upheld a $100,000 fine and twelve-month prison sentence for violation of the federal Protection of Children Against

---

[2] *Fort Wayne Books, Inc. v. Indiana,* 489 U.S. 46 (1989).
[3] *Alexander v. United States,* 509 U.S. 544 (1993).

Sexual Exploitation Act.[4]

Supreme Court rulings in obscenity law fall into two basic areas. First, the Court interprets federal statutes and regulations that control or prohibit the creation and distribution of erotic material. This body of law includes the Federal Communications Act, rules and regulations of the Federal Communications Commission and U.S. Postal Service, laws controlling imports and exports, and regulations governing interstate commerce. Obscenity laws, like statutes on almost any subject, contain vague provisions that courts must interpret. For example, if U.S. Customs agents in New York City intercept pornographic films shipped from Germany to New Hampshire, what laws and standards apply — those of New York, Germany or New Hampshire? If federal statutes are silent on such issues, federal appellate courts must divine rules of law by relying on other legal precedents.

More importantly, the Supreme Court decides how far federal and state governments may go in restricting erotic speech. More than sixty years ago, the Court said in *Near v. Minnesota* that obscenity was one of those classes of speech not protected by the First Amendment.[5] *Near* provided no guidelines, however, and it would be another twenty-six years before the Court began the difficult task of drawing the line between obscene and non-obscene material.

State legislatures and supreme courts are also sources of obscenity regulation. And local police and prosecutors are the major source of enforcement, or lack of enforcement, of state obscenity law. Neither the First Amendment nor federal statutes mandate that states enact and implement obscenity laws. State judges in Oregon and Hawaii, for example, have exercised their option to decriminalize the sale of obscenity to adults. And in some metropolitan areas, political liberalism and a profit motive discourage the enforcement of obscenity laws. By contrast, a few cities — like Cincinnati — vigorously prosecute obscenity.

When state and local governments control obscenity, they rely on a general authority of the states called the police power. The term is not what it sounds like; it has little to do with the official duties of police officers. This broad legal power allows states to prohibit all things inimical to the comfort, safety, health and welfare of society. The police power authorizes the legislative branch of state governments to enact laws to protect the peace, good order, morals and health of communities. Of course, state and federal constitutions limit how far states may go in exercising their police powers.

---

4 *United States v. X-Citement Video, Inc.*, 513 U.S. 64 (1994).
5 283 U.S. 697 (1931).

OBSCENITY AND SOCIETY

But is pornography clearly a threat to public safety, health and morality? The creation and sale of pornography traditionally have been entangled with other fringe and illicit services such as gambling, prostitution and drugs. But times change. Video rental stores located in malls and suburban neighborhoods isolated from illegal drugs and prostitution derive substantial revenue from X-rated videos that are not legally obscene.

Sociologists and political activists are divided on whether adult pornography is harmful. Theoretically, private behavior should not be criminalized unless it is harmful to specific individuals. But researchers and political groups disagree about the effects of pornography. Two presidential commissions have studied the issue. President Lyndon Johnson created the Commission on Obscenity and Pornography in 1968. Two years and thousands of dollars later, during the Nixon Administration, the commission concluded that neither hard-core nor soft-core pornography leads to antisocial behavior and thus should not be prohibited. Eighteen years later, however, the Attorney General's Commission on Pornography, called the "Meese Commission" for then Attorney General Edwin Meese, concluded that pornography is pervasive in society and recommended vigorous enforcement of obscenity laws.

Many people, including a number of social scientists who have researched obscenity, oppose obscenity laws. They see erotica as a private, moral issue that exists beyond the reach of government. They argue that, in fact, moderate consumption of erotica — like wine, ice cream or even marijuana — is compatible with physical and mental health. Sallie Tisdale defended pornography for women in a 1992 *Harper's* magazine article and in a 1994 book.[6] She wrote: "I want never to forget the bell curve of human desire, or that few of us have much say about where on the curve we land." And Canadian philosopher F. M. Christensen provided a reasoned defense of pornography in his 1990 book, *Pornography: The Other Side*, in which he argued, "We constantly hear about sex criminals found to own pornography — ignoring all those who do not, and all the noncriminals who do. Similar stories of rapists and murderers who were Bible readers can equally well be found."[7]

Proponents of strict enforcement of obscenity laws cite history

---

6 Sallie Tisdale, "Talk Dirty to Me: A Woman's Taste in Pornography," *Harper's*, February 1992, p. 37; Sallie Tisdale, *Talk Dirty to Me: An Intimate Philosophy of Sex* (New York: Doubleday, 1994).

7 F.M. Christensen, *Pornography: The Other Side* (New York: Praeger, 1990), p. 126.

and opposing research to defend their position. They point out that many cultures traditionally have controlled erotic expression. The Bible may include bawdy tales of prostitutes and adulterers, but they are told discretely without close-ups of genitals. They point to studies demonstrating that men exposed to explicit videos become more callous in their attitudes toward women and to a study that shows a strong correlation between the consumption of men's girlie magazines and the incidence of sex crimes against women. Two feminists, Catherine MacKinnon and Andrea Dworkin, have been particularly active in fighting pornography, which they define as the graphic, sexually explicit subordination of women. They argue that it presents women "as sexual objects for domination, conquest, violation, exploitation, possession, or use, or through postures or positions of servility or submission or display."[8] A 1984 ordinance in Indianapolis adopted this argument, but the Seventh U.S. Circuit Court of Appeals found it to be unconstitutional.[9]

Some federal judges, however, support attempts by states to control pornography and public nudity. Supreme Court Justice Antonin Scalia observed in 1991 that Indiana's nudity law would be violated "if 60,000 fully consenting adults crowded into the Hoosier Dome to display their genitals to one another, even if there were not an offended innocent in the crowd."[10]

OBSCENITY AND THE SUPREME COURT

Justice Scalia's colorful observation — part of a lively history of Supreme Court jurisprudence in the area of erotic speech — is from a concurring opinion in a case involving nude dancing. Darlene Miller, a dancer at the Kitty Kat Lounge in South Bend, Indiana, argued that nude dancing was a form of protected expression. Indiana, however, said the state had a right to require all public performers to at least wear pasties and G-strings, and the Supreme Court agreed in a decision that is representative of the Court's history in pornography law.

In his majority opinion, Chief Justice William Rehnquist insisted that Indiana had a right to combat public nudity, conceding that nude dancing was "expressive conduct within the outer perime-

ters of the First Amendment." But, Rehnquist observed, "It is possible to find a kernel of expression in almost every activity a person undertakes."[11] Justice Byron White, joined by three other justices, dissented, arguing that non-obscene, nude dancing performed before consenting adults was protected expression. Justice David Souter joined Scalia in his attack on the concept that consent should affect the outcome of the case.

This kind of fragmentation — and worse — dominated Supreme Court jurisprudence in obscenity law for more than thirty years. Typical was a 1966 case, *Memoirs v. Massachusetts*,[12] in which Justice William Brennan presented a three-part test to determine whether a work was obscene: (a) the dominant theme of the material taken as a whole must appeal to a prurient interest in sex; (b) the material must be patently offensive because it affronts contemporary community standards relating to the representation of sexual matters; and (c) the material must be utterly without redeeming social value. Two justices signed the plurality opinion holding that the 1749 novel, *Memoirs of a Woman of Pleasure*, was not obscene; two justices voted to overturn the conviction for other reasons; and three justices wrote separate, dissenting opinions.

William Douglas, a staunch First Amendment supporter, concurred in the judgment, he wrote, because the First Amendment absolutely protected obscene speech: "Publications and utterances were made immune from majoritarian control by the First Amendment, applicable to the States by reason of the Fourteenth. No exceptions were made, not even for obscenity."[13] But Justice Tom Clark disagreed with Douglas and with Brennan. The new test, he wrote, "gives the smut artist free rein to carry on his dirty business" and "preying upon prurient and carnal proclivities for its own pecuniary advantage."[14]

The *Memoirs* definition of obscenity, which was an expansion of a definition in the 1957 case of *Roth v. United States*,[15] made it difficult to prosecute erotic works because they were judged:

* on the basis of average persons and not the most sensitive or conservative persons,
* on the basis of contemporary community standards and not on the standards of someone's grandparents,
* and on the basis of the dominant theme of the entire work and not on isolated scenes or passages.

---

[8] Andrea Dworkin and Catherine MacKinnon, *Pornography & Civil Rights: A New Day for Women's Equality* (Minneapolis: Organizing Against Pornogarphy, 1988), p. 113-14.

[9] *American Booksellers Association v. Hudnut*, 771 F.2d 323 (7th Cir. 1984).

[10] *Barnes v. Glen Theatre*, 501 U.S. 560, 575 (1991)(Scalia, J., concurring).

[11] *Id.* at 570.

[12] 383 U.S. 413 (1966).

[13] *Id.* at 427 (Douglas, J., concurring).

[14] *Id.* at 441-42 (Clark, J., dissenting).

[15] 354 U.S. 476 (1957).

But the requirement that prevented most obscenity prosecutions was that works be "utterly without redeeming social value." Most films or books contain a kernel of a story line or a smidgen of nonsexual plotting that amounts to some social value.

The social value test was suggested in *Roth* and formally adopted nine years later in *Memoirs*. Under the combined *Roth/Memoirs* test, other appellate courts found most erotic materials to be non-obscene and thus protected by the Constitution. Adult bookstores and theaters proliferated; two presidential commissions studied pornography; and the Supreme Court generally ruled in favor of free speech on obscenity matters. Judges, however, were divided on how to define obscenity and whether they should be spending so much time perusing erotic materials. For example:

- In 1964, the Court invalidated the $2,500 fine of a Cleveland Heights theater manager for showing *Les Amants*. Justice Potter Stewart conceded that he could not intelligibly improve on the legal definition of obscenity: "But I know it when I see it, and the motion picture involved in this case is not that."[16]
- In 1966, Justice Hugo Black objected to "saddling this Court with the irksome and inevitably unpopular and unwholesome task of finally deciding by a case-by-case, sight-by-sight personal judgment of the members of this Court what pornography (whatever that means) is too hard core for people to see or read."[17]
- In 1967, the Court reversed obscenity convictions from New York, Kentucky and Arkansas for distributing the publications *High Heels, Gent, Swank, Lust Pool* and *Shame Agent*. The justices disagreed on what rule of law to apply but deemed the material protected "whichever of these constitutional views is brought to bear."[18]
- In 1968, a justice noted that the Court had published fifty-five separate opinions for 130 obscenity cases since *Roth*, that this was a "chaotic state of affairs" that was "unmatched in any other course of constitutional adjudication."[19]
- And in 1970, Chief Justice Warren Burger complained about assuming the role of a "supreme and unreviewable board of censorship for the 50 states."[20]

The struggles the Court had in defining and regulating obscenity were mirrored throughout the judicial system. Some scholars, attorneys and judges joined Justices Black and Douglas in their opposition to all obscenity laws, but most jurists and observers agreed that the task was unavoidable. Indeed, many so-called absolutists who believe that consenting adults have a right to view whatever they desire, agree that lines must be drawn for material aimed at children, for required reading materials for juveniles in public high schools, or for material that is obtrusive and unavoidable, such as billboards.

If lines must be drawn, the predominant question becomes, "Where are those lines drawn?" Federal District Court Judge Bruce Jenkins emphasized the difficulty in such line drawing in a 1982 decision, in which he declared the Utah cable obscenity statute to be unconstitutional:

I'm an old legislator. I am appreciative of the legislative process. I was President of the State Senate some years ago. I respect those who participate in the legislative process very, very much. Nevertheless the extremely difficult drafting problems that exist in any effort to deal with the areas of expression requires exquisite care by the legislature and conscientious conformity to exacting constitutional standards. Free expression is so important to the well being of our whole social structure that any limitations must be viewed by the most critical of legislative eyes.[21]

In 1973, the fragmentation on the Supreme Court abated when five judges, for the first time since *Roth*, agreed on where some of those lines should be drawn. The definition of obscenity established in *Miller v. California*[22] continues to be the law today.

Miller v. California

Marvin Miller sent a mass mailing to California residents, promoting four illustrated books — *Intercourse, Sex Orgies Illustrated, Man-Woman* and *An Illustrated History of Pornography* — and a film — *Marital Intercourse*. A restaurant owner and his mother in Newport Beach who received copies of the brochure complained to police. Miller was eventually charged with violating California's obscenity statute.

The Supreme Court described the brochure as consisting primarily of "pictures and drawings very explicitly depicting men and

---

16 *Jacobellis v. Ohio,* 378 U.S. 184, 197 (1964).

17 *Mishkin v. New York,* 383 U.S. 502, 516-17 (1966).

18 *Redrup v. New York,* 386 U.S. 767, 771 (1967).

19 *Interstate Circuit v. Dallas,* 390 U.S. 676, 707-04 (1968)(Harlan, J., concurring and dissenting).

20 *Walker v. Ohio,* 398 U.S. 434, 443 (1970)(Burger, C.J., dissenting).

21 *Home Box Office v. Wilkinson,* 531 F. Supp. 986, 995 (D. Utah 1982).

22 413 U.S. 15 (1973).

women in groups of two or more engaged in a variety of sexual activities, with genitals often prominently displayed." Five justices, in an opinion written by Chief Justice Warren Burger, found the brochure obscene under the Court's new definition:

(1) whether the average person, applying contemporary community standards, would find that the work, taken as a whole, appeals to the prurient interest;

(2) whether the work depicts or describes, in a patently offensive way, sexual conduct specifically defined by applicable state law;

(3) whether the work, taken as a whole, lacks serious literary, artistic, political, or scientific value.

The first two parts of the *Miller* obscenity test were quite similar to the first two parts of the *Memoirs* test. In part three of the *Miller* test, however, the Court rejected the requirement that a work be utterly without redeeming social value and replaced it with the more restrictive requirement that the work lack serious value. In addition, the *Memoirs* definition used the broad adjective "social" to qualify value; the *Miller* test specified that the value be literary, artistic, political or scientific, omitting, for example, entertainment value. Thus, the *Miller* test appeared to make obscenity prosecutions easier by changing the third part of the *Memoirs* test.

On the same day that the Court decided *Miller*, it decided four other obscenity cases, all by 5-4 votes, clarifying a variety of constitutional provisions in obscenity law. Justice Douglas dissented in all cases, reiterating his position that the First Amendment protects even obscene material; Justice Brennan, joined by Thurgood Marshall and Potter Stewart, dissented, arguing that "obscenity" could not be defined sufficiently to give notice to producers of explicitly sexual material and, therefore, should be decriminalized.

In *Kaplan v. California* the Court decided that photographs and drawings were not necessary for a work to be obscene; words alone are sufficient.[23] *Kaplan* involved *Suite 69*, a book sold by the Peek-A-Boo Bookstore, one of 250 adult bookstores in Los Angeles. The Court described the book as consisting "entirely of repetitive descriptions of physical, sexual conduct, 'clinically' explicit and offensive to the point of being nauseous." The Court said the book contained almost every conceivable variety of sexual contact, homosexual and heterosexual, regardless of whether a reader sampled every fifth, tenth or twentieth page, and regardless of the page upon which the reader started.

In *Paris Adult Theatre I v. Slaton*, the Court confirmed that adult movies were obscene, even when they were marketed discretely.[24] The Court described the Atlanta adult movie house as having a "conventional, inoffensive theatre entrance, without pictures." And the entrance door had the sign, "Adult theatre — you must be 21 and able to prove it. If viewing the nude body offends you, please do not enter." The fact that the theater had a tasteful, non-exploitative exterior and that it restricted its clients to interested adults did not exempt it from obscenity prosecution.

Finally, the Court upheld a prosecution for importing obscene material into the United States for private, personal use and the right of the federal government to prosecute for the transportation of obscene material in common carriers in interstate commerce.[25]

Miller Part 1: The Prurient Interest Test

The first prong of the *Miller* test — "Whether the average person, applying contemporary community standards, would find that the work, taken as a whole, appeals to prurient interest" — is the easiest to satisfy. It requires that an erotic work be judged according to average persons — not particularly susceptible and sensitive persons or totally insensitive persons. And the work is judged according to local contemporary standards, which may vary from community to community. Wrote the *Miller* majority:

It is neither realistic nor constitutionally sound to read the First Amendment as requiring the people of Maine or Mississippi to accept public depiction of conduct found tolerable in Las Vegas or New York City.... People in different states vary in their tastes and attitudes, and this diversity is not to be strangled by the absolutism of imposed uniformity.[26]

The first part of the *Miller* test requires that the overall work have a prurient appeal, that is, the work arouses an immoderate or unwholesome interest in sex. The work, however, is judged on its entirety, not on isolated or fleeting passages or scenes that contain sexual descriptions or images. When a Cincinnati art museum was prosecuted for exhibiting photographs by Robert Mapplethorpe, the judge required the 175-photo exhibit to be judged on the basis of seven controversial photos that had been isolated from the others in the exhibit, violating the intent of the *Miller*

---

23 413 U.S. 115 (1973).

24 413 U.S. 49 (1973).

25 *United States v. 12 200-Ft. Reels of Super 8mm Film,* 413 U.S. 123 (1973); *United States v. Orito,* 413 U.S. 139 (1973).

26 413 U.S. at 32-33.

test.[27]

Judges have conducted crude content analyses to determine the appeal of the overall work. One federal district court judge in Georgia concluded that an issue of *Penthouse* magazine satisfied the first part of the *Miller* test because most of the pages were devoted to photos emphasizing the genitals of nude women. The judge noted: "The magazine's overwhelming effect, obviously planned, is to create sexual excitement and stimulation, to scratch the itch—or to create the itch itself—of prurient interest."[28]

Miller Part 2: The Patently Offensive Test

The second prong of the *Miller* test is "Whether the work depicts or describes, in a patently offensive way, sexual conduct specifically defined by the applicable state law."

The same federal judge who found that *Penthouse* appealed to a prurient interest in sex also found that it satisfied the second part of the *Miller* test: The sexual portrayal was sufficiently graphic to be considered patently offensive. Ordinary photographs or drawings of nudes would not satisfy such a requirement, but the 108 photographs in the five photo features went beyond nudity. The judge noted that eighty-seven photos included exposed breasts, buttocks or genitals; nine included actual or simulated lesbian, oral sex; seven alluded to masturbation through the location of fingers in or near genitals; and sixteen photos showed legs spread to expose genitals, with six of those "close-up photographs showing nothing but women's groins."[29]

The patent offensiveness requirement separates hard-core sexual portrayals from other erotic expression. In order for a sexual portrayal to be obscene, it must be specifically described in state law. In *Miller,* the Court said that such portrayals were of ultimate sexual acts, normal or perverted, actual or simulated, including masturbation, excretory functions and the lewd exhibition of genitals. State statutes that define the human behaviors whose portrayals may be obscene read like a catalog of sexual practices for heterosexual and homosexual couples and individuals.

Thus communities are restricted in obscenity prosecutions to works containing explicit portrayals of hard-core sex acts. One year after *Miller,* the city of Albany, Georgia, fined theater manager Billy Jenkins $750 and sentenced him to twelve months of probation for showing the movie *Carnal Knowledge.* Some critics listed

the film as among the ten best movies of 1971, and Ann-Margret received an Academy Award nomination for her performance. The Supreme Court reversed the obscenity conviction and pointed out that juries do not have "unbridled discretion in determining what is 'patently offensive.'" Sexuality may have been the major theme of the movie, the Court said, but it was not obscene: "There is no exhibition whatever of the actors' genitals, lewd or otherwise, during these scenes. There are occasional scenes of nudity, but nudity alone is not enough to make material legally obscene under the *Miller* standard."[30] The case, *Jenkins v. Georgia,* is a strong reminder to those individuals who mistakenly believe that *Miller* gave communities unlimited power to regulate erotic material.

Subjectivity, imprecision and unpredictability occur in all three parts of the *Miller* test. Complicating this subjectivity, tolerance for erotic materials varies from community to community. The concepts of patently offensive and prurient interest vary according to community norms, which are reflected in the attitudes of court jurors.

Miller Part 3: Serious Value Test

The third and final determinant of obscenity is "Whether the work, taken as a whole, lacks serious literary, artistic, political or scientific value."

Even if a work appeals to the prurient interest and is patently offensive under state law, it must satisfy the third part of the *Miller* test to be obscene and lie outside the protection of the First Amendment. In effect, the third part forces judges to play the role of artistic or social critics and evaluate the aesthetic merit of works containing sexual content. Often prosecution and defense attorneys call expert witnesses who describe the social value of the work for the jury. The Court ruled in 1987 that the third part of *Miller* involves national rather than community standards.[31]

The presence of a substantial amount of serious, nonsexual material may salvage a work that contains graphic sex, but the amount of nonsexual material must be substantial. One judge has cautioned: "A quotation from Voltaire in the flyleaf of a book will not constitutionally redeem an otherwise obscene publication."[32] Although some judges have classified *Penthouse* as obscene because of the quantity of explicit, erotic photographs, others have judged it non-obscene because of its serious articles. The Louisi-

---

[27] *Cincinnati v. Contemporary Arts Center,* 57 Ohio Misc.2d 15, 566 N.E.2d 214 (1990).

[28] *Penthouse v. Webb,* 594 F. Supp. 1186, 1198 (N.D. Ga. 1984).

[29] *Id.*

[30] *Jenkins v. Georgia,* 418 U.S. 153, 161 (1974).

[31] *Pope v. Illinois,* 481 U.S. 497 (1987).

[32] *Kois v. Wisconsin,* 408 U.S. 229, 231 (1972), quoted in *Miller,* 413 U.S. at 25, n. 7.

ana Supreme Court in 1980 found that the 228-page, June 1980 issue of *Penthouse* satisfied the first two parts of *Miller*, and that ninety-six pages of photo essays of women satisfied the third part because they constituted hard-core sexual conduct. However, the magazine as a whole was redeemed by sixty-seven pages of articles that clearly had serious value: "These articles convey ideas, and purport to convey serious information. They do not lack serious political and scientific value, nor even serious literary value."[33]

Similarly, in 1979 a Boston Municipal Court judge upheld First Amendment protection for the film *Caligula* by a legal thread. He found that the film lacked social value because it "does not lift the spirit, does not improve the mind, nor does it enrich the human personality or develop character." But a political scientist had testified that the film had a serious political theme about absolute power corrupting absolutely, and no rebuttal witness was presented on the issue. The judge ruled that the movie was protected because the government had failed to prove beyond a reasonable doubt that the film lacked serious political value.[34]

Judges are not free to serve as their own fact finders on the issue of social value. A federal district court judge found to be obscene the lyrics of the 2 Live Crew album "As Nasty As They Wanna Be," but he ignored the testimony of critics who said that the music had political significance and literary conventions, and the government presented no evidence on the issue of artistic value. The Eleventh U.S. Circuit Court of Appeals reversed the ruling, rejecting the argument that "simply by listening to this musical work, the judge could determine that it had no serious artistic value."[35]

A federal district judge demonstrated in 1991 that a modicum of political or literary value can salvage a work. The judge ruled that a truck driver's bumper sticker, "How's my driving? Call 1-800-EAT-SHIT," had serious literary value because it parodied bumper stickers that encouraged drivers to call truck companies with comments about the driving habits of truck drivers. The judge also said the bumper sticker had serious political value because it protested the "Big Brother" mentality that is promoted by serious versions of the sticker, and it did not satisfy the first two parts of *Miller* because it was not erotic.[36]

Other judges are not so quick to find serious value in sexually explicit material. In 1977, the Kentucky Supreme Court upheld an obscenity conviction and accompanying $4,000 fine against the Paducah Fourth Street Cinema for showing *Deep Throat*. After viewing the movie, the court held that it lacked serious value: "The story line consists entirely of the sexual activities of Miss Linda Lovelace. We failed to find any serious literary, artistic, political or scientific value in this motion picture."[37] A federal district court four years later similarly failed to find serious value in the film *Cinderella-96*, which was described as a translation of the fictional character, Cinderella, into a bawdy, lusty tale of recurring homosexual and heterosexual encounters. The judge said the "sum and substance of the movie is the almost unbroken string of sexual acts depicted." He concluded that the movie was obscene even though it contained no sexual penetration or ejaculation. And he said it lacked serious literary and artistic value even though it may be entertaining and enjoyable to some viewers.[38]

OBSCENITY AND PUBLIC OPINION

Miller v. California should have increased obscenity convictions and diminished the availability of erotica. It didn't. Indeed, obscenity convictions decreased and more erotica became available after 1973. Why?

Because the public is apparently unwilling for obscenity laws to be strictly enforced. Most prosecutors and judges — those people responsible for enforcing obscenity law — are elected. And members of the public serve on the juries that decide criminal obscenity cases. Studies show that these people use erotica themselves or tolerate its use by others. A 1992 study, for example, reported that forty-one percent of men and sixteen percent of women questioned said they had purchased autoerotic materials during the previous twelve months. Twenty-three percent of the men had watched X-rated movies, twenty-two percent had visited clubs with erotic dancers and sixteen percent had purchased sexually explicit books or magazines. Only thirty-four percent of all subjects said they believed there should be laws prohibiting the sale of pornography to adults.[39]

Other studies report similar results. An Indiana survey found that fifty-four percent of all adults questioned had watched X-rated videos or movies at least once.[40] And a 1991 Gallup poll found

[33] *Louisiana v. Walden Book Co.,* 386 So.2d 342, 346 (La. 1980).

[34] *Massachusetts v. Saxon Theatre Corp.,* 6 Media L. Rep. (BNA) 1979 (Boston Mun. Ct. 1980).

[35] *Luke Records, Inc. v. Navarro,* 960 F.2d 134, 138 (11th Cir. 1992).

[36] *Baker v. Glover,* 776 F. Supp. 1511 (N.D.Ga. 1991).

[37] *Western Corp. v. Kentucky,* 558 S.W.2d 605, 607 (Ky. 1977).

[38] *Septum, Inc. v. Keller,* 7 Media L. Rep. (BNA) 1664 (N.D.Ga. 1981).

[39] Robert Michael, John Gagnon, Edward Laumann and Gina Kolata, *Sex in America: A Definitive Survey* (New York: Little, Brown and Company, 1994).

[40] June Reinisch and Ruth Beasley, *The Kinsey Institute New Re-*

that fifty-three percent of adults either opposed tightening standards in their communities for the sale of sexually explicit material or wanted the standards to be less restrictive. In addition, more than fifty percent of adults said magazines with nudity, magazines that show adults having sexual relations, theaters showing X-rated movies, and X- rated video rentals should be available to adults without restrictions or without public displays.[41]

These attitudes translate into high demand for erotic material. The Kinsey Institute estimated in 1990 that thirty-five million copies of "girlie" magazines are distributed each month.[42] The 1994 Standard Rate and Data Services reports that *Playboy* has a monthly circulation of 3.4 million with an advertising rate of $49,000 per page and *Penthouse's* monthly circulation is 1.2 million with an advertising rate of $28,000 per page.[43] *Writer's Market* does not list *Playboy* or *Penthouse* as welcoming submissions from freelance writers but does list eighteen magazines under its "men's magazine" category, including *Climax* (83,000 circulation), *Screw* (125,000), *Gallery* (500,000) and *Thigh High* (89,000). *Playboy* is rated the most tasteful of the top three girlie magazines (*Playboy, Penthouse* and *Hustler*), but a content analysis of *Playboy* centerfolds from 1953 to 1990 found that the portrayals became more explicit from 1971 to 1985. Explicitness was defined as the showing of pubic hair and opened legs.[44]

Reliable statistics on the sale of X-rated movie tickets or the rental of adult videos are unavailable, but the proliferation of home VCRs has played a major role in making erotic films more available to interested adults. The number of households with VCRs has increased from less than one percent in 1978 to seventy-three percent in 1992, and the availability of erotic videos has skyrocketed.

The proliferation of girlie magazines, increased explicitness of the major men's magazines, growing availability of VCRs and erotic videos are developments that reflect a public that consumes more erotic material and is increasingly tolerant of erotica. This is a public that balks at obscenity prosecutions. Law professor Robert Riggs counted the number of obscenity cases appealed to higher courts before and after *Miller* and found a sharp upward trend

from 1969 to 1974, the year after the decision, and an "almost equally sharp down turn" after 1974.[45] Political scientist Harold Leventhal detected similar trends when he surveyed local prosecuting attorneys about obscenity enforcement before and after *Miller.* Although prosecutors reported an increase in the quantity of obscenity in their communities after 1973, they reported a lower priority for prosecuting obscenity and a drop in the number of obscenity cases. Leventhal concluded that *"Miller* failed to spur more obscenity prosecutions."[46] Similarly, University of Chicago law professor Cass Sunstein observed in 1993 that "realistically speaking, most people involved in the production of sexually explicit work have little to fear from the *Miller* test."[47]

Jurors are more tolerant of erotica than they are of censorship. This was one lesson from the obscenity trial of the Contemporary Arts Center in Cincinnati. However, it was an expensive lesson, costing the museum more than $300,000 in legal fees. The trial involved seven homoerotic photos from a 175-photo art exhibit by Robert Mapplethorpe. Cincinnati had a tradition of cracking down on erotica; it had no adult bookstores, nude dance establishments or X-rated cable networks. Early motions in the obscenity trial posed a special threat to civil liberties. First, jurors were denied access to the full exhibit and were only exposed to the controversial photos. This violated the spirit of two parts of the *Miller* test that require that obscene material be judged on the basis of the entire work. Second, jurors were selected from the entire county and not just from within the city limits of Cincinnati where public opinion was more liberal. Despite these setbacks, at the end of the trial and following two hours of deliberations, the four-man, four-woman jury ruled in favor of the art museum and freedom of expression.

So, while the three-part *Miller* test and the wording of some local obscenity statutes theoretically have made it easier to prosecute obscenity, the public has grown increasingly tolerant of erotic material and has reduced political pressures on elected officials to enforce obscenity laws. And members of that public have difficulty when they serve as jurors and are asked to punish magazines or films similar to those the jurors may have rented or purchased recently.

---

port on Sex (New York: St. Martin's Press, 1990).

[41] *The Gallup Poll Monthly,* October 1991.

[42] Samuel Janus and Cynthia Janus, *The Janus Report on Sexual Behavior* (New York: John Wiley and Sons, Inc., 1993).

[43] *Consumer Magazine and Agri-Media Source* (Willmette, Ill.: Standard Rate and Data Services, 1994).

[44] Anthony Bogaert and Deborah Turkovich, "A Content Analysis of Playboy Centerfolds From 1953 Through 1990: Changes in Explicitness, Objectification, and Model's Age," *The Journal of Sex Research* 30 (May 1993): 135.

---

[45] Robert Riggs, *"Miller v. California:* An Empirical Note," *Brigham Young University Law Review* 1981: 247.

[46] Harold Leventhal, "An Empirical Inquiry into the Effects of *Miller v. California* on the Control of Obscenity," *New York University Law Review* 52 (1977): 810.

[47] Cass Sunstein, *Democracy and the Problem of Free Speech* (New York: Macmillan, 1993).

THE LIMITED TRADITION OF PROTECTING OBSCENITY

Miller and its companion cases were aimed at restricting the transportation and sale of explicit erotica, but what of the possession of sexually explicit material? Coexisting with the doctrine that obscenity may be regulated is a second doctrine at the core of which is the concept that when persons are in the privacy of their homes, the government may not interfere with their personal thought process or their perusal of words or pictures. Under this doctrine, the private possession of erotica is legal.

This concept that the mere possession of obscenity for private use is beyond the reach of government was articulated best, probably, by Justice Thurgood Marshall in *Stanley v. Georgia,* a 1969 case.[48] When police searched the home of Robert Eli Stanley for bookmaking equipment, they found no gambling devices but discovered three reels of sexually explicit 8mm film.

In his majority opinion overturning Stanley's conviction, Justice Marshall found that the mere private possession of obscene matter could not be a crime under the Constitution. The state has no right "to control the moral content of a person's thoughts," Marshall wrote, and the right to receive information and ideas is critical. Wrote Marshall:

If the First Amendment means anything, it means that a state has no business telling a man, sitting alone in his own home, what books he may read or what films he may watch. Our whole constitutional heritage rebels at the thought of giving government the power to control men's minds.[49]

Stanley was as much a victory for home sanctity as for free expression. A year later the Supreme Court upheld homeowner prerogatives in another case involving erotica. In *Rowan v. U.S. Post Office* the Court gave homeowners "complete and unfettered discretion" to prohibit a pornography distributor from mailing erotic material to a homeowner's address. "[W]e are often 'captives' outside the sanctity of the home and subject to objectionable speech," the Court said. But that does not mean "we must be captives everywhere." The homeowner has sole discretion in deciding whether mailed material is erotically arousing or sexually provocative and can require the postal service to notify the mailer to stop sending the material to the homeowner.[50] Theoretically, a homeowner could judge a gun catalog or jewelry brochure, even one lacking human models, as erotic and order the distributor to cease further mailings.

State legislatures and supreme courts have minimized obscenity prosecutions. A state high court can do so by finding an obscenity statute unconstitutional as the Wisconsin Supreme Court did in 1980.[51] As long as the legislature remains inactive in redrafting a statute, obscenity prosecution is stymied. Similarly, in 1979 the Arkansas Supreme Court reversed a $1,000 fine and one-month jail term for the possession of one obscene film in a home.[52] And, as the result of the Iowa legislature, the dissemination and ownership of obscene material was legal for adults in Iowa from 1974 to 1976. In 1976 the Iowa legislature changed the law to make the sale of obscenity a misdemeanor.[53] For twelve years, 1973 to 1985, there were no obscenity prosecutions in North Carolina because of the complexity of state law. A specific work could not be the target of a criminal obscenity prosecution until it first had been declared obscene in an advisory hearing.[54]

It is difficult for state legislators to get elected on a platform of decriminalizing obscenity. In 1990 a federal district court judge in Florida told opponents of obscenity laws: "In sum, if persons subscribe to the view that obscenity should be legalized, they should take their petitions to Tallahassee, the Florida capital, not to the steps of the U.S. courthouse."[55] But most state legislatures have been unsympathetic.

Most actions to abolish obscenity laws come from state supreme courts, which are more independent of voters than state legislatures. The most dramatic example is Oregon. In 1987, the Oregon Supreme Court voted unanimously to decriminalize the sale or ownership of obscenity for consenting adults.[56] State law, however, continued to prohibit the sale of obscenity to unwilling viewers, captive audiences or minors. The court reversed the conviction of Earl Henry, the operator of an adult bookstore in Redmond, Oregon, ruling that the free expression clause of the state constitution was broader than the First Amendment and protected obscenity. The court reasoned that territorial law existing in

---

[48] 394 U.S. 557 (1969).

[49] *Id.* at 565.

[50] 397 U.S. 728, 737 (1970).

[51] *Wisconsin v. Princess Cinema,* 96 Wis. 2d 646, 658, 292 N.W.2d 807, 807 (Wis. 1980).

[52] *Buck v. Arkansas,* 265 Ark. 434, 578 S.W.2d 579 (1979).

[53] *Chelsea Theater Corp. v. Burlington,* 258 N.W.2d 372 (Iowa 1977).

[54] Samuel Currin and Robert Howers, "Regulation of Pornography — The North Carolina Approach," *Wake Forest Law Review* 21 (1986): 263.

[55] *Skywalker Records, Inc. v. Navarro,* 739 F. Supp. 578, 587 (S.D. Fla. 1990).

[56] *State v. Henry,* 302 Or. 510, 732 P.2d 9 (1987).

1857, when the state constitution was adopted, only prohibited the distribution of obscenity to minors. The court concluded: "In this state any person can write, print, read, say, or sell anything to a consenting adult even though the expression may be generally or universally considered 'obscene.'"[57]

Obscenity protection made other inroads in the Western United States. The Hawaii Supreme Court ruled that the right of privacy, which had been incorporated in its state constitution nine years earlier, protected adult possession of obscenity. "Since a person has the right to view pornographic items at home," the court said in a unanimous opinion, "there necessarily follows a correlative right to purchase such materials for this personal use, or the underlying privacy right becomes meaningless."[58] The court indicated in a footnote that it was not deciding the issue of child pornography, the sale to minors, the obtrusive public display of pornography, the showing of obscenity to a captive audience, or films that depicted actual killings.

The Oregon obscenity doctrine almost crossed the Columbia River into Washington. There, the state's supreme court voted 5-4 that the Washington constitution did not afford obscenity greater protection than the federal constitution. The four-judge minority favored Oregon's approach.[59] One vote made the difference in public policy between the two Pacific Northwest states.

PROTECTING CHILDREN AND JUVENILES

Even when obscenity is decriminalized for consenting adults, courts recognize the need to restrict obscene material from juveniles and children. The exception has two manifestations. First, federal and state law strictly prohibits the distribution of materials portraying children or juveniles in sexually explicit situations. Second, federal and state laws prohibit the sale of sexual materials to minors.

These laws don't merely ban the sale of legally obscene materials to minors; they ban the sale of sexual materials that clearly would be legal if sold to adults. This concept has been called "variable obscenity." Government may be stricter in prohibiting the sale of sexual materials to juveniles than to adults.

In 1968, the Supreme Court upheld a New York statute that made it a crime to sell materials containing nudity to anyone under the age of sixteen. Sam Ginsberg, the owner of a Bellmore, Long Island, luncheonette, sold two girlie magazines to a sixteen-year-

old on two different occasions. The magazines contained pictures of nude women that were clearly not obscene.[60] The Court upheld the conviction and denied that the statute lacked a rational justification, even though studies neither proved nor disproved a causal link between erotic material and the ethical and moral development of youths.

The Federal Communications Commission has applied the same logic in prohibiting the use of indecent language on commercial radio. The Supreme Court has said radio may be censored more than print media because of its intrusiveness and its accessibility to children.[61] The case began when WBAI broadcast a twelve-minute monologue by George Carlin, "Filthy Words," at 2 p.m. Though the station preceded the monologue with an advisory that the Carlin routine contained offensive language, a man who was driving with his young son missed the advisory and tuned in to the middle of the monologue. He was offended and complained to the FCC.

The Supreme Court voted 5-4 to uphold possible civil sanctions against the radio station, but the decision was based on the fact that radio is "uniquely available to children." The majority said the decision balanced the significant interests of listeners in their homes against the broadcasters' interests. A concurring opinion indicated that the ruling did not apply to the isolated use of an offensive word in a broadcast. Eleven years later, in 1989, the Supreme Court underscored the importance of the intrusiveness factor and invalidated a ban on telephone indecency. The FCC was attempting to control the dial-a-porn business that made sexually oriented messages available to people who called 900 numbers. The Court indicated that the telephone was not nearly as intrusive as the radio: "Placing a telephone call is not the same as tuning in a radio and being taken by surprise by an indecent message."[62]

From 1989 to 1993, while Alfred Sikes was FCC chairman, the commission actively enforced radio's prohibition against indecency and levied fines of from $2,000 to $600,000. Most notorious was shock-jock Howard Stern, who drew the $600,000 fine for his off-color morning commentary. He was cited for his numerous and explicit references to masturbation, fornication, excretory functions and sexual organs.

The Court indicated in 1975 that there were limits to how far it would go to shelter children and disinterested adults from offen-

---

[57] 302 Or. at 525, 732 P.2d at 18.

[58] *State v. Kam,* 69 Haw. 483, 748 P.2d 372, 373 (1988).

[59] *State v. Reece,* 110 Wash. 2d 766, 757 P.2d 947 (1988).

[60] *Ginsberg v. New York,* 390 U.S. 629 (1968).

[61] *FCC v. Pacifica Foundation,* 438 U.S. 726 (1978).

[62] *Sable Communications v. FCC,* 492 U.S. 115, 128 (1989).

sive speech that was not legally obscene.[63] The Court ruled that a city ordinance prohibiting the showing of films with nudity in drive-in theaters with screens visible from streets or public places was unconstitutional. The theater was prosecuted for the R-rated film, *Class of '74.* The outdoor screen was visible from two city streets and a church parking lot. The majority said that the censorship was not justified by the limited privacy interests of persons on public streets who could simply look away when confronted by offensive material. The Court said that "clearly all nudity cannot be deemed obscene even as to minors."[64] Such a rule would bar films with pictures of baby's buttocks, nude bodies of war victims, cultures in which nudity is indigenous, the opening of art exhibits and bathers on a nude beach.

The Supreme Court applied similar logic when it invalidated the Communications Decency Act of 1996. The act made it a crime to communicate indecent material on the Internet to persons 17 or younger. The act defined "indecency" as patently offensive descriptions of sexual or excretory activities or organs. The Supreme Court said that the act would allow Internet users to be punished for disseminating such things as the seven "dirty words" of the George Carlin monologue, discussions of prison rape or safe sexual practices, artistic images that include nudity or arguably the card catalog of the Carnegie Library. The Court concluded that the Internet was not as available to children as radio and television and that it was unconstitutional to deprive adults of sexual matter that was indecent but not obscene. The court said that banning such material from the "vast democratic for a of the Internet" was like "burning the house to roast the pig."[65]

Films or media that portray minors in erotic or suggestive poses are quite another matter. The Supreme Court, Congress, state supreme courts and state legislatures have been unequivocal in supporting the criminalization of what is known as "child pornography." In 1982, the Supreme Court upheld a state statute that prohibited the dissemination of material with sexual performances by children under the age of sixteen. *New York v. Ferber*[66] involved a Manhattan store that sold to an undercover police officer films of young boys masturbating. The Court conceded that material depicting children in sexual situations could be prosecuted even if the material would not be obscene had it depicted adults in the same situations. But, in reversing the highest appellate court

in the state, the Court said that the paramount concern in such cases was protecting children who were portrayed in such materials from psychological, emotional and mental harm. This was clearly a compelling state interest that justified some limits on expression.

Eight years later, the Supreme Court upheld an Ohio child pornography law that prohibited the possession of materials depicting nude children unless they served a bona fide artistic, scientific or educational purpose.[67] Clyde Osborne was sentenced to six months in prison for the possession of four photographs of juvenile, nude males in sexually explicit positions. The Court said that the gravity of the state interest in protecting victims of child pornography justified the limits on free expression. The Ohio Supreme Court specified that it was limiting its ruling to the lewd exhibition or graphic focus on genitals to prevent punishment for possession of innocuous photographs of naked children.

Thus child pornography joins fighting words as one of the few categories of legally taboo speech in American society.

PANDERING AND ZONING

Most of this chapter has analyzed the definitional approach for controlling obscenity. Zoning laws and the concept of pandering are other approaches for controlling explicit material. The more obscure of the two is pandering.

Pandering. The classic pandering case is *Ginzburg v. United States.* Ralph Ginzburg was sentenced to five years in federal prison and fined $42,000 because of the method he used to promote his erotic but non-obscene books and periodicals. What was thought to be a liberal Supreme Court upheld the conviction by a 5-4 vote. Earl Warren and William Brennan voted to uphold the conviction because of Ginzburg's blatant pandering: "The business of purveying textual or graphic matter openly advertised to appeal to the erotic interest of their customers."[68]

Ginzburg — a former articles editor for *Esquire* and staff writer for NBC and *Reader's Digest* — mailed nine million copies of a brochure to promote the book, *The Housewife's Handbook on Selective Promiscuity;* the newsletter, *Liaison;* and the hardcover quarterly devoted to love and sex, *Eros.* The mailings generated 150,000, $25 subscriptions to *Eros.*

The Supreme Court said Ginzburg's method of promotion could be used to judge the content of the works: "Where the pur-

---

[63] *Erznoznok v. Jacksonville,* 422 U.S. 205 (1975).

[64] *Id.* at 212.

[65] *Reno v. American Civil Liberties Union,* 117 S.Ct. 2329, 2343 (1997).

[66] 458 U.S. 747 (1982).

[67] *Osborne v. Ohio,* 495 U.S. 103 (1990).

[68] 383 U.S. 463, 467 (1966).

veyor's sole emphasis is on the sexually provocative aspects of his publications, that fact may be decisive in the determination of obscenity."[69] Ginzburg had highlighted the erotic nature of his publications by mailing the promotions from cities whose names had sexual connotations: Intercourse and Blue Ball, Pennsylvania, and Middlesex, New Jersey.

The Court's decision was denounced by civil libertarians who pointed out that none of Ginzburg's publications were even close to satisfying the court's own definition of obscenity. *Eros* had received a number of national graphics awards, including one from the National Society of Art Directors. In order to secure a conviction, federal prosecutors had moved the trial from New York City to the more conservative Philadelphia, where the mayor had narrowly won election on a promise to rid the city of smut, and the police department's obscenity control squad recently had arrested twenty-two magazine dealers and confiscated seventeen vanloads of magazines. Ginzburg's appeal to the Supreme Court was supported by briefs of the American Civil Liberties Union, the Authors League of America and a group of writers that included Joseph Heller, James Jones, Norman Mailer and Arthur Miller.

Zoning. A decade after *Ginzburg*, the Supreme Court approved another non-content approach for the control of pornography. In *Young v. American Mini Theatres, Inc.,* the Court allowed cities to use zoning laws to limit the location and concentration of businesses that specialize in erotic media.[70] The Pussy Cat, an adult theater in what had been a corner gas station, challenged a Detroit ordinance. The law said that an adult business could not be located within 1,000 feet of two other adult businesses, or within 500 feet of a residential neighborhood. Adult businesses included pool halls, pawnshops and adult bookstores and theatres. The intent of the ordinance was to prevent the concentration of such businesses on one street.

In an opinion by Justice John Paul Stevens, the Court upheld the Detroit ordinance. Stevens said the ordinance did not impose content limitations on the creators of adult movies or significantly restrict the viewing of such movies. Stevens concluded that the impact of the ordinance on free expression was at most incidental and minimal. He attempted to create a doctrine granting erotic speech less protection than political speech, noting that "it is manifest that society's interest in protecting this type of expression is of a wholly different, and lesser, magnitude, than the interest in untrammeled political debate."[71] But only a minority of justices joined him on that point.

The advent of the VCR and the proliferation of video rental stores with adult movie sections, and the growth of cable TV with its adult networks, have diminished the significance of the *Young* decision. Adult theatres are a dying business.

RATINGS AND LABELING

Young helped to shield disinterested adults from unwanted, erotic media. It empowered cities to isolate adult businesses from homes, schools and churches and made it easier for disinterested adults to avoid such businesses. Offensive businesses that are unobtrusive and easily avoided are easier to tolerate. The voluntary labeling of movies, recordings and video games has had the same effect. It gives adults fair warning about the explicit content of media and assists them in avoiding material they find offensive for themselves or their children.

The most successful of the rating systems was initiated by the Motion Picture Association of America after Jack Valenti took over as president in 1966. That year a new kind of frankness emerged in movies. *Who's Afraid of Virginia Woolf* included the word "screw" and the phrase "hump the hostess." More movies contained nudity. Because of the fear of government censorship, the movie industry decided to create its own system for rating films. The system has changed over the years. As it exists today, the system has five categories:

- *G — General Audiences.* All ages are admitted. The film contains nothing in language, nudity and sex, or violence that would offend parents whose children view the film. Snippets of language may go beyond polite conversation, but they are common, everyday expressions.
- *PG — Parental Guidance Suggested.* Some material may not be suitable for children. There may be some profanity, violence or brief nudity, but these elements are not intense. There is no drug use content.
- *PG-13 — Parents Strongly Cautioned.* Some material may be inappropriate for children under 13. The rating is required for drug use content or use of harsher, sexually derived words.
- *R — Restricted.* The admission of people under age 17 requires accompanying parent or adult guardian. The movie contains some adult material: hard language, tough violence, nudity within sensual scenes or drug abuse.
- *NC-17 — No Children Under 17 Admitted.* The content of the movie is patently inappropriate for youngsters. The rating does not necessarily mean the content is obscene or pornographic.

---

69 *Id.* at 470.

70 427 U.S. 50 (1976).

71 *Id.* at 70.

It can mean the presence of violence or sex or aberrational behavior or drug use that is too strong and therefore off-limits for viewing by children.

Leaders in the motion picture industry consider the movie rating system a success. The system has been embraced by the National Association of Theater Owners and by the Video Software Dealers Association. Polls conducted by the Opinion Research Corporation of Princeton, New Jersey, show that three-quarters of parents with children find the system very useful or fairly useful in selecting movies for their children.

Ratings also have been adopted by the recording and video games industries, but in a more limited way. In 1985, the Recording Industry Association of America agreed to encourage its members to place the warning "Explicit Lyrics — Parental Advisory," on recordings containing explicit sex, violence or substance abuse. Instead of the warning, song lyrics may be printed on the back of the album cover. In 1994, the Software Publishers Association, following threats from Congress, agreed to encourage its members to label computer and video games. Games are labeled for age appropriateness and for the explicitness of violence, nudity or sex, and language. The major advantage of movie, record and video game ratings is that, because they alert consumers to content, they tend to discourage the involvement of government in controlling that content.

SUMMARY

The centrist decision in *Miller v. California* displeased liberals, conservatives, civil libertarians and religious fundamentalists. The decision did not achieve the hoped-for effect of reducing the availability of erotica. In fact, explicit erotica has grown in popularity since *Miller,* thanks in part to changes in media technology and the developments with VCRs, cable and the Internet. The increase in erotica has occurred despite the actions of virtually every state legislature to draft restrictive statutes to comply with *Miller.* Erotica also has become quite commonplace in Canada, which has an eighty-five-store chain called "Adults Only Video." Under Canadian Supreme Court rules, portrayals of explicit sex are legal if they do not include degradation or violence.

Why has erotica prospered while laws have become more restrictive? The answer is public opinion, which has grown quite tolerant of unobtrusive erotica. For example, a 1990 survey in Orlando found that only a minority wished to ban erotica: twenty-eight percent for sexually explicit videos, thirty-two percent for sexually explicit movies and twenty-five percent for magazines that show nudity. Larger percentages wanted to ban violence or the combination of sex and violence.[72] Liberal public opinion translates into less pressure on prosecutors and police to enforce obscenity laws. The concept of jury nullification also limits obscenity convictions: Jurors make their decisions based on conscience and overall justice and not on the law.

FOR ADDITIONAL READING

Christensen, F. M. *Pornography: The Other Side.* New York: Praeger, 1990.

Dworkin, Andrea and Catharine A. MacKinnon. *Pornography & Civil Rights: A New Day for Women's Equality.* Minneapolis: Organizing Against Pornography, 1988.

Lewis, Felice Flanery. *Literature, Obscenity, & Law.* Carbondale: Southern Illinois University Press, 1976.

Linz, Daniel. "Estimating Community Standards: The Use of Social Science Evidence in an Obscenity Prosecution," *Public Opinion Quarterly* 55 (Spring 1991): 80-112.

MacKinnon, Catharine A. *Only Words.* Cambridge: Harvard University Press, 1993.

Michael, Robert T., et al. *Sex in America: A Definitive Survey.* New York: Little, Brown and Company, 1994.

Strossen, Nadine. *Defending Pornography: Free Speech, Sex, and the Fight for Women's Rights.* New York: Scribner, 1995.

---

[72] Randy Fisher, Ida Cook and Edwin Shirkey, "Correlates of Support for Censorship of Sexual, Sexually Violent, and Violent Media," *The Journal of Sex Research* 31 (1994): 229.

Libel: The Plaintiff's Case

By Kyu Ho Youm

Freedom of speech is not absolute. It must be balanced against other competing social interests. One area in which such balancing must occur is that of defamation. The U.S. Supreme Court has said, "[A]bsolute protection for the communications media requires a total sacrifice of the competing value served by the law of defamation."[1]

The libel law of a society indicates to a large extent how society balances the importance of reputational interests with freedom of speech. Harm to reputation has been a criminal offense or a civil wrong since civilization's earliest days, but the social and cultural approach to reputation as a value varies from society to society. Professor Robert C. Post elaborates:

Defamation law would operate differently in a deference society than in a market society. In the latter, reputation is a quintessentially private possession; it is created by individual effort and is of importance primarily to those who have created it. Reputation's claim to legal protection is neither greater nor less than the claim to public protection of similar private goods. The preservation of honor in a deference society, on the other hand, entails more than the protection of merely individual interests. Since honor is not created by individual labor, but instead by shared social perceptions that transcend the behavior of particular persons, honor is "public good, not merely a private pos-

session."[2]

In the United States, defamation was one of the earliest legal actions available against the press, and it is still the most common legal danger to the media. Libel is clearly an occupational hazard for professional communicators: Seventy percent of all libel actions are filed against the mass media; at least two-thirds of those are brought against newspapers.

Libel, then, has the very real possibility of chilling speech, particularly when one considers the ramifications of a libel suit. As attorney Barbara Dill writes:

Libel law in the United States is at a critical juncture. The old broken formula of sue-and-be-sued is not working well for anyone but lawyers. It costs too much, takes too long, and clogs the courts with fencing matches that end most often in technical decisions that bypass the fundamental issues and satisfy neither side.[3]

The chill caused by libel law is clearly an irony in the United

---

[1] *Gertz v. Robert Welch, Inc.,* 418 U.S. 341, 341 (1974).

[2] Robert C. Post, "The Social Foundations of Defamation Law: Reputation and the Constitution," *California Law Review* 74 (1986): 702.

[3] Barbara Dill, "Libel Law Doesn't Work, But Can It Be Fixed," in Martin London and Barbara Dill, *At What Price? Libel Law and Freedom of the Press* (New York: Twentieth Century Fund Press, 1993), p. 35.

States, where press freedom is protected as a constitutional right, but reputation is not. In many ways, First Amendment scholar Frederick Schauer writes, "the American approach ... reflects a society in which the press is considered to occupy a much more important role in the resolution of public issues. The press occupies a special position in the American system, a position that accounts for its strong protection against inhibiting defamation laws."[4]

Although libel suits are common, and while there are no guarantees, professional communicators can be proactive in an attempt to stay out of trouble and to provide themselves with more protection should they be sued.

This chapter reviews libel law from the plaintiff's perspective. It focuses on the elements of a cause of action for libel and related areas, including the technological impact of cyberspace. It also explores the policy justifications underlying the law of defamation. Chapter 7 provides an overview of libel defenses.

DEFAMATION DEFINED

Defamation — the publication of material that would tend to hold one up to hatred, ridicule, contempt or spite — consists of twin torts: libel and slander. In general, libel is the publication of defamatory matter by written or printed words or by some other physical form. Slander is defamatory communication by spoken words, gestures or other transitory means.[5]

The distinction between libel and slander originated when relatively few people could read and the spoken word was more credible. Since then, the written word has gained more credibility and defamation by writing is perceived to cause greater harm. More recently, however, new modes of communication have developed that often make the distinction between libel and slander obsolete. Defamation by means of television or radio, for example, might have more impact and greater reach than that by a small newspaper. Modern legal guides suggest that, instead of the form of communication medium, courts should consider the area of dissemination, the deliberate and premeditated character of a publication and the persistence of the defamation when classifying a defamatory statement as libel or slander.[6]

Jurisdictions often disagree whether defamation by electronic means should be defined as libel or slander. Most states do not distinguish libel from slander with regard to broadcasting, but four, including California, treat defamatory radio and television broadcasts as slander, and thirteen states, including New York, treat it as libel. A New York court explained its rationale:

When account is taken of the vast and far-flung audience reached by radio today, often far greater in number than the readers of the largest metropolitan newspaper, it is evident that the broadcast of scandalous utterances is in general as potentially harmful to the defamed person's reputation as a publication by writing. That defamation by radio, in the absence of a script or transcription, lacks the measure of durability possessed by written libel, in nowise lessens its capacity for harm.[7]

Some states — Connecticut and Tennessee are two — make a distinction between a statement broadcast from a script — libel — and that which is ad-libbed — slander. An appellate court in Georgia, noting that television broadcasting contains both libel and slander, coined the word "defamacast" to describe broadcast defamation. The court said, "Perhaps the most perplexing problem is whether defamatory material shown on television should be classified as a libel, a slander or in some third category." The court decided to classify this type of material: "Believing as we do that the common law must adapt, and classically has adapted, to meet new situations, we now make that 'frank recognition...' that defamation by radio and television falls into a new category, thus completing the triptych. In this category, defamation by broadcast or 'defamacast' is actionable per se."[8]

While debate on the issue continues, an increasing number of jurisdictions are accepting the position that, because of the wide dissemination and the increased power of the broadcast media, defamation by electronic means is closer to libel than slander.

THE RATIONALE AND REACH OF LIBEL LAW

Libel law protects the reputational interests of individuals because it involves statements about them made by others. Legal scholar David Anderson has identified four types of reputational harm in the context of relational interest. The defamation may (1) interfere with the plaintiff's existing relationships with other people; (2) in-

---

[4] Frederick Schauer, "Social Foundations of the Law of Defamation: A Comparative Analysis," *Journal of Media Law and Practice* 1 (May 1980): 3.

[5] See *Restatement (Second) of Torts,* secs. 568(1) and 568(2) (1977).

[6] *Id.* at sec. 568(3) (1977).

---

[7] *Shor v. Billingsley,* 4 Misc.2d 857, 158 N.Y.S.2d 476, 484 (Sup. Ct. 1956).

[8] *American Broadcasting-Paramount Theatres, Inc. v. Simpson,* 106 Ga. App. 230, 240, 126 S.E.2d 873, 876, 879 (1962).

terfere with future relationships; (3) destroy a favorable public image; (4) create a negative public image for a person who previously had no public image at all.[9]

Libel law also serves other important societal interests. It attempts to compensate for economic and emotional injury and promotes human dignity by providing a civilized forum in which a dispute is settled.

More importantly, however, libel law acts as a deterrent on the publication of false and injurious speech through the award of damages. The Supreme Court has noted, for example, that a state "may rightly employ its libel laws to discourage the deception of its citizens."[10] In addition, libel law serves a vital social interest by providing a check on media power. It opens the news-gathering and decision-making process of the media to public scrutiny and accountability. A federal judge in a libel action against *Time* magazine explained:

> *Time* has refused to issue any correction or to print plaintiff's denial. Only through the litigation process has plaintiff been able to uncover and publish the evidence from which *Time* claimed to have learned the contents of the [a secret document] relating to the Beirut massacre in 1982]. And only through this avenue has he been able to bring to light the process by which the allegedly offending statement came to be written, including evidence of the possible motivations and truthfulness of its author. That this process has proved enormously expensive, and painfully contentious, is as much the product of *Time's* all-out litigation strategy as of any plan by plaintiff to intimidate the press.[11]

Libel, Constitution and State Law

Even though reputational rights are not explicitly recognized by the Constitution, the value of a good name has often been noted by American courts. In an often quoted opinion, Justice Potter Stewart characterized an individual's right to protection of reputation as "a concept at the root of any decent system of ordered liberty." Justice Stewart continued: "The protection of private personality, like the protection of life itself, is left primarily to the individual States under the Ninth and Tenth Amendments. But this does not mean that the right is entitled to any less recognition by

this Court as a basic of our constitutional system."[12] Therefore, the Supreme Court has recognized that "society has a pervasive and strong interest in preventing and redressing attacks upon reputation."[13]

The Constitution, of course, is not the only source of law to be used in balancing free speech and reputational rights. State constitutions and common law play a significant role in protecting press rights and in allowing individuals to protect their reputations. In addition, state statutes can affect libel conflicts. Statues of limitations — laws that prevent stale lawsuits from being adjudicated — and retraction statutes — which can mitigate or eliminate some damages—are examples of state laws that directly affect libel.

In addition, the First Amendment principle that prior restraint is presumptively unconstitutional applies to attempts to restrain material because it may be defamatory. State courts have rejected attempts to halt the publication of material because it may be defamatory. However, one state supreme court did not rule out a possibility of defamatory statements being to subject to prior restraint in limited circumstances. The Nebraska Supreme Court held in 1997: "[A]bsent a prior adversarial determination that the complained of publication is false or a misleading representation of fact, equity will not ... enjoin a libel or slander, unless such libel or slander is published (1) in violation of a trust or contract, or (2) in aid of another tort or unlawful act, or (3) injunctive relief is essential for the preservation of a property right."[14]

Criminal Libel

Twenty-one states have statutes that allow the government to prosecute people for defaming public officials, libeling the dead and using racial or ethnic epithets. These statutes are rarely used today, but the Supreme Court has not yet repudiated criminal libel. Indeed, the Court, in *Garrison v. Louisiana*,[15] extended the actual malice rule — knowledge of falsity or reckless disregard of the truth—rule to criminal libel.

Criminal libel had its genesis in *De Libellis Famosis*, an English case in which Lord Coke delineated the principal points of the action:

---

[9] David A. Anderson, "Reputation, Compensation, and Proof," *William & Mary Law Review* 25 (1984): 765-66.

[10] *Keeton v. Hustler*, 465 U.S. 770, 776 (1984).

[11] *Sharon v. Time*, 559 F. Supp. 538, 556 (S.D.N.Y. 1985).

[12] *Rosenblatt v. Baer*, 383 U.S. 75, 92 (1966).

[13] *Milkovich v. Lorain Journal Co.*, 497 U.S. 1, 22 (1990), quoting *Rosenblett v. Baer*, 383 U.S. 75, 86 (1966).

[14] *Sid Dillon Chevrolet-Oldsmobile-Pontiac, Inc. v. Sullivan*, 251 Neb. 722, 732, 559 N.W.2d 740, 747 (1997).

[15] 379 U.S. 64 (1964).

Every libel is made either against a private man, or against a magistrate or public person. If it be against a private man it deserves a severe punishment, for although the libel be made against one, yet it incites all those of the same family, kindred or society to revenge, and so tends *per consequens* to quarrels and breach of the peace, and may be the cause of the shedding of blood and greater inconvenience; if it be against a magistrate, or other public person, it is a greater offense; for it concerns not only the breach of the peace, but also the scandal of Government; for what greater scandal of Government can there be than to have corrupt and wicked magistrates to be appointed by the King to govern his subject under him.[16]

In 1991, a U.S. district court struck down the 1912 criminal statute of South Carolina, finding the statute unconstitutional because it allowed liability upon a showing of common law malice — ill will, spite or hatred — rather than actual malice.[17] Four years later, however, the Tenth U.S. Circuit Court of Appeals upheld the Kansas criminal defamation statute of 1988. The federal appeals court held that the Kansas statute is not unconstitutional on its face because it requires establishment of actual malice in libel cases involving matters of public concern.[18]

THE LIBEL ACTION

Before the Supreme Court constitutionalized libel law in 1964 with *New York Times Co. v. Sullivan,*[19] the basic requirements for a plaintiff in making a case for defamation were proof that the defendant published a statement about the plaintiff that had a tendency to harm the plaintiff's reputation in the community or to discourage other people from associating or dealing with the plaintiff. The burden was on the plaintiff to prove three essential elements: identification of the plaintiff, publication of the allegedly defamatory statement and the defamatory nature of the statement.

But the requirements in a modern libel action are not that simple. To win damages, especially in libel actions against the media, a plaintiff must establish that: (1) a false *and* defamatory statement of fact concerning the plaintiff was published to a third party, (2) the publication was not privileged and was made with fault on the part of the publisher, and (3) the publication caused actual injury.

Falsity

Under the common law, when a libel action was filed, statements upon which the action was based were presumed to be false. As a matter of constitutional law, however, that presumption of falsity has been rejected. Libel plaintiffs today must prove the statements are false, even if the statements were made with ill will.

Media attorneys Robert Sack and Sandra Baron, in the highly acclaimed *Libel, Slander, and Related Problems,* wrote that under the constitutional rule, "Truth is usually now not a defense. Proof of falsity is instead part of the plaintiff's case, at least in defamation suits brought by public officials, or involving communications about public issues, or both."[20]

Defamation

In addition to being false, offending material must be defamatory. Identifying defamatory language is the first order of business in libel law. As one scholar wrote, however, "words are not single faced. They have many facets and may have many interpretations. Their values change with time, with place, and with association. Whether or not a word has a libelous connotation will therefore require analysis and perception in terms of its milieu and period."[21] Supreme Court Justice Oliver Wendell Holmes also observed: "A word is not a crystal, transparent and unchanged; it is the skin of a living thought and may vary greatly in color and content according to the circumstances and the time in which it is used."[22] Thus, the same words may communicate different meanings in different contexts.

Socialism, love, democracy, communism and other words are capable of as many connotations and interpretations as there are situations in which they can be used. Consequently, words can be ambiguous. One cannot say with assurance that a word is or is not defamatory unless it has been placed in time, in location and in association so that its meaning can be determined. As the Hawaii Supreme Court said, whether a statement is defamatory "depends, among other factors, upon the temper of times, the current of contemporary public opinion, with the result that a word, harmless in one age, in one community, may be highly dam-

---

[16] 77 Eng. Rep. 250, 251 (1609).

[17] *Fitts v. Kolb.,* 779 F. Supp. 1502 (D.S.C. 1991).

[18] *Phelps v. Hamilton,* 59 F.3d 1058 (10th Cir. 1995).

[19] 376 U.S. 254 (1964).

[20] Robert D. Sack and Sandra S. Baron, *Libel, Slander, and Related Problems,* 2d ed. (New York: Practising Law Institute, 1994), pp. 171-72.

[21] Philip Wittenberg, *Dangerous Words: A Guide to the Law of Libel* (New York: Columbia University Press, 1947), p. 11.

[22] *Towne v. Eisner,* 245 U.S. 418, 425 (1918).

aging to reputation at another time or in a different place."[23]

Though time, place and context are important, some legal commentators have compiled lists of words and expressions that have been held by various courts to be defamatory. Attorney Bruce Sanford has listed a number of so-called "red flag," words: addict, adultery, AIDS, alcoholic, atheist, bankrupt, bigamist, blacklisted, blackmail, bribery, cheater, child abuse, con artist, coward, crook, deadbeat, drug abuser, drunkard, ex-convict, fraud, gangster, gay, Herpes, hypocrite, incompetent, infidelity, Jekyll-Hyde personality, kept woman, Ku Klux Klan, Mafia, mentally ill, Nazi, neo-Nazi, peeping Tom, perjurer, plagiarist, prostitute, rapist, scam, scoundrel, seducer, shyster, slacker, stool pigeon, suicide, swindle, thief, unethical, unmarried mother, unprofessional, unsound mind, villain.[24]

Again, compendiums of words cannot be considered a foolproof formula to divining how courts will rule on similar language. Sanford's list, however, is based on the eight categories of words that are especially sensitive.[25] They are words that:

- impute to another a loathsome disease;
- accuse another of serious sexual misconduct;
- impugn another's honest or integrity;
- accuse another of committing a crime or of being arrested or indicted;
- allege racial, ethnic or religious bigotry;
- impugn another's financial health or credit-worthiness;
- accuse another of associating with criminals or others of unsavory character;
- assert incompetence or lack of ability in one's trade, business, profession or office.

Interpreting Defamation. Defamation is recipient-oriented. That is, it hinges on how the language is interpreted by its recipients. Thus, the first step in analyzing the defamatory nature of a statement is determining whether the recipients could interpret the words to be defamatory and whether they did so. The value judgments, knowledge and background of recipients will affect their interpretation of statements. For example, people who support abortion as a constitutional right of privacy would not consider it defamatory for a person to be depicted as being "pro-choice." In contrast, those who view abortion as morally reprehensible might lose their reputations among a certain group by be-

ing depicted as "pro-choice." So, whose understanding of a defamatory statement is used in establishing the defamatory nature of the statement?

The *Restatement (Second) of Torts,* a legal tract designed to explain the law, states that "[i]t is enough that the communication would tend to prejudice [the plaintiff] in the eyes of *a substantial and respectable minority"* of the community, and "it is not enough that the communication would be derogatory in the view of a single individual or a very small group of persons, if the group is not large enough to constitute a substantial minority."[26]

As an example, a prison inmate was unsuccessful in maintaining a libel action when he was identified as an FBI informant, because, the court said, he was not accused of unlawful or improper conduct. Noting that the defamatory statement must expose the plaintiff to public ridicule "in the minds of 'right thinking persons' or among 'a considerable and respectable class of people,'" the court stated: "It is true that a charge of informing may bring opprobrium from one's·fellow inmates in the prison community. However, it is not one's reputation in a limited community in which attitudes and social values may depart substantially from those prevailing generally which an action for defamation is designed to protect."[27]

Rules of Construction. Most states use the reasonable construction rule to determine the defamatory nature of a statement. Under the rule, the meaning of a communication, according to the *Restatement,* "is that which the recipient correctly, or mistakenly but reasonably, understands it was intended to express." The rule does not allow a strained interpretation. The Alabama Supreme Court provided a good explication of the rule:

[T]he printed words are to be taken in their natural meaning, and according to the sense in which they appear to have been used and the idea they are adapted to convey to those who read them. A forced construction is not to be put upon them in order to relieve the defendant from liability, nor are they to be subjected to the critical analysis of a trained legal mind, but must be construed and determined by the natural and probable effect on the mind of the average lay reader.[28]

By contrast, the innocent construction rule, which is applied in a few states, requires a statement "to be considered in context,

---

[23] *Beamer v. Nishiki,* 66 Haw. 572, 580, 670 P.2d 1264, 1271 (1983).

[24] Bruce W. Sanford, *Libel and Privacy,* 2d ed. (Englewood Cliffs: Aspen Law & Business, 1998), sec. 4.13.

[25] Neil J. Rosini, *The Practical Guide to Libel Law* (New York: Praeger, 1991), p. 9.

[26] *Restatement (Second) of Torts,* sec. 559 comm. e (1977) (emphasis added).

[27] *Saunders v. WHYY,* 382 S.2d 257, 259 (Del. Super. Ct. 1978).

[28] *Kelly v. Arrington,* 624 So. 2d 546, 548-49 (Ala. 1993).

with the words and the implications therefrom given their natural and obvious meaning; if, as so construed, the statement may reasonably be innocently interpreted or reasonably be interpreted as referring to someone other than the plaintiff it cannot be actionable per se."[29]

The *Restatement* indicates that a report of a single act of misconduct by a person in the course of the person's business, trade, profession or office may be sufficient to support a libel action, even though the charge does not imply a habitual course or conduct. A number of states, however, have adopted the single instance rule, which provides that a charge of ignorance or a mistake on a single occasion is not actionable unless special damages can be shown. The rule is based on the common-sense premise that people make mistakes, and to state that a professional has made a mistake in a specific instance should not cause damage because the statement only implies that the person is human.

Implication. Defamation by implication occurs when false impressions arise from truthful statements. It demonstrates the larger problem of determining the meaning of an allegedly defamatory communication by examining the words in context. One example of defamation by implication is a story published by the *Memphis Press-Scimitar*. The story reported that Mrs. Ruth A. Nichols was treated for a bullet wound she received when another woman found Mrs. Nichols with the woman's husband in the Nichols home. According to witnesses, the woman fired at her husband, then at Mrs. Nichols. The story was true. The Tennessee Supreme Court held, however, that the story was defamatory because it omitted crucial facts.[30] What the newspaper did not report was that Mrs. Nichols and the suspect's husband were not alone in the Nichols home; Mrs. Nichols's husband and two neighbors were also there, and Mr. Nichols had attempted to prevent the shooting.

Defamation through implication often arises in one of three contexts: (1) when a writer tries to guide a reader to a conclusion without stating the conclusion; (2) when a writer is ambiguous, offering multiple meanings, at least one of which is defamatory; (3) when a writer juxtaposes one message with another, creating an implication that is not necessarily intended.

An important tract on the law of torts has explained that proof of defamation by implication requires a combination of elements, defined by the terms "inducement," "innuendo" and "colloquium," explained here:

If the plaintiffs themselves are not directly named they must show by "colloquium" that the statements were "of and concerning" them. If it is still not clear how the plaintiffs have been defamed, they must plead extrinsic facts that would permit a defamatory meaning to be applied to defendants' words. This allegation of extrinsic facts is called the "inducement...." Where a statement is not clearly defamatory on its face it is the function of the innuendo to assert the meaning that plaintiff attaches to the passage and any additions by colloquium and inducement. The innuendo is not a fact but is the plaintiff's assertion of how the passage would be understood by those who heard the defendant's words and knew the additional unstated facts.[31]

To state, for example, that John Doe ran his car into an utility pole is not defamatory since he has every right to do so. But when it is specifically pleaded as "inducement" that Doe insured the car and, as "innuendo," that the statement is construed to mean that he was defrauding the insurance company, a charge of property damage is clearly implied, which is defamatory.

The Supreme Court has not addressed the issue of whether those who defame through implication are liable for damages. Several lower courts, however — including courts in Minnesota, Louisiana, Tennessee and Michigan — have declined to recognize liability for defamatory implications. The basis for the rulings appears to be this premise:

If unrestrained ... the theory of libel by implication would allow a jury to draw whatever inferences it wished, truthful or otherwise, from statements of fact. It would thereby permit liability for the mere tone of a publication, for statements that are in substance opinion or true, or for statements about public persons that do not pass the "actual malice" test because they do not constitute knowing falsity or "reckless disregard for the truth."[32]

The California Supreme Court, for example, has noted that a false and defamatory meaning cannot be based on "the fact that some person might, with extra sensitive perception, understand such a meaning.... Rather, the test ... is whether by reasonable implication a defamatory meaning may be found in the communication."[33]

---

[29] *Chapski v. Copley Press,* 8 Media L. Rep. (BNA) 2403, 2406 (Ill. 1982).

[30] *Memphis Publishing Co. v. Nichols,* 569 S.W.2d 412 (Tenn. 1978).

[31] T. Barton Carter, *et. al., The First Amendment and the Fourth Estatae,* 7th ed. (Westbury, Ct.: Foundation Press, 1997), p. 91.

[32] Sack and Baron, *supra* note 20, at 85.

[33] *Forsher v. Bugliosi,* 26 Cal. 3d 792, 805-06, 608 P.2d 716 (1980).

Libel per se and libel per quod. A statement that is libelous *per se* is defamatory on its face. That is, the defamation is apparent in the statement. If additional information is required before a statement is defamatory, the statement is libelous *per quod,* and a plaintiff must prove special damages — that there was, in fact, a loss of money — before the plaintiff can recover.

The distinction between libel *per se* and libel *per quod* was weakened in 1974 when, in *Gertz v. Robert Welch, Inc.,*[34] the Supreme Court required plaintiffs to prove damages before recovering, but in many jurisdictions, the distinction remains as a rule of law. The Missouri Supreme Court no longer recognizes a distinction between libel *per se* and libel *per quod.* That court stated that the rule created unjustifiable inequities by requiring a higher standard of proof for certain defamations. "[I]n defamation cases the old rules of *per se* and *per quod* do not apply and plaintiff need only to plead and prove the unified defamation elements," the Missouri high court held. "In short, plaintiffs need not concern themselves with whether the defamation was *per se* or *per quod,* or with whether special damages exist, but must prove actual damages in all cases."[35]

By contrast, Illinois is one of the jurisdictions where the *per se/per quod* distinction is still recognized. In *Bryson v. News America Publications, Inc.,*[36] for example, the Illinois Supreme Court held that a statement is defamatory *per se* if it falls into one of five statutorily defined categories: (1) commission of a crime; (2) infection with a type of communicable disease that could cause the infected person to be avoided; (3) malfeasance in the performance of a job; (4) unfitness for one's profession or trade; and (5) if the statement falsely accuses plaintiff of "fornication or adultery."[37]

The plaintiff in *Bryson* sued the publisher of *Seventeen Magazine* for an article in which she was described as a "slut." She claimed that the article was libelous per se. The Illinois Supreme Court agreed, stating that the article's reference to the plaintiff as a slut fell within the Illinois libel statute's classification of words that "amount to charge any person with having been guilty of fornication or adultery."[38]

Statements of Fact

For an allegedly defamatory statement to be actionable — that is, for a lawsuit to be based upon the statement — the statement must be one of fact rather than of opinion. In *Gertz,* the Supreme Court said: "Under the First Amendment there is no such thing as a false idea. However pernicious an opinion may seem, we depend for its correction not on the conscience of judges and juries but on the competition of other ideas. But there is no constitutional value in false statements of fact."[39] And in *Milkovich v. Lorain Journal*[40] the Court held that for a statement to be actionable, it must be provably false.

The threshold question facing the opinion defense is how to distinguish fact from opinion. These issues are discussed in detail in Chapter 7. Whether a statement is a statement of fact or opinion is decided by the judge. If the judge cannot determine whether a particular statement constitutes fact or opinion, the determination is made by the jury.

Identification

In order to win a libel action, a plaintiff must prove that he or she was identified, that is, that the defamation was "of and concerning" the plaintiff. Identification has nothing to do with the intent of the publisher of the defamation. As one writer put it, "The test is not whom the story intends to name but who a part of the audience may reasonably think is named — 'not who is meant but who is hit.'"[41]

Identification does not always mean that the plaintiff must be named. The plaintiff can be identified by other information within the published material or by extrinsic facts not included in the published material. And the plaintiff need not show every viewer or reader of the material identified the plaintiff, but that some significant number did.

A landmark Illinois case, *John v. Tribune Co.,*[42] provides a good example of how identification can cause unique problems. The case began when the *Chicago Tribune* reported on a police raid on a prostitution operation in an apartment house. Two articles about the raid identified the arrested owner as Dorothy Clark, also known as "Dolores Reising, 57, alias Eve Spiro and Eve John."

---

[34] 418 U.S. 323 (1974).
[35] *Nazeri v. Missouri Valley College,* 860 S.W.2d 303, 313 (Mo. 1993)(en banc).
[36] 174 Ill. 2d 77, 672 N.E.2d 1207 (1996).
[37] 174 Ill. 2d at 89, 672 N.E.2d at 1215.
[38] 174 Ill. 2d at 102, 672 N.E.2d at 1221.

[39] 418 U.S. at 339-40.
[40] 497 U.S. 1 (1990).
[41] Paul P. Ashley, *Say It Safely,* 4th ed. (Seattle: University of Washington Press, 1969), p. 30
[42] 24 Ill. 2d 437, 181 N.E.2d 105 (1962).

By sheer coincidence, a woman whose maiden name was Eve Spiro and whose name at the time of the raid was Eve John was living in the basement of the raided building at the time of the raid. The basement dweller was a practicing psychologist and was not involved with the prostitution operation. She sued for libel.

The Illinois Supreme Court said that "the alias names ... cannot be read as identifying the 'of and concerning' or 'target' name of the publication," because they do not change the subject of the publication but only disclose the subject's false name or names.[43] Thus, there was no identification of the plaintiff in the *Tribune* story.

Fictitious names can also create headaches for media. In April 1982, *TV Guide* published an ad for an upcoming television documentary series on teenage pregnancy. The heading of the advertisement asked in large, bold letters: "GUESS WHAT LORI FOUND OUT TODAY." In the middle of the advertisement was a photograph of a diary that contained the handwritten entry: "Dear Diary: I found out today that I'm pregnant. What will I do now?" Directly below the diary was a photograph of a teenager embracing a young man.

Libby Sue Chumley sued the publisher of *TV Guide* for a false implication that she was pregnant. She claimed she was the girl in the picture and that she was not and had never been pregnant. She further asserted that she never engaged in sexual relations with the young man in the photograph or with anyone else.

In 1984, the Georgia Supreme Court ruled that the ad was "of and concerning" Chumley. The court rejected the argument that the advertisement did not identify Chumley because "Lori" was the name used in the ad even though the photograph of the advertisement was Chumley. The court reasoned that the bold print of the advertisement and the strategic placement of the photo made it possible for people to interpret Chumley to be "Lori," a pregnant teenager.[44]

The Supreme Court has said that races or other large groups of people cannot win libel actions because individual members of the large groups have not been identified. The *Restatement* delineates the "group libel doctrine" this way:

> One who publishes defamatory matter concerning a group or class of persons is subject to liability to an individual member of it if, but only if: (a) the group or class is so small that the matter can reasonably be understood to refer to the member; or (b)

the circumstances of publication reasonably give rise to the conclusion that there is a particular reference to the member.[45]

The rationale for the rule is that, "First, defamatory statements do little damage to the reputation of any member of a group larger than twenty-five if the defamation refers to all members of the group.... Second, the price to be paid by making such statements actionable is simply too high" for freedom of expression.[46]

The cut-off point for identification probably ranges from about twenty-five to about one hundred. Indeed, a class of 637 commercial net fishermen was certainly too large for any individual net fisherman to sustain a libel action against two television stations. The Florida Circuit Court that ruled in the case noted that the group libel doctrine is "deeply entrenched" in the common law and "almost never operates to create liability when the allegedly defamed group is greater than twenty-five individuals.... No case has been reported that has ever applied the principle to a group larger than 60 individuals."[47]

While members of groups can be defamed if the groups are small enough, it is almost impossible for family members to be defamed based on the activities of other members of the family. A father cannot be defamed, for example, because of a report that his son was charged with some crime.[48]

Publication

Publication is essential to a libel plaintiff's case. It is probably the easiest element to prove when the lawsuit involves the media, but legally, "publication" is a term of art. It occurs when defamatory material is intentionally or negligently disseminated to someone other than the person defamed. As one court put it, "A defamatory writing is not published if it is read by no one but the one defamed. Published it is, however, as soon as read by anyone else."[49]

The form of publication is irrelevant. Defamatory material can be published in written or spoken form or on computer bulletin boards. Especially noteworthy, however, is the congressional at-

---

[43] 24 Ill. 2d at 442, 181 N.E.2d at 108.

[44] *Triangle Publications v. Chumley*, 253 Ga. 179, 182, 317 S.E.2d 534, 537 (1984).

[45] *Restatement (Second) of Torts*, sec. 5645a (1977).

[46] Rex S. Heinke, *Media Law* (Washington, D.C.: Bureau of National Affairs, 1994), p. 101.

[47] *Adams v. WFTV, Inc.*, 24 Media L. Rep. (BNA) 1350, 1351 (Fla. Cir. Ct. 1995).

[48] Apparently only one Puerto Rico case violated this tenet of libel law. Compare *Torre-Silva v. El Mundo, Inc.*, 106 P.R.R. 415 with *Rodriguez v. El Vocero De Puerto Rico, Inc.*, 22 Media L. Rep. (BNA) 1495 (P.R. 1994).

[49] *Ostrowe v. Lee*, 256 N.Y. 36, 37, 175 N.E. 505, 505 (1931).

tempt to immunize online publication of defamatory statements from liability. In 1996, Congress enacted the Communications Decency Act, which provides in part that "No provider or user of an interactive computer service shall be treated as the publisher or speaker of any information provided by another information content provider."[50] Thus, the federal law protects online service providers from state law causes of action for defamation.[51] And, while repetition of a defamation generally consists of a new and separate libel, repetition by the defamed person generally does not constitute publication. Similarly, while each person involved in the publication of defamatory material may be sued, unless the involvement is direct, there is not likely to be liability. News vendors, book sellers and libraries, for example, are not subject to liability for "publishing" defamatory material, if they had no reason to suspect that the material was defamatory.

The accurate republication of defamatory statements within quotation marks is automatically a republication. And, since accuracy is not necessarily the equivalent of truth, simply reporting what another person has said is no defense except where the "neutral reportage" doctrine is recognized.[52]

Once, each separate publication of a defamatory statement could prompt a cause of action. For example, if a newspaper sold 500,000 copies of an edition containing a libelous statement, a plaintiff could bring 500,000 different lawsuits. But courts have recognized the inherent unfairness of such a rule, and many have adopted the single-publication rule. The rule requires a plaintiff to recover all damages suffered from a libel published in any one edition of a magazine or newspaper in one action.

The date of publication of an alleged libel is important, because courts do not like to hear old lawsuits. Therefore, each jurisdiction in the United States has a statute of limitations, which bars legal actions after certain periods of time. The statute of limitations for libel actions in most states is one or two years. The key, therefore, is determining the actual date of publication of the libel. If each republication constitutes a new publication, therefore, a new statute of limitations applies to each republication.

Courts that have applied the single publication rule, however, have held that the statute of limitations begins to run with the first publication. In addition, courts have distinguished between a "republication" and a "repetition" of the libel, the latter not being a publication for purposes of a lawsuit. An example of a repetition would be the distribution of a syndicated column. The publication occurred, one court held, with the distribution of the column, and each printing of the column thereafter was a repetition, not a republication. The statute of limitations of the state where the column first appeared should apply, the court held.[53]

Fault

U.S. libel law is exceedingly complex, and one of the best examples of that complexity might be the various degrees of fault that are applied. Public figures and public officials are required to prove actual malice — knowledge of falsity or reckless disregard for the truth — before they can win libel actions. Private persons, on the other hand, must only prove negligence in most states in order to win, but must prove actual malice if they want to win punitive damages or presumed damages.

The actual malice rule, which originated for constitutional purposes in *New York Times Co. v. Sullivan*,[54] is derived from the constitutional right of American people to express themselves about matters of public concern. Against the background of "a profound national commitment to the principle that debate on public issues should be uninhibited, robust, and wide-open," the Supreme Court declared, "erroneous statement is inevitable in free debate, and ... it must be protected if the freedoms of expression are to have the 'breathing space' that they 'need to survive.'"[55]

Times v. Sullivan arose from an advertisement published in the March 29, 1960, issue of the *New York Times*. The full-page advertisement, entitled "Heed Their Rising Voices," was designed for civil rights advocates to raise funds. The editorial advertisement, which was for an organization called the Committee to Defend Martin Luther King and the Struggle for Freedom in the South, focused on the civil rights movement in the South. It started thusly: "As the whole world knows by now, thousands of Southern Negro students are engaged in widespread non-violent demonstrations in positive affirmation of the right to live in human dignity as guaranteed by the U.S. Constitution. In their efforts to uphold these guarantees, they are being met by an unprecedented wave of terror by those who would deny and negate that document which the

---

[50] 47 U.S.C. 230(c)(Supp. 1996).

[51] For a discussion of judicial interpretations of the Communication Decency Act on libel, see Chapter 7.

[52] For discussion of the neutral reportage doctrine, see Chapter 7.

[53] *Givens v. Quinn*, 877 F. Supp. 485, 490 (W.D. Mo. 1994).

[54] 376 U.S. 254 (1964). For excellent discussions of *New York Times Co. v. Sullivan*, see Anthony Lewis, *Make No Law: The Sullivan Case and the First Amendment* (New York: Random House, 1991), and W. Wat Hopkins, "Justice Brennan, Justice Harlan and *New York Times Co. v. Sullivan*: A Case Study in Supreme Court Decision Making," *Communication Law and Policy* 1 (1996): 469.

[55] 376 U.S. at 270-72.

whole world looks upon as setting the pattern for modern freedom...."

The advertisement alleged repressive actions taken by local authorities against civil rights demonstrations in the South: "In Montgomery, Alabama, after students sang 'My Country, 'Tis of Thee' on the State Capitol steps, their leaders were expelled from school, and truckloads of police armed with shotguns and teargas ringed the Alabama State College Campus. When the entire student body protested to state authorities by refusing to re-register, their dining hall was padlocked in an attempt to starve them into submission."

The advertisement, without naming any individuals or organizations, asserted that "the Southern violators of the Constitution" were "determined to destroy the one man who, more than any other, symbolizes the new spirit now sweeping the South — the Rev. Dr. Martin Luther King, Jr., world-famous leader of the Montgomery Bus Protest." It continued: "Again and again the Southern violators have answered Dr. King's peaceful protests with intimidation and violence. They have bombed his home almost killing his wife and child. They have assaulted his person. They have arrested him seven times — for 'speeding,' 'loitering' and similar 'offenses.' And now they have charged him with 'perjury' — a felony under which they could imprison him for ten years...."

L.B. Sullivan, Commissioner of Public Affairs for Montgomery, sued the New York Times Co. for libel. He claimed that because he was responsible for supervision of the Montgomery police, the advertisement's allegations of police wrongdoing libeled him as commissioner. He sought damages of $500,000, and a jury awarded him the entire amount. The Alabama Supreme Court affirmed the judgment, holding that the *Times* was irresponsible in publishing the false advertisement, because the paper could have verified the allegations in the advertisement by checking its own files prior to publication. The Alabama court curtly rejected the *New York Times'* argument that the advertisement was protected by the U.S. Constitution. It reasoned in a single sentence that "The First Amendment of the U.S. Constitution does not protect libelous protection."[56]

The New York Times Co. appealed the decision to the U.S. Supreme Court. On March 9, 1964, the U.S. Supreme Court reversed the Alabama court decision unanimously. It was a stunning victory for free press and free speech in America. Alexander Meiklejohn, who had argued for years that political expression relating to the government should be immune from punishment, character-

ized the *Times* decision as "an occasion for dancing in the streets."[57]

Justice William Brennan, who wrote the opinion for the Court began with the "general proposition that freedom of expression upon public questions is secured by the First Amendment." Noting the First Amendment's guarantee of freedom of expression as a right of Americans citizens, Justice Brennan said that the *Times* case should be examined "against the background of a profound national commitment to the principle that debate on public issues should be uninhibited, robust, and wide-open, and that it may well include vehement, caustic, and sometimes unpleasantly sharp attacks on government and public officials." Justice Brennan wrote that the advertisement in question was "an expression of grievance and protest on one of the major public issues of our time" and thus entitled to the constitutional protection. However, "The question is whether it forfeits that protection by the falsity of some of its factual statements and by its alleged defamation of respondent."[58]

Justice Brennan answered by stating that "the First Amendment guarantees have consistently refused to recognize an exception for any test of truth." He recognized the flexibility of the concept of truth and warned against the chilling effect of penalizing honest mistakes: "A rule compelling the critic of official conduct to guarantee the truth of all his factual assertions — and to do so on pain of libel judgment virtually unlimited in amount — leads to a comparable 'self-censorship.'"[59]

Therefore, the Court established that a public official could win a libel action based upon criticism of official conduct, only if the official could prove actual malice, defined as knowledge of falsity or reckless disregard for truth or falsity. "Actual malice" does not mean hatred, ill-will or spite, which is the definition of common law malice.

The Supreme Court has specifically said that actual malice is a subjective rather than objective standard. That means that the standard reflects an attempt by a publisher to, as Justice Brennan said in *New York Times*, injure through knowing or reckless falsehood. Thus, the conduct of a libel defendant is often examined to determine whether there is objective evidence of the subjective standard. One way a plaintiff can prevail in a libel action, therefore, is to demonstrate that there was knowledge of falsity or

---

[56] *Id.* at 264, quoting *New York Times Co. v. Sullivan,* 144 So. 2d 25, 40 (Ala. 1962).

[57] Harry Kalven, Jr., "The New York Times Case: A Note on 'The Central Meaning of the First Amendment.'" *Supreme Court Review* (1964): 199.

[58] *Id.* at 271.

[59] *Id.* at 279.

reckless disregard for the truth.

Knowledge of Falsity. Actual malice is proved much more often by showing reckless disregard on the part of the defendant than by showing knowing falsity. One reason — perhaps the foremost reason — is that professional communicators rarely publish anything knowing it is false. But there are exceptions. One was when Ralph Ginzburg published in *Fact* magazine that some psychiatrists he surveyed found Republican presidential candidate Barry Goldwater to be mentally unstable. Goldwater sued for libel, and his attorneys were able to show that the survey results were actually very favorable toward Goldwater, but Ginzburg ignored the positive comments and focused on only the negative. In addition, there was evidence that the publishers of the article knew before the survey was distributed what the tenor of the article would be. Goldwater was able to meet the actual malice standard by showing that, although the statements Ginzburg made were true individually, collectively they misrepresented the truth; that is, they were false and that the author knew this but published them anyway.[60]

While knowledge of falsity can be easily applied, it's not easily proved. Because "[t]he knowledge of falsity prong of the Times Rule Actual Malice is based on a determination of what the publisher knew or did not know at the time of publication," one scholar wrote, the defendant's state of mind at the time of publication is key.[61] Proving state of mind with convincing clarity can be challenging at the least. Rarely will a libel defendant admit knowledge of falsity, so, most often, plaintiffs must use objective evidence. That's difficult, but it can be done. When editorial writers at a newspaper asserted that a public official was a liar, for example, but articles in the same newspaper demonstrated that the official had not lied, the editorial writers were found to have acted with actual malice — they *knew* their statements were false.[62]

A plaintiff's claim that a publication is false, while signaling that a publisher should investigate further, is not sufficient, standing alone, to show knowledge of falsity, particularly in the face of evidence from reliable, objective sources. If the evidence from those reliable sources raised questions about the truth of the material to be published, it's a different story. As one scholar wrote, "To publish in the face of such evidence would be to publish with knowledge of falsity. Similarly, to publish charges with little or no support for those charges has also been determined to be publishing with knowledge of falsity, as has the selective use of information to the detriment of the plaintiff."[63]

Thus, the determination of knowledge of falsity rests on what the libel defendant knew at the time of publication. And what the publisher knew often rests on the extent of the investigation before publication, along with the interpretation, editing and presentation of the material. In *Herbert v. Lando*,[64] for example, the Court concluded that a plaintiff could inquire as to a defendant's state of mind while preparing a report. Questions about why the defendant believed and disbelieved certain sources, why the defendant used some material over other material and like issues were permissible, Justice Byron White wrote for the majority.

Former Army Col. Anthony Herbert contended that he was defamed in a *60 Minutes* segment. Producer Barry Lando and correspondent Mike Wallace argued that the First Amendment protected them from testifying as to their thought processes or state of mind at the time the segment was being edited and produced. The Supreme Court disagreed, finding that state of mind was central to actual malice. In a previous case, the Court had held, "There must be sufficient evidence to permit the conclusion that the defendant in fact entertained serious doubts as to the truth of his publication."[65] The assertion by a defendant that he or she believed the publication to be true is inadequate standing alone, but may be sufficient when not refuted by the plaintiff.

What a libel defendant knew at the time of publication was also central to the 1984 case *Bose Corporation v. Consumers Union of United States*.[66] Bose filed suit against the publisher of *Consumer Reports* magazine for statements critical of stereo speakers developed by the company. Bose convinced a jury that the magazine had published false statements with actual malice. The U.S. Court of Appeals for the First Circuit reversed, however, and the Supreme Court upheld the reversal. Bose had succeeded in showing that the author of the critical report might have not expressed himself well and might have attempted, at trial, to cover up for that poor expression. That proof, the Court said, however, was irrelevant. What was important was the author's "state of mind when he wrote his initial report, or when he checked the article against that report."[67]

In short, it becomes essential to explore the libel defendant's

---

[60] *Goldwater v. Ginsburg*, 414 F.2d 324 (2d Cir. 1969).

[61] W. Wat Hopkins, *Actual Malice Twenty-Five Years After Times v. Sullivan* (New York: Praeger, 1989), p. 144.

[62] *Costello v. Capital Cities Communications*, 153 Ill. App. 3d 956, 505 N.E.2d 701 (1987).

[63] Hopkins, *supra* note 61, at 138.

[64] 441 U.S. 153 (1979).

[65] *St. Amant v. Thompson*, 390 U.S. 727, 731 (1968).

[66] 446 U.S. 485 (1984).

[67] *Id.* at 495.

state of mind at the time of the preparation and publication of the defamation in order to learn whether actual malice existed. The libel defendant should recognize that these are likely to be probed and should be prepared to justify both the actions and the state of mind that led to the choices made.

The publisher's state of mind toward the investigation and the material that is eventually published is also key to the question of knowledge of falsity. Indeed, the publisher's state of mind toward the *subject* of the report may be irrelevant because ill will toward the plaintiff is not sufficient to demonstrate actual malice. Ill will, however, may be introduced to demonstrate a defendant's motive for lying or publishing with reckless disregard for the truth. As one court noted, while "the concepts underlying malice and actual malice are not the same ... this does not preclude a relationship between them."[68] When courts permit evidence of ill will, hatred or spite to be introduced for their bearing on the actual malice question, they usually admonish juries that those elements, standing alone, can never establish actual malice.

Courts have also indicated that knowledge of falsity can be demonstrated by the way material is written, edited or presented. This may be particularly true with headlines. Wrote First Amendment scholar W. Wat Hopkins:

When large headlines are not literally defamatory, for example, but raise the implication of wrongdoing not supported by the texts of the articles over which they appear, a libel verdict for a public official can stand because of sufficient evidence that the headlines were published with actual malice. When the headlines are merely ambiguous, however, there is no knowledge of falsity. Similarly, ambiguous language or internal inconsistencies in news stories, standing alone, are insufficient evidence of actual malice.[69]

In addition to a media defendant's state of mind, the editorial policies that govern or guide actions can play a role in the determination of predisposition. The idea that a media defendant preconceived a story line, then proceeded to skew reporting to fit that preconception, is evidence of knowledge of falsity. In *Burnett v. National Enquirer,* for example, the trial court suggested that the *Enquirer's* editorial predisposition may have contributed to its judgment. Entertainer Carol Burnett argued that she had been falsely portrayed by the *National Enquirer* as being "drunk, rude,

uncaring, and abusive" in a Washington restaurant.[70] At trial, a reporter for the *Enquirer* testified that the article about Burnett was published even though he was unable to verify its accuracy.

Similarly, *Tavoulares v. Washington Post Co.*[71] resulted in some troubling law that courts may believe they need to follow. A *Washington Post* article implied that William Tavoulares, the president of Mobil Oil Co., misused his corporate position by setting up his son to head an international tanker fleet. A federal jury awarded Tavoulares $2 million in damages. Before the verdict was overturned by the full Court of Appeals for the District of Columbia,[72] a panel of that court had held that the *Post's* predisposition toward "hard-hitting investigative journalism" could be considered as evidence relevant to actual malice.[73] The suggestion that a practice generally revered in journalism could be used against a libel defendant sent shock waves throughout the field. Those feelings were eased, however, when a full-panel rehearing by the District of Columbia Circuit reversed, throwing out the $2 million verdict, ruling that actual malice had not been proven. Adding to the relief was the court's assertion that a media organization's reputation for aggressive reporting was not to be taken as evidence of actual malice.

Pressure exerted by newsroom supervisors to produce high-impact stories may also be construed as a predisposition toward certain kinds of stories with specific plot lines. Such pressure may contribute to reporters skewing facts to fit such predilections. First Amendment scholar and libel expert Rodney Smolla places this phenomenon within the context of freedom of expression:

At the very core of our first amendment jurisprudence lies the elemental wisdom that government has no business prescribing what is orthodox, genteel, or polite in politics and culture. A publication or broadcast outlet is not to be penalized because of its unique boldness, style, or flair. Indeed, in an era in which one of the great *economic* tendencies in the media is toward consolidation and centralization, often resulting in "play it safe" editorial styles that make all news sound the same, the first amendment's protection for those media outlets with special courage or uniqueness is more vital than ever. To actually preconceive a story is one thing — such an act is quite properly probative of actual malice — but merely to have an editorial im-

---

[68] *DiLorenzo v. New York News,* 81 A.D.2d 844, 847, 432 N.Y.S. 2d 483, 486 (1981).

[69] Hopkins, *supra* note 61, at 141-42.

[70] 144 Cal. App. 3d 991, 1014, 193 Cal. Rptr. 206 (1983).

[71] 759 F.2d 90 (D.C. Cir. 1985).

[72] *Tavoulares v. Washington Post Co.,* 817 F.2d 762 (D.C. Cir. 1987).

[73] *Tavoulares v. Washington Post Co.,* 759 F.2d 90, 121 (1985).

age or slant is quite another.[74]

Thus, when circumstances permit, proving falsity can be easier than exploring a defendant's state of mind. It simply stands to reason that it is much more difficult to prove a particular state of mind compared to presenting evidence that suggests reckless oversights. But what happens when a defendant admits to altering an interviewee's quotations? Arguably, that is an example of knowing falsity. That is, if quotations were knowingly altered to the extent that their meaning is materially transformed, then the journalist must have been aware of the fact that they are false. Traditionally, journalistic practice suggests that words bracketed by quotation marks are taken to be the exact words of the person to whom they are attributed. When a journalist knowingly changes this material, the quoted information arguably has been knowingly falsified.

While that might be the case, publishing knowing falsehoods is only one element of a public figure's burden of proof. In *Masson v. New Yorker Magazine, Inc.,* the Supreme Court ruled that even the deliberate misquotation of a public figure cannot be libelous unless the wording materially changes the meaning of what was really said.[75] The Court said that, in *Masson,* the meaning had not been transformed. On remand, a federal district court jury ruled in favor of the journalist, even though she had admitted to condensing certain statements by the plaintiff.[76]

In his dissenting opinion, Justice Byron White addressed the issue of knowing falsehoods: "[T]he reporter ... wrote that Masson said certain things that she knew Masson did not say. By any definition of the term, this was 'knowing falsehood.'"[77] He was right, but the final word on this issue was in favor of the defendant, based on the statements at issue being substantially true.

Reckless Disregard. Reckless disregard for whether material is true or false, like knowledge of falsity, is a subjective test. But it can often be determined by the conduct of the publisher rather than by examining thought processes, state of mind, or predisposition at the time of publication. Knowledge of falsity focuses on what the publisher knew; reckless disregard focuses on what the publisher reasonably *should have known*. The focus of the actual malice inquiry, as one scholar has written, "is on a defendant's attitude toward the truth or falsity of the publication," on "sub-jective awareness of its probable falsity" and on "actual doubts as to its accuracy." The "inquiry in 'actual malice' focuses largely on the defendant's belief regarding truthfulness."[78]

For recklessness to rise to the level of actual malice, it must be significant — it must be tantamount to lying; it must be obvious that the publisher did not care about the truth of the published information. When publishers have demonstrated adequate investigation of potentially libelous charges, courts have typically ruled that there was no reckless disregard. Therefore, a plaintiff cannot prove reckless disregard if the defendant can show the statements were adequately investigated prior to publication.

The seriousness of the charges being made is also weighed. The more serious the material in question, the more detailed an investigation into its truth should be. In addition, reckless disregard is more likely to be found when sources for published material are anonymous, biased or of questionable reputation. Courts look to the number of reputable sources when determining whether a sufficient investigation was conducted.

The Supreme Court has provided some guidance as to the meaning of reckless disregard. It has, for example, called reckless disregard publishing with a "high degree of awareness of probable falsity."[79] And, the Court has said, for reckless disregard to exist, "there must be sufficient evidence to permit the conclusion that the defendant in fact entertained serious doubts as to the truth of his publication."[80] Whether a defendant had such serious doubts can be established by circumstantial evidence including determining what the defendant's thoughts were leading up to publication of the challenged statements.

The mere failure to investigate charges is not sufficient, standing alone, to prove reckless disregard. Publishers often rely on the work of reputable writers. If there is no reason to doubt the truth of material submitted by those writers, it is not necessary for publishers to have conducted independent investigations. If plaintiffs can show that publishers had doubts about the truth of such material or reasonably should have had doubts, however, that's a different story. In such cases, the question of reckless disregard may be open. In short, a publisher must be able to demonstrate a reasonable belief in the truth of the published material. That may sometimes require an investigation into the facts, but the belief may also be based on the reputation of the original author. As Rodney Smolla wrote:

---

[74] Rodney A. Smolla, *Law of Defamation* (Deerfield, Ill.: Clark Boardman Callaghan, 1997), sec. 3.20[7](emphasis in original).

[75] 501 U.S. 496, 516 (1991).

[76] *Masson v. New Yorker,* 832 F. Supp. 1350 (N.D. Cal. 1993).

[77] *Masson,* 501 U.S. at 526 (White, J., dissenting).

[78] Smolla, *supra* note 74, at sec. 3.14[1].

[79] *Garrison,* 379 U.S. at 74.

[80] *St. Amant,* 390 U.S. at 731.

In winning in libel cases through establishment of actual malice, plaintiffs should go beyond proving that a reporter failed to show significant initiative in corroborating, verifying, or further investigating the defamatory story at issue. The mere failure to investigate, even when that failure to investigate is less than reasonable or responsible journalism, does not in and of itself meet the actual malice test. There must be some evidence of subjective suspicion that further investigation is needed. That evidence, of course, can be met by circumstantial data, including such things as the reliability or unreliability of the source or the inherent implausibility of the allegation, but something other than the stark failure to pursue investigation must be established.[81]

Negligence. At a minimum, the Supreme Court said in *Gertz v. Welch,* private persons seeking damages for the publication of false defamations must prove negligence. As a result, most states have ruled that negligence is the standard of fault for private-person libel plaintiffs.

Negligence has been defined in a variety of ways, but it is generally defined as failure to act as a reasonably careful or ordinarily careful person would act under similar circumstances. A second definition — known as "journalistic malpractice" — is failure to adhere to standards of reporting and writing that are common to the news industry.

The reasonable care standard requires a libel plaintiff to establish that a libel defendant did not operate in a reasonable way, that is, that a reasonable person would have operated in a way significantly different from that of the defendant. The Arizona Supreme Court, for example, defined negligence as, "conduct which creates an unreasonable risk of harm. It is the failure to use that amount of care which a reasonably prudent person would use under like circumstances. The question which the jury must determine from the preponderance of the evidence ... is whether the defendants acted reasonably in attempting to discover the truth or falsity or the defamatory character of the publication."[82]

Most states have adopted the reasonable person definition of negligence, but some — including Iowa, Kansas and Oklahoma — define negligence as journalistic malpractice. The *Restatement* defines journalistic malpractice this way:

The defendant, if a professional disseminator of news, such as a newspaper, a magazine or a broadcasting station, or an employee, such as a reporter, is held to the skill and experience normally possessed by members of that profession.... Customs and practices within the professional are relevant in applying the negligence standard, which is, to a substantial degree, set by the profession itself, though a custom is not controlling.... If the defendant is an ordinary citizen, customs of the community as a whole may be relevant.[83]

Regardless of the definition of negligence, some factors seem common when courts have ruled that defendants published material negligently. In his in-depth study of negligence as an actionable standard in post-*Gertz* cases, media law scholar W. Wat Hopkins identified three general negligence rules:

(1) [I]f there is a discrepancy between what a reporter says he was told by a source and what the source said he told the reporter, the court is more likely to believe the source and find that negligence is likely; (2) courts are likely to rule that negligence could be established if media representatives make little or no effort to contact a person against whom accusations are made or if a medium bases a story later found to be false upon a single source; (3) courts are likely to rule that negligence could be established if media fail to get all the information they should.[84]

Actual Injury

Even if libel plaintiffs can prove they were identified in false, defamatory publications, and even if they can prove the requisite degree of fault, they must still prove actual injury in order to recover damages.

Warning against the "danger of media self-censorship" resulting from jury discretion in assessing punitive damages, the Court said that "punitive damages are wholly irrelevant to the state interest that justifies a negligence standard for private defamation actions. They are not compensation for injury. Instead, they are private fines levied by civil juries to punish reprehensible conduct and to deter its future occurrence." The Court noted, however, that the private libel plaintiff who establishes liability under a less demanding standard than actual malice may be limited to recovery of "only such damages as are sufficient to compensate him for actual in-

---

[81] Smolla, *supra* note 74, at sec. 3.17[1].

[82] *Peagler v. Phoenix Newspapers, Inc.,* 114 Ariz. 309, 315, 560 P.2d 1216, 1222 (1977).

[83] *Restatement (Second) of Torts* sec. 580B comment g (1977).

[84] W. Wat Hopkins, "Negligence Ten Years After *Gertz v. Welch*," *Journalism Monographs* 93 (August 1985): 19.

jury."[85]

In a libel action, four types of damages are recognized.

Nominal damages are awarded to plaintiffs who have not suffered from provable injury to their reputations. They are granted in very small amounts, usually $1, and are awarded where a plaintiff does not seek compensation for loss, but a vindication of reputation in the form of a declaration that a published statement is false.

Compensatory damages are awarded for actual injury. They compensate, not for out-of-pocket loss, but for harm to reputation, humiliation, suffering and mental anguish. Awards of compensatory damages must be based upon the evidence, but if the damages are not outrageous, a jury can award damages in its own discretion. Compensatory damages are sometimes called "general damages."

Special damages are designed to compensate for actual pecuniary loss. Evidence of special damages will demonstrate an actual amount of money the plaintiff lost as a result of the defamation.

Punitive or exemplary damages are designed to punish the defendant for outrageous and willful defamation. They are designed to deter the defendant and others from repeating similar actions. Actual malice must be proved for recovery of punitive damages. Four states — Michigan, Oregon, Massachusetts and Washington — do not recognize punitive damages in libel cases. But some states require that both actual malice and common law malice be established in seeking punitive damages for libel.

PUBLIC PERSONS

The Supreme Court has established that two categories of libel plaintiffs — public officials and public figures — must prove actual malice in order to win libel actions.

Public Officials

Public officials for purposes of the actual malice rule are persons in government who are in policy-making roles. The Supreme Court has indicated that "the 'public official' designation applies at the very least to those among the hierarchy of government employees who have or appear to the public to have, substantial responsibility for or control over the conduct of governmental affairs."[86] The trial judge determines whether a plaintiff is a public official.

The parameters of "official conduct" are almost as broad as those of "public officials." Anything that affects an official's ability to carry out official duties is included. Said the Supreme Court:

The New York Times rule is not rendered inapplicable merely because an official's private reputation, as well as his public reputation, is harmed. The public-official rule protects the paramount public interest in a free flow of information to the people concerning public officials, their servants. To this end, anything which might touch on an official's fitness for office is relevant.[87]

Public Figures

In 1967, the actual malice rule was expanded to include public figures. In *Curtis Publishing Co. v. Butts,* the Court established that there was little legal difference between persons who have widespread fame and notoriety — public figures — and public officials. "Many who do not hold public office at the moment," wrote Chief Justice Earl Warren, "are nevertheless intimately involved in the resolution of important public questions or, by reason of their fame, shape events in areas of concern to society at large."[88]

The rule was established in a roundabout way. Justice John Marshall Harlan had written a plurality opinion differentiating between public officials and public figures, but he also differentiated between the rule that should apply to each category. Chief Justice Warren wrote that the actual malice rule should apply to both categories of libel plaintiffs, and a sufficient number of justices joined his opinion so as to establish that rule.

The actual malice rule was extended in 1971 to any defamatory story involving matters of public or general interest, but the expansion was short-lived. In *Rosenbloom v. Metromedia, Inc.,*[89] a plurality of the Court had favored a rule that required private people involved in matters of public interest to prove actual malice when suing for libel based upon discussion of those matters.

The so-called "Rosenbloom Rule" lasted only three years. In 1974, a 5-4 majority of the Court definitively rejected the rule by overruling *Rosenbloom* in *Gertz v. Robert Welch, Inc.*[90] The *Gertz* case started when *American Opinion,* a monthly published by the John Birch Society, a far-right organization founded by Robert

---

[85] *Gertz,* 418 U.S. at 350.
[86] *Rosenblatt v. Baer,* 383 U.S. 75, 85 (1966).

[87] *Garrison v. Louisiana,* 379 U.S. 64, 77 (1964).
[88] 388 U.S. 130, 163 (1967)(Warren, C.J., concurring).
[89] 403 U.S. 29, 43 (1971).
[90] 418 U.S. 323 (1974). For a detailed account of the *Gertz* case, see Elmer Gertz, *Gertz v. Robert Welch, Inc.: The Story of a Landmark Libel Case* (Carbondale: Southern Illinois University Press, 1992).

Welch, published an article critical of a respected Chicago civil liberties lawyer, Elmer Gertz, in its April 1969 issue. The article said of Gertz: "The file on Elmer Gertz in Chicago Police Intelligence takes a big Irish cop to lift.... He has been an official of the Marxist League for Industrial Democracy, originally known as the Intercollegiate Socialist Society, which has advocated the violent seizure of our government.... In fact, the only thing Chicagoans need to know about Gertz is that he is one of the original officers, and has been Vice President, of the Communist National Lawyers Guild ... which probably did more than any other outfit to plan the Communist attack on the Chicago police during the 1968 Democratic Convention."

The *American Opinion* article also claimed that Gertz, who was retained by the family of a young man shot and killed by a Chicago policeman, Richard Nuccio, for a wrongful death suit against the city of Chicago and Nuccio, was the architect of the "frame-up" in the earlier prosecution of Nuccio for second-degree murder. It further maintained that the prosecution was part of a Communist effort to discredit the Chicago police.

Gertz sued Robert Welch, Inc., publisher of *American Opinion*, for libel. He said that all the statements about him in the article at issue were all false. He had no criminal record, contrary to the defamatory implications of the article. He was not a member of he Marxist League for Industrial Democracy. Further, although he was a member of the National Lawyers Guild 15 years earlier, the Guild was not a communist organization. Neither had he anything to do with the prosecution of Nuccio for murder.

In his complaint, Gertz claimed: "As a result of the said article, plaintiff has been, and is, or may be, injured in his good name, credit and reputation, both as an individual and as an attorney at law. At the present time plaintiff does not know how much actual damage he has suffered as a result of this said article, and, therefore, seeks only nominal actual damages. However, the actual malice and viciousness of said article, entitles plaintiff to a large amount of punitive damages."[91] He claimed $100,001 in actual damages and $500,000 in punitive damages.

In 1970, Gertz won a jury verdict of $50,000 in damages against the publisher, but the trial judge set aside the verdict because, he said, since the article discussed Gertz's public activity, the actual malice rule should apply. Gertz appealed, but the U.S. Court of Appeals for the Seventh Circuit applied *Rosenbloom* and affirmed the trial judge's ruling, stating that there was no clear and convincing evidence of actual malice.

In his appeal to the U.S. Supreme Court, Gertz argued in part:

"Is every attorney, representing a client, to be exposed to the most scurrilous attacks, with absolutely no recourse? May a defamer concoct wholly fictitious stories about such an attorney which have no legitimate connections with the matter at hand? Are the members of the legal profession such public figures that they imperil their very livelihood to all unfounded attacks with absolutely no recourse? These issues must be considered very carefully and fully, not in an offhand manner."[92]

In *Gertz*, the Supreme Court held that the actual malice rule applies only to private person libel plaintiffs who want to win presumed or punitive damages. Other than that, the Court said, states could determine the fault standard for private person libel plaintiffs, so long as states did not allow liability without some degree of fault. The Court explained the distinction between public and private persons:

Public officials and public figures usually enjoy significantly greater access to the channels of effective communication and hence have a more realistic opportunity to counteract false statements than private individuals normally enjoy. Private individuals are therefore more vulnerable to injury, and the state interest in protecting them is correspondingly greater. More important than the likelihood that private individuals will lack effective opportunities for rebuttal, there is a compelling normative consideration underlying the distinction between public and private defamation plaintiffs. An individual who decides to seek governmental office must accept certain necessary consequences of that involvement in public affairs. he runs the risk of closer public scrutiny than might otherwise be the case.[93]

Gertz, the most important libel case since *New York Times Co. v. Sullivan*, also established a new set of guidelines for balancing the constitutional right of free speech against concerns for reputational interests.

First, the Court reaffirmed that public figures, along with public officials, must prove actual malice in libel cases involving matters of public concern.

Second, the Court held that "so long as they do not impose liability without fault, the states may define for themselves the appropriate standard of liability for a publisher or broadcaster of a defamatory falsehood injurious to a private individual," at least where the content of the defamatory statement "makes substan-

---

[91] Gertz, *supra* note 86, at 40.

[92] *Id.* at 85-86.
[93] *Gertz*, 418 U.S. at 344-45.

tial danger to reputation apparent."[94]

Third, the Court stated that presumed or punitive damages may not be awarded absent a showing of actual malice. Those who cannot prove actual malice, the Court said, may be compensated only for actual injury.[95] In a later case, the Court held that the actual malice requirement for punitive damages does not apply to material "of purely private concern."[96]

As a result of *Gertz*, thirty-four states have established negligence as the private-person fault standard; five states have adopted a variation of the Rosenbloom Rule; and one state, New York, requires gross irresponsibility when matters of public concern are involved.

SUMMARY

Defamation law is designed to protect reputations so that individual relational interests are not harmed, while the guarantees of free expression are designed to promote the gathering and dissemination of information. Reputational rights are recognized in every society as a significant interest, but the degree of protection by law or custom varies greatly from country to country.

In the United States, though free expression is vigorously protected, libel law is one of the most visible legal restraints on expression. In recent years, the chill on expression caused by libel law has been a growing concern for the media. On the other hand, those critical of the excesses of the press welcome some degree of press chill. Notwithstanding the debate, there is no denying that libel law serves as a necessary mechanism for the balance between reputational rights and press freedom.

There are two types of defamation: libel, or written defamation, and slander, or spoken defamation. The traditional distinction between libel and slander is not as clear-cut as it once was because of new modes of communication. Broadcast defamation, for example, is more often than not treated as libel.

Nearly all libel cases in the United States are civil actions, in which plaintiffs claim monetary damages for reputational harm from the publication of defamatory statements. Libel is still recognized as a crime in some jurisdictions, but criminal libel statutes are rarely invoked.

To establish a cause of action against a non-media libel defendant, a plaintiff must prove that he or she was identified in a statement that was published to some third person, and that the statement was defamatory, that is, that it injured the plaintiff's reputation. When a media organization is the defendant, the plaintiff must establish two additional elements: (1) that the publication resulted from fault on the part of the defendant and (2) that the plaintiff suffered actual injury from publication of the defamatory statement.

Libel as a tort — a civil wrong — is premised on the requirement that a libelous statement be false and defamatory. Thus, falsity is essential to a libel claim. Only because statements of fact can be proved true or false, there cannot be a libel claim for a statement of opinion which cannot be proved to be true or false.

"Truth" in libel law is not synonymous with "accuracy." Verbatim quotations in a news story may be accurate, but may not necessarily be true. "Truth" means that the substance of the quoted statement is factually verifiable.

It is difficult to determine when some language is defamatory; other language is clearly defamatory. The meaning of words changes with the time, place and manner in which they are used. In some jurisdictions, the libel *per se* and libel *per quod* rules are still followed. Libel *per se* refers to words and phrases that are defamatory on their face and need no additional information. Libel *per quod* refers to a statement that is not defamatory in and of itself but that can be made defamatory if additional facts are known.

Family members or relatives of libel plaintiffs can rarely claim damages for libels unless they can individually establish that they suffered from damage to their reputations because of the publication of defamatory statements about them. Identification is not necessarily the specific reference to a plaintiff by name. If a plaintiff is identifiable to those who were exposed to the publication, the identification requirement is met. Individuals who are members of groups have increasing difficulty proving they were identified as the size of the group grows.

Publication has little to do with the ordinary meaning of printing or broadcasting a defamatory statement. Instead, it means that defamatory material is disseminated to someone other than the defamed person. Publication is rarely an issue in media libel actions because defamatory statements are usually disseminated to a wide audience when they are published by the media. Republication of a libelous statement can constitute a cause of action separate from the original publication. Whoever is substantially and directly involved in publishing a defamatory statement is liable and thus can be sued.

Libel plaintiffs must prove fault, but the degree of fault depends upon the status of the plaintiff. In most jurisdictions, private per-

---

[94] *Id.* at 347-48.

[95] *Id.* at 349-50.

[96] *Dun & Bradstreet, Inc. v. Greenmoss Builders, Inc.,* 472 U.S. 749, 759 (1985).

sons are required to prove negligence in order to win compensatory damages. Public figures and public officials must prove actual malice in order to win compensatory damages. In addition, every libel plaintiff must prove actual malice in order to win punitive or presumed damages.

FOR ADDITIONAL READING

Bezanson, Randall P., Gilbert Cranberg and John Soloski. *Libel Law and the Press: Myth and Reality*. New York: Free Press, 1987.

Dennis, Everette E. and Eli M. Noam. *The Cost of Libel: Economic and Policy Implications*. New York: Columbia University Press, 1989.

Elder, David A. *Defamation: A Lawyer's Guide*. Deerfield, Ill.: Clark Boardman Callaghan, 1997.

Gertz, Elmer. *Gertz v. Robert Welch, Inc.: The Story of a Landmark Libel Case*. Carbondale, Ill.: Southern Illinois University Press, 1992.

Gillmor, Donald M. *Power, Publicity, and the Abuse of Libel Law*. New York: Oxford University Press, 1992.

Hopkins, W. Wat. *Actual Malice Twenty-Five Years After Times v. Sullivan*. New York: Praeger, 1989.

Lewis, Anthony. *Make No Law: The Sullivan Case and the First Amendment*. New York: Random House, 1991.

London, Martin and Barbara Dill. *At What Price?: Libel Law and Freedom of the Press*. New York: Twentieth Century Fund Press, 1993.

Metcalf, Slade R. *Rights and Liabilities of Publishers, Broadcasters and Reporters*. 2 vols. New York: McGraw-Hill, Inc., 1994.

Rosini, Neil J. *The Practical Guide to Libel Law*. New York: Praeger Publishers, 1991.

Sack, Robert D. and Sandra S. Baron. *Libel, Slander, and Related Problems*, 2d ed. New York: Practising Law Institute, 1994.

Sanford, Bruce W. *Libel and Privacy*, 2d ed. Englewood Cliffs, N.J.: Aspen Law & Business, 1998.

Smolla, Rodney A. *Law of Defamation*. Deerfield, Ill.: Clark Boardman Callaghan, 1997.

Soloski, John and Randall P. Bezanson, eds. *Reforming Libel Law*. New York: Guilford Press, 1993.

7

Libel: Defense Issues and Strategies

By Joseph A. Russomanno

To some degree, defending a libel suit involves turning the definition of libel inside out. That is, by taking those elements of libel explained in Chapter 6 and proving their inverse, a defendant attempts to demonstrate that there is no liability for publishing the statement at issue. While the plaintiff must prove every element of the burden of proof, a successful defense need refute only one.

Libel law serves to check the power of the media by opening their news-gathering and decision-making processes to public scrutiny and accountability. While the best cure for bad speech may be more speech, contemporary American society is often unwilling to let corrective speech work.

Libel law is one of the checks and balances. The rights of individuals to be secure in their reputations are weighed against the rights of others to be heard on issues of importance to self-government. Libel defendants typically argue that the importance of issues of public concern should be debated in a free, open and uninhibited manner, a position that was one of the underpinnings of Justice William Brennan's opinion in *New York Times Co. v. Sullivan*,[1] the landmark case that pulled libel law within constitutional scope. A libel suit today, thanks to the precedent established by *New York Times Co. v. Sullivan*, may be defended on constitutional grounds as well as through the common law.

THE CONSTITUTIONAL DEFENSE

Chapter 6 explains that the burden of proof in establishing fault is on the plaintiff. Nevertheless, fault is still an integral part of a defendant's case since the defendant can present evidence to refute a plaintiff's claims. Not only must the plaintiff bear the burden of proving fault, but when the fault level is actual malice, the U.S. Supreme Court said in *New York Times Co. v. Sullivan* that it must be shown with convincing clarity. The proof of actual malice, therefore, must go beyond the "preponderance of evidence" standard typical in civil litigation. While convincing clarity must be strong, positive and free from doubt, it is still less than proof beyond a reasonable doubt, which is required in criminal cases.

The freedoms of speech and press are protected by the First Amendment. Therein lies the heart of the so-called "constitutional defense" in libel law. The Supreme Court has recognized that free speech is vital because it ensures individual self-fulfillment and that it is a social good because it helps in the search for the truth. The First Amendment "rests on the assumption that the widest possible dissemination of information from diverse and antagonistic sources is essential to the welfare of the public."[2] Moreover, as Justice Louis Brandeis wrote during the era in which the Court truly began to interpret the meaning and scope of the First Amendment, "freedom to think as you will and speak as you think

---

[1] 376 U.S. 254 (1964).

[2] *Citizen Publishing Co. v. U.S.*, 394 U.S. 131, 139-40 (1969).

are means indispensable to the discovery and spread of political truth."[3]

Thus, a libel defense, of sorts, has developed out of the notion that contributing significantly to a body of knowledge is important, and freedom of expression is a key element in that process: "The First Amendment serves not only the needs of the polity but also those of the human spirit — a spirit that demands self-expression."[4] Limiting expression is antithetical to this philosophy.

The question becomes, "Does the speech contribute to the 'profound national commitment to the principle that debate on public issues should be uninhibited, robust, and wide-open?'"[5] At a base level, a media organization's defense of libel on constitutional grounds is a claim that limiting its ability to convey information is an abridgment of the First Amendment guarantees of free speech and press. Carrying this argument to its logical conclusion, then, finding a media defendant guilty of libel is unconstitutional because doing so limits constitutionally protected freedoms. Moreover, knowing that such a verdict is possible in the wake of critical or less-than-positive statements about an individual may also limit freedom by producing a chilling effect. That is, the media may be less inclined to publish information containing critical statements knowing that they may be held liable for false, though well-intentioned, publications.

The ability to criticize the government and those in government was central to *New York Times Co. v. Sullivan.* Behind Justice Brennan's opinion was the notion that statements about public officials — people who hold important positions in government — are most deserving of constitutional protection. The ability to be critical of government and government officials, after all, was the basis and justification for the First Amendment's protection of speech and the press from interference by the state. Some scholars, in fact, have taken an unconditional approach to the issue. Philosopher Alexander Meiklejohn, for example, has written that speech relevant to self-government is absolutely protected under the First Amendment.[6] And Harry Kalven, Jr., wrote that the central meaning of the First Amendment is uninhibited discussion of governmental affairs: "Political freedom ends when government can use its powers and its courts to silence its critics."[7] By grant-

ing protection to the citizen-critic of government and its officials, Kalven wrote, "The theory of the freedom of speech clause was put right side up for the first time."[8]

Given this sanctity bestowed on the ability of citizens to criticize government and government officials, Justice Brennan created the new standard that had to be met before public officials could recover damages for libel: actual malice. The scope of the standard was soon thereafter expanded to apply to more than public official plaintiffs.

Extending Actual Malice to Public Figures

The Supreme Court has also applied the actual malice standard of and concerning public *figures,* that is, individuals who either possess widespread fame or notoriety or who have thrust themselves into a public controversy in order to influence its outcome.

As indicated in Chapter 6, the actual malice rule was extended to public figures in 1967 with *Curtis Publishing Co. v. Butts,* in which the Supreme Court also decided *Associated Press v. Walker.*[9] In *Associated Press*, retired Maj. Gen. Edwin Walker was at the University of Mississippi when rioting occurred over the enrollment of James Meredith, the first African American to attend that university. An Associated Press story reported that Walker had taken command of a violent crowd, personally leading a charge against federal marshals and encouraging the crowd to use violence. Walker sued AP and a number of media outlets that used the story.

The *Butts* case began when an insurance salesman claimed that, while making a pay telephone call, he was mysteriously patched into a conversation between University of Georgia athletic director Wally Butts and University of Alabama football coach Paul "Bear" Bryant. The two men were allegedly conspiring to fix an upcoming football game between the two schools. The salesman took the information to the *Saturday Evening Post,* which, months later, ran a story about the alleged fix. Butts sued, winning at trial. The *Post* appealed, arguing that Butts, as a public official, was required to prove actual malice. The Court disagreed, but held that both Butts and Walker were public figures. That was important because a majority of the justices agreed that public figures should also have a heightened burden of proof. In the words of Chief Justice Earl Warren, public figures are "intimately involved in the resolution of

[3] *Whitney v. California,* 274 U.S. 354, 375 (1927)(Brandeis, J., concurring).

[4] *Procunier v. Martinez,* 416 U.S. 396, 427 (1974)(Marshall, J., concurring).

[5] *New York Times,* 376 U.S. at 270.

[6] Alexander Meiklejohn, *Political Freedom* (New York: Harper, 1960), pp. 20-27.

[7] Harry Kalven, Jr., "The New York Times Case: A Note on the 'Central Meaning of the First Amendment,'" *Supreme Court Review* 1964: 205.

[8] *Id.* at 208.

[9] 388 U.S. 130 (1967).

important public questions or, by reason of their fame, shape events in areas of concern to society at large."[10]

In the plurality opinion, Justice John Marshall Harlan attempted to require public figures to prove that media, in effect, were guilty of journalistic malpractice in order to show liability. More justices joined Chief Justice Warren's concurring opinion, however, establishing actual malice as the standard for public figures. Warren justified the extension, writing that the "differentiation between public figures and public officials and adoption of separate standards of proof for each have no basis in law, logic, or First Amendment policy."[11] Thus, *Butts* and *Walker* established the principle that many people who do not hold governmental office are nevertheless intimately involved in the resolution of public issues and that public individuals — officials or figures — are required to show actual malice when suing for libel.

The Public/Private Distinction

Because of the dramatic difference in the level of fault required of public person and private person libel plaintiffs, defendants often exert great effort to demonstrate that plaintiffs are public persons. This effort, of course, while not purely a defense, is considered part of the so-called "constitutional defense" given that it stems from the actual malice concept.

Determining just who qualifies as a public official is reasonably, but not entirely, clear-cut. In a 1979 case, the Supreme Court made it clear that "public official" is not synonymous with "public employee."[12] Though the matter is less than entirely settled, two guidelines may be whether a public employee is in a position to make policy and whether the employee has ready access to the media. Anything that touches on an official's fitness for office is relevant.[13]

A person remains a public official for the purposes of the actual malice rule even after leaving office, at least with regard to stories that refer to conduct while in office. The passing of time, however, eventually may erode public interest in the office-holder's conduct so that the *New York Times* rule would no longer apply. There may be cases "where a person is so far removed from a former position of authority that comment on the manner in which he performed his responsibilities no longer has the interest necessary to

justify the *New York Times* rule."[14] But this exception is rare — so rare as to be virtually nonexistent.

A public official must also establish that a defamatory statement was directed at the official, rather than at the official's government unit. This is at the heart of First Amendment philosophy — that under the Constitution there is no such thing as libel against the government; there is no seditious libel.

Demarcating between public and private figures is not an easy task. As one court noted, it "is much like trying to nail a jelly fish to the wall."[15] The requirement is that a public figure must have widespread fame or notoriety, or must have voluntarily entered a matter of public controversy, attempting to affect the outcome of the controversy. The application of the rule is not nearly as clear-cut as the definition.

The defining case is *Gertz v. Robert Welch, Inc.*,[16] described in Chapter 6. In *Gertz*, the Supreme Court differentiated between two types of public figures. General or all-purpose public figures are persons who have achieved pervasive fame or notoriety in their communities or are pervasively involved in the affairs of society. It is not easy to become an all-purpose, or universal, public figure. The category is generally reserved for people whose names have become household words. While specific circumstances may vary — creating nuances — various courts have held that a political candidate, an entertainer, a social activist, a writer and columnist, a political adviser and a religious leader qualify as public figures. Certainly, not all people within each of these categories would qualify as universal public figures. Some have risen to such positions of prominence, however, to render them public for all situations.

Far more common than the all-purpose public figure is the limited-purpose public figure. Limited-purpose public figures have "thrust themselves to the forefront of particular controversies in order to influence the resolution of issues involved."[17] This means, first, a public controversy must exist and, second, the nature and extent of the plaintiff's participation in the controversy must be determined. While it is clear that newsworthiness and public-figure status are not synonymous, some courts have held that a person who creates a public controversy in order to affect the outcome of some public issue has met the limited-purposes criteria.

The *Gertz* Court saw a relationship between public figures and

---

[10] *Id.* at 164 (Warren, C.J., concurring in the result).

[11] *Id.* at 163 (Warren, C.J., concurring in the result).

[12] *Hutchinson v. Proxmire*, 443 U.S. 111, 119 n. 8 (1979).

[13] See *Rosenblatt v. Baer*, 383 U.S. 75, 85 (1966), and *Garrison v. Louisiana*, 379 U.S. 64, 77 (1964).

[14] *Rosenblatt*, 383 U.S. at 87 n. 14.

[15] *Rosanova v. Playboy Enterprises, Inc.*, 411 F. Supp. 440, 443 (S.D. Ga. 1976).

[16] 418 U.S. 323 (1974).

[17] *Id.* at 345.

public officials, in part, because individuals in both groups tend to have access to the media and, therefore, have the ability to set the record straight. Private figures, on the other hand, usually have limited access and are, therefore, more vulnerable to irreparable injury. In addition, there is a certain degree of risk that accompanies those in the public. While public officials "must accept certain necessary consequences [regarding their] involvement in public affairs," they also "run the risk of closer public scrutiny than might otherwise be the case.... Those classified as public figures stand in a similar position.... [T]he communications media are entitled to act on the assumption that public officials and public figures have voluntarily exposed themselves to increased risk of injury from defamatory falsehoods concerning them."[18] The Court said in *Gertz* that society's stake in news about private figures is not as great as when public people are involved. Society places a high value in protecting private figures against libel, so the level of fault they are required to meet is less demanding than it is for public people.

A number of cases illustrate the Court's delineation of public people. They demonstrate that being in the public eye and being a public figure are not the same. The case of Mary Alice Firestone is one example. She was married to the heir to the Firestone Rubber Co. fortune, was a prominent member of Palm Beach society and even subscribed to a clipping service so she could keep track of all the news published about her. In addition, when she and her husband became involved in a well-publicized divorce proceeding, Mrs. Firestone held daily press conferences. When she sued *Time* for incorrectly reporting that her husband was granted a divorce because of her adultery and extreme cruelty — rather than because "neither party is domesticated" — many assumed she would be a categorized as a public figure for libel purposes. But the Supreme Court said no. The Court said that while a large number of people might be interested in the problems of the extremely wealthy, those were not the kinds of matters the Court had in mind when it referred to a public controversy.[19]

Similarly, the Court held in *Wolston v. Reader's Digest*[20] that mere involvement in judicial proceedings or in alleged criminal activity does not necessarily make one a public figure. Ilya Wolston had been cited for, but not found guilty of, contempt of court when he failed to appear before a grand jury during Senator Joseph McCarthy's Communist-scare frenzy. Years later he was named in a book as being among those who were identified as Soviet agents

or had been found guilty of perjury or contempt in connection with spying charges. He sued for libel, and the Supreme Court ruled that he was not a public figure. First, the Court said, he had done nothing voluntarily to thrust himself into the controversy over Soviet espionage. Instead, he had been brought into the controversy by the FBI and a grand jury — a grand jury he did not appear before because he was ill. Second, the Court said Wolston was not a public figure just because news stories were published about the grand jury incident. *Reader's Digest* had thrust the plaintiff back into the public spotlight, in spite of the fact that Wolston chose not to appear before a grand jury and was then the subject of several newspaper articles. Wolston, the Court ruled, had been "dragged unwillingly" into the controversy. He remained a private individual, therefore, and did not have to prove actual malice on the part of *Reader's Digest.*

Thus, a plaintiff cannot be made public merely by the defendant's actions. This was further illustrated by the Court's decision in *Hutchinson v. Proxmire.*[21] Ronald Hutchinson was a researcher who had received $500,000 in grants from the Department of Defense and NASA to study stress in monkeys. In an effort to highlight what he perceived to be wasteful allocation of federal funds, Senator William Proxmire gave his "Golden Fleece" award to Hutchinson's funding agencies. Hutchinson contended that Proxmire's award subjected him to public derision and sued for libel. The Supreme Court said Hutchinson was not a public figure because his work was of limited interest and was not controversial until Proxmire's award made it so. Hutchinson had not voluntarily thrust himself into the public eye to influence others.

This and similar cases illustrate what has come to be labeled as "bootstrapping." Bootstrapping occurs when media defendants attach (or bootstrap) themselves onto the protection of the actual malice standard by citing media coverage — including their own — of the plaintiff as evidence that the plaintiff is a public figure. The Court said, "Clearly, those charged with defamation cannot, by their own conduct, create their own defense by making the claimant a public figure."[22] As a result, courts have said that the public controversy at issue must have existed before the publication upon which the defamation is based. A court, however, that rigidly applies the pre-existing controversy requirement may punish legitimate reporting that uncovers specific acts of wrongdoing. Courts, therefore, attempt to strike a delicate balance between which came first — the controversy or the story about the controversy.

But, just as a media organization is not permitted to bootstrap

---

[18] *Id.*
[19] *Time Inc. v. Firestone,* 424 U.S. 488 (1976).
[20] 443 U.S. 157 (1979).

---

[21] 443 U.S. 111 (1979).
[22] *Id.* at 135.

itself into creating its own defense, a plaintiff may not be permitted to avoid the actual malice standard by claiming that the attention was unwanted. The proper question is not whether the plaintiff volunteered for the publicity but whether the plaintiff volunteered for an activity from which publicity would foreseeably arise.

Even if an individual is not active within a particular sphere, the mere presence within the sphere may satisfy a court's public figure requirements: Where a person has "chosen to engage in a profession which draws him regularly into regional and national view and leads to fame and notoriety in the community, even if he has no ideological thesis to promulgate, he invites general public discussion.... If society chooses to direct massive public attention to a particular sphere of activity, those who enter that sphere inviting such attention overcome the *Times* standard."[23] Thus, voluntary entry into a sphere of activity, the court reasoned, is sufficient to satisfy the "voluntariness" element of the public figure inquiry.

But merely being an executive within a prominent and influential company does not by itself make one a public figure. Professionals are typically not public figures, but under certain circumstances they can be. For example, voluntary use of controversial or unorthodox techniques may be enough to confer public figure status. Publicly defending such methods or adopting other controversial stands also tends to bring about public status. So, a doctor who had written extensively on health issues as a newspaper columnist, who was also the author of various journal articles, and who had appeared on at least one nationally broadcast television program discussing health and nutrition issues was held to be a public figure for a limited range of issues — those pertaining to health and nutrition.[24]

An individual may assume public figure status within small publics but may revert to being a private figure in larger spheres. For example, a university professor may be a public figure on campus and in the adjacent academic community but a private person beyond those boundaries. The professor, therefore, may be a public figure for purposes of an article in the university newspaper but not for purposes of a regional newspaper or a national magazine. Similarly, an individual can attain the status of an all-purpose public figure within a particular geographical area.[25]

In *Gertz*, the Supreme Court acknowledged that involuntary limited public figures may exist theoretically but that such cases would be rare. Yet, an individual could be thrust into a matter of public controversy not merely through voluntary actions but also through bad luck. It is possible to become a public figure through no purposeful action. *Dameron v. Washingtonian Magazine, Inc.*[26] is a good example.

Merle Dameron was the only air traffic controller on duty at Dulles Airport near Washington, D.C., when a plane crashed nearby killing ninety-two people. Eight years later, following another crash in Washington, *The Washingtonian* magazine examined the issue of air safety, noting that air traffic control systems had rarely been at fault in major air accidents. Dameron claimed that the magazine libeled him because, although he had not been identified by name, prior publicity had linked his name with the Dulles tragedy that was mentioned in the contested article. He also claimed he was a private person. The District of Columbia Circuit Court of Appeals disagreed, ruling that a clear public controversy existed surrounding the accident and the article — although eight years after the fact — centered on issues pertinent to that controversy. Moreover, the court said that Dameron had played a central role in the controversy even though his involvement lacked the usual elements of "activity and injection."[27] Although he had not sought the public eye, Dameron's involvement was so central to the controversy that he had become identified with the case, therefore assuming the role of public figure.

The passage of time may theoretically permit some people who were once public figures to regain private figure status. To revert to private figure status, the likelihood is that a plaintiff would need to demonstrate that the original status as a public figure was not connected to events or controversies that have become part of the permanent historical consciousness of the country.

Whether a governmental entity should assume public status and therefore be subject to the actual malice standard was at issue in a 1994 California case. The University of California sued David Nadel and Carol Ruth Denney for violent and destructive conduct during a protest. In the course of the litigation, the university issued news releases that Nadel and Denney said defamed them.[28] They claimed that, though they were public figures, the actual malice standard should not apply when the government is the defendant. Their rationale was that the First Amendment is not meant to protect government from citizens, only citizens from the government. While the court considered the argument, it ruled that the actual malice standard should be extended to cases in which

---

[23] *Chuy v. Philadelphia Eagles Football Club,* 431 F. Supp. 254, 276 (E.D. Pa. 1977).

[24] *Renner v. Donsbach,* 749 F. Supp. 987 (W.D. Mo. 1990).

[25] See, e.g., *Williams v. Pasma,* 656 P.2d 212 (Mont. 1982).

[26] 779 F.2d 736 (D.C. Cir. 1985).

[27] *Id.* at 741.

[28] *Nadel v. Regents of the University of California,* 24 Cal. App. 4th 1251, 34 Cal. Rptr. 2d 188 (1994).

governmental entities are defendants because that promotes the free exchange of ideas.

The Supreme Court has said that a public figure is one with widespread fame or notoriety, so prominence is important in determining public figure status. Moreover, that prominence may apply to a narrowly drawn context.

In sum, the public/private distinction is vital in libel law. How a libel suit unfolds hinges on this determination. Public officials and public figures are required to show the defendant acted with actual malice; private individuals are not. For those plaintiffs who are not required to demonstrate that actual malice occurred, showing only some other, lesser level of fault — usually negligence — is required. Thus, integral to a defense strategy is the goal to have plaintiffs categorized as public persons — either officials or figures.

The Nature of the Statement

Not only is the categorization of the plaintiff meaningful to the libel defendant, so is the nature of the statement that the defendant allegedly published. In *Dun & Bradstreet v. Greenmoss Builders*[29] a private-person plaintiff contended that he was defamed by material the Supreme Court said was a matter of private concern. A Dun & Bradstreet credit report that was sent to five subscribers inaccurately reported that Greenmoss Builders had declared bankruptcy. Justice Lewis Powell, for the majority, wrote that the purpose of the speaker and the nature and size of the audience are among the criteria for determining when speech involves matters of public concern.[30] Rodney Smolla adds a note of caution in understanding this standard:

> It is extremely important to keep the "matters of public concern" standard articulated in *Dun & Bradstreet* separate from the term of art "public controversy" used as part of the vortex public figure test in *Gertz*. By definition, any person who is a private figure plaintiff has already failed to voluntarily thrust himself into a public controversy; otherwise, that plaintiff would be deemed a public figure. If anyone who did not fall into the public figure classification could automatically claim that the speech involved did not implicate matters of public concern, then the negligence standard in *Gertz* would never apply as a constitutional minimum — the case would be either tried under the actual malice test or under common law strict liability. *Dun & Bradstreet* clearly had no such thing; it did not establish an all

or nothing regime. Rather, *Dun & Bradstreet* subdivided the universe of cases involving private figures into those containing defamatory speech about matters of public concern, and those not containing defamatory speech about matters of private concern. This means that the "public concern" standard may include speech that is "public" even when the plaintiff is "private." The public controversy formulation is linked to the plaintiff's voluntary participation in the public arena, but the public concern test looks primarily to the speech itself.[31]

Thus, the Court sought to establish minimal standards of fault not only depending on the status of the plaintiff but also according to the nature of the subject matter.

Neutral Reportage

Neutral reportage is also a defense with a constitutional foundation. First enunciated in 1977 in *Edwards v. National Audubon Society, Inc.,*[32] neutral reportage protects accurate, unbiased news reporting of accusations made against public figures by prominent, responsible persons. It recognizes that the actual malice rule does not protect a media defendant from reporting false, defamatory statements that are newsworthy if the defendant knows those statements are false. The Second U.S. Circuit Court of Appeals — and other courts that have adopted the neutral reporting rule — believed that such statements, when made by public figures, are newsworthy and should be protected provided that they are reported accurately and objectively. The *Edwards* court overturned a jury verdict against the *New York Times,* saying it was constitutionally impermissible to hold the newspaper liable for publishing such statements:

> [W]hen a responsible, prominent organization ... makes serious charges against a public figure, the First Amendment protects the accurate and disinterested reporting of those charges, regardless of the reporter's private views of their validity.... We do not believe that the press may be required under the First Amendment to suppress newsworthy statements merely because it has serious doubts regarding their truth.[33]

Since the Supreme Court has said that serious doubts about a

---

[29] 472 U.S. 749 (1985).
[30] *Id.* at 783.

[31] Rodney A. Smolla, *Law of Defamation,* 11th ed. (Deerfield, Ill.: Clark Boardman Callaghan, 1996), at 3-15 (footnote omitted).
[32] 556 F.2d 113 (2d Cir. 1977).
[33] *Id.* at 120.

statement's truth constitutes actual malice, *Edwards* seemed to fly in the face of precedent. Clearly, it seemed, neutral reportage would create yet even greater breathing space for a media industry already provided latitude *via* the actual malice standard. Indeed, Rodney Smolla has called the emergence of the neutral reportage privilege "one of the most significant developments in the law of defamation today."[34]

A dozen years later, in his concurring opinion in *Harte-Hanks v. Connaughton*,[35] Justice Harry Blackmun called a newspaper unwise for abandoning the neutral reportage defense, suggesting that the Court may have been ready to adopt, or at least consider, the doctrine. Blackmun noted that the newspaper had accurately reported newsworthy allegations about a political candidate and his response. "Were this Court to adopt the neutral reportage theory," Blackmun wrote, "the facts of this case arguably might fit within it. That question, however, has also not been squarely presented."[36] Aside from that brief statement, the U.S. Supreme Court has not addressed neutral reportage and whether the doctrine is a viable libel defense.

A case that, as this book went to press, was pending in the California Supreme Court could shed additional light on neutral reportage. In *Khawar v. The Globe*,[37] a tabloid newspaper was sued for libel for writing that Khalid Khawar was the person who assassinated Sen. Robert Kennedy in 1968. A jury found for Khawar and awarded him $1.175 million in damages. But *The Globe* appealed, using the neutral reportage defense. It claimed its report was based solely on a book titled *The Senator Must Die* that made the same claim. *The Globe* said it was merely reporting what had already been reported elsewhere. The appeals court rejected those claims,[38] but *The Globe* appealed again, this time to the California Supreme Court, and was supported in its claim of neutral reportage by major news organizations including *The New York Times, The Los Angeles Times*, ABC, CBS, and NBC. The ruling was expected in the spring of 1999.

In the two decades since its inception, ten states — Alabama, California, Florida, Georgia, Illinois, Louisiana, Ohio, Oklahoma, Vermont and Washington — and the District of Columbia have adopted neutral reportage. In addition, the Third, Seventh and Tenth U.S. Circuit Courts have joined the Second in recognizing the privilege. While it remains a part of the libel defendant's strat-

egy, therefore, the inconsistent manner in which courts have accepted neutral reportage makes it an unreliable defense.

Opinion

The opinion defense has both constitutional and common law elements, causing discussion of this complex area of the law to become even more muddled. Traditionally, opinion as a libel defense stemmed from the common law. But the ability to voice opinions, particularly about issues of public concern, has been recognized as also being at the heart of the First Amendment's protection of freedom of expression. Constitutional derivations of the opinion defense are analyzed here; the common law components of opinion follow.

When statements are pure opinion — that is, when they cannot be proved to be true or false — those statements are protected, though the protection has come in a round-about way. To attempt to separate statements of fact from statements of opinion is to venture onto one of the law's slipperiest of slopes, yet to do so is vital in establishing the boundaries of the protection. In addition, state-to-state variations make the distinction all the more difficult.

The role of *Gertz* in constitutional protection of opinion cannot be underestimated. The significance — and sometimes confusion — stems from Justice Lewis Powell's seemingly offhanded observation in his majority opinion: "Under the First Amendment there is no such thing as a false idea. However pernicious an opinion may seem, we depend for its correction not on the conscience of judges and juries but on the competition of other ideas."[39] The *dicta* made it appear that the common law defense in opinion cases had been superseded by a constitutional overlay. Opinion, it seemed, had been provided blanket protection. Indeed, many courts used *Gertz* as the basis of absolute protection for expression of opinion.

The problem came in attempting to distinguish statements of fact from statements of opinion. Statements of opinion were defined as statements that could not be proved to be true or false. A Massachusetts court, for example, said a company spokesperson's explanation that an employee was terminated because of sloppy and irresponsible techniques represented an expression of opinion.[40] Similarly, writing that a judge is one of the ten worst in New York and should be removed from office, and calling one in-

---

[34] Smolla, *supra* note 31, at 4-17, 4-72.
[35] 491 U.S. 657 (1989).
[36] *Id.* at 694-95 (Blackmun, J., concurring).
[37] 923 P.2d 766 (Cal. 1996)(granting petition for review).
[38] 51 Cal. App. 4th 14 (1996).

[39] 418 U.S. at 339-40.
[40] *Cole v. Westinghouse Broadcasting Co., Inc.*, 386 Mass. 303, 309, 435 N.E.2d 1021, 1025 (1982).

dividual a liar and another a fascist all have been ruled to be expressions of opinion and, therefore, not libelous.[41]

A defining case in this area of the law is *Ollman v. Evans.*[42] A college professor sued two columnists who wrote that he had no status within the profession, and that he used his classroom as an instrument to prepare for a Marxist revolution. The U.S. Court of Appeals for the District of Columbia Circuit was split in its decision. Then-Judge Antonin Scalia decided that the columnists wrote a "classic and cooly crafted libel,"[43] but the court's majority, led by then-Judge Kenneth Starr, found the column to be opinion protected by the First Amendment and the principles enunciated in *Gertz.* Moreover, Judge Starr noted the difficulty in distinguishing opinion from fact, and attempted to simplify the task by establishing a four-part test, now known as the *Ollman* test:[44]

1. What is the common usage or meaning of the words?
2. Is the statement verifiable — "objectively capable of proof or disproof?" That is, can the statement be proven either true or false?
3. What is the linguistic or journalistic context in which the statement occurs? The entire article or column must be considered as a whole. "The language of the entire column may signal that a specific statement which, standing alone, would appear to be factual, is in fact a statement of opinion."
4. What is the "broader social context into which the statement fits?"

Opinion came to be granted a wide berth of protection. *Newsweek,* for example, was vindicated in publishing a reference to a false accusation that former South Dakota governor William Janklow had sexually assaulted a teenage girl. The words might appear to constitute a statement of fact, but the court found them to be "imprecise, unverifiable" and "presented in a forum where spirited writing is expected and involves criticism of the motives and intentions of a public official."[45] Other plaintiffs who sued because they were called unscrupulous charlatans, neo-Nazis, sleazebags, and ignorant and spineless politicians lost their cases because these charges were determined to be statements of opinion rather than statements of fact.[46] In short, *Gertz* seemed to establish nearly absolute protection for the expression of opinion.

But then came *Milkovich v. Lorrain Journal,*[47] a case that put Justice Powell's "no such thing as a false idea" language into context and, by so doing, reframed what had appeared to be an absolute opinion defense. It also forced recognition of the notion that where pure opinion may not exist, mixed opinion may. In *Milkovich,* a high school wrestling coach sued when a local newspaper columnist indicated that the coach lied under oath about his role in a brawl during a wrestling match. The Supreme Court, for the first time, addressed Powell's "false idea" statement. "[W]e do not think this passage from *Gertz* was intended to create a wholesale defamation exemption for anything that might be labeled 'opinion,'" Chief Justice William Rehnquist wrote for the Court. "Not only would such an interpretation be contrary to the tenor and context of the passage, but it would also ignore the fact that expressions of 'opinion' may often imply an assertion of objective fact."[48] Rehnquist wrote that facts can disguise themselves as opinions, and, when they do, they imply a knowledge of hidden facts that led to the opinion. Moreover, he expressed a desire to avoid drawing lines between opinion and fact. In short, while *Milkovich* holds that opinion is not protected as a category of speech, it provides a framework in which opinion *is* protected. That is, since an opinion cannot be proved to be false, it cannot be the basis for a successful libel action.

Milkovich has become one of the Court's most frequently cited cases. One recent case is a good example. In *Moldea v. New York Times Co.,* author Dan Moldea sued the *New York Times* for a reviewer's criticisms of his book. Among other things, the reviewer wrote that the book contained "too much sloppy journalism to trust the bulk of [its] 512 pages including its whopping 64 pages of footnotes."[49] A federal judge granted summary judgment for the *New York Times,* holding that the reviewer's statements were not actionable because they were statements of opinion and, therefore, unverifiable.

The D.C. Circuit Court of Appeals reversed, finding that some of the statements in the review to be verifiable.[50] After rehearing the case, however, the court held that the review was not defamatory, ruling that the genre of the writing and the context within which it appears must be considered:

---

[41] *Rinaldi v. Holt, Rinehart & Winston, Inc.,* 42 N.Y.2d 369, 366 N.E. 2d 1299 (1977).

[42] 750 F.2d 970 (D.C. Cir. 1984).

[43] *Id.* at 1038.

[44] *Id.* at 979-983.

[45] *Janklow v. Newsweek,* 788 F.2d 1300, 1305 (8th Cir. 1986).

[46] *Spelson v. CBS, Inc.,* 581 F. Supp. 1195 (N.D. Ill. 1984); *Anderson v. Liberty Lobby, Inc.,* 746 F.2d 1563 (1984), *aff'd on other grounds,* 477 U.S. 242 (1986); *Henderson v. Times Mirror Co.,* 669 F. Supp. 356 (D.

Colo. 1987); *Dow v. New Haven Indep., Inc.,* 41 Conn. Supp. 31, 549 A.2d 683 (1987).

[47] 497 U.S. 1 (1990).

[48] *Id.* at 18.

[49] 793 F. Supp. 335, 337 (D.D.C. 1992).

[50] 15 F.3d 1137, 1146-48 (D.C. Cir. 1994).

In contrast to the situation in *Milkovich,* the instant case involves a context, a book review, in which the allegedly libelous statements were evaluations quintessentially of a type readers expect to find in that genre.... [T]here is a long and rich history in our cultural and legal traditions of affording reviewers latitude to comment on literary and other works. The statements at issue in the instant case are assessments of a book, rather than direct assaults on Moldea's character, reputation, or competence as a journalist.... [W]hile a critic's latitude is not unlimited, he or she must be given the constitutional "breathing space" appropriate to the genre.[51]

As noted above, opinion defenses are not limited to the constitutional category. Defenses such as "fair comment and criticism" and "letters to the editor" are common law libel defenses, and are discussed below.

COMMON LAW DEFENSES

Libel defendants also have defenses that originated with the common law. Traditional state rules governing libel largely stem from laws and principles handed down through generations of legal precedent, mainly from English law. Early in the Sixteenth Century, the common law courts began to recognize a claim for defamation and, with it, various defenses. These grew out of the recognition that there is sometimes an interest in the free flow of information that is so important that some allowance for error and damage to reputation must be made.

Fair Comment and Criticism

Fair comment and criticism is a common law privilege that protects critics from lawsuits brought by individuals in the public eye. A "critic" can be anyone who comments on these individuals, and being "in the public eye" is not the same as being a public figure for purposes of actual malice. A person in the public eye is anyone who enters a public sphere: artists, entertainers, dramatists, writers, members of the clergy, teachers — anyone who moves in and out of the public eye, either professionally or as an amateur. The privilege also protects commentary on institutions whose activities are of interest to the public or where matters of public interest are concerned.

Fair comment and criticism protects criticism based on facts that are stated, privileged or otherwise known to be available to the public. But if the challenged statement conveys or implies a defamatory message, the defense may be lost and the implication may be the basis of a libel suit.

The principle of fair comment and criticism extends at least to a turn-of-the-century case in which a court ruled that a venomous newspaper review was not libelous. The *Des Moines Leader* republished a review of an act by "The Cherry Sisters." The reviewer, among other things, described one sister as "an old jade," a second as "a capering monstrosity" and the three of them as "strange creatures." When the sisters sued for libel, the Iowa Supreme Court accepted the *Leader's* defense of fair comment:

One who goes upon the stage to exhibit himself to the public, or who gives any kind of a performance to which the public is invited, may be freely criticised [sic].... [E]ntire freedom of expression is guarantied [sic] to dramatic critics, provided they are not actuated by malice or evil purpose in what they write.[52]

Thus began the development of the fair comment and criticism doctrine. Originally the privilege provided only modest coverage, protecting commentary only when it was based on true facts, but over time it has expanded. Still, to qualify for the privilege, commentary must be fair, it must be made without common law malice, and it must accurately reflect the opinion of the commentator.

Truth

Truth is a complete defense in a libel case because, if it can be proved, there can be no liability. This, of course, is common sense. But there are a number of misconceptions about the truth defense, and the defense is not easy to maintain.

One of the first and best-known uses of truth as a successful libel defense was in the 1735 trial of printer John Peter Zenger. Zenger had printed, in his *Weekly Journal,* criticisms of the governor of New York. Under the law, truth was no defense, but the jury in the case accepted the argument of Zenger's attorney that one should not be punished for publishing true statements, refused to follow the instructions of the judge in the case and acquitted Zenger. Although the verdict failed to establish an immediate precedent, it did sow the seeds of press and speech freedoms, specifically the notion of truth as a legitimate defense in libel trials. It was not until 1790 that Pennsylvania became the first state to formally recognize truth as a defense. New York followed in 1805.

---

[51] 22 F.3d 310, 315 (D.C. Cir. 1994).

[52] *Cherry v. Des Moines Leader,* 114 Iowa 298, 86 N.W. 323, 325 (1901).

For years, truth was considered a noble defense. After all, the media are supposed to be in the business of rooting out and publishing the truth. A turnabout in the law, however, has turned the truth-falsity distinction on its ear. In modern libel law, the burden of proof in this area lies with the plaintiff, not the defendant.

The change began in 1964 with the actual malice rule. By establishing that public officials persons must prove actual malice, the Supreme Court implied that those plaintiffs must also prove falsity. How does one prove reckless disregard for the truth or knowledge of falsity without proving falsity? Then, in *Philadelphia Newspapers, Inc. v. Hepps,*[53] the Court said specifically that, when the defamatory material involves matters of public concern, the libel plaintiff must prove that the material is false. This has caused some courts to hold that truth is no longer an affirmative defense.

Hepps left open the specific question of the burden of proof in non-media cases. Presumably, in such cases with public plaintiffs, the burden would remain on the plaintiff, but the Court has not addressed where the burden lies in cases contested by non-media defendants and private-figure plaintiffs. Moreover, when the statement at issue does not involve a matter of public concern, the question of the burden of showing truth or falsity is open. It is difficult to imagine a media case that does not involve a matter of public concern, however, given that, virtually by definition, material published in a media outlet qualifies as being of public concern.

A libel defendant does not stand idly by just because the burden of proof lies with the plaintiff. The defendant's attorneys will attempt to demonstrate that the disputed material is true. The attorneys will do this by cross-examining the plaintiff's witnesses and, possibly, by producing evidence of truth.

In such circumstances — and even when a defendant advances a defense of truth — the defendant need not demonstrate that a defamatory statement is completely true in order to maintain the defense. Substantial truth is all that is required. As one court said, "Slight inaccuracies of expression are immaterial provided that the defamatory charge is true in substance."[54] The Supreme Court has agreed:

[Substantial truth] would absolve a defendant even if she cannot justify every word of the alleged defamatory matter; it is sufficient if the substance of the charge be proved true, irrespective of the slight inaccuracy in the details.... Minor inaccuracies do not amount to falsity so long as the substance, the gist, the sting of the libelous charge can be justified.[55]

Substantial truth means, for example, that if a newspaper reported that an individual was in custody when, in fact, the individual had been released on bail, the story would be substantially true, because the individual had been in custody and it was only a quirk in time that had caused the mistake. If, however, a newspaper published that an individual had been charged with a crime when the individual had only been questioned and released, the story would not be substantially true.

It is worthwhile to note a growing trend in lawsuits against media defendants. Plaintiffs are circumventing the issue of truth in the defendant's reports by filing suit for transgressions other than libel. A good example is *Food Lion v. Cap Cities/ABC,*[56] in which a supermarket chain that was unhappy with a television news magazine segment on its food preparation practices sued, not for libel, but because of the techniques used in gathering the information. This strategy enabled Food Lion to entirely bypass any obligation of proving that the broadcast was false. Thus, whereas libel once may have been the preferred sword for plaintiffs in cases like this, lawyers are more frequently advising their clients to avoid the realm in which media defendants have the shield of both Constitutional and common law protection at their disposal.

Fair Report Privilege

Within some spheres of society, it is so vitally important that people be allowed to speak without fear of being sued for libel that they are granted immunity from liability. This privilege — called "absolute privilege" — typically occurs within the context of carrying out the business of government. Nothing a government official says that is relevant to the official's duties can be the subject of a successful libel suit. In an open society, policy demands that the public have access to information relating to government proceedings. It logically follows, then, that people reporting on these proceedings also have the protection of privilege. As representatives of the public, the media are granted a "qualified privilege" to report on governmental proceedings. This privilege, however, is conditioned on the fair and accurate reporting of the proceeding and is sometimes referred to as the "fair report" privilege.

The privilege is lost if the allegedly defamatory material is pub-

[53] 475 U.S. 767 (1986).
[54] *Liberty Lobby v. Dow Jones & Co., Inc.,* 838 F.2d 1287, 1296 (D.C. Cir. 1988).
[55] *Masson v. New Yorker Magazine,* 501 U.S. 496, 516-17 (1991).
[56] 116 F.3d 472 (4th Cir. 1997), 984 F. Supp. 923 (M.D.N.C. 1997), 951 F. Supp. 1217 (M.D.N.C. 1996), 887 F. Supp. 811 (M.D.N.C. 1995).

lished with common law malice, if it is not accurate and fair, if the gist of the article is not substantially correct or if the author draws conclusions or adds comments to the official report. Sometimes referred to as the "official report privilege," it proves to be an exception to the rule of republication (see below). This privilege protects media reports of official government actions, regardless of possible defamatory elements in those reports. The rationale is that citizens in a participatory democracy are entitled to such information. But that entitlement does not extend to official reports issued by governments other than those in the United States.[57]

The privilege covers officials and proceedings in the executive, judicial and legislative branches of state, local and federal governments and, often, private individuals communicating with the government.

Executive Branch. Reports on the official statements and proceedings of people in the administrative — or executive — branch of government are typically privileged. The reports and hearings administrators are required by law to prepare and conduct are covered, particularly when the information contained therein has been made available to the public.

When an Oklahoma newspaper was sued for libel because of its report of a conversation between two undercover narcotics agents, the Oklahoma Supreme Court said the report was privileged.[58] A county district attorney had distributed a transcript of the conversation at a news conference, which, the court said, was conducted as part of the official duties of the district attorney's office. The newspaper had published the transcript verbatim.

Law enforcement agencies are part of the executive branch of government, so reports of police activity are conditionally privileged. Official reports and statements by police officials and officers qualify. Not every statement by a police officer is privileged, however. The Idaho Supreme Court, for example, refused to apply the privilege to statements made by a police officer to a reporter during an interview.[59] These were not considered to be part of the officer's official duties, which is a key determinant in deciding whether the privilege applies.

Legislative Branch. Reports about the proceedings of Congress, state legislatures and local governing bodies are privileged. In addition, reports on documents — petitions and complaints, for example — that are filed with or submitted to these bodies are also privileged. It is important to remember, however, that documents coming from legislative meetings are not privileged until officials take possession of them.

Judicial Branch. As a Massachusetts judge, Oliver Wendell Holmes, Jr. was among those who reasoned that the public should be provided with information about judicial proceedings because "those who administer justice should act under a sense of public responsibility."[60] Nearly a century later, another Massachusetts court echoed Holmes and held that the value of granting privilege to media reports about the courts is "the security which publicity gives for the proper administration of justice."[61]

Reports about judicial activities — the courts — are conditionally privileged. Therefore, media accounts of testimony, depositions, attorney arguments, trials, verdicts, opinions and orders — those aspects that are typically open or available to the public — are among the proceedings covered. Documents that relate to the judicial branch are also typically privileged. Conversely, those parts of the judicial process that are closed are not privileged.

Non-Publication and Republication

Since a plaintiff in a libel case must prove that a defamatory statement was published, a defendant may prevail by showing that the statement was not published by the defendant or, failing that, that the statement was not understood by a third party.

Since republication is generally considered tantamount to publication, there is virtually no defense in arguing that the defendant merely repeated a defamatory statement. As one court ruled, "one who republishes a defamatory statement 'adopts' it as his own and is liable in equal measure to the original defamer."[62] Moreover, media organizations are especially prone to libel suits for repeating defamatory statements, because plaintiffs sue defendants who are best able to pay damages. Neither the original publisher nor a reporter is as likely to be as financially capable as a media organization.

Letters to the Editor

Letters to the editor demonstrate the absence of republication as a defense. Newspapers publish letters to the editor and are liable when those letters are defamatory. But most letters are viewed as expressions of opinion rather than statements of fact, and, possi-

---

[57] See, e.g., *Lee v. Dong-A Ilbo,* 849 F.2d 876 (4th Cir. 1988).

[58] *Wright v. Grove Sun Newspaper Co., Inc.,* 873 P.2d 983 (Okla. 1994).

[59] *Weimer v. Rankin,* 117 Idaho 566, 790 P.2d 347 (1990).

[60] *Cowley v. Pulsifer,* 137 Mass. 392, 394 (1884).

[61] *Liquori v. Republican Co.,* 8 Mass. App. Ct. 671, 396 N.E.2d 726, 728 (1979).

[62] *Liberty Lobby v. Dow Jones & Co., Inc.,* 838 F.2d at 1298 .

bly for that reason, newspapers and magazines have won most cases based on the publication of letters to the editor. Courts have apparently sought to provide protection for the publication of letters, often viewing them as part of an open forum for the general public.

The placement of a letter can have a bearing in determining whether it qualifies as opinion. That is, by appearing within a section of a newspaper that is clearly set aside for letters expressing opinions, a letter is much more likely to be viewed by a court as an expression of opinion.

This issue of context is particularly important in jurisdictions that apply the innocent construction rule. First set forth by the Illinois Supreme Court in 1962, the rule provides that allegedly defamatory publications are to be read as a whole and the words should be given their natural and obvious meaning.[63] This libel defense can be particularly useful for publishers of letters to the editor, and, especially, where hyperbolic expressions are involved. For example, in 1989 an Illinois appellate court invoked this common law rule in construing a letter to the editor at issue as "hyperbolic rhetoric."[64] The court said that "commie" was a figurative expression and that the depiction of the plaintiff as a "guy [who] isn't travelling with a full set of luggage" was "mere name-calling."[65] Cases involving the application of the innocent construction rule have seen mixed results for media defendants, but the rule remains a viable libel defense, especially in a number of jurisdictions. (See Chapter 6 for additional explanation of innocent construction.)

Courts have held that some letters to the editor have been expressions that mixed opinion and facts. Often cases based on such expressions are resolved in favor of libel plaintiffs. For example, a Florida appellate court ruled that a letter questioning a child psychologist's qualifications was defamatory because it was just such a mixed expression and, therefore, not privileged.[66]

Perhaps the most noteworthy case involving a letter to the editor was *Immuno A.G. v. Moor-Jankowski* [67] in 1991. Dr. Jan Moor-Jankowski, the founder and editor of the *Journal of Medical Primatology,* received a letter that was critical of the Immuno A.G. Corp. and its establishment of a facility in West Africa that used chimpanzees for hepatitis research. Dr. Moor-Jankowski submit-

ted the letter to Immuno to provide it an opportunity to respond. The response included both claims that statements in the letter were inaccurate, unfair and reckless, and a threat of legal action if the letter was published before Immuno had a meaningful chance to reply. Nearly one year later, having not heard again from Immuno or its lawyers, Moor-Jankowski decided to print the letter in the journal, complete with an editorial note explaining the chronology of events. Immuno sued for libel, naming several defendants; all but Dr. Moor-Jankowski settled out-of-court.

A trial court rejected the defense claim that the letter was constitutionally protected opinion, holding instead that the statements at issue were expressions of fact. An appellate court reversed, ruling that the letter was either opinion, and therefore absolutely privileged under the First Amendment, or that the plaintiff failed to prove the falsity of the letter.[68] Then in its analysis, the New York Court of Appeals, that state's highest court, labeled the letter to the editor "a special type of expression," saying that because such letters are generally not published on the authority of a newspaper or journal, "any damage to reputation done by a letter to the editor generally depends on its inherent persuasiveness and the credibility of the writer, not on the belief that it is true because it appears in a particular publication." The court also suggested that the average reader would interpret the letter as an expression of opinion rather than a statement of fact. And in its most sweeping statement, the court suggested that media should be granted wide latitude to publish letters to the editor that focus on matters of public concern, to the extent that they should be "free of defamation litigation."[69]

In 1991, after the Supreme Court agreed to hear *Immuno,* then remanded it, the New York Court of Appeals reconsidered its decision in light of *Milkovich.* It decided that statements in the letter would be actionable if they were false, but that the plaintiff had failed to meet its burden of establishing falsity. The court also re-examined the case with the overlay of state law, noting that the New York Constitution provides for even broader protection than that guaranteed by the First Amendment. In addition, the court took into account its belief that the average reader would not view the letter as conveying actual facts about the plaintiff, and that it therefore constituted a protected expression of opinion in a forum dedicated to airing public opinion. Neither the *Milkovich* ruling nor the Court's requirement that *Immuno* be re-examined in light

---

[63] *John v. Tribune Co.,* 24 Ill. 2d 437, 181 N.E.2d 105 (Ill. 1962).

[64] *Haberstroh v. Crain Publications, Inc.,* 189 Ill. App. 3d 267, 271, 545 N.E.2d 295, 298 (1989).

[65] 189 Ill. App. 3d at 271-72, 545 N.E.2d at 298.

[66] *Madsen v. Buie,* 454 So. 2d 727, 729 (Fla. Dist. Ct. App. 1984).

[67] 77 N.Y.2d 235, 567 N.E.2d 1270 (1991).

[68] *Immuno A.G. v. Moor-Jankowski,* 145 A.D. 2d 114, 537 N.Y.S. 2d 129, 135 (1989).

[69] *Immuno A.G. v. Moor-Jankowski,* 74 N.Y. 2d 548, 560, 549 N.E.2d 129 (1989).

of *Milkovich* materially changed the New York Court of Appeals' view. The letter to the editor was still regarded as opinion.

The Wire Service Defense

One exception to the republication rule is the publication of information from a business that expressly provides information to news organizations. The so-called "wire service defense" is available to libel defendants if four factors are met: (1) the defendant received the copy in which the defamatory statements are contained from a reputable news gathering agency, (2) the defendant did not know the story was false, (3) nothing on the face of the story could have reasonably alerted the defendant that it may have been incorrect, and (4) the original wire service story was republished without substantial change. In short, the wire service defense holds that the accurate republication of a story provided by a reputable news agency does not constitute fault as a matter of law.

The wire service defense originated with a 1933 case, *Layne v. Tribune Co.* The Florida Supreme Court held that republication of wire service reports could not be libelous unless the publisher acted in a negligent, reckless or careless manner. "No newspaper could ... assume in advance the burden of specially verifying every item of news reported to it by established news gathering agencies," the court held.[70]

The wire service defense has succeeded even when a newspaper published a story that relied on past wire-service articles[71] and when a CBS affiliate broadcast network news reports.[72] Though by no means universally accepted, at least thirteen jurisdictions have adopted the wire service defense: Alaska, the District of Columbia, Florida, Georgia, Hawaii, Kentucky, Louisiana, Massachusetts, Missouri, New York, North Carolina, Wisconsin and Puerto Rico.

On-Line Republication

The publication of on-line computer material is related to publication and republication. The issue in libel law is whether an on-line service can be held liable for defamatory statements that are published through that service. That is, who is really the publisher of on-line material? Three cases have helped clarify the parameters in this area of the law.

In *Cubby v. CompuServe*,[73] a federal court held that CompuServe could not be held liable for statements published by the service unless it knew or had reason to know the nature of the statements. While a defense of republication is generally unsuccessful, the court noted that vendors, book stores and libraries are not subject to liability if they neither know nor have reason to know of the defamation. The court said "a computerized database is the functional equivalent of a more traditional news vendor."[74] CompuServe, the court ruled, had no more editorial control over the statements at issue than a library does over the contents of its books.

In a 1995 case, however, a state court ruled for the first time that an on-line service may be held liable for a defamatory statement that appeared on one of its bulletin boards. In *Stratton Oakmont, Inc. v. Prodigy Services Co.*,[75] the court ruled that Prodigy was liable for defamatory statements because Prodigy marketed itself as a moderator of its bulletin boards by screening and editing content.

The case stems from messages posted by an unidentified user of one of Prodigy's bulletin boards, "Money Talk," which stated that the securities firm Stratton Oakmont committed criminal fraud, that its president was "soon to be proven a criminal" and that the firm was a "cult of brokers who either lie for a living or get fired."[76]

Relying on *Cubby*, Prodigy defended itself by claiming that it was not the publisher of these defamatory statements but acted merely as a passive conduit and was, therefore, more like a library or database. The court, however, ruled that Prodigy *was* the publisher. Because Prodigy had promoted itself as a family-oriented computer network that carefully screened the content of its messages through both manual and technology-based means, and because it also exercised content control by urging users to refrain from posting insulting and offensive messages, it created for itself a high level of liability, the court said. Prodigy acknowledged that manually reviewing the 60,000 bulletin board messages it posts each day was unfeasible. It also urged the court not to set a precedent that would chill speech within a new and developing medium. But the court did not accept these defense arguments.

But the defining case in this area of the law is *Zeran v. America*

[70] 108 Fla. 177, 146 So. 234, 239 (1933)(en banc).

[71] *McKinney v. Avery Journal, Inc.*, 99 N.C. App. 529, 393 S.E.2d 295 (1990).

[72] *Auvril v. CBS*, 140 F.R.D. 450 (E.D. Wash. 1991).

[73] 776 F. Supp. 135 (S.D.N.Y. 1991).

[74] *Id.* at 140.

[75] 1995 N.Y. Misc. LEXIS 229, 1995 WL 805178, 23 Media L. Rep. (BNA) 1794 (N.Y. Sup. 1995).

[76] 23 Media L. Rep. at 1795.

Online.[77] This case also dealt with the issue of an on-line service as publisher, but did so in light of the passage of the Communications Decency Act of 1996. Kenneth Zeran sued America Online when the server included his name and telephone number in a series of bulletin board notices that advertised T-shirts and other items glorifying the 1995 bombing of a federal building in Oklahoma City. The inclusion of Zeran's name was part of a hoax performed by an unknown individual. A relevant section of the CDA stipulates that no provider of an interactive computer service can be treated as the publisher of any information provided by some entity other than the provider. A U.S. District Court ruled that, while the CDA does not preempt all state law actions of this nature, it did preempt Zeran's claim because his claim that AOL was negligent conflicted with both the language and purposes of the CDA.[78] On appeal, the Fourth U.S. Circuit Court of Appeals ruled that this section of the CDA "plainly immunizes computer service providers like AOL for liability for information that originates with third parties."[79] Thus, an on-line libel defendant may be able to utilize the CDA when similar circumstances present themselves.

The Libel-Proof Plaintiff

A libel defendant may be able to invoke the concept of the "libel-proof plaintiff." When an individual's reputation in the community is so bad that even a false accusation could not further harm that reputation, the individual is considered to be libel-proof and cannot win a defamation suit. The libel-proof doctrine was first articulated as a libel defense in *Cardillo v. Doubleday Co., Inc.,* a 1975 case.[80] Since then, two separate prongs of the libel-proof doctrine have developed — incremental harm and issue-specific publication.

Incremental Harm. If an individual is identified in an article as a thief, child molester and tax evader, and if all of those charges are true, does it make any difference if the individual is also identified falsely as a kidnapper? The doctrine of incremental harm says no. In such a case, the defendant-publisher could probably win, arguing that the false statement causes harm that is merely incremental beyond what already exists and, therefore, is not grounds for a libel suit. In short, the false statement causes no harm to the

reputation beyond the harm caused by the true statements, which are protected.

One of the leading incremental harm cases is *Herbert v. Lando.*[81] Herbert, a retired Army officer, sued over statements made about him during a segment of *60 Minutes.* The segment questioned the validity of Herbert's claim that the U.S. Army had punished him for trying to disclose information about massacres by American forces in South Vietnam. The Second U.S. Circuit Court of Appeals ruled that, if the charge that Herbert lied about reporting war crimes was not actionable, "other statements, even those that might be found to have been published with actual malice should not be actionable if they merely imply the same view, and are simply an outgrowth of and subsidiary to those claims upon which it has been held there can be no recovery."[82]

In several cases, however, the incremental harm doctrine has failed as a libel defense. A particularly noteworthy example was the outright rejection of the doctrine in *Liberty Lobby, Inc. v. Anderson.*[83] Journalist Jack Anderson described the founder of Liberty Lobby as a racist, fascist, anti-Semitic and neo-Nazi, and wrote that Liberty Lobby was founded to pursue his goals. Anderson argued that previous publications had already so irreparably tarnished the plaintiff's reputation that the libel-proof doctrine should apply. In an opinion written by then-Judge Antonin Scalia, the court rejected the claim, ruling that "we cannot envision how a court would go about determining that someone's reputation had already been 'irreparably' damaged — i.e., that no new reader could be reached by the freshest libel."[84]

More recently, the Ninth U.S. Circuit Court of Appeals also rejected the incremental harm doctrine, in part because it is not required by the First Amendment.[85] Nevertheless, the doctrine remains a valuable defense weapon, particularly against frivolous libel suits, and especially given the Supreme Court's opinion that states are free to adopt the incremental harm doctrine as they see fit.

Issue-Specific Publication. Libel claims pursued in the issue-

---

[77] 129 F.3d 327 (4th Cir. 1997).

[78] 958 F. Supp. 1124, 1135 (E.D. Va 1997).

[79] 129 F.3d 327, 328 (4th Cir. 1997).

[80] 518 F.2d 638 (2d Cir. 1975)(ruling that the passages of a book whose authors wrote that a habitual criminal was involved in various other criminal activities did not constitute actual malice).

[81] 781 F.2d 298 (2d Cir. 1986), *aff'g* in part, *rev'g* in part, and *remanding* 596 F. Supp. 1178 (S.D.N.Y. 1984). The case and its facts had been thoroughly explored by the courts on several previous occasions. See *Herbert v. Lando,* 73 F.R.D. 387 (S.D.N.Y.), *rev'd,* 568 F.2d 974 (2d Cir. 1977), *rev'd* 441 U.S. 153 (1979).

[82] *Id.* at 312.

[83] 746 F.2d 1563, (D.C. Cir. 1984), *rev'd on other grounds,* 477 U.S. 242 (1986).

[84] *Id.* at 1568.

[85] *Masson v. New Yorker Magazine, Inc.,* 960 F.2d 896 (9th Cir. 1992), *rev'd on other grounds,* 501 U.S. 496 (1991).

specific context present the question of whether previous publicity or criminal convictions have so tarnished the plaintiff's reputation that the plaintiff should be barred from receiving a damage award. That is, courts recognizing the issue-specific doctrine have found that plaintiffs with reputations tarnished in one area are libel-proof *with respect to that area*.

Two cases demonstrate how this prong of the libel-proof doctrine can actually tend to limit its scope. First, in *Logan v. District of Columbia*,[86] the plaintiff challenged a newspaper report that he had tested positively for drug use. The court found that, while the report was incorrect, the plaintiff was libel-proof regarding this specific issue because he had previously admitted using drugs. Then in *Wynberg v. National Enquirer, Inc.*,[87] the *Enquirer* had published an article stating that the plaintiff had used his relationship with Elizabeth Taylor for financial gain. The court ruled that the plaintiff had a "reputation for taking advantage of women generally, and of Miss Taylor specifically." The ruling went on to say that "[a]n individual who engages in certain anti-social or criminal behavior and suffers a diminished reputation may be 'libel-proof' as a matter of law, as it *relates to that specific behavior.*"[88]

Thus, the doctrine of the libel-proof plaintiff may serve a defendant who has published otherwise defamatory statements about an individual whose reputation is already so sullied as to render additional accusations moot, regardless of their falsity. The doctrine may apply to accusations of any nature or to those that relate only to a specific issue.

OTHER DEFENSE ISSUES

While not purely defenses, several other strategies can have a bearing on—and even strengthen—a libel defense.

Responsible Reporting

As part of a defense strategy a libel defendant may attempt to demonstrate to a court that it conducted itself in a responsible way. This demonstration may come within the context of attempts to disprove that employees acted with reckless disregard of the truth.

In attempting to prove that a libel defendant acted with reckless disregard, a plaintiff is likely to attempt to build a case bit by bit, demonstrating irresponsibility or carelessness in publishing.

Courts have said that no single element is sufficient to prove clearly and convincingly that a defendant acted with actual malice, but they can be used as evidence. A libel defendant who is aware of certain claims of irresponsibility or carelessness, therefore, can be prepared to refute them. Some of the claims might be:

- failure to investigate sufficiently;
- failure to interview parties who have knowledge of facts related to the story, including the subject of the report;
- reliance on previously published material;
- reliance on biased stories;
- inaccurate reporting;
- reporting from a specific point of view in an investigative story;
- refusal to retract or correct if the facts warrant;
- absence of a demonstrable deadline;
- ill-will or hatred toward the plaintiff;

Even if media defendants are unable to escape liability altogether, by refuting these points, and demonstrating responsible reporting, they are likely to mitigate damages.

Retractions, apologies and corrections for reputation-damaging reports can also be considered "responsible reporting." In the eyes of the law, their impact varies greatly from state to state. In some states, a prompt and complete apology, correction and retraction will protect a defendant from punitive damages. In other states, retractions are merely considered by jurors in determining the amount of damages awarded.

While a retraction or apology is not a libel defense, a potential libel defendant is advised to correct possibly libelous errors due to the correction's ability to alleviate the statement's defamatory sting in the eyes of a court. And, of course, admitting errors in such circumstances is an aspect of responsible reporting. Moreover, many states have retraction laws that provide varying degrees of protection. Typically, they require a plaintiff to give a publisher an opportunity to retract a libelous statement prior to initiating a libel suit. If the publisher honors the request in a timely manner, the retraction may reduce the damages that the plaintiff may later seek should a lawsuit be filed.

Summary Judgment

A summary judgment is just what the name implies: A judge summarily decides certain points of a case and issues a judgment dismissing the case. It can occur at any of several points in litigation.

A judge may issue a summary judgment on grounds that there is no genuine issue as to any material fact. Generally, this is a result of a plaintiff clearly being unable to meet at least one element

---

[86] 447 F. Supp. 1328 (D.D.C. 1978).

[87] 564 F. Supp. 924 (C.D.Cal. 1982).

[88] *Id.* at 928 (emphasis added).

in the plaintiff's burden of proof. In a 1962 case, the Supreme Court said that when considering motions for summary judgment, courts "must view the facts and inferences to be drawn from them in the light most favorable to the opposing party."[89] The rationale behind this view is, if the summary judgment is granted, the plaintiff's opportunity to prove a case is ended, but if the defendant's motion for summary judgment is denied, the defendant still has an opportunity to prove its case.

Summary judgments have been seen as important tools for protecting free expression, particularly in an environment when plaintiffs have harrassed the media by filing frivolous lawsuits. As one federal judge explained:

> In the First Amendment area, summary procedures are even more essential. For the stake here, if harassment succeeds, is free debate. One of the purposes of the *Times* principle, in addition to protecting persons from being cast in damages in libel suits filed by public officials, is to prevent persons from being discouraged in the full and free exercise of First Amendment rights with respect to the conduct of their government. The threat of being put to the defense of a lawsuit brought by a popular public official may be as chilling to the exercise of First Amendment freedoms as fear of the outcome of the lawsuit itself, especially to advocates of unpopular causes.[90]

Until 1979, summary judgment was a preferred method of dealing with libel cases involving actual malice. When the defense submitted a motion for summary judgment — based on the contention that the plaintiff could not prove actual malice — the judge would either grant or deny it. If granted, the case was over; if denied, the case went to trial.

In 1979, Chief Justice Warren Burger cast doubt on the appropriateness of summary judgment in libel cases because, he argued, any examination of actual malice "calls a defendant's state of mind into question." Such a circumstance, Burger argued, "does not readily lend itself to summary disposition." [91] While some lower courts took Burger's admonition to heart — using it as a basis for denying summary judgment — motions for summary judgment are granted more often than not. Then, in 1986, Justice Byron White wrote that in deciding whether to grant motions for summary judgment, trial judges should decide whether public plaintiffs can meet the actual malice standard by "clear and convincing evi-

dence." If not, summary judgment should be granted.[92] In short, this tempered Burger's words, suggesting that summary judgment remains a viable option.

Today, judges may be more apt to grant motions for summary judgment in an effort to curtail the increasing cost of defending libel suits. About eighty percent of libel insurance costs are incurred, not through the compensation of injured plaintiffs, but merely in defense costs. Estimates regarding the average libel defense cost vary, but typically range from $100,000 to $200,000. In major cases, defendants have spent millions of dollars to defend themselves. Moreover, libel defendants have discovered that juries are increasingly unsympathetic toward them. The median jury award has increased from $200,000 in the early 1980s to an average of $1.5 million a decade later. According to the Libel Defense Resource Center, libel judgments against the media averaged $2.8 million in 1996.[93] In fact, juries tend to be striking some libel defendants — especially the *National Enquirer, Hustler, Penthouse* and other publications that jurors seem to find distasteful — particularly hard with punitive damages. Jury verdicts can reach into the millions, making it appear that juries base their decisions at least in part on the unsavory nature of the defendant. In the wake of these awards, one scholar wrote, "The ability of juries to punish unpopular speakers by awarding punitive damages in ruinous amounts flies in the face of the First Amendment which protects unorthodox as well as mainstream speech."[94]

While approximately two-thirds of jury verdicts in media libel cases are rendered against media defendants, about seventy-five percent of those are reversed or reduced on appeal. The bottom line — and not necessarily a reassuring one — for those facing a libel suit may be that in short, media defendants tend to win on the law rather than having to rely on the often emotion-based conclusions of jurors.

SUMMARY

Libel defendants have at their disposal a variety of tools they can use to defend themselves. Typically, their first option is to seek summary judgment. If there is reason to believe that the plaintiff is unable to prove all the elements of the burden of proof — whether on constitutional or common law grounds — a defense attorney

---

[89] *U.S. v. Diebold, Inc.,* 369 U.S. 654, 655 (1979).

[90] *Washington Post Co. v. Keogh,* 365 F.2d 965, 968 (D.C. Cir. 1966).

[91] *Hutchinson,* 443 U.S. at 120, note 9.

[92] *Anderson v. Liberty Lobby,* 477 U.S. 242, 244, 256 (1986).

[93] *Editor & Publisher*, 8 March 1997, p. 50.

[94] Nicole B. Casarez, "Punitive Damages in Defamation Actions: An Area of Libel Law Worth Reforming," *Duquesne Law Review* 32 (1994): 687.

may be able to prevail with a summary judgment.

When a case goes to trial, libel defendants can use both constitutional and common law defenses. At the heart of the constitutional defense is the notion that there is a First Amendment value embedded in the media's freedom to express themselves. The creation of actual malice was designed to provide an additional layer of protection for media defendants in reporting about public officials. The doctrine was later extended to public figures. Thus, establishing the nature of the plaintiff is key. Libel defendants seek to have plaintiffs categorized as public because the plaintiffs then have to prove the defendant acted with actual malice — knowledge of falsity or reckless disregard for the truth.

Media organizations have the right to express opinions, and that right has its roots, in part, in the First Amendment freedom of the press. However, defining what qualifies as opinion has been a challenge, and largely rests with the four-part *Ollman* test. The protection of opinion is also derived from the common law. Those who are in the public eye subject themselves to fair comment and criticism by the media.

Other common law defenses for media defendants include the privilege of reporting the proceedings of all government branches. The privilege is qualified on the reporting being fair and accurate.

To some extent, defending a libel accusation involves refuting the elements of the plaintiff's case — that is, contesting the plaintiff's attempts to prove that the definition of libel were met. Given that one of those elements is that the statement at issue is false, if the defendant can prove that it is true, the defense is successful. Similarly, because publication is an element of the plaintiff's case, a defendant may attempt to prove that its publication qualifies as one of the exceptions to the republication rule — neutral reportage, the wire service defense, or on-line republication.

Finally, media defendants want to portray themselves as reliable and trustworthy organizations that conduct themselves responsibly. While not a defense, per se, this representation can only help the defendant's image in the eyes of the court and jury. Moreover, journalistic integrity is simply the proper way to conduct business, and often tends to be the best way to avoid libel suits in the first place — and that may be the best defense.

FOR ADDITIONAL READING

Gilles, Susan M. "Taking First Amendment Procedure Seriously: An Analysis of Process in Libel Litigation," *Ohio State Law Journal* 58 (1998): 1753.

Kite, Kevin L. "Incremental Identities: Libel-Proof Plaintiffs, Substantial Truth, and the Future of the Incremental Harm Doctrine," *New York University Law Review* 73 (1998): 529.

"The Libel-Proof Plaintiff Doctrine," *Harvard Law Review* 98 (1985): 1909.

Logan, David A. "Of 'Sloppy Journalism,' 'Corporate Tyranny,' and Mea Culpas: The Curious Case of Moldea v. New York Times," *William & Mary Law Review* 37 (1995): 161.

Martin, John C. "The Role of Retraction in Defamation Suits," *University of Chicago Legal Foundation* 1993 (1993): 293.

Murchison, Brian C., John Soloski, Randall P. Bezanson, Gilbert Cranberg, Roselle L. Wissler, "Sullivan's Paradox: The Emergence of Judicial Standards of Journalism," *North Carolina Law Review* 73 (1994): 7.

Russomanno, Joseph A. and Kyu Ho Youm. "'Neutral Reportage' and Its Second Decade: A Marketplace Perspective," *Communication Law and Policy* 3 (1998): 439.

Simon, Todd F. "Libel as Malpractice: News Media Ethics and the Standard of Care," *Fordham Law Review* 53 (1984): 449.

Smolla, Rodney A. *Law of Defamation*, 11th ed. Deerfield, Ill.: Clark, Boardman, Callaghan, 1997.

Weaver, Russell L. and Geoffrey Bennett. "Is the New York Times 'Actual Malice' Standard Really Necessary? A Comparative Perspective," *Louisiana Law Review* 53 (1993): 1153.

8

Intellectual Property

By Dorothy Bowles

The U.S. legal system conveys certain rights to property owners. Generally, they may modify, sell, rent or give away their property. Patent, trademark and copyright laws provide similar rights to people who own "intellectual property" — original literary, musical or graphic works or unique devices, identifying words, phrases or symbols. Copyright and, to a lesser extent, trademark law most directly impact communications and the media and, therefore, are the primary topics of discussion here.

A hypothetical situation is a good starting point. Suppose several young musicians form a heavy metal band named "Skool of Hard Nocks" and begin practicing together in hopes of hitting the big time. The group sings original songs as well as popular songs by well-known artists. During a practice session in the garage one night, the musicians notice that a particular series of sounds on the synthesizer causes mice to rush from their hiding places and congregate in one corner. After experimenting a bit, the musicians invent what they call "Hard Nocks Mouse Trap," a contraption consisting of two boxes designed to be placed in opposite corners of a room. One tiny box emits the synthesizer sounds, and, shortly thereafter, the second, much larger box springs shut to capture the mice that huddle within it.

Do the songs or the mouse trap qualify for protection under intellectual property laws? Yes to both counts. If the group has gone beyond merely playing the songs and has taken the extra step of fixing the music and lyrics in tangible form, such as writing them on paper or making an audio tape, the works are protected, even if they are not published. Protection begins as soon as the songs are fixed in tangible form.

In addition, if a review of existing patents shows that the Skool of Hard Nocks has indeed invented a better mouse trap, the group can patent it to protect its right to potential profits. The patenting process, however, is likely to be long and drawn out, requiring the services of an attorney specializing in patent law.

The names "Skool of Hard Nocks" and "Hard Nocks Mouse Trap" might eventually become trademarks, but, unlike copyright protection, trademark protection is not automatic upon creation. Only if the names are unique and are used so that the public comes to identify them with the band or the mouse trap, do they become trademarks.

Certainly, Skool of Hard Nocks should seek these protections. On the flip side of the coin, Skool might be guilty of infringing someone else's copyright by performing songs from radio play lists. So long as that playing is confined to private practice sessions, no problems exist. If, on the other hand, the band performs those songs publicly without paying royalty fees or receiving permission from the copyright owners, Skool of Hard Nocks is guilty of copyright infringement.

Congress's right to enact patent and copyright laws derives from what is called "the interstate commerce clause" of Article I, Section 8 of the Constitution. This is the same section that gives Congress the power to collect taxes, provide for the common defense, regulate commerce, coin money and declare war. The pertinent sentence is:

> The Congress shall have power ... To promote the progress of science and useful arts, by securing for limited times to authors and inventors the exclusive right to their respective writings and discoveries.

The Supreme Court has interpreted the phrase "to promote" as being synonymous with the phrases "to stimulate," "to encourage" and "to induce."[1]

Intellectual property laws both hinder and help the mass media. On the one hand, copyright and trademark laws give news and entertainment companies an economic incentive to create material, knowing they can reap financial rewards from works their employees create and that others cannot steal the fruits of their labors. On the other hand, the media must take care not to publish material that infringes the intellectual property ownership rights of others. The limited monopoly bestowed by copyright is intended to serve the ultimate goal of stimulating activity and progress in the arts and sciences and thus enriching the public. As the Supreme Court has noted, the Copyright Act is intended to increase rather than impede the harvest of knowledge.[2] The Act protects only the manner of expression, not ideas, so other people face no barriers to creating their own expressions about ideas in the marketplace. The limited copyright monopoly rewards the individual author in order to benefit the public. By this reasoning, copyright and trademark law can co-exist with the First Amendment.

ELEMENTS OF COPYRIGHT LAW

The first federal copyright law in the United States was enacted in 1790, within two years of ratification of the Constitution. The law has been amended many times, and Congress passed major revisions about every forty years until 1909. Then it was roughly seventy years before Congress passed its last major revision of copyright law. Today copyright is governed by the Copyright Act of 1976,[3] which went into effect January 1, 1978. It, too, has been amended several times since its passage.

Until 1955, U.S. authors had little protection from international

pirates because the United States had not signed the major international copyright treaties. Today, works copyrighted in the United States are generally protected from infringement in some eighty nations that agree to two multilateral treaties: the Universal Copyright Convention and the Berne Convention for the Protection of Literary and Artistic Property. The United States joined the Berne Union in 1989. Members of the union agree to a certain minimum level of copyright protection and agree to treat nationals of other member countries like their own for purposes of copyright. A work first published in the United States or another Berne Union country (or first published in a non-Berne country, followed by publication within thirty days in a Berne Union country) is eligible for protection in all Berne member countries.

Industries that create copyrighted works represent a major stake in the U.S. economy, with recent studies placing the amount generated by these businesses at $238.6 billion per year with an additional $120 billion annually coming from related industries, such as those that distribute copyrighted works. Between 1991 and 1993, while the entire U.S. economy grew at an annual rate of approximately 2.7 percent, the core copyright industries grew twice as fast, at the rate of 5.6 percent. Furthermore, the employment generated by these industries grew at four times the annual rate of the whole economy between 1988 and 1993.[4]

Protected Works

The Copyright Act protects original works of authorship fixed in any tangible medium of expression, from which they can be perceived, reproduced or otherwise communicated, either directly or with the aid of some device. The medium of expression may be existing or yet to be developed. Works of authorship include
(1) literary works;
(2) musical works, including any accompanying words;
(3) dramatic works, including any accompanying music;
(4) pantomimes and choreographic works;
(5) pictorial, graphic and sculptural works;
(6) motion pictures and other audiovisual works;
(7) sound recordings; and
(8) architectural works.
These categories are illustrative, not limitative, and they are interpreted broadly. For example, the Act defines literary works as

[1] *Goldstein v. California*, 412 U.S. 546 (1973), *reb'g denied* 414 U.S. 883 (1973).

[2] See *Sony Corp. of America v. Universal City Studios, Inc.*, 464 U.S. 417 (1984), and *Harper & Row v. Nation Enterprises*, 471 U.S. 539 (1985).

[3] 17 U. S. C. §101 et.seq.

[4] Information Infrastructure Task Force, "Intellectual Property and the National Information Infrastructure: The Report of the Working Group on Intellectual Property Rights" (Washington, D. C.: Office of Legislative and International Affairs, September 1995).

"works, other than audiovisual works, expressed in words, numbers, or other verbal or numerical symbols or indicia, regardless of the nature of the material objects, such as books, periodicals, manuscripts, phonorecords, film, tapes, disks, or cards, in which they are embodied." Telephone directories, therefore, and expressions used by computer programers are copyrightable as "literary works," although processes used in developing computer programs are not within the scope of copyright protection.[5] Coin-operated electronic video games are copyrightable under the category "audiovisual works."[6] Maps may be registrable as "pictorial, graphic, and sculptural works," as may advertisements, floral arrangements, bumper stickers, fabric, wallcovering designs, patterns for sewing and stained glass designs.

Courts have distinguished among three separate concepts — originality, creativity and novelty. A work is "original" if it is the independent creation of its author. A work is "creative" if it embodies some modest amount of intellectual labor. A work is "novel" if it differs from existing works in some relevant respect. For a work to be copyrightable, it must be original and creative, but need not be novel. This contrasts with patent law where novelty is a requirement.

In a case involving telephone directories published by rival telephone companies, the Supreme Court said the level of creativity required to meet the originality requirement is extremely low.[7] The Court said the time-honored tradition of compiling facts in alphabetical order did not possess the minimal creative spark required for protection under the Copyright Act. As a result, the Copyright Office no longer registers claims to the white pages of telephone books. However, a telephone directory or other compilation satisfies the "original work of authorship" requirement if the authors independently made subjective decisions regarding layout and design of pre-existing information.[8]

Just as the arrangement of facts in a telephone directory may be sufficiently creative to qualify for copyright protection,[9] facts and ideas "authored" by celestial beings rather than humans can become the basis for a copyrightable compilation.[10] The Urantia Foundation registered the Urantia Book with the Copyright Office, describing its as having been created at the instance of "planetary celestial supervisors." These spiritual entities revealed their teachings through a psychiatric patient, whose doctor later formed a Contact Commission that discussed the revelations, compiled them and transferred ownership to the Urantia Foundation. A copyright infringement suit arose after Kristen Maaherra, who described herself as a long-time avid reader of the Book, copied it and distributed a computerized disk version of it. Maaherra answered the suit with the argument that no valid copyright in the Book could exist because it lacked the requisite ingredient of human creativity. The appeals court upheld the lower court[11] in ruling that although the facts themselves were not copyrightable, the human beings who compiled, selected, coordinated and arranged the teachings exercised enough creativity to meet copyright requirements. The fact that Maaherra's computer disk was a verbatim copy rather than an original and creative use of facts made known through celestial revelations is an important distinction. In an earlier copyright infringement case, a court held that a defendant who wrote an original text using facts revealed by a divine spirit was not guilty of infringing an earlier work based on those same revelations.[12]

As early as 1884, courts recognized that photographing a person or filming an event involves creative labor.[13] Abraham Zapruder's film of the assassination of President John F. Kennedy in 1963 was held copyrightable because it embodied many elements of creativity. Among other things, Zapruder selected the kind of camera (movies, not snapshots), the kind of film (color), the kind of lens (telephoto), the area in which the pictures were to be taken, the time they were to be taken and (after testing several sites) the spot on which the camera would be operated.[14] Similarly, a court said the many decisions made during the broadcast of a baseball game — camera angles, types of shots, the use of instant replays and

---

[5] *Southern Bell Telphone and Telegraph Co. v. Associated Telephone Directory Publishers*, 756 F.2d 801 (11th Cir. 1985); *Gates Rubber Co. v. Bando Chemical Industries, Ltd.*, 9 F.3d 823 (10th Cir. 1993); *Atari Games Corp. v. Nintendo of America Inc.*, 975 F.2d 832 (9th Cir. 1992).

[6] *Midway Mfg. Co. v. Dirkschneider*, 543 F. Supp. 466 (D.C. Neb. 1981).

[7] *Feist Publications, Inc. v. Rural Telephone Service Company, Inc.*, 499 U.S. 340 (1991).

[8] *Southern Bell Telphone and Telegraph Co. v. Associated Telephone Directory Publishers*, 756 F.2d 801 (11th Cir. 1985).

[9] *Feist Publications, Inc. v. Rural Telephone Service Company, Inc.*,

[9 cont.] 499 U.S. 340 (1991).

[10] *Urantia Foundation v. Maaherra*, 25 Media L. Rptr. (BNA) 1873 (9th Cir. 1997).

[11] *Urantia Foundation v. Maaherra*, 895 F. Supp. 1347 (D. Ariz. 1995).

[12] *Oliver v. Saint Germain Foundation*, 41 F. Supp 296 (S.D. Calif. 1941).

[13] See *Burrow-Giles Lithographic Co. v. Sarony*, 111 U.S. 53, 60 (1884).

[14] *Time, Inc. v. Bernard Geis Associates*, 293 F. Supp. 130 (S.D.N.Y. 1968).

split screens and shot selection — supply the creativity required for the copyrightability of the telecasts.[15]

In the 1976 Copyright Act, Congress expressly afforded copyright protection to simultaneously recorded broadcasts of live performances such as sports contests,[16] but the protection does not extend to the underlying events. The National Basketball Association sought to stop Motorola and its sports reporting partner company from selling pagers and SportsTrax, a service that provides subscribers with almost up-to-the-minute information about NBA games in progress.[17] Among the NBA's six claims for relief was federal copyright infringement on the grounds that it owned the basketball games and could control real-time transmission of information about those games. The professional baseball, football and hockey leagues filed friend-of-the-court-briefs in the case.

Both a New York federal district court and the Second U.S. Circuit Court of Appeals held that the sports events do not constitute "original works of authorship." The appeals court noted that despite considerable preparation for games, they are not "authored" in any common sense of the word; they have no scripts like movies, plays and many other forms of entertainment. Developments like the T-formation in football or new movements and techniques in figure skating, gymnastics or wrestling cannot be copyrighted, prohibiting other athletes from attempting to duplicate the feats, the court wrote.[18] Some legal scholars promote the idea that routine-based athletic performances, such as figure skating and gymnastics, comply with the requirements of the Copyright Act because they are original and creative and may be fixed in a tangible medium of expression.[19]

In other cases, courts have said:
• The video display for Breakout, a game in which a "rectangular paddle" directed a "circular ball" into colored rectangular "bricks" while accompanied by audio signals, was lacking in the minimal artistic expression necessary for a copyright;[20]
• Acrylic panels used in a decorative supermarket display were sufficiently original and expressive;[21]
• The phrase "alpine Goldilocks" in a travel guide description of the average skier was an analogy constituting expression of original insight and thus protectable under the Copyright Act.[22]

Although the creativity threshold is low for copyright, independent authorship, rather than copying, is absolutely essential. This does not mean, however, that variations on existing works may never be copyrighted. So long as the variation goes beyond merely trivial, the added elements to the original may be copyrighted.[23]

Unprotected works

Items not eligible for copyright protection include
• an idea, procedure, process, system, method of operation, concept, principle or discovery, regardless of the form in which it is described, explained, illustrated or embodied;
• facts or other works consisting entirely of information that is common property and containing no original authorship;
• works that have not been fixed in a tangible form of expression;
• names, short phrases and slogans; familiar symbols or designs; mere variations of typographic ornamentation, lettering or coloring; mere listings of ingredients or contents;
• works produced by the U.S. government;
• works that are in the public domain.

Ideas and Facts. A key copyright principle is that no person can own an idea or a fact. Our hypothetical Skool of Hard Nocks band, for example, may compose as many songs about the topic of love as it wishes, so long as it expresses its own sentiments about love, rather than copying someone else's words. Other authors are likewise free to write about love.

One way to illustrate the difference between a fact or idea and protected expression — not always a clear-cut distinction — is to consider a court case involving two books and a movie about the tragic explosion of the Hindenburg. The colossal dirigible, built in Germany during Hitler's reign, burst into flames over a New Jersey landing site in 1937 before scores of onlookers. Thirty-six people perished in the fire. The explosion received widespread news coverage with no copyright problems — a news event cannot be copyrighted, but the way the event is described in stories can be.

---

[15] *Baltimore Orioles, Inc. v. Major League Baseball Players Assn.*, 805 F.2d 663 (7th Cir. 1986).

[16] 17 U.S.C. Sec. 101.

[17] *National Basketball Association and NBA Properties, Inc. v. Motorola, Inc. and Sports Team Analysis and Tracking Systems, Inc.*, 105 F.3d 841 (2d Cir. 1997).

[18] *Id.* at 846.

[19] See, e.g., William Tucker Griffith, "Note and Comment: Beyond the Perfect Score: Protecting Routine-Oriented Athletic Performance with Copyright Law," *Connecticut Law Review* 30 (1998): 675.

[20] *Atari Games Corp. v. Oman*, 693 F. Supp. 1204 (D.D.C. 1988), *rev'd* 888 F.2d 878 (1988).

[21] *Designer's View, Inc. v. Publix Super Markets, Inc.*, 764 F. Supp 1473 (S.D. Fla. 1991)

[22] *Feder v. Videotrip Corp.*, 697 F. Supp. 1165 (D. Colo. 1988).

[23] *Merritt Forbes & Co. Inc. v. Newman Inv. Securities, Inc.*, 604 F. Supp. 21 (D.N.Y. 1985).

The official blame for the disaster was placed on static electricity igniting the hydrogen-filled airship. A different theory — that the Hindenburg was sabotaged — emerged from years of investigation by author A. A. Hoehling, who, in 1962, published a book arguing that a crew member, seeking to impress his anti-Hitler girlfriend in Germany, planted a bomb aboard the dirigible, intending for it to explode after everyone had disembarked. Bad weather had delayed the flight, causing the premature detonation of the bomb, according to Hoehling's theory.

Would Hoehling's research and his new theory about the cause of the explosion be copyrightable? Hoehling thought so and brought a copyright infringement suit when Universal City Studios released a motion picture based on the theory. The acknowledged source for the movie was a 1972 novel by Michael Mooney, who used Hoehling's theory as the basis for his fictionalized account of the Hindenburg tragedy. Mooney was also named as a defendant in the infringement suit. A district court judge ruled for the defendants and an appeals court affirmed, because neither research nor ideas are copyrightable.[24]

Another suit, brought by the widow of author Richard Wright, best known for *Native Son* and *Black Boy,* also turned, in part, on the fact-expression distinction. After Wright's death, a biography was written by one of his acquaintances, Dr. Margaret Walker, and published in 1988 by Warner Books. Wright's widow refused to give the biographer permission to use material from Wright's journals and letters and sued for copyright infringement.

A three-judge panel for the Second U.S. Circuit Court of Appeals examined ten journal entries and six letters, considering as a threshold matter whether that material as quoted or paraphrased in Walker's book bore "the stamp of the author's originality," making it copyrightable, or whether the material communicated facts or ideas.[25] Ultimately, the court determined that only three of the journal entries "under a generous reading of expression, adopt Wright's creative style." Of ten quoted sections from the six letters, the court said "four bear Wright's stamp of creativity and meet the threshold test of copyright protection. The other six tersely convey mundane details of Wright's life and serve only to illustrate Dr. Walker's friendship with Wright."[26] These three paraphrased sections of Wright's journals and four quoted portions of letters became the basis for the court's determination of whether the "fair use" defense against copyright infringement applied in the case.

Fair use will be discussed later in this chapter. The letters at issue in the Wright case were written by Richard Wright to Margaret Walker. Although she was the recipient of the letters, Walker did not own the manner of expression contained within them. Richard Wright, and later his widow, retained ownership of the original expression contained in the letters.

Useful Articles. A procedure, process, system, method of operation, concept, principle or discovery, regardless of the form in which it is described, explained, illustrated or embodied in such a work may be eligible for a patent, but not a copyright. While pictorial, graphic and sculptural works may be copyrighted, the mechanical or utilitarian aspects of such works are not copyrightable.

The Copyright Act defines a "useful article" as an article having an intrinsic utilitarian function that is not merely to portray the appearance of the article or to convey information. Examples are clothing, furniture, machinery, dinnerware and lighting fixtures. An article that is normally part of a useful article may itself be classified as a useful article, such as an ornamental wheel cover on a vehicle. Yet, a useful article may have both copyrightable and uncopyrightable features. For example, the design of a piece of furniture may qualify for protection under patent law while unique ornate carvings on the furniture may be copyrightable.

The copyrightable work must be capable of existing independently of its utilitarian aspects. In a case where the form of a bicycle rack was inspired by a sculpture, the sculpture was eligible for copyright, but the bicycle rack was not because it was influenced in significant measure by utilitarian concerns. Therefore, its aesthetic elements could not be said to be conceptually separable from utilitarian elements.[27] However, a copyrighted work of art does not lose its protected status merely because it subsequently is put to functional use.

Clothing, even that based on elaborate designs of high fashion industry, is utilitarian and not copyrightable. Even when a designer claimed Halloween costumes were "soft sculptures," equally adaptable as wall hangings or decorations, courts disagreed. One court said the artistic elements of the costumes advanced the utilitarian purpose of enabling wearers to masquerade, and the designer's artistic judgment was not exercised independently of functional influences.[28] On the other hand, decorative belt buckles used principally for ornamentation have been considered jew-

---

[24] *Hoehling v. Universal City Studios,* 618 F.2d 972 (2d Cir. 1980).

[25] *Wright v. Warner Books, Inc. and Margaret Walker,* 953 F.2d 731 (2d Cir. 1991).

[26] *Id.* at 736.

---

[27] *Brandir Intern, Inc. v. Cascade Pacific Lumber Co.,* 834 F.2d 1142 (2d Cir. 1987).

[28] *Whimsicality, Inc. v. Rubie's Costumes Co., Inc.,* 721 F. Supp. 1566 (E.D.N.Y.), *aff'd in part, vacated in part,* 891 F.2d 452 (2d Cir. 1989).

elry sufficiently original for copyright protection.[29] Not all jewelry meets originality standards for copyright. A particular ring design, for example, was ruled ineligible for copyright protection because it was not exceptional, original or unique.[30] Copyright protection does not encompass games because they consist of abstract rules and play ideas.

Works Produced by the U.S. Government. Works created by the federal government are in the public domain with the exception of standard reference data produced by the U.S. Secretary of Commerce under the Standard Reference Data Act.[31] The federal government, however, can have an existing copyright assigned to it. If an independent government contractor — a postage stamp designer, for example — produces a work, it is copyrighted, and nothing prevents that contractor from assigning the copyright back to the government. In addition, the arrangement and pagination of government documents — if they reflect skill, discretion and effort — are copyrightable. Someone else could use the government material, but they could not use the particular layout.[32]

Works created by state governments are subject to copyright. Each state decides whether to retain the copyright or place the works in the public domain. No statute, case or regulation indicates that a state cannot copyright its laws, but the U.S. Copyright Office takes the position that a state's laws may not be copyrighted. The Compendium of Copyright Office Practices (Compendium II) states, "Edicts of government, such as judicial opinions, administrative rulings, legislative enactments, public ordinances, and similar official legal documents are not copyrightable for reasons of public policy. This applies to such works whether they are Federal, State, or local as well as to those of foreign governments." Although the Compendium II does not have force of law, apparently any state trying to register its laws for copyright would be refused registration by the Copyright Office.

Works containing material produced by the federal government published before March 1, 1989, when the United States became a party to the Berne Convention, were required to carry a notice. The notice is no longer required, but the Copyright Office strongly recommends it in order to defeat a claim of "innocent infringement," meaning that defendants in an infringement suit did not know the material they used was protected by copyrighted. The Copyright Office suggests this copyright notice for works containing government material:[33]

Copyright 1996 Jane Doe. Copyright claimed in Chapters 7-10, exclusive of U.S. Government maps.

Works in the Public Domain. If a particular work is in the public domain, it is not copyrighted and can be used without securing permission. In addition to works produced by the federal government, works that were never copyrighted or ones for which the copyright period has expired are in the public domain. The duration of copyright protection will be discussed later in this chapter.

Exclusive Rights of Copyright Holders

If our hypothetical Skool of Hard Nocks heavy metal group has copyrighted its original musical compositions, it has exclusive rights

(1) to reproduce the copyrighted work;

(2) to prepare derivative works based upon the copyrighted work;

(3) to distribute copies or phonorecords of the copyrighted work to the public by sale or other transfer of ownership, or by rental, lease or lending;

(4) to perform the copyrighted work publicly;

(5) to display the copyrighted work publicly.

These rights are separate and distinct from each other, so Skool of Hard Nocks can authorize one company to reproduce its music and a different company to distribute the copies. Yet, if either of those companies prepared derivative works or sponsored public performances of the music without authorization, that company would be guilty of the crime of copyright infringement.

Derivative Works. The copyright owner of a work has the right to make or authorize new works that are based on the original, such as translations, dramatizations, fictionalizations, motion picture versions, sound recordings, art reproductions, abridgments, condensations or any other forms of the work. A work consisting of editorial revisions, annotations, elaborations or other modifications that, as a whole, represent an original work of authorship is a derivative work.

A work will not be considered derivative unless it substantially

---

[29] *Kieselstein-Cord v. Accessories By Pearl, Inc.,* 632 F.2d 989 (2d Cir. 1980).

[30] *DBC of New York, Inc. v. Merit Diamond Corp.,* 768 F. Supp 414 (S.D.N.Y. 1991).

[31] 15 U.S.C. 290e.

[32] *West Pub. Co. v. Mead Data Cent., Inc.,* 616 F. Supp 1571 (D.C.Minn. 1985), *aff'd* 799 F.2d 1219 (8th Cir. 1986), *cert. denied* 479 U.S. 1070 (1987)

---

[33] *Copyright Basics* (Washington, D.C.: United States Copyright Office, 1994).

copies from the original, copyrighted work. Copyright infringement charges against makers of the popular play and screenplay *Driving Miss Daisy* were not justified, a court held, even though an earlier play titled *Horowitz and Mrs. Washington* was also about an elderly, white, Jewish woman who eventually became close friends with a black assistant. The court said that despite similarities, the works differed in their themes, settings and tone, plot and character development, so *Driving Miss Daisy* was not a derivative work.[34]

Public Performance or Display. Only a copyright owner can authorize the public performance or display of the work. After purchasing one or more copies of a work, a video store, for example, may rent those copies. It would be a copyright violation, however, for a video store owner to set up a projector and screen a film for the public or make additional copies of it. It is not considered a public performance for a hotel to provide audiovisual materials for use in guest rooms. Similarly, one could play Skool of Hard Nocks music for the enjoyment of family and social acquaintances, for religious services at a place of worship or for face-to-face teaching activities at a non-profit educational institution without violating copyright, but could not play it in a business to entertain customers without receiving permission, which generally includes paying a fee. A restaurant or other business is allowed to play radio music over a single receiver and speakers of a kind commonly used in private homes.[35] For a business to connect a radio receiver to speakers placed throughout the store and transmit it beyond the normal area of a single radio and its speakers, however, constitutes a public performance and a copyright violation.[36] Firms that play tapes or CDs rather than home-style radios must pay royalties.

What about broadcast stations that play recorded music; isn't that a public performance? Yes, and those stations pay music licensing organizations — the two best-known are the American Society of Composers, Authors and Publishers (ASCAP) and Broadcast Music Inc. (BMI) — for the right to broadcast music.

But the music industry is mired in other performance and copyright questions. Who actually controls performance rights among the many people involved in the creative process of getting a piece of music from the mere idea for a song to the physical medium upon which it is fixed? Who — the composer, the record producer, the performer — shares licensing fees? Do musicians and others participating in the production of sound recordings have the right to prevent particular people or companies from performing their works?

The answers to these and other copyright questions in the complex music industry are discussed later in the "compulsory licensing" section of this chapter.

Does the use of a copyrighted visual work within another visual work constitute a display subject to unlawful infringement? Case law on this question is not clear-cut. One court held that the use of an architectural drawing in a film was an infringement,[37] while another court denied an injunction to bar the showing of a film that included copyrighted film clips.[38] In a 1997 case, the Second U.S. Circuit Court of Appeals said a jury or other fact-finder, rather than summary judgment, was necessary to determine whether the use of a copyrighted poster as set decoration in a television show constituted infringement.[39] The poster in question was visible in the background from 1.86 seconds to 4.16 seconds during several scenes in the show. A federal regulation[40] provides that public broadcasting entities will pay royalty fees for the use of published pictorial and other visual works. The regulation distinguishes between a "featured" display, a "full-screen or substantially full screen display for more than three seconds," and a "background" display, one that is less than full-screen or substantially less or one that is full-screen but visible for less than three seconds.

Moral Rights. In addition to the five exclusive rights belonging to all copyright owners, a limited category of visual artists received more protection in a 1990 amendment to the Copyright Act.[41] Creators of visual art — paintings, drawings, prints, sculptures or photographic images, existing in up to 200 copies — received what are referred to as "authors' rights" or "moral rights." These rights prevent the use of an author's name on works that he or she did not create. The act also prevents the use of an author's name on a work that has been distorted, mutilated or otherwise modified so the use prejudicial to the author's honor or reputation.

---

[34] *Denker v. Ubry*, 820 F. Supp 722 (S.D.N.Y. 1992), *aff'd* 996 F.2d 301 (2d Cir. 1993).

[35] *Cass Country Music Co. v. Vasfi Muedini*, 821 F. Supp. 1278 (E.D. Wis. 1993).

[36] *Sailor Music v. Gap Stores, Inc.*, 668 F.2d 84 (2d Cir. 1981), *cert. denied* 456 U.S. 945 (1982).

[37] *Woods v. Universal City Studios, Inc.*, 920 F. Supp. 62 (S.D.N.Y. 1996).

[38] *Monster Communications, Inc. v. Turner Broadcasting System, Inc.*, 935 F. Supp. 490 (S.D.N.Y. 1996).

[39] *Ringgold v. Black Entertainment Television, Inc.*, 25 Media L. Rptr. (BNA) 2387 (2d Cir. 1997).

[40] 37 C.F.RF. Sec.253.8 (1996).

[41] Visual Artists Rights Act, 17 U.S.C.A. Sec. 106a.

Copyright Ownership

Initial copyright ownership is vested in the author or authors of a work as soon as the work is created in a tangible form.

Joint Works. The authors of a joint work are co-owners of the copyright. A joint work is one prepared by two or more authors with the intention that their contributions will be merged into inseparable or interdependent parts of a whole. Ownership of a copyright may be transferred in whole or in part or bequeathed by will to someone else.

Works Made for Hire. Journalists and other media employees generally do not own the copyright to articles, photographs or other works they produce as part of their jobs. Unless an agreement between the employee and employer specifies otherwise, employees usually produce what are known as "works made for hire," with the employer owning the copyrights. Journalists working on a made-for-hire basis do not have any rights over those works without permission from the copyright owner.

Copyright disputes between employers and employees sometimes turn on whether a work was produced within the scope of employment or whether a work was produced separate from the normal duties on the job. Major league baseball players tried to argue that telecasts of games amounted to a misappropriation of their names, pictures and performances, but a court rejected the argument and held that the players were employees and their performances before broadcast audiences were within the scope of their employment, so the telecasts of major league baseball games were works made for hire.[42]

The 1976 Copyright Act also defines as a work made for hire one "specially ordered or commissioned for use as a contribution to a collective work, as a part of a motion picture or other audiovisual work, as a translation, as a supplementary work, as a compilation, as an instructional text, as a test, as answer material for a test, or as an atlas, if the parties expressly agree in a written instrument signed by them that the work shall be considered a work made for hire." This is the condition under which a freelancer typically works. Unless agreed to by a contract, a commissioned work is not a work-made-for-hire, and a freelancer maintains copyright ownership.

As might be expected, these issues have prompted a considerable number of lawsuits. In a 1989 case, the Supreme Court said that factors to consider in making this distinction include, but are not limited to, the skill required; the amount of supervision; whether the hired worker set his or her own hours, owned equipment or tools needed for the job or received employee fringe benefits; how payment was made; how taxes were paid and whether the hired party independently hired and fired assistants.[43] The Supreme Court has said these factors should be considered as a whole with no single one being determinative.

Collective Works. Magazines, anthologies or encyclopedias are examples of collective works in which a number of separate and independent articles are assembled into a whole. The 1976 Copyright Act says that each separate contribution to a collective work is distinct from the whole, and copyright belongs to the author of the contribution. Unless the parties make other arrangements, the owner of the copyright of the collective work is presumed to have acquired only the privilege of reproducing and distributing the contribution as part of the whole, any revision of the collective work, and any later collective work in the same series. The Supreme Court has made clear that the party paying a fee is buying first-time rights.[44] The freelance author or artist retains other rights as well as the right to future uses of the material.

Freelance writers were unsuccessful, however, in a 1997 lawsuit against numerous newspaper and magazine publishers that had reproduced articles from their hard-copy publications as part of electronic databases without paying authors for the use.[45] The district court held that publishers exercise creativity in their selection of articles for printed versions of their publications and that creative selection aspect is preserved in the electronic version, which is substantially similar to the original. In mid-1998 the case was under appeal, with the authors arguing in their brief[46] to the Second U.S. Circuit Court of Appeals that the lower court interpreted the term "revision" in the Copyright Act too broadly, thus giving publishers to right to creat new anthologies in express conflict with Congress's intent and depriving authors of the right to share in revenues produced by the electronic databases.

Duration of Ownership. Recall that the purpose of intellectual property law is to promote the progress of science and useful arts, by securing for limited times to authors and inventors the exclusive right to their respective writings and discoveries. The framers of the Constitution recognized that it would not best

---

[42] *Baltimore Orioles, Inc. v. Major League Baseball Players Assn.*, 805 F.2d 663 (7th Cir. 1986).

[43] *Community for Creative Non-Violence v. Reid*, 490 U.S. 730 (1989). See also, *Marco v. Accenty Pub. Co., Inc.*, 969 F.2d 1547 (3d Cir. 1992).

[44] *Id.*

[45] *Tasini et al. v. New York Times Company et al.* 25 Med. L. Rptr. (BNA) 2056 (S.D.N.Y. 1997).

[46] *Tasini et al. v. New York Times Company et al.*, No. 97-9181 (2nd Cir., appellants' brief filed Feb. 3, 1998).

serve public policy for protection to continue forever. After a term of protection expires, copyrighted works become part of the public domain, freely available for anyone.

When Congress rewrote copyright law in the 1970s, it changed the time when protection began (to the time the work was fixed in tangible form rather than from the time it was first published or registered as an unpublished work) and also the number of years that copyright protection lasted. Therefore, when deciding whether a particular work is still protected, it is important to consider whether it was protected under the current Copyright Act, which went into effect on January 1, 1978, or under the law in effect before 1978.

For works created under present law, copyright protection continues for the lifetime of the author plus fifty years. If the copyright is held by joint authors, protection continues for fifty years after the last author dies. Works made for hire and anonymous or pseudonymous works (unless the author's identity is revealed in Copyright Office records) are protected by copyright for seventy-five years from the date of publication or 100 years from the date of creation, whichever is shorter. These same terms apply for works that had been created before January 1, 1978, but never published or registered for copyright by that date.

Under the pre-1978 copyright statute, protection did not begin upon a work's creation, but began on the date the work was published or the date the work was registered in unpublished form. In either case, the copyright term was for twenty-eight years. During the twenty-eighth year of the term, the copyright owner could apply for a twenty-eight-year extension, making the total length of protection fifty-six years. If the copyright owner failed to apply for renewal, the work fell into the public domain. In order to bring about better conformity between current and previous law, the Copyright Act of 1976 extended the renewal term from twenty-eight to forty-seven years for copyrights that existed on January 1, 1978. This makes those works eligible for a total term of seventy-five years. Further, in 1992, Congress amended the Copyright Act to make renewal automatic so that owners do not have to file for an extension in order to extend the original twenty-eight-year term to the full seventy-five years.

Infringement

Anyone who violates the rights of a copyright owner may be found guilty of copyright infringement. "Piracy," "bootleg" and "plagiarism" are informal, nonlegal synonyms for "copyright infringement." The statute of limitations on infringement actions is three years. In order to prove infringement, the copyright owner must be able to prove that (1) the defendant had access to the copyrighted work and (2) the two works are substantially similar.

One who successfully establishes infringement may recover monetary damages, obtain an injunction against further infringing and, if the court so directs, collect attorneys' fees. Monetary awards may be in the form of either actual or statutory damages. Actual damages are out-of-pocket losses the copyright owner can prove resulted from the infringement. Often it is difficult to pinpoint actual damages, so the copyright owner can ask for statutory damages, which range from $500 to $20,000, as determined by the judge. If the infringer can prove that the infringement was unintentional, the court may lower damages to $200 per infringement. On the other hand, if the plaintiff proves that the defendant's infringement was "committed willfully," the judge may award damages to as high as $100,000 per infringement.

Registering a Work

Any work fixed in tangible form is automatically protected under copyright law, so it is no longer necessary to register a work with the Copyright Office. There are advantages to doing so, however. With some exceptions, a copyright owner may not sue for infringement unless the work is registered, but one may register after the infringement occurs. Registering before infringement allows the copyright owner additional remedies that are not available if registration takes place after an infringement, namely, statutory damages and attorneys' fees.

To register a copyright, a person must send a $20 registration fee along with the appropriate form to the U.S. Copyright Office. For most types of work, two copies of a published work or one copy of an unpublished work must be deposited with the Copyright Office for the use of the Library of Congress. These three items — application form, fee and deposit material — should be sent in the same package to the Copyright Office, Library of Congress, Washington, D.C. 20559. Strictly speaking, the deposit is not a requirement for copyright, but failing to make the deposit at the time of publication can result in fines. Some works are exempt from the deposit requirement.

As of March 1, 1989, the effective date of the Berne Convention Implementation, no notice is required to retain copyright, but a notice prevents a defendant in an infringement suit from pleading "innocent infringement" to mitigate actual or statutory damages. A proper copyright notice consists of three things:

(1) © (the letter "C" in a circle) or the word "Copyright" or the

abbreviation "Copr." (Use the letter "P" in a circle for a sound recording);

(2) the year of first publication;

(3) the name of the copyright owner.

An inadvertent mistake on a copyright registration certificate will not invalidate a copyright and thus bar an infringement action unless the alleged infringer has relied to its detriment on the mistake, or unless the claimant intended to defraud the Copyright Office by making the misstatements.[47] For example, in the divine authorship case discussed earlier in this chapter, the defendant unsuccessfully argued that the Foundation intended to defraud the Copyright Office when it stated that the Book was a "work made for hire," fearing that the application would be rejected if it were known that the authors were celestial beings. The court concluded that there had been no fraud on the Foundation's part and no prejudicial reliance on the defendant's part.[48]

COPYRIGHT AND FAIR USE

The bundle of rights that belongs to a copyright holder is referred to in Copyright Act of 1976 as "exclusive rights," but the act also places some limitations on those rights.

Perhaps the most controversial of these limitations is the fair use doctrine, created by the courts, but codified in the 1976 statute. The fair use doctrine is designed to balance the rights of the copyright holder with the public's interest in dissemination of information affecting areas of universal concern, such as art, science and industry. It allows the use of copyrighted material in a reasonable manner without the consent of the copyright owner. Fair use has been justified this way:

> Notwithstanding the need for monopoly protection of intellectual creators to stimulate creativity and authorship, excessively broad protection would stifle, rather than advance, the objective. First, all intellectual creative activity is in part derivative. There is no such thing as a wholly original thought or invention. Each advance stands on building blocks fashioned by prior thinkers. Second, important areas of intellectual activity are explicitly referential. Philosophy, criticism, history, and even the natural sciences require continuous reexamination of yesterday's theses.[49]

For these reasons, the Copyright Act of 1976 provides that the fair use of a copyrighted work for purposes such as criticism, comment, news reporting, teaching (including multiple copies for classroom use), scholarship or research is not an infringement of copyright. As in many areas of law, a definitional problem exists. The legislative history of the 1976 act makes it clear that "since the doctrine is an equitable rule of reason, no generally applicable definition is possible, and each case raising the question must be decided on its own facts."[50] There is no simple definition of "fair use," and Congress did not include one in the definitions section of the Copyright Act. Drawing on analyses used in court cases before the new statute was enacted, Congress listed four factors for determining whether the use of a work was a fair use:

(1) the purpose and character of the use;

(2) the nature of the copyrighted work;

(3) the amount and substantiality of the portion used; and

(4) the effect of the use upon the potential market for or value of the copyrighted work.

A 1992 amendment to the Copyright Act makes fair use applicable for both published and unpublished work.

Courts have made it clear that the four factors must be explored together, rather than in isolation, that no one of the factors is determinative, and that the line between fair use and infringement must be drawn on a case-by-case basis.

Purpose and Character of the Use

A key consideration here is whether the secondary use is of a commercial nature or is for nonprofit educational purposes. However, the analysis is more complex than this. Educational purposes or lack of commercial motive does not justify wholesale copying. In weighing this factor, courts will consider whether the secondary use of the copyrighted material serves the public interest by stimulating creativity as copyright law intended. Courts will also ask other questions: Does the secondary use do more than paraphrase or repackage the original? Does it have what judges have referred to as "transformative" value; that is, does the secondary use add value to the original?

Examples of transformative uses would be critical reviews of quoted material or summarizing material in the original in order to comment on it. In an infringement case involving a parody, the Supreme Court held that the more transformative the new work is, the less significant are other factors, like commercialism, that

---

[47] *Urantia Foundation v. Maaherra*, 25 Med. L. Rptr. (BNA) at 1880 (9th Cir. 1997) (quoting from Nimmer, Sec. 7.20 at 7-201 and n. 6).

[48] *Id*. at 1881.

[49] Pierre N. Leval, "Commentary: Toward a Fair Use Standard,"

Harvard Law Review 103 (1990): 1105.

[50] House of Representatives Report No. 94-1476, p. 65 (1976).

might weigh against the finding of fair use. In that same case, the Court has said transformative works lie at the heart of the fair use doctrine's guarantee of breathing space within the confines of copyright although transformative use is not absolutely necessary for a finding of fair use.[51]

Nature of the Copyrighted Work

That courts explore the nature of the copyrighted work implies that certain kinds of works are more amenable to fair use than others. Fair use is more likely to protect copying from an out-of-print work, for example, than from one that may still be purchased. And if a work is designed to be used only once — a workbook, for example — the commercial impact will be great if a teacher makes multiple copies of workbook exercises. Whether the original work is fictional or factual influences judgments of fair use. A federal district court in Illinois noted that public interest in dissemination becomes progressively stronger as we move along the spectrum from fancy to fact.[52] Whether the work copied was published or unpublished has been an important consideration. Courts have held that copying from unpublished work tends to negate the defense of fair use;[53] the fair use section of the Copyright Act was amended in 1992, however, making fair use applicable for both published and unpublished works.[54]

Amount and Substantiality of Portion Used

This factor calls for both a quantitative and qualitative assessment of material used. If a large amount of the original copyrighted work or the most significant part of it is taken, the fair use defense may not protect the secondary use. No specific formula exists to determine how much of an original work can be used without defeating the fair use defense.

Courts must consider the interaction between this factor and the first and fourth factors. In some instances, the transformative nature of the secondary use may justify taking only a small part of the original, whereas in other situations, a larger amount of copying may be essential to accomplish the transformative purpose of the secondary work. A court ruled, for example, that a teacher's "learning activity package" about cake decorating, consisting of about fifty percent of a copyrighted booklet on the subject, contained virtually no additional information and amounted to substantial quantitative and qualitative copying and, thus, was not fair use.[55]

But there are occasions on which use of an entire work might qualify as fair use. If, for example, the transformative purpose is a lengthy critical study analyzing the structure, symbolism and meaning, literary antecedents and influences of a single poem, fragments of the poem dispersed throughout the work of criticism could encompass the entire original work without compromising its market value. The impact on the market value of the original in such an example might be nil, assuming that potential buyers would prefer to purchase the poem alone or as part of a collection of poems rather than buying a lengthy critical study.

Effect on Potential Market or Value

Although all four factors are weighed in determining whether a use is fair, courts give special attention to the effect of the secondary use upon the potential market for or value of the copyrighted work. Several court opinions, including that of the Supreme Court in *Harper & Row Publishers, Inc. v. Nation Enterprises*, indicate that this is the single most important factor in analyzing the fair use defense.[56]

News Reporting and Fair Use

The 1985 *Harper & Row* case, which involved copying from former President Gerald Ford's unreleased memoirs, illustrates how the Court applies the four fair use factors and how slippery interpretation of the fair use concept can be, even for judges. The Court was split 6-3, with the majority analyzing each of the four factors and holding that *The Nation*, a political commentary magazine, exceeded the limits of fair use. Meanwhile, three dissenting justices

---

[51] *Campbell v. Acuff-Rose Music, Inc.*, 510 U.S. 1164 (1994).

[52] *National Business Lists, Inc. v. Dun & Bradstreet, Inc.*, 552 F. Supp. 89 (D.C. Ill. 1982). See also *New Era Publications International v. Carol Pub. Group*, 729 F. Supp. 992 (S.D.N.Y. 1990); *aff'd in part, rev'd in part on other grounds* 904 F.2d 152 (2d Cir. 1990), *cert. denied* 498 U.S. 921 (1990).

[53] *Harper & Row, Publishers, Inc. v. Nation Enterprises*, 471 U.S. 539 (1985); *Salinger v. Random House, Inc.*, 811 F.2d 90 (2d Cir. 1987), *cert. denied* 484 U.S. 890 (1987); *New Era Publications International v. Carol Pub. Group*, 729 F. Supp. 992 (S.D.N.Y. 1990); *aff'd in part, rev'd in part on other grounds* 904 F.2d 152 (2d Cir. 1990), *cert. denied* 498 U.S. 921 (1990).

[54] Pub. L. No. 102-492 (1992), amending 17 U.S.C. 107.

---

[55] *Marcus v. Rowley*, 695 F.2d 1171 (9th Cir. 1983).

[56] 471 U.S. 539 (1985). See also *Association of American Medical Colleges v. Cuomo*, 928 F.2d 519 (2d Cir. 1991), *cert. denied* 502 U.S. 862 (1991).

reasoned that the magazine's 2,250-word article, appropriating some 300 words of the total 200,000 words in the manuscript, did not constitute an unfair taking of a copyrighted work.

President Ford left the White House in January 1977 and a month later contracted with Harper & Row and *Reader's Digest* to publish his yet-unwritten memoirs. Ford's book, eventually titled *A Time to Heal: The Autobiography of Gerald R. Ford,* was to contain previously unpublished information about the Watergate crisis, White House discussions in the days before former President Richard Nixon's resignation, Ford's pardon of Nixon and Ford's reflections on this period in U.S. history and the morality and personalities involved. In addition to the right to publish the Ford memoirs in book form, Harper & Row owned the exclusive right to license prepublication excerpts, known in the publishing industry as "first serial rights."

In 1979, when the memoirs were nearly completed, Harper & Row negotiated a prepublication licensing agreement with *Time* magazine, which would pay $25,000 — half in advance and the other half at publication — for the right to excerpt 7,500 words from Ford's account of the Nixon pardon. The magazine excerpts were to appear approximately one week before shipment of the book version to bookstores. Exclusivity was an important consideration, and Harper & Row instituted procedures designed to maintain the confidentiality of the manuscript. In addition, *Time* retained the right to renegotiate the second payment if the material appeared in print before the *Time* excerpts.

Two to three weeks before the scheduled *Time* article, an unidentified person secretly delivered a copy of the Ford manuscript to Victor Navasky, editor of *The Nation.* According to the district court trial transcript, Navasky, knowing that he was unauthorized to possess the manuscript and that he needed to work quickly to return it to his source, hastily put together a story composed of quotes, paraphrases and facts drawn from the manuscript. He included no independent commentary, research or criticism in the 2,250-word article.

Immediately after *The Nation* article appeared, *Time* cancelled plans to publish its own excerpts and refused to pay the second half of the $25,000 fee. Harper & Row brought suit against *The Nation's* parent company, alleging, among other things, a violation of the Copyright Act. At trial, *The Nation* argued that the information it published was of great public interest, that much of it was news or facts ineligible for copyright and that the article made fair use of the original manuscript. The district court rejected the arguments and awarded Harper & Row $12,500 in actual damages.[57]

A divided Court of Appeals for the Second Circuit reversed the district court decision. The majority said the lower court erred in assuming that the coupling of Ford's verbatim reflections with uncopyrightable facts transformed that information into a copyrighted totality. The majority held that when the uncopyrighted material was stripped away, *The Nation* article contained, at most, about 300 words that were copyrightable. The court of appeals focused on those words in its analysis of the four fair use factors, concluding that (1) the purpose of *The Nation* article was news reporting, (2) the Ford book was essentially factual in nature, (3) the 300 words appropriated were insubstantial in relation to the whole 2,250-word article, and (4) the impact on the market was minimal because the court was not convinced that *Time's* decision not to publish the excerpts resulted from *The Nation's* scoop. The court of appeals was especially influenced by the politically significant nature of the subject matter and its conviction that it is not "the purpose of the Copyright Act to impede that harvest of knowledge so necessary to a democratic state" or "chill the activities of the press by forbidding a circumscribed use of copyrighted works."[58]

The Supreme Court disagreed and reversed the appeals court decision. Justice Sandra Day O'Connor, writing for six members of the Court, acknowledged the factual nature of Ford's book but said "creation of a nonfiction work, even a compilation of pure fact, entails originality."[59] Further, she noted that the copyright principle of rewarding the individual author in order to benefit the public applies equally to works of fiction and nonfiction. Without the incentive guaranteed by copyright protection, Ford and other public figures might never document their reflections and unique perspective on historical facts. Justice O'Connor wrote that *The Nation's* use of excerpts from Ford's unpublished manuscript effectively usurped the right of first publication, an important marketable subsidiary right.

Then the opinion turned to a lengthy discussion of the fair use defense, tracing its legislative and judicial history, before applying each of the four fair use factors to the facts of the case. The purpose of *The Nation* article, the majority said, agreeing with the court of appeals, was news reporting, and *The Nation* had every right to seek to be the first to publish information. But, wrote Justice O'Connor, "*The Nation* went beyond simply reporting uncopyrightable information and actively sought to exploit the headline value of its infringement, making a 'news event' out of its unauthorized first publication of a noted figure's copyrighted ex-

[57] 557 F. Supp. 1067 (S.D.N.Y. 1983).

[58] 723 F.2d 195, 208-09 (2d Cir. 1983).
[59] *Harper & Row,* 471 U.S. at 547.

pression."[60] *The Nation's* stated purpose was to scoop the forthcoming hardcover and *Time* abstracts. Thus, "*The Nation's* use had not merely the incidental effect but the *intended purpose* [emphasis in the original] of supplanting the copyright holder's commercially valuable right of first publication."[61] The defendant's conduct is also relevant in analyzing the character and purpose of the use, the majority said, noting that the trial court had found that *The Nation* knowingly exploited a purloined manuscript.

The nature of the copyrighted work, the majority held, was an unpublished historical narrative or autobiography; copyright law generally recognizes a greater need to disseminate factual works than works of fiction or fantasy. The Court said the fact that a work is unpublished is a critical element of its nature, and the right of first publication encompasses not only the choice of whether to publish at all but also the choices of when, where and in what form first to publish a particular work. Noting that Harper & Row's contract with *Time* magazine required the abstract to be submitted to the copyright holder for prepublication review, the Court said, "*The Nation's* clandestine publication afforded no such opportunity for creative or quality control," a situation "difficult to characterize as 'fair.'"[62]

Justice O'Connor admitted that the amount and substantiality of the portion of *A Time to Heal* used by *The Nation* might appear to be insubstantial. Qualitatively, however, the taking was essentially the heart of the book. The portion of the book about the pardon of former President Nixon was "the most interesting and moving parts of the entire manuscript." Victor Navasky, editor of *The Nation*, testified that he had selected the most powerful passages in those chapters and had quoted them verbatim to best convey Ford's distinctive expression.

Finally, the majority opinion focused on the effect *The Nation's* article had on the market, labeling this factor "the single most important element of fair use" and rejecting the circuit court's finding of no casual relationship between *The Nation* article and *Time's* refusal to pay. For the majority at the Supreme Court, there was "clear-cut evidence of actual damage." In addition to money lost from *Time* magazine, the Court considered harm to the *potential* market to the original copyrighted work as well as derivative works.[63]

Justice Brennan, joined by Justices White and Marshall, dissented, arguing that the majority opinion applied a constricted reading of the fair use doctrine. On the threshold copyrightability question, the dissenters noted that the Copyright Act limits protection to literary form and precludes any claim of copyright in facts, including historical narration. Brennan's dissent also noted that infringement must be based on a *substantial* appropriation of literary form, which is determined by examining *how closely* the second author tracked the first author's particular language and structure of presentation and *how much* of the first author's language and structure was used (emphasis in the original).

Reasoning that, apart from the direct quotations, virtually all of *The Nation's* article dealt with noncopyrightable information, the dissent said infringement would have to be based on too close and substantial a tracking of Ford's expression. But a comparison of the two works, Brennan said, revealed linguistic similarities insufficient to constitute infringement for three reasons:

First, some leeway must be given to subsequent authors seeking to convey facts because those "wishing to express the ideas contained in a factual work often can choose from only a narrow range of expression." Second, much of what *The Nation* paraphrased was material in which Harper & Row could claim no copyright. Third, *The Nation* paraphrased nothing approximating the totality of a single paragraph, much less a chapter or the work as a whole. At most *The Nation* paraphrased disparate isolated sentences from the original. A finding of infringement based on paraphrase generally requires far more close and substantial a tracking of the original language than occurred in this case.[64]

Further, the dissent argued that the article's structure of presentation did not mimic the Ford book in that information in the article was drawn from scattered parts of the unpublished book rather than in the same sequence. While some of the article's discussion of the Nixon pardon roughly tracked the original, Brennan said Ford had presented these historical facts in chronological order and could not claim infringement when a subsequent author similarly presented the facts of history in a chronological order. Further, Brennan considered it "difficult to suggest" that a 2,000-word article could bodily appropriate the structure of a 200,000-word book.

After considering the threshold question of copyrightability, Brennan's dissenting opinion discussed each of the four fair use factors and concluded that the magazine's quotation of 300 words was fair use. The dissent shared the majority view that the effect

---

[60] *Id.* at 540.
[61] *Id.* at 562.
[62] *Id.* at 564.
[63] *Id.* at 567.

---

[64] *Id.* at 585 (Brennan, J., dissenting).

on the market was the single most important element of fair use but disagreed with the Court that *Time* backed out on its deal with Harper & Row because *Time* magazine could no longer be first with excerpts of literary form. The market in this instance was the noncopyrightable information known only to Ford, the dissent argued, not literary expression of that factual information. Brennan accused the majority of jeopardizing the robust public debate essential to self-government by giving former public officials too much control on information about their terms of office.

Another case concerning news reporting and fair use revolved around the widely circulated videotape of the beating of Reginald Denny during the April 29, 1992, riots in Los Angeles in the aftermath of a jury verdict in favor of police officers accused of using excess force to subdue Rodney King, a criminal suspect. The Los Angeles News Service (LANS) shot the dramatic tape from a helicopter, broadcasting the scene "live" over a LANS licensee station. The news service then licensed the tape to the media, and other stations aired it later that evening. KCAL-TV aired the tape without a license and without credit a number of times on the following day and thereafter. The district court that originally heard the copyright infringement suit granted summary judgment in KCAL's favor, holding that the doctrine of fair use exempted KCAL because the Denny videotape was unique and newsworthy and had significant public interest and concern; KCAL used portions for the purposes of news reporting; LANS failed to identify a commercial loss because of KCAL's conduct. The Ninth Circuit Court of Appeals analysis' of the four factors of the fair use doctrine led it to reverse the district court and remand the case for further proceedings.[65]

Concerning the purpose and character of use, the court said that although KCAL had not scooped LANS, as had *The Nation* in *Harper & Row*, this did not mean that "KCAL's use of the Denny tape had neither the effect nor purpose of depriving LANS of its also valuable right of licensing its original videotape which creatively captured the Denny beating in a way that no one else did."[66] The second factor — nature of the copyrighted work — weighed in favor of KCAL, the court said, because of the informational and factual nature of the tape. The third factor — amount and substantiality of what was used — weighed against fair use because although KCAL used only 30 seconds of the four minute, 40-second videotape, it was the "heart" or most valuable segment of the original. Regarding the fourth factor — effect on the market — the appeals court wrote, "This case doesn't fit neatly into a tra-

ditional niche because 'news' isn't normally thought of as having a secondary market."[67] The court noted, however, that there was evidence that KCAL's use of LAN's product without a license would destroy LANS's primary market. In considering impact on the market, courts must consider "whether unrestricted and widespread conduct of the sort engaged in by the defendant ... would result in a substantially adverse impact on the potential market for the original."[68]

Fair Use and Classroom Copying

The fact that a copyrighted work is copied for educational use rather than for profit does not insulate the user from a finding of infringement. The fair use section of the Copyright Act, however, specifically lists teaching (including multiple copies for classroom use) as one example where certain uses of copyrighted works may qualify as a fair use. But Congress did not intend for classroom copying to substitute for the purchase of materials. Copying from works intended to be consumable — workbooks, exercises, standardized tests, test booklets and answer sheets, for example — is specifically prohibited. Further, separate guidelines were adopted for copying from books and periodicals and copying from musical or audiovisual works.

For use in scholarly research or for instruction, teachers may make a single copy of a chapter from a book, an article from a periodical or newspaper, a short story, short essay, short poem, chart, graph, diagram, drawing, cartoon or picture from a book, periodical or newspaper. Multiple copies for classroom use (not to exceed more than one copy per student in a course) may be made, provided that the copying meets specific tests of brevity and spontaneity and each copy includes a copyright notice. The brevity guidelines are:

Poetry: (a) A complete poem if less than 250 words and if printed on not more than two pages or, (b) from a longer poem, an excerpt of not more than 250 words.
Prose: (a) Either a complete article, story or essay of less than 2,500 words, or (b) an excerpt from any prose work of not more than 1,000 words or ten percent of the work, whichever is less, but in any event a minimum of 500 words.

The use of multiple copies must be spontaneous, meaning that the decision to use the work and the moment of its use for maxi-

---

[65] *Los Angeles News Service v. KCAL-TV Channel 9*, 25 Media L. Rptr. (BNA) 1506 (9th Cir. 1997).
[66] *Id.* at 1508

[67] *Id.* at 1509.
[68] *Id.* (quoting Nimmer, Sec. 13.05{A}{4}, p. 113-102.61).

mum teaching effectiveness are so close in time that it would be unreasonable to expect a timely reply to a request for permission. In addition, there must be no more than nine instances of such multiple copying for one course during one class term. The legislative history of the Copyright Act indicates that Congress intended for similar guidelines to apply for the use of music for instructional purposes.

Courts have held that coursepacks compiled by university instructors for reproduction and distribution by commercial copy centers exceed the brevity and spontaneity tests.[69] To avoid illegally infringing copyrights on photocopied compilations, copy shops must obtain permissions from the various copyright holders and pay them license fees. These costs are passed along to students, of course, but the alternative for students is to buy entire volumes of multiple works. At this writing, the only federal appeals court to have considered this issue was sharply divided, voting 8-5 that coursepacks did not qualify as fair use, despite their educational use.

Parody and Fair Use

Material that mimics or makes fun of a copyrighted work may be protected by the fair use defense. The decision often turns on the third factor — the amount and substantiality of the portion. To be effective, a parody must copy enough to conjure up the original. Even more extensive use might be ruled fair, provided that the parody builds on the original, using it as a known element of modern culture and contributing something new for humorous effect or commentary.

Several court cases have involved advertising parodies. "McDonaldland" television commercials were ruled an infringement on a children's television show, *H.R. Pufnstuf*.[70] On the other hand, *Screw* magazine's spoof of "Poppin' Fresh," a copyrighted trade character owned by Pillsbury Company, was considered a fair use. The magazine said its character, "Poppie Fresh," was meant to poke fun at Pillsbury's advertising campaign and corporate image in general. The district court opinion concluded that the magazine's use was more like an editorial or social commentary than an attempt to capitalize financially on the original, despite the commercial nature of the magazine.[71]

In another case, the Dr Pepper Company, which spent approximately $100 million between 1978 and 1981 on its "Be A Pepper" campaign, was not amused when Sambo's Restaurants mimicked the campaign with its "Dancing Seniors" television commercials. "Wouldn't you like to be a Pepper too?" the soft drink commercials asked the viewing audience. The invitation from the restaurant chain was "Don't you want to be a Senior, too?" Applying the four fair use factors, a district court in Texas noted several similarities between the commercials and concluded that Sambo's copied the essence of the Dr Pepper commercial and jingle, distracting from the uniqueness and originality of the "Be A Pepper" commercials and thus logically shortening the life of the campaign and the business goodwill it had brought the company.[72]

In 1995 the Supreme Court decided a parody case involving the rap music group 2 Live Crew and one of the music industry's leading publishers, Acuff-Rose, Inc. Luther Campbell, a 2 Live Crew member, wrote a satirical version of "Oh, Pretty Woman," a hit song from the 1960s by Roy Orbison and William Dees. Both the rap and the rock versions of the song opened with the line "Pretty Woman, walking down the street." Beyond that line, the two songs bear little resemblance. Whereas in the Orbison and Dees version the singer seeks the attention of a woman described as looking "lovely as can be," the sexually suggestive 2 Live Crew song is about a "bald headed, two timin' woman." One of the appellate court judges characterized the rap song as "clearly intended to ridicule the white-bread original" and said it "reminds us that sexual congress with nameless street-walkers is not necessarily the stuff of romance and is not necessarily without its consequences. The [rap] singers have the same thing on their minds as did the lonely man with the nasal voice [Orbison], but here there is no hint of wine and roses."[73]

The manager for 2 Live Crew contacted Acuff-Rose Music, the copyright owner, offering to pay a fee for use of the song and enclosing a copy of the lyrics and a recording of the rap parody, but Acuff-Rose refused permission. Nonetheless, in mid-1989, 2 Live Crew released records, cassette tapes and compact discs of "Pretty Woman" in a collection of songs titled "As Clean As They Wanna Be." The albums and compact discs identified the authors

---

[69] *Basic Books, Inc. v. Kinko's Graphics Corp.*, 758 F. Supp. 1522 (S.D.N.Y. 1991); *Princeton University Press v. Michigan Document Services, Inc.*, 99 F.3d 1381 (6th Cir. 1996), *cert. denied* 117 S.Ct. 1336 (1997).

[70] *Sid & Mary Krofft Television Productions, Inc. v. McDonald's Corp.*, 562 F.2d 1157 (9th Cir. 1977).

[71] *Pillsbury Co. v. Milky Way Productions, Inc.*, 8 Media L. Rep. (BNA) 1016 (N.D. Ga. 1981).

[72] *Dr. Pepper Co. v. Sambo's Restaurants, Inc.*, 517 F. Supp. 1202 (N.D. Tex. 1981).

[73] *Acuff-Rose Music, Inc. v. Campbell*, 972 F.2d 1429, 1442 (6th Cir. 1992), *rev'd*, 510 U.S. 569 (1994).

of the original "Pretty Woman" as Orbison and Dees and its publisher as Acuff-Rose. Almost a year later, after nearly a quarter of a million copies of the recording had been sold, Acuff-Rose sued 2 Live Crew and its record company, Luke Skyywalker Records, for copyright infringement.

The district court granted summary judgment for 2 Live Crew, reasoning that the commercial purpose of 2 Live Crew's song was no bar to fair use; that 2 Live Crew's version was a parody, which "quickly degenerates into a play on words, substituting predictable lyrics with shocking ones" to show "how bland and banal" the rap group thinks the Orbison song is; that 2 Live Crew had taken no more than was necessary to "conjure up" the original in order to parody it; and that it was "extremely unlikely that 2 Live Crew's song could adversely affect the market for the original."[74]

The Court of Appeals for the Sixth Circuit reversed and remanded. Although it assumed for the purpose of its opinion that 2 Live Crew's song was a parody of the original, the court of appeals thought the district court had put too little emphasis on the commercial use of the rap version, and it held that "the admittedly commercial nature" of the parody weighed against a finding of fair use. The court of appeals also said that, by "taking the heart of the original and making it the heart of a new work," 2 Live Crew had, qualitatively, taken too much. Finally, after noting the effect on the potential market for the original, as well as the market for derivative works, the appeals court faulted the district court for "refus[ing] to indulge the presumption" that "harm for purposes of the fair use analysis has been established by the presumption attaching to commercial uses."[75]

The Supreme Court reversed, with Justice David Souter writing for a unanimous Court and noting that this was the Court's first opinion on the question of whether fair use could protect a parody from a copyright infringement claim. Justice Souter wrote:

Suffice it to say now that parody has an obvious claim to transformative value, as Acuff-Rose itself does not deny. Like less ostensibly humorous forms of criticism, it can provide social benefit, by shedding light on an earlier work, and, in the process, creating a new one. We thus line up with the courts that have held that parody, like other comment or criticism, may claim fair use....[76]

The Court cited lower court cases holding that a song titled "When Sonny Sniffs Glue" parodying "When Sunny Gets Blue" was a fair use,[77] as was the *Saturday Night Live* television show skit featuring "I Love Sodom," a takeoff on the New York City tourism campaign song "I Love New York."[78] The Court also said that parody, like any other use, has to be judged on a case-by-case basis according to the four factors of fair use.

The Court applied the four factors to "Pretty Woman." First:

While we might not assign a high rank to the parodic element here, we think it fair to say that 2 Live Crew's song reasonably could be perceived as commenting on the original or criticizing it, to some degree.... The Court of Appeals, however, immediately cut short the enquiry into 2 Live Crew's fair use claim by confining its treatment of the first factor essentially to one relevant fact, the commercial nature of the use. The court then inflated the significance of this fact by applying a presumption ... that every commercial use of copyrighted material is presumptively unfair [citations omitted]. In giving virtually dispositive weight to the commercial nature of the parody, the Court of Appeals erred. The language of the statute makes clear that the commercial or nonprofit educational purpose of a work is only one element of the first factor enquiry into its purpose and character.[79]

The second factor — the nature of the copyrighted work — is not much help, the Court said, "in separating the fair use sheep from the infringing goats in a parody case, since parodies almost invariably copy publicly known, expressive works."[80]

For its analysis of the third factor — the amount and substantiality of the portion used in relation to the copyrighted work as a whole — the Court turned its attention "to the persuasiveness of a parodist's justification for the particular copying done," recognizing "that the extent of permissible copying varies with the purpose and character of the use." Souter wrote:

Parody presents a difficult case. Parody's humor, or in any event its comment, necessarily springs from recognizable allusion to its object through distorted imitation. Its art lies in the tension between a known original and its parodic twin. When parody

[74] *Acuff-Rose Music, Inc. v. Campbell,* 754 F.Supp. 1150, 1158 (M.D. Tenn. 1991).

[75] *Acuff-Rose Music,* 972 F.2d at 1439.

[76] *Campbell v. Acuff-Rose Music, Inc.,* 510 U.S. 569, 579 (1994).

[77] *Fisher v. Dees,* 794 F.2d 432 (9th Cir. 1986).

[78] *Elsmere Music, Inc. v. National Broadcasting Co.,* 482 F. Supp. 741 (S.D.N.Y. 1980), *aff'd,* 623 F.2d 252 (2d Cir. 1980).

[79] *Campbell,* 510 U.S. at 583-84.

[80] *Id.* at 586.

takes aim at a particular original work, the parody must be able to "conjure up" at least enough of that original to make the object of its critical wit recognizable [citations omitted]. What makes for this recognition is quotation of the original's most distinctive or memorable features, which the parodist can be sure the audience will know. Once enough has been taken to assure identification, how much more is reasonable will depend, say, on the extent to which the song's overriding purpose and character is to parody the original or, in contrast, the likelihood that the parody may serve as a market substitute for the original. But using some characteristic features cannot be avoided. We think the Court of Appeals was insufficiently appreciative of parody's need for the recognizable sight or sound when it ruled 2 Live Crew's use unreasonable as a matter of law. It is true, of course, that 2 Live Crew copied the characteristic opening bass riff (or musical phrase) of the original, and true that the words of the first line copy the Orbison lyrics. But if quotation of the opening riff and the first line may be said to go to the "heart" of the original, the heart is also what most readily conjures up the song for parody, and it is the heart at which parody takes aim. Copying does not become excessive in relation to parodic purpose merely because the portion taken was the original's heart. If 2 Live Crew had copied a significantly less memorable part of the original, it is difficult to see how its parodic character would have come through [citations omitted]. This is not, of course, to say that anyone who calls himself a parodist can skim the cream and get away scot free. In parody, as in news reporting [citing *Harper & Row v. The Nation*] context is everything, and the question of fairness asks what else the parodist did besides go to the heart of the original. It is significant that 2 Live Crew not only copied the first line of the original, but thereafter departed markedly from the Orbison lyrics for its own ends. 2 Live Crew not only copied the bass riff and repeated it, but also produced otherwise distinctive sounds, interposing "scraper" noise, overlaying the music with solos in different keys, and altering the drum beat. This is not a case, then, where "a substantial portion" of the parody itself is composed of a "verbatim" copying of the original. It is not, that is, a case where the parody is so insubstantial, as compared to the copying, that the third factor must be resolved as a matter of law against the parodists. Suffice it to say here that, as to the lyrics, we think the Court of Appeals correctly suggested that "no more was taken than necessary," but just for that reason, we fail to see how the copying can be excessive in relation to its parodic purpose, even if the portion taken is the original's "heart." As to the music, we ex-

press no opinion whether repetition of the bass riff is excessive copying, and we remand to permit evaluation of the amount taken, in light of the song's parodic purpose and character, its transformative elements, and considerations of the potential for market....[81]

Regarding the fourth fair use factor — the effect of the use upon the potential market for or value of the copyrighted work — the Supreme Court said the appeals court erred in concluding that the commercial nature of 2 Live Crew's parody rendered it presumptively unfair. The Court noted that a parody is unlikely to act as a substitute for the original because the parody and the original usually serve different market functions. In moving for summary judgment at the district court level, however, 2 Live Crew attorneys confined arguments to uncontroverted submissions that there was no likely effect on the market for the original, but they did not address the effect the "Pretty Woman" parody had on the market for rap derivatives. The Supreme Court said this "evidentiary hole" disentitled 2 Live Crew from summary judgment and should be "plugged" when the case was reheard at district court.

The publishers of an illustrated book about the infamous O.J. Simpson murder trial unsuccessfully argued that the book was a parody of Dr. Seuss' *The Cat in the Hat* and a fair use of Theodor S. Geisel's book for children.[82] The defendant's book was titled *The Cat NOT in the Hat! A Parody by Dr. Juice* and was described in promotional literature as telling "... the whole story in rhyming verse and sketches as witty of Theodore [sic] Geisel's best. This is one parody that really packs a punch!" The district court and the Ninth Circuit Court agreed that ordinary reasonable people would perceive that a substantial similarity existed between the two works.

Further, in applying the four-part fair use test, the appeals court drew from Justice Arthur M. Kennedy's concurring opinion in the 2 Live Crew parody of "Oh, Pretty Woman," noting that "The parody must target the original, and not just its general style, the genre of art to which it belongs, or society as a whole."[83] Despite its claim in the title and its broadly mimicking of Dr. Seuss's characteristic style, *The Cat NOT in the Hat!* was not a parody, the appeals court said, because it did not hold Seuss's style up to ridicule. The court quoted from Justice Souter's majority opinion in *Acuff-Rose*

---

[81] *Id.* at 588-89.

[82] *Dr. Seuss Enterprises L.P. v. Penguin Books USA, Inc.,* 25 Med. L. Rptr. (BNA) 1641 (9th Cir. 1997).

[83] *Id.* at 1646, quoting from *Acuff-Rose,* 502 U.S. at 597 (Kennedy, J., concurring).

in concluding that the author and illustrator of the infringing work merely used the Cat's stove-pipe hat, the narrator ("Dr. Juice") and the title "to get attention" or maybe even "to avoid the drudgery in working up something fresh."[84] While Simpson was depicted thirteen times in the Cat's distinctively scrunched and somewhat shabby red and white hat, the substance and content of *The Cat in the Hat* was not conjured up by the focus on the Brown-Goldman murders or the O.J. Simpson trial, the appeals court wrote, concluding that the infringing work did not create a transformative work with new expression, meaning or message.

MUSIC, BROADCASTING AND DEVELOPING TECHNOLOGIES

Copyright law takes some different twists for music, broadcasting and developing technologies.

Compulsory Licensing for Music and Broadcasting

Just as copyright law authorizes fair use as a limitation on the five exclusive rights of a copyright owner, compulsory licensing limits those rights for five types of uses: (1) phonorecords of musical works, (2) musical works on jukeboxes, (3) cable television, (4) certain works on public broadcasting and (5) satellite retransmissions to the public for private viewing. Generally, compulsory licensing is a system that compels the owner of certain types of intellectual property to allow others to use that property for a reasonable fee set by the government. The Library of Congress and the Copyright Office administer a series of Copyright Arbitration Royalty Panels that periodically review and set rates for licensing fees, collect the fees annually and distribute them to representatives of copyright owners.

Music and Copyright. Recall that a copyright bestows five exclusive and divisible rights — to reproduce, to prepare derivative works, to distribute copies, to perform and to display the work. These rights have been compared to owning a stick of salami, which can be sold in its entirety or cut into several pieces, each sold or given away separately. Compulsory licensing means that owners of copyrighted musical works do not have the exclusive right to decide who may perform or display their works, because the law allows anyone who pays a royalty fee to use them.

It is also important to understand that the law recognizes protection for three different aspects of music: compositions, sound recordings and phonorecords. A musical composition consists of music, including any accompanying words. Sound recordings are defined in the law as "works that result from the fixation of a series of musical, spoken, or other sounds, but not including the sounds accompanying a motion picture or other audiovisual work." Generally, copyright protection extends to the contribution of the performers whose performances are captured on the recording and to the contribution of the person or persons responsible for capturing and processing the sounds to make the final recording. The right to make a recording of a musical work is referred to in copyright law as a mechanical right. A sound recording is not the same as a phonorecord, which is simply the physical object, such as a cassette tape, CD, LP or 45 r.p.m. disk, containing the recording and its underlying musical composition. This means that three entities — the composer, the producer/performer and the manufacturer of the phonorecord — may own separate copyrights for various aspects of a single phonorecord.

Musical compositions have always been eligible for copyright protection, but sound recordings and phonorecords did not receive federal protection until 1972, although common law and some state laws provided limited protection. The rationale for this lack of protection, predating the 1909 Copyright Act, was that piano rolls used to activate pianos were not copies of the underlying musical composition because they could not be read or deciphered by the naked eye.[85] With the 1909 Act, Congress gave recordings less than complete copyright protection, providing composers with the right to authorize or not the public distribution of sound recordings. "Demo" records did not trigger the compulsory license. If, however, the owner of the copyright in an underlying composition allowed a producer to release a sound recording of the piece of music, then permission to make a recording could not be denied to anyone else willing to pay the composer a fee set by law. The fee established in the 1909 statute was two cents "on each such part manufactured," which was construed by the music industry as two cents per composition, not two cents per copy. The second producer could simply copy, or pirate, the original recording with no obligation to the first producer or to the performers. Finally, in 1972, Congress allowed the originally authorized producer of sound recordings to file infringement suits against pirating companies.

The present copyright law, effective January 1, 1978, gives sound recordings fixed on or after February 15, 1972, greater protection than the 1972 law, but copyright owners still may not exclude others from performing their recordings publicly. This means that the hypothetical Skool of Hard Nocks band could take legal action if it

---

[84] *Id.* at 1647, quoting from *Acuff-Rose,* 502 U.S. at 580-81.

[85] *White-Smith Music Publishing Co. v. Apollo Co.*, 209 U.S. 1 (1908).

owned the copyright on a sound recording and someone duplicated or reproduced it in the soundtrack or audio portion of a movie, but the group could not prevent someone from deliberately imitating it for a public performance or from making a separate sound recording. If the band owned a copyright on the underlying composition, it could collect royalties for the use of that music every time it was performed, but it could not collect by virtue of owning rights to a sound recording.

How much will Skool of Hard Nocks make from royalty fees paid to publicly perform its copyrighted sound recordings, and how does it go about collecting those fees? The hundreds of broadcast stations and other entities that perform or display Skool of Hard Nocks music will not deal individually with the band. Instead, the band will join one of the performance rights organizations such as ASCAP or BMI and grant it the right to license the band's songs. The Copyright Arbitration Royalty Panels, will collect licensing fees for distribution to performance rights organizations, which will in turn pay royalties to members. The amount of royalty fees members receive is based on the frequency their music is performed. As of November 1, 1995, the rate was at least 8.25 cents per work or 1.31 cents per minute, whichever was greater. Rates are adjusted periodically.

It would be impractical for broadcast stations, night clubs and other businesses using music to keep track of each time each recording is used, so these firms buy a blanket license, paying an annual fee to the performance rights organization that controls the right to the recording. The fee varies according to the gross receipts of the station or business. Broadcasters do not like these blanket licenses, arguing in numerous lawsuits over the years that they are monopolistic and violate the Sherman Antitrust Act. Eventually, ASCAP and BMI agreed to permit members to negotiate directly with broadcasters and others seeking licenses, but generally performers and composers prefer to leave the matter to ASCAP and BMI.

Broadcasters also object to the industry practice by which producers of syndicated programming sell those programs to stations without synchronization rights — the right to reproduce music in conjunction with video. This means that in addition to buying the programming, broadcasters have to pay ASCAP or BMI for "performance" rights. Broadcasters say their costs would be reduced if producers of the programming negotiated with copyright owners for both synchronization and performance rights, but under the present system, copyright owners, or their ASCAP or BMI representatives, knowing that broadcasters cannot air the programming without performance rights, have little incentive to bargain

with broadcasters. In a 1984 lawsuit, hundreds of independent television stations presented this "lack of incentive to bargain" argument in court, but the Second U.S. Circuit Court of Appeals did not think a lack of bargaining incentive was sufficient to rule the blanket licensing procedure an illegal restraint of trade.[86]

Another historically controversial copyright issue involves coin-operated phonorecord players or jukeboxes. The 1909 Copyright Act exempted jukebox operators, so, until the present law went into effect in 1978, they had free use of phonorecords. Apparently, music publishers did not oppose the exemption in 1909 because they saw jukebox plays as a way to increase the popularity of songs and to increase sheet music sales, and jukeboxes brought in relatively little income. As jukebox revenues became increasingly significant, however, music publishers and other copyright holders took a very different position. During copyright law revision discussions in the 1970s, they denounced the jukebox exemption as an anachronistic historical accident that was unconscionable, indefensible, totally unjustified and grossly discriminatory.

After much controversy and many proposals in Congress, the 1976 Copyright Act established a compulsory license requirement with the fee set at $8 per year per jukebox, subject to periodic review and adjustment by the Copyright Arbitration Royalty Panels. One legal scholar called the requirement "one of the greatest failures of the 1976 Act, entirely due to deliberate lawlessness by the majority of jukebox operators."[87] Barely one-fourth of the jukeboxes in operation were licensed in 1978, and the number steadily declined between then and 1989, despite thousands of infringement suits brought by ASCAP, BMI and other performing rights organizations. Civil suits did not succeed in requiring licenses, and despite requests from the Copyright Office, the Justice Department did not take criminal action against the worst offenders.

In order for the United States to join the Berne Convention and have a measure of international copyright protection, the jukebox licensing situation demanded change. After some four years of deliberations, the compulsory license provision for jukeboxes in the 1976 Copyright Act was suspended to allow the trade association representing jukebox operators, the Amusement and Music Operators Association, to negotiate licensing agreements with ASCAP, BMI and the Society of European Stage Actors and Composers. The initial ten-year agreement lasts until 1999 and is scheduled for automatic renewal from year to year thereafter. In 1994, jukebox

---

[86] *Buffalo Broadcasting Co., Inc. v. ASCAP*, 744 F.2d 917 (2d Cir. 1984).

[87] William F. Patry, *Copyright Law and Practice,* vol. 1 (Washington, D.C.: The Bureau of National Affairs, Inc., 1994), p. 982.

licensing fees were $287 for the first jukebox, $54 for each additional jukebox up to ten, and $46 for each one after that. Failure to execute a license agreement and display a certificate on the jukebox is grounds for infringement.

Copyright and TV Signals. Like jukebox operators, cable television system owners paid no fees for using copyrighted material until 1978. Broadcasters paid royalties for programming they aired, but cable owners retransmitted that programming at no cost. Copyright infringement suits against cable operators were unsuccessful; the Supreme Court twice held that retransmission did not constitute a "performance."[88] Now cable system operators participate in a compulsory licensing procedure that permits them to use copyrighted material without securing permission, but also requires them to pay royalties. Those fees are based on a rather complex formula that considers the gross revenues subscribers pay for the basic retransmissions, plus the number of distant television station signals retransmitted and whether those distant stations are independent or network affiliated. The copyright fee structure for cable systems influences programming choices for viewers because the more nonlocal stations, such as "superstations," a system retransmits, the greater the system's expenditures for royalty fees.

Home satellite dishes were new and expensive items when the Copyright Act was passed in 1976. By the mid-1980s, however, more than a million and a half U. S. homes were receiving broadcasts via satellites. Copyright owners received no royalties on these retransmissions and sought help from Congress. One result was a provision in the 1984 revision of the Communications Act that encouraged the scrambling of broadcast signals so that home satellite dish owners could not receive signals without paying annual fees. In 1988 Congress passed the Satellite Home Viewer Act, which applied a compulsory licensing system to satellite carriers who retransmit unaltered superstations and network stations to home satellite dishes for private home viewing. Fees were based on the number of subscribers.

Developing Technology — VCRs

In a sense, all copyright law has been in response to developing technology. After all, unauthorized copying was hardly a problem when each new copy required laborious hand lettering. Infringement concerns began with the inventions of movable type and multiplied with succeeding generations of faster, more efficient printing presses. The development of each new medium for fixing works in tangible form — photography, moving pictures, sound recordings, digital imaging — as well as each new means of reproducing or transmitting works — radio, television, photocopying machines, video tape recorders, satellites, fax machines, pagers, computer networks — challenged lawmakers and judges.

One such challenge was the claim by movie studios that their copyrights were being infringed by the use of video tape recorders to copy movies transmitted by broadcast stations. The stations, of course, paid royalties for the right to broadcast the movies, but home viewers paid no fees for copying those over-the-air performances. Recall that under the doctrine of "first sale," movie studios receive no royalties from the rental of a film after it is sold, although a video store may recoup its purchase price many times over through repeated rentals of a single film. Home recording of movies broadcast over television further decreased the opportunity for studios to make that first sale.

Recognizing the futility of collecting fees from individuals who taped in their homes, Universal Studios and Walt Disney Productions attempted to hold the manufacturers of taping equipment responsible for what they considered to be the illegal use of the video recorders. The studios filed suit in 1976 in a federal district court in California, arguing that the manufacturer and sales of taping equipment contributed to copyright infringement. Sony, one manufacturer of video tape recorders, was named as defendant in the suit. The studios pointed out that the fair use doctrine had not been interpreted as protecting the copying of an entire copyrighted work where no transformational value was added. During a lengthy trial, both parties introduced survey results showing that the primary use of tape recorders was for taping a television program for later viewing, referred to as "time-shifting." The surveys also showed that most viewers erased tapes and reused them.

The district court ruled in favor of Sony, concluding that noncommercial home recording of off-the-air broadcasts was a fair use. Considering the four factors of the fair use doctrine, the court emphasized that the material was broadcast free to the public at large and that home taping was a private, noncommercial activity conducted entirely within the home. Further, the court reasoned that the purpose of this use served the public interest in increasing access to television programming. The district court said that even if time-shifting were considered an infringement, Sony and other video tape recorder manufacturers could not be held liable as contributory infringers for merely selling a "product capable of a vari-

[88] *Fortnightly Corp. v. United Artists Television, Inc.*, 392 U.S. 390 (1968); *Teleprompter Corp. v. Columbia Broadcasting System*, 415 U.S. 394 (1974).

ety of uses, some of them allegedly infringing."[89]

The movie studios appealed, and the Ninth U.S. Circuit Court of Appeals reversed, reasoning that home taping of entire broadcasts was not a "productive use" and that it was therefore unnecessary for the studios to prove any harm to the potential market for their copyrighted works.[90] A sharply divided Supreme Court reversed the court of appeals. The Court held that Sony was not guilty of contributory infringement where there was a significant likelihood that substantial numbers of copyright holders who sold stations or networks the right to broadcast performances would not object to time-shifting by private viewers. The Court said there was no showing that time-shifting would cause significant harm to the potential market for the movies and other taped material. Four justices dissented, expressing the view that time-shifting was not a fair use and that the recorder manufacturers were guilty of inducing and materially contributing to the infringement.[91]

The case applies to home taping intended for private use. It does not extend to commercial uses of a home-taped movie — selling it or charging admission for a public performance, for example. Likewise, the decision does not protect a clipping service that tape records newscasts for sale to subjects of the broadcasts.[92]

Before the Sony case, some industry representatives suggested that consumers pay surcharges on video tape recorders and blank tapes to compensate copyright owners for over-the-air broadcasts. Congress never acted on the suggestion, which was opposed on the grounds that recorders and tapes were used for purposes other than copying protected movies. Perhaps because they acted while digital audio recording equipment was relatively unknown in the United States, and that industry was without lobbying power, proponents of this method of generating royalty revenue successfully lobbied Congress to enact the Audio Home Recording Act of 1992. The Act requires manufacturers of digital audio recorders for home use to make the equipment incapable of "serial copying," meaning making a copy from a copy. In addition, manufacturers must pay royalty fees on both the taping devices and the blank tapes, costs that typically are passed along to consumers. This law applies to digital audio equipment and tapes alone, not video taping devices or blank video tapes.

---

[89] *Universal City Studios, Inc., et al. v. Sony Corporation of America, et al.*, 480 F. Supp. 429, 460 (D. Calif. 1979).

[90] *Universal City Studios, Inc., et al. v. Sony Corporation of America, et al.*, 659 F.2d 963 (9th Cir. 1981).

[91] *Sony Corporation of America, et al. v. Universal City Studios, Inc., et al.* 464 U.S. 417 (1984).

[92] *Georgia Television Co. v. TV News Clips of Atlanta, Inc.*, 718 F. Supp. 939 (N.D. Ga. 1989).

Developing Technology —
Computers and Computer Networks

Copyright questions raised by video and audio tape recorders pale in comparison to the avalanche of legal problems prompted by the development of affordable personal computers and ingenious software that enable users to infringe on the rights of copyright owners with relative ease. With a few keystrokes, deft maneuvering of a mouse or skilled use of computerized drawing tools, a copyrighted work can be reproduced or derivative works made and displayed via the Internet to literally millions of people connected by computer networks around the globe. Each of those recipients has the capabilities to further manipulate, copy and display those same electronic images along even more avenues on the information superhighway.

Should the transmission of a work in digital form be governed as a public performance or as a reproduction and distribution? Can it be all at the same time? How do rules concerning the right of importation of copyrighted works from foreign nations apply in a digital environment? It is far beyond the scope of this book to discuss all the statutory and common law already on the books to address computers and copyright issues, much less legal problems under discussion or those not yet anticipated, but several issues affecting mass media will be addressed.

Anyone who wrestles with shrink wrapping on a computer software program receives notice that, by virtue of opening the package, he or she agrees to abide by copyright statutes protecting the enclosed disks. In 1980, President Jimmy Carter signed legislation making it legal for the owner of a lawful copy of a computer program to load the program into a computer and modify it as necessary. The revision of the Copyright Act also made it legal for the owner to create a backup copy, but only for archival purposes. Unless the copyright owner has authorized public distribution as "shareware," it is illegal to make multiple copies of computer software for friends or co-workers. Companies and educational institutions often purchase site licenses authorizing the production of a specified number of copies for office or classroom use. A computerized database is also eligible for copyright protection as a "literary work" to the extent that it incorporates style rather than merely ideas or facts. And while labor involved in typing factual information into a compilation does not constitute original expression and therefore is not copyrightable, the Supreme Court has held that the specific selection and arrangement of facts, such as the layout and design of a database, may entail a minimal degree of creativity sufficiently original for copyright protection.[93]

Posting digital reproductions of copyrighted photographs on computer bulletin board systems without authorization is an infringement. A company operating such a system made digital reproductions of 170 photographs from *Playboy* magazine and distributed the high-quality computerized images to subscribers. A court rejected a fair use defense, noting that the use was clearly commercial; that the originals were for entertainment, not factual, purposes; and that, if widespread, such conduct would adversely affect the magazine's market.[94] In addition, the use of the magazine's trademarks "Playboy" and "Playmates" as file descriptors on the bulletin board system was held a violation of the Lanham Act, the federal law protecting trademarks. In another lawsuit, Playboy Enterprises Inc. won copyright infringement damages in excess of $1.1 million against a company that produced and sold CD-ROM disks containing photographs downloaded from the Internet.[95] The defendants' claim that they did not know the photographs were copyrighted and thought them to be in the public domain was called "willful ignorance" by the district court, which wrote: "To think that you can go to a bulletin board and pull down material and then sell that and not have any idea that you are violating any laws is just incredible to the court."[96]

One federal district court has said an Internet service provider does not share in the liability for copyright infringement by its subscribers, so long as the ISP had not undertaken any affirmative action that directly resulted in copying.[97] In that particular case, involving the Church of Scientology as the plaintiff, the decision held that "although copyright is a strict liability statute, there should still be some element of volition or causation which is lacking where a defendant's system is merely used to create a copy by a third party."[98] This lack of involvement by the ISP differs from the bulletin board service operators in the Playboy Enterprises cases and another BBS operator who encouraged customers to download Sega video games into their computers after an unidentified subscriber made the games available on the bulletin board. Further, the BBS offered to sell subscribers an alternative to Sega's

video cartridges. The *Sega* court found the BBS operator guilty of contributing to copyright infringement although a subscriber rather than the operator originally uploaded the video games.[99]

Other computer-related copyright debates and ethical dilemmas spring from digital manipulation of images. Is a black and white movie that has been colorized or is a photograph that has been altered a derivative work that is eligible for copyright protection? Does such doctoring of images infringe the copyright owner's right to control derivative works?

Turner Network Television set off a firestorm of protest in some quarters when it used computer technology to colorize classic Hollywood films, including *Casablanca* and *It's a Wonderful Life*. Turner was not infringing copyright because the company had purchased rights to the movies, but protesters decried what they viewed as mutilation of cultural heritage. Prominent Hollywood figures urged Congress to protect the integrity of movies, painting the specter of digital imaging run amok, altering films to replace actors with "fresher faces" or to change the movement of speakers' lips to conform to new dialogue. The upshot was The National Film Preservation Act of 1988, termed by copyright expert William Patry "one of the silliest pieces of legislation ever to pass Congress."[100] The Act establishes a board authorized to designate as many as twenty-five films each year for registration as classical films, a label denoting that the films are materially unaltered. Meanwhile, the Copyright Office passed a regulation requiring the deposit of the black-and-white version as well as the colorized version when copyright registration is sought for the newer version.

Digital technology has created yet another problem for the music industry. The technology allows sounds to be converted to digital bits and manipulated by a recording engineer. Sounds from copyrighted songs, perhaps just a single note or distinctive few notes, can be mixed and remixed and combined with other sounds, to create a new song. Courts have held that this musical "sampling" infringes copyright if the copying is sufficiently significant to result in a substantially similar work. The two musical works do not have to be substantially similar; there is infringement if there is similarity between qualitatively important portions of the two works.[101]

The ease and convenience of digital scanning technology brings with it increasing legal concerns for photographers, particularly

---

[93] *Feist Publications, Inc. v. Rural Telephone Service Col, Inc.*, 499 U.S. 340 (1991).

[94] *Playboy Enterprises, Inc. v. Frena*, 22 Media L. Rep. (BNA) 1301 (M.D. Fla. 1994).

[95] *Playboy Enterprises, Inc. v. Starware Publishing Corp.*, 23 Med. L. Rptr. (BNA) 2420 (S.D. Fla. 1995).

[96] *Id.* at 2427.

[97] *Religious Technology Center v. Netcom On-Line Communications Services, Inc.*, 907 F. Supp 1361 (N.D. Calif. 1995).

[98] *Id.* at 1370.

[99] *Sega Enterprises v. MAPHIA*, 857 F. Supp. 679 (N.D. Calif. 1994).

[100] Patry, at 101 n. 388.

[101] See *Grand Upright Music Ltd. v. Warner Bros. Records*, 780 F. Supp. 182 (S.D.N.Y. 1991) and *Jarvis v. A&M Records*, 827 F. Supp. 282 (D.N.J. 1993).

freelancers. While direct copying of photographs and other visual images without authorization — such as downloading an image from the Internet and displaying it on a Web page — is illegal, does infringement occur when portions of one or more photographs are digitally reproduced and combined to create a new photograph? Should fair use principles apply to such derivative works so long as the new work is sufficiently transformative? As of mid-1998 there had been no reported cases dealing with these questions, and scholars differ in their legal analyses. Some commentators argue that the mere act of scanning a copyrighted photograph without permission is copyright infringement, while others maintain that new images created from bits and pieces of scanned images should be eligible for copyright protection. Other writers call upon Congress or the courts to clarify the legal ambiguities.[102]

Yet another potential legal situation involving copyright and the Internet is the increasingly widespread practice of directly linking one Web site to another one.[103] While most Web enthusiasts probably view hyperlinking as analogous to recommending a book at the local library or citing a copyrighted source, certainly not actions requiring permission or a fee, at least one legal scholar asserts that increasing business use of the Internet will promote "linking rights," which will depend upon the business-oriented laws of unfair competition and intellectual property, not any free

and uninhibited 'right' to link.[104] He predicts that "contrary to the original ethos of Internet use, which celebrated hyperlink technology and encouraged everyone to use it to the greatest extent possible, in the era of business use of the Internet, linkages will often be scrutinized and controlled — and sometimes discouraged, litigated, or penalized."[105]

To date little case law has developed in the United States on linking one Web site to another, but several news organizations, including The Washington Post Co., reached an out-of-court settlement with Total News, Inc., a company whose advertising-filled Web site included "framed" pages of news from other sites.[106] The plaintiff publishers claimed that their own advertising banners were displaced by the Total News ads, actionable as common law misappropriation, federal and state trademark dilution, unfair competition, trademark infringement, copyright infringement and tortious interference. The plaintiffs did not object to the hyperlinks *per se* but to the way they were viewed within a Total News frame, thus blocking plaintiffs' advertising. The cased was settled with Total News agreeing to a licensing arrangement with specified conditions for displaying pages from the publishers' Web sites.

To deal with developing information technology, President Clinton formed the Information Infrastructure Task Force in 1993, to articulate and implement the administration's vision for the National Information Infrastructure. The task force, led by the secretary of commerce, included representatives of federal agencies that play a role in advancing the development and application of information technologies. Working with the private sector, public interest groups, Congress and state and local governments, the task force issued a "White Paper" in 1995, recommending changes to U.S. intellectual property law and policy.[107] Since then, the World Intellectual Property Organization, known as WIPO, adopted two new international treaties that would facilitate protection of copyrighted works in cyberspace and limit the liability of online service providers for copyright infringement in certain circumstances. In 1988, the U.S. House and Senate passed slightly different versions of the Digital Millennium Copyright Act, designed to modify U.S. copyright law to achieve compliance with the WIPO treaties. As of

[102] For discussions of legal issues involving digital photography, see Michael S. Oberman and Trebor Lloyd, "Copyright Protection for Photographs in the Age of New Technologies," *Boston University Journal of Science and Technology Law* 2 (1996): 10; Patricia Krieg, "Copyright, Free Speech and the Visual Arts," *Yale Law Journal* 93 (1984): 1568; Jonathan A. Franklin, "Digital Image Reproduction, Distribution and Protection: Legal Remedies and Industrywide Alternatives," *Computer & High Tech. Law Journal* 10 (Nov. 1994): 347; Wilson Lowrey, "When News Artists Take Without Asking: Digital Photo Collage as Transformative Commentary," paper presented for the Law Division, Association for Education in Journalism and Mass Communication annual convention, Baltimore, Md., August 1998.

[103] For a discussion of potential legal problems involving Internet material, see generally, April M. Major, "Copyright Law Tackles Yet Another Challenge: The Electronic Frontier of the World Wide Web," *Rutgers Computer & Technology Law Journal* 24 (1998): 75; Stephen Fraser, "The Conflict Between the First Amendment and Copyright Law and Its Impact on the Internet, *Cardozo Arts and Entertainment Law Journal* 16 (1998): 1; David J. Loundy, "Revising the Copyright Law for Electronic Publishing," *John Marshall Journal of Computer & Information Technology* 14 (1995): 1; Michael D. McCoy and Needham J. Boddie, II, "Cybertheft: Will Copyright Law Prevent Digital Tyranny on the Superhighway?" *Wake Forest Law Review* 30 (1995): 173.

[104] Mark Sableman, "Link Law: The Evolving Law of Internet Hyperlinks," paper presented for the Law Division, Association for Education in Journalism annual convention, Baltimore, Md., August 1998.
[105] *Id.* at 2.
[106] *The Washington Post Co. v. Total News, Inc.,* 97 Civ. 1190 (PKL) (S.D.N.Y. filed February 20, 1997).
[107] Information Infrastructure Task Force, *Intellectual Property and the National Infrastructure: The Report of the Working Group on Intellectual Property Rights,* 1995.

September 1998, a joint House-Senate conference committee had not yet met to iron out differences in the two bills,[108] but action was expected before the 105th Congress adjourned.[109] In addition, legislation to expand the fair use doctrine to include uses by analog or digital transmission in connection with teaching, research and other specified activities was introduced in the 105th Congress, but was still in committee as of this writing.[110]

TRADEMARKS

Trademarks, service marks and trade names, like copyrighted works, are types of intellectual property protected by law. A federal statute defines a trademark as "any word, name, symbol or device or any combination thereof, adopted and used by a manufacturer or merchant to identify its goods and distinguish them from those manufactured or sold by others."[111] The term "service mark" is used for distinctive identifiers for a service rather than a product. A trade name is defined by statute as "any name used by a person to identify his or her business or vocation."[112] Proctor & Gamble is the trade name of a business that identifies its products with many different trademarks, including Ivory soap, Tide detergent and Crest toothpaste. A single word — Sears, for example — may be used for all three purposes: to identify products, to identify services and to identify the company that produces those products and services. In this section of the chapter, the term "trademark" is used to refer to all three forms of protected property. Examples of trademark symbols are the peacock feathers identifying the National Broadcasting Company and the golden arches of McDonald's. Even a color can be a trademark, the Supreme Court said in a 1995 ruling, if that color has attained a secondary meaning and therefore identifies and distinguishes a particular brand and thus indicates a source.[113]

In addition to identifying sources of goods and services, trademarks function to warrant that goods coming from a particular source — even though consumers may not know the identity of that source — will be of consistent and desirable quality. The instant recognition value of trademarks permits companies to use shortcuts in advertising. Companies recognize the tremendous value of their trademarks and work zealously to protect them from infringement and from falling into generic use.

Celebrities sometimes sue for trademark infringement to prevent the use of their name or likeness without permission. For instance, in May 1998, attorneys for the estate of Princess Diana filed a suit against an American firm, the Franklin Mint, for selling an assortment of dolls, plates, jewelry and other items in memory of the former Princess of Wales. The estate was not deterred from its suit by the defendant's pledge that a portion of the proceeds would benefit the late Princess' charities. Golfer Tiger Woods had earlier won a financial payment and a permanent injunction against the Franklin Mint.[114]

Trademark Registration

Registration is not essential for protection from the tort of trademark infringement, but it is recommended in order to give notice that the owner has the right of exclusive use of the mark for marketing purposes and to establish the date of inception of the use. In addition, a mark must be registered in order to bring an infringement lawsuit in federal courts. A trademark registered with the U.S. Patent and Trademark Office should be accompanied by ® (an *R* in a circle) as notice. An unregistered trademark may use ™ as a notice.

Under the Trademark Revision Act of 1989, a trademark no longer has to be in use before an application for registration is filed. An "intent to use" application gives the applicant six months (or up to three years under some circumstances) to begin using the mark. The mark is not actually registered until it is placed into use, but the "intent to use" provision protects it from infringement by someone else who has neither used the mark previously nor applied for it. Unlike copyright law, which protects a work from the moment it is fixed in tangible form even if it is never published, trademark law requires that a trademark be used in commerce. Further, for protection to continue, commercial use of the mark must continue. If a company ceases to use its trademark, it loses legal protection. Registration is renewable every ten years for as long as the mark remains in use.

State governments, usually through the secretary of state's office, also register trademarks to give notice of valid ownership. Companies marketing goods or services with national or international distribution often forego the state registration process be-

---

[108] H.R. 2281 and S. 2037.

[109] "Guarding Intangible Property in a New, Intangible Realm: Intellectual Property," *National Law Journal,* 3 August 1998, p. C8. See also, "House Passes WIPO Bill, But Senate Debate to Come," *Publishers Weekly,* 10 August 1998, p. 233.

[110] H.R. 3048.

[111] 15 U.S.C. Sec. 1121.

[112] 15 U.S.C. Sec. 1127.

[113] *Qualitex Co. v. Jacobson Products Co.,* 514 U.S. 159 (1995).

[114] "Di's Estate Sues Franklin Mint over Items; Company Accused of Ignoring Trademarks," *Newsday,* 19 May 1998, p. A41.

cause the marks have federal protection. State registration is more important for companies doing businesses within a single state.

Protection of Rights

There is no dearth of trademark disputes. Groups recently involved in such disputes include the U.S. Olympic Committee, Nike, Ford Motor Company, Marvel Comics Ltd., Levi Strauss & Co., American Angus Association, Playboy Enterprises, Twin Peaks Productions Inc., Stern's Miracle-Gro Products, Kohler Co., Wachovia Bank & Trust Co. and Walt Disney Co. Legal action generally comes after a trademark is threatened by the likelihood of confusion with another mark or by dilution.

Likelihood of Confusion. To determine whether consumers are likely to be confused as to the source, sponsorship or approval of a product, courts consider these factors:

- strength or weakness of the plaintiff's trademark, based on its distinctiveness;
- similarity of the plaintiff's and defendant's trademarks;
- the differences in the products or services being marketed under the same trademark;
- whether the original owner is likely to bridge the gap between the the competing products or services;
- presence of actual confusion among consumers;
- whether the defendant had acted in good faith in adopting the mark;
- the quality of the defendant's products or services;
- the sophistication of potential consumers;
- the trade channels for the products or services;
- the similarity of the advertising media.

Like the four factors in the fair use defense in copyright, each of these factors must be examined individually, and no single factor is determinative. And the factors must be applied on a case-by-case basis.

Mead Data Central, for example, sought to prevent Toyota Motor Sales from naming its luxury automobile Lexus, arguing likelihood of confusion with LEXIS, a computerized legal research service. The court denied the claim on the basis that the LEXIS trademark was not known to the general public and that attorneys, the primary customers for LEXIS research service, were unlikely to be confused because of their "recognized sophistication."[115]

McDonald's Corporation went to court in Canada in 1994 trying to prevent Coffee Hut Stores Ltd. from registering "McBeans" as a trademark for coffee, coffee beans, coffee makers and accessories. McDonald's had more than thirty registered trademarks with the prefix "Mc" combined with a food or food-type item, and in U.S. courts the company had successfully prevented a variety of firms from using the prefix, ranging from "McSleep" for a motel chain to "McTooth" for a dental practice. The Canadian court, however, ruled in favor of Coffee Hut, determining that McDonald's and McBeans were different kinds of businesses and there was no likelihood of confusion.

Where one company's parody of another company's trademark leads to an infringement lawsuit, the likelihood of confusion rationale applies. As one authoritative source puts it: "Some parodies will constitute an infringement, some will not.... [T]here are confusing parodies and non-confusing parodies. All they have in common is an attempt at humor through the use of someone else's trademark. A noninfringing parody is merely amusing, not confusing."[116]

Trademark infringement was charged in the Dr. Seuss's *The Cat in the Hat* case discussed earlier in this chapter, and the parody argument did not protect the defendant publishers. The district court's preliminary injunction, upheld by the appeals court, was based in part on a finding that the good will and reputation associated with *The Cat in the Hat* character and title, the name "Dr. Seuss," and the cat's hat outweighed the expenses incurred by the defendants in publishing their book about the O. J. Simpson trial.[117]

The appeals court in that case cited examples from several cases in which courts have held, in effect, that poking fun at a trademark is no joke and have issued injunctions. Examples include: a diaper bag with green and red bands and the wording "Gucchi Goo," allegedly poking fun at the well-known Gucci name and design mark;[118] the use of a competing meat sauce of the trademark "A.2" as a pun on the famous "A.1" trademark.[119] The Hard Rock Cafe corporation won a trademark infringement suit against a company using a "Hard Rain" logo. The claim of parody is no defense, the court said, "where the purpose of the similarity is to capitalize on a famous mark's popularity for the defendant's own commercial

[115] *Mead Data Central, Inc. v. Toyota Motor Sales, Inc.*, 875 F.2d 1026 (2d Cir. 1989).

[116] *McCarthy on Trademarks*, Sec. 31.38[1], at 31-216 (rev. ed. 1995).

[117] *Dr. Seuss Enterprises L.P.*, 25 Media L. Rptr at 1651.

[118] *Gucci Shops, Inc. v. R.H. Macy & Co.*, 446 F. Supp. 838 (S.D.N.Y. 1977).

[119] *Nabisco Brands, Inc. v. Kaye*, 760 F. Supp. 25 (D. Conn. 1991).

use."[120]

Dilution. Even where there is no likelihood of consumer confusion or no competition or relationship between the goods or services involved, at least half of the states have laws allowing a trademark owner to get an injunction to stop another party from diluting the distinctive quality of a trademark. Generally, this protection is available only to those marks that have acquired strength through long and substantial use or that were particularly distinctive to begin with, at least with a certain group of people, product line or territory.

Trademarks are categorized according to distinctiveness, ranging from coined or fanciful marks at the high end of the spectrum to marks that are merely descriptive at the low end of the continuum. Coined or fanciful marks are those created solely for the purpose of serving as trademarks. Examples are EXXON and Kodak, which, as created, had no relationship to the products they represent. At the other end of the trademark distinctiveness continuum are those that are merely descriptive of the quality or characteristic of the goods or service they represent, such as Handyman for a carpenter service or Shine for a floor polish. Geographic names and surnames used as trademarks are also considered merely descriptive, and companies operating within the same location or with the same surname would be free to use them.

A classic example of the potential of a trademark being diluted by having its image tarnished was the sale of a poster reading "Enjoy Cocaine" in flowing red and white script identical to that used in labels and posters for Coca-Cola soft drinks. A court granted the soft drink company an injunction against sale of the poster.[121] Ringling Brothers' slogan The Greatest Show on Earth was found illegally diluted by a car dealer using the slogan The Greatest Used Car Show on Earth.[122]

In January 1996 the doctrine of trademark dilution became part of federal law when President Bill Clinton signed the Federal Trademark Dilution Act of 1995[123] to protect famous trademarks from subsequent uses that blur the distinctiveness of the mark or tarnish or disparage it, even in the absence of a likelihood of confusion. Before then, such protection was based on state law, which was inconsistent from state to state and not recognized in some states. Contrary to the patent and copyright arena, where federal law controls, the legislative history behind the Dilution Act specifically indicates that the Dilution Act was not meant to preempt existing state dilution statutes.[124] The Act also made U. S. law consistent with the international obligations of the United States in the trademark area.

Trademark owners successfully used the Federal Trademark Dilution Act of 1995 to stop others from using their trademarks as Internet domain names.[125] A defendant in several such cases had registered multiple domain names based on trademarks and trade names, including: aircanada.com, anaheimstadium.com, australiaopen.com, camdenyards.com, deltaairlines.com, eddiebauer.com, flydelta.com, frenchopen.com, lufthansa.com, neiman-marcus.com, panavision.com, northwestairlines.com and yankeestadium.com.

Generic Terms. A generic term — one that designates the substance or "genus" of the product — cannot be used as a trademark. Anyone is free to use words like *automobile, car, soft drink* and *computer*. Even if there were only one manufacturer of a particular product and the public associated only that manufacturer with that particular product, the name of that product would still be generic.

Some trademarks have become generic because of their use — or misuse — by the public. The King-Seeley Thermos Company, for example, originated the term "thermos" for vacuum-insulated containers during the 1920s, but the word fell into general use so that King-Seeley was unsuccessful in its attempts to prevent Aladdin Industries from referring to its vacuum-insulated products as "thermos" bottles.[126] Other examples of former trademarks that are now generic are *aspirin, cellophane* and *yo yo*.

To protect their marks from falling into generic use, trademark owners take steps — like advertisements — to educate the public that the mark should not be used in a generic sense. Companies also write warning letters to journalists and others who used trademarks incorrectly, such as using them as nouns or verbs, as in "Xerox this document" or "make a Xerox." Correct usage for

---

[120] *Hard Rock Cafe Licensing Corp. v. Pacific Graphics, Inc.*, 776 F. Supp. 1454, 1462 (W.D. Wash. 1991).

[121] *Coca-Cola Co. v. Gemini Rising, Inc.* 346 F. Supp. 1183 (E.D.N.Y. 1972).

[122] *Ringling Bros. — Barnum & Bailey Combined Shows, Inc. v. Celozzi-Ettelson Chevrolet, Inc.*, 855 F.2d 480 (7th Cir. 1988).

[123] 15 U.S.C. 1125.

[124] Susan L. Serad, "Comment: One Year After Dilution's Entry Into Federal Trademark Law," *Wake Forest Law Review* 32 (1997): 215.

[125] For a discussion of these cases and others arising out of the Act during the first year after its passage, see Serad, *id.* For information about various methods a company can utilize to curb Internet name poaching, see Stacy B. Sterling, "Comment: New Age Bandits in Cyberspace: Domain Names Held Hostage on the Internet," *Loyola of Los Angeles Entertainment Law Journal* 17 (1997): 733.

[126] *King-Seeley Thermos Co. v. Aladdin Industries*, 321 F.2d 577 (2d Cir. 1963).

trademarks is as adjectives followed by a noun: Xerox® copier, a Xerox® copy, Kleenex® tissue, Teflon® coating, Jeep® vehicle, Weed Eater® trimmer. Trademarks should be differentiated typographically from words around them by capitalization, italics, bold, quotation marks or some other special type. Registered marks should be indicated with ® (an R in a circle), and the ™ symbol should follow unregistered trademarks. Plural forms should not be used. "She uses Kleenexs" is incorrect; the correct form is "she uses Kleenex tissues." Trademarks should not take the possessive form, as in "the Jeep's windshield." Instead, "the windshield on a Jeep® sport utility vehicle" is correct.

SUMMARY

Intellectual property laws both hinder and help the mass media by providing media companies an economic incentive to create material, knowing it is protected from infringement, but at the same time such laws prevent the media from publishing material owned by others. The Copyright Act protects original works of authorship fixed in any tangible medium of expression, now known or later developed, from which they can be perceived, reproduced or otherwise communicated, either directly or with the aid of a machine or device. A key copyright principle is that expression or style, not ideas or facts, is protected.

A copyright owner has this exclusive bundle of rights that may be exercised separately or as a package: (1) to reproduce the work in copies or phonorecords, (2) to prepare derivative works, (3) to distribute copies or phonorecords, (4) to perform the work publicly, (5) to display the work publicly. The fair use doctrine and compulsory licensing are limitations on these rights.

The development of each new medium for fixing works in tangible form — photography, moving pictures, sound recordings, digital imaging — as well as each new means of reproducing or transmitting works — radio, television, photocopying machines, video tape recorders, satellites, fax machines, computer networks — has challenged lawmakers and judges to amend or interpret copyright law to accommodate the new medium. Networked computers comprising the Internet currently pose copyright concerns and questions. In addition to copyrighted works, other legally protected types of intellectual property include trademarks, service marks and trade names.

FOR ADDITIONAL READING

Branscomb, Anne Wells. *Who Owns Information?* New York: Basic Books, 1994.

Copyright Law Symposium. New York: Columbia University Press. Published annually. Award-winning research papers in program sponsored by the American Society of Composers, Authors and Publishers (ASCAP).

Office of Technology Assessment. *Finding a Balance: Computer Software, Intellectual Property and the Challenge of Technological Change.* Washington, D.C.: U.S. Congress, 1992.

Goldstein, Paul. *Copyright's Highway: From Gutenberg to the Celestial Jukebox.* New York: Hill and Wang, 1994.

Kurz, Raymund A. *Internet and the Law: Legal Fundamentals of the Internet.* Rockville, Md.: Government Institutes.

Patry, William F. *Copyright Law and Practice,* 3 Vols. Washington, D.C.: The Bureau of National Affairs, Inc., 1994.

Patterson, L. Ray and Stanley W. Lindberg. *The Nature of Copyright.* Athens, Ga.: University of Georgia Press, 1991.

Thorne, Robert and John David Vlera, eds. *Entertainment, Publishing and the Arts Handbook.* New York: Clark Boardman Callaghan (annual).

Regulating Advertising and Public Relations

By Greg Lisby

The economy — the foundation and fiber of the United States — is based upon the exchange of goods and services. In no other country does capitalism exist as such a crucial part of society. In the United States, the ability of individuals to succeed is equaled only by their corresponding ability to fail. In such a society, perception is almost as important as fact.

To complicate matters, corporate entities have many of the same rights and privileges as persons under the Constitution, especially in the area of free expression, even though they might be considered artificial persons at best.[1] Both corporations and people, for example, have the right to advertise their positions about issues they believe to be important — especially political positions. But no person — genuine or artificial — can be forced to disseminate a view with which that person disagrees. In addition, both have the right of self-promotion and the right to make money off their likenesses and activities.[2] That is, they have the right of publicity.

Historically, there were few restrictions on these marketplace rights. *Caveat emptor* — let the buyer beware — was the rule. That is not the case today; both advertisers and public relations practitioners have legal responsibilities to the public.

ADVERTISING AND PUBLIC RELATIONS LAW DEFINED

Advertising and public relations law has been described as business law with a heavy sheen of First Amendment jurisprudence. In fact, neither was considered related to the First Amendment until the middle of the twentieth century. While companies have been concerned about their reputations and the reputations of their products at least since the development of mass production, in 1942 the Supreme Court said purely commercial advertising lay outside the protection of the First Amendment.[3] The assumption was that neither commercial nor economic expression was vital to the nation's well-being. Only expression contributing to informed self-government was thought to fit that description.

Justice Harry Blackmun once wrote that a consumer's "interest in the free flow of commercial information ... may be as keen, if not keener by far, than his interest in the day's most urgent political debate."[4] Even so, commercial speech — which may be defined as expression which "propose[s] a commercial transaction"[5] — has not received the protection of political expression, but it has been

---

[1] *First National Bank of Boston v. Bellotti,* 435 U.S. 765 (1978).
[2] *Zacchini v. Scripps Howard Broadcasting Co.,* 433 U.S. 562 (1977).

[3] *Valentine v. Chrestensen,* 316 U.S. 52 (1942).
[4] *Virginia Board of Pharmacy v. Virginia Citizens Consumer Council,* 425 U.S. 748, 763 (1976).
[5] *Pittsburgh Press Co. v. Pittsburgh Commission on Human Relations,* 413 U.S. 376, 385 (1973).

recognized as a significant form of speech, and First Amendment claims are being heard more and more frequently in this area of law.

ACCEPTED TIME, PLACE AND MANNER RESTRICTIONS

No one has ever successfully contended that the First Amendment protects one's right to say anything, at any time, at any place. Consequently, time, place and manner restrictions — as long as they are content neutral — may be used to balance opposing rights. The restrictions may not single out a particular type of expression, though they may incidentally restrict or inhibit expression, and they must serve some significant governmental interest. These restrictions usually involve the maintenance of peace and quiet in a neighborhood or park, litter-free public areas, uninterrupted traffic flow and the like.

Unfortunately, the doctrine can only be applied at the most superficial levels: Does the importance of free expression outweigh the social interests furthered by the regulation being proposed? How does one, for example, determine the exact noise level at which an ordinance regulating the use of loud speakers at public events denies a speaker freedom of expression? Or, how small or unintrusive must a billboard or banner be before its message will not disrupt the accident-free flow of traffic? Clearly, answers to these and similar questions are complex and, possibly, not subject to uniformity or consistency. Answers may depend upon individual situations.

Size and Location of Expression

Public safety, aesthetics and other community concerns may take precedence when courts consider the right to communicate through commercial speech. Atlanta, for example, was the scene of a debate on this very issue in its preparation for the 1996 Summer Olympics. Corporate Olympic sponsors sought the right to erect billboards as large as ten-story buildings for the duration of the games. Opponents of the billboards argued that the signs would be unsightly and would create hazardous traffic flow. While billboard opponents prevailed, the issue was not the content of the billboards' messages but the place and manner of their expression.

Lobbying, Petitioning, Protesting

Public relations practitioners need to know the regulations gov-

erning a variety of activities, including where lobbyists must register, what lobbying activities are legally permissible, where to obtain proper permits for collecting signatures and how to stage rallies and protests.

An employer, for example, has a free speech right to communicate his views to his employees but may not disseminate an expression containing material misrepresentations of fact or prejudicial racial appeals.[6] On the other hand, many union organizing and election restrictions — permissible in a labor relations context — would be inappropriate in a political context. And in many cases permits are required prior to some expressive activities.

UNPROTECTED ADVERTISING ACTIVITIES

Commercial speech, the Supreme Court has said, has less protection under the First Amendment than political speech. In addition, the Court has also said that certain expressive activities — specifically deceptive and unfair advertising — lie wholly outside the protection of the First Amendment.

Deceptive Advertising

Advertising is considered deceptive if (1) it is likely to deceive (2) a reasonable consumer (3) with an omission or material representation of fact so significant that it has the capacity to affect a decision to purchase. For example, an advertisement's claim that a particular brand of air conditioner assures cooling on extra hot, humid days would be a material claim, since purchasing decisions might be affected by it. Similarly, the declaration that aspirin relieves pain better than other pain relievers and the proclamation that a skin cream contains aspirin are examples of material claims. But it would not be material to say in a car commercial that the car's manufacturer has its main office in a building of modern architectural design when, in fact, it is in a colonial building, because the style of the building would not be germane to a consumer's decision to buy a car. Material claims have included omissions or claims about health, safety, durability, performance, warranties, efficiency, cost and quality.

Deception may take place through express falsehoods or false implications. It might even take place through an omission, if the consumer needs the omitted information to form an impression.

An expressly false statement would be that a piece of furniture is an antique when it is simply old, that coffee is caffeine-free when it is low caffeine, that leather is genuine when it is imitation or that

---

[6] *NLRB v. Gissel Packing Co.,* 395 U.S. 575 (1969).

certain material is fireproof when it is fire resistant. False implications include statements that create a false impression by implication, such as a consumer's assumption that claims about a company's tires are backed by scientific tests when persons clad in white technicians' jackets make such statements without offering additional scientific evidence.

Advertising puffery, on the other hand — statements about subjective matters, such as taste, smell, appearance and feel — are not improper. The Federal Trade Commission assumes that consumers do not take puffery seriously, until advertising claims falsely imply material assumptions of superiority. For example, the claim that a sports car is the "sexiest" car on the road or that Bayer aspirin "works wonders" is acceptable. A claim that a television antenna was an "electronic miracle," however, was held by the FTC to go beyond acceptable puffery because the statement, taken with a series of other claims, could lead consumers to believe falsely that the antenna was generally superior to others. Puffery becomes deceptive when exaggerated claims falsely imply material assumptions of superiority.

An advertisement does not actually have to deceive someone to be improper. Taken as a whole, the advertisement only has to be likely to or have a tendency or capacity to mislead, regardless of the advertiser's intent, a substantial number of reasonable consumers — those in the target group at whom the advertisement is directed, "acting reasonably in the circumstances." On the other hand, the FTC closely examines advertising aimed at children, who are not able to understand the possibility that advertising claims may not be factually accurate. Where the deception is not fully clear, the FTC relies on expert testimony and the results of consumer surveys to assess the likelihood of deception. In addition, advertising acceptable in certain circumstances may not be proper in others. For example, an advertisement exaggerating the medicinal powers of a product might not deceive average, healthy adults but could be deemed deceptive if directed to the terminally ill who are desperately seeking solutions. Also, misleading promises of easy weight loss might not deceive the consumer of average weight but could deceive a chronically obese consumer.

A classic example of deceptive advertising is a Rapid Shave advertisement broadcast in the early 1960s. Colgate-Palmolive attempted to demonstrate that its shaving cream was so effective that it would make sandpaper shavable. The company faced problems when it attempted to demonstrate the claim in a television commercial, however.

First, the company found that sandpaper looked plain, brown and unattractive under bright television lights. Second, the paper

did not hold up well to the ingredients in the shave cream during the making of the commercial. The company solved these two problems by substituting a piece of Plexiglas with sand affixed for the demonstration. The FTC found the demonstration a fraudulent misrepresentation because the sand-covered Plexiglas had to be coated with Rapid Shave for about eighty minutes before it could be shaved. The fact that Colgate-Palmolive did not intend to deceive consumers did not matter. The stated claim — that Rapid Shave could be used to shave sandpaper — was material and could not be substantiated, said the FTC. The Supreme Court agreed that, without some form of disclosure of elapsed time, the thirty-second television commercial could not accurately depict the demonstration being attempted.[7]

All fifty states have enacted legislation that, unlike the FTC Act, prohibits unfair competition, unfair acts and practices, and allows citizens and companies to sue over deceptive advertising. Under many state laws, consumers (as well as competitors) can also sue to recover damages and attorney's fees.

Unfair Advertising.

More broadly, while a number of federal and state statutes govern advertising do's and don'ts,[8] the FTC also has the authority to define and control unfair practices in the marketplace, though primarily after the fact. While its effectiveness has varied greatly over the years as a result of differing political attitudes, the agency — which consists of five members, only three of whom may have the same political affiliation, who serve five-year terms — has the power to ban types of advertising and to order that certain advertising be altered so it is no longer improper. Required alterations may include warnings, disclosures and corrections of earlier deceptive advertising. The FTC's rulings and reports not only determine the scope of federal regulation but also set standards for stand and industry regulatory bodies.

This authority has evolved slowly. While early judicial decisions raised questions about the extent of the FTC's power over advertising, the Supreme Court in 1922 backed a broad interpretation of its ability to define false advertising as an unfair means of competi-

---

[7] *FTC v. Colgate-Palmolive,* 380 U.S. 374 (1965).

[8] These laws include the Sherman Anti-Trust Act of 1890, 15 U.S.C. 1; the Clayton Act of 1914, 15 U.S.C. 12; the Wheeler-Lea Amendment of 1938, 15 U.S.C. 53; and the Consumer Product Warranties and Federal Trade Commission Improvements Act of 1975 (also known as the Moss-Magnuson Act), 15 U.S.C. 57.

tion.[9] The Court subsequently brought advertising excesses within the FTC's power to regulate unfairness in 1937,[10] and Congress responded the following year with an amendment to the FCT Act, which allowed the agency to act to protect consumers as well as competing businesses from unfair advertising. In the 1970s, Congress authorized to the FTC to seek injunctive relief against advertising which violates federal law and later to regulate advertising affecting all commerce, not just interstate commerce.

Section 5 of the FTC Act defines "unfairness" very broadly: It is the extent to which a practice offends public policy, is immoral or unethical, or causes substantial injury to consumers or businesses.[11] The FTC has generally narrowed the focus of its unfairness inquiries to examine whether advertising practices cause substantial injury that is not outweighed by offsetting benefits to consumers or competitors who cannot reasonably avoid the injury. Thus, the concept of unfairness may most easily be seen in a company's treatment of its customers. The harm must be substantial and, more often than not, monetary, as when sellers coerce consumers into purchasing unwanted goods or services. However, the unfair treatment may not be unsubstantiated or trivial. One cereal advertisement involving naturalist Euell Gibbons was determined by the FTC to be unfair because of its potential to influence the uneducated to eat poisonous wild berries by mistake. But the commission has also found unfairness in certain promotional practices that bring with them unwarranted safety or health risks to consumers, such as the inclusion of free sample razor blades in copies of a newspaper.

PROTECTED ADVERTISING ACTIVITIES

In *Valentine v. Chrestensen,* the Court ruled in 1942 that purely commercial advertising did not enjoy First Amendment protection, a decision that has long troubled many with its emphasis on New York City's regulation of advertising handbills as litter and the lack of any separate opinions from the Court's First Amendment protectors, Justice Hugo Black and William Douglas. [12] Perhaps even more difficult to accept was the evident lack of First Amendment protection which a political protest handbill appeared to have when printed on the back of an advertisement. In 1964, the Court began to back off this absolute. In a libel case, the Court ruled that public officials could collect damages for defama-

tory criticisms of their official conduct only if they could also prove that the criticism was made with actual malice.[13]

What sometimes is overlooked is that the public official in that case was defamed in an advertisement. The Court concluded that the advertisement was tantamount to a petition for redress of grievances — a political expression — and, therefore, was entitled to First Amendment protection because it "communicated information, expressed opinion, recited grievances, protested claimed abuses, and sought financial support on behalf of a movement whose existence and objectives are matters of the highest public interest and concern."[14]

In 1975, the Court affirmed and expanded its 1964 conclusion that advertisements dealing with matters of public concern are protected. But in *Bigelow v. Virginia,*[15] a case involving advertisements for out-of-state abortion clinics, the Court still distinguished between mere commercial advertising and advertising on issues that were newsworthy or of public concern. The case came two years after *Roe v. Wade*[16] and, based on the earlier ruling, should have been no surprise. If a woman has a constitutional right to an abortion based on her right of personal privacy, it follows that she also has the right to receive information about such services. The advertisement in question, the Court held, "did more than simply propose a commercial transaction. It contained factual material of clear 'public interest.'"[17]

Commercial Speech Doctrine

The next year, in *Virginia State Board of Pharmacy v. Virginia Citizens Consumer Council,*[18] the Supreme Court established what is now known as the "commercial speech doctrine." The doctrine provides First Amendment protection for truthful advertising of legal products and services. The advertisement at issue dealt with prices of prescription drugs. The fact that "the advertiser's interest is a purely economic one," the Court said, "hardly disqualifies him from protection under the First Amendment."[19] In addition, the Court concluded, the First Amendment protection for advertising was based on the consumer's right to receive commercial information:

---

[9] *FTC v. Winstead Hosiery Co.,* 258 U.S. 483 (1922).

[10] *FTC v. Standard Educational Society,* 302 U.S. 112 (1937).

[11] 15 U.S.C. sec 45(a)(1) (1988).

[12] 316 U.S. 52 (1942).

[13] *New York Times Co. v. Sullivan,* 376 U.S. 254 (1964).

[14] *Id.* at 266.

[15] 421 U.S. 809 (1975).

[16] 412 U.S. 113 (1973).

[17] *Bigelow,* 421 U.S. at 822.

[18] 425 U.S. 748 (1976).

[19] *Id.* at 762.

Advertising, however tasteless and excessive it sometimes may seem, is nonetheless dissemination of information as to who is producing and selling what product, for what reason, and at what price. So long as we preserve a predominantly free enterprise economy, the allocation of our resources in large measure will be made through numerous private economic decisions. It is a matter of public interest that those decisions, in the aggregate, be intelligent and well informed. To this end, the free flow of commercial information is indispensable. And if it is indispensable to the proper allocation of resources in a free enterprise system, it is also indispensable to the formation of intelligent opinions as to how that system ought to be regulated or altered. Therefore, even if the First Amendment were thought to be primarily an instrument to enlighten public decision-making in a democracy, we could not say that the free flow of information does not serve that goal.[20]

By the late 1970s, the Court appeared to be applying a sort of "public interest" test to determine what commercial expression was constitutionally protected and what was not. This seems especially apparent in the Court's ruling in *First National Bank of Boston v. Bellotti*.[21] There, agreeing that corporate speech was constitutionally protected, the sharply divided Court took pains to point out that the advertisement involved — which stated the bank's position on a proposed amendment to the Massachusetts constitution — was

the type of speech indispensable to decision-making in a democracy, and this is no less true because the speech comes from a corporation rather than an individual. The inherent worth of the speech in terms of its capacity for informing the public does not depend upon the identity of its source, whether corporation ... or individual.[22]

Based upon *Virginia State Board of Pharmacy* and *First National Bank of Boston*, then, determining the extent of First Amendment protection for advertising appeared to be a simple matter of determining the extent to which a given advertisement dealt with an issue of public interest and contributed to the free flow of ideas. Thus, advertisements of political protest; for constitutionally protected rights such as abortion; for commercial price information, the public interest in which is "as keen, if not keener

by far, than [its] interest in the days most urgent political debate;"[23] and about corporate positions on election issues are constitutionally protected. By the end of the decade, and without much guidance for potential advertisers, the Court had extended constitutional protection to advertising by attorneys, to the advertising of contraceptives, to "For Sale" signs in the yards of private homes and to promotions by an electrical utility included in customers' monthly bills.[24]

The Central Hudson Test

In the last of these cases, *Central Hudson Gas & Electric Corporation v. Public Service Commission of New York*, and in an apparent attempt to provide more predictability in commercial speech law, the Court established a four-part test for determining when an advertisement may be regulated:

(1) Is the advertisement in question protected by the First Amendment? An advertisement is not protected by the First Amendment if it advertises a product or service that is not legal or if it contains false information. If the advertisement is not protected by the First Amendment, the regulation is clearly acceptable. If the advertisement is truthful, however, and is for legal products or services, the next part of the test must be applied.

(2) Does the regulation serve a legitimate or substantial government interest? (If the regulation is aimed at political expression, by comparison, the government must demonstrate a compelling interest.) This governmental interest may be in the public's health, safety or welfare, secured through its police powers. State interests could also include public morality, traffic flow and community aesthetics, among others. If the government's interest is not legitimate, any regulation is unacceptable. But if it is substantial, the third part of the test is be applied.

(3) Does the regulation directly advance the government's interest? This condition is difficult to meet, for no other reason, than it assumes advertising is effective. In *Central Hudson*, the Court concluded that there was an "immediate connection between advertising and the demand for electricity."[25] Thus, conservation of electricity could be promoted by a reduction in advertising pro-

---

[20] *Id.* at 765. Citations and references omitted.
[21] 435 U.S. 765 (1978).
[22] *Id.* at 777.

[23] *Virginia State Board of Pharmacy v. Virginia Citizens Consumer Council*, 425 U.S. 748, 763 (1976).
[24] *Bates v. State Bar of Arizona*, 433 U.S. 350 (1977), and *Zauderer v. Office of Disciplinary Counsel*, 471 U.S. 626 (1985); *Carey v. Population Services International*, 431 U.S. 678 (1977); *Linmark Associates v. Township of Willingboro*, 431 U.S. 85 (1977); *Central Hudson Gas & Electric Corp. v. Public Service Commission*, 477 U.S. 577 (1980).
[25] *Central Hudson*, 477 U.S. at 569.

moting its use — although the public service commission's regulation here did not even allow advertising promoting the efficient use of electricity. If the regulation does not directly advance the government's interest, it is unacceptable. If it does, then the final part of the test must be applied.

(4) Is the restriction of expression minimal? Is the regulation no broader than necessary to accomplish the desired result? This final part of the *Central Hudson* test was modified by the Court in 1989 to require only a reasonable fit between state interests and the regulatory methods used to protect them.[26] Thus, if the regulation is broader than necessary, it runs counter to the constitutional protection afforded advertising. If it is not broader than necessary, the regulation is constitutional and does not violate the First Amendment.

The first hint that the *Central Hudson* test could be used to restrict truthful advertising about legal activities, which were previously thought to be fully protected by the First Amendment, came six years later. In *Posadas de Puerto Rico v. Tourism Co.,*[27] the Court applied the test to a Puerto Rican statute restricting the advertising of casino gambling within the commonwealth to decrease gambling among Puerto Ricans. The Court concluded that the restrictions were a legitimate exercise of the commonwealth's police power to protect its citizens from gambling's harmful effects, including prostitution, organized crime and gambling addiction. Because the statute did not prohibit Puerto Ricans from gambling — still a lawful activity in Puerto Rico — and was the least restrictive means of accomplishing this goal, it was upheld.

Subsequently, the Court struck down bans on the distribution of free-circulation, commercial magazines from free-standing racks on public property[28] concluding that the city's interest in preventing litter did not outweigh the First Amendment principles at stake. But the same year it upheld federal legislation generally prohibiting the broadcasting of lottery advertisements while at the same time allowing the advertising of state-run lotteries by broadcasters licensed in states with such lotteries.[29] In this last case, more than ninety percent of a North Carolina broadcaster's audience was in neighboring Virginia, yet the broadcaster could not accept advertising for Virginia's lottery.

Clearly, the primary danger in the application of the *Central Hudson* test is that all advertising potentially may be regulated. Af-

ter the Court's decision in *Posadas,* some even took the position that courts should always defer to legislative advertising regulation of "vices" and other "harmful" social activities. However, during the 1995-96 term, the Court in three rulings corrected that misconception, reaffirming that the simple "labeling" of an activity as "harmful" without sufficient reason was adequate to justify the regulation of its advertising.

- In *Rubin v. Coors Brewing Co.*, the Court overturned a section of the Federal Alcohol Administration Act that prohibited brewers from displaying and publishing alcohol content on their beer labels. The government had argued that the ban was necessary to prevent "strength wars" in which brewers would seek marketplace advantaged based on the potency of their products and, in turn, could lead to increased alcoholism.[30]

- In *Florida Bar v. Went For It, Inc.,*[31] the Court upheld thirty-day limitations following an accident or disaster on direct-mail solicitations to victims or relatives by personal injury attorneys, even though both the lower federal district and circuit courts had overturned the ban, relying on an earlier Supreme Court decision. The Court concluded that the limits protected the privacy and tranquillity of victims and relatives while preventing the continued erosion of confidence in the legal profession as a whole.

- Finally, in *44 Liquormart v. Rhode Island,*[32] the Court — following its *Virginia Board of Pharmacy* decision regarding prescription drug prices — struck down a state statute that completely banned the advertising of retail liquor prices because it did not directly advance Rhode Island's asserted interest in the promotion of temperance. The justices splintered in four directions in their attempts to find a common legal rationale, however, leading some scholars to predict more instability in this area of law twenty years after the Court's decision in *Virginia Board of Pharmacy.*

This predicted uncertainty seemed to be confirmed two years later when the Court, in *Glickman v. Wileman Brothers & Elliott, Inc.,* disagreed over whether First Amendment advertising rights — and incidently the freedom from compelled speech — were even implicated, determining instead that the 1937 federal requirement that agricultural commodity producers fund generic advertising campaigns promoting their fruits was only one of ordinary business regulations affecting economic policy.[33]

---

[26] *Board of Trustees of the State University of New York v. Fox,* 492 U.S. 469 (1989).

[27] 478 U.S. 328 (1986).

[28] *El Vocero de Puerto Rico v. Puerto Rico,* 508 U.S. 147 (1993).

[29] *U.S. v. Edge Broadcasting Co.,* 509 U.S. 418 (1993).

---

[30] 514 U.S. 476 (1995).

[31] 515 U.S. 618 (1995).

[32] 517 U.S. 484 (1996).

[33] 117 S.Ct. 2130 (1997).

The Court's recent decisions have raised the question of the extent to which minors may constitutionally be shielded from certain advertising, while at the same time the advertising rights of alcohol and cigarette manufacturers, for example, be protected. Regulatory fears may not be entirely unfounded, given recent discussions between Congress and the tobacco industry over the industry's legal liability for the harm caused by its product and the Food and Drug Administration's announced intent to consider regulating nicotine in cigarettes as a drug, thereby restricting cigarette advertising as a result. It cannot be seriously argued that minors — who have fewer legal rights than adults because of their legal status as minors and are thus entitled to greater protection under the Constitution — cannot be shielded from certain advertising messages, as when the Federal Communications Commission acted at Congress' direction to limit television andvertising aimed at children, as a result of the Children's Television Act of 1990.[34] The question is not "whether" such advertising may be restricted; it certainly may be constitutionally regulated. The question is only "how" and "when."

ADVERTISING THAT MAY BE REFUSED

With very few exceptions — notably broadcast advertising for legally qualified candidates for public office, which is regulated by the Federal Communications Commission — the mass media may refuse commercial messages, if no contract has been signed. (The media are also subject to normal laws of business, such as antitrust regulations, and thus could not conspire to deny advertising space or time to someone.) As former Chief Justice Warren Burger noted, "For better or worse, editing is what editors are for; and editing is selection and choice of material."[35]

ADVERTISING THAT MUST BE REFUSED

The media must refuse advertising for illegal products and services. This rule is implicit in the first part of the *Central Hudson* test. Commercial expression, which is entitled to First Amendment protection, must itself promote lawful products and services. Thus, advertising for criminal activities or obscene materials must be refused, as must advertising that advocates unnecessary discrimination by gender in classified listing of job openings and all real estate sale or rental racial preferences in violation of the federal Fair Housing Act.[36] Even advertising the illegal uses of products that are otherwise lawful must be rejected.[37] As a voluntary aid in determining whether to accept or reject certain national advertising messages, the Council of Better Business Bureaus established the National Advertising Review Board in the 1970s as an agency to investigate grievances about national advertising.

ADMINISTRATIVE REGULATIONS

The stock market crash of 1929 ushered in a new type of American law, specifically designed to deal with the growing complexities and technical intricacies of the Twentieth Century marketplace. Administrative law is different from other types of law, because it is not based on the separation of powers, in which the legislative branch of government makes the law, the executive branch enforces the law and the judicial branch interprets the law. In developing administrative law and the accompanying administrative agencies, Congress and the states, in essence, called upon experts to administer a whole new set of rules.

Administrative Law and Administrative Agencies

The so-called "alphabet agencies" — the IRS, FDA, FCC, FAA and others — are unique in that the rules of traditional separation of powers do not apply. Each agency makes its own regulations, enforces them and provides initial judicial review. The result is that it is almost impossible to beat administrative agencies at their own game. Generally, courts defer to the expertise of these appointed specialists, except when they (1) overstep the boundaries of their authority or (2) violate their own internal procedures.

Agencies that directly affect advertising and public relations include the Federal Communications Commission, the Federal Trade Commission,[38] the Food and Drug Administration[39] and

---

[34] 47 U.S.C. sections 303a, 303b, 394. The Act limited weekday television advertising aimed at children to ten and one-half minutes per weekdays and to twelve minutes per hour of weekends. It also required the FCC to police the extent to which broadcasters met children's educational programming needs.

[35] *CBS v. Democratic National Committee,* 412 U.S. 94, 124 (1973).

[36] *Pittsburgh Press Co. v. Pittsburgh Commission on Human Relations,* 413 U.S. 376 (1973).

[37] *Hoffman Estates v. Flipside, Hoffman Estates,* 455 U.S. 489 (1982).

[38] Of recent concern to the FTC is the extent to which companies' claims of environmentally friendly products are fact-based and meet the FTC's so-called "green guidelines." See Michael C. Lasky, "PR and Legal Issues: Earth-Friendly PR Claims Must Meet FTC's 'Green' Guidelines," *O'Dwyer's PR Services Report* (February 1995): 51.

[39] Advertisements and press releases by pharmaceutical companies, for example, must be submitted to the FDA for its approval prior

the Securities and Exchange Commission. The SEC is particularly concerned with the regulation of the buying and selling of stocks and bonds and with the corporate communication surrounding that buying and selling. Its guiding principle was stated by the late President Franklin Roosevelt, following the stock market crash of 1929: "No essentially important element [may] be concealed from the buying public."[40] The purpose of the agency and the myriad of securities laws enacted in the early 1930s, the Court said, is "to substitute a philosophy of full disclosure for the philosophy of *caveat emptor* and thus to achieve a high standard of business ethics in the ... industry."[41]

Important Concepts and Definitions

While, arguably, it is impossible for a public relations practitioner to have a complete knowledge of every federal and state agency with a regulatory interest in a particular corporate or public communication, the practitioner should be aware of certain important concepts and definitions. Among them are the following:

Timely Disclosure. Companies must disclose, in a timely manner, important financial information that reveals a full and complete understanding of their fiscal condition — every "essentially important element," in Roosevelt's words. Failure or delay in doing so can be evidence of deceptive or misleading actions on the part of the company or even proof of an intent to defraud. On the other hand, the information:

... must be "available and ripe for publication" before there commences a duty to disclose. To be ripe under this requirement, the content must be verified sufficiently to permit the officers and directors to have full confidence in [its] accuracy. It also means ... that there is no valid corporate purpose which dictates the information not be disclosed. As to the verification of the data aspect, the hazards which arise from an erroneous statement are apparent, especially when it has not been carefully prepared and tested. It is equally obvious that an undue delay not in good faith in revealing facts can be deceptive, mis-

leading, or a device to defraud....[42]

Material Information or Facts. Corporate communication may not omit any "material" or significant fact or claim to the buying public, defined as reasonable and objective persons and investors making purchasing decisions. The claim need not actually influence an investor's decision to buy, nor must the investor actually lose money for the claim to be considered deceptive. The material fact must only have the capacity to affect an investor's choices. Such an omission — however inadvertent — makes the information false and misleading, according to the Securities and Exchange Commission. According to the Supreme Court:

An omitted fact is material if there is a substantial likelihood that a reasonable shareholder would consider it important in deciding how to vote.... Put another way, there must be a substantial likelihood that the disclosure of the omitted fact would have been viewed by the reasonable investor as having significantly altered the "total mix" of information available.[43]

Such extensive disclosure requirements reinforce Congress's belief that "there cannot be honest markets without honest publicity. Manipulation and dishonest practices of the marketplace thrive on mystery and secrecy."[44]

Knowingly False and Misleading Information. As in the area of advertising, corporate release of knowingly false and misleading information may be equated with fraudulent misrepresentation. In such instances, "the seller is made to assume the burden of proving lack of scienter," defined as guilty knowledge that the information is false and misleading.[45] Information may be fraudulently misrepresentative when a corporation uses "indefinite and unverifiable" terms — such as "high value" or "fair" — in its public communication. In fact, "such conclusory terms in a commercial context are reasonably understood to rest on a factual basis that justifies them as accurate, the absence of which renders them misleading." Corporate expression "should be to inform, not

---

to their placement or release.

[40] Message of the President to Congress, House of Representatives Report No. 85, 73rd Congress, 1st Session 2 (March 29, 1933).

[41] *SEC v. Capital Gaines Research Bureau*, 375 U.S. 180, 186 (1963). Those laws include the Securities Act of 1933, 15 U.S.C. 78; the Securities Exchange Act of 1934, 15 U.S.C. 78; the Public Utility Holding Company Act of 1935, 15 U.S.C. 79; the Trust Indenture Act of 1939, 15 U.S.C. 77; and the Investment Company Act of 1940, 15 U.S.C. 80.

[42] *Financial Industrial Fund v. McDonnell Douglas Corp.*, 474 F.2d 514, 519 (10th Cir. 1973).

[43] *TSC Industries v. Northway*, 426 U.S. 438, 449 (1976). The falsehood's materiality is its "natural tendency to influence, or [capacity] of influencing, the decision of the... body to which it was addressed," *Kungys v. U.S.*, 485 U.S. 759, 770 (1988).

[44] House of Representatives Report, No. 1383, 73rd Congress, 2d session 11 (1934).

[45] *Wilko v. Swan*, 346 U.S. 427, 430 (1953).

to challenge, the reader's critical wits."[46] Disclosure that is made with honesty of purpose and freedom from fraudulent intent, without the knowledge of any circumstances that would cause a reasonable individual to inquire further, is good faith disclosure.

In Connection With. Everything used in connection with the sale or purchase of securities in a manner "reasonably calculated to influence the investing public" is inappropriate and subject to SEC sanction. This would include false financial statements, deceptive corporate press releases or incomplete public communication by the corporation.

Duty to Correct. A company may have a legal responsibility to remove material errors from non-corporate reports. It must do so if it has become so involved in the preparation of the reports — projections by others outside the company — that there is "an implied representation that the information ... is true or at least in accordance with the company's views." Such involvement "is a risky activity, fraught with danger; management must navigate carefully between ... misleading stockholders and the public by implied approval of reviewed analyses and ... tipping material inside information by correcting statements which it knows to be erroneous."[47] However, there is no duty to correct erroneous reports if the company has a policy of refraining from commenting on earnings forecasts.

Mere Agent/Reasonable Investigation. A mere agent is one acting on behalf of or representing another, but acting without the insight or influence into the affairs of the employer. The time-worn attitude that public relations is simply a conduit for corporate expression is no longer workable. Public relations practitioners are not considered by the Securities and Exchange Commission and the courts to be mere publicists with no responsibility for the accuracy of corporate financial statements, although neither are they guarantors of such information. The courts require them to make fair, proper and appropriate investigations as to the accuracy of such statements.

Insider. In modern corporate law, the term "insider" is generally defined as one who has company information that is not available to the general public; that is, one who normally is involved in confidential relationships in the conduct of business. Corporate officers obviously fall into this category. Public relations practitioners, at times, also may be so classified. An insider, however, must act for personal gain in order to be in violation of the law. In addition, one has a duty to disclose information in one's possession to the public if the information in question could change the mind of an average individual making an investment decision. This tendency to change an investor's mind meets the standard of materiality discussed earlier. In a seminal case from the late 1930s, the federal courts held that the SEC could release sales, cost and gross profit data filed with the agency by the American Sumatra Tobacco Company, because the data were in the public interest, even though the release could put the company at a competitive disadvantage in the marketplace.[48] Only if disclosure would so seriously affect the company as to wreck its business would release of the information not be required.

But the mere possession of non-public market information does not necessarily require its disclosure. For example, it must be noted that one who has no connection with a company has no concomitant duty to disclose information in his or her possession.

However, under the SEC's "misappropriation theory," even someone who is not a true company insider may still be restricted as an insider would be from taking advantage of market information obtained from sources outside the company itself. The theory has been the core of some of the most highly visible insider-trading cases of the 1980s, including the prosecution of takeover specialist Ivan Boesky and junk-bond kind Michael Milken. In 1997, the Supreme Court refused to restrict the SEC's regulatory direction, reviving a federal lawsuit against a Minneapolis attorney who had been convicted of making more than $4.3 million by trading on confidential information about a planned takeover bid for Pillsbury Company, even though he had no formal connection with or legal obligation to the company or its shareholders.[49] The attorney was a partner in the firm which had been retained to represent Pillsbury's interests in the takeover offer, but did no work on the representation himself. Yet the Court concluded that he knew or should have known that the information he used had been obtained from an insider or someone working on that person's behalf. The SEC may thus prohibit actions which are not in and of themselves fraudulent if its prohibition is "reasonably designed" to prevent actions which are fraudulent, such as insider trading based on non-public information.

Reasonable Basis For Projections. There must exist a fact-based, supported basis for all business reports and projections issued by a corporation. As a rule of thumb, anything other than objectively verifiable statements of fact are presumptively misleading. The corporation, however, has no legal responsibility for in-

---

[46] *Virginia Bankshares v. Sandberg,* 501 U.S. 1083, 1097 (1991).
[47] *Elkind v. Liggett & Myers,* 635, F.2d 156, 163 (2d Cir. 1980).

[48] *American Sumatra Tobacco Corp. v. SEC.,* 110 F.2d 117 (D.C.App. 1940).
[49] *U.S. v. O'Hagan,* 117 S.Ct. 2199 (1997).

dependent reports and projections.

Mere Disbelief. Disbelief or undisclosed belief or motivation as to the reality of a situation does not require the corporate officer or public relations practitioner to disclose the information unless the disbelief is accompanied or supported by factual evidence.

BUSINESS LAW REGULATION OF PUBLIC RELATIONS

Because public relations may be defined as the explanation of business concerns, the marketing of corporate ideas and ideals, and the defense of commercial actions and transactions, a close, symbiotic relationship exists between business law and public relations law. Public relations practitioners must understand the extent to which the general laws of business also govern their field.

Letters of Agreement/Employment Contracts

Agreements and contracts spell out the responsibilities of both parties in a relationship:
- to the public relations practitioner: the terms of work to be produced, timeliness, deadlines, billing routines, the use of free-lancers through sub-contracting and other pertinent data;
- of the employer or client: the terms of supplying information, turn-arounds on review of work, and payment schedules.

These should be thoroughly understood before either side agrees.

Hold-Harmless Clauses

Letters of agreement and employment contracts should include hold harmless/duty to read or indemnification clauses. Such a clause should clearly state that the public relations practitioner shall not be held responsible for any material approved by the client or corporate officers for public dissemination that results in negative or otherwise unwanted publicity or legal action. Such a clause would generally be unenforceable if it (1) is unconscionable, (2) is a violation of public policy or (3) lacks true mutual and informed assent. A successful challenge to such clauses could arise if one party to the agreement unfairly shifts the burden of responsibility for any act of wrongdoing to the weaker party, wrongly taking advantage of that party.

Such a clause might say:

```
I hereby release and agree to hold harmless all
such persons and entities from any liability
connected with the use and results of such mate-
rial as has been approved by the corporation or
its corporate officers.
```

Another version might read:

```
The corporation agrees to indemnify and hold
harmless from and against any and all losses,
claims, damages, liabilities, and/or expenses
which [public relations practitioner's name] may
incur based upon information, data, or represen-
tations furnished by the corporation to the ex-
tent that the material was furnished, prepared,
or approved by the corporation for use by
[public relations practitioner's name].
```

In some instances, provisions might also include payment of legal costs and damages if the covered individual is sued.

No-Compete Clauses

Letters of agreement and employment contracts may also include no-compete clauses, which restrict the employment of the public relations practitioner by a company's competitors. Public policy concerns have historically and still generally disfavor restraints of trade and favor an individual's right to work. Thus, despite the individual's freedom to make a contract, no-compete clauses in employment agreements are generally unenforceable, unless four requirements are met:
- the clauses are in writing;
- the clauses are part of the contract at the initial time of employment or change in the employee's status and involve consideration or payment;
- the clauses are reeasonable in both duration (time) and space (geography); and
- the clauses are reasonably necessary to protect the business interests or activities of the employer. Reasonableness is a determination to be made by the court as a matter of law, not a factual determination for the jury.

Despite the centrality, the obvious importance of the fourth element — especially when one realizes that the employee is usually at a disadvantage both procedurally (such as, the potential for unfairness in the "process" of making the bargain) and substantively (such as, the potential for unfairness in the terms or "outcome" of the agreement) when contracting for employment — most debate focuses on the third element. The test is whether the restraint of trade is unreasonable. Is the time or geographic limitation greater than required to protect the employer's interests? Do the limitations impose an undue hardship on the employee's ability to profit from his skills? Are either limitation injurious to the public's interest, which favors free competition in the market?

The traditional disfavor in which such agreements are usually held means that courts construe them against the party — the employer—seeking to enforce them. Thus, the initial burden is on the employer to prove that the no-compete clause is reasonable, and is fairly related to and is necessary for the employer's business interests or activities. The employer is not entitled to protection against ordinary competition in the market. For example, even if a business were national in scope, an agreement not to compete anywhere in the nation would be unreasonable.

When examining covenants "not-to-compete," courts tend to apply one of three strategies: the "all-or-nothing" approach, the "blue line" method, or the "rule of reasonableness." With the "all-or-nothing" approach, if any part of the employment contract is objectionable, then it is completely unenforceable. (The legal trend has been steadily away from this tactic toward one of the two following forms of judicial modification.) With the "blue line" method, courts mark out what is objectionable in the contract, and what is left is enforceable. Using the "rule of reasonableness," courts assume that the parties to the agreement intended some type of restriction, absent any evidence of "bad faith" on the part of either party, and then modify the problematic parts of the contract as best they can to match that intent.

Confidentiality Agreements

Because public relations professionals — unlike doctors, attorneys, ministers and, in some cases, journalists — cannot claim that a legally privileged relationship exists between themselves and their clients, some corporations require agreements forbidding any sharing of information outside the organization. A typical agreement might read:

```
I understand and agree that certain corporate
information to which I have access may be confi-
dential or proprietary in nature. I will not
disclose such information to others, except as
approved by corporate officers for the purposes
of the corporation's public communication pro-
gram.
```

If there is a difficulty with these agreements, some public relations practitioners recommend involving the company's attorney, when necessary, in public relations discussions and creating a privileged relationship in that manner. Evidence that the problem of confidentiality is taken seriously in the modern business world may be found in the wording of confidentiality statements on fac-simile cover sheets:

```
The information contained in this facsimile mes-
sage may be legally privileged and contain con-
fidential information. It is intended only for
the use of the individual or entity named [in
the Recipient area] below. If you are not the
intended recipient, you are notified that any
dissemination, distribution, or copying of this
facsimile is strictly prohibited. If you have
received this facsimile in error, please notify
the sender immediately by telephone and return
the facsimile to the sender at his corporate ad-
dress via the United States Postal Service.
```

Some companies also offer to reimburse the recipient of an erroneously transmitted fax for any costs incurred in notifying and returning it to the sender.

Work-for-Hire by Independent Contractors

The Supreme Court ruled in 1989 that, unless an express agreement exists to the contrary, free-lancers own the copyright to the works they create.[50] So corporations and public relations practitioners should agree to the ownership of public relations plans or programs in specific terms.

Ownership of Proposals/Ideas

Because prospective clients can easily use part or all of a proposal after having seen it during a presentation, a statement of ownership should be included on the proposal's title page:

```
The information and ideas in this proposal were
developed by and are the property of
_____[NAME]_____. We are furnishing them solely for
the corporation's use in the selection of a pub-
lic relations and/or advertising firm. We have
an implicit agreement between the two of us that
the corporation will not make any use of these
proposals and/or ideas in any way contrary to
our interests.
```

AVOIDING LITIGATION

A few simple and practical actions can help corporations, public relations practitioners and other business communicators avoid

---

[50] *Community for Creative Non-Violence v. Reid,* 490 U.S. 730 (1989).

lawsuits.

Recording Interviews

Corporate clients should be advised to tape-record all interviews with journalists. Deliberate misquoting that materially changes the meaning of what was said can be the legal equivalent of actual malice, which is an essential element in some libel suits, and a tape recording can demonstrate the changes.[51] Tape recording is also a good policy in any antagonistic situation, although care must be taken not to violate state laws governing consensual monitoring. Some states allow recording with the consent of one party; others require the consent of both parties.

Careful Public Actions

Public relations practitioners and their corporate clients should never do or say anything they do not want disseminated by the media, especially if they are engaged in some newsworthy activity. They should remember that courts generally allow the media broad leeway in defining newsworthiness.

Consent Agreements/Release Forms

Many types of consent agreements may be necessary to effective public relations and advertising. Although releases may not be necessary in every situation, the basic rule of thumb is that if the use is commercial — if it is for purposes of trade — releases are necessary. While the following list of releases is not necessarily complete, these examples demonstrate the concerns that must be addressed in advertising and public relations. A model consent release should be in writing and contain these elements: (1) consideration or exchange of value, (2) identification of parties' names and ages, (3) a statement as to the agreement's scope and duration, (4) words binding one's representatives and (5) a statement that the agreement is the full agreement, that no promises were made not plainly stated in the release. It might also be wise to tie the agreement to one that has a purpose much broader than consent, but minimally open-ended consent/release agreements should be obtained to protect future uses of the material. Some sample consent forms follow.

---

[51] *Masson v. New Yorker*, 501 U.S. 496 (1991).

Consent to publication by print media:

On [DATE] , I,   [NAME]   , carefully reviewed (CHECK ONE): ____a transcript of an interview, ____an article, ____a photograph, or ____other (please describe) _____ involving (check one): ____me, ____my business, or ____other (please describe) _____, which is attached to this consent form. I hereby freely and without duress of any kind give my consent for the attached article, transcript, or photograph to be published as is. I have authority to give this consent on behalf of _____[NAME OF BUSINESS OR CORPORATION, IF APPLICABLE]_____ .

Consent of publication by electronic media:

On [DATE] , in the company of _____[NAME OF WITNESS]_____ , I (check as many as apply): ____listened to a tape, ____viewed a videotape, ____reviewed a transcript, or ____other (please describe)_____ of an anticipated publication involving (check one): ____me, ____my business, or ____other (please describe) _____. I hereby freely and without duress give my consent to the publication of such material as is. I have the authority to give this consent on behalf of _____[NAME OF BUSINESS OR CORPORATION, IF APPLICABLE]____ .

Conditional consent:

On [DATE , I, _____[NAME]   , was interviewed by [NAME OF JOURNALIST/PUBLIC RELATIONS PROFESSIONAL . The subject of the interview was (please describe): _____. I was informed that the results of this interview might be (check as many as apply): ____published, ____broadcast, ____other as follows: ____[DESCRIBE INTENDED PROGRAM OR MEDIA OF PUBLICATION . I hereby freely and without duress give my consent for the interview results to be published, on the express basis that such publication will be limited to the subject and to the program/media specified.

Release for photographs, films, videotapes and audiotapes:

In exchange for [AMOUNT] dollars and other good and valuable consideration I have received, the recipient of which is acknowledged hereby, I certify that I am over 21 years of age and give ____[NAME]___, his or her associates, as well as his or her employer,publisher, station, network, film company, and any other person or entity with whom he or she may contract for the use of the product covered in this release, the absolute right and permission to use without restriction -- including reproducing, copyrighting, publishing, or circulating -- any photographs or likenesses of me (whether by means of still, film, audio, or video) recording, which were taken on __[DATE]__ at _____[LOCATION]_____. I also consent to the use of any printed matter in conjunction therewith. I also give all such persons and entities the right to use such photographs, film, videotape, and/or audiotape throughout the world, as well as my name, likeness and biography, in connection with the production, exhibition, advertising, promotion, or other exploitation of the following: _____[NAME OF PROGRAM OR EXHIBITION]_____ for a period of __[NUMBER]__ years or for as long as I am an employee of _____[ORGANIZATION]_____. I hereby release and agree to hold harmless all such persons and entities from any liability connected with an accidental or intentional distortion of said photographs, film, videotape, and/or audiotape that may occur in the recording detailed above, in the subsequent processing thereof, or in its use. I hereby waive any right I may have to inspect and/or approve the finished product which results from said photographs, film, videotape, audiotape, or the use to which they are put. I understand that by signing this form I am waiving my right of privacy which might be infringed upon as a result of the publication or use of said photographs, film, videotape, and/or audiotape. I make this authorization, release and agreement on the basis of the representation by _____[NAME]_____, that the photographs, film, videotape, and/or audiotape is intended for the following purpose (please be specific): _____. I have read the above authorization, release, and agreement prior to signing it and am fully familiar with its contents. I certify that this agreement fully represents all terms and conditions and no other documents, statements, or promises have been made to me.

Of course, the parents or guardians of minors must enter into such agreements on the behalf of those minors.

In situations where photographs, film, videotape and/or audiotape are acquired from other sources and come with releases, the public relations practitioner should determine what limitations, if any, exist on those releases. It is possible that the supplier does not have a release sufficient to cover the planned use to protect the purchaser. To protect against such situations, the PR practitioner could order the items on the following conditions:

This order is placed only on the condition that the supplier has complete, fully effective, and legally enforceable releases and/or consent agreements necessary for all uses of the material ordered. By accepting this order, the supplier agrees to defend at his own expense any legal actions against the purchaser or his client, and to pay in full any sums finally awarded to any and all parties in such a lawsuit.

The bottom line is this: Whenever there is any doubt as to the origin of any material to be used in a commercial campaign, copies of all consent agreements or releases should be obtained to protect against corporate liability from improper use of the material.

Trademark/Service Marks/Copyright Restrictions

Corporations and public relations practitioners should be extremely careful when "taking off" or adapting ideas, slogans, images or logos that might be protected by trademark or copyright law. Minimally, the corporate attorney should conduct a trademark search to determine if a similar logo or company name is already in use by a company in a similar line of business. Failure to do so could expose the corporation or public relations practitioner to a lawsuit seeking to prevent the use of the logo or mark, even though it is already in use and developing business and goodwill for the company.

Off-the-Record Remarks

The rules for off-the-record remarks are difficult to understand simply because they are almost always unwritten. Indeed, each individual journalist or media organization may have its own understanding of what the so-called "rules" are. It is always best to clarify rules or expectations at the beginning of a conversation with any member of the media. Conversations are generally considered to fall into one of these categories:

- *On the record.* Every comment made by a corporate employee may be attributed to the employee through either direct quotations or paraphrases.
- *For background.* The corporate employee may be quoted directly, but his name may not be used.
- *For deep background.* The information may be used but may not be attributed to the individual.
- *Off the record.* The reporter may not use the information.

Promises of Confidentiality

A reporter's verbal promise of confidentiality is enforceable under the principle of *promissory estoppel*. It is wise in such situations to have the reporter repeat the confidentiality agreement and to use the word "promise." For this reason, corporate officers and public relations practitioners should tape record all conversations with reporters in case the promise of confidentiality is broken.

FOR ADDITIONAL READING

Lamb Robert, William Armstrong and Karolyn Morigi. *Business, Media, and the Law: The Troubled Confluence.* New York: New York University Press, 1980.

Moore, Roy, Ronald Farrar and Erik Collins. *Advertising & Public Relations Law.* Hillsdale, N.J.: Lawrence Erlbaum, 1997.

Rohrer, Daniel. *Mass Media, Freedom of Speech and Advertising.* Dubuque, Iowa: Kendall/Hunt, 1979.

Simon, Morton. *Public Relations Law.* New York: Appleton-Century-Crofts, 1969.

Stevenson, Russell. *Corporations and Information: Secrecy, Access and Disclosure.* Baltimore: Johns Hopkins University Press, 1980.

Walsh, Frank. *Public Relations and the Law.* Sarasota, Fla.: Institute for Public Relations Research and Education, 1992.

10

Broadcast Regulation

By Milagros Rivera-Sanchez

Broadcast regulation is one of the most complex areas of communication law. Essential to understanding how broadcasting came to be regulated as it is today is an understanding of its history.

THE DEVELOPMENT OF BROADCAST REGULATION

Few people involved in radio's development, which began more than one hundred years ago, foresaw its becoming a form of mass communication. Radio initially was used to communicate with ships. Only much later did it become a mass medium.

Broadcasting's Early History

Guglielmo Marconi, generally considered to be the first to send radio signals without wires, believed his "wireless radio," used for ship-to-shore and ship-to-ship radio transmissions, would be commercially successful. He competed fiercely with rival companies to retain rights to his invention. Employees of Marconi Wireless Company of America, for example, refused to recognize signals sent to shore from ships using equipment manufactured by other firms. Concern that distress signals might be ignored led Congress to adopt the Wireless Ship Act of 1910, which required large ships

to have wireless equipment and a radio operator on board. The law also made it illegal not to retransmit or answer wireless transmissions from ships. The 1910 law was the first American regulation of devices using the electromagnetic spectrum, a natural resource through which radio signals are transmitted.

When ships began using wireless equipment, many radio signals filled the spectrum. Signals would interfere with each other, so only static was heard, causing problems not only for U.S. vessels but for ships throughout the world. In an effort to deal with the problem, representatives from a number of countries met to establish certain standards of radio use. They also insisted that individual nations adopt laws requiring that the standards be followed. This agreement and one tragic event led to the United States replacing the 1910 law with the Radio Act of 1912.

The Radio Act of 1912

The tragedy was the sinking of the *Titanic*. The supposedly unsinkable passenger ship hit an iceberg in the Atlantic Ocean, and more than 1,500 people died. The irony that tied the *Titanic* tragedy to broadcast regulation was the fact that a ship only a few miles from the sinking could have saved many lives. No one on the nearby ship knew of the Titanic's desperate radio transmissions, however, because, even though the ship met the provisions of the 1910 act and possessed the required radio equipment, the radio operator had gone off duty, so there was no one to receive the *Ti-*

The author would like to thank Robert Trager, who wrote the broadcast regulation chapter for the 1998 edition of *Communication and the Law* and who allowed that chapter to become the framework for this revision.

tanic's pleas for help. While the 1910 act required radio equipment, it did not require a radio operator to be on duty twenty-four hours a day.

The *Titanic* tragedy focused public and congressional attention on radio legislation. Congress adopted the 1912 act, which, in addition to closing some of the loopholes of the 1910 act, became the first law directly affecting commercial radio. Among other provisions, it allowed the U.S. Secretary of Commerce to award licenses for radio stations and to assign the spectrum frequencies those stations would use. But there was a serious problem with the 1912 law — it did not allow the secretary to reject license applications. All the secretary could do was award a license to anyone who applied for one, if there would be no interference with another licensee's transmissions.

As commercial radio began to develop, then, the government granted and registered licenses, but could neither refuse a license to an applicant nor limit the purposes for which radio stations were used. The secretary of commerce faced other limitations as well. Station operators would unhesitatingly change the frequencies and transmission powers. An operator might even move a station to a different city. Under the 1912 statute, federal courts ruled,[1] Secretary of Commerce Herbert Hoover had no power to control these actions, and the U.S. Attorney General agreed.[2]

World War I spurred radio's development. America's war effort required the most modern and efficient radio equipment. U.S. companies built the needed manufacturing plants, but when the war ended in 1918 the military no longer needed new radio supplies. General Electric, Westinghouse, American Telegraph and Telephone and other firms turned to building and marketing radio sets for the general public, but company officials knew people would not purchase them unless radio signals could be heard without interference. In addition, by 1920 many serious broadcasters, not just hobbyists, believed radio was doomed as a public medium unless the government was able to control both the number of radio stations on the air and the frequencies used.

In an attempt to deal with the chaos on the airwaves, Hoover convened several radio conferences between 1922 and 1926 but could not convince radio station owners to cooperate with one another. At first, Congress ignored calls to adopt legislation controlling radio broadcasting. In most major cities, interference constantly interrupted radio stations' signals. Eventually, the problem became so serious that Congress cooperated.

Radio Act of 1927

Recognizing radio's importance to the public and the country's commerce, and realizing the need to control spectrum use, Congress adopted the Radio Act of 1927. The act established a five-member Federal Radio Commission, each commissioner representing a different region of the country. The FRC was given the power to grant and deny radio station licenses, assign frequencies and prevent spectrum interference, but not to censor content.

The 1927 act was important because it was the initial law giving the U.S. government, through the FRC and Congress, control over radio broadcasting to the public. The act also established definitively that the electromagnetic spectrum belonged to the public, that it was not to be privately owned. And it required the FRC to act in the "public interest, convenience or necessity," the standard still used by the Federal Communications Commission. The 1927 law did not explicitly give Congress complete jurisdiction over broadcast regulation, but the Supreme Court later interpreted it as doing so and as forbidding the states from interfering.[3] Each of these points continues to be an important element in regulating broadcasting.

Communications Act of 1934

In adopting the 1927 act, Congress expected that the FRC could be disbanded after completing its task of allocating licenses to radio stations, but it soon became apparent that somehow the federal government would need to oversee broadcasting on a continuing basis. Another problem was that the 1927 act had added yet another federal agency, the FRC, to the list of bureaucracies — including the Interstate Commerce Commission, the Department of Commerce and the Postmaster General's Office — with control over spectrum use and telephony. To continue jurisdiction over broadcasting, but also to simplify the regulatory process, Congress adopted the Federal Communications Act of 1934, establishing the Federal Communications Commission and giving it jurisdiction over "radio and wire communication service," that is, broadcasting and long distance telephone service. The 1934 act replaced the 1927 law, and the FCC superseded the FRC.

In the more than sixty years since the adoption of the act, the FCC has had to decide how to deal with satellites, cellular telephones and other new technologies that use the spectrum but which, of course, were not mentioned in the act and were not imagined by any member of Congress in 1934. Because of this, and

---

[1] *Hoover v. Intercity Radio Co.,* 286 F. 1002 (D.C. Cir. 1923); *United States v. Zenith Radio Corp.,* 12 F.2d 614 (N.D. Ill. 1926).

[2] Ops. Atty. Gen. 126(1)-(c) (1926).

[3] *Federal Radio Comm'n v. Nelson Bros.,* 289 U.S. 266 (1933).

for political reasons, there have been many suggestions to completely revise the 1934 act. Congress has adopted some major amendments, such as a new section on regulation of cable television, first added in 1984 and significantly amended in 1992. Then, in 1996, Congress adopted and President Bill Clinton signed into law major changes to the Communications Act. The Telecommunications Act of 1996 altered many rules regarding broadcasting, as well as cable, telephone service, satellite television transmission and other communications media. (Cable regulation and the Telecommunications Act are discussed in Chapter 11.)

RATIONALES FOR BROADCAST REGULATION

The First Amendment states that the government "shall make no law ... abridging the freedom of speech, or of the press...." Does that mean broadcasters are fully protected, having the same First Amendment rights as publishers of the print media? The Supreme Court has said "no," holding that various mass media may be treated differently under the First Amendment and that broadcasters' rights are not equal to those of the print media.[4]

Print v. Broadcast

When the Supreme Court began making rulings involving broadcasting, it had precedent for not treating the industry the same as the print industry. From 1915 until 1952, the Court held that motion pictures were entertainment and, therefore, not entitled to First Amendment protection.[5] As radio developed into a major mass medium, it primarily offered entertainment. By the mid-1930s, First Amendment rights essentially had been applied only to the print media, and courts found no reason to extend free speech protection to broadcasting. For example, just one year after the Supreme Court ruled in *Near v. Minnesota* [6] that a state could not stop a newspaper from printing "malicious, scandalous, and defamatory" attacks on public officials, a federal appellate court upheld the FRC in denying a radio license renewal to a church whose minister, Dr. Robert Shuler, used the station to attack government officials, labor unions and religions other than his own.[7]

Three decades later, the Supreme Court took the same approach. In 1964, a small Pennsylvania radio station carried a fifteen-minute program in which the Rev. Billy James Hargis attacked Fred J. Cook, the author of *Goldwater — Extremist on the Right.* Hargis said Cook was fired as a newspaper reporter because he made false charges against city officials, that Cook had worked for a Communist publication, had denounced former FBI chief J. Edgar Hoover and the Central Intelligence Agency, and set out to "destroy Barry Goldwater," Republican presidential candidate in 1964. When Cook learned of the broadcast, he asked the station for free time to reply under the FCC's Personal Attack Rule. The station refused. Cook complained to the FCC, which ordered the station to offer Cook time. The station appealed to the courts.

In 1969 the Supreme Court found in *Red Lion Broadcasting Co. v. FCC* that "those who are licensed stand no better than those to whom licenses are refused. A license permits broadcasting, but the licensee has no constitutional right ... to monopolize a radio frequency to the exclusion of his fellow citizens." Therefore, said the Court, the First Amendment does not prohibit "requir[ing] a broadcaster to permit answers to personal attacks occurring in the course of discussing controversial issues...."[8]

Five years later, the Supreme Court heard a case in which a newspaper refused to abide by a state statute that required the newspaper to provide free space for a candidate it had criticized. The *Miami Herald* had published an editorial highly critical of a candidate for the Florida House of Representatives. When the candidate demanded space for a response under Florida law and the newspaper refused, the candidate sued. The Supreme Court, in *Miami Herald Publishing Co. v. Tornillo,* held that it is unconstitutional for a government to force a newspaper to publish anything it chooses not to. The Court said that a "responsible press is an undoubtedly desirable goal, but press responsibility is not mandated by the Constitution and like many other virtues it cannot be legislated."[9]

The Court apparently thought of "press" as "print media," not broadcasting. *Red Lion* required a radio station to provide a right of reply, while the Court held in *Tornillo* that the same requirement could not be applied to newspapers. This does not mean broadcasters have no First Amendment rights; the Supreme Court has found that they do. The Court has also said, however, that "of all forms of communication, it is broadcasting that has received the most limited First Amendment protection."[10] Courts have

---

[4] See, e.g., *Red Lion Broadcasting Co. v. FCC,* 395 U.S. 367 (1969) (upholding limits on broadcasters' First Amendment rights).

[5] *Joseph Burstyn, Inc. v. Wilson,* 343 U.S. 495 (1952); *Mutual Film Corp. v. Industrial Comm'n of Ohio,* 236 U.S. 230 (1915).

[6] 283 U.S. 697 (1931). *Near v. Minnesota* and prior restraint are discussed in Chapter 4.

[7] *Trinity Methodist Church, South v. Federal Radio Comm'n,* 62 F.2d 850 (D.C. Cir. 1932), *cert. denied,* 288 U.S. 599 (1933).

[8] 395 U.S. at 389, 392.

[9] 418 U.S. 241, 256 (1974).

[10] *FCC v. Pacifica,* 438 U.S. 726, 748 (1978).

used several rationales for the proposition that print media have greater First Amendment rights than broadcasters.

Spectrum Scarcity

The electromagnetic spectrum is the array of energy that includes radio waves.[11] Other portions of the spectrum are identified as "infrared," "X-rays," "gamma rays" and "ultraviolet." Radio and television stations use transmitters to send radio waves to receiving antennas. Transmitters radiate several thousands or millions of radio waves per second. This is the "frequency" at which the station is broadcasting. The FCC assigns frequencies to stations and requires them to transmit only on those frequencies.

Groups of frequencies can be used only for certain types of broadcasting. FM radio stations are assigned frequencies within a certain portion of the spectrum, as are AM radio stations and UHF television stations. VHF television stations are found in three sections of the spectrum — channels 2, 3 and 4 are located in one portion, channels 5 and 6 in a second portion and channels 7 to 13 in a third part. Because of the way the federal government has allocated the spectrum for broadcasters' use, a limited number of radio and television stations can be on the air. Therefore, only a relatively few people or companies may use the spectrum for broadcasting. In addition, the spectrum belongs to the public, and broadcasters are permitted to use only limited portions of it — assigned frequencies — in limited geographic areas for several years before they must renew their licenses. So there is a spectrum scarcity: There are not enough frequencies to allow all who want to broadcast to do so. Courts have decided that Congress may impose certain obligations to the public on those fortunate enough to have broadcast licenses.

However, in most cities there are more radio and television stations than newspapers. Where, then, is the scarcity? As the courts see it, this is not simply a matter of numbers. There are so few newspapers because a newspaper is very costly to begin and operate, and advertisers and subscribers for competing newspapers are limited. This is an economic limitation, the courts say, while spectrum scarcity is a physical and technical limitation, that is, a limitation of nature. No matter how much money might be available to begin a new broadcast station, if there is no room on the spectrum — if a station cannot be added without causing signal interference with other stations — the new station may not go on the air.

Therefore, those who are awarded broadcast licenses are considered to be granted privileges. Another person or company who wants to communicate to the community by owning a broadcast station simply may not do so if no frequencies are available in the area.

The Supreme Court adopted the spectrum scarcity rationale in 1943. The Court was straightforward, stating that radio's "facilities are limited; they are not available to all who may wish to use them; the radio spectrum simply is not large enough to accommodate everybody. There is a fixed natural limitation upon the number of stations that can operate without interfering with one another."[12] The Court echoed the point twenty-six years later in *Red Lion*: "[I]t is idle to posit an unabridgeable First Amendment right to broadcast comparable to the right of every individual to speak, write, or publish."[13]

The broadcast station ownership pattern in the United States is unusual. In most countries, broadcasting is controlled and stations are owned by the government, though some private stations now exist in economically advanced countries. In the United States, nearly all commercial stations are privately owned. But because the spectrum remains in the government's hands, those who are given licenses hold portions of the spectrum in trust for the public, that is, they are public trustees. The courts have said that Congress and the FCC may require broadcasters to operate in the public interest if they are to be granted the privilege of holding a broadcast license. The Supreme Court has accepted this approach, stating in *Red Lion*:

> There is nothing in the First Amendment which prevents the Government from ... requiring a licensee to ... conduct himself as a proxy or fiduciary with obligations to present those views and voices which are representative of his community.... [T]he people as a whole retain their interest in free speech by radio and their collective right to have the medium function consistently with the ends and purposes of the First Amendment. It is the right of the viewers and listeners, not the right of the broadcasters, which is paramount.... Licenses to broadcast do not confer ownership of designated frequencies, but only the temporary privilege of using them.[14]

Four years after deciding *Red Lion*, the Court wavered on this

---

[11] For a detailed, clear explanation of broadcast technology, see F. Leslie Smith, Milan Meeske and John Wright, *Electronic Media and Government* (White Plains, N.Y.: Longman, 1995), pp. 110-142.

[12] *National Broadcasting Co. v. FCC*, 319 U.S. 190, 213 (1943).
[13] 395 U.S. at 388.
[14] *Id.* at 394.

point. The CBS television network refused to accept advertisements from the Business Executives' Move for a Vietnam Peace, which, together with the Democratic National Committee, asked the FCC to rule that broadcasters could not "refuse to sell time to responsible entities ... for comment on public issues."[15] The Commission rejected the groups' request. The Supreme Court ruled that broadcasters did not have to take any and all advertisements. *Red Lion,* which held that a radio station must give time for an individual to reply to a personal attack, and the CBS case, which held that broadcasters need not sell time for commercials about public issues, may not be as contradictory as they appear. The two decisions suggest that there is no general right for the public to have access to broadcast stations. But Congress may require access under certain circumstances, such as when a person is attacked during discussion of a controversial issue. This still leaves broadcasters less protected under the First Amendment than are the print media.

The spectrum scarcity and public trustee rationales have been attacked often as being unsupportable. By the mid-1980s, even the Supreme Court suggested that it would consider a "signal from Congress or the FCC that technological developments have advanced so far that some revision of the system of broadcast regulation may be required."[16] That is, the Court recognized that, since audiences may receive video signals from cable television, satellites, microwave transmissions and other new technologies, the scarcity of spectrum space for broadcast stations may not limit communication with the public through the electronic media. Also, technologies exist to put more stations on the AM and FM bands without causing interference. In 1983, for example, the FCC adopted a spectrum allocation for FM radio intended to add 1,000 stations nationwide.[17]

A former chair of the FCC has argued that even if there is a spectrum scarcity, all goods are scarce to some degree.[18] Newsprint is scarce and increasingly expensive, for example. Does that justify government ownership of all newspapers or limits on the First Amendment rights of newspaper publishers?

Pervasiveness

Another rationale courts use to justify differential First Amendment treatment of broadcasters is that radio and television are ubiquitous — they are heard and seen in homes, stores and in many other places, and are constantly intrusive, especially on the lives of children. Further, a listener or viewer has no idea what is being broadcast until a receiver is turned on.

Exactly that kind of confrontation was at the center of a case in which the Supreme Court noted that broadcasting is different. In *FCC v. Pacifica,*[19] a child inadvertently was exposed to indecent language when his father turned on the car's radio. The Court said that with many forms of speech — like movies or words on jackets[20] — people have a responsibility to avoid the communication; they can turn their heads, for example. But, the Court said, radio and television are omnipresent; they are intruders rather than forms of communication people invite into their lives. The Court was particularly concerned that when radio or television comes into the home children may be exposed to material their parents don't want them to see or hear. Broadcasting's intrusiveness and omnipresence make it unique among mass media, the Court said. The characteristics justify treating radio and television differently than print media under the First Amendment.

Special Impact

A few courts have added a third rationale for broadcast regulation. They suggest that radio and television have a greater impact on audiences than do print media.[21] Considering a law forbidding cigarette and small cigar advertising on television, a federal appellate court, without clearly explaining the grounds for its assertion, stated that "an ordinary habitual television watcher can avoid these commercials only by frequently leaving the room, changing the channel, or doing some other such affirmative act. It is difficult to calculate the subliminal impact of this pervasive propaganda, which may be heard even if not listened to, but it may reasonably be thought greater than the impact of the written word."[22]

[15] *Columbia Broadcasting System v. Democratic National Comm.,* 412 U.S. 94, 98 (1973).

[16] *FCC v. League of Women Voters of California,* 468 U.S. 364, 376 n.11 (1984).

[17] *Modification of FM Broadcast Station Rules to Increase the Availability of Commercial FM Broadcast Assignments,* 94 F.C.C. 2d 152 (1983).

[18] Mark Fowler and Daniel Brenner, "A Marketplace Approach to Broadcast Regulation," *Texas Law Review* 60 (1982): 207.

[19] 438 U.S. 726 (1978).

[20] *Erznoznik v. Jacksonville,* 422 U.S. 205 (1975); *Cohen v. California,* 403 U.S. 15 (1971).

[21] See, e.g., *Robinson v. American Broadcasting Co.,* 441 F.2d 1396 (6th Cir. 1971); *Banzhaf v. FCC,* 405 F.2d 1082 (D.C. Cir. 1968), *cert. denied,* 396 U.S. 842 (1969).

[22] *Banzhaf,* 405 F.2d at 1101.

THE FEDERAL COMMUNICATIONS COMMISSION

The FCC is the government agency responsible for regulating broadcasting, other spectrum uses and long-distance telephone service.

Structure of the FCC

The FCC is one of the federal government's independent agencies, similar in that respect to the Securities and Exchange Commission or the Federal Trade Commission. But the FCC cannot be considered truly independent. Congress allocates the FCC's budget in a bill that must be signed by the president. The Commission's five members are selected by the president and approved by the Senate; they serve five-year terms and can be reappointed.[23] The president decides which of the five commissioners will be chair. While the FCC is not intended to be political, only three of the five commissioners can be from the same political party, and political considerations play a part in the appointment process. In many ways, then, the FCC is imbued with politics.

The FCC employs more than 2,000 staff members in six bureaus and several offices and divisions. Of particular relevance to broadcasters are the Mass Media Bureau, which deals with broadcast networks, broadcast stations and new electronic technologies; and the Compliance and Information Bureau, which, among other duties, investigates violations of FCC technical rules.

The FCC deals with broadcast matters in two primary ways. First, when it awards licenses that allow companies to operate stations, or considers taking other actions that affect particular licensees or those who want to be licensees, it acts much as a court does. If more than one company wants a license, for example, the FCC must choose between them — it must choose a winner, the way a court might decide which party wins a civil lawsuit. Competitive license hearings and other cases dealing with individual parties are decided initially by administrative law judges within the Commission. An ALJ will hold a hearing that might look much like a trial. A losing party may appeal an ALJ's decision through the FCC to the five commissioners.

The FCC also acts much as a legislative body, adopting policies affecting an entire industry. The legislative process often begins when the commissioners consider an issue — how to define the quality or "character" a broadcast licensee must possess, for ex-

ample. FCC staff members prepare a Notice of Proposed Rule Making stating what regulations the FCC is considering adopting, changing or rescinding, and explaining the reasons behind the new regulations. When the commissioners agree on the NPRM's language, they make it public. Members of the public, although that usually means corporations and lobbying groups representing companies that may be affected by the rules, submit comments to the FCC. The Commission makes the comments public and then accepts reply comments — written arguments supporting or rebutting the initial comments. The staff and commissioners review the comments and replies, discuss the proposed rules and finally adopt a Report and Order. The regulations in the Order may be the same as in the NPRM, or they may be different, based on the public's suggestions or changes made by commissioners for other reasons. After an order is released, members of the public may ask the FCC to reconsider the decision, which the Commission may or may not do.

The FCC may impose an array of penalties to enforce its decisions, rules, regulations and policies — from a letter of reprimand inserted into a licensee's file, to a fine, to renewing a license for less than a full term, to revocation or non-renewal of a license. Short-term license renewals and non-renewals are harsh penalties, and the Commission normally prefers to impose no more than a fine, called a "forfeiture," on licensees found to have violated FCC rules. But the threat of losing a license generally keeps broadcasters in line.

Commission decisions, whether rule makings, license awards or other determinations, may be appealed to a federal appellate court. Most appeals from FCC decisions are taken to the U.S. Court of Appeals for the District of Columbia Circuit. The case may then be appealed to the Supreme Court which, of course, may grant or deny *certiorari*. An appellate court is to give deference to the FCC's interpretation of the Communications Act.[24] And when the FCC rules on a factual matter — whether a licensee lied to the Commission, for example — a court can overturn the FCC's decision only if it was "arbitrary, capricious [or] an abuse of discretion."[25]

The Public Interest Standard

In both the 1927 and the 1934 acts, Congress required the Commission to regulate broadcast licensees so that they function in

---

[23] The FCC initially had seven commissioners instead of the FRC's five, since the FCC had more responsibilities. Congress reduced the number of commissioners to five in 1982.

[24] *Chevron U.S.A., Inc. v. Natural Resources Defense Council*, 467 U.S. 837 (1984).

[25] 5 U.S.C. § 706(2)(A).

the "public interest, convenience and necessity."[26] The public interest standard, adopted from the 1890 Interstate Commerce Act, is the policy that is intended to govern Commission decisions. The law does not define the term, leaving it to the FCC and the courts to give it substance. This allows the Commission much flexibility in establishing policies and deciding cases under the Communications Act. There are several problems with this scenario. The FCC may give the words different meanings at different times, for example, depending upon its make-up. The FCC has used the standard both to adopt and later reject the same regulation, and the Commission and the courts cannot always agree on what the term means.

The "public interest" standard has been in use since the Federal Radio Commission was established. In 1928 the FRC issued a statement providing certain technical and content guidelines for radio that it believed were required to meet the public interest.[27] Later it used a 1929 case involving a dispute among three Chicago area stations to further amplify its understanding of the public interest.[28] These suggestions included ways to limit spectrum interference, provide radio signals to much of the country, limit the private use of commercial radio frequencies and provide well-rounded programming. The FRC also recommended that it would be in the public interest for stations to limit the "use of phonograph records" as program material.

In addition, the FRC applied its public interest standard to broadcast content. For example, in the 1920s Dr. John R. Brinkley aired a program called the

"medical question box," devoted to diagnosing and prescribing treatment of cases from symptoms given in letters.... Patients are not known to the doctor except by means of their letters.... The doctor usually advises that the writer of the letter is suffering from a certain ailment, and recommends the procurement from one of the members of the Brinkley Pharmaceutical Association, of one or more of Dr. Brinkley's prescriptions.... [For instance,] "Sunflower State, from Dresden Kans[as]. Probably he has gall stones. No, I don't mean that, I mean kidney stones. My advice to you is to put him on Prescription No. 80 and 50 for men, also 64. I think that he will be a whole lot better. Also

drink a lot of water."[29]

The FRC refused to renew the station's license, stating that Dr. Brinkley's programs did not serve the public interest. On appeal, the court agreed that Brinkley operated the station only to earn revenue for himself and that public health was being endangered. Brinkley argued that his First Amendment rights were being abridged, but the court found that the Commission "has merely exercised its undoubted right to take note of appellant's past conduct, which is not censorship."[30]

Similarly, the FRC refused to renew a radio station licensed to a church. When evaluating the station's renewal application, the FRC found that the Reverend Robert Shuler used his access to the airwaves to issue attacks against public officials and various religious groups. On appeal, the court upheld the FRC's decision finding that "the evidence abundantly sustains the conclusion of the Commission that the continuance of the broadcasting programs is not in the public interest.... [I]t is manifest, we think, that it is not narrowing the ordinary conception of 'public interest' in declaring his broadcasts — without facts to sustain or to justify them — not within that term."[31]

The FCC often has discussed its understanding of the public interest in its policymaking rulings affecting entire broadcast industries, but also has done so in its licensing decisions. And the interplay between the FCC and the courts also has helped define the public interest. For example, the Supreme Court agreed with the FCC that the Commission could not take into consideration any possible impact on an existing radio station's revenues when it granted a license for a new station in the same city.[32] The public interest meant being concerned with the public, not the licensee, the Court said. Three years later the Supreme Court reinforced this interpretation in *National Broadcasting Co. v. FCC*: "The 'public interest' to be served under the Communications Act is ... the interest of the listening public...."[33] The Supreme Court has held that judges have limited powers to overturn a Commission public interest determination. If the FCC balances the various interests at stake, it is up to the Commission to define the public interest.[34]

---

26 See, e.g., 47 U.S.C. §§ 302(a), 307(d), 309(a) and 316(a).

27 *Public Interest, Convenience, or Necessity,* 2 F.R.C. Ann. Rep. 166 (1928).

28 *Great Lakes Broadcasting Co.,* 3 F.R.C. Ann. Rep. 32 (1929), *rev'd on other grounds,* 37 F.2d 993 (D.C. Cir.), *cert. dismissed,* 281 U.S. 706 (1930).

29 *KFKB Broadcasting Association v. Federal Radio Commission,* 47 F.2d 670, 671 (D.C. Cir. 1931).

30 *Id.* at 672.

31 *Trinity Methodist Church, South v. Federal Radio Comm'n,* 62 F.2d 850, 852 (D.C. Cir. 1932), *cert. denied,* 288 U.S. 599 (1933).

32 *Sanders Bros. Radio Station v. FCC,* 309 U.S. 470 (1940).

33 319 U.S. 190, 216 (1943).

34 *FCC v. WNCN Listener's Guild,* 450 U.S. 582 (1981).

In 1946 the FCC attempted to give station licensees better guidance about how to operate in the public interest. A set of informal programming guidelines, known as the "Blue Book" after the color of its cover, suggested that stations broadcast nonsponsored programs, live programs originated locally and programs "devoted to public discussions."[35] The Blue Book also urged stations to limit the number of commercials and be careful of their content. Although broadcasters feared the Blue Book was an attempt by the FCC to scrutinize programming practices, the fact is that the Commission never denied the renewal of a station's license for violation of the Blue Book guidelines.[36]

In 1960 the FCC replaced the Blue Book with a formal programming statement that specified fourteen program categories as "the major elements usually necessary to meet the public interest."[37] The categories included children's, religious, educational, public affairs, agricultural, news, sports, entertainment and weather programs, and "opportunit[ies] for self-expression," "the development and use of local talent" and "service to minority groups."

After decades of protecting the public interest by imposing regulations on broadcast stations and networks, the FCC in the 1980s moved toward a marketplace approach. The Commission said that competition among stations and from other forms of electronic media would be sufficient to ensure that licensees operate in the public interest and that extensive regulation would be unnecessary.

The FCC took significant steps to deregulate radio in 1981[38] and television in 1984.[39] In these and other actions the Commission eliminated a number of programming guidelines; requirements for surveying community leaders, interest groups and individuals to ascertain programming needs and preferences; most limits on how much time could be used for commercials; complex license renewal processes; certain technical rules; and a number of more minor regulations. But the Commission left many other broadcasting rules in place.

---

[35] FCC, Public Service Responsibility of Broadcast Licensees (Mar. 7, 1946).

[36] See *Hearst Radio, Inc. (WBAL)*, 15 F.C.C. 1149 (1951).

[37] *En Banc Programming Inquiry*, 25 Fed. Reg. 7291 (1960), *aff'd*, *Suburban Broadcasters v. FCC*, 302 F.2d 191 (D.C. Cir.), *cert. denied*, 371 U.S. 821 (1962).

[38] *Deregulation of Radio*, 84 F.C.C. 2d 968 (1981), *aff'd in part, remanded in part sub nom. Office of Communication of the United Church of Christ v. FCC*, 707 F.2d 1413 (D.C. Cir. 1983).

[39] *Commercial Television Stations*, 98 F.C.C. 2d 1076 (1984).

Broadcast Networks

Most programs carried by broadcast television stations are, or once were, network shows. The same was true of radio from 1930 to 1952. A "network" distributes programs to stations, and the stations broadcast the programs. For example, NBC will send *The Tonight Show* to more than two hundred stations throughout the country, all of which receive the program the same evening, although networks send programs at several different times to accommodate the country's different time zones. That makes NBC a network, as are ABC, CBS, Fox, UPN and WBN. Most of the stations receiving the programs from the networks are known as affiliates because they have contractual obligations to carry the programming distributed by the networks. Some stations, however, are licensed to the networks and are known as O & O — owned and operated by the networks.

The FCC licenses only broadcast stations. "Broadcasting" means sending a signal intended for general reception. The signals a network sends — via satellite today, formerly by telephone wires — are meant only for the stations affiliated with the network, not for the general public. Therefore, networks do not "broadcast" and are not licensed by the FCC. Each of the major networks has licenses for several television stations it owns and operates. So in a way the FCC, which licenses those stations, has indirect control over the networks. Also, courts have allowed the FCC to set certain rules for the networks because of the networks' contractual relations with the broadcast stations over which the Commission does have jurisdiction.[40]

STATION LICENSING

In large part, the Federal Radio Commission was created to ensure that stations broadcast without interfering with other stations' signals. That responsibility continues, but today the FCC's duties extend much farther. The Communications Act of 1934 gives the FCC the authority to allocate frequencies, that is, to assign frequencies to companies that the Commission has decided may operate radio and television stations. The act requires that the FCC do this in a "fair, efficient and equitable" manner.[41]

The Commission first must decide which portions of the spectrum will be used for what purposes. How much of the spectrum will be used for satellite transmissions, or AM radio, or cellular radio, or for police and fire department purposes? Then, within each

---

[40] See, e.g., *National Broadcasting Co. v. FCC*, 319 U.S. 190 (1943).

[41] 47 U.S.C. § 303 and § 307(b).

portion of the spectrum assigned to a particular use, the FCC selects who will be given the right to use a particular frequency. The Federal Radio Commission had assigned four experimental television frequencies in 1928. The FCC established standards for television and allocated experimental television channels in the 1930s. But the Commission waited until 1941 to adopt the first nationwide television allocation plan.[42] The plan allowed interested individuals and companies to apply for permission to operate television stations in the cities to which the Commission allocated frequencies. However, U.S. involvement in World War II stopped station licensing and construction.

In 1945, the FCC assigned VHF channels to individual cities, being certain that broadcasting on a frequency — say, channel 2 — in one city did not interfere with a channel — for example, channel 3 — in the same city or in a neighboring community. Los Angeles, then, could have a station broadcasting on channel 2, but not on channel 3. Neither could a city close to Los Angeles have a station on channel 3, since its transmitter would be close enough to interfere with channel 2's broadcasting in Los Angeles.

In 1948, the FCC decided to use the portion of the spectrum it had designated "channel 1" for purposes other than VHF television. Therefore, today the VHF channels in use are 2-13; there is no frequency called "channel 1." The Commission soon recognized that basing the country's television allocations on twelve VHF frequencies, instead of UHF (ultra high frequency) with its dozens of frequencies, limited the number of stations that could be on the air. In 1948, it stopped awarding television licenses and did not resume until 1952. During that time it considered the role UHF stations should play and the technical standard to use for color television and other issues.

When the license freeze ended, the Commission established new television allocations, added seventy UHF channels and set aside certain frequencies for noncommercial television stations.[43] Congress later helped to foster UHF stations by adopting the All-Channel Receiver Act, requiring that all television sets sold in the United States allow viewers to easily tune in UHF channels.[44]

The FCC's 1997 order requiring television stations to move toward providing digital television signals will affect station allocations and is discussed in Chapter 11.

---

[42] 6 Fed. Reg. 2284 (1941).
[43] 17 Fed. Reg. 3905 (1952).
[44] 47 U.S.C. § 303(s).

Awarding Station Licenses

The Communications Act of 1934 makes it illegal to operate a radio or television station in the United States without a license from the FCC. Stations operating without license — known as pirate stations — can be subject to civil fines, court injunctions and seizures of their radio equipment. Although there have always been pirate stations, in recent years the Commission has cracked down on numerous illegal stations across the country. A key concern is that pirate stations can interfere with licensed broadcast stations and even with aircraft, police and fire communications, creating a potential for harm to public safety.

Obtaining a license begins with submitting an application to the FCC. Until recently, if an applicant sought a new station, the request would be for a construction permit, which meant permission to build the station, but the Telecommunications Act of 1996 allows the FCC to grant a broadcast license without first awarding a construction permit. The applicant must give notice to the public that the application was submitted. The application is processed by the FCC staff, and, barring objections or challenges to the application by the staff or the public, it will be approved.

Any company wanting a radio or television station license (for legal, tax and other reasons, most licensees are companies rather than individuals) first must meet a set of basic qualifications established by the Communications Act and the FCC. Whether the company is the only applicant for a license or is competing with others for the license, it is required to meet the basic criteria.

The first criterion is U.S. citizenship. The Communications Act forbids granting a broadcast station license to foreign governments or alien individuals, or their representatives, or to foreign corporations. In addition, no more than twenty percent of the stock of a corporation holding a broadcast license may be owned by foreign interests. For a corporation that is controlled by another corporation, the controlling entity may not have more than twenty-five percent of its stock owned or voted by foreign interests. In 1995 the FCC waived this last rule to allow Rupert Murdoch and his companies to continue owning Fox television stations and the Fox television network. Murdoch had changed his citizenship from Australian to American in order to own television stations in the United States. But, in fact, his Australian company, News Corporation, was the owner of the Fox properties. Because Murdoch controls News Corporation, however, and because changing Fox's ownership structure might have caused economic harm sufficient to damage the network's attempt to compete with ABC, CBS and NBC, the FCC granted the waiver, finding it was in the public interest.[45]

Second, the FCC will determine if an applicant is of good character. For example, the Commission will not award licenses to companies run or controlled by individuals who have engaged in fraudulent conduct, or who have been convicted of felonies or of violating antitrust laws involving the mass media.[46] The FCC is particularly concerned with applicants who have lied or made misrepresentations to the Commission.

Third, an applicant must have access to technical expertise sufficient to operate the station. That means having sufficiently planned for the equipment and engineering personnel needed.

Fourth, an applicant must demonstrate sufficient financial backing, through funds on hand or loan commitments, to run the station for the first three months without advertising or other income.

Fifth, most license applicants must provide a plan designed to meet the FCC's equal employment opportunity rules, which are intended to ensure that licensees act in good faith to provide employment possibilities for minorities and women.

Sixth, an applicant must show an awareness of the community's programming needs and interests. Formal ascertainment of the community's preferences, through surveys and interviews, no longer is required. Today, an applicant is permitted to use any method to determine a community's needs. And applicants must commit to offering programming to meet community needs.

The final basic criterion for license applicants is the most complex — concentration of media ownership.[47] The FCC long has acted on the assumption that the public interest is best served when many different licensees operate stations. For decades it has limited the number of stations, as well as other media outlets, a single owner can control. Although the FCC may waive its ownership limits, without a waiver there are absolute barriers to certain combinations of media ownership. Often, situations that existed when a rule was adopted or changed were allowed to continue although they would violate the rules.

These restrictions have been adopted over time, some have changed since they first were added, and the Telecommunications Act of 1996 sharply modified some ownership limits. At one time, the duopoly rule limited a licensee to only one station in a market in the same service. (AM radio, FM radio and television each is a "service.") Currently, a licensee may control only one commercial television station per market. But the Telecommunications Act of 1996 instructs the FCC to consider changing the rule and allowing one company to have licenses for one VHF and one UHF television station in each market. Only in unusual circumstances would the FCC permit ownership of two VHF television stations in the same market.

The limit on radio stations depends on the number of stations in the market:

- In communities with up to fourteen radio stations, a licensee can have no more than five radio operations, no more than three of which may be AM or FM stations, and no single licensee can control more than half of the total radio stations in a market.
- In markets with fifteen to twenty-nine radio stations, one owner may control up to six radio stations, but no more than four AM or four FM stations.
- In communities with thirty to forty-four radio stations, one owner may control up to seven radio stations, but no more than four AM or four FM stations.
- In markets with forty-five or more radio stations, one owner may control up to eight radio stations, but no more than five AM or five FM stations.

The Commission may waive any of these limitations if doing so will allow more radio stations to be on the air, but the Justice Department may question whether a company's radio station holdings violate antitrust laws, which make it illegal to attempt to monopolize a business. For example, even if a company complies with the limits on the number of stations that can be owned in a city, there may be an antitrust concern if the firm controls too much of the total radio advertising revenue in the market.

The "one-to-a-market" rule forbids owning both a commercial television station and any radio station in the same market. Under the Telecommunications Act of 1996, however, the FCC is to waive this rule in the country's fifty largest markets if the Commission finds it in the public interest to do so. The FCC also is to consider allowing television-radio ownership in smaller markets if there still would be a sufficient number of different media owners.

There also is a restriction on owning television stations throughout the country. Under the Telecommunications Act of 1996, one licensee cannot control television stations capable of reaching more than thirty-five percent of the country's households with television sets. The percentage rises somewhat if the additional stations are minority-controlled.

One company may own as many radio stations throughout the

[45] Fox Television Stations, Inc., 78 Rad. Reg. 2d (P & F) 1294 (1995).

[46] Character Qualifications in Broadcast Licensing, 5 F.C.C. Rcd. 3252 (1990); Character Qualifications in Broadcast Licensing, 102 F.C.C. 2d 1179 (1986).

[47] 47 C.F.R. § 73.3555.

country as it wants; the rules only restrict ownership within each market. In 1996, Westinghouse Electric Corporation and Infinity Broadcasting Corporation merged, forming the country's largest radio owner. In 1997, Westinghouse bought American Radio System Corporation's 98 stations and became and even larger radio licensee. Thus, it appears that the trend is for station groups to become larger and larger, which in turn raises concerns about potential anti-trust problems.

FCC rules forbid a cable system and a television station in the same community to be jointly owned. The 1996 act rescinded the statutory ban on such combinations but left the Commission's rule in place.

Finally, there cannot be common ownership of a daily newspaper and any commercial broadcast station — radio or television — in the same community. In one instance, the FCC granted temporary waivers to Fox Television, controlled by Rupert Murdoch, to purchase television stations in Boston and New York City, although Murdoch also owned a newspaper in each city. The Commission's apparent concern was that if Murdoch had to choose, he would retain ownership of the television stations, not the newspapers, and the papers might be forced to close. Congress adopted legislation effectively forcing the FCC to lift the waivers, but a federal appellate court overturned the action, holding that Congress had singled out Murdoch without "any legitimate public purpose."[48] That would not have been in the public interest, according to the court.

The Commission is discussing whether to waive the newspaper-broadcast cross-ownership ban to allow newspaper companies to own radio stations in large markets or where there are many media outlets. Under the current rules, however, the FCC would not allow the Walt Disney Co. to own a daily newspaper and radio stations in both the Detroit and Dallas-Ft. Worth metropolitan areas after Disney purchased Cap Cities/ABC in 1995. The company was required to divest either the newspaper or radio station in each city.

Congress has suggested that the Commission consider waiving the newspaper/broadcast station ban in any of the twenty-five largest markets in which there are at least thirty different broadcast licensees, and the FCC has done so several times.

Comparative Hearings

If two or more applicants for the same broadcast license meet the basic criteria, the FCC must choose among them. In 1965 the

Commission established a set of comparative standards that assist in determining which applicant will best serve the public interest,[49] but in 1993 a federal appellate court rejected one of the comparative factors the FCC had been using.[50] Since then the Commission has not begun any comparative hearings and has been considering whether to revise its comparative criteria to meet the court's objections.[51]

The factor to which the District of Columbia Circuit objected is called "integration." For nearly thirty years the Commission had said the public interest was best served if the station owner were involved in the station's day-to-day management. For several years before the court's decision invalidated this factor, many comparative hearing decisions had turned on the integration criterion. But the court held that the FCC had offered no proof that the integration of ownership and management had led to better broadcast service than absentee ownership, and therefore no evidence that using the factor was in the public interest.

Other criteria used in comparative hearings include each applicant's proposed programming and the likely reach of the station's signal. The FCC also considers an applicant's status as a minority. The Commission has acknowledged that minorities are underrepresented as station licensees. Congress has agreed and essentially ordered the FCC to increase minority ownership.[52] Thus, the Commission has given a preference to minority applicants, an approach upheld by the Supreme Court in 1990. In 1995, however, the Court issued a decision that limited the FCC's ability to grant preferences on the basis of race.[53] The Commission also has argued that women are underrepresented as station owners and, for a time, awarded a preference to female applicants. But the District of Columbia Circuit found that the FCC had not presented sufficient evidence that giving female applicants a preference helped to increase the level of programming across the country devoted, or of interest, to women and ordered the FCC to stop giving preferences to women.[54]

For more than two decades, the FCC's comparative hearing process for awarding broadcast licenses when there is more than one qualified applicant has been heavily criticized. Even the Com-

[48] *News America Pub. v. FCC,* 844 F.2d 800, 814 (D.C. Cir. 1988).

[49] *Policy Statement on Comparative Hearings,* 1 F.C.C. 2d 393 (1965).

[50] *Bechtel v. FCC,* 10 F.3d 875 (D.C. Cir. 1993); *Bechtel v. FCC,* 957 F.2d 873 (D.C. Cir. 1992), *cert. denied,* 506 U.S. 816 (1992).

[51] See, e.g., *Reexamination of the Policy Statement on Comparative Broadcast Hearings,* 9 F.C.C. Rcd. 2821 (1994).

[52] See *Metro Broadcasting, Inc. v. FCC,* 497 U.S. 547, 563 (1990).

[53] *Adarand Constructors, Inc. v. Pena,* 515 U.S. 200 (1995).

[54] *Lamprecht v FCC,* 958 F.2d 382 (D.C. Cir. 1992).

mission has criticized its own method as one that "can be described most charitably as laborious, exceedingly time consuming, expensive and often resulting in choices based on, at most, marginal differences."[55] Others have suggested that it is highly discretionary, inconsistent, unpredictable and an inadequate way to award radio and television licenses that may earn millions of dollars for those who receive them.

License Renewals

Both radio and television station licenses are awarded for eight-year periods, after which the licenses must be renewed. Until recently, competitors were allowed to challenge license renewal, forcing the station owner to compete against a challenger, and forcing the FCC to determine whether to grant renewal or award the license to the competitor. Broadcasters have long complained about this system, arguing that there would be no point in a station owner undertaking the considerable expense of improving programming, equipment and personnel, and investing money in the community if at the end of a few years that owner would have no better chance than anyone else to continue operating the station. Congress seemed to listen to these concerns.

The Telecommunications Act of 1996 requires the FCC to take a two-step approach to broadcast license renewal. First, the Commission must decide whether to renew the current license holder, without considering whether the public interest would be better served by a different licensee. The Commission must renew the license unless it finds that the broadcaster has not operated in the public interest, has committed serious violations of the Communications Act or FCC rules, or in any other way has shown a pattern of abusing the law or Commission regulations. The Commission also is to consider any comments submitted by the public to the station or the FCC about any violent programming aired by the station. The 1934 act allows the Commission to consider other comments from the public about a licensee's performance. If the FCC decides under these standards that a broadcast license should not be renewed, the Commission then will move to the second step. It will consider which new applicant should be given the license that has been taken away from the current broadcaster. While the Telecommunications Act of 1996 seems to ensure that broadcast licenses will be renewed, the FCC still may refuse to renew a license on grounds that the station owner has not operated in the public interest.

Public Involvement in Licensing

It may seem obvious that since the FCC's standard is the public interest, the public should have a voice in the Commission's decision-making process. It took a court decision, however, to require the FCC to allow public involvement. The Commission assumed it had the authority and responsibility to determine how the public interest standard applied to broadcasters. In essence, it presumed that it represented the public and, therefore, that the public need not be involved.

In 1964, a public interest group accused television station WLBT in Jackson, Mississippi, of selecting its programming based on racial bias. The FCC would not allow the group to participate in the Commission's license renewal proceeding for WLBT, but a federal appellate court held that members of the public had a right to be part of the process.[56] Then, after the FCC renewed WLBT's license, a court overturned the Commission's decision. The court said that when the public participates in FCC proceedings, it only has to draw the Commission's attention to pertinent issues; the public is not required to prove the charges are true.[57] The Commission must investigate the claims, if it decides they have credence.

Since 1966, then, members of the public have been able to participate in licensing proceedings. The FCC may set certain limits, such as allowing participation only by groups representing listeners or viewers who actually will be affected by the Commission's action. The usual method of public participation at the FCC level is the filing of a "petition to deny" the granting of a construction permit, broadcast license or license renewal. The Commission may reject the petition, or attempt to gather additional information needed to make a decision on the petition's complaint.

Another broadcast station may intervene in the licensing process also, either because it believes its signal will be degraded if the FCC grants or renews a license, or because it claims it will suffer financially. But a claim that it will lose revenues only allows a station to be involved in the license proceeding; it is not sufficient grounds for denying or not renewing a license.[58] The FCC is not required to protect other broadcasters' economic interests from competition by a new or renewed station.

---

[55] *Random Selection (Lottery)*, 4 F.C.C. Rcd. 2256 (1989).

[56] *Office of Communication of the United Church of Christ v. FCC*, 359 F.2d 994 (D.C. Cir. 1966).

[57] *Office of Communication of the United Church of Christ v. FCC*, 425 F.2d 543 (D.C. Cir. 1969).

[58] *FCC v. Sanders Bros. Radio Station*, 309 U.S. 470 (1940).

Transferring Broadcast Licenses

A broadcast station's facilities — its transmitter, compact disk players, desks and trucks — belong to the station owner and can be sold to anyone at any time. But the facilities are useless without a license allowing the new owner to broadcast. The license belongs to the federal government and is given to a licensee for a specified period of time. If the licensee — the station owner — wants to sell the station, it is unlikely anyone would purchase it without also being able to use the station's license, and that requires asking the FCC to transfer the license. Generally, the FCC will transfer a license upon request if the new licensee meets the basic criteria.

At one time, a broadcaster could not transfer a license within three years of receiving or renewing it. The purpose of the rule was to prevent trafficking in licenses, that is, obtaining a broadcast license for the sole purpose of selling the station. The restriction was repealed in 1982. Now, a broadcaster may transfer the license at any time upon permission from the FCC, with one exception: A license received through a comparative hearing process must be held for at least one year before it can be transferred. Currently, more than three-quarters of broadcast licenses are held by companies other than the ones to which the licenses first were granted.

Cost of Licenses

For seven decades, broadcasters paid essentially nothing to the federal government for their licenses. The cost of obtaining a license may be substantial, but the costs were for engineering studies and attorneys' fees to assist with the application process; the government did not charge a fee for licenses. Today, there still is no cost to obtain a license, but broadcast stations and many other users of the electromagnetic spectrum must pay regulatory fees, which for broadcasters amount to several hundred dollars to tens of thousands of dollars per year, depending on the type of service — AM, FM, VHF, UHF — and size of the market in which the station operates.[59] This is Congress's method of reimbursing the federal government for the cost of regulating spectrum users.

Licensing Reform

Awarding initial licenses for broadcast stations, or dealing with challenges to license renewals, can be a complex, expensive pro-

cess. That process is designed to ensure that the public interest is met when licenses are awarded. There are arguments, however, that the current method does not necessarily achieve its goal. In 1982 Congress gave the FCC permission to choose licensees for a number of different communication services by lottery. The Commission, then, awards some licenses — certain cellular telephone licenses, for example — by lottery, but has decided not to do so for broadcast stations. In addition, Congress has allowed the FCC to grant certain licenses by auctioning them to the highest qualified bidder, but the Commission is not permitted to auction broadcast licenses.

REGULATION OF BROADCAST PROGRAMMING

The Communications Act forbids the FCC from censoring broadcast programming, but that has not prevented the FCC and Congress from adopting a number of regulations and laws affecting broadcast content. Some broadcasters argue that these limitations amount to censorship, but courts generally have allowed content requirements and restrictions.

Formats

While most broadcast television stations offer a broad selection of programming, radio stations adopt formats that provide a relatively limited range of content. A radio station's format may be country and western music, adult-oriented albums, oldies or another sub-genre of rock, sports or news and talk. Listeners tune to a radio station because of its particular programming and may be upset if the station changes formats. This is particularly true if the format is unusual — jazz, classical music or children's programming, for example. Indeed, courts told the FCC that the public interest requires the Commission to give approval, and to allow citizens' groups to have an opportunity to express their views, before a station could change a unique format.[60]

The rulings didn't stand, however. Several years later, the Commission decided stations should be able to choose their formats without FCC approval, based upon the rationale that market forces should determine the formats of the large number of stations on the air, and the Supreme Court upheld that decision.[61] Stations now may change formats at will, no longer needing FCC

---

[59] 47 U.S.C. § 159.

[60] *Citizens Comm. to Save WEFM v. FCC,* 506 F.2d 246 (D.C. Cir. 1973); *Citizens Comm. to Preserve the Voice of the Arts in Atlanta v. FCC,* 436 F.2d 263 (D.C. Cir. 1970).

[61] *FCC v WNCN Listeners Guild,* 450 U.S. 582 (1981).

permission. The FCC believes that if a sufficient number of listeners will support a station offering a particular format, a station in the market will respond to that consumer demand.

Fairness Doctrine

Broadcasters have argued that many rules and laws affecting programming conflict with their First Amendment rights, but the fairness doctrine particularly nettled them. The FCC eliminated the doctrine in 1987, a decision that was upheld on appeal. Some public interest groups, however, continue to press Congress to codify the doctrine.

The FCC developed the fairness doctrine in a number of decisions beginning in 1949. The doctrine required broadcasters to inform their audiences about controversial issues of public importance in the stations' license areas and to present contrasting viewpoints about those issues. This was to be done in overall programming, not necessarily through any individual program.[62] The Supreme Court, in the *Red Lion* case, effectively upheld the FCC's right to impose fairness requirements. Many observers assumed that a series of amendments to section 315 in 1959 — amendments establishing certain exemptions to the definition of "use" for political broadcasting — established the fairness doctrine as law rather than FCC principle. If so, only Congress could repeal it. But if the doctrine was no more than an FCC creation, the Commission could rescind it without congressional approval.

In 1986, the U.S. Court of Appeals for the District of Columbia ruled that Congress had not adopted the fairness doctrine as part of the 1959 amendments.[63] A year earlier, the FCC had questioned whether it needed the doctrine, since the number of broadcast and other outlets available to most people for dissemination of news and opinions about controversial issues had grown significantly. In 1987, as an appellate court required,[64] the Commission considered whether the fairness doctrine abridged broadcasters' First Amendment rights and concluded that it did. On that basis, the FCC rescinded the doctrine, a decision upheld on appeal.[65]

While remnants of the fairness doctrine may remain — the Zapple, political editorial and the personal attack rules — the fairness

requirements, which had been in effect for forty years, are gone. Congress once tried to bring them back, adopting a law requiring the FCC to impose the fairness doctrine, but President Ronald Reagan vetoed the bill. Subsequent efforts to reimpose the doctrine have failed.

Indecent Programming

No form of electronic media, including broadcasting, may carry obscene material. Obscenity on radio or television is no more protected by the First Amendment than in any other mass medium (see Chapter 5). In addition to possibly violating criminal laws, broadcasters who air obscene material are subject to stiff fines for not complying with FCC rules. Broadcasters, however, are also forbidden from airing "indecent or profane" programs,[66] a restriction not placed on other mass media. While the FCC has not attempted to control profane programming, the question of indecent material has become a continuing source of controversy.

For broadcasting's first fifty years, no station was punished solely on grounds that it aired indecent material.[67] But in the 1970s, the face of radio was changing, and some stations allowed — indeed, encouraged — on-air personalities to discuss sexual topics in a joking way, often at times when children could be listening.[68] Reacting to complaints from the public, the FCC fined some stations and stated that it expected such programming to stop.[69]

Then, in 1973, the FCC was faced with what it considered an egregious example of indecent material. During a weekday mid-afternoon, a father and son driving through New York City turned on the car radio and heard on WBAI, an FM station licensed to the Pacifica Foundation, a portion of an album by comedian George Carlin. Recorded live, the twelve-minute routine was based on Carlin's list of seven words "you can't say on the public, ah, airwaves." The father complained to the FCC, and, after a hearing, the Com-

---

[62] *Editorializing by Broadcast Licensees,* 13 F.C.C. 1246 (1949).

[63] *Telecommunications Research and Action Center v. FCC,* 801 F.2d 501 (D.C. Cir. 1986), *cert. denied,* 482 U.S. 919 (1987).

[64] *Meredith Corp. v. FCC,* 809 F.2d 863 (D.C. Cir. 1987).

[65] *Syracuse Peace Council v. FCC,* 867 F.2d 654 (D.C. Cir. 1989), *cert. denied,* 493 U.S. 1019 (1990); *Arkansas AFL-CIO v. FCC,* 11 F.3d 1430 (8th Cir. 1993).

[66] 18 U.S.C. § 1464 (a provision of the United States Criminal Code); 47 U.S.C. §§ 312(a)(6), 503 (b)(1)(D).

[67] But see *Robinson v. FCC,* 334 F.2d 534 (D.C. Cir. 1964), *cert. denied,* 379 U.S. 843 (1964) (The FCC found that a disk jockey told indecent jokes on air, but did not renew the license on grounds of the station management misleading the FCC).

[68] *Sonderling Broadcasting Corp.,* 41 F.C.C. 2d 777 (1973) (for example, a caller saying, "... I used to spread [peanut butter] on my husband's privates.... [W]omen should try their favorite...," and the announcer replying, "Whipped cream, marshmallow....").

[69] See *Illinois Citizens Committee for Broadcasting v. FCC,* 515 F.2d 397 (D.C. Cir. 1974).

mission warned Pacifica that if it broadcast indecent programming again, the Commission could impose sanctions. Pacifica appealed to the Supreme Court, which upheld the Commission.[70]

The Court adopted the FCC's definition of indecent communication as words that "describe, in terms patently offensive as measured by contemporary community standards for the broadcast medium, sexual or excretory activities and organs, at times of the day where there is reasonable risk that children may be in the audience."[71] The Court recognized that the restriction on indecent programming limited broadcasters' First Amendment rights but found the restriction acceptable because (1) broadcasting is pervasive, and (2) the Carlin monologue was aired at a time children likely could be listening. Both points were important.

First, the Court assumed that people could be exposed to radio or television at any time, in any place, with little control over what they would hear or see. Because broadcasting differs in this regard from print media, which normally require a decision to purchase and a conscious effort to read, broadcasters' First Amendment rights could be narrowed. Second, since the primary concern was preventing children from being exposed to indecent programming, the FCC and Supreme Court did not hold that stations never could carry such material. Rather, they could not air indecent material when children were likely to hear or see it.

From the time of *FCC v. Pacifica Foundation* through the late 1980s, the FCC chose not to examine specific broadcast programming to determine if indecency existed, even in the face of public complaints, unless the type of words used in the Carlin recording constantly were repeated. In 1987 Congress made clear that it wanted the Commission to take action against a broader range of programming. The FCC agreed[72] and, for example, from 1987 through mid-1995, fined Infinity Broadcasting a total of $1.7 million for carrying the Howard Stern program, which included material the FCC found to be indecent.

Also, as a way to balance broadcasters' First Amendment rights and public concerns about preventing children from being exposed to indecent material, the Commission decided to encourage the channeling of indecency into periods of the broadcast day when it was unlikely many children would be in the audience.[73]

The FCC first chose 10 p.m. to 6 a.m. as a "safe harbor" during which broadcasters would be permitted to carry indecent programming, but then changed to midnight to 6 a.m. The decision was challenged by groups arguing that the Commission was censoring broadcast programming carried between 6 a.m. and midnight. A federal appellate court agreed with the FCC that it had the right to channel indecent broadcast material but held that the Commission had not sufficiently justified a particular safe harbor period.[74] Congress entered the fray by passing a law requiring the Commission to eliminate the safe harbor and make indecent programming impermissible at any time.[75] The FCC, obeying the congressional mandate, adopted such a rule, which was also challenged in court. The court ordered the FCC not to impose a 24-hour ban, but allowed the Commission to continue enforcing the safe harbor standard.[76] The FCC studied the issue further, lost another court challenge[77] and continued to battle with Congress over what a proper safe harbor should be.[78]

Under another congressional mandate, the Commission, in 1993, set the safe harbor period at midnight to 6 a.m., with the period beginning at 10 p.m. for public stations that went off the air at midnight or earlier.[79] Two years later, the District of Columbia Circuit Court ruled that (1) limitations on when indecent material could be broadcast were constitutional, (2) certain limits on airing indecent programming did not violate broadcasters' First Amendment rights, (3) a complete ban on broadcasting indecent programs would violate the First Amendment, and (4) it was not rational to distinguish between stations going off the air prior to midnight and those that did not. Therefore, the court held, the FCC should set the safe harbor at 10 p.m. to 6 a.m. for all broadcast stations if it were going to restrict indecent programming at all.[80] Currently, then, broadcasters are forbidden to air indecent material from 6 a.m. to 10 p.m.

By 1998, the FCC had issued almost fifty fines against broadcast

---

[70] *FCC v. Pacifica Foundation,* 438 U.S. 726 (1978).

[71] *Id.* at 732.

[72] *Pacifica Foundation, Inc.,* 2 F.C.C. Rcd. 2698 (1987); *The Regents of the University of California,* 2 F.C.C. Rcd. 2703 (1987); *Infinity Broadcasting Corporation of Pennsylvania,* 2 F.C.C. Rcd. 2705 (1987).

[73] *Indecency Enforcement Standards,* 62 Rad. Reg. 2d (P & F) 1218 (1987).

[74] *Action for Children's Television v. FCC,* 852 F.2d 1332 (D.C. Cir. 1988).

[75] Pub. L. 100-459, 102 Stat. 2186, § 608 (1988).

[76] *Action for Children's Television v. FCC,* No. 88-1916 (D.C. Cir. Jan. 23, 1989).

[77] *Action for Children's Television v. FCC,* 932 F.2d 1504 (D.C. Cir. 1991), *cert. denied,* 503 U.S. 913 (1992).

[78] See Public Telecommunications Act of 1992, Pub. L. 102-356, 106 Stat. 954 § 16(a) (1992); *Broadcast Indecency,* 8 F.C.C. Rcd. 704 (1993).

[79] *Broadcast Indecency,* 8 F.C.C. Rcd. 704.

[80] *Action for Children's Television v. FCC,* 58 F.3d 654 (D.C. Cir. 1995) (en banc), *cert. denied,* 116 S. Ct. 701 (1996).

stations for violation of the indecency rules. While the FCC receives hundreds of complaints against radio and television stations, the Commission has only issued one fine against a television station.[81] The rest of the fines have been issued against radio stations, mostly for broadcasts involving live shows that feature sexually graphic or suggestive discussions, lewd songs or expletives.

Children's Programming

For decades Congress and the FCC have fought with the broadcast television networks over children's programming. Early on, the battle involved excessive violence in shows children watched. Later, advocates for better children's television programming convinced Congress that there simply were not enough shows that helped children learn about themselves and their world. Congress held a number of hearings about children's television and tried to convince broadcast network executives to pay more attention to the quality of children's programs. In addition, public interest groups tried to tie license renewal to television stations offering quality children's shows.[82]

Finally, in 1990, Congress adopted a law requiring broadcast stations to provide certain types of children's programs, which essentially meant that networks and syndicators would need to supply the shows.[83] The statute also limited the amount of commercial time that could be inserted before, during and after children's programming on broadcast or cable.

The Children's Television Act requires all broadcast television stations to provide programming intended for children sixteen years old or younger that will serve their "educational and information needs."[84] The law also encourages stations to offer educational and information programming that is meant for families — adults, as well as children. Nature programming might be an example of programming that could be educational for both adults and children. Additionally, the act suggested that television stations could show their concern about children's programming in other ways. They could air announcements for children's shows on public television, for example, or they could help pay for study guides for educational and information programs.[85] The law did

not specify how much programming aimed at children would be required for a station to be in compliance. The voluntary activities, then, could help convince the FCC that a station meets the requirements.

By the mid-1990s, several FCC commissioners and some members of Congress had said that television broadcasters were not fulfilling their responsibilities under the Children's Television Act. To give the law more teeth, in 1996 the Commission adopted rules making it clear what stations would have to do. Specifically, stations were to broadcast three hours per week of programs specifically designed to serve children's intellectual/cognitive and social/emotional needs. The programs are required to be at least thirty minutes in length, regularly scheduled on a weekly basis and broadcast between 7 a.m. and 10 p.m. These rules establish what is termed "core programming," and stations' compliance with the rules is considered at license renewal.

A station that does not broadcast quite three hours of core programming can still have its license renewed by airing public service announcements, programs fewer than thirty minutes in length and programs not scheduled weekly, all of which are designed to meet children's intellectual and emotional needs and which the station persuades the FCC are equivalent to meeting the three-hour requirement. Stations not coming within either of these categories will have to convince the FCC commissioners that they deserve to have their licenses renewed.

A recent study found that stations are either meeting or exceeding the FCC's three-hour standard. But the same study found that there was a significant drop in the amount of "highly educational" programs aired by television stations in 1997. In addition, many of the networks appeared to be preempting children's shows for sports programs during the weekend. However, the FCC rules require that preempted children's shows be rescheduled.

While the programming requirements apply to broadcast television stations and not to cable systems, the Children's Television Act has commercial limits that apply to both. The act restricts advertising time before, during and after programming specifically directed at children twelve years old and younger. Commercials are limited to twelve minutes per hour during the week and ten and one-half minutes per hour on Saturdays and Sundays. These limits are prorated; a half-hour program could carry only six minutes of commercials on Thursday afternoon, for example. The FCC has fined several television stations thousands of dollars for exceeding these limits. After reviewing recent license renewal applications, the FCC found that about twenty-six percent of all television sta-

---

[81] *Grant Broadcasting System II, Inc.,* 12 F.C.C. Rcd. 8277 (1997).

[82] See *Washington Association for Television and Children v. FCC,* 712 F.2d 677 (1983).

[83] Children's Television Act, Pub. L. 101-437, 104 Stat. 996 (1990).

[84] 47 C.F.R. §§ 73.520, 73.671.

[85] *Children's Television Programming,* 6 F.C.C. Rcd. 2111 (1991);

Children's Television Programming, 6 F.C.C. Rcd. 5093 (1991).

tions have exceeded the commercial limits. In response, the FCC announced its intention to conduct unannounced audits to identify violators. The Commission also has ruled that characters in children's programs cannot appear in commercials before, during or after those programs.[86]

Some groups have called for reinstituting a family viewing hour, once suggested to television stations by the National Association of Broadcasters, an industry group. Programs shown in the hour prior to prime time and in the first hour of prime time—6-8 p.m.—were to have a reduced level of sex and violence. The standard was challenged in federal court,[87] but the NAB already had dropped its suggestion. Nevertheless, the networks voluntarily continued the family viewing hour for several more years before abandoning it in 1983.

V-Chips & Television Program Ratings

In the mid-1990s, rumblings from the public and politicians about the perceived amount of violence and sex on television rose to a roar. Congress addressed the complaints in the Telecommunications Act of 1996, which requires that, beginning in 1998, all television sets sold in the United States include a means for viewers to prevent certain programs from being seen on the sets. A microprocessor chip—called a "v-chip"—within the set will pick up an electronic signal embedded within certain television programs. The signal will indicate the program's rating. The v-chip in a set may be instructed to prevent programs rated for mature audiences, for example, from being seen on that set.

Congress encouraged the television industry to develop a rating system for television programs and required the FCC to establish a committee to do so if the networks refused, or if they failed to meet the Commission's standards for rating programs. The four major broadcast networks chose Jack Valenti, head of the Motion Picture Association of America, to chair a group devising a ratings system. The committee adopted an age-based system much like that used by movie studios and administered by the MPAA.

After mounting criticism by some members of Congress and various consumer groups that the age-based ratings did not provide parents with enough information, the television industry agreed to modify the ratings system. The new ratings system is a combination of the age-based ratings and letters that identify various types of content. For example, "V" stands for violence, "FV" for fantasy

violence, "S" for sexual material, "L" for strong language, and "D" for suggestive dialogue.

Many critics continue to question the usefulness of the program ratings. Some research studies suggest that while the ratings may be useful, their utility may be limited if broadcasters do not make an effort to display the ratings. For example, a recent study by the Kaiser Family Foundation found that more than half of 1,358 parents surveyed said they use the tv ratings system to guide their children's television viewing. On the other hand, a study by the Annenberg Public Policy Center found that seventy-five percent of children's programs that contain a lot of violence are not carrying the "FV" rating.

While the law does not require a rating to be applied to any individual program, once a program is rated the rating must be imbedded on the signal carrying the show.

Political Broadcasting

The political broadcast rules, which also apply to cable television, are found in section 315 of the Communications Act. In addition, Section 312(a)(7) of the act adds that broadcast stations, but not cable systems,[88] must provide "reasonable access" for candidates for federal offices—Congress and the presidency.

Section 315. Under section 315, once a legally qualified candidate for an elective office has used a station or cable system—has been given or sold time—all other legally qualified candidates for the same office must be given an equal opportunity. That is, candidates for the same office have the right to approximately the same amount of time during a period of the day when they are likely to be seen or heard by the same size and type of audience. Section 315 applies to legally qualified candidates running for all types of elective office—local, state or federal.

Section 312(a)(7). While the FCC has held, essentially, that the public interest requires candidates to be given access to broadcast stations, Congress made certain of that for those running for federal offices. Section 312(a)(7) of the Communications Act requires broadcast stations (the provision does not apply to cable systems) to give federal candidates "reasonable access" to radio and television audiences. The term "reasonable access" is interpreted liberally. In 1980 the Carter-Mondale Committee asked the three broadcast networks to sell it thirty minutes of time. The networks refused, and the Supreme Court upheld the FCC's decision that the refusal violated section 312(a)(7).[89] The Commission

---

[86] *Children's Television Programming,* 6 F.C.C. Rcd. 7199 (1990).

[87] *Writers Guild of America, West, Inc. v. FCC,* 609 F.2d 355 (9th Cir. 1979), *cert. denied,* 449 U.S. 824 (1980).

[88] *Political Programming Policies,* 7 F.C.C. Rcd. 4611 (1992).

[89] *CBS, Inc. v. FCC,* 453 U.S. 367 (1981).

also has stated that "reasonable access" does not mean free time for federal candidates; stations may charge at the lowest unit rate.[90]

Section 312(a)(7) guarantees that a candidate for federal office cannot be denied time on broadcast stations. Otherwise, federal candidates are subject to the provisions of section 315, just as are candidates for non-federal offices.

Legally Qualified Candidate. A legally qualified candidate, first, has announced publicly that she or he is running for an office. This means more than telling a few friends. The person must have made a widely disseminated statement. Second, the person must meet qualifications for the office — age or residency, for example. Third, the person must either (a) have qualified for a place on the ballot, usually by having a sufficient number of registered voters sign a nominating petition or being nominated by a political party, or (b) be a publicly committed write-in candidate. Independent candidates can be legally qualified, and even candidates with no reasonable chance of winning the election can insist upon equal opportunity.

A candidate claiming equal opportunity in reaction to another candidate's appearance must be running for the same office. Clearly, two candidates seeking the mayor's seat or two candidates seeking the senate seat are running for the same office. But other scenarios are not so clear. Assume two Republicans are running in a primary election for mayor, as are two Democrats. A Republican buys a minute of time on a radio station, and one of the Democrats insists on a similar purchase. Under section 315, the station need not sell time to the Democrat. The FCC has ruled that the Democrat and Republican are not running for the same "office"; the Democrat is running for the Democratic nomination, and the Republican is running for the Republican nomination. If both these candidates were to win their primary races and face each other in the general election, they would be running for the same office, and so would any third-party or independent candidates for mayor.

A station could avoid all these problems by not selling advertising time to any candidates for state and local offices, although the FCC has indicated it would frown on such action. But the requirement under section 312(a)(7) that broadcast stations offer reasonable access for federal candidates essentially means that a station must sell time to even the first candidate for a federal office asking to run an advertisement.

Use. "Using" a station or cable system, which triggers section 315 for competing candidates, happens when a candidate, the candidate's picture or the candidate's identifiable voice appears on the air. This can be a campaign commercial, or it can be an appearance on a station's cooking show with no mention of the election. There is no use if the appearance is disparaging, which would occur, for example, if the candidate's opponent used the candidate's picture in a belittling way.

In 1959, Congress amended section 315 by specifying four exemptions to the "use" rule. In these instances, even if a candidate's voice or picture is used on the air, section 315 does not apply because there has been no use under the law. Congress's intent was to be certain that section 315 did not artificially limit coverage of political campaigns and candidates. First, on-the-spot coverage of a news event will not trigger section 315. The FCC and courts have ruled that press conferences, speeches and debates among candidates generally will be considered news events, and coverage of them will not constitute a use. For example, President Jimmy Carter, running for re-election, used a press conference to attack Edward Kennedy, one of his opponents for the Democratic nomination. Kennedy demanded time to reply, but the FCC and the courts found that a press conference is a *bona fide* news event and, therefore, is an exception to section 315.

Similarly, debates among candidates are news events and, therefore, exempted from section 315 regardless of who sponsors the debates — the candidates, broadcasters or a nonpartisan group.[91] It isn't required, therefore, for all candidates for an office to be included in a debate, and those who are excluded cannot claim time under section 315.[92] In 1998, the U. S. Supreme Court said that even state-owned public television stations may exclude minor political candidates from on-air debates. The 6-3 opinion said that public stations could exercise their "journalistic discretion" as long as the exclusion of minority candidates was not based on the candidate's views.[93]

In 1996, the FCC allowed three television networks (ABC, Fox and the Public Broadcasting Service) to provide free time for the major party presidential candidates.[94] The Commission said that the candidates' appearances would be exempt from the equal opportunities requirement of section 315 as coverage of a *bona fide*

---

[90] *Kennedy for President Committee v. FCC,* 636 F.2d 417 (D.C. Cir. 1980).

[91] *League of Women Voters Educ. Fund v. FCC,* 731 F.2d 995 (D.C. Cir. 1984) (without opinion).

[92] *Johnson v. FCC,* 829 F.2d 157 (D.C. Cir. 1987).

[93] *Arkansas Educational Television Commission v. Forbes*, 118 S. Ct. 1633 (1998).

[94] *Fox Broadcasting Co., Public Broadcasting Service, and Capital Cities/ABC,* 11 F.C.C. Rcd. 11101 (1996).

news event.

Second, an appearance by a candidate on a regularly scheduled newscast is not considered a use. This could be an interview with a candidate, coverage of a candidate's campaign activities or any other appearance. Courts have interpreted this exception broadly. Candidates appearing on *The McLaughlin Group*, for example, a television program featuring discussions among panelists as well as presentations of news events, are considered to be involved in news coverage, even though the appearance was not in a typical newscast.[95]

The FCC does not interpret the broadcast exemption broadly in relation to on-air personalities who are running for office. While it may seem, for example, that a news program anchor would come under the newscast exemption if he is a political candidate, the Commission has held otherwise.[96] Congress recognized that the broadcasting of news about candidates for public office is important to viewers, so it amended section 315 to exclude appearances by candidates in newscasts. Appearing in a news story, however, and appearing on a news program as a reporter or anchor are not the same. A person presenting the news does not help the public learn more about the campaign; it simply gives that candidate an unfair opportunity to become known by voters. Therefore, a news anchor on a Sacramento station who was a candidate for town council in a nearby community had to choose between being on the air or being a candidate during the campaign period. Had he been both, the station would have been required to offer more than thirty hours of free time to other candidates for the same office to comply with the requirements of section 315.

Third, a candidate's appearance on a regularly scheduled news interview program is not a use and does not trigger section 315. Interview programs like *Meet the Press* and *Issues and Answers* are exempt. The FCC has extended the definition of a "news interview program" to include *The Today Show, Entertainment Tonight* and similar programs.[97] Even call-in talk shows can be exempt. To fall under the exemption, the program must have been regularly scheduled beginning well before the election period, and the station or cable system must control the content, format and guests.

Fourth, a candidate's appearance on a news documentary program is not a use if the appearance is incidental to the campaign. For example, a water engineer who is running for governor could be in a documentary about water conservation in the state. But a documentary about the political views of a mayoral candidate would not qualify under the exemption.

Application Time of Section 315. Section 315 applies whenever there are two or more legally qualified candidates for the same elective office. That may be only a short time before an election, or months prior to an election.

Requesting Time. Under section 315, a candidate whose opponent has used a broadcast station or cable system must ask for equal opportunity. Neither the station nor system has an obligation to notify candidates. Information about candidates who have requested time and who have appeared must be kept in public files available at stations and systems. Requests for time must be made within seven days of the appearance that triggered section 315.

Lowest Unit Rate. Under section 315, candidates purchasing time for political commercials must be charged no more than the station's or cable system's most-favored advertiser would pay. That is, whatever the rate would be for the advertiser who purchases the most minutes during the year on a station is the rate a candidate would be charged. This is true even if that minute is the only time the candidate will purchase during the entire campaign. This is called the "lowest unit rate."[98] But if the appearance triggering section 315 was free to the first candidate — a candidate appears on a local children's program only to read a story aloud — opponents may demand equivalent free time.

The lowest unit rate provision takes effect forty-five days before a primary election and sixty days before a general election. Outside those periods, stations and cable systems may charge political candidates what any other advertiser would be charged (not just their best advertiser) for a comparable purchase of advertising time.

Content of Political Commercials. Broadcast stations and cable systems cannot edit or censor political advertisements, nor can they refuse to run a candidate's commercial because they believe their audience will be offended by the message. At the same time, stations and systems are not liable for anything said or shown in political commercials. Broadcasters and cable operators cannot be sued for libel, invasion of privacy or any other tort based on material in a candidate's presentation under section

---

[95] *Telecommunications Research and Action Center,* 7 F.C.C. Rcd. 6039 (1996).

[96] *Branch v. FCC,* 824 F.2d 37 (D.C. Cir. 1987), *cert. denied,* 485 U.S. 959 (1988).

[97] See, e.g., *Paramount Pictures Corp.,* 3 F.C.C. Rcd. 245 (1988) ("Entertainment Tonight"); *Multimedia Entertainment,* 56 Rad. Reg. 2d (P & F) 143 (1984) ("Donahue").

---

[98] See *Political Programming Policies,* 7 F.C.C. Rcd. 678 (1991).

315.[99]

The general rule that political advertisements cannot be censored was severely tested in the 1990s when some candidates chose to show aborted fetuses as part of their commercials. A Georgia candidate for the U.S. House of Representatives, for example, included in a commercial depictions of "the actual surgical procedure for abortion ... [including] graphic depictions and descriptions of female genitalia, the uterus, excreted uterine fluid, dismembered fetal body parts, and aborted fetuses."[100] The FCC held that while such commercials are not indecent, stations and cable systems may decide to carry such advertisements only in the safe harbor hours used for indecent programming if they find that the commercials could be "harmful to children."[101] But a federal appellate court found that this would permit "broadcasters to take the content of a political advertisement into account" in determining whether to confine the commercial to the safe harbor period, allowing broadcasters "standardless discretion."[102] The court said that, on balance, candidates' rights as specified in sections 315 and 312(a)(7) of the Communications Act took precedence over concerns about children being exposed to possibly offensive material.

Zapple Rule. While not a part of section 315, a Commission doctrine known as the "Zapple rule" applies to political appearances.[103] Originally a part of the fairness doctrine, the Zapple rule takes effect when a candidate's supporters, but not the candidate (or the candidate's picture or voice), use a station. For example, a candidate's campaign manager might appear in a commercial supporting the candidate's election; the mere mentioning a candidate's name is not a use. Under the Zapple rule, however, the station then must offer comparable time to supporters of the candidate's opponent, but not to the opponent. The doctrine applies only to major candidates in a campaign and is subject to the same "use" exemptions as Congress adopted for section 315.

The Zapple rule, named for a congressional staff member who first brought the issue to the FCC's attention, does not apply to independent political committees, sometimes called "political ac-

tion committees." Stations and cable systems are not required to sell time to these groups. If they do sell them time, they need not do so at the lowest unit rate.

Political Editorials. Also part of the now defunct fairness doctrine, the political editorial rule requires that if a member of a station's management team, such as the general manager, delivers an editorial supporting one candidate for a public office, the station must notify that candidate's opponents and offer them free time (since the first candidate did not pay) to appear on the station. Broadcasters have been trying to have this rule repealed for over a decade, along with the personal attack rule, which is discussed later.

Ballot Issues. Section 315, the Zapple rule and the political editorial rule apply only to candidates for public offices; they do not apply to ballot issues. Supporters and opponents of such issues may purchase broadcast or cable time if they wish, but there is no requirement that such time be sold or that equal opportunities be provided.

Other Programming Requirements

The FCC has imposed on broadcasters several other rules affecting program content. When those rules have been challenged as violating broadcasters' First Amendment rights, courts have upheld them, although that may change in the future.

Personal Attacks. The personal attack rule requires action by a station carrying a personal attack on the honesty or character of an individual or group. The station must, within one week, notify the person or group of the attack; provide a tape, script or summary of the remarks, and provide free time for reply. The rule applies only if the attack is made during a discussion of a controversial issue of public importance; it does not apply to attacks on political candidates or foreign individuals or groups, nor does an attack during a news program trigger the rule.

The rule, originally part of the fairness doctrine, remains intact even though that doctrine has been rescinded. It was upheld in *Red Lion*. However, various groups, including the Radio and Television News Directors Association and the National Association of Broadcasters are pushing for the elimination of the rule. The FCC is deadlocked on whether the personal attack rule, along with the political editorials rule, should be eliminated. The RTNDA and the NAB have asked the U.S. Court of Appeals for the D. C. Circuit to treat the FCC's deadlock as a formal rejection of RTNDA's petition to abolish the rules, so the court can review the case.

Lotteries. FCC rules and federal criminal laws have long re-

---

[99] *Farmers Educational & Cooperative Union of America v. WDAY,* 360 U.S. 525 (1959).

[100] *Gillette Communications of Atlanta v. Becker,* 807 F. Supp. 757 (N.D. Ga. 1992) (finding the commercial to be indecent), *dismissed without opinion and remanded,* 5 F.3d 1500 (11th Cir. 1993).

[101] Section 312(a)(7) of the Communications Act, 9 FCC Rcd. 7638 (1994) (disagreeing with the *Gillett* decision that such commercials are indecent).

[102] *Becker v. FCC,* 95 F.3d 75, 81 (D.C. Cir. 1996).

[103] *Letter to Nicholas Zapple,* 23 F.C.C. 2d 707 (1970).

stricted the information cable systems and broadcasters may carry about lotteries, except for state-run lotteries in states where the systems or stations were located or in neighboring states. Congress changed all that in 1990.[104]

A lottery is a contest that has a prize of more than token value, uses chance rather than skill to determine winners and requires some form of consideration — like the purchase of a ticket — to enter.

Broadcasters and cable operators may carry information about certain lotteries. As before, they can provide facts about state lotteries if the station or system is located in a state that has a lottery. They may also carry news or advertisements for gaming conducted by Native American tribes under federal laws allowing such gambling. And they may provide information about a lottery legal in the state where it is conducted and that is offered by a governmental or nonprofit organization or is sponsored by a person or company not primarily in the business of sponsoring lotteries.[105] Thus, reports or advertisements for bingo games at churches or a cereal company giving away an automobile are acceptable if permitted by law. Stations and cable systems cannot carry information or advertisements for gambling casinos or sports betting.

Two federal appellate courts have come to opposite conclusions on the constitutionality of the restriction on broadcasters carrying lottery advertisements. In 1996, the Fifth Circuit found that the law does not abridge broadcasters' First Amendment rights.[106] The court found the government had an interest in reducing "public participation in commercial gambling" and the social ills that stem from that gambling. It said that the law furthered that interest in a reasonable way.

The Ninth Circuit took a different approach.[107] It said that if the government's goal was to minimize problems caused by people engaging in commercial gambling, the law at issue did a poor job. According to the court, the government still allows advertising of lotteries by not-for-profit groups, governmental organizations and Native American tribes. Also, the court said that the government failed to show that reducing advertising for casino gambling would reduce the number of people who gamble at casinos.

While the decisions are in obvious conflict, the Fifth Circuit's

decision is void because the Supreme Court ordered the court to reconsider its holding based on *44 Liquormart v. Rhode Island*.[108] In *44 Liquormart*, the Court said the government must present evidence that limiting advertising will further the government's interest. The Fifth Circuit will decide whether to reinstate its 1995 decision or to hold that the government did not present evidence sufficient to meet the *44 Liquormart* standard.

Sponsorship Identification. Broadcasters and cable operators must identify clearly any individual or group providing money, or anything else of value, in return for the dissemination of a message. The purpose of the rule is to ensure that viewers and listeners will not confuse paid advertisements with entertainment or news programs. If the sponsor is obvious — a cereal, a laundry detergent, a fast food restaurant — the requirement is met. Other messages are not so clearly identifiable. If, for example, a local company provides funds for a "Clean Up The Parks" advertising campaign, those ads must carry the company's name as a sponsor.

Hoaxes And News Distortion. The FCC prohibits the broadcasting of hoaxes. Under the regulation, a hoax occurs when a station knowingly broadcasts false reports of crimes or catastrophes that "directly cause" foreseeable "immediate, substantial and actual public harm."[109]

WALE-AM radio in Providence, Rhode Island, perpetuated a hoax in 1991 when the news director announced over the air that a WALE talk show host had been "shot in the head" while outside the station's studio. About ten minutes later, the station stated that the "shooting" had been a dramatization. Before the second announcement, several police officers rushed to the scene, as did several members of the media. WALE apologized to the media and offered to repay the Providence Police Department for any costs resulting from the hoax. The FCC admonished the station's owner, citing the Commission's policy "requiring licensees to program their stations in the public interest." [110]

The Commission also has a policy against news distortion. One example of distortion occurred when a Chicago television station had a group of people stage a gathering at which marijuana was smoked in order to film a "pot party." The FCC expressed its concern about manufacturing news but did not threaten action against the station.[111] In another instance, the CBS documentary "Hunger in America" showed a child said to be suffering from mal-

---

[104] 18 U.S.C. § 1307.

[105] *United States v. Edge Broadcasting Co.,* 509 U.S. 418 (1993).

[106] *Greater New Orleans Broadcasting Association v. United States,* 69 F.3d 1296 (5th Cir. 1995), *vacated and remanded,* 117 S. Ct. 39 (1996).

[107] *Valley Broadcasting Co. v. United States,* 107 F.3d 1328 (9th Cir. 1997).

[108] 116 S.Ct. 1495 (1996).

[109] *Broadcast Hoaxes,* 7 F.C.C. Rcd. 4106 (1992).

[110] *Letter to WALE-AM,* 7 F.C.C. Rcd. 2345 (1992).

[111] *WBBM-TV,* 18 F.C.C. 2d 124 (1969).

nutrition but who was afflicted with a different illness.[112] The commission took no action against CBS but used the case to establish a policy forbidding intentional news distortion. The Commission, however, distinguishes deliberate distortion from a mistake or negligent reporting.

Cigarette Advertising. Concerned with the costs to public health caused by cigarette smoking, Congress made it "unlawful to advertise cigarettes on any medium of electronic communication" after January 1, 1971.[113] The law was upheld despite a challenge based on broadcasters' First Amendment rights.[114]

Distilled Spirits Advertising. A more recent controversy arose when, in 1997, a television station aired an advertisement for *Seagrams.* The ad represented a departure from a four-decade long, self-imposed ban of hard liquor advertising on television. While few stations have agreed to carry the ads, Congress and the FCC became concerned that the distilled spirits industry was going to begin advertising on television on a regular basis. The FCC, along with some members of Congress, began to discuss whether there should be a statutory ban on such ads. While the ban on cigarette advertising provides a precedent for a potential ban on distilled spirits on television, the current issue is complicated by the fact that beer and wine ads appear regularly on television. Thus, the issue then becomes whether the government can constitutionally ban the advertising of some types of alcohol products on television — such as distilled spirits — while allowing others — such as beer and wine.

Prime Time Access and "Fin-Syn" Rules

The FCC's rescission of two rules affecting programming has broadened the networks' roles in television program production. Both the prime time access rule and the financial interest and syndication rules — called "fin-syn rules" — had restricted the amount of programming that the broadcast networks could produce, own and syndicate. When the rules were in place, most shows carried by the networks were produced by Hollywood movie studios and other companies independent of the television networks. This began to change in the 1990s.

The prime time access rule limited the amount of network programming commercial television stations owned by or affiliated with a broadcast television network and located in the country's fifty largest markets could carry. The purpose was to limit the networks' control of television programming and encourage stations to carry children's and public affairs shows in the hour that could not be used for network programming. Instead, most stations carried independently produced game and talk shows and tabloid-style news programs in the extra hour, known as the "access" period. In 1995, the FCC rescinded the rule, based on the development of three new networks — Fox, Paramount and Warner Brothers — the growth of independent television stations and the number of new outlets for non-network programs, including cable television, satellite services and wireless cable.[115]

Financial interest and syndication rules were adopted in 1970 to limit broadcast networks' control over television programming. Under the fin-syn rules, broadcast television networks could not own any financial interest in most programs they carried. In particular, they were not allowed to sell programs as re-runs after the shows no longer were on a network's schedule. The FCC then rescinded the rules, and they were no longer in effect by late 1995.

In addition, certain agreements the networks signed with the federal government under court supervision (consent decrees), which also limited the amount of programming the broadcast television networks could produce, have ended. With the consent decrees, the fin-syn rules and the PTAR gone, networks now have much more freedom to produce, own and syndicate the programs they carry.

NONCOMMERCIAL BROADCASTING

Certain parts of the broadcast spectrum are set aside for use by noncommercial stations. Radio broadcasting was using the AM band before any government agency could consider whether to reserve frequency assignments for noncommercial uses. The FCC, however, was able to set aside portions of the FM band and reserve certain television frequencies for use by nonprofit organizations, usually educational institutions and state governments, but also religious groups. The Commission recognized that some educational institutions might be tempted to sell their stations to commercial broadcasters, in part because of the high costs of keeping a station on the air, unless certain frequencies were reserved only for nonprofit, educational use.

In 1967, Congress aided noncommercial broadcasting by adopting the Public Broadcasting Act, which established the Corporation for Public Broadcasting, an agency through which federal government and other funding is used to produce programming for

[112] *Hunger in America,* 20 F.C.C. 2d 151 (1969).

[113] 15 U.S.C. sec. 1335.

[114] *Capital Broadcasting Co. v. Mitchell,* 333 F. Supp. 582 (D.C. 1971), *aff'd without opinion,* 405 U.S. 1000 (1972).

[115] *Prime Time Access Rule,* 11 F.C.C. Rcd. 546 (1995).

noncommercial stations. The FCC has no jurisdiction to enforce any provisions of the Public Broadcasting Act,[116] such as that requiring "strict adherence to objectivity and balance in all programs or series of programs of a controversial nature"[117]

One section of the act insisting on objectivity and another forbidding noncommercial stations from supporting political candidates raise questions of First Amendment protection for public stations. The Supreme Court rejected the provision forbidding public stations from supporting political candidates and the Public Broadcasting Act's ban on noncommercial stations editorializing. The Court recognized "the substantial abridgment of important journalistic freedoms which the First Amendment jealously protects" even for public stations.[118]

Most public stations receive federal and possibly state funds, and many are owned by government agencies. The tension between the public nature of noncommercial stations and First Amendment freedoms was reflected in the "Death of a Princess" case. The docu-drama, intended for showing on public television, portrayed the execution in Saudi Arabia of a woman and her lover accused of adultery. There had been "strong ... objections by the government of Saudi Arabia" to broadcasting the program, and several public television stations decided not to carry it. Viewers took government-owned stations in Alabama and Houston, Texas, to court, hoping to force them to broadcast the program.[119] In part, the suits claimed that the public stations were arms of the government and were engaging in censorship, as well as violating viewers' First Amendment rights. A federal appellate court found that, as licensees under the Communications Act, the stations were permitted to use their editorial judgment in selecting what programs to carry.[120]

EQUAL EMPLOYMENT OPPORTUNITIES

The FCC, in conjunction with the Equal Employment Opportunity Commission, a federal agency established in 1964, requires that broadcasters not discriminate in hiring, promoting or firing on the basis of race, gender, religion, color or national origin. While the EEOC is expected to notify the FCC of any discrimination complaints filed against broadcast licensees, the FCC also enforces its own equal employment rules.[121]

Generally, broadcasters are required to establish procedures to ensure nondiscrimination and to notify employees and employee groups of these procedures. Licensees are to establish requirements for each job category, such as general manager and sales manager, and be certain that all employees are aware of job openings and qualifications to apply for them. Broadcasters are to publicize employment opportunities at their stations by informing minority organizations and organizations for women. Stations are to assess their efforts to recruit, hire and promote minorities and women, and remedy any shortcomings in their equal opportunity hiring. Licensees also must file an equal opportunity report annually with the FCC and place in their public inspection files a number of documents relating to their employment practices.

The Commission has proposed simplifying its EEO rules and reporting requirements in some ways, while retaining its goals of increasing employment of minorities and women in broadcasting.[122] However, in 1998 the EEO rules suffered a major setback when Court of Appeals for the D.C. Circuit declared them unconstitutional.[123] Reviewing sanctions the FCC imposed on a Missouri station, the court found that the rules were not narrowly tailored. The FCC argued that its EEO regulations were aimed at fostering "diverse programming," but the court said that such an interest was too abstract to be meaningful. The FCC has asked the court to reconsider its decision.

FOR ADDITIONAL READING

Bittner, John R. *Law and Regulation of Electronic Media.* Englewood Cliffs, N.J.: Prentice-Hall, 1994.

Creech, Kenneth C. *Electronic Media Law and Regulation.* Boston: Focal Press, 1993.

Goodale, James C., ed. *Communications Law.* New York: Practicing Law Institute, 1997.

Krattenmaker, Thomas G. and Lucas A. Powe, Jr. *Regulating Broadcast Programming.* Cambridge, Mass.: MIT Press, 1994.

---

[116] *Accuracy in Media, Inc. v. FCC,* 521 F.2d 288 (D.C. Cir. 1975), *cert. denied,* 425 U.S. 934 (1976).

[117] 47 U.S.C. § 396(g)(1)(A).

[118] *FCC v. League of Women Voters of California,* 468 U.S. 364, 402 (1984).

[119] In Alabama, all public stations operate under a statewide agency; in Texas, the public television stations operate independently of one another.

[120] *Muir v. Alabama Educational Television Commission,* 688 F.2d 1033 (5th Cir. 1982) (en banc), *cert. denied,* 460 U.S. 1023 (1983).

---

[121] 47 C.F.R. § 73.2080.

[122] *Modification of Equal Employment Opportunity Requirements,* 11 F.C.C. Rcd. 5154 (1996).

[123] *Lutheran Church-Missouri Synod v. FCC,* 141 F.3d 344 (D.C. Cir. 1998).

Lipschultz, Jeremy H. *Broadcast Indecency: F.C.C., Regulation and the First Amendment.* Boston: Focal Press, 1997.

Minow, Newton N. and Craig L. LaMay. *Abandoned in the Wasteland: Children, Television, and the First Amendment.* New York: Hill and Wang, 1995.

Smith, F. Leslie. *Perspectives on Radio and Television: Telecommunication in the United States,* 3d ed. New York: Harper & Row, 1990.

Smith, F. Leslie, Milan Meeske and John W. Wright, II. *Electronic Media and Government: The Regulation of Wireless and Wired Mass Communication in the United States.* White Plains, N.Y.: Longman Publishers, 1995.

11

Regulating New Communication Technologies

By Susan Dente Ross

From a regulator's perspective, the term "new communication technologies" is applied to mass media developed after broadcast television. The oldest of these is cable television, developed in the late 1940s. Other new technologies include wireless cable, direct broadcast satellites and the Internet. And some observers predict that technological developments and market pressures eventually will result in the convergence of television, telephones and computers into a single service offered through a single link to a multipurpose computer monitor or television set.

These new technologies are not mentioned in the First Amendment, and courts have been forced to consider how specific constitutional protections for speech and press apply. The U.S. Supreme Court has recognized that the unique traits of each mass medium permit different constitutional standards.[1] Yet the unique characteristics of a new communication technology often are not apparent until the public has adopted the technology and adapted its use. Thus, the Federal Communications Commission, Congress and the courts must choose either to regulate an emerging technology before it is well understood or to attempt to formu-

late logical and consistent regulatory schemes after the technology is in general use and it is too late for policy makers to direct the technology's development in the public interest. For example, cable television has been in existence for more than fifty years, and the Supreme Court continues to struggle to establish the constitutional standards for its regulation.[2]

CABLE TELEVISION

When cable television was developed, it was welcomed by broadcasters because it expanded the audience for local broadcast stations. Cable providers erected tall antennas to pick up local television signals, then transmitted the signals through coaxial cables to homes unable to receive them clearly over the air. During this era, television stations saw cable as an ally.

Beginning in the mid-1950s, these community area television — CATV — systems began using microwave technology to import and distribute signals from distant television stations. Local broadcasters recognized that cable could compete for viewers, resulting in smaller audiences and, therefore, lost revenue. They sought Federal Communication Commission control of cable sys-

---

The author would like to thank Robert Trager, who wrote the chapter on regulating new technologies for the 1998 edition of *Communication and the Law* and who allowed that chapter to become the framework for this revision.

[1] See, e.g., *Times Film Corp. v. Chicago,* 365 U.S. 43 (1961).

---

[2] *Turner Broadcasting Sys., Inc. v. FCC,* 512 U.S. 622 (1994); 520 U.S. 180 (1997).

tems.

But what regulatory framework would work for cable systems? The systems need government permission to use public rights-of-way and utility poles to string their cables, but unlike telephone systems, they are not common carriers transmitting the messages of all users. Instead, cable operators select the programs they provide much as newspaper editors control the content of news columns. The content of cable systems is similar, if not identical, to that of broadcaster stations, but a cable system operates differently from a broadcast station. The differences are significant for regulatory purposes. Cable systems receive programming from local broadcasters, through cable connections, by capturing signals from satellites and from videotapes and original programming. A cable operator brings all this programming together in the system's control room, called a "headend," and then transmits the programming through coaxial cables, optical fibers or both. In contrast, a broadcast station transmits its signal from its transmitting tower over the scarce public airwaves to receiving antennas attached to television sets. The courts have relied upon this use of the scarce electromagnetic by broadcasters, as discussed in Chapter 10, as a rationale to support more extensive regulation of broadcast stations than is permitted of the print media. But spectrum scarcity does not apply to cable television, which is not permitted to use the spectrum or to have signals (called "radio frequency" or "RF") that may cause interference with other communications leak from their cables. Until the 1980s, no federal statute clearly established the framework or purpose for cable regulation.

Early Federal Regulation of Cable Television

When Congress adopted the federal Communications Act of 1934, it could not have envisioned, and did not mention, cable television. Consequently, the FCC initially said the law gave the Commission no jurisdiction over cable; the Commission's jurisdiction was limited to radio, broadcast television and other technologies using the electromagnetic spectrum. Through the 1950s, the FCC refused to assume control over cable, even at the request of broadcasters.[3]

In fact, the Communications Act of 1934 does not provide clear justification for the FCC's jurisdiction over cable. One portion of the law gives the FCC power over common carriers — companies that allow anyone to use their facilities and do not limit or control the content that can be transmitted. Another portion of the act puts broadcasting under the Commission's jurisdiction. However,

as the FCC noted, cable is not a broadcast medium.

So, to justify its jurisdiction over cable, the FCC broadly interpreted the general language of the Communications Act. The act gives the Commission power over "interstate ... communication by wire" and the responsibility to adopt rules and regulations to "make available ... [an] efficient ... radio communication service ..." in the "public interest, convenience and necessity." The FCC, beginning in 1962, decided, therefore, that because cable involves interstate communication by wire, it must be regulated to serve the public interest.[4] In fact, cable systems — like broadcast stations — pay fees to the FCC to compensate for the cost of regulating them. The FCC's focus was not on cable television but on the survival of local broadcasting. The Commission suggested that television stations, particularly in smaller markets, could be harmed financially, even driven off the air, if viewers switched away from local stations to stations imported by cable from other cities.

The Supreme Court, ruling that because the Communications Act of 1934 gave the FCC responsibility for fostering the growth of broadcast television, the Commission could regulate cable as long as the regulation was "reasonably ancillary" to the Commission's jurisdiction over broadcast television.[5]

In addition to rules limiting the number of distant broadcast signals cable systems could import, the FCC adopted rules requiring cable systems to carry all local broadcast signals.[6] The FCC also issued an expansive order in 1972 covering many facets of cable regulation.[7] The Commission required larger cable systems to produce local programming. The Supreme Court upheld that decision, but the Commission removed the requirement shortly thereafter.[8] Later, the FCC required systems to make channels available to the public, government officials and school administrators, and to provide cameras and other equipment for those who wanted to use these access channels. This time the Supreme Court said the FCC had gone too far, that the Communications Act did not allow the Commission to force cable systems to open

---

[3] *Frontier Broadcasting Co. v. Collier,* 24 F.C.C. 251 (1958).

[4] *Carter Mountain Transmission Corp.,* 32 F.C.C. 459 (1962), *aff'd, Carter Mountain Transmission Corp. v. FCC,* 321 F.2d 359 (D.C. Cir. 1963), *cert. denied,* 375 U.S. 951 (1963).

[5] *United States v. Southwestern Cable Co.,* 392 U.S. 157 (1968).

[6] *First Report and Order in Dockets 14895 and 15233,* 38 F.C.C. 683 (1965); *Second Report and Order,* 2 F.C.C.2d 725 (1966).

[7] *Cable Television Report and Order,* 36 F.C.C. 2d 143, *recon.,* 36 F.C.C. 2d 326 (1972), *aff'd sub nom. American Civil Liberties Union v. FCC,* 523 F.2d 1344 (9th Cir. 1975).

[8] *United States v. Midwest Video Corp.,* 406 U.S. 649 (1972) *(Midwest Video I).*

their channels to everyone.[9]

In the mid-1970s cable television began offering programming—HBO and ESPN, for example — not available on either local or distant broadcast stations. Programmers' signals were sent from a transmitter on the ground to a satellite which retransmitted the signals to ground receiving dishes owned by cable systems which then distributed the signals to cable customers. In addition, the FCC spurred the growth of pay cable, and consequently of all cable television, with its so-called "open skies" policy, which eliminated many of the regulations formerly imposed on satellite transmission and reception.[10]

Local Regulation of Cable Television

Between 1975 and 1985, the number of cable subscribers skyrocketed, and cable operators, franchising authorities, broadcasters and program producers disagreed about who should regulate cable and how it should be regulated. Each group lobbied the FCC and Congress for federal rules that favored that group. During the period, the FCC prevented city and state authorities from regulating pay television. Yet states, counties and local governments imposed extensive requirements on cable systems through an elaborate franchising process.

Cable systems must run their wires from the headend to subscribers' homes over (or sometimes under) streets and other public land. Local authorities control this use of public rights-of-way and, therefore, can impose conditions, in the form of franchise agreements, on cable operators. A franchise is essentially a contract between the two parties. Many franchising authorities wanted to control the programming carried by cable, the rates cable systems charged, the customer services provided by cable systems and other aspects of the cable business. Franchising authorities also wanted to be paid a portion of cable systems' revenues in return for permission to use public rights-of-way.

Then, in 1984, the Supreme Court held that the FCC had broad powers regarding cable and that certain regulatory powers belonged to the Commission alone, not to state or local authorities.[11] At the same time, broadcasters didn't like the fact that cable retransmitted broadcast signals to subscribers without permission or payment. Historically, broadcast stations have been the most watched channels on cable systems. Carrying broadcast stations, then, has been important to the success of cable systems. On the one hand, broadcasters were glad to reach cable subscribers, on the other hand, they competed with cable operators for audiences, advertising revenue and programming.

Congress eventually had to act to accommodate the competing interests of cable operators and broadcasters.

The Cable Acts and The Telecommunications Act

In 1984, Congress determined that the fifty-year-old Communications Act needed to be amended to incorporate cable regulation. Congress adopted the Cable Communications Policy Act of 1984[12] to clarify the areas of responsibility of local and federal authorities. The act deregulated the prices cable operators could charge subscribers and forced cable systems to provide service to their entire franchise area. The law also limited the fees local franchising authorities could charge cable operators and prevented franchisers from arbitrarily refusing to renew a cable operator's franchise. By clarifying the regulatory situation of cable television, the act permitted increased growth of cable.

But soon complaints arose that a larger, powerful cable television business was concerned more with profits than with customer service. Customers complained about rapidly increasing prices. Localities complained about unfulfilled franchise obligations. So Congress, believing the 1984 cable act had eliminated too much cable regulation, again amended the 1934 Communications Act with the Cable Television Consumer Protection and Competition Act of 1992.[13] Among other provisions, the 1992 law gave television broadcast stations the choice of requiring cable systems to carry their signals (must-carry) or to insist on payment or other compensation for being carried (retransmission consent); regulated rates for many cable services; and required the FCC to adopt rules that would allow cable television's competitors to have access to much of the same programming that cable television carries. Federal courts have upheld several of the act's provisions.[14]

Four years later, again changing its mind, Congress passed the Telecommunications Act of 1996, which limited some regulations and eliminated others affecting cable television.[15] The 1996 law fo-

---

[9] *FCC v. Midwest Video Corp.*, 440 U.S. 689 (1979) *(Midwest Video II)*.

[10] *Domestic Communications-Satellite Facilities*, 35 F.C.C. 2d 844, 38 F.C.C. 2d 665 (1972).

[11] *Capital Cities Cable, Inc. v. Crisp*, 467 U.S. 691 (1984).

[12] 47 U.S.C. §§ 601-639.

[13] Pub. L. No. 102-385, 106 Stat. 1460 (1992); 47 U.S.C.S. § 543 (1996).

[14] *Time Warner Entertainment Co. v. FCC*, 93 F.3d 957 (D.C. Cir. 1996); *Time Warner Entertainment Co. v. FCC*, 56 F.3d 151 (D.C. Cir. 1995), *cert. denied*, 516 U.S. 1112 (1996).

[15] 104 Pub. L. 104, 110 Stat. 56 (1996), 47 U.S.C. §§ 251 et seq. (1996).

cused on increased competition – rather than federal regulation – to assure communications services in the public interest. The Telecommunications Act sought to encourage competition by allowing local telephone companies, long distance telephone companies and cable companies into each others' businesses. Instead of competition, however, the law prompted mergers and buyouts among cable and telephone companies.[16] The Telecommunications Act also maintained existing cable system content requirements but prohibited the FCC from imposing new content obligations on cable operators.

Cable Television System Ownership

At one time, federal law and FCC rules designed to prevent concentration of media ownership prohibited the owner of a broadcast television station from owning a nearby cable system. The so-called "cross-ownership rule" first adopted by the FCC in 1970 and later made part of the 1984 cable act, aimed to protect diversity of ownership and content. The ban on broadcast-cable cross-ownership was intended to prevent a broadcast owner from favoring his own station and refusing to carry competing broadcasters on the cable system. In 1992, the FCC recommended that Congress repeal the cross-ownership ban, and Congress took that action in the Telecommunications Act of 1996. However, the FCC cross-ownership ban remains in place.

Another cross-ownership rule imposed by the 1992 cable act generally prohibited a cable operator from owning a wireless cable or a satellite master antenna television system, both discussed later in this chapter, in the same area served by the cable system. The 1996 act removes that joint ownership ban if the cable system faces competition from another company providing multichannel video service.

There are no restrictions on cable systems being owned by citizens of other countries, owners of newspapers in the areas the cable system services or other print media owners.

Video Services and Telephone Companies

There have been arguments for decades about whether companies providing local telephone service should be allowed to own cable systems or offer video programming. Under the Communications Act of 1934, telephone companies are common carriers that must provide non-discriminatory services at similar rates to anyone wishing to send messages over their systems.

Different portions of the Communications Act govern telephone companies, broadcast stations and cable systems, which makes the act a cumbersome vehicle for regulating telephone companies' provision of video services. More importantly, for a number of years many government regulators believed that telephone companies would use their large size, their universal penetration and their economic power to drive other multichannel video providers out of business. Telephone company behavior prior to 1970 supported this concern.

American Telephone & Telegraph dominated local and long-distance telephone service in the United States during the first seven decades of the Twentieth Century. The dominance was so great that the federal government filed lawsuits against AT&T in 1914 and again in 1956. The government charged that AT&T violated antitrust laws by attempting to monopolize local and national telecommunications markets for service and equipment. Each time, AT&T signed a consent decree, promising that it would no longer engage in the impermissible actions.

Similar concerns arose during the early years of the cable industry, when telephone companies could own cable systems. Cable systems often need to string their lines above ground, but government officials may refuse to allow cable operators to erect their own poles. It also is expensive and inefficient to put up poles when existing telephone poles frequently have the capacity to carry cable system lines. Cable operators, then, often rented space on existing poles owned by telephone or power companies. However, from cable's earliest days through the 1960s, the FCC heard many complaints that cable operators not affiliated with telephone companies were not being allowed to rent space on poles. In 1960, the FCC responded by adopting the telephone-cable cross-ownership ban to eliminate the incentive for telephone companies to discriminate against cable competitors.

In 1974, the U.S. Department of Justice filed a third antitrust suit against AT&T, claiming that, despite the 1956 consent decree, the company continued efforts to monopolize long-distance telephone service and the manufacture of telephone equipment. The government and AT&T agreed to settle the case by modifying the 1956 consent decree. The new agreement, settled in 1982, became known as the "Modification of the Final Judgment," or the "MFJ."[17]

---

[16] See, e.g., "Whitacre Explains Ameritech Purchase at Senate Hearing," *Communications Daily,* 20 May 1998; "SBC Would Create Biggest LEC in $62-Billion Stock Deal for Ameritech," *Communications Daily,* May 12, 1998; Kevin Fong, "The Urge to Converge will Mark the Year Ahead," *Network World,* 23 February 1998, p. 42.

[17] *United States v. Western Elec. Co.,* 552 F. Supp. 131 (D.D.C. 1982).

Among many other provisions, the MFJ forced AT&T to sell off its local telephone service divisions. AT&T became a long-distance provider. The newly-formed regional and local phone companies were limited to local telephone services and could not offer "information services," which included cable television programming, anywhere in the United States.

Two years later, Congress adopted the FCC's cross-ownership ban as part of the 1984 cable act. The law prevented telephone companies in the United States — including the approximately 2,500 independent telephone companies not formerly affiliated with AT&T — from owning or operating cable systems.[18]

The companies divested from AT&T in 1982 — called "RBOCs" for "Regional Bell Operating Companies" — are the country's largest providers of local telephone service.[19] The RBOCs chafed at many restrictions in the MFJ, including the ban on "information services." In 1991, Judge Harold Greene, the federal district court judge overseeing the consent decree, essentially removed the "information services" ban.[20] But that left in place the 1984 cable act ban on telephone-cable cross-ownership. Several RBOCs brought lawsuits and argued in court that their First Amendment rights to free speech were being abridged by the cable act ban. Beginning in 1993, every court hearing such a case agreed and overturned the ban.[21]

While the RBOCs were in court challenging the cable act ban, the FCC also gave telephone companies a way to be involved in video. In 1992 the Commission allowed the RBOCs to offer a common carrier video service called "video dialtone" or VDT.[22] With VDT, a telephone company would use its wires and support services to carry the video signals of any other program provider to subscribers' homes. The telephone company was required to provide the service on a non-discriminatory, first-come-first-served basis. The company also could offer its own video services over its VDT system on a limited basis. VDT systems did not require local franchises because neither the telephone company nor any of the programming services met the legal definition of a cable system.[23] Cable companies opposed VDT systems and argued that the absence of franchising requirements gave VDT systems an unfair advantage in the market.

The Telecommunications Act of 1996 resolved the complex questions about telephone companies offering video services. The law eliminated the telephone-cable cross-ownership ban and allowed local telephone companies to provide video programming in one of four ways:

- A firm offering local telephone service may own a cable system as a separate subsidiary company. Telephone-owned cable systems must comply with all the laws and franchise requirements that pertain to any cable operator.

- A telephone company may operate a common carrier video service similar to VDT, although that term is no longer used on a first-come-first-served basis. Under this approach, the telephone company's video service would be regulated much as its telephone service, as a common carrier.

- The telecommunications act created a new way for telephone companies to offer video — the "Open Video System." OVS providers serve both as common carriers of others' programming and as program providers as well. If outside demand for video service exceeds system capacity, then the OVS provider can program no more than one-third of the channels. The other two-thirds must be offered to other video providers on a first-come-first-served basis. The systems are not required to obtain a franchise, but local governments may require OVS fees equivalent to the franchise fees of a cable operator. In exchange for acting as video common carriers, OVS providers are absolved of some regulatory obligations imposed on cable television systems.

- A telephone company may offer video services through a "wireless cable" system. Wireless cable is discussed later in this chapter.

Under the 1996 act, a telephone company generally is not permitted to purchase an existing cable system located in the telephone company's service area. Nor is a cable system allowed to

---

[18] 47 U.S.C. § 613(b).

[19] The RBOCs are Ameritech Corporation, Bell Atlantic Corporation, BellSouth Corporation, Nynex Corporation, Pacific Telesis Group, SBC Communications Inc. (formerly Southwestern Bell Corporation) and U S West. SBC Communications Inc. and Pacific Telesis Group have announced they will merge, as have Bell Atlantic Corporation and Nynex Corporation.

[20] *United States v. Western Elec. Co.,* 900 F.2d 283 (D.C. Cir. 1990); *United States v. Western Elec. Co.,* 767 F. Supp. 308 (D.D.C. 1991).

[21] *Chesapeake & Potomac Tel. Co. v. United States,* 830 F. Supp. 909 (E.D. Va. 1993), *aff'd* 42 F.3d 181 (4th Cir. 1994), *vacated and remanded* 516 U.S. 415 (1996). After adoption of the Telecommunications Act of 1996, 104 Pub. L. 104, the Supreme Court found this series of decisions moot, since Congress had answered the question of whether telephone companies could offer video services. *United States v. Chesapeake & Potomac Tel. Co. of Virginia,* 516 U.S. 415 (1996).

[22] *Telephone Company-Cable Television Cross-Ownership Rules,* 7 F.C.C. Rcd. 5781 (1992).

[23] *National Cable Television Ass'n v. FCC,* 33 F.3d 66 (D.C. Cir 1994).

buy a telephone company where both provide service. A rule adopted by the FCC before passage of the 1996 act prohibits any cable system operator from passing its wires by more than thirty percent of all homes passed by cable in the United States, or up to thirty-five percent if the company is minority controlled.[24] A federal appellate court ruled that a challenge to this regulation was not yet ready to be heard by the courts.[25]

The RBOCs also are challenging provisions of the 1996 law. The companies have begun to argue that the law unfairly punishes them by requiring them to wait until competition exists before providing certain services. In 1998, one federal circuit court upheld the FCC's effective competition standard before allowing an RBOC to offer long-distance services.[26] The same court later rejected another RBOC's constitutional challenge to the telecommunications act's mandate that Bell companies provide electronic publishing only through separate affiliates.[27] The court said the rule was a well justified, content-neutral mechanism to prevent monopolies and unfair competition.

Even before the 1996 act was adopted, U S West had invested in Time Warner. Shortly after the act's passage, U S West agreed to acquire Continental Cablevision for $5.3 billion. Through these two transactions, U S West has a potential reach of more than sixteen million customers, approximately one of every four cable subscribers. In 1997, the FCC approved another major merger between British Telecom and MCI Communications. At the same time, concerns about unfair competition persist. In 1997, the Supreme Court refused to review a circuit court of appeals ruling granting a small telephone provider $1.54 million and possible punitive damages as a result of AT&T's unfair and anti-competitive treatment of the company.[28]

Cable System Franchises

The 1984 cable act made clear that local authorities have a right to grant cable franchises and that a cable system must have a franchise in order to offer service. Some states grant franchises; in other states, franchises are awarded by cities or counties and must be approved by the state; most frequently, however, franchises are granted exclusively by cities or counties.

In awarding a franchise, a city will ask interested companies to submit proposals outlining details about the system to be installed, the kinds of programming to be carried and information about customer service. The 1992 cable act forbids franchising authorities from awarding exclusive franchises. That is, they cannot agree to grant one, and only one, franchise. Although most communities have franchised only one company to offer cable service, the exclusive franchise exists because other companies have not sought franchises; they do not want to invest the large amounts of money necessary to build competing cable systems. However, more areas soon may have competing cable companies now that telephone companies are allowed to offer cable service. At least two Bell operating companies, U S West and Ameritech, have begun to offer competing cable services in the western United States but do not expect the systems to be profitable for several years.

A city also can own a cable system, even in competition with a cable company offering service in the municipality. Courts have held that a franchising authority can build a system and compete with an existing cable operator in the city[29] and even grant a city agency a cable franchise with better terms than the company against which the city will compete.[30] The 1992 act allows cities to operate their own cable systems without a franchise.

Pole Attachment Agreements

To attach their cables to poles or run them through underground conduits owned by telephone or electric companies, cable operators must have a contract with the pole or conduit owners. To prevent telephone companies from charging unreasonably high rental prices or refusing cable use altogether, Congress adopted the Pole Attachment Act in 1978. The act gives the FCC authority to regulate the rates, terms and conditions of agreements between most pole owners and cable systems. In addition, the Telecommunications Act of 1996 requires pole operators to allow cable companies to rent pole or conduit space. The act also extends the pole attachment provisions to cable operators' use of poles or conduits for non-video services — such as data or voice transmissions — that compete with telephone offerings.[31] The law permits

[24] *Horizontal and Vertical Ownership Limits, Second Report and Order*, 8 F.C.C. Rcd. 8565 (1993).

[25] *Time Warner Entertainment Co. v. FCC*, 93 F.3d 957 (D.C. Cir. 1996).

[26] *SBC Communications v. FCC*, 138 F.3d 410 (D.C. Cir. 1998).

[27] *BellSouth v. FCC*, No. 97-1113 (D.C. Cir., May 15, 1998).

[28] *Central Office Telephone v. American Telephone & Telegraph*, 108 F.3d 981 (D.C. Cir. 1997), *cert. denied* 118 S.Ct. 644 (1997).

[29] See *Warner Cable Communications, Inc. v. City of Niceville*, 911 F.2d 634 (11th Cir. 1990), *cert. denied*, 501 U.S. 1222 (1991).

[30] See *Paragould Cablevision, Inc. v. City of Paragould*, 930 F.2d 1310 (8th Cir.), *cert. denied*, 502 U.S. 963 (1991).

[31] 47 U.S.C. § 224; see also *Texas Utilities Electric Co. v. FCC*, 997 F.2d 925 (D.C. Cir. 1993); *Heritage Cablevision v. Texas Utilities Electric Co.*,

a state, rather than the FCC, to oversee pole rental contracts within the state. Nearly twenty states have decided to do so.

But the FCC is struggling to determine the fees cable Internet service providers should be charged for pole use and the status of wireless carriers that attach their equipment to poles. Early in 1998, the FCC established a formula for fees for pole attachments by cable and wireless telephone services unable to negotiate terms in states that do not regulate pole attachments.[32] Internet services carried by cable will be charged at the rate applied to cable services, which currently is half the rate applied to telephone services. These rules have been challenged.

A federal district court issued a summary judgment rejecting an electric utility company's claim that mandatory pole access requirements were an unconstitutional taking of private property without just compensation.[33] The court agreed that mandatory access was a form of taking but said companies were fairly compensated for the use.

Cables on Private Property

While a franchise allows a cable operator to use public rights-of-way, and a pole attachment contract allows the use of privately-owned poles and conduits, cable wires often must run over private property. When a homeowner asks for cable service, part of the agreement allows cables to pass over the homeowner's yard to reach the house. But if the potential subscriber lives in an apartment or in a private development, for example, the customer does not own the property over which cables will pass.

Courts generally have found that nothing in the 1984 or 1992 cable acts gives cable operators the right to use private property without permission of the property owner, and nothing requires the owner to give permission.[34] An owner may demand a high payment from a cable company for permission, or may choose to have a different provider offer video services. An exception under the cable acts occurs when a private property owner has given permission for all public utilities to use the property. In that case, cable may use the property without seeking additional permission, even though cable television is not a "public utility" under the ca-

ble acts. But if a property owner has specified which particular utilities may use the property, or has not allowed any utilities to do so, cable must receive permission before crossing the private property. Some fifteen states have adopted laws that, to some degree, allow cable operators access to apartment buildings. Cable systems are required to pay for this access, but in some instances the payment may be only $1.[35]

Cable Franchise Provisions

Franchises can be short or hundreds of pages long, depending on the complexity of the agreement. Certain provisions will be found in most franchises.

For decades, franchising authorities have required cable systems to pay a franchise fee as part of the agreement to use public rights-of-way. At one time, franchise fees would be set as high as thirty-six percent of a cable system's revenues. In 1972, however, the FCC limited franchise fees, and the 1984 cable act set a franchise fee ceiling of five percent of gross annual revenues. The 1984 cable act does not define "gross annual revenues," allowing cable operators and franchising authorities to negotiate a definition with respect to franchise fees.

Some cable operators have argued that having to pay any franchise fees violates their First Amendment rights, but most courts hearing such cases have decided that cable's use of public rights-of-way justifies imposing franchise fees.[36]

The 1984 cable act allows franchising authorities to specify broad categories of video programming that a cable operator will be required to carry, such as movies, children's programming, news and public affairs and sports, but franchisers are not permitted to specify which programming services a cable system must provide or to forbid a cable operator from offering specific services.

Franchises also specify the duration of the agreement, which typically is from eight to fifteen years. There are no cable act or FCC requirements.

Prior to 1992, franchising authorities and cable operators negotiated customer service requirements as part of the franchise agreement. The 1992 cable act, however, required the FCC to establish a minimum level of customer service and permitted franchising authorities to determine customer service standards. The Commission adopted a number of requirements concerning, for

---

6 F.C.C. Rcd. 7099 (1991).

[32] *Amendment of the Commission's Rules and Policies Governing Pole Attachments, Report and Order,* 11 P&F Rad. Reg. 79 (1998).

[33] *Gulf Power Co. v. United States*, No. 3-96-CV-381/LAC (N.D. Fla., March 6, 1998).

[34] See, e.g., *TCI of North Dakota v. Schriock Holding Co.,* 11 F.3d 812 (8th Cir. 1994).

[35] *Loretto v. Teleprompter Manhattan CATV Corp.,* 458 U.S. 419 (1982).

[36] See, e.g., *Group W Cable, Inc. v. City of Santa Cruz,* 679 F. Supp. 977 (N.D. Cal. 1988).

example, when cable system offices must be open, how quickly a system must answer telephone calls and when service outages must be repaired. Franchising authorities may impose the FCC standards or stricter requirements on cable operators. Franchising authorities also may change customer service requirements when they choose.

Most franchises specify that the cable operator must ask the franchising authority's permission to transfer or sell the franchise to a new owner. Under the 1992 cable act, the franchising authority must decide whether to grant a transfer request within 120 days or transfer permission is presumed. The Telecommunications Act of 1996 removed the 1992 cable act rule forbidding franchise transfers within three-years from the time the system was built or most recently purchased. The limitation had been designed to hold down the sale prices of cable systems, which tend to increase each time a system is sold, because cable operators often raise subscribers' rates to recoup the cost of the system purchase. Cable operators now may sell systems at any time.

The FCC sets technical standards, which affect the quality of picture and sound of cable transmissions. Franchising authorities are not permitted to determine the type of subscriber equipment or transmission technology a cable system uses.

Cable Franchise Renewals

Most cable owners invest heavily in the equipment needed to operate their systems and hope to renew franchises and continue providing service beyond the initial franchise period. The 1984 cable act establishes a franchise renewal process.

A cable operator and a franchising authority negotiate a franchise renewal without reference to the 1984 cable act's renewal provisions unless they cannot come to agreement. If the franchising authority decides not to renew, the 1984 cable act gives cable operators some protection by establishing a formal renewal process and specifying a limited number of grounds on which renewal can be denied. The formal steps begin thirty to thirty-six months before franchise expiration when the cable operator notifies the franchising authority in writing of the desire to begin the formal renewal process. Alternatively, the franchising authority can initiate the process.

Within six months of notification, the franchising authority must begin a study of: (1) the quality of the cable operator's performance during the franchise period and (2) the cable-related needs of the area's residents in the coming franchise period. There is no deadline for completing this study. In response to the com-

pleted study, the cable operator may, or must if the franchising authority insists, give the franchising authority a renewal proposal much like a proposal for a new franchise. The franchising authority may set a deadline for the cable operator to submit the proposal. No later than four months after receiving the proposal, the franchising authority must make a decision to renew or preliminarily to deny renewal. Denial is preliminary because the cable operator may insist upon a review hearing.

Under the cable act, the franchising authority may deny renewal only for one or more of four reasons: (1) the cable operator did not substantially comply with the important terms of its franchise and with laws that apply to the operator, (2) the operator's customer service or overall program offerings were inadequate, (3) the operator does not have the financial, legal and technical ability to provide the services promised in its renewal proposal, or (4) the operator's renewal proposal was not a reasonable attempt to meet the community's cable-related needs and interests as established in part by the franchising authority's stated preferences in the initial study.

The hearing is intended to be formal, much like a civil trial, with attorneys, witnesses and evidence. The purpose is to record the franchising authority's reasons for denying renewal and the cable operator's objections to the reasons. The cable operator may appeal a formal denial of renewal to the courts.

Cable and the First Amendment

The Supreme Court has addressed the franchising question only indirectly, indicating that some regulations of cable systems do raise constitutional concerns. In 1986, the Court held for the first time that cable operators clearly had First Amendment interests and enjoyed some level of protection. In *Los Angeles v. Preferred Communications, Inc.,* the Court said cable television operators engage in "some of the aspects of speech and the communication of ideas as do the traditional enterprises of newspapers and book publishers...."[37] The Court said a franchising authority could not use the franchising process to grant a cable monopoly. Instead, the Court held that Los Angeles was required to show that its interests in refusing to issue a competing franchise outweighed the First Amendment interests of the cable applicant.

In 1991 the Court said in *Leathers v. Medlock* that cable operators are "engaged in 'speech' under the First Amendment."[38] Even so, the Court held that a state could tax cable system revenues,

---

[37] 476 U.S. 488, 494 (1986).
[38] 499 U.S. 439, 444 (1991).

even if other mass media aren't taxed, because the tax was unrelated to speech and was a non-discriminatory, property and service tax applied to a large number of other businesses. In neither of these cases did the Court specify what standards courts should use to determine whether a cable operator's First Amendment rights had been abridged.

The Court did so in *Turner Broadcasting Sys., Inc. v. FCC.* [39] In response to a First Amendment challenge to the must-carry provisions of the 1992 cable act, the Court drew a distinction between content-based and content-neutral regulations but did not determine the constitutionality of the must-carry rules. The Court held that the First Amendment is to be applied to cable television in two ways. First, governmental regulations directed toward the content of cable television programming must pass the strict scrutiny test to be constitutional. That is the government must show that the restriction is needed to protect a compelling governmental interest of the highest order.

But if the governmental regulation is not directed at content and imposes only an incidental burden on a cable operator's speech, the Court held that the regulation need be tested only under the intermediate First Amendment standard established in *United States v. O'Brien* and *Ward v. Rock Against Racism.* [40] Intermediate scrutiny of content-neutral regulations requires the government to show that the government regulation is a reasonable way of achieving an important or substantial government interest.

Using this strategy, the Court found the must-carry rules content-neutral in 1994 but did not determine the constitutionality of the law. The Court remanded *Turner* to a lower court, which found the must-carry rules constitutional in 1995.[41] The Supreme Court agreed, finding the must-carry rules to be a narrowly tailored, content-neutral means to protect the broadcast industry from extinction.[42] By a 5-4 vote, the Court said the rules, which require cable systems to carry the signals of local broadcasters, were an appropriate means by which the government assured that cable operators did not force broadcasters out of business.

Four members of the majority said Congress had justified the rules for three reasons: (1) they protect the strength of local television broadcasting, enhancing the diversity of content available to viewers; (2) they ensure that viewers who are not cable sub-scribers have access to local news, information and opinions; and (3) they promote competition for the delivery of video programming. They found the rules did not impermissibly favor broadcast programming but were a content-neutral means to protect the broadcast industry and enhance competition. The four justices said the must-carry rules were a reasonable way to achieve important government interests, and the rules had no greater impact on cable operators' and programmers' free speech rights than was necessary to achieve their goals.

Justice Stephen Breyer provided the fifth vote affirming the constitutionality of the must-carry rules but based his opinion on the need to protect local and educational broadcast programming not on the majority's premise that the rules promote competition in the video-delivery market. The dissenting justices said Justice Breyer's opinion actually supported their argument that the must-carry rules were designed to favor specific content and were, therefore, unconstitutional.

Content and Programming Regulations

Congress and the courts have placed a variety of content regulations upon cable television.

Leased Access Channels. The 1984 cable act requires large cable systems to provide channels for purchase by commercial users and allows franchising authorities to negotiate with cable systems to offer channels for use by the public and educational and governmental organizations. Requirements for commercial, leased-access channels and public, educational and governmental access channels do not violate cable operators' First Amendment rights, according to a federal appellate court.[43]

Under the 1984 act, cable systems with fewer than thirty-six channels are not required to offer commercial, leased-access channels. Cable systems with thirty-six to fifty-four channels must designate ten percent of their channels for this purpose, and systems with fifty-five or more channels must set aside fifteen percent of their channels. These channels may be leased for a fee by anyone who wants to put programming on the cable system. The FCC has jurisdiction over the rates, terms and conditions of commercial, leased-access contracts.

Congress probably expected these channels to provide viewers with access to full-time programmers not carried on the local cable system. In reality, the channels more often are leased by a person,

---

[39] 512 U.S. 622 (1994).

[40] 391 U.S. 367 (1968) and 491 U.S. 781 (1989).

[41] *Turner Broadcasting Sys., Inc. v. FCC*, 910 F. Supp. 734 (D.D.C. 1995).

[42] *Turner Broadcasting Sys., Inc. v. FCC*, 520 U.S. 180 (1997).

[43] *Time Warner Entertainment Co. v. FCC*, 93 F.3d 957 (D.C. Cir. 1996).

company or organization that wants to have a limited amount of time on a cable system. So in the 1992 act, Congress specifically said the leased-access channels were intended, in part, to promote competition in the delivery of video programming.

Generally, cable systems use these channels for purposes other than leased access, such as carrying cable network programming, until they are requested. Under the 1992 cable act, a cable system may use up to one-third of its leased-access channels for certain educational or minority cable programming services, and the channels will be counted as being used for leased access.

Cable operators act as common carriers of commercial, leased-access channels, but in the 1992 act, Congress gave cable systems the right to reject leased-access programming that the operator "reasonably believes describes or depicts sexual or excretory activities or organs in a patently offensive manner as measured by contemporary community standards."[44] The 1996 act also permits a cable system operator to refuse to carry a program or portion of a program "which contains obscenity, indecency or nudity" on a commercial leased access channel.

Congress also developed a complex method of segregating indecent leased-access material that operators carried. Operators were required to put all such programming on a separate channel that was scrambled or blocked in some way. A subscriber was required to ask in writing for the channel to be unblocked and, later, could also may ask for the channel to be re-blocked. The cable operator has thirty days to comply with a written request for unblocking or re-blocking.

In 1996, a divided Supreme Court reviewed a First Amendment challenge to the law's indecency and obscenity restrictions and upheld the provision permitting cable operators to reject obscene programming, but the Court rejected the parts of the law requiring operators to segregate indecent material and required subscribers to request it.[45] Several justices noted that, unlike obscenity, indecency is protected by the First Amendment. They said alternative means that would interfere less with viewers' First Amendment rights could still protect children and sensitive viewers from the material. In addition, the justices expressed concern that cable customers who wanted access to some or all of the segregated programming might hesitate to request access in writing for fear their names would be released.

PEG Access Channels. The 1984 cable act permits, but does not require, franchising authorities to negotiate with cable operators to provide access channels for members of the public, educational institutions and governmental bodies. The agreements need not require all three types of programming and a system might devote one channel to multiple purposes. For example, a system could use one channel for educational access during daytime hours and for governmental access during the evening.

Access channels grew out of competitive offerings from cable operators attempting to land franchises in large cities. Beginning more than thirty years ago, cable operators promised PEG access and other features as a means of winning franchises. Then, in 1969, the FCC encouraged cable operators to offer PEG channels[46] and in 1972 required systems to do so.[47] In 1979, the Supreme Court ruled that the Commission did not have the authority to require PEG channels,[48] but the ruling did not prevent cable systems and franchising authorities from agreeing to have channels. Finally, the 1984 cable act gave franchising authorities the right to negotiate with cable operators to have PEG channels.

Cable operators have very limited control over the content of PEG channels and are not liable for material they cannot prohibit. This means a cable system cannot eliminate specific programming or public access provisions to exclude ideas it dislikes or disfavors. For example, when the Ku Klux Klan attempted to offer a program on the Kansas City, Missouri, cable system's public access channel, the city council removed the public access channel requirement from the city's cable franchise. With the requirement gone, the operator stopped providing the channel, and the Klan had no way to offer its program. The Klan sued the cable system. A federal district court ruled in favor of the Klan because the city could not show that it had not eliminated the channel requirement as a way to limit the Klan's First Amendment rights to free speech.[49] The city re-established the public access provision, and the Klan presented its program.

The 1984 cable act says franchising authorities and cable systems can agree that cable services — including PEG channels — will not present material that is "obscene or otherwise unprotected by the United States Constitution."[50] The 1992 cable act went further. It allowed cable operators to prohibit "obscene ma-

---

[44] 47 U.S.C. § 532(h). See also *Indecent Programming, First Report and Order,* 8 F.C.C. Rcd. 998, 1003 (1993).

[45] *Denver Area Educational Telecommunications Consortium, Inc. v. FCC,* 518 U.S. 727 (1996).

[46] *Community Antenna Television Sys.,* 20 F.C.C. 2d 201 (1969).

[47] *Cable Television Report and Order,* 36 F.C.C. 2d 143 (1972).

[48] *FCC v. Midwest Video Corp.,* 440 U.S. 689 (1979) (*Midwest Video II*).

[49] *Missouri Knights of the Ku Klux Klan v. Kansas City,* 723 F. Supp. 1347 (W.D. Mo. 1989).

[50] 47 U.S.C. § 544(d).

terial or sexually explicit content or material soliciting or promoting unlawful conduct" on PEG channels and withdrew operators' protection against lawsuits based on their presentation of such material. The Supreme Court found this provision violated the First Amendment.[51] The Court said both public and private groups provided sufficient oversight of public access channels to exclude the type of material to which Congress objected. Moreover, the government had not provided sufficient evidence to demonstrate that further control by the cable operator was required to protect children from indecent material. The Court also said cable operators permitted to exclude programming from public access channels likely would restrict borderline material that otherwise might be protected under the First Amendment.

Sexually Explicit Programming on Other Channels. While the Court said cable operators could not prohibit indecent programming, the Court permitted cable operators to use discretion to voluntarily adopt and enforce written policies on segregating, blocking, scrambling and time-channeling of adult-oriented programming.[52]

The 1996 Telecommunications Act required the FCC to establish rules regarding sexually explicit programming on channels used primarily for such material.[53] The Commission issued a regulation that these channels would have to be scrambled or blocked, unless a subscriber chose to receive them. If cable operators do not scramble such channels, they must provide a safe harbor free of sexually-oriented programming from 6 a.m. until 10 p.m. Although a federal district court issued a temporary restraining order to prevent enforcement of the provision, a permanent injunction was denied, and the Supreme Court affirmed that denial.[54] The FCC restated its support of voluntary content controls in 1997.[55]

Carrying Broadcast Stations. Broadcast programming is protected under copyright law, which (as discussed in Chapter 8) requires that permission be obtained for its material. Broadcast television stations, or the networks with which the stations are affiliated, routinely sign contracts with program producers or syndi-cators allowing the stations to carry certain shows. Similarly, when cable systems began to retransmit local broadcast signals, program producers argued that cable television was required to obtain permission. Producers said they had sold their shows to broadcast television, not to cable. Broadcast stations also argued that cable should be required to obtain permission to carry local programming — like evening news shows — for which local stations held the copyrights.

In 1968, and again in 1974, the Supreme Court said a cable system's retransmission of a broadcast station's signal did not violate the copyright law.[56] Program producers and broadcasters reached a compromise with cable operators that Congress adopted as part of the Copyright Act of 1976.[57] The law's "compulsory copyright license" for broadcast television and radio programs, permits cable operators to carry such programming for a fee without asking permission.[58] A complex formula determines the amount each cable system must pay, but the fee likely is less than the system would pay if it negotiated separately with the copyright holder of each individual program. Cable payments are made to a fund administered through the Copyright Office, which distributes the money to the copyright holders.

Television broadcasters also were concerned about the effect cable retransmission would have on their audience size and advertising revenues. Broadcasters argued that because retransmission of broadcast channels helped cable operators attract viewers and revenues away from broadcast stations, cable should be required to obtain permission to carry broadcast programming. And smaller stations with fewer or less-loyal viewers believed they would not have large enough audiences to stay in business if they were not carried by cable systems. Nearly two-thirds of viewers watch television *via* cable, and the smaller stations said cable systems should be required to carry their broadcast programming to protect the availability of that programming to the public.

Although the FCC began in 1965 to adopt various rules forcing cable to carry broadcast stations, federal appellate courts twice ruled that the must-carry rules unconstitutionally infringed cable operators' First Amendment rights.[59] The courts did not say the must-carry rules could never be applied to cable operators, but

---

[51] *Denver Area Educational Telecommunications Consortium, Inc. v. FCC*, 518 U.S. 727 (1996).

[52] *Id.*

[53] 47 U.S.C. 561.

[54] *Playboy Entertainment Group, Inc. v. United States*, 918 F. Supp. 813 (D. Del. 1996); *Playboy Entertainment Group, Inc. v. United States*, 945 F. Supp. 772 (D. Del. 1996), *aff'd*, 117 S.Ct. 1309 (1997).

[55] *Indecent Programming and Other Types of Materials on Cable Access Channels*, Memorandum Opinion and Order, 12 F.C.C. Rcd. 6390 (1997).

[56] *Fortnightly Corp. v. United Artists Television, Inc.*, 392 U.S. 390 (1968); *Teleprompter Corp. v. Columbia Broadcasting Sys.*, 415 U.S. 394 (1974).

[57] Pub. L. No. 94-553, 94 Stat. 2541, 17 U.S.C.S. §§ 101 et seq. (1976).

[58] 17 U.S.C. § 111.

[59] *Century Communications Corp. v. FCC*, 835 F.2d 292 (D.C. Cir. 1987), *cert. denied*, 486 U.S. 1032 (1988); *Quincy Cable TV, Inc. v. FCC*, 768 F.2d 1434 (D.C. Cir. 1985), *cert. denied*, 476 U.S. 1169 (1986).

both said the FCC had not adequately demonstrated why it favored broadcasters' concerns over cable operators' rights. In the 1992 cable act, Congress attempted to resolve the problem by allowing a television station either to choose must-carry status with the local cable system or to negotiate with the cable operator on the terms for retransmitting the broadcaster's signal. The latter option is called "retransmission consent." In adopting these provisions, Congress presented more than a dozen rationales to justify imposing must-carry rules.

In 1994, the Supreme Court held that must-carry rules serve an important governmental interest by protecting free local television. However, the Court sent the case back to lower court to determine if, in fact, local television stations would be in danger of going out of business in the absence of must-carry rules. After eighteen months of additional fact finding, a three-judge federal district court, in a 2-1 decision, found that the must-carry rules do not violate the First Amendment. The Supreme Court agreed.[60]

Generally, the must-carry rules apply to all except the smallest cable operations. Systems with twelve or fewer channels must carry at least three eligible television stations, and systems with more than twelve channels must devote up to one-third of their channels to carrying eligible stations. All full-power commercial stations located in the community served by a cable system may demand to be carried. Rules also require non-commercial stations to be carried, but they cannot choose to negotiate for carriage under the retransmission consent rules.[61]

Under the law, every three years commercial television stations choose whether to negotiate terms for carriage or require carriage under the must-carry standards. Originally many cable operators refused to consider paying to carry broadcast stations. Operators that owned multiple cable systems, on the other hand, negotiated non-monetary deals with companies that owned a number of television stations. For example, some cable operators agreed to carry the then-new Fx network, if Fox would permit the operators to retransmit television stations Fox owned. Similarly, Capital Cities/ABC agreed to allow carriage of television stations it owns in exchange for cable systems carrying ESPN2, the sports cable network owned in part by ABC.

Carrying Cable Networks. In the 1990s, Congress raised concerns about increased ownership of cable programming networks by cable system operators. For example, two of the coun-

try's largest cable system owners, TCI and Time Warner Inc., were investors in the company that owns TNT, CNN and other cable networks. Then Time Warner purchased the company in 1996. During debate of the 1992 cable act, Congress expressed concern that such cable companies might carry primarily the networks they own, excluding others from reaching viewers. In response, a provision of the 1992 cable act ordered the FCC to adopt rules to limit the number of cable networks in which a cable owner had invested that the owner could carry on her cable system.

The FCC ruled that no more than forty percent of a system's first seventy-five channels may be used for programming affiliated with the system's owner. Sixty percent of the channels must be available to carry broadcast television stations and cable programming in which the system's owner has no more than a five percent interest.[62] Slightly more of a system's channels may be used for cable programming in which the system owner has an interest if the services are controlled by minority individuals or businesses. Local and regional cable networks are exempt from this rule. If a system has more than seventy-five channels, those additional channels are not affected by the regulation. The rules did not stop Time Warner from purchasing TNT, CNN and other cable networks in 1996.

Nonduplication Rules. The FCC has adopted two other rules designed to protect broadcast stations from cable competition — syndicated exclusivity and network nonduplication. Syndicated programming is sold by exclusive contract to individual television stations in different cities. These programs are not provided by a network, although many are reruns of once-popular network programs. Many talk shows and some dramatic series are produced to be sold through syndication and are not carried first by broadcast networks.

When cable systems import distant broadcast stations' signals, those signals may include the same syndicated programming being shown by a local station under an exclusive contract. To address this duplication and protect local stations, the FCC adopted syndicated exclusivity rules in 1972.[63] These rules permitted a local station to require a cable system to black out any syndicated program on an imported signal that also was being carried by the local station. The Commission rescinded the rules in 1980 but reinstated them in 1988,[64] and they continue in force and have

---

[60] *Turner Broadcasting System, Inc. v. FCC,* 910 F. Supp. 734 (D.D.C. 1995), *aff'd Turner Broadcasting System, Inc. v. FCC,* 520 U.S. 180 (1997).

[61] 47 U.S.C. § 535.

[62] *Development of Competition and Diversity in Video Programming Distribution and Carriage,* 8 F.C.C. Rcd. 8565 (1993); 47 U.S.C. § 536.

[63] *Cable Television Report and Order,* 36 F.C.C. 2d 143 (1972).

[64] *Syndicated Exclusivity Rules,* 79 F.C.C. 2d 663 (1980); *Rules Re-*

been upheld as content-neutral by the U.S. Court of Appeals for the D.C. Circuit.[65]

Similar rules for network programming allow television stations affiliated with a broadcast network to demand that a cable system black out network programming being carried on an imported station.[66] Small cable systems are exempt from both the syndicated exclusivity and network nonduplication rules.

Similarly, FCC blackout rule permits a professional team to require a cable operator to black out the local telecast of a local sports event involving that team if tickets are not sold out.[67] A blackout cannot be required, however, if a television station in the same area as the cable system and the sports event is showing the event. The National Football League has agreed that its team owners will not ask for a blackout if a game is sold out seventy-two hours prior to game time.

Cable Networks. The 1992 cable act requires companies that supply cable systems with programming also to offer such programming to cable's competitors.[68] The act prevents cable systems and programmers from entering into exclusive agreements or in other ways limiting access to programming by such multichannel video distributors as direct broadcast satellite systems. The purpose is to allow cable's competitors to offer popular programming services to potential customers.

Other Programming Laws and Rules. Cable systems also must comply with certain federal laws and FCC rules that apply to broadcasters (see Chapter 10) regarding political cablecasting, bans on carrying obscene material, limitations on information about lotteries and sponsorship identification rules. Cable systems must comply with the limits on commercial time during children's programs but are not governed by the children's television programming requirements.

Rate Regulation

For decades, cable television operators, the FCC and franchising authorities have received complaints about rates charged for cable services. Attempts to limit cable service prices have competed with concerns that cable's growth as a business would be stunted if government interfered by setting prices. In 1971 the FCC prohibited franchising authorities from regulating rates for pay-per-channel services but did not address rate regulation for other cable services.[69] The 1984 cable act set rates for basic cable service in communities without competing cable systems, but the FCC's implementation of the rules effectively exempted most cable systems from rate regulation. As rates continued to climb, Congress adopted the 1992 cable act, which required the Commission to establish rules that would regulate many rates. Responsibility for cable rate regulation is shared between franchising authorities and the FCC.

Cable systems with what the Commission calls "effective competition" do not face rate regulation. There is "effective competition" if any one of several circumstances exists: (1) fewer than thirty percent of the households in the cable system's service area subscribe to the system, (2) at least fifteen percent of households subscribe to competing multichannel video providers, (3) the franchising authority itself operates a competing multichannel video service available to at least fifty percent of the area's households, or (4) a telephone company offers video programming comparable to that provided by cable.

Few cable systems have effective competition under that standard, and therefore most operators face rate regulation, with certain exceptions for small systems. Cable operators must charge reasonable rates for cable programming services. Rates are considered reasonable if they are roughly equivalent to the average per-channel rates charged by cable systems that face effective competition. Alternatively, cable systems may attempt to show that their rates are reasonable because of higher-than-average costs of providing service.

Rate regulation for small cable systems ended in February 1996. Rate regulation for other cable operators was set to end March 31, 1999, under the Telecommunications Act of 1996.

Cable Companies as Telephone Providers

The Telecommunications Act of 1996 opened local telephone service to competition. For nearly 100 years, residential telephone users could obtain service from only one local company. But the 1996 act permits any firm to offer local telephone service and requires telephone companies to make their facilities available, on a nondiscriminatory basis, to others who want to compete in the

---

lating to Program Exclusivity in the Cable and Broadcast Industries, 3 F.C.C. Rcd. 5299 (1988).

[65] *United Video, Inc. v. FCC,* 890 F.2d 1173 (D.C. Cir. 1989).

[66] *First Report and Order in Dockets 14895 and 15233,* 38 F.C.C. 683 (1965); *Rules Relating to Program Exclusivity in the Cable and Broadcast Industries,* 3 F.C.C. Rcd. 5299 (1988).

[67] 47 C.F.R. sec. 76.67 (Michie 1995).

[68] 47 U.S.C. § 548; *Time Warner Entertainment Co. v. FCC,* 93 F.3d 957 (D.C. Cir. 1996), *request for rehearing en banc denied,* 105 F.3d 723 (D.C. Cir. 1997).

[69] *Time-Life Broadcasting, Inc.,* 31 F.C.C. 2d 747 (1971).

local telephone market. In return, local telephone companies will be allowed to offer long-distance service.

In 1996, the FCC began implementing the law by specifying how local telephone companies should permit competitors to connect to their telephone networks. A federal appellate court stayed and later overturned the portion of the FCC order that provided guidelines to states about the connection rates local phone companies could charge other local telephone providers.[70]

Congress incorrectly expected cable to seize the opportunity provided by the 1996 Act to rush into and provide competition in the lucrative local telephone market. After all, local telephone service providers earn more than $66 billion a year, nearly three times the $23 billion in revenues earned from cable television service. Moreover, cable operators — already in nearly two-thirds of American homes and passing more than ninety-five percent of homes — were permitted to carry a full range of communications services: local telephone, Internet access, cable video and online banking. services. But such communications packages required fiber optic cables, and many cable operators hesitated to make the major investment necessary to upgrade coaxial lines. Other cable operators entered the telephone market cautiously and selectively because they lacked experience or expertise in interactive services billed by usage.

To avoid the cost of cable upgrades, some cable companies plan to offer telephone and other services through personal communications systems, a network similar to cellular telephone service, by sending signals over the air initially and then through wires over a local telephone system's facilities. Wireless telephone revenues are more than $20 billion per year. The FCC has used auctions to award portions of the spectrum to be used for personal communications services, thus far raising $20 billion in successful bids. In its 1997 year-end report to Congress, the Commission said it intended to auction additional spectrum for PCS use.

Cable Customer Privacy

In the 1984 cable act, Congress reacted to a concern that cable companies could collect private information about their customers and share that information with others without subscribers' permission. Congress particularly focused on cable company access to customer information through cable's two-way capabilities, such as banking-from-home. Most of these two-way services have not fully developed, but cable systems are limited in the

---

[70] *Iowa Utilities Board v. FCC,* 109 F.3d 418 (8th Cir. 1996), *amended, on reh'g,* 120 F. 3d 753 (8th Cir. 1997).

information they can gather and release about their customers.

Private information includes the customer's name, address, telephone number, cable services taken and other information that identifies a particular subscriber. Cable systems annually must inform customers in writing what private information the system collects, what use the system makes of the information, to whom the information is disclosed and why, how long the information will be kept by the system, when and where the customer may see the information the system keeps, the limits placed by law on the system's right to collect and disclose private information, and what steps the customer may take if the cable system violates those limitations.

Without a customer's permission, a cable operator may collect only the private information needed to offer cable or other services ordered by the customer and to be certain customers are not stealing services. Similarly, a cable operator may not release private information to others without permission except as needed to provide services to the customer or for the system's legitimate business needs, such as giving information to a company that sends the cable system's monthly bills.

Equal Employment Opportunity Requirements

The FCC has had equal employment opportunity rules for broadcasters and cable systems in place for twenty-five years, but the 1984 and 1992 cable acts codify these rules into law for cable systems and other multichannel video programming providers. Generally, the law forbids cable systems and their corporate owners from discriminating on the basis of national origin, race, color, age, religion or gender in employment. The rules require that the employees in certain job categories, such as managers and technicians, reasonably reflect the makeup of the pool of possible employees in the cable system's area. Further, cable systems and their owners must establish programs to ensure that no discrimination occurs in any phase of employment, including hiring, training, promotions and firing. These programs must be reviewed for effectiveness periodically.

Theft of Cable Service

Theft of cable service costs cable companies billions of dollars each year. Thieves tap into cable wires to obtain service without being subscribers or use illegal set-top boxes to receive premium channels. The 1984 cable act forbids intercepting or receiving any cable service, or assisting anyone in doing so, without the cable company's permission. The law also forbids the manufacture and distribution of equipment intended to be used to steal cable service. Another section of the Communications Act makes it illegal to intercept signals not intended for the general public and to manufacture or sell equipment used to intercept such signals. Additionally, more than forty states have laws that may be used to prosecute theft of cable service.

OTHER NEW ELECTRONIC MASS MEDIA

While cable systems provide service to nine of the country's ten multichannel video customers, other technologies also send video signals to viewers. Some members of Congress and federal regulators hope several of these will provide serious competition to cable and that this competition will improve cable operators' customer service, reduce prices and increase programming diversity.

Direct-to-Home Services

In 1934, when Congress passed the Communications Act, it did not envision satellites circling the earth and remaining in fixed positions relative to cities below. This concept — known as geosynchronous satellites — was first put forth by the science fiction writer Arthur C. Clarke in 1945.[71] It uses modern technologies such as digital band compression to beam down more than 100 channels of video programming. It is not surprising, then, that the Communications Act does not mention direct broadcast satellites and that provisions in the Communications Act do not precisely fit DBS. However, the FCC clearly has jurisdiction over DBS because satellites use the electromagnetic spectrum to send signals to receiving dishes. The FCC licenses all DBS operations.

In 1982, when the Commission faced regulation of DBS, it realized that the service could be seen as (1) a broadcasting service, distributing signals to terrestrial antennas, just as broadcast stations do, or (2) a service much like local telephone companies, renting space on the satellite to anyone who wants to send signals. The Commission chose not to clearly classify DBS and to adopt simplified, flexible regulations to allow DBS to develop.[72] Broadcasters challenged the fairness of this approach, and a federal appellate court disagreed, in part, with the Commission's

strategy.[73] The court found that DBS met many of the legal characteristics of a broadcast medium and could be regulated in a new way only to the extent that the FCC could justify such distinctions. The court said DBS could be regulated as a non-local broadcast service without the "localism" obligations the Commission places on broadcasters. A later court decision held that DBS was more like subscription services than broadcasting because DBS does not use the spectrum to transmit to the general public.[74] The confusion, which arose partly because of the different ways in which satellites may be used to provide services, caused the FCC to reconsider its terminology as well as its regulatory approach.

The Commission now uses the term "direct-to-home" to comprise services sending video signals to receivers in the United States. One type of DTH service is DBS, the service sending transmissions to receiving dishes eighteen to twenty-four inches in diameter. Operators such as DirecTv and U.S. Satellite Broadcasting offer this service using high-power signals. Another company, PrimeStar, offers DBS service using medium power. DBS is becoming increasingly popular. The FCC informally refers to a second type of satellite service as "home satellite dish." Its proper name is "fixed satellite service." This service requires a receiving dish approximately four- to eight-feet in diameter. The larger receiver is necessary because HSD uses a lower power signal than does DBS, requiring a larger surface to capture the signal. The Commission intended to create DBS in 1982, but HSD was the first to develop commercially.

Under international agreements, the United States has eight positions for DTH satellites in the geosynchronous orbit. Each position may utilize up to thirty-two transmission channels. But with digital signal compression, a technology allowing several signals to be transmitted in the portion of the spectrum previously needed for a single signal, each of the thirty-two channels can offer five to seven signals, or 150 to more than 200 from one satellite. Newer technologies soon may bring that to twenty signals per channel, or more than 600 from a satellite. In the past, the Commission awarded the orbital positions through competitive hearings or by lottery. Now it auctions orbital slots. One DBS license auctioned in 1996 for $682.5 million.[75]

Satellite operators must comply with federal laws and FCC regu-

---

[71] Arthur C. Clarke, "Extra-Terrestrial Relays — Can Rocket Stations Give World-Wide Radio Coverage?" *Wireless World,* October 1945, p. 305.

[72] *Direct Broadcast Satellites,* 90 F.C.C. 2d 676 (1982).

---

[73] *National Association of Broadcasters v. FCC,* 740 F.2d 1190 (D.C. Cir. 1984).

[74] *National Association for Better Broadcasting v. FCC,* 849 F.2d 665 (1988).

[75] See *Time Warner Entertainment v. FCC,* 93 F.3d 957 (D.C. Cir. 1996).

lations, but they also must operate under standards adopted by the International Telecommunications Union, the worldwide body overseeing spectrum use. U.S. satellite operators need not strictly comply with ITU rules, but ultimately the ITU must approve the deviations from its standards, or the operators must come into compliance.

The 1992 cable act required the FCC to establish certain public interest obligations of satellite operators, such as rules regarding political communication, retransmission consent — but not the must-carry rules — and equal employment opportunities.[76] Broadcasters and cable operators since have argued that DBS has an unfair competitive edge and should be subject to government mandated must-carry rules. In 1998, the FCC announced its intention to conduct a rulemaking to examine whether must-carry rules should be applied to DTH services.

Additionally, the 1992 act requires DBS service providers to devote four to seven percent of their channel capacity to "noncommercial programming of an educational or informational nature."[77] The FCC has interpreted the 1992 act as applying these requirements to DBS operators, but not to HSD services. Also, a federal appellate court has held that satellite operators may use the compulsory copyright license, just as cable television does.[78]

Under the 1992 cable act, the Commission also was instructed to determine whether DBS operators should be subject to local programming rules similar to those broadcasters face. However, the FCC could not determine how a service that sends a signal nationally and offers a wide variety of programming options could be concerned with localism in the same way as a local broadcaster.

When satellite operators act as conduits, they provide channels on which others put programming or other services. To apply localism rules, the FCC would regulate the licensed satellite operator, who would need to ensure that the programmer complied with the public interest requirements. Alternatively, a satellite operator itself could be the program provider and would need to comply with the requirements. Or possibly a satellite operator would act like a commercial broadcaster, providing service to anyone with an antenna but without requiring subscriptions. Then the operator would have to comply with all the rules and regulations applied to over-the-air broadcast stations.

The 1996 telecommunications act limited the ability of cities, homeowners' associations and others to place restrictions, such as zoning laws or appearance requirements, on satellite receiving dishes. Congress's intent was to ensure that the growth of DBS would not be stymied by limitations on satellite receivers that potential subscribers want to install. In 1998, the FCC announced plans to consolidate and streamline regulation of DBS and direct-to-home services as a means to encourage and speed growth of the services and to promote competition with cable, whose rates continued to climb.[79]

Satellite Master Antenna Television Systems

A satellite master antenna television system, also called "private cable," is essentially a cable system contained within an apartment building or several buildings. Similar to cable, a SMATV system collects local television signals through an antenna and satellite signals through receiving dishes, all placed on top of the building. It sends these signals through wires that run through the building and into individual apartments. The SMATV system may serve other commonly owned buildings on the same plot of private land, and the system's wires will run to and through each building. If the wires go across public rights-of-way, such as crossing a public street, the operation becomes a cable, not a SMATV, system.[80]

The FCC has chosen to impose few regulatory burdens on SMATV systems, thus allowing SMATV systems to develop into competition for cable. Further, the Commission has held that there can be no local or state regulation of SMATV.[81] As a result, SMATV systems must comply with the FCC's equal employment opportunity rules — unless they serve fewer than fifty subscribers — but do not face rate regulation, franchise fees, customer service standards or most of the other regulatory requirements imposed on cable systems.

Wireless Cable

In 1970 the FCC dedicated part of the spectrum to a service for business communications. By 1974, the Commission realized that

---

[76] See *Implementation of Section 25 of the Cable Television Consumer Protection and Competition Act of 1992,* 8 FCC Rcd. 1589 (1993).

[77] 47 U.S.C. § 335(b)(1); *Time Warner Entertainment v. FCC,* 93 F.3d 957 (D.C. Cir. 1996).

[78] *National Broadcasting Corp. v. Satellite Broadcast Networks,* 940 F.2d 1467 (11th Cir. 1991); *National Association for Better Broadcasting v. FCC,* 849 F.2d 665 (1988).

[79] *Policies and Rules for the Direct Broadcast Satellite Services,* Notice of Proposed Rulemaking, FCC 98-26, IB Docket No. 98-21 (Feb. 26, 1998).

[80] *FCC v. Beach Communications, Inc.,* 508 U.S. 307 (1993).

[81] *New York State Commission on Cable Television v. FCC,* 669 F.2d 58 (2d Cir. 1982).

part of the spectrum could be used to send video signals to subscribers and established the Multipoint Distribution Service. The FCC permitted two video channels to be provided in the country's fifty largest markets and one video channel in other markets. It increased the number of available channels in 1983, then again in 1991.[82] The business became known as "multichannel multipoint distribution service," or MMDS.

Today, it is called "wireless cable," and it sends as many as thirty-three channels by microwave signals to small antennas on subscribers' homes. The signals then are sent by wire from the antenna to a television set. Wireless cable uses microwaves, part of the electromagnetic spectrum, and therefore it is licensed and regulated by the FCC. Because wireless cable does not cross public rights-of-way, it is not a cable system and does not require a local franchise.

Wireless cable became a viable business when the FCC permitted wireless cable operators to combine their spectrum allocations with other portions of the spectrum dedicated to other types of wireless services. By combining spectrum allocations, wireless cable systems can compete with cable systems in some cities. Wireless cable was helped by the 1992 cable act requirement that cable networks offer their programming to wireless cable and other multichannel multipoint video providers. The FCC does not permit cities or states to regulate wireless cable operations, and, as with satellite operators, the Commission allows wireless operators to act as conduits for other video programmers or to themselves provide programming.[83] In either case, the Commission imposes very few regulatory requirements on wireless cable, but the Commission must approve any non-subscription service supplied by MDS or MMDS.[84] As with DBS, wireless cable services must comply with the retransmission consent rules requiring operators to obtain permission from any broadcast stations the wireless cable service carries. This, too, was expected to be reviewed by the FCC in 1998.

The FCC has used auctions to award hundreds of wireless cable licenses. As technological advances soon will enable wireless cable operators to offer a number of video signals on each of their thirty-three channels through digital signal compression, wireless cable licenses have become more valuable. Several telephone companies have expressed an interest in purchasing wireless cable

operators because the 1996 telecommunications act permits telephone companies to provide video services through wireless cable. In 1997, the FCC began a proceeding to adopt more flexible regulation of wireless cable and to encourage use of the medium for interactive services. That same year, the FCC issued its first rulings preempting restrictions on the installation and use of satellite dishes imposed by local governments and homeowners associations in four states.

In 1998, the Commission auctioned spectrum to be used for local multipoint distribution service, which uses transmitters to send voice, data or video within a six-mile radius. The FCC awarded more than 859 LMDS licenses and raised approximately $580 million. The FCC is not expected — for several years at any rate — to permit local telephone companies or cable companies to bid for most LMDS licenses within their service areas, hoping that other companies will develop LMDS to compete with local telephone and cable services. In 1998, the FCC adopted more flexible LMDS rules to encourage small businesses to enter the market.[85]

Digital Television

"Digital television" is a term applied to a technological standard for a new form of television, affecting both the transmission and display of television signals. Other terms, such as "advanced television" and "high definition television," also are used to refer to these new standards. The transmission standard currently in use in the United States is called "NTSC," for the National Television System Committee, adopted by the FCC in 1941.

A DTV standard would improve significantly on NTSC transmissions by providing better pictures, compact disk-like sound and a picture shaped more like a movie theater screen than current screens. Any of the electronic mass media — broadcasting, cable, SMATV, wireless cable, satellite — could transmit DTV programming, but existing television sets will not be able to receive DTV signals and translate them into viewable pictures.

DTV development, initially called HDTV, began in Japan in the mid-1960s. Later work was undertaken in Europe on a different HDTV standard not compatible with the Japanese technology. The United States began HDTV development late, but the delay allowed American companies to use a digital rather than an analog transmission scheme. In 1987, the FCC established the Advisory Committee on Advanced Television Systems to coordinate Ameri-

---

[82] *Private Video Distribution Systems,* 6 F.C.C. Rcd. 1270 (1991).

[83] *Multipoint Distribution Service,* 2 F.C.C. Rcd. 4251 (1987).

[84] *Revisions to Part 21 of the Commission's Rules regarding the Multipoint Distribution Service,* Second Report and Order, FCC 98-70, CC Docket No. 86-179 (April 14, 1998).

[85] *Rulemaking to Establish Rules and Policies for Local Multipoint Distribution Service and for Fixed Satellite Services,* Fourth Report and Order, FCC 98-77, CC Docket No. 92-297 (May 6, 1998).

can HDTV research. After years of work, several companies that had been competing to develop DTV agreed upon a standard, called the "Grand Alliance," that is different from the Japanese and European standards.

In 1996 the FCC approved a compatible standard for signal transmission protocols, giving television set manufacturers the confidence to manufacture sets able to receive DTV signals. Televisions compatible with both the Grand Alliance and the FCC standards are expected to reach the market in the late 1990s, when various programming providers plan to begin transmitting both digital and analog programs. Computer companies also plan to build what are being called PC-TVs or PC-Theater machines that will display DTV programs as well as act as computer terminals.

In 1997, the Commission decided to give full-power television broadcasters a second channel to use for DTV. It expected large, major market stations to offer DTV by late 1998, with other stations to begin doing so within another five years. During that time, stations would be expected to offer programming on both NTSC/analog and digital channels, so that existing television sets still could be used. In 1998, the FCC affirmed its commitment that conversion to DTV be completed by the year 2006, when analog channels would go dark, broadcasters would return one channel to the FCC, and only DTV would be available.[86]

While it is expected the transition periods may take longer than the FCC foresees, quite early in the Twenty-First Century consumers who want to watch broadcast television will need television sets capable of receiving digital signals, or set-top boxes that will convert digital signals to analog but without HDTV-quality pictures and sound.

The digital channels allocated in 1997 could be used for high definition television, or for "multiplexing," that is, offering up to four television signals that would be an improvement on current quality but not up to the level of HDTV. Using digital compression, several television signals, plus data and other services, such as paging, could be provided on the spectrum space now devoted to one channel. The 1996 act states that if broadcasters are given a second channel, and they use it to provide services for which they charge a fee, they must compensate the federal government for using that channel.

President Clinton urged the FCC to impose certain public interest obligations on broadcasters in return for the new digital channels. The president appointed a committee to consider what those should be, with suggestions ranging from free air time for political candidates to not carrying hard liquor advertisements.

Interactive Video and Data Services

Interactive Video and Data Services combine data transmission and interactivity to permit home shopping, banking and other services. Some IVDS providers enter the business by buying available spectrum through FCC auctions that offer preferences for women and minorities. In 1997, a federal circuit ruled that a constitutional challenge to these preferences must be reviewed on its merits by the FCC.[87] The IVDS provider argued that the preferences unconstitutionally favored select groups and inflated auction prices. Indeed, the FCC has been concerned by the number of auction and lottery winners who have defaulted on their payments. Observers are watching the case carefully to determine whether it may effectively eliminate all FCC minority and female ownership preferences.

THE INTERNET

The Internet has become a means for tens of millions of people to be entertained, to exchange electronic mail and to access information through the World Wide Web. Anyone connected to this international grouping of computer networks can become a publisher, sending material to millions of people in many countries. Called the "national information infrastructure" or the "information superhighway" in the United States, the Internet already is being connected to television sets through cable systems and telephone companies. The Internet could be part of the convergence of telephone, television and computers, providing an extensive, international broadband network. Some analysts predict that a single broadband network could replace television, radio, telephones, mail, newspapers and other forms of communication.

The Internet presents legal problems, some familiar and some new. For example, communication through the Internet can be undertaken anonymously, copyrighted material can be distributed without the copyright holder's permission, and information stored on computers can be obtained by people with no right to it. As a new medium of communication, the Internet's legal status is unclear. The courts must determine how existing law will apply to the Internet and whether new laws intended specifically for the Internet will withstand constitutional challenge.

---

[86] *Advanced Television Systems and their Impact upon Existing Television Broadcast Service,* Memorandum Opinion and Order, FCC 98-24, MM Docket No. 87-268 (Feb. 23, 1998).

[87] *Graceba v. FCC,* 115 F.3d 1038 (D.C. Cir. 1997).

The Internet and Indecency

A portion of the Telecommunications Act of 1996 called the Communications Decency Act made it illegal to knowingly send or make available to minors any indecent or obscene material. [88] In 1997, the Supreme Court found the Communications Decency Act's indecency provisions unconstitutional. In *Reno v. ACLU*, [89] the Court acknowledged Congress's concern with preventing children from being the targets of, or having access to, sexually explicit communications. But the Court said the CDA's ban on indecency was both vague and overbroad. The law did not define indecency in a way that conformed to previous Court decisions. Thus, the law impermissibly prohibited expression that is protected for adults, the Court said.

In its ruling, the Court distinguished the Internet from broadcasting because the Internet does not use the limited public spectrum, and because people are not likely to be exposed inadvertently to sexually explicit material on the Internet as they might be on broadcast stations. Accordingly, Internet users should not suffer the reduced First Amendment protections that apply to radio and television station operators, the Court reasoned. The Court noted, however, that obscene material may be banned from the Internet because the First Amendment does not protect any obscene messages, regardless of medium.

The Court issued a similar ruling in 1989, when it said Congress may prohibit obscene telephone communications but may not impose a complete ban on indecent "dial-a-porn" messages available *via* telephone for a fee. [90] Although the Court ruled in 1979 that the FCC could constitutionally restrict indecency on broadcast stations, [91] it found in *Sable Communications v. FCC* that telephones are markedly different from broadcasting. Stations are ubiquitous, uniquely powerful and easily available to children. In contrast, a person must consciously and actively choose to access a dial-a-porn telephone service providing indecent material.

Congress later adopted a law requiring dial-a-porn businesses to make their services available only through a presubscription arrangement, credit card payment or other method that would make it difficult for children to gain access to the indecent messages.

While courts use the *Miller v. California* [92] definition of obscenity for print and visual media, questions exist about applying it to the Internet. For example, the Sixth Circuit upheld the conviction on federal obscenity charges of two people who operated a computer bulletin board from their California home. [93] The service offered sexually-explicit materials only to those who subscribed. The bulletin board owners were able to accept or deny requests for subscriptions.

The couple was charged in Memphis, Tennessee, with transmitting obscene material. A postal official had subscribed to the bulletin board, obtained computer files and ordered six videotapes, all containing sexually explicit material. A jury found that the material violated the "local, contemporary community standards" of Memphis and convicted the couple of transporting obscene images across state lines *via* the Internet.

The lower court rejected arguments that the ruling effectively established a national standard for obscenity, contrary to the Supreme Court's *Miller* test, or that upholding the conviction would mandate that all material sent over the Internet be no more explicit than permitted by the most restrictive community. The court said the defendants could, and should, have made certain when screening subscribers that their materials would not be received in restrictive communities.

Libel on the Internet

Portions of the Communications Decency Act not struck down by the Supreme Court's ruling in *Reno v. ACLU* have been used to protect Internet service providers from liability for libel and other civil torts. A federal district court in 1998, for example, rejected a libel suit brought by a Clinton administration official and his wife against the Drudge Report, an online publication carried by America Online. The couple sued after the report said the husband had a history of spousal abuse.

In *Blumenthal v. Drudge*, [94] the court relied on a section of the CDA that protects providers of interactive services from liability for the content of third-party materials. The court said even though America Online exercises some editorial control and is more than a passive carrier, the law dictates that online providers be protected from liability.

---

[88] 104 Pub. L. 104, tit. 5, 110 Stat. 56 (1996).

[89] 117 S.Ct. 2329 (1997).

[90] *Sable Communications v. FCC*, 492 U.S. 115 (1989).

[91] *FCC v. Pacifica Foundation*, 438 U.S. 726 (1979).

[92] 413 U.S. 15 (1973).

[93] *United States v. Thomas*, 74 F.3d 701 (6th Cir. 1996); see Pamela A. Huelster, "Cybersex and Community Standards," *Boston University Law Review* 75 (1995): 865.

[94] *Blumenthal v. Drudge*, 992 F. Supp. 44 (D. D.C. 1998). See also *Zeran v. America Online*, 129 F.3d 327 (4th Cir. 1997);

Copyright on the Internet

The Internet also presents questions about protection of intellectual property rights for computer originated and transmitted material. Original material is protected by copyright upon its creation, and the creator has exclusive rights to reproduce and distribute the work, as well as the right to create other works derived from the original. (See Chapter 8.) Therefore, uploading a document, copying an Internet posting and retransmitting the posting without permission all could violate copyright law.[95] Even browsing through material on a computer, which causes a temporary copy of the digital information to be held in the screen memory, could possibly constitute illegal copying. Alternately, this might be interpreted as the digital form of reading a book in a library or a magazine at a newsstand, and not a copyright infringement.[96]

The growth of Internet sites that "link" to or "frame" a small section of another site's content raises a new question of copyright infringement. In 1997, the *Washington Post* and five other news organizations charged a group of Internet news sites with copyright infringement for republishing and repackaging the media Web pages for profit.[97] The media organizations charged that the news sites copied their trademarks for use as links and republished their copyrighted material with advertising that generated revenue for the pirates rather than the copyright holders. The suit was settled out of court when the news sites agreed to provide links but not to frame any content from the news organizations' sites.

Other questions surround the copyright protection of computer-generated materials. To qualify for copyright protection, material must be fixed in a tangible medium as well as be original. Therefore, if an online document is a copy of material that already exists on paper, it is unclear whether the online document should be considered "original" and therefore protected. Additionally, it remains to be determined whether material created and transmitted electronically is "fixed in a tangible medium."

For example, a live television broadcast is not fixed in a tangible medium and, therefore, is not protected, unless, for example, it is simultaneously put on videotape. In contrast, a document put on a floppy or hard disk or a CD-ROM is fixed.[98] The question then is whether material created on a computer, sent over the Internet and then not "saved" on the computer is fixed in a tangible medium and thus subject to copyright protection. One court has held that material in a computer's random access memory is sufficiently fixed to be protected.[99]

The copyright liability of online service providers also is unclear. If a subscriber uses one of these services to send material that clearly is protected under copyright, is the service as well as the user guilty of copyright violation? For example, a company could print a hard copy of a magazine and then put the magazine's contents online. A Compuserve user could copy a story from the online magazine and send it to millions of other Internet users. Who is liable?[100] Two courts have found online service providers liable for their subscribers' copyright infringements,[101] and one has found to the contrary.[102] A key factor affecting the court rulings was whether the online provider had, or should have had, prior knowledge of the infringement. Online providers who electronically screen or preview material may be held accountable for copyright infringements while providers who act as common carriers may not.

The 1995 report of a committee organized by the United States Patent and Trademark Office to consider copyright questions on the Internet failed to resolve these issues.[103] While the committee suggested that computer transmissions should be considered "copies" similar to a photocopy of a book page, it decided that existing copyright law was generally adequate to deal with the Internet.

The Internet and Privacy

Privacy also is an Internet concern. At work, employees who occasionally use the Internet for personal reasons could find that their employers have access to everything sent and received online. People using the Internet from home for such services as banking or shopping and for sending e-mail messages could find they have less privacy protection than when engaging in such activities by

---

[95] See *Playboy Enterprises, Inc. v. Frena*, 839 F. Supp. 1552 (M.D. Fla. 1993).

[96] *Religious Technology Center v. Netcom On-Line Communications Services*, 907 F. Supp. 1361, 1378 n. 25 (N.D. Cal. 1995).

[97] *Washington Post Co. v. Total News Inc.*, No. 97 Civ. 1190 (S.D. N.Y., complaint filed Feb. 20, 1997).

[98] *Mai Systems Corp. v. Peak Computer, Inc.*, 991 F.2d 511, 518 (9th Cir. 1993), *cert. dismissed*, 510 U.S. 1033 (1994).

[99] *Id.* at 518; *Triad Sys. Corp. v. Southeastern Express Co.*, 64 F.3d 1330 (9th Cir. 1995).

[100] See *Playboy Enterprises v. Frena*, 839 F. Supp. 1552 (M.D. Fla. 1993).

[101] *Id.*; *Sega v. MAPHIA*, 857 F. Supp. 679 (N.D. Cal. 1994).

[102] *Religious Technology Center v. Netcom On-Line Communications Services*, 907 F. Supp. 1361 (N.D. Cal. 1995).

[103] Working Group on Intellectual Property Rights, Information Infrastructure Task Force, *Intellectual Property and the National Information Infrastructure* (1995) (White Paper).

mail or in person.

Privacy becomes a question when law enforcement authorities want to tap into computer transmissions the way they do telephone calls. While a court order would be required for either, it may be possible for computer users to encrypt their transmissions in ways that make it very difficult for law enforcement authorities to understand what is being sent. In 1993, the National Security Agency proposed a "Clipper Chip," a technology to allow government decoding of encrypted telephone, fax and some modem messages. A similar technology is being developed for computer messages. There is disagreement over whether the government should have such power.

FOR ADDITIONAL READING

Brock, Gerald W. *Telecommunication Policy for the Information Age: From Monopoly to Competition.* Cambridge, Mass.: Harvard University Press, 1994.

Crandall, Robert W. *Cable Television: Regulation or Competition.* Washington, D.C.: Brookings Institution, 1996.

Ferris, Charles D., et al. *Cable Television Law.* New York: Mathew Bender, 1984-1998.

Hanson, Jarice. *Connections: Technologies of Communication.* New York: HarperCollins, 1994.

Huber, Peter W., et al. *The Telecommunications Act of 1996: Special Report.* Boston: Little, Brown, 1996.

Pool, Ithiel de Sola. *Technologies of Freedom.* Cambridge, Mass.: Belknap Press, 1983.

Rosston, Gregory L. and David Waterman, eds. *Interconnection and the Internet.* Mahwah, N.J.: Lawrence Erlbaum Associates, 1997.

12

Regulating Student Expression

By Thomas Eveslage

Thirty years ago, the U.S. Supreme Court said that students do not "shed their constitutional rights to freedom of speech or expression at the schoolhouse gate."[1] Since then, however, it's become clear that not all schoolhouse gates are the same. Some have narrow passages. Others remain guarded by over-protective gatekeepers.

Yet the Supreme Court's premise remains: Students are citizens even when they're on school property. The high court said that no mental detector should prevent students from bringing their beliefs into the schools and expressing them. Educational institutions, the Court implied, can be laboratories for young citizens trying to grasp the First Amendment's meaning and applications.

High schools and universities are microcosms of society — with government-like figures of authority; with co-existing organizations, social classes and races; and with student media trying to interpret and help their audiences understand their learning communities. An examination of freedom of speech and press within the educational environment is a lesson in the scope and boundaries of individual liberties.

Just as all citizens discover that freedom of expression has strings attached, student journalists learn that they do not have the absolute freedom to say anything they want, anywhere they want. Courts have ruled that the First Amendment lets government officials regulate in a reasonable way where, when and how

citizens speak, as long as those officials have valid reasons and are not suppressing ideas just because the government does not like them.

Student journalists, especially those on college publications, have many of the freedoms accorded their professional counterparts. Both groups face similar legal obligations and are subject to the same standards regarding libel, privacy, copyright and even the more peripheral student media concerns of free press/fair trial, broadcast regulation and confidentiality of sources.

Student status and the educational setting allow authorities some latitude when regulating speech on school property, but these factors are dealt with quite differently in high school and college settings. Because their learning environments are different, as are the age and maturity of their students and the responsibilities of those in charge, the freedom available and school officials' ability to restrict that freedom vary from high school to college.

Some free-speech concerns — especially prior restraint and access to information — pose special problems for the student press. Denial of press access to crime statistics and disciplinary proceedings have, in recent years, led to conflicts with college administrators. Censorship has been more of a problem to the high school press, primarily because courts give public officials more latitude when protecting children from potentially harmful material. Recently, fear and uncertainty regarding the Internet and public concern with press responsibility has chilled serious, sometimes heated, discussion of controversial topics on high school

---

[1] *Tinker v. Des Moines Ind. School Dist.*, 393 U.S. 503, 506 (1969).

and university campuses.

This chapter reviews principles of free expression as they extend to students. Court cases affecting the student media reveal legal arguments used to limit students' freedom of speech and how the physical environment, the age of young citizens and societal interests affect the expressive rights of students.

A FRAMEWORK FOR STUDENT EXPRESSION

Most Americans understand that citizens are not free to speak or publish anything they want, that there are limits and penalties, that circumstances affect constitutional liberties. To understand that concept better, college students only have to look around and think back to their high school days. Whether individually or as student journalists, they experience some of the societal tensions that influence free expression.

School as Society

At least in *public* colleges and high schools, a microcosm of American society exists that can help young citizens learn and appreciate what free speech and a free press mean. This society has organizations and social classes, rules established to benefit all citizens, a government that makes and enforces the regulations, and various outlets for expression.

When the abstract principle of free expression becomes real in the educational laboratory, high school and college journalists learn what professionals know — there is no special free-speech privilege for the press. Law and ethics must be balanced to maintain credibility and public support.

The college campus more closely parallels society than does the high school, where students today often must express themselves responsibly or risk losing their freedom of expression. Adults, including college students, don't face that limitation. In fact, as will be demonstrated, courts consider college campuses to be public forums where the exchange of ideas is central to the educational mission. Just as government officials have little power to stop or punish professional journalists who express unpopular or embarrassing ideas, college administrators have little control over content of the student press. There still are efforts to control expression — by enforcing campus speech codes, by denying the student press access to information about crime on campus even by equating high school and college.

The Legal Foundation

Students and educators have asked the courts to address two central questions: How does one balance the competing interests of individual freedom and institutional responsibility? And, how much intellectual freedom do young citizens have while in the high school and at college? A review of court guidance reveals common ground for the First Amendment in high school and college and beyond those institutions' boundaries. The foundation was laid more than fifty years ago.

As early as 1943, the Supreme Court told students that they bring the right of free expression with them to school. In *West Virginia State Board of Education v. Barnette*[2] it applied the longstanding free speech concept that government should neither require nor suppress expression. A high school policy requiring students to pledge allegiance to the flag unconstitutionally forced them to express beliefs they did not hold, the Court ruled. When sitting in silent protest does not interfere with other students' rights, school officials may not punish this expression.

Despite the *Barnette* ruling, the prevailing judicial sentiment for the next quarter century would be that public school officials have a parent-like role that entitles them discretion in their control of high school students. First Amendment cases with a college setting did not reflect this attitude, however. Differences in the environment, maturity of students and educational function led courts to view public-college administrators as facilitators rather than parents.

Strengthening the Foundation

High school *and* college students, including young journalists, received a boost when the high court revisited the public school twenty-six years after *Barnette* and stated more emphatically that constitutional rights extend to students, even when they're on public-school property. *Tinker v. Des Moines Independent School District*[3] focused on the limits that public school officials have in the regulation of student expression. What the Court said about students, administrators and the educational environment had sweeping implications that touched all young citizens, including student journalists.

Mary Beth and John Tinker and their friend Christopher Eckhardt wore black armbands to school in December 1965 to express their opposition to the Vietnam war. Their form of silent

---

[2] 319 U.S. 624 (1943).
[3] 393 U.S. 503 (1969).

protest clashed with a hastily prepared school policy. Officials thought that such expression was conduct and would disrupt the school. When the students refused to remove the armbands, they were suspended and sent home.

Legal action challenging the suspensions raised larger questions about whether fundamental First Amendment principles the Court applied outside of the school setting would pertain in school as well. Some questions were:

* Would any special circumstances justify different standards for regulating student expression?
* Is it protected symbolic speech or unprotected action to wear an armband to school?
* Will public school officials have to meet the same burden that courts have placed on other government regulators?
* What overriding interests would justify suppressing student expression?

Federal district and circuit court rulings in *Tinker* upheld the suspensions, reflecting the prevailing view that school officials should be given broad authority. The Supreme Court disagreed, ruling 7-2 that students, even when they're in school, share First Amendment protection with other citizens. The freedom has limits, but, the Court ruled, public school officials who wish to restrict expression must meet the burden of other government decision-makers and must justify suppressing or punishing speech.

Officials obligated to maintain an orderly learning environment can control student behavior inside the high school. The *Tinker* Court, however, ruled that wearing an armband is not conduct but a symbolic form of speech that can be stopped or punished only when educators can show that such expression would cause a "substantial disruption of or material interference with school activities."[4]

Tinker tells us that, whether on or off school grounds, public officials are not to stop or punish speech solely because they find it offensive. In the words of Justice Abe Fortas, writing for the Court:

> Students in school as well as out of school are "persons" under our Constitution.... In our system, students may not be regarded as closed-circuit recipients of only that which the State chooses to communicate. They may not be confined to the expression of those sentiments that are officially approved. In the absence of a specific showing of constitutionally valid reasons to regulate their speech, students are entitled to freedom of expression of their views.[5]

The Supreme Court placed the burden on school officials but offered several valid reasons that would justify regulation. The most common, and the one most often challenged in court, is the school's claim that expression would disrupt the educational process. A reasonable forecast of disruption justifies suppression of speech, the Court said, but officials must show a factual basis for their prediction. The structure and close supervision common to most secondary schools have given officials confidence in their claim of substantial disruption.

Another argument used to restrict student expression is that *Tinker* does not protect speech that is an invasion of the rights of others. High school officials have used this to justify censorship of defamatory material or, as in *Hazelwood School District v. Kuhlmeier*, discussed later in this chapter, because of fear that content invades someone's privacy. Because libel and privacy are defined no differently inside the school than outside, the student press and professional media are equally vulnerable and share the same legal defenses.

The Tinker *Philosophy*

The Supreme Court brought the First Amendment onto school grounds with *Tinker* because educational institutions are appropriate laboratories for learning the marketplace-of-ideas philosophy. "Freedom of expression would not truly exist," the Court said in *Tinker*, "if the right could be exercised only in an area that a benevolent government has provided as a safe haven for crackpots."[6]

The Court knew the risks of free speech but was willing to take those risks with young people. As Justice Fortas wrote:

> Any word spoken in class, in the lunchroom, or on the campus, that deviates from the views of another person may start an argument or cause a disturbance. But our Constitution says we must take this risk.... Our history says that it is this sort of hazardous freedom — this kind of openness — that is the basis of our national strength and of the independence and vigor of Americans.[7]

The Student Press Law Center, an Arlington, Virginia-based

---

[4] *Id.* at 514.

[5] *Id.* at 510.
[6] *Id.* at 513.
[7] *Id.* at 508.

source of legal advice and support for student journalists, considers *Tinker* "undoubtedly the most important student First Amendment case in the nation's history."[8] Little wonder. State and federal courts have cited *Tinker* in hundreds of high school and college cases. Free-speech advocates value the Court's emphasis on individual liberties and its assertion that speech — even on school property — is protected unless officials can demonstrate a reason to restrict it. With *Tinker,* a free-speech philosophy applied to all citizens embraced high school students. And the case provided a solid foundation for a long line of higher-education cases that declare college students to be adults worthy of all rights accorded citizens off campus.

Tinker was not a student press case, but during the next nineteen years more and more lower courts adopted the *Tinker* philosophy and applied it to cases involving student publications. Courts saw public high school and college students as citizens, and officials in all public institutions as arms of the government.

Limitations in Private Schools

It's different in private institutions. The First Amendment does *not* tell private citizens that they *must* speak or what they must say *if* they speak; it tells government not to interfere with citizens' expressive rights. The First Amendment applies, therefore, when there is government involvement or what is called "state action." When taxpayers are not heavily funding an educational institution or dictating its policies, and those making decisions for the school are not elected by, paid by or working for taxpayers, there is no state action. The assumption is that private-school officials are not obligated to abide by First Amendment constraints on government.

Students in private institutions, then, do not have First Amendment protection within those institutions. But that does not mean that students cannot be *given* the "right" to express themselves. Where a private school's promotional material or written philosophy, policies and practices promise certain freedoms, students may argue that reneging on those promises constitutes breach of contract.

A state's constitution or its legislature may be an additional vehicle for private-school students to obtain free-speech rights. In February 1995, a California superior court upheld what then was the only state law in the country that extended First Amendment protection to students at private post-secondary schools. In

Corry v. Stanford University[9] the court found the university's speech code unconstitutional and rejected Stanford's argument that as a private school it was not bound by the First Amendment. The state's content-neutral 1992 Leonard Law extended First Amendment protection to more California citizens (those on private-college campuses), the court said. It does not require a university to express ideas or to provide a platform for speech, the court added, nor would it lead the public to associate a college with ideas expressed on its campus.

Despite this recent ruling, the reality is that beyond the walls of California colleges, First Amendment protection extends to private-school students only when those who operate the schools allow it or a state constitution provides it. If private-school practices and stated policies permit expression, students can benefit from that freedom. If restrictions abound, students may stay at the school and abide by its rules or transfer to a public institution or a more permissive private school.

THE COLLEGE ENVIRONMENT

It may have surprised some people when a California judge in *Corry* upheld the state law that imposed First Amendment obligations on the managers of private institutions. But the court's unwillingness to distinguish between First Amendment protection on and off campus did not surprise those familiar with free-speech cases involving college students. With few exceptions, courts have equated the university campus with a public forum open to as far-reaching a collection of ideas as one might expect in a public park, and judges have given post-secondary students the adult-citizen status they would have if they were not in college. (A lone, recent exception is *Kincaid v. Gibson,* a federal district court case discussed later in this chapter.)

Distinguishing Student Expression

The factors courts normally consider when they address student expression make it easier today to distinguish between high school and college cases than to distinguish between cases involving college students and those affecting citizens beyond campus boundaries.

Three factors have been central to the court's reasoning in cases concerning regulation of student expression:

(1) The Age of the Speaker and Audience. When calls to "protect the children" accompany efforts to regulate cyberspace

---

[8] *Law of the Student Press,* 2nd ed. (Arlington, Va.: Student Press Law Center, 1994), p. 27.

[9] No. 740309 (Cal. Super. Ct., Santa Clara Cty., Feb. 27, 1995).

and computer access to sexual material, the courts are asked to reconcile another legal dilemma that has distinguished high school and college students. Courts for years have ruled that children are more vulnerable and deserve more protection than adults. This has led to different legal standards for sexual material and indecent, over-the-air broadcasts. Judges have said that high school students more comfortably qualify for the special protection of children than do college students, who are legally adults.

A three-judge federal court in Pennsylvania, when it enjoined enactment of the Communications Decency Act in June 1996, and the Supreme Court, when it held the act unconstitutional a year later, were both careful not to refute the notion that children deserve to be shielded from indecency. Both courts held that regulation must not be so sweeping that it prohibits adults from obtaining or disseminating material that is legally protected for adults.[10] This is particularly true, the Court has said, when alternative means are available to shield children from objectionable material.[11] The adult status accorded college students in a First Amendment context seemed to spare universities the task of monitoring cyberspace to the extent required of high school officials striving to shield minors. But the case of access to a broad range of on-line information and unresolved questions about liability have led to close monitoring and tighter regulation on some university campuses.

(2) Where the Speech Occurs. The public school is a different setting than either a college campus or a public street. High school students are closer to a captive audience, with less freedom to come and go. Judges have given broad regulatory latitude to public school officials who argue that discipline and control of behavior are necessary to provide an effective learning environment. Because the university is more open and enrollment is voluntary, judges have been reluctant to give college officials more regulatory authority than city officials would have over a public demonstration or parade.

(3) The Educators' Responsibilities. The Supreme Court, during the past fifteen years, has given high school officials more discretion when regulating speech they believe is inconsistent with educational goals and moral values. During this time, the gap has widened between freedom of speech in high school and in college because courts have *not* changed their view that the university should be a forum for exchanging ideas and college officials should encourage, not interfere with, that process.

The Legal Arguments

In general, five topics must be addressed in determining the status of speech in the college environment.

Lack of Disruption. *Tinker* has been cited to support college free-speech positions because it solidified the "substantial disruption" standard applied even earlier in a college press case. In that 1969 case, editor Gary Dickey was suspended from Troy State College for his published protest of student newspaper censorship. The Alabama federal district court judge who lifted the suspension in 1967 said that only reasonable regulations needed to maintain order and to operate "in a manner conducive to learning" are appropriate. Officials may infringe on students' rights only with evidence of material and substantial interference with such discipline, the court ruled.[12]

After the Supreme Court reinforced the disruption standard in *Tinker*, the Court applied it to the college setting with two decisions in the early 1970s. In *Healy v. James*[13] and *Papish v. Board of Curators of the University of Missouri*[14] the Court said there is no less need for order in schools than elsewhere in society, but that there also is no less First Amendment protection. That means, the Court said, that school officials may not silence a student organization just because it has a philosophy of disruption and violence (as in *Healy*) or suspend a graduate student just because the alternative newspaper she was distributing contained offensive language (as in *Papish*). In both instances, the Court ruled, such speech is consistent with the notion that universities are forums for exchanging ideas, and expression may be restricted only if officials can show that the learning process is substantially disrupted.

Public Forums. Sidewalks and parks traditionally have been public forums for sharing ideas, and the government has no authority to be selective about who speaks there. Not all public property is automatically a forum, but may become one, as when a city-owned building becomes a civic center open to community groups. The purpose of utility poles is not to carry signs, but if a city lets citizens post notices, the poles have been designated a public forum and officials may not arbitrarily allow some messages and prohibit others.

The public-forum doctrine is an important concept that distinguishes free-speech and free-press rights in high school and col-

---

[10] *Reno v. American Civil Liberties Union*, 929 F. Supp. 824 (E.D. Pa. 1996); 117 S.Ct. 2329 (1997).

[11] See *Sable Communications v. FCC*, 492 U.S. 115 (1989).

[12] *Dickey v. Alabama State Board of Education*, 273 F. Supp. 613 (M.D. Ala. 1967).

[13] 408 U.S. 169 (1972).

[14] 410 U.S. 667 (1973).

lege. A public high school is not traditionally a place for all citizens, or even all young people, to exchange ideas. Nor is all of a high school a public forum. And a student newspaper may not be a public forum because its function may not be to allow all students to express themselves; the newspaper must clearly be identified, by practice or policy, as a public forum.

The university press has not faced such rigid restrictions. Courts often have found the state university campus, by the nature of its mission and environment, to be a public forum. A federal district court in Utah said as much when it allowed a student group to construct shanties on the grounds of the University of Utah to protest apartheid and the university's South African investment policies.[15] And a federal appellate court in 1992 ruled that policy and practice at Southwest Texas State University clearly established all outdoor grounds "owned or controlled by the university" as a public forum.[16] Similarly, courts have said that once a university has established a newspaper, it has created a limited forum for the exchange of ideas,[17] but a forum where student editors retain control over content.[18]

A Kentucky federal district court judge late in 1997 took a different position of great interest to the collegiate press. The lower court has ruled that administrators at Kentucky State University could refuse to distribute the student-produced yearbook and could remove the faculty advisor who refused to force editors to print positive stories about the university. Students argued that university censorship based on dissatisfaction with negative newspaper stories and with the yearbook's content and the color of its cover abridged the students' First Amendment rights. In a ruling for the university, Judge Joseph M. Hood became the first federal judge to apply to a college case the Supreme Court's decision in the high school case of *Hazelwood v. Kuhlmeier*.[19]

Rejecting student arguments that the newspaper and yearbook are public forums, Judge Hood, instead, cited *Hazelwood* and deferred to the "intent of the publisher," in this case a university administration that the judge said did not intend to open the pages but retain them as "an educational tool."

Students sought a review of the November ruling, but Judge Hood in March affirmed his decision, noting that *Hazelood* is "the starting point in an analysis of whether a publication is a public forum, regardless of the fact that *Hazelwood* purely dealt with a high school publication." An appeal is pending before the Sixth U.S. Circuit Court of Appeals.

Current Campus Issues. The Student Press Law Center concluded in 1995 that "First Amendment protections for college students ... appear as strong today as they were 25 years ago."[20] The *Kincaid v. Gibson* ruling and renewed assaults by zealous college officials have tempered this optimistic assessment, but most courts continue to strike down sweeping, well-intentioned restrictions. For evidence, one need look no further than the past decade's cases involving speech codes created to curb hate speech on campus.

When college officials were faced with an increase in incidents of bigotry and racism on campus, the officials tried to curb verbal harassment rather than do nothing and appear to condone such incidents. Aware that courts had given broad protection to on-campus speech, officials attempted to equate verbal abuse with easier-to-control conduct and with unprotected fighting words. But the codes clearly focused on offensive expression, and when they were challenged, courts continued to hold that on-campus speech restrictions were no more permissible than off-campus restrictions.

A federal court, for example, found that a University of Michigan policy was so vague and sweeping that it punished constitutionally protected speech, even though the university's motive was to provide a comfortable learning environment for all students.[21] Even a more focused policy in the University of Wisconsin system was declared overbroad in 1991 and sent back to the Board of Regents for revision. Designed to punish only those who directed racial slurs or epithets at specific individuals, the code went beyond restricting fighting words and also restricted speech that created an undefined "intimidating, hostile or demeaning environment for education."[22] And, two years later, a federal judge in Michigan found another speech code, this one at Central Michigan University, to be unconstitutionally vague and overbroad.[23]

In 1996, a federal appellate court ruled against a San Bernardino community college after school officials reprimanded an English

---

[15] *University of Utah Students Against Apartheid v. Peterson,* 649 F. Supp. 1200 (D. Utah 1986).

[16] *Hays County Guardian v. Supple,* 969 F.2d 111 (5th Cir. 1992).

[17] See *Bazaar v. Fortune,* 489 F.2d 225 (5th Cir. 1973).

[18] See *Lee v. Board of Regents of State Colleges,* 441 F.2d 1257 (7th Cir. 1971); *Mississippi Gay Alliance v. Goudelock,* 536 F.2d 1073 (5th Cir. 1976); *Sinn v. The Daily Nebraskan,* 829 F.2d 662 (8th Cir. 1987); *Leeds v. Meltz,* 85 F.3d 51 (2d Cir. 1996).

[19] See *Kincaid v. Gibson,* Civ. No. 95-98 (E.D. Ky., Nov. 14, 1997), *aff'd* March 5, 1998.

[20] *Law of the Student Press,* p. 51.

[21] *Doe v. University of Michigan,* 721 F. Supp. 852 (E.D. Mich. 1989).

[22] *UWM Post., Inc. v. University of Wisconsin Board of Regents,* 774 F. Supp. 1163, 1165 (E.D. Wis. 1991).

[23] *Dambrot v. Central Michigan University,* 839 F. Supp. 477 (E.D. Mich. 1993).

professor whose classroom discussions allegedly violated an anti-sexual harassment policy. The controversial class discussions were protected from punishment and the instructor was the victim of an unconstitutionally vague policy, the court ruled.[24]

The court's message once again was that there would be no First Amendment exceptions on college campuses. When the Supreme Court unanimously rejected a *city's* hate-speech ordinance as unconstitutional, it seemed unlikely that a campus speech code could withstand a court challenge.[25] Many campuses either abandoned efforts to draft speech codes, chose to keep them but not enforce them or decided to punish hate speech only when it was tied to a criminal action.[26]

Courts clearly have continued to equate college students with adults and hold public-university administrators to the same First Amendment strictures as off-campus government officials. The contrasting atmosphere for free expression at the high school and university levels will be clearer after the next section's discussion of the Supreme Court's *Hazelwood* ruling.

Access to Crime Reports. College journalists share the First Amendment freedom of professional journalists but face similar struggles to exercise those freedoms. One of the students' major battles in the 1990s has been over access to campus crime information.

Professional journalists know that once they have information, the First Amendment makes it hard for government to stop publication. But it is just as clear that the First Amendment does not require government agencies to release information. State and federal legislation can call for the release of such information, as the Freedom of Information Act and other access legislation have done. Journalists use these tools to joust with public officials over access to information some government employees would prefer to keep quiet.

Some university officials react with the same reservations when student journalists seek details about the types and extent of crimes on campus. Traci Bauer, while editor-in-chief of the Southwest Missouri State University newspaper, was the first to win a federal court decision granting access to incident reports from the campus police. A Missouri judge rejected the university's argument that police reports were education records that the Buckley Amendment of the Family Education Rights and Privacy Act required be closed to protect the students' privacy. Judge Russell Clark, in *Bauer v. Kincaid,* cited the First Amendment and the Missouri Sunshine Law when he granted students access to the same type of information other police departments in Missouri must provide.[27]

Colleges and universities continued to resist the release of crime information, and the U.S. Department of Education fueled this tension by rejecting the judge's interpretation in *Bauer*. It wasn't until the Student Press Law Center intervened and federal legislation was passed in 1992 that crime records were released from the bonds of Buckley Amendment secrecy.[28]

This did not end legal struggles for campus crime information, however. The Federal Campus Security Act of 1990 requires that colleges and universities receiving federal aid publish annual figures for the number of crimes reported on campus. Instances of incomplete or misleading reports of campus crime prompted the U.S. House of Representatives to unanimously pass a resolution late in 1996 urging the U.S. Department of Education to monitor crime reports more closely.

Matters did not improve, and in February of 1997 the DOE reported to Congress that sixty percent of postsecondary institutions required by law to compile and report crime statistics on their campuses admitted that they do not follow federal guidelines defining campus crimes. The report fueled additional congressional activity that by late 1998 had produced a number of bills related to campus security. Access to campus police logs, better disclosure of crime on campus, and more access to student disciplinary records and proceedings are parts of the amendments to the Higher Education Act overwhelmingly approved by the U.S. House and Senate and signed into law by President Clinton in early October.

Some legislation is a direct response to an access battle college journalists have repeatedly and successfully fought in court. At the University of Georgia, student journalists spent more than five years in court seeking entry to university disciplinary board hearings and records. Twice in 1993 the state supreme court cited Georgia's open meeting and open-records laws and released the records from a hearing involving fraternity hazing[29] and from a dif-

---

[24] *Cohen v. San Bernardino Valley College,* 92 F.3d 968 (9th Cir. 1996), *cert. denied* 117 S.Ct. 1290 (1997).

[25] See *RAV v. St. Paul,* 505 U.S. 377 (1992).

[26] See Scott Jaschik, "Campus 'Hate Speech' Codes in Doubt After High Court Rejects a City Ordinance," *Chronicle of Higher Education,* 1 July 1992, p. A19.

[27] 759 F. Supp. 575 (W.D. Mo. 1991).

[28] Mark Goodman, "Campus Records Fight Continues Despite Bauer Win," *Quill,* May 1992, pp. 14-15.

[29] *Red & Black Publ. Co. v. Board of Regents, University of Georgia,* 262 Ga. 848, 427 S.E.2d 257 (1993).

ferent hearing about a gay-bashing incident.[30] In July 1997, the Ohio Supreme Court ruled that Miami University of Ohio officials were wrong to consider disciplinary records from the campus court to be "education records" and thus deny student journalists access to them. Records of the proceedings are not prodected by the Buckley Amendment's privacy provisions, the court said.[31]

Despite these rulings, student journalists in other states may have to wait for federal legislation granting comparable access.[32] Although the U.S. Supreme Court refused to hear the Miami University of Ohio case, the U.S. Department of Education continues to oppose disclosure. In January 1995, the DOE said state open-meeting laws may provide access to campus judicial proceedings and colleges may open their disciplinary proceedings. But the department also said that all disciplinary records, even those related to criminal misconduct, remain "educational records" subject to the Buckley Amendment.[33] Early in 1998 the DOE sought a court order to prevent Ohio State University and Miami University of Ohio from releasing unedited campus disciplinary records. Legislation has been proposed, but not yet passed, removing student disciplinary records from the Buckley Amendment's privacy umbrella.

Special Press Problems. College journalists face a few free-speech problems the professionals are spared:

- Student fees often underwrite part of a campus newspaper's publishing costs. Student governments usually have a hand in dispersal of this money and occasionally try to place content requirements on the newspaper as a condition of funding.[34]

- When university officials have inappropriately withheld funds from the student newspaper because of disagreement with its content, courts have had to intervene.[35]

- Student newspaper advisers in increasing numbers are finding their jobs at risk because college administrators want fewer

controversial stories and more positive news published.[36]

- Students continue to steal and destroy campus newspapers as a means of expressing dissatisfaction with content or policies. College officials have been reluctant to bring criminal charges.[37]

- With reports of binge drinking and alcohol use on campus, college newspapers have been the target of efforts to ban ads for alcoholic beverages. In Pennsylvania, the Liquor Control Board threatened to revoke the liquor licenses of any establishment advertising in a college newspaper.[38]

Notwithstanding these special concerns, the college press is far closer to equal First Amendment footing with the professional press than the high school press is.

REGULATING HIGH SCHOOL EXPRESSION

During the 1970s and much of the 1980s, lower courts, with increasing regularity, stressed the *Tinker* testament to individual expression. They made it hard for school officials to censor the student press, telling them to write guidelines before regulating expression. And courts rejected vague and overbroad guidelines that allowed administrators to suppress material that, while embarrassing or disturbing to school officials, was neither substantially disruptive nor infringed on the rights of others.[39] In the mid-1980s, however, the Supreme Court began signaling a shift that would make it far harder for high school journalists to exercise the constitutional rights acknowledged in the *Tinker* decision.

Tinker, with its inspirational free-speech rhetoric, remains good law today for *individual* expression in the high school. However, the many students in supervised speech-related activities, such as student publications, now have less First Amendment protection. This is because the Supreme Court has refocused its attention in high school cases.

---

[30] *John Doe v. Red & Black Publ. Co.,* 437 S.E.2d 474 (Ga. 1993).

[31] *Miami Student v. Miami University of Ohio,* 79 Ohio St. 3d 168, 680 N.E.2d 956 (1997), *cert. denied* , 118 S. Ct. 616 (1997).

[32] In *Community College of Philadelphia v. Brown,* 674 A.2d 670 (Pa. 1966), the Pennsylvania Supreme Court denied the student newspaper access to campus crime records. Pennsylvania's open records act does not apply to the state's educational institutions, the court said, because they are not agencies performing an "essential governmental function."

[33] See Mac McKerral, "Changes to Buckley Amendment Keep Campus Crime Reports Hidden," *Quill,* May 1995, p. 17.

[34] Claire Goldstein, "College Newspapers Face Attempts at Content Control by Campus Groups," *Quill,* June 1995, p. 61.

[35] See, e.g., *Stanley v. Magrath,* 719 F.2d 279 (8th Cir. 1983).

[36] Leo Reisberg, "When Student Newspapers Offend, Advisers May Pay With Their Jobs," *Chronicle of Higher Education,* 17 July 1998, pp. A53-54.

[37] See "Getting the Message Out," Legal Analysis, *Student Press Law Center Report,* Winter, 1993-94, pp. 22-27; Michael Koster, "The New Campus Censors," *Columbia Journalism Review,* September/October 1994, p. 19; M.L. Stein, "Stealing and Trashing Student Newspapers is Current Campus Craze," *Editor & Publisher,* 3 Sept. 1994, p. 13; and "Newspaper Thefts Spark New Solutions," *Student Press Law Center Report,* Spring 1997, pp. 28-30.

[38] "Alcohol-Related Ads Banned," *Student Press Law Center Report,* Fall 1997, p. 19.

[39] See *Nitzberg v. Parks,* 525 F.2d 378 (4th Cir.1975); and *Gambino v. Fairfax County School Board,* 564 F.2d 157 (4th Cir. 1977).

A *Shift in First Amendment Philosophy*

Instead of concentrating on students and viewing constitutional freedom as an instrument to help those in high school learn societal values, the Supreme Court has turned its attention to school officials and what they must do to meet their responsibility to instill those values in the young. School officials now have more latitude, and the burden has shifted to students, who more easily can be silenced in public schools because of who they are, where they are and why they're there.

A 1986 Supreme Court case introduced this philosophy and foreshadowed a landmark high school newspaper case two years later. *Bethel School District v. Fraser* [40] began when a student gave a two-minute campaign speech during a school-sponsored assembly. Matthew Fraser used no four-letter words, but he did use sexual innuendo. He described the candidate as "firm — he's firm in his pants, he's firm in his shirt, his character is firm" and as one who "takes his point and pounds it in.... He doesn't attack things in spurts; he drives hard, pushing and pushing until finally — he succeeds."

Several students in the audience of 600 hooted during the speech, but when Fraser finished, the candidate spoke briefly and the end-of-school assembly concluded. The next day, several teachers complained, and Fraser was suspended for three days. He filed suit and won when federal district and appellate courts agreed that because it was not substantially disruptive, his speech was protected.

But the Supreme Court disagreed. The disruption standard stemmed from *Tinker*, which dealt with students who wore armbands as individuals expressing political beliefs. Because circumstances are different in *Bethel*, the Court said, a different standard applies. First, school officials have more control over the content of a school-sponsored assembly than over what a student says in the corridors. Second, school officials should see that public education instills moral values and encourages civility. To do this, the Court said, school officials must be free to disassociate the school from "vulgar and lewd speech" that undermines the educational mission and is "inconsistent with the 'fundamental values' of public school education." The Court said it was more important that school officials have discretionary power to identify and inculcate "fundamental values" than that they establish and follow narrow regulations.[41]

Although the Court said that *Bethel* did not overturn *Tinker*, it

was not clear until two years later whether the Court intended the *Tinker* standard to remain in place for serious idea speech (similar to that of a war protest) or whether *Tinker* was to apply only to speech not under the control of school officials. In 1988, the Court's *Hazelwood School District v. Kuhlmeier*[42] ruling clarified this: *Tinker* would apply when students spoke on their own in school, but a different set of rules applied to students using a school-sponsored vehicle such as the student newspaper.

The Hazelwood *Standard*

The *Spectrum* was very much a part of Hazelwood East High School. Its adviser taught most staff members, who were in their second journalism course at the suburban St. Louis, Missouri, school. The student newspaper had covered serious topics in earlier issues and put together a spring edition that included two pages featuring stories on teenage concerns, including pregnancy and divorce.

It was established practice to let Hazelwood East principal R.E. Reynolds review page proofs before publication. He objected to two stories. In one, three unnamed students described their pregnancies. In the other, students were quoted discussing the impact of their parents' divorces. Concerned that these stories might offend young readers and invade students' and parents' privacy, Reynolds pulled the two pages that included the offending articles. Three staff members who learned of the censorship when the printed paper was delivered filed suit.

A federal district court said that the principal's actions were reasonable and that he had authority because the newspaper was part of the school curriculum instead of a public forum. The Eighth U.S. Circuit Court of Appeals said *Spectrum* was part of the curriculum but *also* a public forum. The appellate court built its decision on a number of student-press cases grounded in *Tinker* and concluded that school officials had no reason to forecast substantial disruption and no liability for any libel or invasion of privacy suit.

The same day the Eighth Circuit ruled in favor of the Hazelwood East students, the Supreme Court ruled in *Bethel v. Fraser*. Six months later, the Court agreed to review *Hazelwood*.

The Supreme Court almost effortlessly applied its *Bethel* rationale to *Hazelwood*. In reversing the Eighth Circuit ruling, the Court described a high school setting and citizenry in stark contrast to those of the university or society at large.[43] As it had done

---

[40] 478 U.S. 675 (1986).
[41] *Id.* at 685-86.

[42] 484 U.S. 260 (1988).
[43] In footnote 7 of the *Hazelwood* decision, the Supreme Court

two years before, the Court stressed the obligation school officials have and the authority they need to educate youth. The content of the censored *Spectrum* stories was less important than whether the principal's actions were reasonable.

The Educator's Role. A public-school official doesn't quite have the autonomy of a true publisher but does have more control over expression than do most government officials. The Court came close to granting public school administrators the same unquestioned authority of a private newspaper's owner.

State or local government officials and public university administrators have strict limits on their censorship power and must justify restrictions. High school officials also have to defend any censorship, but today that is much easier. The tone and substance of the *Hazelwood* decision encourage close scrutiny of student expression. School officials may regulate "in any reasonable manner" the content of any "supervised learning experience," the Court said. In the words of Justice Byron White: "[E]ducators do not offend the First Amendment by exercising editorial control over the style and content of student speech in school-sponsored expressive activities so long as their actions are reasonably related to legitimate pedagogical concerns."[44] These concerns include "speech that is ... ungrammatical, poorly written, inadequately researched, biased or prejudiced, vulgar or profane, or unsuitable for immature audiences."[45] The school does not need specific written guidelines in order to control school-sponsored publications, the Court said, and violates the First Amendment only when censorship has no valid educational purposes.

The Learning Environment. The *Hazelwood* Court also said that a more narrowly defined educational environment and a broader definition of curriculum give officials more regulatory control over student expression in high school than in college.

Hazelwood East students argued successfully at the appellate court level that *Spectrum* was a public forum that should be free of content-based regulation, but the Supreme Court disagreed. It ruled that because the newspaper had not been clearly designated as a public forum, school officials were free to oversee its content.

The Court did not assume what lower courts had come to accept — that the ideas exchanged in the student newspaper made it a public forum. Although it covered controversial issues and carried letters to the editor, *Spectrum* had not become a public forum because no school board policy clearly stated such intent, and the practice of submitting the newspaper for administrative review indicated the school wanted to retain control.

Age and Maturity. When it supported school officials, the Supreme Court in *Hazelwood* applied a legal philosophy built on the premise that, for legitimate reasons, government decision-makers can deny children constitutional rights that adults have. The age and maturity of high school students put their rights of free expression second to the rights of adults responsible for advancing the school's educational goals.

The Court said that school officials could use censorship to protect students from a newspaper story on coping with teenage pregnancy. Then the Court applied the legal rationale it had used in previous rulings to protect children from sexual material.

The Supreme Court earlier had defined and defended "variable obscenity" as a permissible way for government to protect minors from the potential harm of sexual content. In *Ginsberg v. New York*[46] the Court said that when evaluating sexual material available to minors, the test for judging a work as obscene for adults can be modified and the material restricted if it meets a lesser standard. In 1982, the Court unanimously upheld a state child-pornography law directed at material not obscene for adults but illegal because it involved minors. The rationale, once more, was a valid state interest in protecting vulnerable youth.[47] In *Hazelwood* the Court again decided that the First Amendment permits government — in this case, high school officials — to consider the "emotional maturity of the intended audience" when determining "whether to disseminate speech on potentially sensitive topics."

As computers and Internet resources have entered the classroom and become tools for research and learning, school officials have had the added burden of protecting the young from adult material on the net. Even as it ruled the Communications Decency Act unconstitutional, the Supreme Court acknowledged the valid government interest in protecting minors. Today some overly protective school administrators are denying student journalists access to Internet resources useful in reporting, and publication staffs have to resolve privacy concerns before their newspapers are allowed to go on-line.

---

said only, "We need not now decide whether the same degree of deference is appropriate with respect to school-sponsored expressive activities at the college and university level." Although the Court did not foreclose that possibility, it was more than ten years before a federal judge applied the *Hazelwood* standard in a college press rights case, *Kincaid v. Gibson, supra* note 19 and accompanying text.

[44] 484 U.S. at 273.

[45] *Id.* at 271.

---

[46] 390 U.S. 629 (1968).

[47] *New York v. Ferber,* 458 U.S. 747 (1982).

Arguing for Free Speech

The Supreme Court has not left students powerless to speak in the public schools. Valid legal arguments for free expression remain. Some questions that the most persuasive of those arguments address are:

Is There a Legitimate Reason To Regulate? In American society, the government must show that a legitimate public good will occur as a result of any regulation of an individual's speech. It's no different in public educational institutions. In high school, it *is* easier for officials to find valid reasons.

Hazelwood gave school officials more authority over school-sponsored speech than over content students generate on their own. But when a Wisconsin high school student told readers of an underground newspaper how to crack the security of the school's computer system, he was expelled. A federal district judge, applying *Tinker* to the off-campus expression, lifted the expulsion because the article did not cause substantial disruption. On appeal, the Seventh U.S. Circuit Court of Appeals agreed that expulsion was excessive but said punishment was justified because the article was a substantial threat to the school.[48]

The *Hazelwood* ruling has given school officials more control over what teachers say, as well. The most recent case is from North Carolina, where the Fourth U.S. Circuit Court of Appeals upheld sanctions of a drama teacher whose selection of a controversial play led school officials to remove the production from state competition and transfer the teacher to another school. The court said that although the teacher always selects the play, the drama is part of the curriculum that administrators can legitimately control as school-sponsored speech.[49]

But students *have* successfully challenged administrators to demonstrate in court that speech restrictions are reasonably related to educational goals. One such victory came from the New Jersey Supreme Court, which ruled unanimously that the principal of Clearview Junior High School had not met the *Hazelwood* standard when he censored two movie reviews by Brien Desilets. The principal had no problem with the content of the eighth-grader's reviews for the student newspaper but censored them because the films — *Rain Man* and *Mississippi Burning* — are R-rated, which school officials said meant the subject matter was inappropriate for junior-high students. The state supreme court dis-

agreed and concluded that there were insufficient educational grounds to justify the censorship.[50]

Is It School-Sponsored Speech That's Being Regulated?
The *Hazelwood* court clearly gave high school officials more control than they had before over expression that is school-sponsored or supervised by faculty members. Students who speak on their own still have constitutional safeguards in high schools. Before 1988, pre-publication review of school newspapers was permitted in most of the country, as long as constitutional procedureal guidelines existed. The *Hazelwood* majority removed the requirement of guidelines for school-sponsored speech, but said it was not yet eliminating that safeguard for individual expression.

Speech that does *not* come through a faculty-supervised activity has more protection because it is subject to the *Tinker* standard and must be permitted unless school officials can show the speech is substantially disruptive or invades the rights of others. Post-*Hazelwood* cases that support this view deal with students wanting to distribute religious materials or publish alternative student newspapers.

The same year as *Hazelwood*, the Ninth U.S. Circuit Court of Appeals ruled that school officials were wrong to discipline five students who distributed their newspaper at a class picnic without getting prior approval. This court said the school's broad control over curriculum does not extend to a policy controlling content of non-school-sponsored speech.[51] More recently, a federal district court rejected a prior-review policy applied to a religious pamphlet distributed in a Florida elementary school. The judge said school officials showed no evidence that distribution would be disruptive.[52] The *Tinker* disruption standard also was applied in district court cases that supported students' right to distribute religious literature in Texas and Colorado.[53] A school policy in Indiana that set forth conditions for prior review of any written material distributed on school grounds was ruled constitutional because the policy included no content provisions for censorship.[54]

The proliferation of computers and the relative ease with which students can publish on-line and create web sites have given the term "underground press" a new dimension. Until the courts rule otherwise, such off-campus use of the Internet qualifies as indi-

---

[48] *Boucher v. School Board of Greenfield,* 134 F.3d 821 (7th Cir. 1998).

[49] *Boring v. Buncombe County Board of Education,* 136 F.3d 364 (4th Cir. 1998).

[50] *Desilets v. Clearview Regional Board of Education,* 137 N.J. 585, 647 A.2d 150 (1994).

[51] *Burch v. Barker,* 861 F.2d 1149 (9th Cir. 1988).

[52] *Johnston-Loebner v. O'Brien,* 859 F. Supp. 575 (M.D.Fla. 1994).

[53] *Clark v. Dallas Ind. School Dist.,* 806 F. Supp. 116 (N.D. Texas 1992); *Rivera v. East Otero School Dist.,* 721 F. Supp. 1189 (D. Colo. 1989).

[54] *Harless v. Darr,* 937 F. Supp. 1251 (S.D. Ind. 1996).

vidual expression, subject to punishment by school officials only if it can meet the "substantial disruption" standard of *Tinker*.[55]

Is the Newspaper a Public Forum? A city is not required to create a public park or stock one with benches where people can share ideas. But if there *is* a park, public officials can't decide which political ideas may be expressed on a park bench and which may not. Students have used this public forum principle to defend their right to express ideas on school property. While courts consistently have found a public university's campus and student newspaper to be public forums, the courts have not said that about high school corridors and publications. High school students and publication staffs will have more freedom of expression if their newspapers are public forums, but they should not assume a newspaper is a public forum.

The Ninth U.S. Circuit Court of Appeals clarified in 1991 what it means for a school to designate a public forum. A Nevada school district gave principals the authority to set guidelines for acceptable advertising in their student publications and reject ads that did not meet those guidelines. The school set a review procedure and refused to run Planned Parenthood ads considered unsuitable. Before deciding whether the broad administrative discretion of *Hazelwood* applied to this case, the appellate court had to decide whether the publications were public forums, thus limiting administrative control. The court said the newspaper was not a public forum just because it accepted advertising or reported on controversial issues. It was not a forum because school officials, with their policy and practice of prior review, had clearly retained control and had not turned it over to the staff.[56]

Even when school officials allow students to make editorial decisions, it does not mean that the student publications are public forums open to anyone who wants access to the newspaper or yearbook. When the U.S. Supreme Court refused in June 1998 to hear his case, a Massachusetts businessman lost his argument that a high school newspaper had to accept his political advertisement encouraging sexual abstinence. Douglas Yeo wanted the ad in the newspaper and yearbook, but the student editors said no. Yeo rejected the students' offer to write a letter to the editor after they cited an unwritten policy not to accept political or advocacy ads. The First U.S. Circuit Court of Appeals initially ruled for Yeo, but a six-judge panel of the appellate court reheard the case and unanimously ruled for the students. The court ruled that where high school officials (here under the mandate of a Massachusetts statute) grant editorial authority to students, there is "no legal duty here on the part of school administrators to control the content of the editorial judgments of student editors of publications."[57]

Free press advocates have encouraged student journalists to clearly establish their publications as public forums. Where the newspaper is clearly a public forum, and administrators have given students control over content, it is likely that the standard from *Tinker*, not *Hazelwood*, will apply. The newspaper can become a forum through school board policy or an agreement with school officials, reinforced by practice and a staff policy that demonstrate the newspaper is used for an exchange of opinions.

Do Officials Know That Editorial Control Brings Liability? Whether a high school newspaper is, by policy or practice, a public forum is important to students. But school officials also can benefit when they decide not to review copy before publication and give the staff responsibility for newspaper content.[58]

High school or college officials who fear they will be held responsible for harmful expression should be reassured that they will be as liable as a private publisher only if they routinely review and regulate publication content.[59]

Private publishers are legally responsible for defamatory content they print because they and their editors are free to decide what to publish. The Supreme Court, however, said that a television station carrying the defamatory comments of a political candidate was *not* responsible because the station had no editorial control. Broadcasters cannot be held accountable for content that Congress, through Section 315 of the Communications Act, denied station owners the power to edit, the Court said.[60]

School authorities may argue for the same immunity when the student newspaper at their school, "by policy or by practice," has become a public forum and the administration does not review content. In public universities, where administrators have little control over student publication content, it is unlikely that a

---

[55] See "The Other Side of the School Gate," Legal Analysis in *Student Press Law Center Report*, Fall 1997, pp. 20-23.

[56] *Planned Parenthood v. Clark County School Dist.*, 887 F.2d 935 (9th Cir. 1989).

[57] *Yeo v. Lexington*, 131 F.3d 241 (1st Cir. 1997), *cert. denied* 118 S.Ct. 2060 (1998).

[58] See "Fixing the Blame," Legal Analysis in *Student Press Law Center Report*, Winter 1997-98, pp. 24-27.

[59] See *Lentz v. Clemson University*, No. 95-CP-39-66 (Ct. Common Pleas, Pickens County, South Carolina, Dec. 20, 1995); *McEvaddy v. City University of New York*, 633 N.Y.S.2d 4 (N.Y. App. Div. 1995); *Gallo v. Princeton University*, 656 A.2d 1267 (N.J. Super. Ct. A.D. 1995); and *Law of the Student Press*, pp. 159-163.

[60] *Farmers Educational & Cooperative Union of America v. WDAY, Inc.*, 360 U.S. 525 (1959).

court would hold school officials legally liable for what is printed. In the high school, officials have more authority to oversee content but are not required by *Hazelwood* to do so. The more oversight and influence the administration exercises, the more likely it is that the school will be legally liable for what is published. By turning editorial decisions over to a staff and/or faculty adviser, school officials are in a better position to argue for the immunity at least two courts have accorded state universities.[61]

Mark Goodman, executive director of the Student Press Law Center, said in a statement posted on the SPLC web page that one message of *Yeo v. Lexington* is that "as long as they give students editorial independence, school officials will not be held responsible for the content decisions students make. The decision suggests that a 'hands-off' policy ... may actually insulate schools from liability."[62]

Has Law or Policy Given Students More Free-Speech Rights? The Supreme Court has clearly indicated that lawmakers may give citizens *more* First Amendment protection than the Constitution provides. That's what students learned when the Court unanimously upheld their rights under the California Constitution to distribute literature at a privately owned shopping mall.[63]

California also passed a law in 1971 that codified the *Tinker* "substantial disruption" standard and protection for the speech and press rights of high school students. By the early 1980s, federal courts regularly cited and applied *Tinker,* and some free-speech observers thought the California law merely re-stated the Supreme Court precedent.

Then along came the *Hazelwood* decision, and within weeks a high school administrator tried to apply the new ruling and censor a California student newspaper. But the censorship was challenged, and a judge ruled that the state law granting students more free-speech rights takes precedence over the *Hazelwood*-based argument that educational goals justified censorship.[64]

Since then, the Student Press Law Center reports, at least twenty-eight other states have considered or debated legislation on student expression. Massachusetts followed California's lead and enacted legislation in July 1988. Then came Iowa, Colorado,

Kansas and Arkansas. No similar state legislation has been passed since 1995, and some legislators in 1998 tried to give school officials more authority by amending the Kansas Freedom of Student Expression law. But nationwide, other legislative obstacles have discouraged censorship:

- California's "Leonard Law," discussed earlier in connection with campus speech codes, extends First Amendment protection to high school and college students in both public and private schools.
- Students in Oregon and New Jersey have argued that their state constitutions protect student expression.
- The New York Commissioner of Education said that the publication policies of Long Island's Northport High School reveal the school's decision to set free-speech standards more permissive than *Hazelwood's.*
- In its state education code, Pennsylvania's Department of Education used *Tinker* to build a standard for freedom of expression.

SUMMARY

High school and college students today experience quite different First Amendment freedoms and tensions on their campuses. In public institutions, students have many rights other citizens have and administrators are considered public officials subject to some of the same constitutional restrictions all government officials face. But freedoms of speech and press have limits in the schools, just as they have parameters elsewhere in society.

The legal springboard for student free-speech rights is the Supreme Court's 1969 ruling in *Tinker v. Des Moines Independent School District,* which stressed the value of free expression and said that school officials could stop student speech only by showing that the expression would substantially disrupt the school or infringe on the rights of others. Hundreds of high school and college cases during the next seventeen years were based on *Tinker* and its premise that free speech should be encouraged, even in school.

Some educators, especially in high schools, continued to argue for different regulatory standards based on school officials' responsibility to teach the young. That plus the relative immaturity of students and the need for an environment conducive to learning were reasons administrators gave for denying students freedom in school that they might have elsewhere.

The Supreme Court eventually agreed that free-speech distinctions and tighter restrictions are appropriate when dealing with

[61] See *Mazart v. State,* 100 Misc. 2d 1092, 441 N.Y.S.2d 600 (N.Y.Ct.C1. 1981); and *Milliner v. Turner,* 436 So.2d 1300 (La. Ct. App. 1983).
[62] "Court Upholds the Right of High School Editors to Reject Ads," SPLC web page, http://www.splc.org/newsflashes.
[63] *Pruneyard Shopping Center v. Robins,* 447 U.S. 74 (1980).
[64] *Leeb v. DeLong,* 198 Cal. App. 3d 47, 243 Cal. Rptr. 494 (Cal. Dist. Ct. App. 1988).

high school students. Whether the free-speech rationale used in *Bethel* (in 1986) and *Hazelwood* (in 1988) will be applied in college and university cases may depend on the outcome of appeals in *Kincaid v. Gibson,* the first judicial ruling applying *Hazelwood* to the college press. Students in post-secondary schools are considered adults, with the same First Amendment rights accorded adults elsewhere in society.

In the past decade, college students have successfully challenged speech and conduct codes that the courts ruled too broad and restrictive, and college journalists have had some success in the Congress and the courts during frequent battles for access to campus crime reports. High school officials have found it easier to restrict expression, but student journalists have tried to curb censorship by getting the school to recognize the student press as a public forum. Efforts also continue at the state and local levels to enact laws or draft policies to give students more tools to encourage free expression. And the Internet, with its ease of access, wealth of information and potential for abuse and harm, has imposed added responsibility on school officials. Their uncertainty as they balance the learning tool and their obligation to protect vulnerable youth have made school authorities more willing to err on the side of close regulation.

FOR ADDITIONAL READING

Death by Cheeseburger: High School Journalism in the 1990s and Beyond. Arlington, Va.: The Freedom Forum, 1994.

Ingelhart, Louis E. *Student Publications: Legalities, Governance, and Operation.* Ames: Iowa State University Press, 1993.

Law of the Student Press, 2nd ed. Arlington, Va.: Student Press Law Center, 1994.

Student Press Law Center Report. Thrice-yearly magazine of the SPLC, Arlington, Va.

13

Privacy and the Professional Communicator

By Sigman Splichal

Privacy.

The word resonates within American society, its citizens often making social and legal claims based on the belief they have a fundamental right, as Supreme Court Justice Louis Brandeis once put it, "to be let alone."[1] Privacy is a social concept as old as the nation, imbedded in its beginning, from the first settlers drawn to a new land in search of religious and political freedom in the Seventeenth Century to revolutionary patriots affronted by England's cavalier disregard for the autonomy of their businesses and the sanctity of their homes. The concept of privacy can be found in the liberal theories of Enlightenment philosophers, whose emphasis on individual liberties based on natural rights inspired the Founding Fathers' generation as it began to envision a new nation.[2] Indeed essential elements of privacy are woven into the nation's most hallowed documents. Yet, while privacy as a social value was apparent during the nation's formative years, privacy as the basis for *legal* claims remained elusive. Only in the last 100 years has privacy been propelled into the legal mainstream, mainly due to changes in the way Americans live and think.

Privacy is a dynamic value that continues to evolve, as do all social values, norms and customs. To be understood in an information-driven society — both in social and legal contexts — privacy must be viewed as a value that changes as society tries to balance rights of individuals with its needs and desires for information. The Ninth U.S. Circuit Court of Appeals put it aptly in a 1975 privacy case: To resolve privacy claims, courts must consider "the customs and conventions of the community; and in the last analysis what is proper becomes a matter of community mores."[3]

This chapter looks first at the evolution of the concept of privacy in American society. It then focuses on the development of privacy as a distinct legal doctrine and its treatment in the common law of the states. The chapter then discusses the four distinct privacy torts identified by courts: publication of embarrassing private facts, physical and technological intrusion, false-light invasion of privacy and commercialization. It also briefly addresses constitutional and statutory privacy, both of which place limits on government use of personal information — limits that have important implications for journalists, especially in the era of databases, the World Wide Web, the Internet and reporters' growing reliance on computer-assisted reporting. Finally, the chapter looks at the ethical implications of privacy as the rights to gather and receive news are balanced with the rights of individuals to be let alone,

---

[1] *Olmstead v United States*, 227 U.S. 438, 478 (1928). Actually, Judge Thomas M. Cooley had used the term forty years earlier in his *A Treatise on the Law of Torts* 2d ed. (Chicago: Callaghan and Co., 1888), p. 29.

[2] John Locke, *The Second Treatise on Government*, ed. T. Peardon (New York: Liberal Arts Press, 1952).

[3] *Virgil v. Time, Inc.*, 527 F.2d 1122, 1129 (9th Cir. 1975).

and it examines the tort of intentional infliction of emotional distress.

THE EVOLUTION OF A RIGHT TO PRIVACY

The concept of privacy, though never expressed as it is understood today, was not unknown in English common law, the legal system dominant in Colonial America and later adopted by the fledgling nation. Cases dating to the Norman Conquest recognized a value resembling privacy in the property rights of individuals. In 1741, the House of Lords, then England's highest court, invoked a property-rights doctrine to protect contents of personal letters from unauthorized publication.[4] This case, *Pope v. Curl*, is important in the development of privacy in American law because it acknowledged a property right in individuals' retention and control of personal ideas and information in letters sent to others, not only in the letters themselves.

In the development of American social and legal values, the basic characteristics of modern privacy predate the American Revolution. English philosopher John Locke, whose writings influenced Thomas Jefferson and other founders, argued that government had a duty to protect fundamental rights such as life, liberty and property.[5] These inalienable rights were described in the Declaration of Independence, the Constitution and the Bill of Rights. The Supreme Court, almost 200 years later, gleaned from the fundamental concept of liberty a constitutional right of privacy.[6]

In his book *Privacy in Colonial New England*, historian David H. Flaherty explored the precursors to modern privacy. He observed that although privacy as a legal doctrine evolved slowly in Western culture, its underlying values were expressed in colonial customs and in the courts. Courts, he suggested, protected privacy values indirectly by enforcing laws against trespass, by limiting government searches and seizures, by hearing defamation cases and by recognizing privileged communications between wives and husbands. Ironically, as Flaherty pointed out, there was little physical privacy — in the modern sense — in most homes and public accommodations. Homes often lacked individual sleeping quarters, and families congregated in common beds. Communal sleeping arrangements were also common in public inns.[7] Traces of the practice remained as late as 150 years ago: During his early career as a struggling, small-town lawyer, Abraham Lincoln shared a room and bed above his office with a law partner.[8]

Flaherty noted that the concept of informational privacy was officially recognized during Benjamin Franklin's tenure as postmaster general before the American Revolution. Postmasters were required to swear an oath that they would not "wittingly, willingly, or knowingly open ... any letters which shall come into their hands."[9]

Values underlying privacy also were apparent as the Revolutionary War drew near and played a central role in the colonists' growing hostility toward British rule. In 1761, Boston lawyer James Otis, speaking against the practice of general search warrants, noted: "Now one of the most essential branches of English liberty, is the freedom of one's own house. A man's house is his castle; and while he is quiet he is as well guarded as a prince in his castle."[10] On the eve of the Revolutionary War, each colony drew up a list of grievances against the British authorities. Atop each list was concern about general warrants, which authorized government agents to search premises at will without first presenting evidence of a specific violation of the law. After the colonies won independence, James Madison, the major proponent of a bill of rights spelling out individual liberties, introduced a proposal at the Constitutional Convention in 1789 to limit the scope of government searches. That proposal, which established "the right of the people to be secure ... against unreasonable search and seizures," was later adopted as the Fourth Amendment.

Values supporting privacy also found expression in the writings of nineteenth-century English philosopher John Stuart Mill, whose works were widely read in the United States. Mill argued in his influential *On Liberty* that the government should have no say in certain kinds of personal conduct, absent a compelling social interest. Expounding on this concept of personal liberty, he wrote: "The only part of conduct of anyone for which he is amenable to society is that which concerns others. In the part which merely concerns himself, his independence is, of right, absolute."[11]

[4] Morris L. Ernst and Alan U. Schwartz, *Privacy: The Right To Be Let Alone* (New York: MacMillan, 1962), pp. 5-6.

[5] Locke, pp. 55-81.

[6] *Griswold v. Connecticut*, 381 U.S. 479, 486 (1965).

[7] David H. Flaherty, *Privacy in Colonial New England* (Charlottesville, Va.: University Press of Virginia, 1972).

[8] David Herbert Donald, *Lincoln* (New York: Simon & Schuster, 1995), p. 70.

[9] Flaherty, p. 121.

[10] Richard F. Hixson, *Privacy in a Public Society: Human Rights in Conflict* (New York: Oxford University Press, 1987), p. 13.

[11] William Cohen and John Kaplan, *Constitutional Law: Civil Liberty and Individual Rights*, 2d ed. (Westbury, N.Y.: Foundation Press, Inc., 1982), p. 532.

PRIVACY AS A LEGAL RIGHT

Legal concerns related to privacy developed slowly during the nation's first century, in large part because of the agrarian nature of society. Conflicts were as few and far between as the nation's early inhabitants. This physical distance reduced unwanted contacts and intrusions and the need for legal resolutions. Yet cases reflecting privacy concerns did surface. One Nineteenth Century case worth mentioning for its unusual facts is *Demay v. Roberts*. The case arose after a doctor took along an untrained assistant to help deliver a baby. The parents sued when they learned the assistant was not medically trained, arguing their privacy had been violated. The Michigan Supreme Court agreed, holding the mother had a "legal right to the privacy of her apartment at such a time."[12]

The demographics of American society shifted dramatically as the industrial revolution hit full force. Technological developments such as the steam engine led to manufacturing-based cities populated by factory workers. Physical distance between people shrank as populations converged in cities, and those in foreign lands began a flow of immigration to these shores. In those crowded cities, the barriers of time and space common to rural settings no longer insulated individuals from unwanted contacts. Between 1870 and 1900, the population of the United States doubled, and the number of urban residents tripled.

Dramatic technological developments in the Nineteenth Century that threatened privacy were traced by Alan F. Westin in *Privacy and Freedom*, a comprehensive study of privacy issues. Westin noted that several technological developments in the late Nineteenth Century "altered the balance between personal expression and third-party surveillance that had prevailed since antiquity."[13] These innovations were the microphone and telephone in the late 1870s, the Kodak camera with its potential for "instantaneous photographs" in the 1880s and the dictograph recorder in the 1890s.

In 1877, the *New York Times* expressed concern about the effect of new technology on privacy. It called the telephone "a nefarious instrument" with "vast capabilities for mischief" that promised to rob individuals of their personal privacy. Responding to a decision by the city to allow telephone wires to be attached to city lamp posts, the *Times* cautioned:

Every confidential remark made to a lamp-post by a belated Democratic statesman could be reproduced by a telephone connected with any other lamp-post.... Men who had trusted to friendly lamp-posts, and embraced them with the utmost confidence in their silence and discretion, would find themselves shamelessly betrayed, and their unsuspecting philosophies literally reported to their indignant families.[14]

While technology spurred the growth of industrial cities and development of such privacy-altering inventions as the telephone, other innovations — high-speed newspaper presses and advanced photography — spawned an aggressive kind of journalism, a distant cousin to that espoused by the colonial and revolutionary printers who catered to society's well-read and politically astute. New printing processes reproduced newspapers quickly and cheaply, and a new kind of journalism developed that often directed its content at the baser instincts of the swelling numbers of city dwellers. The "penny press" era of the mid-Nineteenth Century later yielded to "yellow journalism," sensationalistic news coverage to boost newspaper circulations that reached its peak toward century's end. Newspaper readers, not so interested in the complexities of politics and other public issues, sought information about misdeeds and travails. This new readership, coupled with journalists armed with cameras intruding into new, heretofore private areas, sometimes brought newspaper practices and privacy concerns into conflict. These conflicts created new social and legal issues to be sorted out.

In 1890, a pair of former law partners and Harvard Law School classmates took issue with the newspaper practices and technologies of the day. Louis Brandeis and Samuel Warren, uppercrust Boston lawyers, penned "The Right to Privacy" for the *Harvard Law Review*. The seminal article would steer the notion of a legal right of privacy toward the mainstream of American law. Attempting to document what they considered a climate of journalistic excess, the authors stated, somewhat hyperbolically: "Instantaneous photographs and newspaper enterprise have invaded the sacred precincts of private and domestic life; and numerous mechanical devices threaten to make good the prediction that 'what is whispered in the closet shall be proclaimed from the housetops.'"[15] Brandeis and Warren argued that individuals possessed certain attributes, such as sentiments and intellect, over which they exercised rights akin to those governing personal property. The authors identified these rights in analogous laws on breach of trust, assault, copyright and defamation.

In 1895, six years after "The Right to Privacy" was published, the

---

[12] 46 Mich. 160, 9 N.W. 146, 148 (1881).

[13] Alan F. Westin, *Privacy and Freedom* (New York: Atheneum, 1967), p. 338.

[14] "The Telephone Unmasked," *New York Times*, 12 Oct. 1877, p. 4.

[15] *Harvard Law Review* 4 (1890): 220.

New York Supreme Court addressed the issue of privacy in *Schuyler v. Curtis*. The family of a prominent woman sued a private organization to halt plans to erect a life-size statue in her memory. The woman had never been a public personality and the statue was an invasion of privacy, her family argued. The court acknowledged there was "no reported decision which goes to this extent in maintaining the right of privacy" and rejected the family's claim. It focused on the fact the woman was dead and concluded that any privacy interest followed her to the grave, thus stopping short of fully exploring the legal issues.[16]

In some early privacy cases, before psychiatry and psychology had gained credence in legal circles, courts expressed fundamental concerns about awarding damages for mental harm. In 1902, for example, the New York Court of Appeals refused to recognize a right of privacy in *Roberson v. Rochester Folding Box Co.*, a case addressed more fully in the discussion of the tort of appropriation. In *Roberson,* the family of a young girl sued a flour company for using the girl's photograph in an advertisement. The family argued the advertisement caused the girl to be "greatly humiliated by the scoffs and jeers of persons who recognized her face and picture." The court, while sympathetic, refused to recognize a legal remedy for an intangible mental harm, fearing such a precedent might trigger similar lawsuits that would clutter the courts. The court also expressed concern that privacy liability would place unreasonable burdens on the press, which often used photographs of individuals without permission.[17]

While New York's highest court was hesitant to embrace privacy, the Georgia Supreme Court was not, reaching the opposite result in a similar case and becoming the first court to recognize unauthorized use of a person's identity as a violation of privacy.[18] The ruling prompted Louis Brandeis to write that he was encouraged to see privacy as a distinguishable legal right recognized by the courts.[19]

In addition to promoting privacy as a legal doctrine, the article by Brandeis and Warren may have helped elevate privacy in public discourse. In 1902, the *New York Times* took issue with new photographic technology, which no longer required willing subjects to sit motionless. Echoing the concerns of Brandeis and Warren, the newspaper complained in an editorial that "Kodakers lying in wait to photograph public figures had become a wanton invasion of

privacy that demands legal control."[20]

While the Brandeis and Warren article nudged the issue of privacy onto the social and legal stage, the development of a unified legal theory remained elusive. In the ensuing decades, the legal contours of privacy developed piecemeal and with many variations. Seventy years after "The Right to Privacy" proposed a separate legal remedy for invasion of privacy, torts expert William Prosser summarized the extent of the common law development of privacy in an article in the *California Law Review*. Titled simply "Privacy," the 1960 article dealt with tort law and not with constitutional or statutory questions of privacy. After reviewing some 200 privacy-related cases, Prosser identified four separate torts: disclosure of embarrassing private facts about individuals; appropriation, or the use of another person's likeness without permission; false light, the intentional dissemination of highly offensive false publicity about another; and intrusion, the physical or technological violation of an individual's privacy.[21]

THE PRIVACY TORTS

American law assumes members of society have certain duties toward one another. These duties, derived from customs, mores and values, are often recognized in common law cases and in various statutes; they form the basis of tort law. Under the theory of tort law, when a member of society violates a duty toward another person that results in an identifiable harm, the injured person may recover damages. One class of duties deals with privacy and the harm — usually mental — that results when it is violated. When the news media are involved, courts have balanced individual privacy with other interests, such as the free flow of information to society about matters of public concern. Since the nature of the harm is usually mental, privacy torts apply only to individuals, not to businesses or corporations that exist merely as creatures of law.

Tort law varies from state to state; so any generalizations are based on trends in cases from the various states. Actual application of law in privacy cases may vary considerably, not only from state to state, but also among judicial jurisdictions within a state. Professional communicators need to be well-versed in the laws and customs where they work.

---

[16] 15 N.Y. Supp. 787, 788, 147 N.Y. 434, 42 N.E. 22 (1891).

[17] 171 N.Y. 538, 64 N.E. 442 (N.Y. 1902).

[18] *Pavesich v. New England Life,* 122 Ga. 190, 50 S.E. 68 (1905).

[19] *Letters of Louis D. Brandeis*, eds. M. Urofsky and D. Levy, vol. 1 (Albany, N.Y.: State University of New York Press, 1971), p. 306.

[20] Westin, p. 338.

[21] William Prosser, "Privacy," *California Law Review* 48 (1960): 383-384.

Embarrassing Private Facts

Definition: The publication of private information that would be highly offensive to a reasonable person and not a matter of legitimate public concern.

The common law acknowledges that some information about individuals should remain beyond the reach of neighbors — and the news media — and that private disclosures normally would lead to unwarranted embarrassment or humiliation. The embarrassing private facts tort rests on several questions, each of which a plaintiff must answer effectively to advance a legal privacy claim:

What is publication? In libel law, "publication" has a specialized meaning. At a minimum, a libel plaintiff must prove a defamatory communication reached at least one person other than the plaintiff and defendant. Under the embarrassing private facts tort, however, "publication" means "publicity," that is, widespread communication. Publication in a newspaper, magazine or other print medium satisfies this requirement, as would dissemination over broadcast or cable. While laws governing libel and privacy in computer communications are still evolving, it is reasonable to assume that widespread communication of private information *via* a commercial database, user groups, bulk e-mail or similar means would meet this requirement.

Is the information private? As a threshold, an embarrassing private facts plaintiff must establish that the information in question is, in fact, private. What happens in public, or what appears in public records, normally, is not considered private. In *Cox Broadcasting Co. v. Cohn*, the U.S. Supreme Court held that the news media are not to be held liable for publication of personal information, even if the media violate a state statute designed to protect rape victims, if they "merely give further publicity to information about a plaintiff which is already public."[22] In *Briscoe v. Reader's Digest Association*, a privacy claim failed because the information was gleaned from public records.[23] A person involved in an automobile accident or the victim of a crime, therefore, cannot claim invasion of privacy based on photographs of or stories about the accident. As a Massachusetts court noted: "Many things which are distressing and lacking in propriety or good taste are not actionable."[24] Likewise, a participant in a public rally or parade cannot

later claim privacy related to those actions.[25] At least one court, however, has said a crime victim's privacy might outweigh newsworthiness and the right to publish, even when the name is a matter of public record. In *Times Mirror Co. v. San Diego Superior Court*, a California appellate court reasoned that a crime witness's safety and the state's interest in prosecuting the crime might outweigh the media's right to publish and the public's right to know the name of the witness.[26]

Even intimate personal information cannot normally be the basis for a privacy claim if it is already widely known, as Oliver Sipple learned after he thwarted an assassination attempt on President Gerald Ford. Subsequent news accounts of Sipple's heroism disclosed that he was a homosexual, a fact already known within the San Francisco gay community.[27]

Consent is also a factor in determining whether personal information should be considered public or private. While the question of consent will be addressed more fully in a later discussion of private facts defenses, it should be noted that a person cannot normally provide information knowingly to the news media and subsequently claim an invasion of privacy, although in some instances consent might be effectively withdrawn.

What kind of information might be considered highly offensive to a reasonable person? A memorable case based on a "Where Are They Now?" story about child prodigy William Sidis offers a definition. Sidis sued for invasion of privacy based on a 1937 article in *The New Yorker*, published more than a quarter century after he made headlines as a pre-teen math whiz. He claimed the magazine's delving into his present life was offensive. On appeal, the Second U.S. Circuit Court of Appeals disagreed, holding that to be sufficiently offensive, a private disclosure must "outrage the community's notions of decency."[28] A more recent California case defined offensiveness differently, suggesting the public's legitimate interest in personal information ends when a publication forgoes legitimate news values and "becomes a morbid and sensational prying into private lives for its own sake."[29]

What kind of disclosure, then, would outrage a community's sense of decency or constitute sensational prying? Another oft-cited case is instructive and suggests that stories dealing with

---

[22] 420 U.S. 469, 494 (1975).
[23] 4 Cal. 3d 529, 483 P.2d 34 (1972).
[24] *Kelley v. Post Publishing Co.*, 327 Mass. 275, 278 (1951).

[25] *Sipple v. Chronicle Publishing Co.*, 104 Cal. App. 3d 1040, 201 Cal. Rptr. 665 (Cal. Ct. App. 1984).
[26] 198 Cal. App. 3d 1420, 244 Cal. Rptr. 556 (Cal. Ct. App. 1988).
[27] *Sipple*, 104 Cal. App. 3d at 1044.
[28] *Sidis v. F-R Publishing Co.*, 113 F.2d 806, 809 (2d Cir. 1940).
[29] *Virgil*, 527 F.2d at 1122, 1129.

medical or other intimate health conditions are most problematic for journalists. Dorothy Barber was dubbed a "starving glutton" in a *Time* magazine article about a bizarre medical condition that caused her to lose weight despite eating large quantities of food. She sued *Time* for invasion of privacy after the magazine published a photograph showing her in a hospital room. The Missouri Supreme Court, citing the long-standing privacy protection accorded doctor-patient relationships, held that disclosure of the unusual eating disorder was embarrassing to Barber and invaded her privacy. The court acknowledged the public's interest in such medical maladies, but reasoned that identifying Barber was not necessary to tell the story about the medical disorder.[30] As a rule, invasive stories or pictures that deal with physical or mental illness, or that expose the intimate parts of the body, require particular caution. The court's reliance on doctor-patient privilege in the Barber case also suggests disclosures that involve information normally protected under common law privileges could be considered highly offensive. *The Restatement of Torts* suggests several problem areas: sexual relations, humiliating illnesses, intimate personal letters, family disputes, details of home life, stolen photos or photos taken in private places, and information from individual tax returns.[31]

A plaintiff must prove the *widespread publicity* of intimately private material that a *reasonable person* would find *highly offensive*, and that the information was *not* related to a *matter of public concern*. At this juncture in most private facts cases involving the news media, plaintiffs fail, because most of what is printed or broadcast is chosen because it *is* newsworthy.

What constitutes a matter of public concern? Even if a plaintiff can establish that disclosure is highly offensive to a reasonable person, the likelihood of winning a privacy suit is slim if the plaintiff has become part of a public event or controversy. Certainly, information related to traditional news values is likely to deal with matters of public concern. Information about politics, law enforcement, crime, domestic violence, suicide, medical advances and social trends falls within the realm of traditional news.

The 1982 case of Hilda Bridges, who became an unintended actor on a very public stage, dramatically underscores the dearth of privacy protection for individuals caught up in news events. Bridges was dragged into a public matter when police officers — and members of the news media — surrounded her apartment af-

ter she was taken hostage by her estranged husband, who forced her to undress to prevent her from fleeing. During a standoff with police, the husband shot himself and police rushed the apartment. Bridges fled naked and distraught into the street, clutching only a hand towel. After *Today* newspaper in Cocoa Beach, Florida, published a revealing photograph, Bridges sued for invasion of privacy and infliction of emotional distress.

Satisfied that such publicity was unwarranted and highly offensive, a Florida jury awarded Bridges $10,000. A Florida appellate court, however, unanimously set aside the award, ruling that the law had not been properly followed. The jury had erred, the court reasoned, because events in question happened in public and because crime was a matter of public concern. Judge James Dauksch noted that privacy at some point must yield to the public interest. "Just because the story and photograph may be embarrassing or distressful does not mean the newspaper cannot publish what is otherwise newsworthy."[32] While publication of the photograph raised numerous ethical questions, Bridges's chances of eventual success were virtually nil because she had become caught up in a public drama. Years earlier in a privacy case, a Florida court had concluded: "Even though the plaintiff's role of 'actor' in an event having news value was not of his own volition ... the fact remains that he was in a public place and present at a scene where news was in the making."[33]

The result was essentially the same when a bystander at a public event thwarted an attempt to assassinate President Gerald Ford during his visit to San Francisco in 1975. As described earlier, Oliver Sipple's act of heroism drew him into the limelight, illuminating his Vietnam war record as well as his homosexuality. Sipple, well known in San Francisco's gay community before the Ford episode, sued the *San Francisco Chronicle* and other newspapers for invasion of privacy. He argued that while his public actions were newsworthy, his private life was not, and that disclosure of his sexual orientation caused him embarrassment because his homosexuality was not widely known. A California appellate court held that both Sipple's heroism and his homosexuality were newsworthy, noting that his heroic behavior cut against stereotypes of gays.

In Florida, a federal district court judge ruled that a suicidal sixteen-year-old girl filmed by a crew from the Fox Television docudrama *Cops* had no right of privacy because the filming resulted

---

[30] *Barber v. Time, Inc.,* 348 Mo. 1199, 159 S.W. 2d 291 (1942).

[31] *Restatement (Second) of Torts* (St. Paul, Minn.: American Law Institute, 1977), sec. 652D, comments b, g.

[32] *Cape Publications, Inc. v. Bridges,* 423 So. 2d 426, 428 (Fla. Ct. App. 1982).

[33] *Jacova v. Southern Radio and Television Co.,* 83 So. 2d 34, 40 (Fla. 1955).

from her call to authorities seeking help. After the call was routed to 911, the film crew, riding with deputies that night, went to the girl's home, where she was videotaped in an open garage. When the footage was televised, the girl's face was blurred by *Cops* producers. The judge said a person who commits public acts that result in police intervention cannot expect such circumstances to remain private.[34]

While much of what is newsworthy deals with matters of social and political importance, any mass communication student knows newsworthiness also can be defined as anything out of the ordinary. Unusual occupations, hobbies, talents and other qualities that attract public attention are newsworthy. Two cases are prime examples. The first was based on a story in *Sports Illustrated* about a California body surfer well known for his derring-do. Michael Virgil sued *Sports Illustrated* for invasion of privacy after the magazine included accounts of his unusual personal behavior in a story about his surfing exploits. The information, discussed freely with a reporter, included his eating insects and burning himself with cigarettes, as well as diving headlong down a flight of stairs to impress women. *Sports Illustrated* included the material despite Virgil's request that personal information not be used. In rejecting Virgil's privacy claim, the Ninth U.S. Circuit Court of Appeals concluded that inclusion of the personal information in the story about the daring body surfer was a "legitimate journalistic attempt" to give a full portrait of the body surfer.[35]

Sidis v. F-R Publishing Corp. began with a *New Yorker* magazine story about a former child prodigy leading a recluse's life in Boston, never having realized his incredible promise. The court rejected Sidis's privacy claim, reasoning that his childhood acclaim gave rise to legitimate public interest about his present accomplishments.[36]

As *Sidis* suggests, newsworthiness normally stands the test of time in privacy actions. The Kansas Supreme Court reached that conclusion in 1975 after a newspaper republished a story about a police officer fired some ten years earlier. Noting that once "facts are in the public domain they remain there," the court held that republication of a newsworthy event was not an invasion of privacy. The court said official government misconduct "is newsworthy when it occurs and remains so for as long as anyone thinks it worth retelling."[37]

In *Forsher v. Bugliosi*, the California Supreme Court stated it another way. Quoting tort expert William Prosser, the court said, "once a man becomes a public figure, or news, he remains a matter of legitimate recall in the public's mind until the end of his days."[38]

What about instances when the subjects of news accounts revealing private information are public officials or public figures? As a rule, most activities of public persons are newsworthy by virtue of their public status. When the *Miami Herald* disclosed that Democratic presidential contender Gary Hart spent the night with a woman who was not his wife, for example, questions were raised about proper bounds of reporting and the *Herald* was criticized, but the legal question of privacy was never raised. Bob Dole, a contender for the Republication nomination at the time, put the privacy issue this way: "Once you stand up and say you're going to be a candidate for president, all bets are off."[39]

Similarly, should former football star and broadcaster Frank Gifford sue the *Globe* for publishing a story and photographs about his being videotaped with a woman not his wife, he would have little legal recourse unless the publication was false. The public's interest in his behavior was heightened by the fact that his wife, talk show host Kathie Lee Gifford, has been an extremely vocal proponent of family values.

Private Facts Constitutional Protections. The news media have some protection under the First Amendment when they publish truthful, lawfully obtained information about matters of public concern. Several cases help define the scope of this protection.

In *Cox Broadcasting Corp. v. Cohn*, parents of a teenage girl who was raped and murdered sued an Atlanta television station after it broadcast the girl's name. The suit was based on a Georgia statute that forbade publication of names of alleged rape victims. The station, WSB-TV, had obtained the victim's name from records provided at an open court hearing. The Georgia Supreme Court upheld the parents' right to pursue the lawsuit, but the U.S. Supreme Court reversed, focusing on the fact the information was revealed in judicial records. The Court said the onus should be on government to ensure privacy by keeping certain information out of the public domain. Allegations of crime and the resulting proceedings, the Court said, "are without question events of legiti-

---

[34] David Kidwell, "Woman Loses Privacy Suit Against TV Crime Show," *Miami Herald*, 13 May 1994, p. 1B.

[35] *Virgil v. Sports Illustrated*, 424 F. Supp. 1286, 1289 (S.D. Cal. 1984).

[36] 113 F.2d 806 (1940).

[37] *Rawlins v. Hutchinson Publishing Co.*, 218 Kan. 295, 543 P.2d 988, 996 (1975).

[38] 163 Cal. Rptr. 628, 638, 608 P. 2d 716, 726 (1980).

[39] Deborah Gersh, "Privacy and the Presidency," *Editor & Publisher*, 13 Oct. 1990, p. 15.

mate concern to the public" that the press has a duty to report.[40]

Similarly, when the *Florida Star*, a small weekly newspaper, published the name of a rape victim as part of its routine police report, copied from a public bulletin board at the Duval County Sheriff's Department, the Court held that the report was protected. The rape victim sued the newspaper, claiming that violation of the state criminal statute barring publication of names of alleged rape victims constituted evidence of breach of duty and that she should be awarded civil damages for invasion of privacy. A jury agreed and awarded her $100,000. The Supreme Court overturned the verdict, holding that the Constitution prevents states from punishing the news media — even by allowing civil damages — for publishing truthful, lawfully obtained information. As in *Cox Broadcasting*, the Court reasoned that the government shoulders the burden in protecting such privacy interests and that news media could be punished for publishing truthful information only when the punishment advanced a "state interest of the highest order."[41] The Georgia Supreme Court, citing the *Florida Star* ruling, overturned a jury verdict awarding damages to a sexual assault victim who shot her assailant. The story identified the victim but never said specifically she had been sexually assaulted. The Georgia Supreme Court said both the state and federal constitutions protected the right of the newspaper to "accurately report the facts regarding the incident," including the name.[42]

Consent as a Defense. Normally, individuals cannot knowingly and willingly disclose personal information and then claim an invasion of privacy. As a rule, the more intimate the information, the more important for the reporter to be sure consent was clearly given, either explicitly or implicitly. Consent is explicit when professional communicators ask a source for permission to use personal information for publication. There are no problems when people providing information know they are speaking for publication and the information is about themselves. Consent must come from someone with authority to provide the information or with the legal capacity to do so. A friend could not give consent for the use of private information about a college roommate. A daycare operator cannot independently give consent for children under his or her care, nor can a hospital official give consent when the privacy of patients is involved. Minor children cannot give legal consent. Consent need not be in written form, but written consent is almost always easier to prove in court than oral consent.

Can explicit consent later be withdrawn? One court has said no — if the person providing information is newsworthy and the private information is used for legitimate journalistic purposes.[43]

The Supreme Court, however, has cast doubt on the freedom of reporters when agreements are made as part of the reporter/source relationship and rise to the level of even rudimentary contracts. In *Cohen v. Cowles Media*, the Court said a reporter's promise to keep a source's name private could be treated by states as an oral contract without violating the First Amendment rights of the journalist. Journalists had argued that the source's name was newsworthy and the ultimate decision to use or not use newsworthy information should reside with the news media.[44] This suggests that journalists should be doubly careful about the terms under which they seek consent to publish private information and about the extent to which they detail the purpose for obtaining the information.

Implied Consent. Reporters frequently talk to sources and use the information without specifically asking for permission to do so. Members of the public generally understand the function of reporters in American society. If journalists identify themselves, and sources talk willingly, there is no problem. But implied consent becomes problematic if private information is obtained from someone who does not understand that the information is likely to be published.[45]

Intrusion

Definition: Intrusion is the highly offensive invasion of another person's solitude, either physically or by use of technological devices.

The fundamental purpose of the tort of intrusion — to protect a person's solitude — can be traced to many of the nation's early values. But the notion of intrusion has gone beyond the traditional legal doctrine of trespass, or physical intrusion, to mechanical and electronic violations of private space. The means by which intrusion occurs certainly have changed over the years, from the "instantaneous photography" that so riled Brandeis and Warren, to today's miniature video cameras that left ABC's *Prime Time Live* reeling from a $3.5 million fraud and trespass verdict. (That verdict was later reduced and remains on appeal.) Whether physi-

---

[40] 420 U.S. at 492.

[41] *Florida Star v. B.J.F.*, 491 U.S. 524, 533 (1989).

[42] *Macon Telegraph Publishing Co. v. Tatum*, 263 Ga. 678, 436 S.E.2d 655, 658 (1993).

[43] *Virgil v. Sports Illustrated*, 424 F. Supp. at 1122.

[44] 501 U.S. 663 (1991).

[45] *Prahl v. Brosamle*, 98 Wis. 2d 130, 295 N.W. 2d 768 (1980).

cal or technological, the tort of intrusion deals with the *process of gathering information*, not the content of the information gathered.

Privacy in Public and Quasi-Public Places. Under common law, people in public places have little expectation of privacy. People engaging in public activities must assume they might be photographed or filmed or that what they say publicly might be recorded.

While people in public places do not forgo all rights to privacy, journalists encounter few legal problems when they photograph or report information on such individuals, so long as they report what would reasonably be considered public. A New Jersey court, for example, granted a newspaper summary judgment in a privacy suit brought by the owner of a historic house when a photograph appeared in the newspaper. The court reasoned that the photograph, taken from a public street, simply recorded what any passer-by might see.[46] A Kentucky court held that a man photographed stepping fully clothed from a portable toilet on a college campus had no basis for a privacy claim, because he was stepping back into public view.[47] Similar reasoning has been applied to individuals on private property that is customarily open to the public, such as malls, restaurants and businesses. One court has held that a dog trainer, waiting backstage to perform his act, was in a public place that afforded little expectation of privacy.[48] However, the Iowa Supreme Court reinstated a lawsuit filed by a woman filmed by a television crew in a pizza restaurant. The restaurant owner had given the crew permission to enter the restaurant. A lower court had dismissed the suit, reasoning that the woman was in public and not cast in a false light, and that the broadcast was for news rather than commercial purposes. The state supreme court disagreed, saying the woman should have an opportunity to present evidence that she was harmed by the telecast.[49]

Courts also have suggested that journalists may be persistent when encountering people in public without invading their privacy, so long as the behavior is not highly intrusive or overzealous. Journalistic behavior that is simply annoying is not necessarily an invasion of privacy.[50] Images come to mind of Mike Wallace doggedly pursuing a reluctant subject across a parking lot or down a public street to get a statement for *60 Minutes*. Persistence in pursuing a story or source is normally considered a virtue in journalistic circles, but behavior can become legally problematic when it is menacing or harassing. Such was the case with paparazzi Ron Galella and his pursuit of Jacqueline Kennedy Onassis, widow of President John F. Kennedy. A federal court, citing Onassis's right to be left alone, ordered Galella to stay at least twenty-five feet away from her in public. At issue was not Galella's right to photograph Onassis in public, but his overly intrusive efforts to obtain exclusive photographs.[51] The death of Princess Diana also spawned efforts to pass restrictive legislation.

Trespass or Physical Intrusion. According to *The Restatement of Torts*, anyone who enters private property without the consent of the owner or possessor commits a trespass.[52] Everyone has seen "No Trespassing" signs posted to warn away unwanted visitors. Private property is protected from intruders under both the common law and statutes, which spell out specific penalties for violators. Entering private property without permission or staying on private or quasi-private property after being asked to leave always poses legal dangers for journalists, whose rights are normally no different from those of any other citizen.

As a rule, a visitor on private property must obtain permission before entry. Permission must be obtained from the possessor of the property, be it the owner or someone with contractual control over the property, such as a renter or tenant. For example, a court held that journalists did not invade the privacy of a farmer when they obtained permission from a caretaker to enter the property and photograph dead cattle.[53]

Consent may be either explicit or implied. Explicit consent occurs when a visitor asks for and is granted permission. A reporter might request an interview at a residence or at a business office, for example. When the purpose of the visit is obscured, however, or when journalists simply lie about their intentions, the question of trespass is much less clear. Two court cases involving the same television news program show how troublesome the question of lawful access to private property can be. In 1997 a North Carolina jury awarded the Food Lion food chain $3.5 million in damages af-

---

46 *Bisbee v. Conover*, 186 N.J. Super. 335, 452 A. 2d 689 (1982).

47 *Livingston v. Kentucky Post*, 14 Media L. Rep. (BNA) 2076, 2077 (Ky. Cir. Ct. 1987).

48 *People for Ethical Treatment of Animals v. Berosini*, 110 Nev. 78, 867 P. 2d 1121 (1994).

49 *Stressman v. American Blackhawk Broadcasting Co.*, 416 N.W. 2d 685 (Iowa 1987).

50 *Dempsey v. National Enquirer, Inc.*, 702 F. Supp. 927 (D. Maine 1988).

51 *Galella v. Onassis*, 353 F. Supp. 196 (S.D.N.Y. 1972).

52 Sec. 158, at 277 (1965).

53 *Wood v. Fort Dodge Messenger*, 13 Media L. Rep. (BNA) 1614 (Iowa Dist. Ct. 1986). See also *Lal v. CBS*, 551 F. Supp. 356 (E.D. Pa. 1982).

ter ABC's *Prime Time Live* carried a report, afforded by hidden video cameras, that Food Lion relabeled and restocked meat after its expiration date. The judge had allowed the jury to consider fraud and trespass charges against ABC without considering the veracity of the network's report on Food Lion's business practices. The jury based its award on the fact that *Prime Time Live* producers had committed a trespass by obtaining access to Food Lion facilities through fraudulent job applications.[54] Even though the Food Lion judgment has been reduced and could be overturned on appeal, it illustrates the dangers reporters face in a society that appears to be growing increasingly wary of certain kinds of reporting techniques.

The Food Lion decision stands in contrast to a ruling by the Seventh U.S. Circuit Court of Appeals in another case involving ABC's *Prime Time Live*. In *Desnick v. ABC*, the court rejected a trespass claim when reporters with hidden cameras posed as patients to obtain information based on claims that a Desnick Eye Center was performing cataract operations unnecessarily. The court drew an analogy between food critics appearing at a restaurant anonymously and unannounced and *Prime Time Live*'s undercover actions, even though *Prime Time Live* had gained the cooperation of the center by promising not to employ undercover tactics.[55]

Technological Intrusion. Modern journalists are armed with an array of devices that enhance newsgathering, from telephoto lenses, to sensitive listening devices, to miniaturized video cameras. Technological intrusion is as old as the discussion of privacy. As noted, in 1890 Brandeis and Warren were concerned about a new kind of "instantaneous" photography that no longer required willing subjects to remain perfectly still. Today the culprit likely would be a miniaturized video camera. As a rule, the use of technology that enhances viewing or listening is legal as long as the device does not effectively let the journalist hear or see what normally could not be observed. If a device simply allows a journalist to see or hear what might be witnessed in public, there is no intrusion. People who go into public places — streets, parks and college campuses, for example — enjoy very little privacy, as long as they are not menaced or harassed. That is, the zone of privacy they enjoy is very small compared to the privacy they can expect in their homes or other strictly private places.

In *Dietmann v. Time, Inc.*,[56] the court awarded $1,000 damages to an unconventional healer when a hidden camera and recording device were taken into his home office. Reporters for *Life* magazine gained entry to Dietmann's home posing as prospective patients and secretly photographed and recorded their conversations as he performed his healing ritual. The Ninth U.S. Circuit Court of Appeals soundly rejected media arguments that subterfuge and secret photographing and recordings were essential to telling the story. "We strongly disagree," the court said, "that the hidden mechanical contrivances are indispensable tools of newsgathering."[57]

In contrast to *Dietmann*, where access was gained by deception, a Kentucky court rejected an intrusion claim after newspaper reporters persuaded a woman indicted on drug charges to secretly record a conversation with her lawyer, whom she said had offered to bribe a judge. In *McCall v. Courier Journal & Louisville Times*, the court noted that the woman had not lied to gain access to her lawyer's office and that the lawyer had waived his privacy when he continued to talk to her even though he suspected he was being taped.[58]

In a more recent case, a federal court found grounds for technological intrusion when the television show *Inside Edition* used a shotgun microphone to eavesdrop on conversations inside a home. The court said use of a sensitive directional microphone, which could pick up conversations sixty yards away, was an invasion of privacy. Journalists for *Inside Edition* were sued by an official of a Pennsylvania health care business who had refused requests to be interviewed for a story on executive salaries. Using a van equipped with the shotgun microphone, reporters waited outside the executive's home in an attempt to obtain information.[59]

Custom and Usage. While explicit consent requires a request of the property owner or possessor, implied consent occurs in a number of ways under a legal doctrine known as "custom and usage." As the name suggests, a degree of access is implied by custom or typical use of private and quasi-private property. It is customary to cross private property to ring someone's doorbell to solicit contributions or sell a product, absent a locked gate, a "No Trespassing" sign or other warning. It is also customary for shoppers and diners to enter stores and restaurants. This kind of access is based on the assumption that the visitor does not engage

---

[54] Estes Thompson, "Jury: ABC Committed Fraud To Get Food Story," *Miami Herald,* 21 Dec. 1996, p. 10A.

[55] 44 F. 2d 1345 (7th Cir. 1995).

[56] 449 F.2d 245 (1971).

[57] *Id.* at 249.

[58] 623 S.W. 2d 882 (Ky. 1981) *cert denied,* 456 U.S. 975 (1982).

[59] *Wolfson v. Lewis,* 924 F. Supp. 1413 (E.D. Pa. 1996).

in unwanted activities and leaves when asked.

The Florida Supreme Court accepted the argument that custom and usage justified a news photographer's entry onto private property with government officials. In *Fletcher v. Florida Publishing Co.*, the mother of a teenager killed in a house fire sued the *Florida Times-Union* for invasion of privacy when it published a photograph, over the caption "Silhouette of Death," showing the outline of where the body of the young victim had lain. The mother learned of her daughter's death from the newspaper account. Complicating the legal reasoning of the case was the fact that the photographer was asked to take photographs for fire officials, thus also acting in a quasi-official capacity. In court, the newspaper successfully argued that it was customary for journalists to accompany officials onto private property where crimes or disasters occurred, a position supported by statements from government officials.[60]

The reasoning of *Fletcher,* however, has not been widely followed. To the contrary, in 1992 a federal court in New York emphatically rejected the *Fletcher* reasoning when journalists for CBS's *Street Stories* accompanied Secret Service agents during a search for documents in a credit card fraud investigation. During the raid, based on a search warrant, CBS employees videotaped a suspect's wife and child despite their repeated requests they not be photographed.[61] The Second U.S. Circuit Court of Appeals upheld a lower court ruling against the Secret Service, underscoring the position that law enforcement officials have no authority to allow journalists into private residences without the owners' permission, even when the property is under police control. Flatly rejecting any constitutional defense to justify the presence of CBS, the court found a clear Fourth Amendment violation by the Secret Service based on the presence of unauthorized journalists during the search. The court concluded that the journalists served no legitimate law enforcement need and that their presence was "calculated to inflict injury on the very value that the Fourth Amendment seeks to protect — the right of privacy."[62] In apparent response to the ruling, the FBI in its *Law Enforcement Bulletin* cautioned local, state and federal law enforcement agencies that "media participation in enforcement activities that occur in private areas should be specifically prohibited, unless the media obtain consent from individuals occupying those areas."[63] But if consent is obtained in such cases, even when it is in writing, some media lawyers advise caution because consent agreements signed when one party is under duress can be legally questionable.

Recording Conversations With Sources. Journalists often record conversations with their sources to create verbatim records of complicated information and lengthy direct quotes. In most states, this practice poses no legal problems because the law assumes that an exact account of a conversation can only benefit all parties involved. Parties to a conversation may legally recount a conversation to others, and the law simply extends this reasoning to allow taped conversations.[64] In some states, however, it is illegal to record a conversation without the consent of *all* parties. In these states, the reasoning assumes that if a person knows a conversation is being taped, the person might behave or respond differently. Perhaps the source would be more cautious or guarded in his or her comments or say nothing at all. Linda Tripp's recordings of her conversations with Monica Lewinsky are a stark illustration. Twelve states require that all parties to a conversation know when the conversation is being recorded. This knowledge can be conveyed in a number of ways. In cases involving personal contact, a journalist either may ask permission or may assume consent if a tape recorder is in full view and turned on. It is always a good idea to state before the conversation begins that it is being taped. This creates a record of consent should the consent later be contested. For telephone conversations, consent should be requested before taping begins and restated at the beginning of the conversation.

In Illinois, where state law requires all parties to agree to recordings, a court has added another legal twist, suggesting that where privacy is not expected, no such right exists. In *Russell v. American Broadcasting Co.*, a court held that ABC's *Prime Time Live* did not violate the privacy of a fish market manager when it secretly taped the manager coaching an undercover reporter about the finer points of selling fish. Because the manager expressed no desire to keep the conversation private, the court reasoned, no privacy right was violated by the taping.[65]

---

[60] *Fletcher v. Florida Publishing Co.*, 340 So. 2d 914 (Fla. 1976), *cert denied* 431 U.S. 930 (1977). See also *Higbee v Times Advocate,* 5 Media L. Rep. (BNA) 2372 (S.D. Cal. 1981).

[61] *Ayeni v. CBS,* 848 F. Supp. 362 (E.D.N.Y. 1994).

[62] *Ayeni v. Mottola,* 35 F.3d 680, 686 (2d Cir. 1994).

[63] "Media Participation in Police Raids May be History," *Florida Press Association Bulletin* (November 1994), p. 3.

[64] Federal law permits any party to a telephone conversation to record it, so long as the recording is not for criminal purposes. However, the Federal Communication Commission, under penalty of lost phone service, requires all parties to consent. See 18 U.S.C.A. sec 2511 (West Supp. 1996).

[65] 23 Media L. Rep. (BNA) 2428 (N.D. Ill. 1995).

False Light

Definition: False light invasion of privacy is the publication of highly offensive false information about an individual with actual malice, that is, knowing the information is false or with reckless disregard for whether it is true or false.

Newsweek's cover on March 28, 1988, showed a young man, hands clasped behind his head, being frisked by police against a backdrop of flashing patrol-car lights. The headlines stated: "The Drug Gangs/Waging War on America's Cities/Anti-Drug Sweep in Los Angeles." On April 25, the photo reappeared on an inside page over the small headline "Correction." A caption explained that the young man in the photo was released without being charged and that *Newsweek* did not mean to suggest that the man was being arrested. It is not known what transpired between *Newsweek* editors and the young man pictured on the cover, but one can suppose the discussion raised the specter of legal action against the news magazine because the man was cast in a false light.

Had the *Newsweek* case resulted in a lawsuit for false light invasion of privacy, the plaintiff would have had some of the same burdens of proof as a libel plaintiff. Consequently, false light cases are often filed in tandem with libel actions. Plaintiffs would have to prove the communication identified them (not always a given in a fictionalization), that it was false, and that the news medium was at fault — typically that it was published recklessly or with knowledge of falsity.

False light plaintiffs, however, would not allege loss of reputation; instead, they would argue that being cast in a highly offensive false light caused some other kind of harm. Also unlike libel, a false-light plaintiff must prove widespread publication — publicity — not just the legal publication.

False Light and Actual Malice.

In most jurisdictions all false light plaintiffs — not just public officials and public figures, as in libel actions — must prove actual malice if involved in matters of public concern, a standard established by the Supreme Court in the 1967 case of *Time, Inc. v. Hill*. The case began in 1952 when three escaped convicts entered the home of James Hill near Philadelphia and held the Hill family hostage for a day. The ordeal received sensational play in Philadelphia newspapers and was the inspiration for Joseph Hayes's *The Desperate Hours*, a novel about the fictional Hilliard family. It was later the basis for a Broadway play and a film starring Humphrey Bogart. In 1955, *Life* magazine published a story titled "True Crime Inspires Tense Play" that purported to describe what actually happened to the Hill fam-

ily. *Life* carried photos from the Philadelphia tryouts for the play, including one of the son being mistreated by a "brutish convict." Another photo showed the daughter biting the hand of an abusive convict. Both photos were embellishments, since the real captors did not harass the family.[66] Arguing that *Life* used the family's name and experience for trade purposes, the Hill family sued for invasion of privacy. They won at trial in 1963, but the Supreme Court set aside the damages in a 5-4 vote, applying the new legal rule that false light plaintiffs involved in matters of public concern must prove actual malice. (A point of interest: The Hills' lawyer was Richard M. Nixon.)

Courts are most likely to find disclosures highly offensive in two ways: (1) Fictionalization is the embellishment or addition of information to an otherwise factual presentation, a device more common to television or stage dramatizations than to news coverage; (2) distortion occurs when elements of a story are deceptively juxtaposed, or when information is omitted, presented out of context or presented in an improper context.

Fictionalizations.

As the *Time, Inc. v. Hill* case suggests, when a drama or novel is modeled on real events, false light problems can arise even when names and other facts have been changed. Fictionalization also can pose problems when the name of a real person is used, but use of a real name normally will not sustain privacy action unless the identity of the person is also appropriated; both a name and facts are usually necessary for there to be legal problems. For example, in *Geisler v. Petrocelli*, a federal judge refused to dismiss a false light claim because characteristics ascribed to the character and plaintiff significantly resembled her.[67] Novels, films and television programs often carry disclaimers, advising readers and viewers that their plots and characters are fictional and that any similarities to real people are coincidental. While disclaimers might prove helpful in marginal cases, they are not a fail-safe way to prevent false-light claims.

Fictionalization also can occur in simple news stories when facts and quotes are added or implied. While such distortions are deplorable as a matter of ethics, they also can also result in legal problems. In *Cantrell v. Forest City Publishing*, for example, the widow of an accident victim successfully sued for invasion of privacy after a reporter for the *Cleveland Plain Dealer* wrote a story that implied he had spoken to the woman at her home. She argued that the story held her and her family up for pity and ridicule, humiliating them and causing mental distress. The Supreme Court

---

[66] 385 U.S. 374, 377 (1967).
[67] 616 F.2d 636 (2d Cir. 1980).

upheld the verdict, agreeing that the family was knowingly cast in a false light by substantial misrepresentations in the story.[68]

To succeed, a false light plaintiff must prove misrepresentations were significant. Minor falsifications, as in libel cases, will not sustain a false light privacy claim.

A plainly unbelievable story — one with facts that defy reason and logic — still can be the basis of a successful false light claim. A 97-year-old Arkansas woman, Nellie Mitchell, won a $1.5 million false light judgment against *The Sun*, a tabloid published by Globe International, after it pulled a ten-year-old photo of her from company files and used it to illustrate an admittedly contrived story under the headline "World's Oldest Newspaper Carrier, 101, quits because she's pregnant." A federal court held the false publication could reasonably be deemed highly offensive and rejected Globe International's contention that it had a First Amendment right to publish an obviously fake story.[69]

Distortions. Until the recent upsurge in so-called television "docudramas" and "infotainment," news organizations were much more likely to find themselves defending false-light lawsuits over instances involving information out of context or inappropriately juxtaposed with other information. The *Newsweek* example is illustrative. The subject, photographed in a public place in the course of a newsworthy event, would have had little recourse if a photo caption simply had said he was being frisked by police during a drug sweep. However, the use of the photo with the various headlines and cutlines implied the subject of the photo was a suspect in a drug sweep that was part of the war on drugs.

Concern about the relationship of photos to text was also evident in a series by the *Miami Herald* titled "Collars for Dollars." The series documented excessive overtime by police officers who attached their names to drunken driving reports so they could earn overtime pay as witnesses. As part of a two-page spread of photos and text, the *Herald* carried this disclaimer: "About the photos. The police officers pictured here were photographed doing their jobs. Some were arresting drunk drivers at roadblocks. Others were at the courthouse, waiting for cases to be heard by a judge. Except where noted, there is no evidence that they are Collars for Dollars cops."[70]

Journalistic use of file photos and video street scenes is commonplace in most news organizations but can pose problems. Such practices should raise red flags when the subject matter is sensitive or individuals might be identified. Editors should take special care when selecting file photos or footage of auto accidents to illustrate stories on drunken driving or using street scenes for hard-to-illustrate stories. When a Washington, D.C., television station broadcast a story about a treatment for the sexually transmitted disease herpes, for example, it used a street scene to provide visuals. The snippet of tape included a clear view of passer-by Linda Duncan as the reporter was saying the following: "For the 20 Americans who have herpes, it is not a cure." Duncan sued, and a court refused to dismiss the action.[71] A jury subsequently awarded her $750, an amount she unsuccessfully challenged in court as grossly inadequate.

Appropriation

Definition: Appropriation is the use of another person's name, likeness or image, without permission, for commercial gain.

Appropriation was one of the first privacy torts to develop, in part because it dealt with a concept resembling property rights — an area of law relevant to Nineteenth Century courts. But it is also a tort that courts initially had difficulty with because it alleged a mental harm based on unwanted publicity. The field of psychology was not highly developed, and the notion that something as intangible as mental suffering could be quantified for the purpose of monetary damages troubled courts.

The turn-of-the-century *Roberson v. Rochester Folding Box. Co.* case, mentioned earlier, illustrates some early problems courts had with mental or psychic damages, as well as newspaper concerns about potential problems associated with the use of personal photos in their news pages. The case began when a New York company that processed baking flour used a picture of young Abigail Roberson in advertisements for its products. Her family sued for invasion of privacy, saying the unwanted attention the girl received in public caused severe embarrassment and humiliation. The court, by a 4-3 margin, rejected the argument that the mental anguish caused by unwanted publicity could give rise to measurable damages. The court's majority was concerned

---

[68] 419 U.S. 245, 253 (1973).

[69] *Peoples Bank & Trust v. Globe International, Inc.*, 786 F. Supp. 791 (W.D. Ark. 1992). A case that creates an interesting contrast is *Pring v. Penthouse*, 695 F.2d 438 (10th Cir. 1982), in which the court found no basis for the plaintiff's claim that a fictional story might be believed when it suggested a beauty queen was able to make sexual partners levitate during sex.

[70] Lisa Getter, Gail Epstein and Jeff Leen, "Cops Cashing In," *Miami Herald*, 14 July 1997, p. 8A.

[71] *Duncan v. WJLA-TV*, 10 Media L. Rep. (BNA) 1395 (D.C.D.C 1984).

about the implications of recognizing damages for such an intangible harm. The court said its understanding of the law "leads us to the conclusion that the so-called right of privacy has not yet found an abiding place in our jurisprudence...."[72]

This case of unwanted publicity generated much publicity of its own, with the public siding with the beleaguered Abigail Roberson. Public sentiment was not lost on the New York legislature, which passed a law prohibiting the commercial use of a person's name or likeness without permission.[73]

While the New York court was unwilling to recognize a legal right of privacy, the Georgia Supreme Court was more receptive. In *Pavesich v. New England Life Insurance Co.*, Georgia's high court, in 1905, became the first to recognize the unauthorized commercial use of one's identity as a violation of privacy. Pavesich sued the insurance company after it used his photograph without permission in a testimonial advertisement that purported to express his sentiments about life insurance. In awarding Pavesich damages, the court focused on the commercial nature of the use.[74] Though private people sometimes make claims of commercial appropriation, most claims deal with celebrities trying to protect the commercial value of their names and likenesses — a more recent legal development.

A Right to Publicity. One issue the Roberson court found troubling was the distinction between public and private individuals. For politicians and celebrities, who seek out and depend on publicity, claims of damages based on mental anguish from unwanted attention would be inconsistent with their *intentional* forays onto the public stage. Courts consistently have balked at the notion that people who seek and depend on public attention could claim a mental harm based on exposure to the public.

While courts are not likely to accord public persons damages for mental harm in appropriation cases, they have recognized a property-like right when the name or likeness of a celebrity or other public person is used without authorization for financial gain.

In some states, this right to publicity can be bartered and inherited. The Georgia Supreme Court blocked the unauthorized sale of plastic models of the Rev. Martin Luther King Jr., holding that the slain civil rights leader's publicity rights could be inherited even if they were not exercised during his lifetime.[75] Similarly, two circuits

of the U.S. Court of Appeals have held that Elvis Presley's right of publicity could be exploited exclusively by his heirs.[76]

Most commercial appropriation cases involve advertising or related enterprises, where the defendant has attempted to capitalize on a celebrity's name and identity. For example, an enterprising portable toilet business borrowed the phrase "Here's Johnny," Ed McMahon's nightly introduction of the star of *The Tonight Show With Johnny Carson,* to advertise its product. To underscore the link, the firm also advertised itself as "The World's Foremost Commodian." Even though neither his complete name nor likeness was used, Carson won his appropriation claim.[77]

The use of celebrity look-alikes and sound-alikes is common practice in advertising and sometimes results in appropriation lawsuits. A jury awarded singer Bette Midler $400,000 after Ford Motor Co. ran ads in which a singer imitated Midler's distinctive style and voice, an award upheld by the Ninth U.S. Circuit Court of Appeals in California, an influential authority on celebrity matters. The court concluded that "to impersonate her voice is to pirate her identity."[78] A few years later, the Ninth Circuit upheld a $2.5 million judgment for singer Tom Waits, whose raspy voice was imitated in an advertisement for Frito-Lays corn chips. The court held that Waits had a property right "to control the use of his identity as embodied in his voice."[79] The court also upheld a portion of the damage award based on mental distress.

Wheel of Fortune letter-turner Vanna White successfully sued an electronics firm for unauthorized use of her likeness. In an advertisement by Samsung Electronics, a well-dressed robot appeared wearing a white wig and turned letters on a giant video board. The Ninth Circuit agreed that Samsung had taken White's identity, observing that the identities of stars "are not only the most attractive for advertisers, but the easiest to evoke without resorting to obvious means such as name or likeness or voice."[80]

It is not a violation of publicity for a news publication to use an individual's name or likeness to promote the news content of the publication. In *Namath v. Sports Illustrated*, for example, the Supreme Court of New York County held that use of photos of

[72] *Roberson,* 64 N.E. at 556.

[73] N.Y. Civ. Rights Law secs. 50-51 (McKinney 1992).

[74] 122 Ga. 190 (1905).

[75] *Martin Luther King, Jr., Center for Social Change v. American*

Heritage Products, Inc., 250 Ga. 135, 296 S.E.2d 697 (1982).

[76] *Factors, Inc., v. Pro Arts, Inc.,* 4 Media L. Rep. (BNA) 1144 (2d Cir. 1978), and *Elvis Presley Enterprises v. Elvis Tours,* 14 Media L. Rep. (BNA) 1053 (6th Cir. 1987).

[77] *Carson v. Here's Johnny Portable Toilets, Inc.,* 698 F.2d 831 (6th Cir. 1983).

[78] *Midler v. Ford Motor Co.,* 849 F.2d 460, 463 (9th Cir. 1988).

[79] *Waits v. Frito-Lays, Inc.,* 978 F.2d 1093, 1100 (9th Cir. 1992).

[80] *White v. Samsung Electronics of America, Inc.,* 971 F.2d 1395, 1399 (1992), *reh'g denied,* 989 F.2d 1512 (1992).

former football star Joe Namath was permissible in promotional ads to establish the news content of *Sports Illustrated*.[81] The Ninth U.S. Circuit Court of Appeals reached a different result when the use of a celebrity's name and photo suggested she endorsed the publication. Actor-singer Cher sued for misappropriation after an interview she granted one publication was sold to another magazine, which used her name and photo for its own advertising. The court upheld a judgment, finding that the advertising implied that Cher endorsed the publication.[82]

In the only appropriation case it has decided, the Supreme Court held that the news exemption did not apply in the case of a performer who earned his living being shot from a cannon. Dubbed the "Human Cannonball," Hugo Zacchini's entire performance from cannon to net lasted fifteen seconds. When a television station broadcast his entire act on a news program, Zacchini sued for appropriation and won. The Supreme Court refused to block a jury trial on the $25,000 damage claim despite its newsworthiness because broadcast of the "entire act poses a substantial threat to the economic value of that performance."[83]

The use of names and likenesses also can pose problems in literary works, films, television and other forms of communication. Obtaining consent or permission is an important defense. In the popular 1997 film *Men in Black,* a spoof on the theory that space aliens reside among us, a TV monitor tracks aliens who, disguised as humans, have become celebrities. To avoid legal problems, director Barry Sonnenfeld said, he obtained permission from Dionne Warwick, Danny DeVito, Sylvester Stallone, Newt Gingrich and other celebrities to use their likenesses.[84] Actress Brooke Shields learned belatedly about the issue of consent when she tried to prevent publication of nude photographs taken of her when she was ten years old. She learned her mother had signed a standard photographic consent agreement that gave the photographer complete control to use or sell the images.[85] Baseball star Orlando Cepeda also learned the hard way that a person's identity can be contracted away. He sued Swift & Co. to stop its use of his name and picture, only to discover he had signed a licensing contract lending his name to the meat company.[86]

Chicago Bulls basketball star Dennis Rodman stopped an en-

trepreneur from marketing a long-sleeve T-shirt bearing images similar to Rodman's numerous upper body tattoos. U.S. District Judge Alfred Wolin granted Rodman's request for a restraining order, ruling that the T-shirt maker appeared to be profiting unfairly from Rodman's fame and tattoos without obtaining his permission.[87]

INTENTIONAL INFLICTION OF EMOTIONAL DISTRESS

The wide berth the First Amendment affords professional communicators makes it difficult for many people who feel harmed by the media to succeed in court. Libel law, discussed in Chapters 6 and 7, requires plaintiffs to prove not only that information is false, but also that the media were at fault — that publication resulted from either negligent or reckless practices or with outright knowledge of falsehood. False light invasion of privacy typically imposes similar burdens on plaintiffs, and plaintiffs under the embarrassing private facts tort have little chance of recovering damages when involved in matters of public concern. As a result, innovative lawyers sometimes file other kinds of legal actions, often in tandem with libel or privacy suits, based on general legal doctrines that have largely developed outside the umbrella of the First Amendment protections.

One such end run approach is the tort of intentional infliction of emotional distress, based on something akin to the common law doctrine of malice, or ill will.[88] The emotional distress tort allows recovery of damages for severe emotional harm or for deliberate or reckless conduct that is deemed outrageous and extreme,[89] a judgment normally determined by the sensibilities of a particular jury.

The leading media case on intentional infliction of emotional distress unfolded in the mid-1980s after a dispute between pornography mogul Larry Flynt, publisher of *Hustler* magazine, and the Rev. Jerry Falwell, a prominent Virginia-based television evangelist. The case was the subject of the critically acclaimed feature film *The People v. Larry Flynt.* Falwell sued Flynt and *Hustler* for libel, invasion of privacy and intentional infliction of emotional distress after the magazine ran a crude take-off of "The first time..." advertising campaign of Campari Liqueur. The campaign focused on celebrities who recalled their first experiences imbibing the upscale

[81] 80 Misc. 2d 531, 363 N.Y. 2d 276 (N.Y. Co. Sup. Ct. 1975).

[82] *Cher v. Forum International,* 692 F.2d 634 (9th Cir. 1982).

[83] *Zacchini v. Scripps Howard Broadcasting,* 433 U.S. 562, 575 (1977).

[84] "Invasion of the Body Snatchers," *Miami Herald,* 12 July 1997, p. 2A.

[85] *Shields v. Gross,* 58 N.Y. 2d 338, 448, 448 N.E.2d 108 (1983).

[86] *Cepeda v. Swift & Co.,* 415 F.2d 1205 (8th Cir. 1969).

[87] Associated Press, "Tattoo T-Shirts Barred, for Now," *Chicago Tribune,* 29 May 1996, p. S5.

[88] William Prosser, "Intentional Infliction of Mental Suffering: A New Tort," *Michigan Law Review* 27 (1939): 874.

[89] *Restatement (Second) of Torts,* sec. 46 comment d (1965).

liqueur. Double-entendre in the interviews gave readers the impression that the celebrities were discussing their first sexual experiences. *Hustler* cast Falwell in one of the "first-time" interviews, ostensibly reporting that his first time sexual encounter with his mother in an outhouse.

The magazine published a disclaimer stating that page was an advertising parody "not to be taken seriously." The Roanoke, Virginia, jury found in favor of *Hustler* on the libel claim, holding that no reasonable person would believe the parody to be true. The judge dismissed the privacy claim, because only appropriation is recognized as an invasion of privacy action in Virginia, and Falwell's identity had not been appropriated for commercial purpose. But the jury awarded Falwell $200,000 on the emotional distress claim. The U.S. Court of Appeals for the Fourth Circuit upheld the judgement, reasoning that the actual malice standard for public figures in libel cases did not apply to emotional distress.[90] Flynt and *Hustler* appealed to the U.S. Supreme Court.

After the lower court rulings, communication professionals had expressed grave concerns, in part because of the unsympathetic character of Flynt and his publication. They feared other public figures could routinely skirt protective libel and privacy laws and win judgments against the media on grounds unrelated to the truthfulness of what was published. Especially troubled were political and social satirists and editorial cartoonists whose purpose often is to hold public figures and institutional up to scorn and ridicule.

Much to their relief, the Supreme Court unanimously overturned the lower courts.

Citing journalism's long history of political caricature and cartooning and its place in the nation's political past and present, Chief Justice William Rehnquist reasoned that allowing public figures to collect damages without proving actual malice would unconstitutionally chill social and political discourse. He noted that the essence of political cartooning often focused on "unfortunate physical traits or politically embarrassing events — an exploration often calculated to injure the feelings of the subject of the portrayal. The art of the cartoonist is often not reasoned or even-handed, but slashing and one-sided." The outrageousness requirement, he noted, was highly subjective and "would allow a jury to impose liability on the basis of the jurors' tastes or views, or perhaps on the basis of their dislike of a particular expression." To prevail, Rehnquist said, public officials or public figures must prove the communication was false and that it was published knowingly, or with reckless disregard for whether it was true or

false.[91]

Private individuals fare better in emotional distress cases. In 1992, the tabloid newspaper *Sun* lost an emotional distress case in an Arkansas court after it published a fabricated story about a 101-year-old woman who became pregnant. To illustrate the story, the *Sun* used a photo of a 96-year-old Arkansas woman from its files, believing the woman had died. Among other things, the jury found the *Sun* guilty of intentional infliction of emotional distress and awarded hefty damages.[92]

A variant of intentional infliction of emotional distress is the tort of outrage, which focuses exclusively on the behavior of the defendant. For example, in 1988 personnel from a Florida television station went to a local police department after officials disclosed that skeletal remains found a year earlier were those of a 6-year-old boy reported missing three years before. A police officer removed the child's skull from a drawer in a laboratory. Images of the skull were broadcast as part of a report on crime. After the family of the boy watched a newscast showing a dramatic close-up of the skull, they filed an invasion of privacy and outrage lawsuit. Trial testimony centered on callous comments made during the television station's newsroom debate over whether to air the close-up footage. A Florida appellate court rejected the privacy claim but held that the newscast showing the skull easily surpassed the outrageousness requirement. The court, in a caustic rebuke of the decision to broadcast the close-up, said that if this case "did not constitute the tort of outrage, then there is no such tort."[93]

Plaintiffs also have been awarded damages in some jurisdictions for negligent infliction of emotional distress, which occurs when media behavior exposes individuals to dangers that the media should have reasonably foreseen. For example, a California court held a radio station responsible after a young driver was killed trying to keep up with a disc jockey who traveled about awarding prizes. The court reasoned that the accident was a foreseeable consequence of the station's promotion, which encouraged prize-seekers to rush from place to place.[94] Other courts, however, have been unwilling to hold the media accountable for the unforeseeable or speculative consequences, such as imitation or copy-cat

---

[90] *Hustler Magazine v. Falwell,* 797 F.2d 1270 (4th Cir. 1986).

[91] *Hustler Magazine v. Falwell,* 485 U.S. 46, 55-56 (1988).

[92] *Peoples Bank & Trust v. Globe International Publishing, Inc.,* 20 Media L. Rptr. (BNA) 2097 (1992).

[93] *Armstrong v. H&C Communications, Inc.,* 575 So.2d 280, 282 (1991).

[94] *Weirum v. RKO General, Inc.,* 123 Cal. Rptr. 468, 539 P.2d 36 (1975). See also "Negligent Infliction of Emotional Distress," *Pepperdine Law Review* 12 (1985): 889.

behavior.[95]

CONSTITUTIONAL AND STATUTORY PRIVACY

The privacy torts do not present the only reasons for special caution when gathering and disseminating information. Constitutional concerns and privacy statutes, which place limits *on government,* still have implications for journalists seeking information under government control. Limits on how government uses personal information indirectly place limits on journalists. And such limits on government use of private information — in this information-soaked era with its headlines about government and private enterprise abuses — are politically attractive to politicians and other policy-makers and record custodians.

Constitutional privacy is especially significant because it provides individuals a constitutional platform from which to challenge journalists in certain situations, potentially offsetting the presumption favoring publication of private facts about matters of public concern. Likewise, statutory privacy designed to protect individuals from government abuse also provides a rationale — sometimes unwarranted — for withholding information from the public and the news media.

Constitutional Privacy

Over time, the Supreme Court has defined a range of constitutional privacy protections. Although the word "privacy" appears nowhere in the Constitution, the Court has nonetheless recognized a right to be free from government intrusion and eavesdropping. For example:

- Reasoning that freedom from intrusion is based on a "zone of privacy" surrounding a person, not a specific place, the Court ruled unconstitutional a government wiretap on a telephone booth.[96]
- In *NAACP v. Alabama*, the Court struck down an Alabama law that required certain organizations, including civil rights groups, to turn over membership rolls to the state. The Court held the rule violated the associational rights of current and potential members of the NAACP, who might not exercise those rights out of fear of government retaliation.[97]
- In *Griswold v. Connecticut*, a case challenging a state law bar-

ring dissemination of birth control information, the Court fashioned a right of decisional privacy based on rights implied in the "penumbra" of various amendments to the Constitution.[98] The case laid the foundation for the controversial *Roe v. Wade* decision that recognized the right of a woman to decide whether to have an abortion.[99]

Most importantly to media professionals, however, has been the recent willingness of the Supreme Court to recognize a constitutional right of informational privacy — the right of individuals to control information about themselves. Concerns about privacy had been raised in several cases addressing government use of computers to gather, store and disseminate information about private individuals.

In 1976, concerns about the effects of new information technologies on privacy were first expressed on the Court by Justice William Brennan. In *United States v. Miller*, the majority held that individuals retained no privacy interest in information voluntarily given to a bank. Cautioned Brennan: "Development of photocopying machines, electronic computers and other sophisticated instruments has accelerated the abilities of government to intrude into areas which a person normally chooses to exclude from prying eyes and inquisitive minds."[100]

A year later, the Court acknowledged a right of informational privacy in upholding a New York state practice of compiling and storing in a computer certain prescription drug records on individuals. Such a practice did not violate individuals' constitutional right of privacy, Justice John Paul Stevens wrote, so long as strict security was in place to ensure the privacy of the information. Wrote Stevens: "We are not unaware of the threat to privacy implicit in the accumulation of vast amounts of personal information in computerized data banks or other massive government files."[101] Justice Brennan, in a concurring opinion, echoed concerns about the threat of computers to privacy, noting prophetically: "The central storage and easy accessibility of computerized data vastly increases the potential for abuse of that information, and I am not prepared to say that future developments will not demonstrate the necessity for some curb on such technology."[102]

In *Justice Department vs. Reporters Committee for Freedom of the Press*, the Court reacted to a long-standing concern about the threat computers pose to personal privacy when it articulated

---

[95] See *Zamora v. CBS,* 480 F. Supp. 199 (S.D. Fla. 1979); *Olivia v. NBC,* 178 Cal. 888 (Cal. App. 1981).

[96] *Katz v. United States,* 389 U.S. 347 (1967).

[97] 357 U.S. 449 (1958).

[98] 381 U.S. 479, 484 (1965).

[99] 410 U.S. 113 (1973).

[100] 425 U.S. 435, 451 (1976).

[101] *Whalen v. Roe,* 429 U.S. 589, 605 (1977).

[102] *Id.* at 607 (Brennan, J., concurring).

the practical obscurity doctrine in response to a news media request for information contained in a government database. In essence, the Court reasoned that computers have obliterated traditional barriers of time and space that once afforded individuals a measure of "practical obscurity" — or distance from their official past. Because of computers, the Court noted, individuals no longer can move to another place to escape past deeds or count on the passage of time to dim official memories. Following this reasoning, the Court suggested that information compiled in central government computers — even information gathered from various *public* records — regained a privacy interest when brought together in one place. In fact, the Court reasoned, if the information were indeed *public*, reporters should have no need to see a government database.[103] Under the reasoning of the *Reporters Committee* case, vast amounts of public-record information about individuals can be shielded from disclosure simply because they existed in a computer database.

The Freedom of Information Act

Since the Great Depression, government's appetite for information has grown steadily, hitting full stride with the Great Society programs of the 1960s that coincided with the growth of systems analysis — a management technique that depended on vast amounts of data. To balance government need for information, much of it personal, statutes were passed to ensure that government gathered information only for specific purposes and that it be used only for those purposes. One of the first such statutes was the federal Freedom of Information Act, passed in 1966 to ensure maximum access to records of federal executive agencies. While the act espouses openness, it also attempts to balance access with competing values. The result was nine exemptions, several of which raise privacy concerns as grounds for withholding information. (See Chapter 16.)

Exemption 3 protects certain kinds of information, as defined by other federal statutes, from disclosure. For a statute to qualify under the exemption, it must specify exactly what information must be withheld and must allow no discretion on the part of agency personnel. Laws governing numerous agencies, including the Internal Revenue Act, which protects personal income tax records, fall into this category. The exemption also covers the Census Bureau, the Consumer Products Safety Commission and the Federal Trade Commission

Exemption 6, which applies to personnel, medical and similar

files, shields information that would "constitute a clearly unwarranted" invasion of privacy. Implicit in this language is the understanding that a balancing process must occur to determine whether withholding would be warranted. The "similar files" wording has been applied to a range of information. The State Department invoked the exemption to successfully withhold disclosure of the citizenship status of individuals. In *Department of State v. Washington Post Co.*, the Supreme Court supported use of the exemption and said information need not be highly personal to be covered. Information could be withheld, the Court said, when disclosure could lead to injury or embarrassment.[104] The Court also upheld the State Department when it argued that the privacy interests of Haitians whose asylum claims were rejected outweighed public interest in disclosure.[105]

Privacy claims also were successfully raised by the National Aeronautics and Space Administration in a successful bid to prevent disclosure of an audio tape of the last communications from the space shuttle Challenger, which exploded after takeoff and killed its seven astronauts, including a high school teacher. In *New York Times Co. v. NASA*,[106] the space agency argued that release of the audiotape, transcripts of which had already been made public, would only add to the anguish of the victims' families. The *Times* countered that background noises and inflections of the astronauts' voices might yield significant information about the tragedy. A federal court rejected that reasoning and adopted the concept of relational privacy that extended protection to family members.

The *Challenger* ruling was cited by a state judge in the murder trial of Danny Rolling, convicted of killing five young people near the University of Florida in 1990. At the behest of prosecutors, Circuit Judge Stan Morris limited public access to graphic autopsy and crime scene photos — evidence jurors viewed before imposing Rolling's death sentence. The photos were public records under Florida law. Faced with the prospect of the photos appearing in print and further traumatizing victims' families, the judge ordered that they be bound in folders and made accessible to the public only under court supervision. Under the ruling, copies of photos could not leave the courthouse.[107]

Exemption 7 covers disclosure of certain law enforcement records, including disclosures that would invade privacy. In the

---

[103] 489 U.S. 749, 780 (1989).

[104] 456 U.S. 595 (1982).
[105] *Department of State v. Ray,* 502 U.S. 164 (1991).
[106] 782 F. Supp. 628 (D.D.C. 1991).
[107] *Florida v. Rolling,* 22 Media L. Rep. (BNA) 2264 (Fla. Cir. Ct. 1994).

Reporters Committee case mentioned previously, the court recognized privacy interests in certain compilations of criminal records — even records that were public at their original source. For example, if a record is contained in a central government database, such as an FBI computer, that record might be considered private. The same record at a courthouse in the jurisdiction where the crime occurred would be a public record. The court said that since the privacy/access balance typically favors withholding records when they are contained in computer compilations, courts need not engage in case-by-case balancing with the public interest in disclosure. The simple determination that a record is in the category of a computer compilation is sufficient to withhold such a record, the Court reasoned.

The Privacy Act of 1974

The Privacy Act was meant to create a "Code of Fair Information Practices" to regulate government agencies. The Senate report on the legislation noted that a purpose of the act was "to promote government respect for the privacy of citizens" by ensuring that executive branch agencies follow certain rules regarding the gathering and disclosing of information.[108] The Privacy Act is most likely to affect requests for information that is not clearly covered by the legislation. In such cases, custodians of records tend to be very cautious because the Privacy Act imposes penalties on custodians who release protected information. Withholding information that should be disclosed, on the other hand, may violate the federal Freedom of Information Act, but that legislation poses no penalties for wrongly withholding information.

Other Privacy Concerns

A number of other federal and state statutes raising privacy concerns can erect barriers to information gathered and kept by government and, in some cases, private institutions.

Driver's Privacy Protection Act. Driver license records have long been a source of useful information for journalists, more so in recent years with the growth of computer-assisted reporting. In 1991, for example, *The Miami Herald* used a computer analysis of state Division of Motor Vehicle records to show that many drunken drivers were being put back on the road. Beginning in September 1997, however, federal legislation began limiting access to such records. The legislation, passed in 1994, was partly in response to the slaying of California actress Rebecca Schaeffer by a fan who located her address through driver records obtained through a private investigator. The intent of the law is to inhibit stalkers and anyone else who might harm an individual after linking a name with an address.[109] The federal legislation contains a provision that allows states to disclose such information if they enact a provision notifying drivers that they have an option to withhold personal information.

The Buckley Amendment. Enacted as the Family Educational Rights and Privacy Act, this federal statute requires educational institutions receiving federal money to keep certain student records private. Directory information such as names, addresses and majors — which appear in most student directories — is not covered. Academic records, including non-criminal disciplinary records, are covered. Before 1992, the Department of Education was advising institutions that campus crime records should be considered student disciplinary records under the Buckley Amendment — a position that was frustrating many news organizations, especially campus newspapers. A 1992 amendment, however, specifically states that crime reports are not educational records and cannot be withheld as disciplinary records.[110]

Rape Shield Laws. Whether to publish the name of a rape victim is a controversial topic, both legally and ethically. Rape shield laws were designed to encourage rape victims to come forward by preventing the additional trauma of publicity. Some courts have specifically upheld rape shield laws.[111] In Florida, however, the state supreme court in 1994 upheld a ruling that the state's law was unconstitutional in a case spawned by the William Kennedy Smith rape trial.[112] The court relied heavily on *Florida Star v. B.J.F.*, which held the news media should not be punished for publishing truthful, lawfully obtained information about matters of public concern absent a state interest of the highest order.[113] The Georgia Supreme Court, also citing *Florida Star*, overturned a verdict against a state newspaper in a civil case based on disclosure of the name of a sexual assault victim.[114]

---

[108] 5 U.S.C. sec. 552a.

[109] Driver's Privacy Protection Act of 1994, 18 U.S.C.S. sec. 2721 (1994).

[110] 20 U.S.C.S. sec. 1232g(a)(4)(B)(ii)(1995).

[111] See, e.g., *Nappier v. Jefferson Standard Life Insurance Co.,* 322 F. 2d 502 (4th Cir. 1963).

[112] *Florida v. Globe Communication Corp.,* 648 So. 2d 110 (Fla. 1994).

[113] 491 U.S. 524 (1989).

[114] *Macon Telegraph Publishing Co. v. Tatum,* 263 Ga. 678, 436 S.E.

Juror Shield Laws. Much has been said and written about protecting jurors' privacy, particularly since the Rodney King police brutality trial and O.J. Simpson murder trial. Since the Supreme Court's ruling in *Press-Enterprise v. Superior Court,* jurors' selection and identity have been presumptively public matters. But after the King and Simpson cases, and the Timothy McVeigh trial in the Oklahoma City bombing, the tide appears to be changing. Citing privacy, judges appear to be routinely impaneling anonymous juries, a practice once reserved for the trials of organized crime kingpins when juror safety was a factor.[115] At least one state, Texas, has passed a law allowing anonymous juries. The law creates a presumption that juries will be anonymous in all criminal trials. Robert Dawson, a University of Texas criminal law professor, believes the 1993 statute was responsible for the growing number of private juries: "Before, a judge would have to go out on a limb to justify such a ruling. Now, he doesn't have to."[116] Jane Kirtley, executive director of The Reporters Committee for Freedom of the Press, says the concept of juror privacy "has become almost epidemic." It is not a question of "media access or exploitation," she says. "It's the notion of public oversight of the system."[117]

Computer Privacy. Journalists depend increasingly on information contained in computer databases and from other computer-based sources, such as the World Wide Web and Internet. Indeed, going online is allowing journalists greater speed and access to more information. Many significant news stories are based on analysis of government databases. Most laws dealing with computer privacy are designed to place limits on government. The Computer Matching and Privacy Act of 1988, for example, limits the ability of government to routinely cross-reference information in various government databases.[118] The Electronic Communications Privacy Act of 1986 made interception of computer communications a crime,[119] and the Computer Crime Act of 1986 made it unlawful to access or disclose certain records in computer form.[120] Many of the laws, reflecting some of the constitutional and statutory concerns discussed previously, treat computerized information as more threatening to privacy than similar information in pa-

per files. Such laws can be vague or over-inclusive in ways that inhibit legitimate journalists.

The computer/privacy debate also has begun to focus on private-sector information practices. A recent survey of Internet users found that fifty-five percent favored privacy limitations.[121] In June 1997, the Federal Trade Commission held four days of hearings that suggested support for the self-regulation of privacy in computer communications. The FTC was expected to make recommendations to Congress regarding the nature and scope of Internet regulation.[122] In what has been viewed as an attempt to head off government regulation of the Internet, Microsoft Corp. and rival computer company Netscape agreed on a standard for privacy software. About 100 computer software companies have endorsed the standard, which would limit how personal information on the Internet is compiled and shared.[123]

SOME FINAL WORDS ABOUT PRIVACY

Despite assaults on their privacy from various quarters — and perhaps in part because of those assaults — Americans remain strong in their belief in the right to be let alone. Privacy concerns are manifested in constitutions, statutes and common law cases that attempt to balance individual rights with competing values, including the right of the news media to publish and the right of the public to be informed. It is to be expected, then, that the rights of individuals and the rights of a free and vigorous press often will clash. In many instances, the balance has traditionally tilted toward the press because of the bedrock principle that a democratic society works best when information flows freely.

Yet journalism in today's information-filled environment is practiced in widely varying ways, from the *National Enquirer* to the *Philadelphia Inquirer*, from *Hard Copy* to *The News Hour*. At times, reporters engage in journalistic behavior that, although technically within the bounds of the law, is ethically questionable. Journalistic excesses are not lost on the public, whose declining opinion of journalism is reflected in some polls. The results of declining confidence in the news media can be reflected in the outcome of court cases, such as the Food Lion case, in which jurors imposed a substantial penalty against ABC despite the fact it had

2d 655 (1993).

[115] Tony Mauro, "Trend to Press Restriction Escalates in Denver," *First Amendment News,* May 1997, p. 1.

[116] Wendy Benjaminson, "Shroud of Secrecy Increasingly Veils Trials in Texas," *Houston Chronicle*, 13 March 1994, p. 1.

[117] Mauro, "Trend to Press Restriction Escalates in Denver," p. 6.

[118] 5 U.S.C. sec. 552a.

[119] 18 U.S.C. sec. 2510.

[120] 18 U.S.C. sec. 1030.

[121] Dan Harrison, "Computer Users Back Net Privacy Law," *DM News,* 16 June 1997, p. 3.

[122] Jaret Seiberg, "Self-Regulation Touted for Net Privacy," *The American Banker,* 12 June 1997, p. 3.

[123] New York Times News Service, "Netscape, Microsoft Bond Over Privacy," *Miami Herald,* 12 June 1997, p. C1.

uncovered apparent wrongdoing. Lack of public confidence in the press also can embolden politicians to pass laws limiting press freedoms in the name of privacy.

Privacy is an important value that the news media must respect —while never losing the responsibility to tell the hard truth whenever necessary.

FOR ADDITIONAL READING

Coleman, A.D. "Private Lives, Public Places: Street Photography Ethics." *Journal of Mass Media Ethics* 2 (Spring/Summer 1997):60.

Ernst, Morris L. and Alan U. Schwartz. *Privacy: The Right to be Let Alone.* New York: Macmillan, 1962.

Flaherty, David H. *Privacy in Colonial New England.* Charlottesville: University Press of Virginia, 1972.

Hixson, Richard F. *Privacy in a Public Society: Human Rights in Conflict.* New York: Oxford University Press, 1987.

Pember, Don. *Privacy and the Press.* Seattle: University of Washington Press, 1972.

Prosser, William. "Privacy." *California Law Review* 48 (1960): 383.

Sanford, Bruce W. *Libel and Privacy,* 2d ed. Englewood Cliffs, N.J.: Prentice-Hall, 1993.

Thomason, Tommy, ed. *Newspaper Coverage of Rape: Dilemmas on Deadline.* Fort Worth: Texas Christian University Press, 1994.

Warren, Samuel D. and Louis D. Brandeis. "The Right to Privacy." *Harvard Law Review* 4 (1890): 220.

Westin, Alan F. *Privacy and Freedom.* New York: Atheneum, 1967.

14

Confidential Sources and Information

By Cathy Packer

The right — or privilege — of a journalist to keep the identities of sources or other information confidential has been a persistent problem for more than a century and an increasingly troublesome one lately. Every year some journalists who refuse to comply with judicial orders to reveal the identities of confidential sources, to hand over work materials or to testify in court are found guilty of criminal contempt and are fined, jailed or ordered to perform community service. Other journalists avoid such penalties but pay a high price in legal fees and time.

Representatives from some 900 newspapers and televisions surveyed by the Reporters Committee for Freedom of the Press reported that they received a total of 3,159 subpoenas in 1993. Three reported that their newsrooms had been searched by law enforcement officials, and three reported that their telephone records were subpoenaed. The Reporters Committee concluded that subpoenas "are not merely a nuisance to the news media — they eat up staff time and resources as well."[1]

More recently the Society of Professional Journalists published a special report documenting an erosion of the reporter's privilege. The report said court decisions are eroding the privilege, especially in states where no shield statutes exist to create a privilege and in cases in which reporters refuse to reveal unpublished and non-confidential information:

Media law experts are not exactly sure why judges have had a change of heart about the reporter's privilege. Some suspect that increasing public scorn for sensational reporting is leading to a bias against journalists by the courts. Others say judges just do not understand the implications of not granting reporters protection.[2]

Problems typically arise when a reporter is served a subpoena to appear at a judicial proceeding to answer questions or provide documents. Ignoring a subpoena may result in a citation for contempt of court; complying may result in the loss of important sources of information.

The Reporters Committee reported that newspapers and television stations responding to its survey fully complied with slightly more than half of the subpoenas issued to them in 1993. In about twenty percent of cases, journalists reported, they were able to persuade the individuals who requested the subpoenas to with-

---

[1] Jane E. Kirtley, Daniel E. Katz and Gregg P. Leslie, eds., *Agents of Discovery: A Report on the Incidence of Subpoenas Served on the News Media in 1993* (Arlington, Va.: The Reporters Committee on Freedom of the Press, 1995), p. 12.

[2] Holli Hartman, *The Erosion of the Reporter's Privilege* (Washington, D.C.: The Society of Professional Journalists, 1997), p. 9.

draw them. In about ten percent of cases, the media challenged the subpoenas, and in seventy percent of those cases they were successful in having the subpoenas quashed.

In mid-1998 the Reporters Committee's web page listed sixteen journalists who had been jailed since 1984. It also listed twenty journalists who had been fined for refusing to reveal the identities of sources or other information.[3]

Journalists who object to testifying or turning over work materials generally claim they are protected from doing so by a reporter's testimonial privilege. The privilege is actually a bundle of privileges including the privilege not to reveal the identity of a confidential source, the privilege to be free from turning over published information or unpublished work materials and the privilege to be free from testifying at judicial proceedings. It also includes protection from newsroom searches by law enforcement agencies. The reporter's privilege is related to the common law doctor-patient, lawyer-client and priest-penitent testimonial privileges that have long granted one party in a relationship the right to refuse to testify against the other. The reporter's privilege, however, has never gained universal acceptance, and the Supreme Court has said it does not exist as a constitutional right.

The reporter's privilege varies dramatically from state to state and among federal jurisdictions. That's because the privilege is based on a patchwork of federal and state constitutional law, federal and state statutes, state common law, judicial rules and attorney general guidelines. The privilege also varies according to the type of proceeding to which a reporter is subpoenaed. For example, while the privilege has been recognized in both criminal and civil cases, a reporter is more likely to be compelled to testify in a criminal case where a defendant has a strong Sixth Amendment right to a fair trial. The privilege also varies according to the nature of what a reporter is being asked to reveal. Reporters are more likely to be compelled to testify about crimes they witnessed, for example, than about crimes of which they have second-hand knowledge.

Before a discussion of these variations, however, it might be helpful to look at a case in which a reporter refused to testify and at the courts' responses.

In a recent and widely publicized case, Graco Children's Products, a manufacturer of infant cradles, subpoenaed outtakes of the NBC program *Dateline*. The manufacturer wanted the network's interviews with Ruth Marden and her attorney to help defend itself from a product liability lawsuit filed by Marden. Marden claimed

that the faulty design of Graco's cradle, which rocked from head to toe rather than from side to side, caused her infant son to suffocate. Graco wanted the outtakes to impeach Marden's testimony and to buttress its position that the Marden child died of Sudden Infant Death Syndrome, not because of the rocking motion of the cradle.

NBC filed a motion asking the court to quash the subpoena. The network claimed a privilege under the New York shield law, the New York Constitution and the First Amendment to the U.S. Constitution. A U.S. District Court denied the motion and held the network in contempt of court for refusing to comply with the subpoena. The court ordered NBC to pay $5,000 a day until it produced all the requested outtakes. The penalty was stayed pending appeal.

The U.S. Court of Appeals for the Second Circuit applied the New York shield law, which granted journalists a partial testimonial privilege, and reversed the decision of the lower court.[4] The court held that the cradle manufacturer failed to establish that the outtakes were "critical or necessary" to the defense as required by the shield law. The court said that in order to find unpublished news to be "critical or necessary" within the meaning of the statute, "there must be a finding that the claim for which the information is to be used virtually rises or falls with admission or exclusion of proffered evidence."[5] Material that might impeach a witness ordinarily is not critical or necessary, the court said. Furthermore, the court held that there was no evidence that the mother would not be able to answer questions by Graco, and that Graco had not shown that the outtakes of the interview with Marden's lawyer were critical or necessary. Because the outtakes had never been aired, the manufacturer had no way of discerning their content. Journalists from NBC were not compelled to testify.

THE PROS AND CONS OF A REPORTER'S PRIVILEGE

A natural question arises in the debate over the benefit of allowing journalists to protect sources and information: Why would a journalist refuse to testify if the journalist had information that would help a court determine the truth in a case? Isn't it the business of journalists to uncover and publish the truth? Certainly it is, but journalists argue that they sometimes need to conceal certain information in order to protect the free flow of other information to the public. That's just one argument that is at the heart of the debate over a privilege of confidentiality for journalists. There are

---

[3] Reporters Committee for Freedom of the Press, *Paying the Price* (visited Sept. 1, 1998) <http//www.rcfp.org/jail.html>.

[4] *In re NBC (Krase v. Graco),* 79 F.3d 346 (2d Cir. 1996).
[5] *Id*. at 347.

others:

- Criminal defense attorneys argue that a client's Sixth Amendment right to a fair trial outweighs the privilege of a journalist to refuse to testify. The criminal defendant's right is characterized as the right to "every man's evidence" to prove innocence. That right is closely tied to the right of the public to fair and effective law enforcement. Courts often emphasize that all citizens — including reporters — are obliged to testify when they have knowledge pertinent to the outcome of a criminal case.

- Journalists counter that they need to be exempt from some of the duties of other citizens. They argue that they should have greater First Amendment protection because they have the difficult task of serving as watchdogs over powerful governments. This raises the question, which will be discussed later in this chapter, of whether the First Amendment provides more protection for journalists than it provides for other citizens.

- If a reporter is forced to reveal the identity of a confidential source, the reporter's supply of confidential sources might dry up, journalists argue. They say sources often have information that the public needs for democratic self-governance — information that cannot be obtained by other means. Furthermore, revealing the identities of sources might subject the sources to harassment or retaliation from those about whom they provided the information. Much important news would go unreported without these sources, the argument goes, and without a guarantee of confidentiality, the sources would not provide information. The common counter argument is that there is no proof of a chilling effect on the gathering and dissemination of the news.

- The burden of having either to testify or to fight a subpoena keeps journalists in court and away from their important jobs, which raises First Amendment concerns. Subpoenas and search warrants also can prompt journalists to censor their writing to avoid being subpoenaed or deter them from recording and preserving their recollections for future use. Journalists say the burden on newsgathering outweighs the public interest in disclosure. Opponents of a reporter's testimonial privilege say the problem of subpoenas being served on journalists only arises when a source is implicated in a crime or possesses information about a crime or other matter being investigated, which does not describe the vast bulk of confidential sources.

- Journalists argue that reporting styles changed in the late 1960s and early 1970s and that there is now more need for confidential sources, particularly when the media seek news about minority cultural and political groups or dissident organizations suspicious of the law and public officials.

- Journalists fear the government might use its subpoena power to harass the news media, to disrupt a reporter's relationships with news sources or to retaliate when the news media are critical of the government. Judges and others counter that rules governing the use of subpoenas are designed to prevent such abuses.

- When police and prosecutors rely on journalists for information, they make the media an arm of law enforcement, which is not their proper role in a democracy and undermines their credibility with sources. Journalists are supposed to be watchdogs of law enforcement. In civil cases, a journalist might be forced into the position of preparing a litigant's case. Also, some journalists argue that if a journalist can find information, police or other investigators should be able to do the same — unless they're just too lazy.

- Journalists argue that law enforcement officials who search newsrooms armed with warrants threaten to interfere with their publication schedules. The government argues that the Fourth Amendment's protection against unreasonable searches and seizures provides ample protection for journalists — the same protection it provides for all citizens. It is the magistrate's job to ensure that a search warrant is not issued without probable cause or in a manner that unnecessarily interferes with publication.

These arguments appear in court opinion after court opinion as reporters resist orders to testify.

THE HISTORY OF THE PRIVILEGE

Reporter's privilege cases are not new. For more than one hundred years, journalists have been resisting judicial — and sometimes Congressional — efforts to compel them to testify, and for most of those years journalists were without any testimonial privilege. In 1873, for example, an editor of the *New York Tribune* was subpoenaed to appear before a New York state grand jury to identify the author of an allegedly libelous article that had been published in the newspaper.[6] The editor appeared but refused to identify the author. Newspaper policy prohibited him from disclosing the identities of any writers, he explained, because the newspaper, not the author, is responsible for the article's contents. The editor was found in contempt of court and sent to the county jail.

Some of the earliest reporter's privilege cases involved Congres-

---

[6] *People ex rel. Phelps v. Fancher,* 2 Hun. 226 (N.Y. Sup. Ct. 1874).

sional subpoenas. The Constitution gives Congress the power to investigate, which is accompanied by the power to subpoena.[7] In the mid-1850s, J.W. Simonton, Washington correspondent for the *New York Times*, reported that certain unnamed congressmen were soliciting bribes to influence their actions regarding the disposal of public lands. Simonton was hauled before the House to divulge the names. When he refused, the House cited him for contempt and imprisoned him for more than two weeks until he decided to testify. After he testified, several congressmen resigned. At the time, the only punishment for an individual who refused a Congressional subpoena was imprisonment during the current session of Congress.[8] Harsher penalties were adopted later.[9]

While no reporter has been found in contempt of Congress for several decades, some have been threatened with contempt citations. In 1992, a special counsel appointed by the Senate wanted to compel Nina Totenberg of National Public Radio and Timothy Phelps of *Newsday* to disclose the sources of stories in which they reported that law professor Anita Hill told Senate investigators she had been sexually harassed by Supreme Court nominee Clarence Thomas. The leadership of the Senate Rules Committee decided not to order the two journalists to testify because of the chilling effect such an act would have on the media.

Year after year, journalists have argued that compelled testimony chills newsgathering, violates their employers' rules and violates professional codes of ethics. Not until 1959, however, did the courts address the question of whether the First Amendment provided reporters with a testimonial privilege. In *Garland v. Torre*, the U.S. Court of Appeals for the Second Circuit refused to exempt the reporter from her obligation to testify but, for the first time, recognized that "compulsory disclosure of a journalist's confidential sources of information may entail an abridgment of press freedom by imposing some limitation upon the availability of news."[10]

The case involved a breach of contract and libel suit filed against CBS by actress Judy Garland. Garland claimed that a network executive made false and defamatory statements about her to *New York Herald Tribune* columnist Marie Torre, who published them. During pre-trial discovery, Garland's legal counsel subpoenaed Torre, who appeared and testified that the statements in her

column were the statements made to her by a CBS informant. But she refused to identify the source, arguing that doing so would violate her promise of confidentiality, even when ordered to do so by a federal judge. The judge held her in contempt of court, and Torre appealed.

Then-Judge Potter Stewart wrote the opinion for the Second Circuit, and later, as a Supreme Court justice, he would use the reasoning from that opinion as the basis for what was arguably the most influential judicial opinion ever written regarding the reporter's testimonial privilege. The Second Circuit ruled that the First Amendment did not exempt the newspaper columnist from her obligation to testify and identify a confidential source. Stewart explained that the court's task was to balance the interest served by compelling the witness to testify against the resulting impairment of First Amendment freedoms. Noting that the balancing was not difficult in this case, Stewart explained that the First Amendment interest was the witness's right to decide whether to speak or remain silent, a privacy right. *If* freedom of the press also is involved, he said, "we do not hesitate to conclude that it too must give place under the Constitution to a paramount public interest in the fair administration of justice. 'The right to sue and defend in the courts is the alternative of force. In an organized society it is the right conservative of all other rights, and lies at the foundation of orderly government.'"[11]

The court suggested limits on the government's power to compel reporters to testify, however. Judge Stewart pointed out that compelling Torre to testify did not involve curtailing unorthodox political, economic or religious views; the wholesale disclosure of a newspaper's confidential sources; or a case in which the identity of the news source was of doubtful relevance. Stewart also said the district court had not abused its discretion in ordering Torre to testify because the court found the deposition was being taken in good faith, was a necessary step in the preparation for trial and was not being taken in a manner as to unreasonably annoy, embarrass or oppress the witness. While ruling against the media, Stewart was planting the seeds for a First Amendment-based qualified testimonial privilege for reporters.

The constitutional question did not come before the Supreme Court until *Branzburg v. Hayes*, fourteen years later. By then, subpoenas were being served on reporters in dramatic numbers. CBS and NBC, for example, received 121 subpoenas in a thirty-month period in the late 1960s and early 1970s, and a *Chicago Sun-Times* reporter was subpoenaed eleven times in eighteen

---

[7] U.S. Const. art. I, §§ 1, 8. See also *McGrain v. Daugherty,* 273 U.S. 135, 174 (1927).

[8] James Hamilton, *The Power to Probe: A Study of Congressional Investigations* (New York: Random House, 1976), p. 91.

[9] 2 U.S.C. 192, 194 (1970).

[10] 259 F.2d 545, 548 (2d Cir. 1958), *cert. denied* 358 U.S. 910 (1958).

[11] *Id.* at 549 (quoting *Chambers v. Baltimore & Ohio R. Co.,* 207 U.S. 142, 148 (1907)).

months. This was the result of tumultuous social and political events that included the Watergate scandal, an increase in investigative reporting, the increased use of confidential sources as the basis for stories and the Nixon administration's desire to maintain law and order in an increasingly unstable society.

BRANZBURG V. HAYES

In 1972 the Supreme Court decided by a 5-4 vote that the First Amendment does not provide journalists with the right to be free from having to appear and testify before a grand jury or at a criminal trial. The landmark opinion in *Branzburg v. Hayes*[12] was a stinging defeat for three reporters who had refused to testify before grand juries. Twenty years later, however, *Branzburg* is widely interpreted by lower courts as providing journalists with a qualified, or conditional, First Amendment-based testimonial privilege. What caused this apparent shift?

Branzburg was actually four separate cases consolidated in one opinion because the four cases raised the same First Amendment issue. Two of the cases involved Paul Branzburg, a reporter for the *Louisville Courier-Journal*. He was first subpoenaed to testify before a grand jury after he wrote a story in which he described watching two people synthesize hashish from marijuana. His second subpoena arrived after he wrote a story detailing the use of drugs in Frankfort, Kentucky, the state capital. In the second story, Branzburg reported that he spent two weeks interviewing dozens of drug users and seeing several of them smoke marijuana. In both stories, Branzburg concealed the identities of his drug-using and manufacturing sources, and, when subpoenaed, he appeared but refused to identify those sources, claiming a testimonial privilege under the Kentucky shield law and the Kentucky and U.S. constitutions. The Kentucky Court of Appeals denied his claims, saying he had no legal right to refuse to testify about crimes he observed.[13]

The third case involved Paul Pappas, a newsman-photographer for a Massachusetts television station. As part of his coverage of civil disorders, he was invited into Black Panther headquarters on the condition that he not disclose anything he saw or heard except those events he might cover in an anticipated police raid. There was no raid, and Pappas reported no story. He was, however, subpoenaed to appear before a state grand jury investigating criminal acts allegedly committed by the Panthers during civil unrest. Pappas testified before the grand jury but refused to say what he saw and heard inside the Black Panther headquarters. The Massachusetts Supreme Judicial Court rejected his claim of a First Amendment privilege,[14] and Massachusetts had no shield law.

The fourth case in the *Branzburg* quartet involved Earl Caldwell, a *New York Times* reporter also covering the Black Panther Party and other black militant groups. He was subpoenaed and told to bring his notes and tape recordings about the aims and activities of the Black Panthers to a federal grand jury investigating crimes allegedly committed by the Black Panthers, including assassination threats against President Richard Nixon.

Caldwell objected to the broad scope of the subpoena, and the district court compromised. The court ordered him to divulge whatever information had been given to him for publication but said that he would not be required "to reveal confidential associations, sources or information received, developed or maintained by him as a professional journalist in the course of his efforts to gather news for dissemination to the public through the press or other news media."[15] The court held that the First Amendment afforded Caldwell a privilege to refuse to disclose such confidential information until the government showed a compelling and overriding national interest in the information that could not be served by any other means. Caldwell, however, objected to having to appear at all. He argued that having to appear before a grand jury, which meets behind closed doors, violated his First Amendment rights and, if enforced, would drive "a wedge of mistrust and silence between the news media and the militants."[16] When Caldwell refused to appear, he was found in contempt. The U.S. Court of Appeals for the Ninth Circuit overturned that decision,[17] ruling that the First Amendment afforded reporters a qualified testimonial privilege and that requiring Caldwell to testify "would deter his informants from communicating with him in the future and would cause him to censor his writings in an effort to avoid being subpoenaed."[18] The government appealed to the Supreme Court.

Justice Byron White, for the Court, declared that the journalists' First Amendment interests were outweighed by the general obligation of each citizen to appear before a grand jury or at a trial and testify. White explained that grand juries, which are mandated by the Fifth Amendment to the Constitution for defendants sus-

---

[12] 408 U.S. 665 (1972).

[13] *Branzburg v. Pound*, 461 S.W.2d 345 (Ky. Ct. App. 1970); *Branzburg v. Meigs*, 503 S.W.2d 748 (Ky. Ct. App. 1971). At the time these cases were decided, the appeals court was Kentucky's highest court.

[14] *In re Pappas*, 358 Mass. 604, 266 N.E.2d 297 (1971).

[15] *Application of Caldwell*, 311 F. Supp. 358, 362 (N.D. Cal. 1970).

[16] *Branzburg v. Hayes*, 408 U.S. at 676.

[17] *Caldwell v. United States*, 434 F.2d 1081 (9th Cir. 1970).

[18] *Branzburg*, 408 U.S. at 679.

pected of a capital or "otherwise infamous crime," are essential to fair and effective law enforcement because they protect a person from having to stand trial unless there is probable cause that the person committed a crime. The journalists' interests, on the other hand, were only slightly affected by this decision, White wrote. He said the Court's decision would have no effect on what journalists can publish and would not affect a large number of their sources; the journalists' argument that having to testify would constrict the news flow from their sources was "to a great extent speculative."[19] History, he said, suggests the press can operate effectively without a testimonial privilege.

Justice White's opinion made it clear that the Court was not about to create a testimonial privilege for journalists that other citizens do not also enjoy. This point goes a long way toward explaining not only why the journalists lost the case, but why, six years later, student journalists would also lose *Zurcher v. Stanford Daily*.[20] In that case, the *Stanford Daily* asked the Court to establish a First Amendment protection against otherwise legal newsroom searches — a protection not afforded to other citizens. In both *Branzburg* and *Zurcher*, the Supreme Court refused to interpret the First Amendment as giving journalists more protection than other citizens. In the view of the Court, the First Amendment applies equally to all citizens, and, furthermore, the Court did not want the task of deciding who is a journalist. This has consistently been the majority view of the Court.

Justice Stewart, for one, disagreed. He argued in a 1974 speech that the press clause was intended to extend rights to the press beyond those of other persons, who are protected by the speech clause. The press clause is needed to enable the media to act as watchdogs of government, he argued, and if the press and speech clauses do not have different meanings, they are no more than "a constitutional redundancy."[21]

When, in 1980, the media again came to the Supreme Court asking for an expanded interpretation of the First Amendment — this time for a right of access to criminal trials — the Court said "yes." The different result in *Richmond Newspapers v. Virginia*[22] undoubtedly was due in large part to the fact that the media requested the right of access for themselves *and* the public; the newspaper did not ask the Court to create a First Amendment protection for journalists beyond that afforded to others.

Also, in *Branzburg* the Court stated that "news gathering is not without its First Amendment protection,"[23] a simple statement that has tremendous potential as a precedent for expanding the traditional scope of First Amendment freedoms. Traditionally the First Amendment has been interpreted as protecting the right to publish the news but not the right to gather it. That changed somewhat in 1980, when the *Branzburg* decision served as a precedent for guaranteeing the media and the public access to criminal trials, as established in *Richmond Newspapers*. But journalists have been unsuccessful in their attempts to have the reach of *Branzburg* extended to include a First Amendment right of access to prisons or jails — places that are not open to the general public and where security is very important.[24]

In *Branzburg*, White also noted that the grand juries in all four cases were conducted properly. Grand juries not conducted in good faith would raise different First Amendment issues, he said. White also warned law enforcement officials that they were not to use subpoenas to harass the media.

Finally, White pointed out that Congress and state legislatures had the power to create testimonial privileges for reporters by statute if they determined they were necessary and desirable. This illustrates the legal principle that while the government cannot take from citizens rights protected by the First Amendment, the government can create rights beyond those provided by the First Amendment. Shield laws do just that, as do state and federal statutes that grant the public and the media rights of access to government meetings and records.

In a three-paragraph concurring opinion, Justice Lewis Powell emphasized the limited nature of the majority opinion and opened the door for lower courts to reinterpret the *Branzburg* decision. "The Court does not hold that newsmen, subpoenaed to testify before a grand jury, are without constitutional rights with respect to the gathering of news or in safeguarding their sources," Powell wrote.[25] He noted that harassment of journalists would not be tolerated and explained that journalists can move to quash a subpoena if their information is only remotely related to a grand jury investigation or if there is no legitimate law enforcement need for the information. He advocated balancing First Amendment and law enforcement interests on a case-by-case basis.

Justice Powell's concurrence opened the door for the reinter-

---

[19]*Id.* at 694.

[20] 436 U.S. 547 (1978).

[21] Potter Stewart, "Or of the Press," *Hastings Law Journal* 26 (1975): 633.

[22] 448 U.S. 555 (1980).

[23] 408 U.S. at 707.

[24] See *Saxbe v. Washington Post Co.,* 417 U.S. 843 (1974); *Procunier v. Pell,* 417 U.S. 817 (1974); *Houchins v. KQED,* 438 U.S. 1 (1978). These cases are discussed in Chapter 16.

[25] *Branzburg,* 408 U.S. at 709 (Powell, J., concurring).

pretation because, although he voted with the majority to deny a First Amendment-based testimonial privilege in the four cases under review, he appeared to support a qualified journalistic privilege — a privilege that would be afforded to journalists if their information were only remotely related to a grand jury investigation or if there were no legitimate law enforcement need for the information. So, when the lower federal and state courts looked beyond who won or lost in *Branzburg* to who supported some degree of First Amendment-based privilege, they added Powell's position to those of the four dissenters. The result was a majority in favor of at least a qualified privilege for reporters.

In light of that reinterpretation, Justice Stewart's dissenting opinion has become enormously important. Arguing that the Court had displayed a "crabbed view" of the First Amendment and "a disturbing insensitivity to the critical role of an independent press in our society,"[26] he proposed a three-part test to determine when a journalist must testify. He proposed that, in order to defeat a reporter's motion to quash a grand jury subpoena, the government must prove each of the following:

- there is probable cause to believe the reporter has information that is clearly relevant to a probable crime;
- the information cannot be obtained by alternative means less destructive of First Amendment rights;
- there is a "compelling and overriding interest" in the information.[27]

These criteria are a version of the qualifications Stewart first suggested in *Garland v. Torre*. From those two media losses came a partial victory.

Most appellate courts have interpreted *Branzburg* as a precedent for a qualified First Amendment-based privilege for reporters and have adopted Stewart's three-part test, or some variation thereof, as criteria for the privilege to stand. That is, the privilege is not absolute. A reporter can successfully claim a First Amendment right not to testify only if the government fails to prove all three parts of the test. If the government is able to prove what the court demands of it, the reporter must testify or chance being cited for contempt of court.

APPLYING THE FIRST AMENDMENT PRIVILEGE

The impact of *Branzburg v. Hayes* is obvious. All but three circuits clearly have interpreted *Branzburg* as a precedent for a First Amendment-based qualified testimonial privilege for reporters.

The Sixth Circuit has ruled that there is no such privilege, at least for grand jury proceedings.[28] The Seventh Circuit has not addressed the issue, although it has supported a district court's decision to quash a subpoena to a reporter.[29] The Eighth Circuit has not yet decided whether a privilege exists.

It is not enough to know which circuits or states recognize the privilege, however. Journalists should be aware that the qualified privilege is formulated differently in different jurisdictions. In most cases, the circuit courts have applied the three-part test from Stewart's dissent in *Branzburg* to decide whether a journalist must testify. Sometimes a fourth prong is added to the test: The underlying claim being litigated must clearly have merit. Other times neither a three- nor a four-part test is used. For example, the U.S. Court of Appeals for the First Circuit employs case-by-case balancing of "the potential harm to the free flow of information ... against the asserted need for the requested information."[30] Usually, however, the application of the three-part test decides a case. Here are examples of how each element of the three-part test has been applied by the circuit courts to protect journalists:

(1) There is probable cause to believe the reporter has information that is clearly relevant to a probable crime. In 1980 the U.S. Court of Appeals for the Fifth Circuit vacated a contempt decree against a reporter who had refused to obey a court order to reveal the identity of a confidential source at an *in camera* hearing.[31] An *in camera* hearing takes place before a judge in chambers and provides an opportunity for the judge to review the reporter's information to decide if it should be revealed in open court. In this case, the subpoena had been sought by a discharged school official who sued the school district for allegedly publicizing false and stigmatizing charges against him and for failing to afford him a hearing in violation of his Fourteenth Amendment due process rights. The discharged school official claimed the defamatory charges had been leaked to the education reporter for the *Dallas Morning News*. He sought the identities of the reporter's confidential sources.

The Fifth Circuit found the reporter had a qualified First Amendment-based right to withhold the identities of confidential sources because their identities were not relevant to what the

---

[26] *Id.* at 725 (Stewart, J., dissenting).

[27] *Id.* at 743 (Stewart, J., dissenting).

[28] *Storer Communications, Inc. v. Giovan,* 810 F.2d 580 (6th Cir. 1987).

[29] *United States v. Lloyd,* 71 F.3d 1256 (7th Cir. 1995), *cert. denied,* 116 S.Ct. 2511 (1996).

[30] *Bruno & Stillman, Inc. v. Globe Newspaper Co.,* 633 F.2d 583, 596 (1st Cir. 1980).

[31] *In re Selcraig,* 705 F.2d 789 (5th Cir. 1983).

court determined to be the only possibly valid claim in the case — that the plaintiff had requested and been refused a hearing. Therefore the reporter could not be compelled to testify until the plaintiff first proved he had indeed been denied a hearing. Then, the court said, the reporter's testimony would be relevant to possible punitive damages.

(2) The information cannot be obtained by alternative means less destructive of First Amendment rights. In 1990, the U.S. Court of Appeals for the D.C. Circuit ruled that the plaintiff in a libel case could not compel a reporter to testify because the plaintiff had not exhausted alternative sources. The plaintiff, a friend of Washington, D.C., Mayor Marion Barry, sued the *Washington Times* for reporting that he waited several hours before calling for help when a woman with whom he was partying collapsed from a drug overdose; the woman subsequently died. The newspaper said the man waited to allow other partygoers time to leave the scene. The plaintiff said he needed to uncover the identities of the newspaper's five confidential sources in order to prove actual malice, the requisite standard of fault in his libel case. The court ruled, however, that he could not defeat the reporter's privilege because he had "utterly failed" to first pursue obvious alternative sources of information.[32] The court did not suggest who those sources might be.

(3) There is a compelling and overriding interest in the information. In 1983, the U.S. Court of Appeals for the Second Circuit allowed *Sports Illustrated* to refuse to comply with a subpoena for documents and tapes related to a story about a basketball point-shaving scandal at Boston College. The defense at the criminal trial resulting from the scandal sought the documents and tapes in order to impeach the credibility of one of the authors of the article, reputed underworld figure Henry Hill. The article was his first-person account of the point-shaving scheme. The court ruled that the magazine had a qualified privilege not to turn over its work materials to the court and that the defense failed to overcome that privilege because it failed to prove that the documents were "necessary and critical" to its case. The court explained that Hill had been thoroughly impeached already and that further evidence against him would serve "a solely cumulative purpose."[33] Hill had admitted under oath that he was a career criminal who had committed robbery, arson, hijacking, extortion and loan sharking and had trafficked in illegal drugs.

THE WHO, WHAT AND WHERE OF THE FIRST AMENDMENT PRIVILEGE

Even when a court recognizes a First Amendment-based testimonial privilege for reporters, the protection afforded to journalists who refuse to testify varies based on three factors: (1) the type of proceeding in which the journalist is subpoenaed to testify; (2) the type of information or material the journalist is being asked to divulge, including whether the journalist is being asked to testify as an eyewitness, whether the journalist promised confidentiality to a source and whether the information sought had been published; and (3) whether the person ordered to testify is, in fact, a journalist.

The Type of Proceeding

Because the Supreme Court said in *Branzburg* that journalists do not have a First Amendment right to refuse to testify before a properly conducted grand jury, journalists today generally have the least protection when called to testify before grand juries. Courts usually interpret *Branzburg* as rejecting a First Amendment privilege unless the grand jury is harassing a witness or otherwise not acting in good faith.

In 1987, for example, the U.S. Court of Appeals for the Sixth Circuit told a Michigan television reporter that he must hand over to a county grand jury videotapes compiled in the course of his reporting about Detroit youth gangs.[34] The grand jury subpoenaed the tapes to assist with an investigation into the murder of a state police officer, allegedly by gang members. The reporter claimed a testimonial privilege under the First Amendment and the Michigan shield law, explaining he had promised gang members that the tapes he made of them would not be used in any manner that could identify any gang member. Subsequently, however, several gang members told police that the police officer's murderers were among those videotaped and that they could identify the assailants from the tapes. The Sixth Circuit wrote that the reporter was asking the court to "restructure" the Supreme Court's holding in *Branzburg* to create a qualified privilege for him.[35] Although it noted that some other courts had reinterpreted *Branzburg*, it declined to do so. Furthermore, the court said the public's interest in effective law enforcement was so strong in the case that it would order disclosure of the videotapes even if *Branzburg* did provide

---

[32] *Clyburn v. News World Communications, Inc.,* 903 F.2d 29, 35 (D.C. Cir. 1990).

[33] *United States v. Burke,* 700 F.2d 70, 77-78 (2d Cir. 1983).

[34] *In re Grand Jury Proceedings (Storer Communications, Inc. v. Giovan),* 810 F.2d 580 (6th Cir. 1987).

[35] *Id.* at 583.

a qualified privilege. The state shield law did not protect the reporter because it did not apply to television reporters.

Some courts use *Branzburg* as a precedent for denying reporters a testimonial privilege in other types of criminal proceedings as well. In such cases, the courts generally conclude that the criminal defendant's Sixth Amendment right to "every man's evidence" outweighs First Amendment interests. For example, in 1988 the U.S. Court of Appeals for the First Circuit enforced a pre-trial subpoena issued to NBC requesting outtakes of an interview with a prospective key witness in the mail and wire fraud trial of Lyndon H. LaRouche and workers in his 1984 presidential campaign. Only a small portion of the interview had been aired. The court decided the case by balancing the journalists' First Amendment interests against the criminal defendants' interests. According to the court, the legitimate First Amendment interests in this case were (1) the threat of administrative and judicial intrusion into the newsgathering and editorial processes; (2) the disadvantage of a journalist appearing to be an investigative arm of the judicial system, the government or a private party; (3) the disincentive to compile and preserve non-broadcast material; and (4) the burden on journalists' time and resources in responding to subpoenas. The defendants' interests, as articulated by the court, were "their constitutional rights to a fair trial under the Fifth Amendment [the right to a grand jury and the guarantee of due process, for example] and to compulsory process and effective confrontation and cross-examination of adverse witnesses under the Sixth Amendment."[36] The weightier were the defendants' interests, the court ruled.

According to the survey conducted by the Reporters Committee, the largest number of subpoenas reported were issued in connection with criminal cases. The second largest category comprised subpoenas served in connection with civil cases. In civil cases, reporters generally have greater success in quashing subpoenas than in criminal cases because no party to the case has a Sixth Amendment fair trial interest. When the management of a Florida television station received a subpoena in a civil case for its audio and videotapes of a county school board meeting, it claimed a qualified privilege under the First Amendment. A U.S. District Court judge granted the privilege because there were no Sixth Amendment interests in the case to outweigh the First Amendment interests. The judge explained: "This Court must only weigh the first amendment interest of the press — the independence in selection and choice of material for publication — against 'the interest served by the liberal discovery provisions embodied in the

Federal Rules of Civil Procedure.'"[37]

A reporter who is a party to civil litigation, however, as in a libel or invasion of privacy suit, is more likely to be ordered to testify than a reporter who is not a party. In a 1974 case, for example, the U.S. Court of Appeals for the D.C. Circuit upheld a lower court's decision that a reporter who was being sued for libel had to disclose the identity of a confidential source. The libel plaintiff was attempting to prove the reporter had not used reliable sources. The plaintiff had to prove actual malice to prevail in the libel case, and there were no other means of proving it. The court explained that although it recognized a qualified privilege, the argument in favor of compelling disclosure was strong because the information sought went "to the heart of the matter."[38]

A reporter's right not to reveal a confidential source in a libel case is further weakened by the Supreme Court's 1979 decision in *Herbert v. Lando*.[39] The Court ruled in that libel case that there is no First Amendment privilege against discovery into the editorial process and, therefore, reporters could be compelled to testify about the details of the newsgathering and writing process. *Herbert* did not involve confidential sources.

Type of Information Sought

Two important considerations in whether a reporter will be ordered to disclose information are whether the information is confidential and whether it has been published. Journalists have greater success in protecting confidential information — especially the identities of confidential sources — than in protecting nonconfidential information and sources. And journalists who object to handing over unpublished work products such as outtakes, notes, unpublished photographs and internal memos generally are more successful than those who object to handing over published work materials such as photographs, stories, audiotape and videotape. Published work products are the most common targets of subpoenas, according to the Reporters Committee study.

Publication and nonconfidentiality were key factors when a U.S. District Court judge ordered reporters to testify in a 1990 case.

---

[36] *United States v. LaRouche Campaign,* 841 F.2d 1176, 1182 (1st Cir. 1988).

[37] *Hatch v. Marsh,* 18 Media L. Rep. (BNA) 1686, 1687 (M.D. Fla. 1990) (quoting *Loadholtz v. Fields,* 389 F. Supp. 1299, 1300 (M.D. Fla. 1975)).

[38] *Carey v. Hume,* 492 F.2d 631, 636 (D.C. Cir.), *cert. dismissed,* 417 U.S. 938 (1974), quoting *Garland v. Torre,* 259 F.2d 545 (2d Cir. 1958), *cert. denied* 358 U.S. 910 (1958).

[39] 441 U.S. 153 (1979).

Newspaper reporters were subpoenaed after they reported statements made by several defendants in a case involving the arson of a bingo hall on a New York state Indian reservation.[40] The U.S. attorney sought to have the reporters testify that the defendants, who were identified in the story, made the statements attributed to them. The reporters moved to quash the subpoenas, claiming a First Amendment privilege. The court said the reporters enjoyed a qualified privilege but that the privilege was diminished by two factors: The information was not confidential, and it had been published. The reporters were required to testify. The court said there was a long list of such diminishing factors, including when the trial before which the reporter is subpoenaed is criminal, when the questions put to a reporter are narrowly limited and when the reporter is subpoenaed to testify about his or her observation of a public place or event.

Reporters must almost always testify if they are eyewitnesses to crimes. A U.S. District Court judge in California ruled, for example, that a television news cameraman's personal observations of force used by San Francisco police officers on a citizen were not privileged. The judge said the cameraman had not been asked to reveal any confidential sources or information, nor had he been requested to produce or discuss any resource materials. Rather, he was requested to disclose information that goes to the "very heart" of the plaintiff's claim that the police violated his rights, the court said, and there is no legal authority to support a testimonial privilege in such a case.[41]

Finally, if a journalist is accused of a crime, usually the only testimonial privilege available is the Fifth Amendment protection against self-incrimination.

Who Asserts the Privilege?

Clearly a full-time professional journalist employed by a print or broadcast outlet can successfully claim a First Amendment-based testimonial privilege if the privilege is recognized in a particular jurisdiction. The protection is not always granted to others who have information they do not want to disclose, however. The general rule is that the witness claiming the privilege must demonstrate that he or she sought, gathered or received the information in dispute with the intent — from the start of the newsgathering process — to distribute it to the public.

The person claiming the privilege need not work for a main-stream or commercial news organization. Medical newsletters, trade association magazines, investment analysts' reports and reports from Standard & Poor's credit rating agency also qualify, as do student publications. Freelance writers and book authors often qualify for the privilege, as well, and pay is not a factor.[42] Scholars have had less success in claiming the privilege.[43] One individual who did not qualify was a personal friend of accused murderer Claus Von Bulow. The U.S. Court of Appeals for the Second Circuit said she could not obtain a privilege merely by claiming she planned to write a book about Von Bulow's trial because she had no contract and had previously published nothing.[44]

OTHER PROTECTIONS AGAINST SUBPOENAS

In addition to First Amendment protections, there is a body of state and federal law that provides reporters with protection from revealing sources and information.

Shield Laws

Maryland adopted the first state shield law in 1896. When *Branzburg v. Hayes* was decided by the Supreme Court in 1972, seventeen states had shield laws. Today the District of Columbia and these thirty states have them: Alabama, Alaska, Arizona, Arkansas, California, Colorado, Delaware, Florida, Georgia, Illinois, Indiana, Kentucky, Louisiana, Maryland, Michigan, Minnesota, Montana, Nebraska, Nevada, New Jersey, New Mexico, New York, North Dakota, Ohio, Oklahoma, Oregon, Pennsylvania, Rhode Island, South Carolina and Tennessee.

But shield laws do not always protect journalists completely; they vary significantly from state to state, and judges often interpret them very narrowly.

One way in which shield laws vary is in whom they protect. Arizona's shield law, for example, specifically applies to persons "engaged in newspaper, radio, television or reportorial work, or connected with or employed by a newspaper, radio or television station."[45] So, when the notes and other documents gathered by a freelance author for a book project were subpoenaed in a criminal case, an Arizona court ruled that the shield law did not apply to

---

[40] *United States v. Markiewicz,* 732 F. Supp. 316 (N.D.N.Y. 1990).

[41] *Dillon v. City and County of San Francisco,* 748 F. Supp. 722, 726 (N.D. Cal. 1990).

[42] James C. Goodale, *et al.,* "Reporter's Privilege," in *Communications Law 1997,* vol. 3 (James C. Goodale, ed., 1997), pp. 438-42.

[43] See *Shoen v. Shoen,* 5 F.3d 1289 (9th Cir. 1993).

[44] *Von Bulow v. Von Bulow,* 811 F.2d 136 (2d Cir.), *cert. denied,* 481 U.S. 1015 (1987).

[45] Ariz. Rev. Stat. Ann. § 12-2237 (1994).

the freelance author. The court said the freelancer did not "gather and disseminate news on an ongoing basis as part of the organized, traditional, mass media."[46] Similarly, Ohio's shield law protects people "engaged in the work of, or connected with, or employed by" newspapers, press associations, or radio or television stations or networks.[47] A federal district court in Ohio refused to extend that law's protection to the publisher of bi-monthly financial reports.[48] The Minnesota law provides broader protection. The law says the testimonial privilege is for any person "directly engaged in the gathering, procuring, compiling, editing, or publishing of information for the purpose of transmission, dissemination or publication to the public."[49]

State shield laws also vary in the strength of the protection they provide. For example, New York's shield law provides absolute protection against having to reveal the identity of a confidential source.[50] Other states — Michigan and Oklahoma are two — have shield laws that offer a qualified privilege. Michigan's law stipulates that in cases involving crimes punishable by life imprisonment, reporters may be compelled to reveal their sources if that information is essential to the proceeding and is not available from another source.[51] Oklahoma's law says a reporter may be compelled to reveal a source if the material sought is relevant to a significant issue in the legal action and not otherwise available "with due diligence."[52] As these examples illustrate, qualified privileges often rely, at least in part, on the three-part test from Stewart's dissent in *Branzburg*.

Furthermore, some shield laws offer the same protection to journalists seeking to conceal the identity of a source and to journalists seeking to conceal other information; other laws distinguish between the two. For example, while the District of Columbia's shield law provides absolute protection for the identities of sources, it provides only qualified protection for news or information.[53]

Also, some states distinguish between situations in which a journalist has promised a source confidentiality and those in which the journalist has not. Rhode Island's shield law, for example, applies only to confidential sources and information,[54] while the District of Columbia law protects journalists who do not want to reveal the identities of sources "whether or not the source has been promised confidentiality...."[55] State shield laws that do not clearly stipulate whether the identity of the source or information must have been received on a promise of confidentiality leave it to the courts to decide that question.

Some state shield laws include a libel exemption, that is, a provision that the testimonial privilege does not apply when the journalist asserting the privilege is a defendant in a libel case and asserts a defense based on the content or source of such information.[56] The logic is clear. A libel plaintiff often needs to know the source of the reporter's allegedly libelous story in order to meet the plaintiff's burden of proof. Denying the plaintiff that information denies the plaintiff the opportunity to prove the source was untrustworthy or ill-informed, which often is held to be evidence of actual malice or negligence, the two most common standards of fault in libel cases. To deny the plaintiff the opportunity to learn the identity of the source of a story would doom the plaintiff's case to failure. Instead, some states with shield laws refuse to let reporters use those laws to conceal the identities of sources of allegedly libelous accusations.

Shield legislation first was introduced in Congress in 1929, and it has been reintroduced periodically since then, but it has never passed. A flurry of activity was prompted by what appeared it be a major news media loss in *Branzburg v. Hayes* and by the Court's suggestion that Congress could create a statutory reporter's privilege. Journalistic organizations drafted model legislation, and bills were introduced. Exhaustive hearings were held in both the House and the Senate in the early 1970s. There were many points of dispute, however. How would the law define who was a member of the press? Should the testimonial privilege only protect the identities of confidential sources? Should the privilege apply in criminal cases in which the constitutional right to a fair trial was at stake? Should a privilege be absolute or qualified? And if Congress could offer a privilege, could it take the privilege away — or something worse? Some journalists objected to encouraging Congress to legislate their rights lest it think it also could legislate controls

[46] *Matera v. Superior Court*, 170 Ariz. 446, 825 P.2d 971, 973 (Ct. App. 1992), *rev. denied without opinion* (Ariz. March 17, 1992).

[47] Ohio Rev. Code Ann. §§ 2739.04 & 2739.12 (Page 1981).

[48] *Deltec, Inc. v. Dun & Bradstreet, Inc.*, 187 F. Supp. 788 (N.D. Ohio 1960).

[49] Minn. Stat. Ann. §§ 595.021-595.025, 595.023 (West 1988 & Supp. 1997).

[50] N.Y. Civ. Rights Law § 79-h (McKinney 1992 & Supp. 1997).

[51] Mich. Stat. Ann. § 28.945(1) (Callaghan 1985 & Supp. 1996).

[52] Okla. Stat. Ann. tit. 12, § 2506, 2506(B)(2) (West 1993 & Supp. 1997).

[53] D.C. Code Ann. §§ 16-4702 & 16-4073 (Supp. 1996).

[54] R.I. Gen. Laws §§ 9-19.1-1 to 9-19.1-3, 9-19.1-2 (1985 & Supp. 1996).

[55] D.C. Code Ann. §§ 16-4702 & 16-4703, 16-4702(1) (Supp. 1996).

[56] See, e.g., Tenn. Code Ann. § 24-1-208, 24-1-208(b) (1980 & Supp. 1996), and Or. Rev. Stat. §§ 44.510-44.540, 44.530(3) (1995).

over the media. Those journalists preferred to persist in the struggle for judicial recognition of a First Amendment-based privilege that would not be subject to political will or whim. Division among members of the media and Congressional opposition to the various proposals ultimately caused the media to abandon their efforts to obtain a federal shield law. By 1974 the issue was virtually dead.

Attorney General's Guidelines

In 1973 the U.S. Department of Justice adopted a policy that limits the authority of federal law enforcement officials to subpoena reporters or their telephone records in criminal or civil cases. The policy explains its purpose this way:

Because the freedom of the press can be no broader than the freedom of reporters to investigate and report the news, the prosecutorial power of the government should not be used in such a way that it impairs a reporter's responsibility to cover as broadly as possible controversial public issues. This policy statement is thus intended to provide protection for the news media from forms of compulsory process ... which might impair the news gathering function.[57]

From 1993 to mid-1998, federal prosecutors sought permission to issue seventy-seven subpoenas to reporters. Of those, fifty-seven were approved, four were not approved, and sixteen were withdrawn.

The policy says that in each case the decision on whether to issue a subpoena for a journalist's telephone records or to obtain information from a journalist should be made by balancing the public's interest in the free flow of information against the public's interest in effective law enforcement and the fair administration of justice. The policy lays out a set of rules federal law enforcement officials must follow in making such decisions. Those rules are similar to Justice Stewart's three-part test for a reporter's testimonial privilege in *Branzburg*:

• All reasonable attempts should be made to obtain information from alternate sources before issuing subpoenas to obtain information from journalists or to obtain their telephone records.

• Negotiations with the news media are to be pursued before seeking subpoenas to obtain information from journalists or to obtain their telephone records. Where the investigation

permits, the policy says, "the government should make clear what its needs are in a particular case as well as its willingness to respond to the particular problems of the media."

• No subpoena shall be issued to obtain information from journalists or to obtain their telephone records without authorization of the U.S. Attorney General. The only exception is when the journalist agrees to provide the information and the information has already been published or broadcast. In that case, authorization can be granted by a U.S. attorney or an assistant attorney general.

• When the attorney general is to decide whether to authorize a subpoena to obtain information from a journalist, six principles apply:

(1) In criminal cases, there must be reasonable grounds to believe — based on nonmedia sources — that a crime has occurred and that the information sought is essential to a successful investigation and will directly establish guilt or innocence.

(2) In civil cases, there should be reasonable grounds — again based on nonmedia sources — to believe that the information sought is essential to the successful completion of the litigation in a case of substantial importance.

(3) The government should first have attempted to obtain the information from alternative, nonmedia sources.

(4) The use of subpoenas to obtain information from journalists should, except in emergencies, be limited to the verification of published information and surrounding circumstances that relate to the accuracy of the published information.

(5) Subpoena authorization requests should be treated with care to avoid harassment of the media.

(6) Subpoenas should, whenever possible, be directed at information on a limited subject, should cover a reasonably limited time period, should avoid requiring a large volume of unpublished material and should give reasonable and timely notice of the demand for documents.

• When the attorney general is to decide whether to authorize a subpoena to obtain a journalist's telephone records, essentially the same principles apply as when the attorney general is deciding whether to issue a subpoena to obtain information directly from a journalist. The notable differences have to do with the guidelines' requirements that the government notify journalists that their telephone records are going to be or already have been subpoenaed. Obviously, when a subpoena is served directly on a journalist, the journalist knows the subpoena has been served. A subpoena for telephone records is

---

[57] 28 C.F.R. § 50.10 (1996).

served on a telephone company, however, and a journalist might never know the records have been obtained by the government or another party in a case. Journalists argue that not knowing deprives them of the opportunity to challenge subpoenas or to warn sources that their identities have been disclosed. In fact, they took that argument to court but lost. In 1978, the U.S. Court of Appeals for the D.C. Circuit, relying on *Branzburg*, rejected reporters' arguments that the Constitution required the government to notify them when their phone records were subpoenaed from phone companies.[58]

The guidelines require that when the government has negotiated with a journalist about telephone records, the journalist shall be given reasonable and timely notice of the attorney general's decision to authorize the subpoena. When that notice is not given, the journalist should be notified as soon as notification will no longer present "a clear and substantial threat to the integrity of the investigation."[59] In any event, the journalist must be notified within forty-five days of the records being turned over to the government unless an assistant attorney general authorizes a forty-five-day delay. Also, the guidelines say that telephone records obtained by the government should be closely held to avoid disclosure to unauthorized persons or use for improper purposes.

Justice Department employees who violate these guidelines are subject to administrative punishment. The guidelines provide no legal recourse to journalists who object to the guidelines or the way they are applied.

State Law and Rules of Evidence

Courts in New York and Wisconsin have recognized a reporter's qualified privilege based on the free press provisions of their state constitutions.[60] In 1980 California's constitution was amended to create an explicit reporter's privilege.[61] In addition, some states have recognized a common-law reporter's privilege.

Finally, Section 403 of the Federal Rules of Evidence allows judges to quash subpoenas if the information sought would duplicate information already available, and New Mexico has a court rule that grants reporters a qualified privilege.[62]

PRACTICAL ADVICE AND ETHICAL CONSIDERATIONS

What should you do if you are served a subpoena? Never ignore it, but never comply without first consulting your editor, who, in turn, should consult the news organization's legal counsel. Never destroy the requested notes or other work materials being subpoenaed. To do so could lead to a finding of contempt of court or obstruction of justice. Also, do not talk to the attorney who is responsible for the subpoena. If you do, you might accidentally waive your reporter's privilege.

Generally your choices will be to move to quash the subpoena, to appear and assert the privilege on a question-by-question basis as necessary or to appear and testify fully. Testifying might be appropriate when no confidential sources are involved or when a reporter is being asked only to confirm that the reporter wrote a particular article and that the information in it is accurate.

Some editors report that their aggressive opposition to all subpoenas served on their reporters eventually results in fewer subpoenas being issued, so fighting the subpoena should always be considered. Furthermore, media attorneys sometimes are successful in talking the party behind the subpoena into withdrawing it by explaining the relevant law and the news organization's intention to oppose the subpoena.

Even before you are confronted with this problem, however, you should be familiar with your news organization's policy regarding the retention of notes, tapes and other work materials. Some news organizations require the destruction of notes and related materials as soon as a story is published. Others wait specified periods of time before destroying these materials. Some routinely destroy photographs of traffic and industrial accidents to avoid having them subpoenaed in civil litigation.[63] One scholar has suggested that any reporter who writes a "controversial or unflattering" story should save the interview notes at least until the required statute of limitations for a libel suit has elapsed and that reporters whose employers resist adopting a document retention policy should develop their own routine for saving and destroying notes.[64]

You should also be aware of your media organization's policy governing the use of confidential sources. Some news organizations require management approval before a reporter can promise

---

[58] *Reporters Comm. for Freedom of the Press v. AT&T,* 593 F.2d 1030 (D.C. Cir. 1978), *cert. denied*, 440 U.S. 949 (1979).

[59] 28 C.F.R. § 50.10 (1996).

[60] *O'Neill v. Oakgrove Const., Inc.,* 71 N.Y.2d 521, 523 N.E.2d 277 (1988); *Zelenka v. Wisconsin,* 83 Wis.2d 601, 266 N.W. 2d 279 (1978); *State v. Knops,* 49 Wis.2d 647, 183 N.W.2d 93 (1971).

[61] Cal. Const. art. I, § 2.

[62] N.M. Sup. Ct. R. of Evidence 11-514.

[63] Kirtley, "Agents of Discovery," *supra* note 1, at 11-12.

[64] Andi Stein, "Taking Note of the Law: A Study of the Legal and Ethical Issues in Cases Involving Reporters' Interview Notes," paper presented to the Association for Education in Journalism and Mass Communication, Anaheim, Calif., 1996.

a source confidentiality. Some policies require reporters to reveal the source's identity to an editor. Others require reporters to tell sources that if a subpoena is served the source will have to come forward. If your organization does not have a policy, you should encourage your editors to consider one.

The code of ethics adopted by the Society of Professional Journalists in 1996 offers additional advice:

- Identify sources whenever feasible. The public is entitled to as much information as possible on sources' reliability.
- Always question sources' motives before promising anonymity. Clarify conditions attached to any promise made in exchange for information. Keep promises.[65]

If you fail in your attempt to have a subpoena quashed by a judge, you might be caught between the ethical mandate to keep your promise to a confidential source and a judge's determination to put you in jail if you do. Nobody can make that choice for you. At this point, however, you might want to ask your source to release you from your promise of confidentiality.

NEWSROOM SEARCHES

Reporters also claim a privilege when law enforcement officials armed with search warrants arrive unannounced to search newsrooms for evidence. There are striking parallels between the law on newsroom search warrants and the law on subpoenas, including the Supreme Court's reasoning in denying a First Amendment privilege, the creation of statutory protection for reporters and the arguments for and against such privileges.

Over the years, journalists have had fewer problems with search warrants than with subpoenas, but search warrants are especially troublesome because they cannot be challenged in court before they are executed. As explained earlier in this chapter, a subpoena commands a reporter to appear at a certain time and place to give testimony and/or to produce certain materials. Thus, the reporter has time to go to court to challenge the subpoena before appearing. Search warrants provide no such option. A search warrant authorizes a law enforcement officer to search for and seize any property that constitutes evidence of a crime. The officer merely shows the warrant at the newsroom door and enters.

Just six years after the Supreme Court decided in *Branzburg v. Hayes* that the First Amendment does not protect reporters from giving testimony, the Court decided in *Zurcher v. Stanford Daily* that the First Amendment does not protect reporters from newsroom searches. Justice White wrote the opinions for the Court in

both cases and, in both, said there was no conclusive evidence that the outcomes of the cases would cause sources to dry up. Justice White suggested — again, in both cases — that Congress and state legislatures could create protection for the media where none exists under the First Amendment. Furthermore, both cases illustrate that the First Amendment protection is the same for all citizens and does not provide special protection for members of the media.

The *Zurcher* case began when nine police officers were injured during a clash between police and student demonstrators at the Stanford University Hospital in California. Two days later, the university's student newspaper, the *Stanford Daily*, published photographs and articles about the violent clash. Investigators obtained a search warrant from the local municipal court to search the *Stanford Daily*'s newsroom for information that would help to identify individuals who had assaulted the police. No newspaper employee was alleged to have committed any crime. Police searched the photo laboratories, filing cabinets, desks and wastepaper baskets. Locked drawers and cabinets were not opened, but police had the opportunity to read reporters' notes and correspondence.

The newspaper sued Zurcher, the local chief of police, claiming that the newsroom search violated its Fourth Amendment protection against unreasonable searches and seizures and its First Amendment free press rights. Reporters said they feared law enforcement officers searching newsrooms would uncover the identities of confidential sources or other sensitive information, causing sources to dry up and interrupting the free flow of information that is essential to a healthy democracy. The paper won in federal district court and the federal court of appeals, but the Supreme Court reversed on a 5-3 vote.

First, the Court said, the lower courts erred when they ruled that the Fourth Amendment prohibited the issuance of search warrants to search the premises of any innocent third parties — parties not suspected of committing crimes. The Court said there was no precedent for such a "sweeping revision" of the Fourth Amendment, noting that search warrants are directed not at individuals but at places. Therefore, it makes no difference whether the person who owns or controls the premises to be searched is suspected of a crime.

The Supreme Court also rejected lower courts' holdings that the First Amendment allows newsroom searches only in the rare circumstances when there is a clear showing that important materials will be destroyed or removed and a restraining order would be futile. Subpoenas, the lower courts had said, were the preferred

---

[65] "Code of Ethics," *Quill,* October 1996, p. 1.

method of obtaining information from news organizations. The Supreme Court, however, said the First Amendment did not create a constitutional barrier against warranted searches of newsrooms. White said the general rules protecting all citizens from improper searches are sufficient protection for the news media as well. "Properly administered," he wrote, "the preconditions for a warrant — probable cause, specificity with respect to the place to be searched and the things to be seized, and overall reasonableness — should afford sufficient protection against the harms that are assertedly threatened by warrants for searching newspaper offices." He noted, however, that the rules must be applied "with particular exactitude when First Amendment interests would be endangered by the search."[66] He said magistrates can guard against searches that might interfere with a newspaper's publication schedule or that might allow police to "rummage at large"[67] through newspaper files.

PRIVACY PROTECTION ACT OF 1980

Congress responded to *Zurcher* by adopting the Privacy Protection Act of 1980, which severely limits the government's power to obtain search warrants for newsrooms. The federal statute, which applies to law enforcement agencies at all levels of government, does not mention newsrooms. Rather the statute makes it illegal for police or other government officials investigating a crime to search for or seize work products or other documentary materials possessed by "a person reasonably believed to have a purpose to disseminate to the public a newspaper, book, broadcast, or other similar form of public communication" when the person is not suspected of a crime.[68]

Four exceptions are spelled out in the law, and they distinguish between work materials and documentary materials. Work materials are defined as materials that are created in anticipation of communication to the public and include impressions, conclusions, opinions or theories of the journalist. Documentary materials are obtained in the course of investigating a story but do not contain a reporter's ideas. They include written or printed materials, photographs, motion picture films, negatives, video tapes, audio tapes and computerized records. Neither type of material includes material evidence — items used in the commission of a crime or possessed illegally.

There are four exceptions to the prohibition against such searches:

(1) Police can use search warrants when a person possessing work products or documentary materials is suspected of a crime related to those materials — that is, when the journalist is not an innocent third party — and when the alleged crime is not related specifically to the handling of the material in question. When the alleged crime is the receipt, possession, communication or withholding of materials, police can use search warrants only if the materials relate to national defense, classified information or restricted data.

(2) Police can use search warrants to obtain work product or documentary materials when there is reason to believe that the immediate seizure of such materials is necessary to prevent death or serious injury.

(3) Police can use search warrants to obtain documentary materials when there is reason to believe the advance notice inherent in the serving of a subpoena would result in the destruction, alteration or concealment of the materials.

(4) Police can use search warrants when documentary materials have not been produced in response to a subpoena and either all appellate remedies have been exhausted or there is reason to believe that the delay caused by further court proceedings relating to the subpoena would threaten the interests of justice. If the latter exception applies, the journalist must be give an opportunity to submit an affidavit opposing the search.

A journalist who believes he or she was the subject of a search in violation of the act can sue the government for damages. But the law stipulates that a law enforcement or other government official who can demonstrate a "reasonable good faith belief in the lawfulness of his conduct" is not liable for damages.

WHICH LAW APPLIES?

The mix of legal protections described throughout this chapter raises the question of which protections apply in which courts. While the answer is not always clear, generally the extent to which a reporter can successfully claim a testimonial privilege hinges on whether the case in which the reporter is being asked to testify is being tried in state or federal court.

In Federal Court

In cases involving questions of federal law, reporters can rely on the First Amendment-based privilege if it is recognized in the jurisdiction where the case is being heard. As previously noted, this

---

[66] *Zurcher,* 436 U.S. at 565.

[67] *Id.* at 566.

[68] 42 U.S.C.S. sec. 2000aa(a).

means a journalist can anticipate a strong privilege in some instances and little or no protection in others. In some cases, a journalist will not know what to expect because the federal court has not decided a reporter's privilege case. Also, some federal courts have turned to state shield laws as guides to help them determine the appropriate scope of the reporter's privilege, but the state law is not binding on the courts.

Federal Rule of Evidence 501 provides that in civil cases in federal court in which the central issue is one of state law, the state law applies. The clearest example of when this rule applies is in a diversity action, in which the case turns on a question of state law but is brought in federal court because the parties reside in different states. In such a situation, the federal court applies the law of the state in which the federal court is situated.

In State Court

In state cases, courts first look to a state shield law for guidance. If there is none, courts then look to the state common law, then to the state's constitution. Finally, state courts consider whether there is a First Amendment privilege.

THE RIGHT TO REVEAL SOURCES

After decades of struggling for the right to honor their promises not to reveal the identities of confidential sources, in the 1980s and 1990s reporters found themselves in court arguing for the right to do just that — to publish the name of a confidential source because they deemed the name newsworthy. In a case that provoked significant disagreement among journalists over the ethics of breaking a promise of confidentiality, the *Minneapolis Star and Tribune* and the *St. Paul Pioneer Press Dispatch* argued unsuccessfully that the First Amendment afforded them the right to publish the name of a confidential source.

The case began in 1982 when Republican Party worker Dan Cohen offered four reporters, including one from the *Pioneer Press Dispatch* and one from the *Minneapolis Star and Tribune*, documents relating to a candidate for state lieutenant governor. Cohen sought and received promises that he would not be identified as the source of the documents, which showed that the candidate had been charged with three counts of unlawful assembly in 1969 and convicted of petit theft in 1970. Further investigation by the media revealed that the unlawful assembly charges, which were dismissed, stemmed from the candidate's participation in a protest against the city's failure to hire minority workers for its construction projects. The petit theft conviction, which was later vacated, was for stealing $6 worth of sewing materials from a store. That incident apparently occurred during a time when the candidate was emotionally distraught.

When the reporters returned to their newsrooms, their editors demanded to know the identity of the confidential source. The editors decided the source's identity was as newsworthy as the political candidate's brushes with the law and published stories identifying Cohen as the source of the information. "The fact that one party was using this tactic to malign the other was as important, if not more important, as the story itself," said the associate editor of the *Star and Tribune*.[69] He also said the newspaper had a clear policy that the decision to conceal the identity of a source was the editor's, not the reporter's.

The advertising agency for which Cohen worked fired him, and Cohen filed suit against both newspapers alleging breach of contract and fraudulent misrepresentation. A jury awarded Cohen $200,000 in compensatory damages and $500,000 in punitive damages. The Minnesota Court of Appeals affirmed the breach of contract finding, but reversed the punitive damage award after concluding that Cohen had failed to establish fraudulent misrepresentation, the only claim that could justify punitive damages.[70] The appeals court found that the reporters had not engaged in fraud because they had entered into their agreement with Cohen with every intention of keeping their promises of confidentiality, had no reason to anticipate their editors would do otherwise and strenuously objected to their editors' decision to publish Cohen's name.

The Minnesota Supreme Court reversed the compensatory damages award, holding that the reporters' promise to keep the source's identity confidential was not a legally enforceable contract. The court explained it was not persuaded that "in the special milieu of media newsgathering a source and a reporter ordinarily believe they are engaged in making a legally binding contract,"[71] but rather are making a moral commitment. The state supreme court also said the First Amendment interest of the newspapers in covering a story involving political sources in a political campaign — "the quintessential public debate in our democratic society" — outweighed the state's common law interest in protecting a promise of confidentiality.[72]

The Supreme Court reversed on a 5-4 vote, rejecting the news-

---

[69] Tony Mauro, "The Name of the Source: Editors Want to Know," *Washington Journalism Review,* September 1987, p. 37.

[70] *Cohen v. Cowles Media Co.,* 445 N.W.2d 248 (Minn. App. 1989).

[71] *Cohen v. Cowles Media Co.,* 457 N.W.2d 199, 203 (Minn. 1990).

[72]*Id.* at 205

papers' argument that deciding the case in favor of Cohen would violate their First Amendment right to publish lawfully obtained, truthful information, absent a need to further a state interest of the highest order. The Court ruled that generally applicable laws, such as those that require an individual to keep a promise, "do not offend the First Amendment simply because their enforcement against the press has incidental effects on its ability to gather and report the news."[73] In this case, the law of general applicability was Minnesota's doctrine of *promissory estoppel*. *Promissory estoppel* is a legal doctrine similar to contract law that holds that when a clear promise is intended to and does induce a specific action, that promise is binding if injustice can be avoided only by enforcing it. The Court said the doctrine required those making promises to keep them. This was the first time the doctrine of *promissory estoppel* had been applied in a case involving the media.

The Court explained that the news media are subject to many generally applicable laws and that the Court has repeatedly refused to interpret the First Amendment as exempting the media from those laws. The Court compared the application of the doctrine of *promissory estoppel* to the media to the application of copyright law, antitrust law, nondiscriminatory taxes and the obligation to testify before a grand jury.

The case was remanded to the Minnesota Supreme Court for a decision under the theory of *promissory estoppel*. The court reinstated the $200,000 verdict in favor of Cohen.[74]

The principle established in *Cohen v. Cowles Media Co.* — that a journalist who breaks a promise to keep the identity of a source confidential is liable for damages that result from breaking the promise — has been applied in several subsequent cases. For example, in another Minnesota case a reporter for *Glamour* magazine was sued by a source who claimed she was identified in a story about therapist-patient sexual abuse after being promised her identity would be concealed.[75] The reporter did not use the source's name in the story but identified her as a Minneapolis attorney who served on a state task force that helped write a state law criminalizing therapist-patient sex. The source said she was identified because she was the only female attorney on the task force. In the story, the source told about incest committed by her father when she was a child and her sexual exploitation by her therapist. The case went up and down through the courts, with the U.S. Court of Appeals for the Eighth Circuit finally deciding the reporter's promise not to identify the source was an enforceable contract under the theory of *promissory estoppel*.

SUMMARY

A reporter who receives a subpoena or whose newsroom is searched by law enforcement personnel needs to be familiar with the patchwork of reporter's privilege law. The law is based on the U.S. and state constitutions, federal and state statutes, common law, judicial rules and law enforcement guidelines. The legal protection afforded to reporters who do not want to testify in judicial proceedings or to turn over work materials varies from jurisdiction to jurisdiction. Within a single jurisdiction, the privilege varies even further according to who is claiming the privilege, the type of proceeding in which a journalist is being asked to testify and the nature of the potential testimony.

One common theme of reporter's privilege law, however, is the qualified privilege suggested by Supreme Court Justice Potter Stewart in his landmark dissent in *Branzburg v. Hayes*. Stewart suggested that in order to defeat a reporter's motion to quash a subpoena, the government must prove each of the following:

- there is probable cause to believe the reporter has information that is clearly relevant to a probable crime;
- the information cannot be obtained by alternative means less destructive of First Amendment rights;
- there is a "compelling and overriding interest" in the information.

Today these three elements are at the core of a widely recognized First Amendment-based reporter's privilege and many state shield laws.

The degree of reporter's privilege is increasingly a subject of legal conflict and controversy, in part because of the important interests at stake. Journalists generally claim that they need to be allowed to refuse to testify in judicial proceedings in order to protect the free flow of information from their sources to the public. That free flow of information, they argue, is essential to a healthy democracy. Judicial and law enforcement personnel and the parties in civil and criminal court cases frequently counter that a reporter's information is crucial to the administration of justice and that a reporter is not exempt from every citizen's duty to testify in a judicial proceeding. These arguments are strongest in criminal cases where the defendant has a Sixth Amendment right to compel testimony that might prove he or she is not guilty. Considering

---

[73] *Cohen v. Cowles Media Co.*, 501 U.S. 663, 669 (1991).

[74] *Cohen v. Cowles Media Co.*, 479 N.W.2d 387 (Minn. 1992).

[75] *Ruzicka v. Conde Nast Publications, Inc.*, 939 F.2d 578 (8th Cir. 1991), *on remand*, 794 F. Supp. 303 (D. Minn. 1992), *vacated* 999 F.2d 1319 (8th Cir. 1993).

the weighty arguments on each side of this debate, a single and simple solution seems highly improbable.

FOR ADDITIONAL READING

Baron, Jerome A. *"Cohen v. Cowles Media* and its Significance for First Amendment Law and Journalism." *William and Mary Bill of Rights Journal* 3 (1994): 419.

Boyd, J. Kirk. "Legislative Response to *Zurcher v. Stanford Daily." Pepperdine Law Review* 9 (1981): 131.

Goodale, James C., *et al.* "Reporter's Privilege." *Communications Law 1997,* vol. 3. New York: Practising Law Institute, 1997.

Levin, Daniel A. and Ellen Blumberg Rubert. "Promises of Confidentiality to News Sources After *Cohen v. Cowles Media Company:* A Survey of Newspaper Editors." *Golden Gate University Law Review* 24 (1994): 423.

Osborn, John E. "The Reporter's Confidentiality Privilege: Updating the Empirical Evidence after a Decade of Subpoenas." *Columbia Human Rights Law Review* 17 (1985): 57.

15

Access to Courts

By Ruth Walden

Like the 1935 trial of Bruno Hauptmann for the kidnapping of the Lindbergh baby and the 1954 trial of Dr. Sam Sheppard for the murder of his wife, the 1995 trial of O.J. Simpson for the murders of his ex-wife Nicole Brown Simpson and her friend Ronald Goldman drew public attention to the free press-fair trial issue. The judge in the Simpson case, Lance Ito, said early in the proceedings that the trial had garnered more media coverage than any other trial in history. That publicity generated concern over whether an impartial jury could be found. Once a jury was selected, it was sequestered to prevent exposure to the ongoing media coverage, and gavel-to-gavel televising of the proceedings caused heated debate over the wisdom and effects of cameras in courtrooms.

The free press-fair trial issue is generally viewed as a conflict between rights guaranteed in two amendments to the U.S. Constitution — the First Amendment right of a free press and the Sixth Amendment right of a criminal defendant to a fair trial by an impartial jury. Some argue that allowing unrestrained media coverage of crimes, arrests, pretrial proceedings and trials seriously threatens defendants' Sixth Amendment rights and that restrictions must be placed on the media to ensure the proper operation of the criminal justice system. Others contend that the First Amendment cannot be subordinated to the Sixth Amendment, that a free press plays a critical role in ensuring the proper functioning of the judicial system and that it is the government's duty to find ways to accommodate both sets of rights.

As the cases discussed in this chapter will demonstrate, the U.S. Supreme Court has adopted a balancing approach in dealing with free press-fair trial conflicts, steadfastly refusing to declare one set of rights more important than the other. Instead, the Court has consistently instructed trial judges to take steps to vigorously protect the rights of defendants without limiting the rights of journalists to attend court proceedings and report on crime and the operation of the court system. In general, the Supreme Court has held that restrictions on the media may be imposed only as the last resort to ensure the defendant's right to a fair trial.

THE NATURE OF THE PROBLEM

Generally the conflict between freedom of the press and the right to a fair trial is manifest in three ways:

1. Pretrial publicity may make it difficult to find impartial jurors who have not made up their minds as to the defendant's guilt — or, in unusual cases, innocence — before the trial begins.

2. During-trial publicity may taint a sitting jury, causing jurors to base a verdict on what they read, see or hear in the media rather than solely on the evidence presented at trial.

3. The presence of journalists and their equipment in the courtroom may cause physical and/or psychological disruption.

Pretrial Publicity

Jurors are supposed to arrive at a verdict based solely on the evidence presented to them in the courtroom. The rules of evidence under which courts operate prevent certain types of information from being presented to the jury. Anyone who has watched a courtroom drama on television — real or fictional — knows that such things as hearsay or the opinions of non-experts are usually inadmissible. But, of course, the media don't follow rules of evidence in deciding what to publish. Thus, considerable information that will never reach the jury in the courtroom could reach potential jurors as they watch television or read newspapers.

The Supreme Court has made it clear that jurors need not be "totally ignorant of the facts and issues involved" in a case to be considered impartial. Exposure to "information about a ... defendant's prior convictions or to news accounts of the crime with which he is charged" are not, standing alone, enough to disqualify a potential juror as biased.[1] The most frequently quoted definition of an impartial juror comes from Chief Justice John Marshall's opinion in the trial of Aaron Burr for treason in 1807. In *United States v. Burr*, Chief Justice Marshall wrote:

Were it possible to obtain a jury without any prepossessions whatever respecting the guilt or innocence of the accused, it would be extremely desirable to obtain such a jury; but this is perhaps impossible, and therefore will not be required. The opinion which has been avowed by the court is, that light impressions which may fairly be supposed to yield to the testimony that may be offered, which may leave the mind open to a fair consideration of that testimony, constitute no sufficient objection to a juror; but that those strong and deep impressions which will close the mind against the testimony that may be offered in opposition to them, which will combat that testimony, and resist its force, do constitute a sufficient objection to him.[2]

The trick, of course, is to determine what types of publicity can result in jurors possessing "strong and deep impressions" that may render them biased. Numerous court decisions, especially those in which criminal convictions have been overturned on appeal, have discussed the types of news stories that can cause prejudice. In addition, the American Bar Association and voluntary bench-press-bar committees in several states have developed guidelines to help identify potentially prejudicial material. Most of these guidelines recognize that reporting the following types of information can create a danger of prejudice:

Prior Criminal Records. This is perhaps the most problematic category of potentially prejudicial information for journalists. In most cases, prior criminal charges and convictions are part of the public record, and journalists may believe it is important for the public to be informed that, say, a person accused of rape and murder had been previously charged with three sexual assaults and convicted once twelve years prior to the current charge. But normally a criminal record is not admitted as evidence at trial since the jury is supposed to base its verdict on evidence relating to the *current* charge only. Officially keeping information about a defendant's past record from jurors may be fruitless if the jurors have unofficially been informed of the defendant's past through the media. It's important to recall, however, that the Supreme Court has said knowledge of a defendant's prior criminal record *alone* is not enough to disqualify a potential juror.

Confessions or Other Admissions by a Defendant. Even today, with the requirement that police "Mirandize" anyone arrested ("You have the right to remain silent...."), criminal defendants sometimes make statements to police that they — and their lawyers — later regret. If a judge can be convinced that a confession or other damaging statement was coerced or obtained before the defendant was informed of his or her rights to remain silent and have an attorney, the statement may be declared inadmissible because of the Fifth Amendment's protection against forced self-incrimination. As with criminal records, jurors who have heard or seen media reports of a confession, or even references to the existence of a confession, may have a hard time forgetting those reports when they deliberate.

The Results of Investigative Procedures or Tests. Reporting the results of fingerprint, DNA, polygraph, blood and ballistics tests or the refusal of the accused to submit to such tests can cause problems. As anyone who paid even the slightest attention to the O.J. Simpson trial knows, the admissibility of test results can often be the basis for a key battle in a criminal case, and such information is often kept from a jury. Reporting that the accused refused to submit to a lie detector test could well leave the impression that the defendant had something to hide.

Opinions Regarding the Character, Personality, Guilt or Innocence of the Accused. As some of the cases discussed later in this chapter will show, it is not unheard of for the media to attach derogatory nicknames to suspects, to report alleged character flaws or unusual lifestyles, or to conduct on-the-street inter-

---

[1] *Murphy v. Florida,* 421 U.S. 794, 799-800 (1975).
[2] 25 Fed. Cas. 49, 50-51 (1807).

views asking about a defendant's guilt or innocence. Furthermore, sometimes officials themselves — police, prosecutors and even judges — make derogatory statements about defendants, which are then reported in the media. Such publicity not only may cause prejudice within a community but also may result in jurors feeling pressured to bring in the verdict they believe the public wants.

Speculation on Evidence or Witnesses. Speculation about potential evidence and opinions as to the credibility or character of prospective witnesses are conjecture, often based on incomplete knowledge, guesswork or even malice. Prospective witnesses who tell journalists what they intend to say in court may change their minds or be prevented from making certain statements in front of the jury. Police officers and lawyers may often be the source of leaks about potential evidence or witnesses, thereby adding a ring of authority to the speculation or opinion.

In addition to those four categories of information, any sensational or inflammatory coverage of a crime and its aftermath is potentially prejudicial. Editorials demanding the arrest of a suspect or suggesting a suspect is getting special treatment because of wealth or position, lurid headlines or gory pictures of victims, and emotional outpourings by victims' friends and families all can stir up emotions in a community that may be inconsistent with the impartiality the Sixth Amendment demands. A look at some cases in which the Supreme Court considered claims that pretrial publicity robbed defendants of their rights to impartial juries provides specific examples of prejudicial coverage as well as an understanding of the types of publicity that may constitute grounds to overturn a conviction.

Irvin v. Dowd,[3] decided in 1961, marked the first time the Supreme Court overturned a state criminal conviction solely because prejudicial publicity interfered with a defendant's right to a fair trial. "Mad Dog" Irvin, as the media dubbed him, was charged with the murder of Whitney Wesley Kerr, who was one of six victims in a series of well-publicized murders that occurred near Evansville, Indiana, beginning December 2, 1954. Although Irvin was being tried for only one murder, police, the prosecutor and media made it clear they believed he was responsible for all six. The Supreme Court described the publicity surrounding the Irvin trial as "a barrage of newspaper headlines, articles, cartoons and pictures." News stories revealed Irvin's juvenile record, his prior convictions for arson and burglary and his court-martial on AWOL charges during World War II. The media also reported that he had

confessed to the six murders and offered to plead guilty if promised a ninety-nine-year sentence. One story characterized Irvin as "remorseless and without conscience."[4]

According to the Court, the effects of this publicity barrage were evident during *voir dire*, the questioning of potential jurors. The court excused 268 of 430 prospective jurors "as having fixed opinions as to the guilt" of Irvin. Almost ninety percent of the potential jurors questioned "entertained some opinion as to guilt — ranging in intensity from mere suspicion to absolute certainty." Of the twelve jurors finally chosen, eight had admitted they thought Irvin was guilty. All twelve, however, told the judge they would be fair and impartial. In reversing Irvin's conviction and death sentence, the Supreme Court said, "With his life at stake, it is not requiring too much that [Irvin] be tried in an atmosphere undisturbed by so huge a wave of public passion and by a jury other than one in which two-thirds of the members admit, before hearing any testimony, to possessing a belief in his guilt."[5] Irvin was retried and again found guilty of murder. He was sentenced to life imprisonment.

Two years after *Irvin*, the Supreme Court again reversed a conviction, this time based on the pretrial broadcast of the defendant's confession. Wilbert Rideau was arrested and charged with bank robbery, kidnapping and murder. Without being informed of his right to remain silent and to have an attorney, he confessed to the crimes — both off and on camera. A twenty-minute film of an interview with Rideau, during which he was "flanked by the sheriff and two state troopers," was broadcast on three consecutive days to estimated audiences of 24,000, 29,000 and 53,000 in Calcasieu Parish, Louisiana, with a population of about 150,000. Rideau's motion for a change of venue was denied, and the trial was held with a jury that included three persons who admitted to having seen the televised confession. Rideau was convicted and sentenced to death.

The Supreme Court ruled that the judge's refusal to move the trial to a community in which Rideau's confession had not been televised violated the defendant's due process rights. "For anyone who has ever watched television," the Court said, "the conclusion cannot be avoided that this spectacle (the televised interview), to the tens of thousands of people who saw and heard it, in a very real sense *was* Rideau's trial — at which he pleaded guilty to murder. Any subsequent court proceedings in a community so pervasively exposed to such a spectacle could be but a hollow formal-

---

[3] 366 U.S. 717 (1961).

[4] *Id.* at 725-26.
[5] *Id.* at 727-28.

ity."[6] On retrial Rideau was once again convicted, and the Louisiana Supreme Court upheld that second conviction.

Among lawyers, judges and journalists, *Sheppard v. Maxwell*,[7] one of the cases mentioned at the start of this chapter, has become synonymous with prejudicial publicity. During the O.J. Simpson trial, repeated comparisons to the Sheppard case appeared in the media, fueled in part by the fact that F. Lee Bailey, the attorney who successfully appealed Sheppard's conviction to the Supreme Court in 1966, was also on the Simpson defense team. The reversal of Sheppard's conviction was based on all three free press-fair trial problems listed earlier in this chapter — prejudicial pretrial publicity, during-trial publicity reaching an unsequestered jury and the activities of journalists in the courtroom. Here the focus will be on the nature and extent of the pretrial coverage.

In the early morning hours of July 4, 1954, Marilyn Sheppard was beaten to death as she lay in bed in her home in Bay Village, a suburb of Cleveland, Ohio. Her husband, Samuel, a surgeon and member of a wealthy, prominent, local family that ran an osteopathic hospital, said he had fallen asleep on the couch downstairs and was awakened by his wife's cries. According to his testimony at trial, Dr. Sheppard ran upstairs to the bedroom, where he saw a "form" by his wife's bed. He was struck on the back of the neck and knocked unconscious. After he came to, Sheppard said he checked his wife's pulse and "felt that she was gone." He next checked his son, who was asleep in another upstairs bedroom, and found him undisturbed. Sheppard said he then went downstairs, saw a "form" running out the door and pursued it to the lake behind his home. He struggled with the person he had chased and was again rendered unconscious. When he awoke, he returned to the house, again checked his wife and determined she was dead. Shortly before 6 a.m. he called a neighbor, who called the police and Sheppard's brother.

The pretrial publicity that followed was relentless and, according to the Supreme Court, virulent. Within days of the murder, the Cleveland newspapers began emphasizing Sheppard's alleged lack of cooperation with the police — which the Supreme Court later indicated was untrue — and refusal to take a lie detector test and be injected with "truth serum." Front-page editorials charged "Somebody's Getting Away with Murder" and demanded an inquest. The inquest, which was promptly called for the day after the editorial appeared, was held in a school gymnasium and broadcast live. During and after the inquest, news stories emphasized incriminating evidence, much of which was never presented at the trial.

The media also focused on Sheppard's personal life, especially his admitted affair with one woman and alleged — but never admitted or proven — affairs with others. A few days after the inquest, a front-page editorial asked, "Why Isn't Sam Sheppard in Jail?" and demanded, "Quit Stalling — Bring Him In." At about 10 p.m. the day that editorial appeared, Sam Sheppard was arrested for the murder of his wife.

Alfred Friendly and John Goldfarb in their book, *Crime and Publicity*, reported that between July 5, when the murder was first reported in the media, and July 30, the day Sheppard was arrested, the *Cleveland Plain Dealer* ran a page-one story about the case twenty-five of the twenty-six days, with twelve of those stories under banner headlines. The *Cleveland Press* ran a page-one story each of the twenty-three days it published during the same period and printed three page-one editorials.[8]

According to the Supreme Court, after Sheppard's arrest "[t]he publicity then grew in intensity until his indictment August 17." In its opinion overturning Sheppard's conviction — eleven and one-half years after the jury verdict — the Court listed numerous examples of prejudicial and sensational coverage, concluding, "There are five volumes filled with similar clippings from each of the three Cleveland newspapers covering the period from the murder until Sheppard's conviction in December 1954." Before jury selection began, all three Cleveland papers published the names and addresses of the people chosen as prospective jurors. "As a consequence, anonymous letters and telephone calls, as well as calls from friends, regarding the impending prosecution were received by all of the prospective jurors." The trial judge, Edward Blythin, who was running for reelection at the time of the trial, refused to grant Sheppard's motion to move the location or delay the start of the trial, despite the fact that all but one of the twelve jurors selected admitted to having read about the case in the newspapers.

Despite the evidence of massive, prejudicial pretrial news coverage, the Supreme Court said that the pretrial publicity alone was not sufficient to prove Sheppard had been denied due process. Instead the Court said its decision was based on the "totality of the circumstances," which included juror exposure to publicity during the trial and disruptions caused by the media.[9] Both of those factors will be discussed in the following sections.

---

[6] *Rideau v. Louisiana*, 373 U.S. 723, 724-26 (1963).
[7] 384 U.S. 333 (1966).

[8] Alfred Friendly and Ronald L. Goldfarb, *Crime and Publicity* (New York: Twentieth Century Fund, 1967), p. 14.
[9] *Id.* at 352.

During-Trial Publicity

The same types of stories that could prejudice potential jurors if published before a trial could also taint a sitting jury. Reading in the newspaper that the person whose guilt or innocence they are supposed to decide has already confessed to the crime or has a record of arrests and convictions for similar crimes could affect jurors' decisions, even if such information is never presented in court. In fact, the Supreme Court has concluded that the effect of highly prejudicial information "may indeed be greater" when it reaches jurors through the media rather than through testimony in court "for it is then not tempered by protective procedures."[10]

Despite its potential for harm, during-trial publicity is usually not considered as serious a problem as pretrial publicity for a number of reasons. First, once a trial begins, the media have the trial itself to cover and are less likely to resort to speculation and prediction. Second, in sensational, widely publicized cases, such as the Simpson trial, jurors are often sequestered and thereby protected from media stories about the case. Finally, even if not sequestered, jurors are routinely instructed by judges not to read, listen to or watch anything about the trial, and studies have found that jurors tend to take such admonitions seriously.

Nonetheless, juror exposure to publicity during trial can and has resulted in the reversal of convictions. It happened in 1959 in *Marshall v. United States*,[11] the first case in which the Supreme Court reversed a federal criminal conviction solely on the basis of prejudicial publicity. (*Irvin v. Dowd* was the Court's first reversal of a *state* conviction due to prejudicial publicity.)

Howard R. Marshall was charged with illegally dispensing drugs to an undercover Food and Drug Administration inspector. During Marshall's trial in federal court, two potentially damaging newspaper articles appeared. One reported that he had two prior felony convictions, had written prescriptions for dangerous drugs and, while serving a forgery sentence in Oklahoma, had told a legislative committee he practiced medicine with a $25 mail-order diploma. The article also stated that Marshall "acted as a physician and prescribed restricted drugs for Hank Williams before the country singer's death in December, 1953." The second article said Marshall had been arrested with his wife, who was convicted of drug charges, and sentenced to jail.

The judge had refused to admit as evidence much of the information published in the two articles specifically because of its highly prejudicial nature. After learning of the articles, the judge questioned each juror individually and learned that seven had seen at least one of the stories. But he received assurances from the jurors that they could continue to be impartial and denied Marshall's motion for a mistrial. The jury brought in a conviction, which was later overturned by the Supreme Court because of the jurors' exposure to prejudicial news stories without the safeguards that generally attend the introduction of evidence at trial.

As previously indicated, during-trial publicity played a major role in the reversal of Sam Sheppard's conviction in 1966. In *Sheppard v. Maxwell*, the Supreme Court gave this summary:

Much of the material printed or broadcast during the trial was never heard from the witness stand, such as the charges that Sheppard had purposely impeded the murder investigation and must be guilty since he had hired a prominent criminal lawyer; that Sheppard was a perjurer; that he had sexual relations with numerous women; that his slain wife had characterized him as a "Jekyll-Hyde"; that he was "a bare-faced liar" because of his testimony as to police treatment; and, finally, that a woman convict claimed Sheppard to be the father of her illegitimate child. As the trial progressed, the newspapers summarized and interpreted the evidence, devoting particular attention to the material that incriminated Sheppard, and often drew unwarranted inferences from testimony. At one point, a front-page picture of Mrs. Sheppard's blood-stained pillow was published after being "doctored" to show more clearly an alleged imprint of a surgical instrument.[12]

The Sheppard jury was not sequestered until it began deliberations, and the judge failed to give adequate instructions regarding juror exposure to the media. The judge suggested and requested that jurors avoid media coverage of the case, but he never ordered them to do so. Several times Sheppard's attorney requested that the judge question jurors about their exposure to specific, highly prejudicial coverage. The judge refused all but once. That one instance resulted from a television and radio broadcast in which Walter Winchell reported that a woman under arrest in New York for robbery said she was Sheppard's mistress and the mother of his child. Two jurors admitted hearing the broadcast — despite the judge's suggestions and requests. After the jurors assured him the broadcast would not affect their decisions in the case, the judge "merely asked the jury to 'pay no attention whatever to that type of scavenging…. Let's confine ourselves to this courtroom, if you please.'" The Supreme Court considered the admonitions in-

---

[10] *Marshall v. United States,* 360 U.S. 310, 313 (1959).
[11] *Id.*

[12] 384 U.S. at 356-57.

sufficient "to protect the jury from outside influence."[13]

The Effects of Publicity

While there is widespread agreement about the types of publicity that are prejudicial, there is significantly less agreement about the actual *effects* of such publicity on jurors. The Sixth Amendment does not guarantee a defendant freedom from inflammatory publicity; it guarantees a trial by an "impartial jury." The key question, then, is whether news coverage of a case, whether pretrial or during trial, actually affects jurors' impartiality. Opinions and evidence are mixed. In all of the cases discussed previously, the jurors told the judges that, despite the publicity, they could be impartial. But Justice Tom Clark, who wrote the opinion of the Court in *Irvin v. Dowd*, voiced skepticism about such claims: "No doubt each juror was sincere when he said that he would be fair and impartial," but "[w]here so many, so many times, admitted prejudice, such a statement of impartiality can be given little weight."[14]

Numerous efforts to measure the effects of publicity on jurors during the past five decades have proved inconclusive. A key problem with empirical studies is that they involve mock trials and juries — experimental simulations rather than real jurors deciding real cases. Real juror deliberations are conducted behind closed doors, and courts fear that allowing researchers to tape deliberations might improperly influence jurors. "Jurors" in the experiments are often exposed to news stories after which the "trial" immediately begins. This ignores the fact that, in real life, exposure to prejudicial coverage may go on for months before the trial actually starts. Real jurors have had the time to either forget much of what they saw in the media or, perhaps because of repeated references, become convinced of its accuracy.

Despite the drawbacks, experimental research and studies of public reaction to news stories are all lawyers, judges and scholars have to help determine the effects of prejudicial publicity. An article in the *Stanford Law Review* summarized the results of empirical studies:

Experiments to date indicate that for the most part juries are able and willing to put aside extraneous information and base their decisions on the evidence. The results show that when ordinary citizens become jurors, they assume a special role in which they apply different standards of proof, more vigorous

reasoning and greater detachment.[15]

This confirms what many judges and lawyers firmly believe: Individuals called to jury duty generally take their responsibility very seriously; they listen to and obey the judge's instructions; they recognize that a human being's liberty and perhaps life are in their hands; and they want to make the right decision based on the evidence and the law.

The 1966 landmark study *The American Jury* reported that not one of 555 judges who had presided over 3,576 criminal cases during the 1950s mentioned prejudicial publicity as a factor affecting a jury's decision.[16] That's largely due to the fact, however, that most criminal cases receive little or no publicity. Trials like those of Sheppard, Irvin, Rideau and Simpson can cause us to lose sight of the fact that "prejudicial publicity is a factor in the rare, sensational case; elsewhere it appears to be close to nonexistent."[17]

Disruption in the Courtroom

Publishing or broadcasting prejudicial material isn't the only way in which the media might interfere with a fair trial. The presence of journalists and their equipment in a courtroom could physically disrupt the proceedings, perhaps distracting jurors and trial participants or creating an atmosphere inconsistent with fairness, calm and reasoned deliberation. Some people, including Supreme Court justices, have argued that the presence of cameras in courtrooms causes psychological disruption sufficient to violate a defendant's Sixth Amendment rights.

The trial of Bruno Hauptmann in 1935 for the kidnapping of Charles and Anne Morrow Lindbergh's eighteen-month-old son is generally cited as one of the earliest examples of journalists disrupting the judicial process and as the reason the American Bar Association recommended in 1937 that cameras be banned from all courtrooms.

Because of the international popularity of Charles Lindbergh, the first person to fly across the Atlantic Ocean nonstop, journalists from around the world crowded into the small town of Flemington, New Jersey, where the trial was held. Estimates of the number of media people present have ranged from about 200 to

---

[13] *Id.* at 348-58.
[14] 366 U.S. at 728.

[15] Rita J. Simon, "Does the Court's Decision in *Nebraska Press Association* Fit the Research Evidence on the Impact on Jurors of News Coverage?" *Stanford Law Review* 29 (1977): 528.

[16] Harry Kalven and Hans Zeisel, *The American Jury* (Boston: Little, Brown, 1966).

[17] Friendly and Goldfarb, *supra* note 8, at 69.

nearly 1,000. While the Hauptmann trial may have been the impetus for the camera ban, the evidence indicates most journalists obeyed the judge's ban on photographing while court was in session. One photographer, however, "muffled his cameras in a soundproof hood, installed in it a recording device with a remote control, and recorded some of the testimony."[18] Apparently more disruptive than the photographers and their cameras were the messengers who ran in and out of the courtroom carrying the reporters' copy to be transmitted back to their newsrooms.

The Hauptmann case has been repeatedly cited as evidence of press misbehavior, but various accounts of the proceedings seem to indicate that court officials and the general public contributed to the lack of decorum as much as, if not more than, the media:

> When the court was not in session sightseers were admitted. Placards were placed around the courtroom showing where principal participants in the trial sat. However, as a sign of decorum, "members of the Rotary Club kept sightseers from cutting their initials in the judge's bench." At the trial, the public applauded state witnesses. The whole proceeding was wild, raucous, and unrestrained. The court itself scarcely attempted to correct it.[19]

Regardless of who was actually to blame for what occurred in the Flemington courtroom, the Hauptmann trial became a frequently mentioned example of media interference with the judicial process.

By the 1960s, when Texas financier Billie Sol Estes went on trial for swindling, two states — Colorado and Texas — permitted televising trials under some conditions. From the outset, Estes' attorney objected to the broadcasting of the judicial proceedings, but the trial judge allowed the pretrial hearing to be broadcast live by both radio and television. According to the Supreme Court, twelve cameramen moved around the courtroom, cables and wires "snaked across" the floor, three microphones were set up on the judge's bench, and "others were beamed at the jury box and the counsel table."

During the trial itself, four cameras — one for each of the three major networks and one for a local station — and camera operators were confined to a booth specially constructed at the rear of the courtroom and painted to blend into the walls. Only the state's opening and closing arguments and the delivery of the jury's verdict were broadcast live with sound. Other portions of the trial, however, were filmed, without sound, and broadcast during regular newscasts.

In the light of the exhaustive, gavel-to-gavel coverage of the Simpson and other trials in the nineties, all of this seems relatively tame and unthreatening. Nonetheless, the Supreme Court voted 5-4 to overturn Estes' conviction, saying he had been deprived of "that judicial serenity and calm to which [he] was entitled."[20] Justice Clark, for the Court, contended that televising trials caused both physical and psychological disruptions and could negatively impact on the jury, judge, witnesses and defendant.

The Sheppard case provides the classic example of disruptions resulting from media presence in the courtroom. Journalists were allowed to literally take over the courthouse. Most of the seats in the 26-by-48-foot courtroom were filled by reporters. The judge allowed about twenty newspaper and wire service reporters to sit at a temporary table inside the bar directly behind the table where Sheppard and his attorney sat, making "confidential talk among Sheppard and his counsel almost impossible during the proceedings. They frequently had to leave the courtroom to obtain privacy." The journalists' frequent movement in and out "caused so much confusion that, despite the loud-speaker system installed in the courtroom, it was difficult for the witnesses and counsel to be heard."

The media were permitted to use and install private telephone lines and telegraphic equipment in all of the rooms on the floor where the courtroom was located. In addition, a radio station set up broadcasting facilities in a room on the third floor next to the jury room. Cameras were not permitted in the courtroom, but "[i]n the corridors outside the courtroom there was a host of photographers and television personnel with flash cameras, portable lights and motion picture cameras." Jurors, witnesses, attorneys and the defendant were repeatedly filmed as they entered and left the courtroom.

The Supreme Court summarized the situation this way: "The fact is that bedlam reigned at the courthouse during the trial and newsmen took over practically the entire courtroom, hounding most of the participants in the trial, especially Sheppard."[21] The existence of this "carnival atmosphere," coupled with the prejudicial publicity that saturated the community before and during the trial, led the Court to reverse Sheppard's conviction. When he was retried a few months later, Sheppard was found not guilty.

---

[18] *Id.* at 12.
[19] *Id.*

[20] *Estes v. Texas,* 381 U.S. 532, 536-37 (1965).
[21] 384 U.S. at 344, 355.

COMPENSATING FOR PREJUDICIAL PUBLICITY

If media coverage of the judicial process can cause problems, the inevitable question is, What can be done to remedy the situation? There are two broad categories of remedies:

1. Measures designed to compensate for the existence of prejudicial publicity.

2. Measures designed to prevent, or at least diminish, prejudicial publicity and to control the presence and/or activities of journalists in the courtroom.

The key difference between the two types of remedies is that the former seeks to mitigate or lessen the *effects* of media coverage without restricting the coverage. Therefore, use of the first category of remedies does not raise First Amendment concerns because no interference with the operations of the press occurs. In contrast, the remedies in the second category are designed to impact journalists and their coverage of trial proceedings. Use of these measures raises serious First Amendment issues.

The Supreme Court has repeatedly declared that the trial judge has the responsibility of protecting a defendant's right to a fair trial. In *Sheppard*, *Estes*, *Rideau* and *Irvin*, the Court indicated its disapproval of and disenchantment with the press's performance. But, more importantly, it focused on what the judges could have and should have done to safeguard the defendants' rights. Some of the remedies it suggested, such as regulating the behavior of journalists in the courtroom and controlling the dissemination of information by police, witnesses and attorneys, will be discussed later. Here the focus will be on the traditional tools that judges can use to compensate for the effects of publicity without restricting publication.

Change of venue means moving a trial to a new location — one in which the publicity has not been as intense and, therefore, potential jurors are less likely to have been influenced by pretrial coverage. Change of venue requires, however, that a defendant give up another Sixth Amendment right — the right to be tried in the "district wherein the crime shall have been committed." Generally this presents no problem since the motion for a venue change comes from the defense attorney.

Whether a change of venue will be effective in mitigating the impact of prejudicial publicity depends on several factors, one being how far the trial is moved. In *Irvin v. Dowd*, the judge agreed to move the trial from Vanderburgh County to neighboring Gibson County. Considering that ninety percent of the prospective jurors questioned said they believed Irvin was guilty, it would appear that moving the trial such a short distance did little to protect Irvin's right to an impartial jury.

If a case is subject to massive, nationwide publicity, like the O.J. Simpson case, it's unlikely that moving it anywhere in the country would make a difference in prospective jurors' exposure to media coverage. Also, there's always the possibility that the publicity will simply follow the trial to its new location. However, sometimes a defendant seeks to move a trial not only because of the potential effects of publicity but also because of the perceived impact of the crime itself on the community in which it occurred. For example, Terry Nichols and Timothy McVeigh, charged with the bombing of the federal building in Oklahoma City April 19, 1995, successfully sought a change of venue to Denver. Their attorneys argued not only that prejudicial publicity was more intense and pervasive in Oklahoma than elsewhere in the country, but also that the bombing had such significant emotional, psychological and economic effects on "every prospective juror in the state" that an impartial jury could not be found anywhere in Oklahoma.[22]

While a change of venue may make it easier to find unbiased jurors, it also increases the costs and inconveniences of the trial; attorneys, police officers and witnesses are forced to travel extra distances. One of the major objections to moving the Nichols and McVeigh trials to Denver was the hardship the move would create for survivors of the bombing and victims' families who wanted to attend the proceedings. In response, Congress passed a law requiring the closed-circuit televising of a federal trial when it is moved from its original location out of the state and more than 350 miles away so that victims and their relatives can view the televised proceedings.[23]

Change of venue can also result in unanticipated drawbacks for a defendant. For example, a judge in Durham, North Carolina, explained why he was reluctant to grant change of venue to a murder defendant. The defendant was accused of murdering her husband, a high school coach, and the case had generated considerable publicity. The judge, however, was familiar with the pattern of jury verdicts in the state and believed that the defendant, if convicted, was less likely to be sentenced to death by a Durham jury than by juries in other communities in the state. He was right. The trial was moved to Fayetteville, and the defendant was convicted and sentenced to death. Her conviction was reversed on appeal. The

---

[22] Motion for Change of Venue and Supporting Brief: Evidentiary Hearing Requested at 2, *United States v. McVeigh and Nichols* (CR 95-110-A) (W.D. Okla. 1995).

[23] Antiterrorism and Effective Death Penalty Act, Pub. L. No. 104-132, § 235, 110 Stat. 1214, 1246-47 (1996).

second trial was held in Durham, where the crime had occurred. She was again found guilty but was sentenced to life in prison.

Change of venire is much less common than change of venue. It entails importing jurors from another community. As with change of venue, this tool only works if the publicity has been confined to the location in which the crime occurred. In addition, it can be an expensive option since it requires the state to pay for transporting, housing and feeding jurors for the duration of the trial.

Continuance means delaying a trial. Like a change of venue, it requires a defendant to sacrifice a constitutional right — the right to a speedy trial — in the hopes of enhancing juror fairness. Postponing a trial may be an effective remedy if publicity surrounding a trial and arrest can reasonably be expected to diminish over time. Studies have shown that people forget much of what they read in newspapers or hear on television and radio, and, especially in large cities, a continuance often means another crime will have taken over the headlines by the time the trial begins. Of course, there's always the possibility that publicity will flare up again once the trial starts. In addition, for defendants who are not granted bail or are unable to pay it, delaying a trial means they must remain in jail longer awaiting trial.

Voir dire is the process of questioning potential jurors to determine if they can be impartial. It is a crucial part of the trial and, in highly publicized, sensational trials, can take weeks, with hundreds of jurors questioned. In the Irvin case, for example, 430 potential jurors were called, and in the O.J. Simpson trial, 304 prospective jurors were questioned in a *voir dire* that took eleven weeks.

Jurors may be questioned not only about their familiarity with the case and opinions regarding the defendant's guilt but also about their occupations, religious beliefs, attitudes towards the death penalty and racial, religious or lifestyle prejudices. They will be asked if they know the defendant, the victim or any of the lawyers in the case. Depending on the nature of the case, they might be asked if they or any members of their families have been victims of sexual abuse, domestic violence or other crimes. In the Simpson case, for example, a juror was dismissed part way through the trial for having lied about whether she had experienced domestic violence.

Both the prosecution and defense can challenge an unlimited number of jurors for cause. It is then up to the judge to determine if there is sufficient reason to believe the potential juror is biased or for some other reason, such as a relationship with the victim or defendant, unsuited to sit on the jury. In the Irvin trial, 268 jurors were dismissed as obviously prejudiced against the defendant.

The attorneys for both sides also can dismiss a limited number of jurors with peremptory challenges. An attorney does not need to state a reason for using a peremptory challenge to dismiss a juror. While lawyers still base many peremptory challenges on instinct, jury selection has now become a form of social science. Law journal articles and books describe the ideal and the worst jurors for particular types of cases. Jury selection consultants can be hired to help lawyers devise the desired juror profile for a specific case. Thus, a lawyer may use peremptory challenges to eliminate from the jury pool people who, because of demographic or socioeconomic factors, are considered less likely to be sympathetic to his or her side of the case.

The number of peremptory challenges available to each side differs depending on the type of case and jurisdiction. For example, in North Carolina each side is entitled to fourteen peremptory challenges in capital cases and six in non-capital cases. In South Carolina, the defense gets ten peremptory challenges in cases involving serious crimes such as murder, rape, arson and burglary, and the prosecution gets five; in cases involving lesser offenses, each side gets five.

Judges, including the Supreme Court justices, place a great deal of faith in the *voir dire* process and believe that, if correctly used, it can be effective in weeding out potentially prejudiced jurors. Critics, however, note that potential jurors can and do hide the truth, either consciously or unconsciously. No doubt it can be difficult for people to openly admit that they have racial or religious prejudices or were so influenced by media coverage of a case that they can no longer be impartial. Sometimes people are not even aware of their own biases. And, as the Simpson case demonstrated, jurors might purposely withhold information, as did the juror who failed to disclose her own history of domestic abuse.

Admonitions to the jury are intended to impress upon the jurors their responsibility to decide the case solely on the basis of the law and evidence presented in court. Typically the judge orders the jurors not to read, watch or listen to any media coverage of or commentary on the trial and not to discuss the trial with anyone except other jurors, and only then when deliberations begin. Failure to follow the judge's orders can result in removal from the jury, citation for contempt of court or both. Recall that in the Sheppard case the Supreme Court found the jury admonitions to be insufficient since the judge merely suggested and requested that the jurors avoid media coverage of the trial. Whether appropriate jury admonitions in the form of direct orders actually prevent juror exposure to media coverage of the trial is open to debate. However, as with *voir dire*, most judges indicate they believe that jury admonitions are effective in most cases.

Sequestration is the most extreme, costly and least seldom used of the remedies designed to shelter jurors from prejudicial publicity. Sequestration means isolating the jury for the duration of the trial. It entails housing the jurors in a hotel, screening their phone calls and monitoring their use of mass media to ensure that they do not see or hear any media coverage of the trial.

While sequestration can be effective in preventing jury exposure to prejudicial publicity, it is a remedy that also has many drawbacks. First, it adds significantly to the cost of the trial because the state must transport, house, feed and guard the jurors. Perhaps more importantly, though, sequestration causes significant disruptions to jurors' lives and effectively eliminates from juries people who cannot leave their families or jobs for weeks at a time. In addition, keeping jurors away from family, friends and normal routines for an extended period of time may have unintended psychological effects, causing jurors to resent the defendant and blame him or her for disrupting their lives.

PREVENTING OR DIMINISHING PUBLICITY

Despite the existence of the traditional remedies, trial judges sometimes try to prevent or diminish the publicity itself. These judicial efforts to control what information journalists have access to and what the media publish or broadcast raise significant First Amendment implications, and during the past twenty years the Supreme Court has severely limited their use. Remedies aimed at eliminating or reducing prejudicial publicity and media interference with fair trial rights fall into six categories: (1) gag orders aimed at the media, (2) restrictions on trial participants, (3) post-publication sanctions, (4) court closures, (5) denials of access to court records and (6) bans or limits on cameras in the courtroom.

Gag Orders on the Media

In *Sheppard v. Maxwell*, the Supreme Court provided a list of tools trial judges could use to protect defendants' fair trial rights. The Supreme Court, however, never suggested judges issue restrictive orders directly prohibiting the media from publishing in-

formation that might be prejudicial. Nonetheless, that's exactly what some judges did. While comprehensive data are not available, a number of sources reported an increase in gag orders on the press during the decade following *Sheppard*. A study by the Reporters Committee for Freedom of the Press identified thirty-nine gag orders directed at the media between 1967 and 1975. What is especially remarkable about the Reporters Committee data is the acceleration in such restraints over time. From 1967 through 1971, the committee identified four gag orders on the press, averaging not even one per year. In the next four years, 1972 to 1975, the committee identified thirty gag orders on the press, reaching a peak of fourteen in 1975.[24] In 1975, Judge Howard Medina, who had headed the New York Bar Association's Special Committee on Radio, Television and the Administration of Justice, wrote in the *New York Times:* "It must be that trial judges like this show of authority. In any event, the number of these omnibus gag orders has vastly increased."[25] The Twentieth Century Fund's Task Force on Justice, Publicity and the First Amendment, in a report issued in 1976, criticized trial judges' "excessive use of restrictive orders."[26]

Journalists and attorneys were as concerned about the absurd nature of some gag orders as they were about the increased numbers. In one case, a judge prohibited publication of a jury verdict entered in open court; in another, the court barred publication of the names of public witnesses for six months; in still another, a judge forbade publication of information about a recent jail break. The excessiveness of trial judges' responses to the "free press-fair trial problem" was illustrated by the results of a 1972 Reporters Committee survey, which showed that in every case in which the media challenged a gag order, the order was struck down by an appellate court.[27] But, as the post-1972 figures demonstrate, lack of success with appeals courts did not deter trial judges from imposing restrictions on the press.

Finally, in 1976, the Supreme Court put a halt to the indiscriminate use of gag orders on the press. The landmark case of *Nebraska Press Association v. Stuart*[28] began on Saturday evening, October 18, 1975, when police arrived at the Henry Kellie home in Sutherland, Nebraska, to find six members of the Kellie family with

---

[24] Jack Landau, "Fair Press and Free Trial: A Due Process Proposal," *American Bar Association Journal* 62 (1976): 55, 57.

[25] "Omnibus 'Gag' Rulings," *New York Times,* 30 November 1975, sec. IV, p. 13.

[26] *Twentieth Century Fund Task Force on Justice, Publicity and the First Amendment, Rights in Conflict* (New York: McGraw-Hill, 1976), p. 4.

[27] Landau, *supra* note 24, at 56, 59.

[28] 427 U.S. 539 (1976).

shotgun wounds to their heads. Five were already dead, and the sixth died later that night. Fear spread through the town of 850. The local radio station reported that an armed murderer was in the area and advised residents to stay indoors and keep their doors locked.

The next day a neighbor of the Kellies, Erwin Charles Simants, 30, was arrested and charged with the six murders. Simants had apparently confessed to his thirteen-year-old nephew and his parents, who called the police. Simants admitted to police that he had killed the Kellies and was arraigned a few hours after his arrest. Reporters learned of Simants' confessions and publicized the information, along with speculation — later confirmed by autopsies — that Simants had sexually assaulted some of the victims after murdering them.

Protecting Simants' right to a fair trial by an impartial jury was complicated by both geography and Nebraska law. The court in which Simants was to be tried was in North Platte, population 19,000, the county seat of Lincoln County, just twenty miles east of Sutherland. Publicity about the crime had, of course, been as widespread in North Platte, the largest city in southwest Nebraska, as in Sutherland itself. Nebraska law severely restricted the use of two traditional techniques for mitigating the effects of prejudicial publicity — continuance and change of venue — by requiring that the accused be brought to trial within six months and allowing a change of venue only to an adjoining county, all of which were smaller than Lincoln County.

On Tuesday, October 21, the county attorney proposed a solution to County Judge Ronald Ruff — a gag order prohibiting publication of potentially prejudicial material. The next day Judge Ruff issued an order barring publication of testimony and evidence presented during the preliminary hearing. In addition, he ordered journalists to abide by the Nebraska Bar-Press Guidelines, a set of voluntary recommendations for minimizing prejudicial publicity. (Bench-bar-press guidelines are discussed later in this chapter.)

The media immediately appealed Judge Ruff's order to District Court Judge Hugh Stuart, who found that there was a "clear and present danger that pre-trial publicity could impinge upon the defendant's right to a fair trial." Judge Stuart vacated Judge Ruff's order and entered his own, which also incorporated the bar-press guidelines and prohibited publication of specific information — including the existence and contents of Simants' confession and information relating to the sexual assaults — until after a jury had been impaneled. Stuart's order also prohibited the media from reporting on the exact nature of the gag order itself.

The media made numerous attempts to have the gag order vacated or stayed. Finally, on December 1, after considerable prodding from Supreme Court Justice Harry Blackmun, who was the overseeing Circuit Justice for the circuit including Nebraska, the Nebraska Supreme Court modified Stuart's order to eliminate references to the bar-press guidelines but continued the ban on reporting confessions and "other facts 'strongly implicative' of the accused." On December 12, 1975, the Supreme Court agreed to review the case; on January 5, 1976, Simants' trial began with jury selection; on January 8, the jury was sworn and sequestered and Stuart's gag order was lifted; on January 16 Simants was found guilty on six counts of first degree murder and sentenced to death; on April 19 *Nebraska Press Association v. Stuart* was argued before the Supreme Court; and on June 30 a unanimous Court held that the Stuart's gag order was a prior restraint on the press that violated the First Amendment. Incidentally, Simants' conviction was eventually overturned on the ground that a sheriff had tried to influence the sequestered jury. On retrial Simants was found not guilty by reason of insanity, which was his original plea.

In *Nebraska Press Association*, all nine justices agreed that the gag order was unconstitutional. They did not all agree, however, on the reasons for their conclusions. In the opinion of the Court, in which four other justices concurred, Chief Justice Warren Burger took a balancing approach, utilizing a variation of the clear and present danger test, which had been developed in the context of sedition cases. After acknowledging that prior restraints "are the most serious and the least tolerable infringement on First Amendment rights," Burger said the constitutionality of a gag order had to be determined by looking at the circumstances of a particular case and deciding whether "'the gravity of the "evil," discounted by its improbability,'" justified a gag order. Burger said three factors must be considered:

(a) the nature and extent of pretrial news coverage;

(b) whether other measures would be likely to mitigate the effects of unrestrained publicity; and

(c) how effectively a restraining order would operate to prevent the threatened danger.[29]

This three-part test is still used by judges to decide whether restrictive orders can be imposed on the media.

Burger said Judge Stuart was correct in concluding there would be intense and pervasive pretrial publicity. However, he failed to consider whether alternative measures might have protected Simants' right to a fair trial. Furthermore, the Chief Justice voiced doubts about the effectiveness of the gag order. Noting the crimes

---

[29] *Id.* at 559, 562 (quoting *United States v. Dennis*, 183 F.2d 201, 212 (2d Cir. 1950), *aff'd*, 341 U.S. 494 (1951)).

took place "in a community of 850 people," Burger said, "It is reasonable to assume that, without any news accounts being printed or broadcast, rumors would travel swiftly by word of mouth. One can only speculate on the accuracy of such reports, given the general propensities of rumors; they could well be more damaging than reasonably accurate news accounts."[30] Thus, Stuart's order failed Burger's balancing test and was declared unconstitutional.

Three justices — Brennan, Marshall and Stewart — were willing to go even further. They concurred in the ruling but said gag orders on the press would always be unconstitutional. Two other justices — White and Stevens — indicated they might agree to an absolute ban on gag orders at a later date.

A year after *Nebraska Press Association*, the Supreme Court underscored the point that gag orders on the media would rarely be constitutional when it struck down an order prohibiting publication of the name and picture of an eleven-year-old charged with murder. The juvenile court judge had allowed journalists to attend the detention hearing for the accused boy but then banned publication of the child's name and the photo, which had been taken outside the courthouse. By the time the judge issued the gag order, the boy's name and picture had already been widely published and broadcast. In *Oklahoma Publishing Co. v. District Court*,[31] the Supreme Court said that once the judge permitted journalists to attend the hearing, he could not prohibit them from publishing the information they gathered while in attendance.

Nebraska Press Association and *Oklahoma Publishing Co.* have made it extremely difficult for a trial judge to justify gagging the press. Periodically judges still try, but such orders are almost always struck down on appeal. For example, appellate courts have struck down gag orders prohibiting publication of the names of jurors,[32] evidence presented in open court but outside the presence of the jury,[33] videotapes made during the government's investigation of alleged drug trafficking,[34] the identities of juve-

nile offenders and victims,[35] and defendants' prior criminal records and nicknames, such as "Quapaw Quarter rapist" and "Sugarhouse rapist."[36]

Television's fascination with "docudramas" based on sensational crimes has led a number of defendants to seek — unsuccessfully — to prevent such broadcasts. One of the best known of these cases involved an attempt by Lyle and Erik Menendez to prevent the broadcast in Los Angeles County of *Honor Thy Father and Mother: The True Story of the Menendez Murders* while the brothers awaited retrial on charges of murdering their parents. The Menendez brothers, who ultimately were convicted, claimed that airing the program in the county would make it impossible to find an unbiased jury. Applying the *Nebraska Press Association* test, a California federal district court disagreed, holding that the trial judge could adequately protect the defendants' fair trial rights through *voir dire* and jury instructions.[37]

In 1996 the Sixth U.S. Circuit Court of Appeals declared unconstitutional an unusual gag order issued in a civil case involving Procter & Gamble Co. and Bankers Trust Co. An attorney who worked for the firm representing Bankers Trust provided a *Business Week* reporter copies of documents relating to the lawsuit. The documents, however, had been sealed by trial Judge John Feikens, a fact apparently unknown to both the attorney who provided the documents and the reporter who received them. Hours before the *Business Week* story based on the documents was to go to press, both Procter & Gamble and Bankers Trust asked Judge Feikens to issue a restraining order barring publication of the story. Without holding a hearing or giving McGraw-Hill, publisher of *Business Week*, a chance to protest, Judge Feikens issued the gag order. A few weeks later, Judge Feikens unsealed the

---

[30] *Id.* at 567.

[31] 430 U.S. 308 (1977).

[32] *Capital Cities Media v. Toole*, 463 U.S. 1303 (Brennan, Circuit Justice 1983); *Times Publishing Co. v. Florida*, 632 So. 2d 1072 (Fla. Dist. Ct. App. 1994); *Des Moines Register & Tribune Co. v. Osmundson*, 248 N.W.2d 493 (Iowa 1976); *New Mexico ex rel. New Mexico Press Ass'n v. Kaufman*, 648 P.2d 300 (N.M. 1982); *Ohio ex rel. Chillicothe Gazette, Inc. v. Ross County Court of Common Pleas*, 442 N.E.2d 747 (Ohio 1982); *Pennsylvania v. Genovese*, 487 A.2d 364 (Pa. 1985).

[33] *Florida ex rel. Miami Herald Pub. Co. v. McIntosh*, 340 So. 2d 904 (Fla. 1976).

[34] *CBS v. District Court*, 727 F.2d 1174 (9th Cir. 1984). This was the well-publicized case involving an FBI sting operation targeting car manufacturer John DeLorean, who was ultimately acquitted.

[35] *KGTV Channel 10 v. Superior Court*, 32 Cal. Rptr. 2d 181 (1994); *Lesher Communications, Inc. v. Alameda County Superior Court*, 22 Media L. Rep. (BNA) 1383 (Cal. Ct. App. 1994); *San Bernardino County Dep't of Public Social Services v. Superior Court*, 283 Cal. Rptr. 332 (1991); *Sarasota Herald-Tribune v. J.T.L.*, 502 So. 2d 930 (Fla. Dist. Ct. App. 1987); *In re a Minor*, 537 N.E.2d 292 (Ill. 1989); *Minneapolis Star & Tribune Co. v. Schmidt*, 360 N.W.2d 433 (Minn. Ct. App. 1985); *Minneapolis Star & Tribune Co. v. Lee*, 353 N.W.2d 213 (Minn. Ct. App. 1984); *New Jersey ex rel. H.N.*, 632 A.2d 537 (N.J. Super. Ct. App. Div. 1993).

[36] *Arkansas Gazette v. Lofton*, 6 Media L. Rep. (BNA) 1535 (Ark. 1980); *KUTV v. Conder*, 668 P.2d 456 (Utah 1983).

[37] *Menendez v. Fox Broadcasting Co.*, 22 Media L. Rep. (BNA) 1702 (C.D. Cal. 1994). See also *Hunt v. NBC*, 872 F.2d 289 (9th Cir. 1989); *Goldblum v. NBC*, 584 F.2d 904 (9th Cir. 1978); *Corbitt v. NBC*, 20 Media L. Rep. (BNA) 2037 (N.D. Ill. 1992); *Clear Channel Communications, Inc. v. Murray*, 636 So. 2d 818 (Fla. Dist. Ct. App. 1994).

documents on which the *Business Week* story was based, making them available to the public. Amazingly, however, the judge still refused to rescind his order barring the magazine from publishing its original article. In March 1996 the U.S. Court of Appeals for the Sixth Circuit ruled that the case involved a "classic case of a prior restraint" in violation of the First Amendment. Judge Feikens had failed to demonstrate that irreparable harm to a substantial government interest would result from publication of the article, the appellate court wrote. Furthermore, he had not provided McGraw-Hill the opportunity to argue the merits of the gag order.[38]

Since *Nebraska Press Association*, only a few gag orders on the media have been upheld on appeal. In one such case, the Utah Supreme Court said an order prohibiting the media from reporting a criminal defendant's alleged ties to organized crime met the three-part test and, therefore, did not violate the First Amendment. The state supreme court said the trial judge had supported "the precise, narrowly drawn order" with facts demonstrating it was necessary to ensure a fair trial and would be effective in preserving the integrity of the jury and that no reasonable alternatives to the gag order existed.[39]

In 1990 the Eleventh U.S. Circuit Court of Appeals refused to lift a temporary gag order prohibiting CNN from disseminating the contents of tape recordings of conversations between deposed Panamanian dictator Manuel Noriega, who was in jail in Miami awaiting trial on federal drug charges, and his lawyers. The tapes were allegedly made by jail officials and were obtained legally by CNN. On a motion from Noriega's attorneys, a U.S. district judge issued a temporary restraining order prohibiting CNN from broadcasting the tapes and ordered the network to submit the tapes to him so he could decide whether their dissemination would present a "clear, immediate, and irreparable danger" to Noriega's fair trial rights and, therefore, should be permanently banned.[40] The next day the judge limited his order to material that was privileged. CNN appealed the judge's order but also disobeyed it by continuing to air the excerpts from the tapes it had broadcast prior to the issuance of the gag order.

The Court of Appeals refused to lift the district court's order, saying CNN's failure to allow the judge to inspect the tapes had made it impossible for the court to balance the network's First Amendment rights against Noriega's Sixth Amendment rights.[41] The Supreme Court denied *certiorari*, despite a vigorous dissent from Justices Marshall and O'Connor, who said the trial judge's order could not be reconciled with *Nebraska Press Association* and the *Pentagon Papers* case.[42] CNN eventually turned the tapes over to the district judge, who, after reviewing them, concluded that broadcast of the remaining unaired portions would not violate Noriega's rights.[43]

Despite the fact that the gag order was ultimately lifted, CNN was found in contempt of court for airing portions of the tapes while the temporary restraining order was in force, fined $85,000 and ordered to broadcast a public apology.[44] This case illustrates an important point that journalists must keep in mind: Even if a court order is eventually declared unconstitutional, a person who violates the order while it is in effect can be found guilty of contempt of court and subject to fines and/or imprisonment. This is known as the "collateral bar rule," which states that a person who disobeys a court order may not collaterally challenge the constitutionality of the order as a defense to the contempt of court charge. The reasoning behind the rule is simple and generally sound: The effectiveness of the entire judicial system would be severely hampered if individuals were free to make their own decisions as to which court orders they would obey and which they would ignore. Under many circumstances, waiting for appellate review of a court order imposes little or no hardship on the individual subject to the order. But the situation changes when gag orders are imposed on the media since timeliness is the essence of news and waiting for an appellate court ruling could change news into history.

A 1972 case decided by the U.S. Court of Appeals for the Fifth Circuit illustrates the traditional strict application of the collateral bar rule. In *United States v. Dickinson*,[45] two Baton Rouge, Louisiana, reporters were held in contempt and fined $300 each for disobeying a federal judge's order not to report on anything that took place during a hearing that had been open to the public. The

---

[38] *Procter & Gamble Co. v. Bankers Trust Co.*, 78 F.3d 219, 225 (6th Cir. 1996).

[39] *KUTV v. Wilkinson*, 686 P.2d 456 (Utah 1984).

[40] *United States v. Noriega*, 752 F. Supp. 1032 (S.D. Fla.), *aff'd sub nom. In re Cable News Network, Inc.*, 917 F.2d 1543 (11th Cir.), *cert. denied*, 498 U.S. 976 (1990).

[41] 917 F.2d 1543, 1544 (11th Cir. 1990).

[42] *New York Times Co. v. United States*, 403 U.S. 713 (1971).

[43] *United States v. Noriega*, 752 F. Supp. 1045 (S.D. Fla. 1990).

[44] *United States v. CNN*, 865 F. Supp. 1549 (S.D. Fla. 1994). Beginning at 6 p.m. on December 19, 1994, CNN broadcast an apology every hour for twenty-two hours. The statement said, in part: "CNN realizes that it was in error in defying the order of the court and publishing the Noriega tape while appealing the court's order. We do now and always have recognized that our justice system cannot long survive if litigants take it upon themselves to determine which judgments or orders of court they will or will not follow."

[45] 465 F.2d 496 (5th Cir. 1972).

hearing was held to investigate the motives of the state in prosecuting a federal volunteer worker charged with conspiring to murder the Baton Rouge mayor. The volunteer contended the charges were brought to harass him because of his civil rights activities. Because the volunteer worker might later be tried on the criminal charges, the U.S. district judge ordered that there be no media coverage of what occurred at the hearing. On appeal, the Fifth Circuit struck down the trial court's gag order as unconstitutional but sustained the contempt convictions of the two reporters. The court wrote:

> We begin with the well-established principle in proceedings for criminal contempt that an injunction ... *must be obeyed*, irrespective of the ultimate validity of the order. Invalidity is no defense to criminal contempt.... "People simply cannot have the luxury of knowing that they have a right to contest the correctness of the judge's order in deciding whether to willfully disobey it.... Court orders have to be obeyed until they are reversed or set aside in an orderly fashion."[46]

While the court recognized that "[t]imeliness of publication is the hallmark of 'news,'" it went on to say: "But newsmen are citizens, too.... They too may sometimes have to wait."[47] It is somewhat ironic that having recognized the importance of timeliness in news reporting, the Fifth Circuit itself took five months to issue an opinion in the case.

More than a decade later, the First U.S. Circuit Court of Appeals adopted a somewhat more flexible approach, ruling that a "transparently invalid" gag order could be violated with impunity as long as the publisher first made "a good faith effort" to have the order reversed by an appellate court. The case resulted from the *Providence Journal's* violation of a judge's order prohibiting publication of information the paper had received from the FBI. The information, which the FBI had gathered through illegal wiretaps in the 1960s, related to reputed organized crime leader Raymond L.S. Patriarca, who died in 1985. In 1976 the *Journal* had sought access to transcripts of the wiretaps under the federal Freedom of Information Act, but the FBI denied the request and a federal court upheld the denial, ruling that release of the transcripts would violate Patriarca's privacy. However, after Patriarca's death, the FBI released the transcripts to the *Providence Journal* as well as other news organizations. After a Providence radio station aired some of the information from the transcripts, Patriarca's son sued to prevent further publication, claiming dissemination of the information would violate his privacy.[48]

On November 13, 1985, Judge Francis Boyle issued an order barring publication of the wiretap information; on November 14 the *Journal* published an article in direct disobedience of that order; on November 19 Judge Boyle vacated his order, acknowledging that it was most likely unconstitutional; and on March 17, 1986, Judge Boyle held the *Journal* and its editor, Charles Hauser, in contempt of court, fining the newspaper $100,000 and giving Hauser an eighteen-month suspended sentence and ordering him to perform 200 hours of community service. The *Journal* appealed, and a three-judge panel of the First Circuit reversed the contempt convictions. While the court recognized that the collateral bar rule is the "general rule," it went on to emphasize that this case involved a prior restraint on speech, which the court said, represents "an unusual class of orders because they are presumptively unconstitutional." The court said the *Nebraska Press Association* test was the standard that applied to evaluating the constitutionality of Judge Boyle's gag order and that it was "patently clear" the order did not meet that test. In fact, the judge had failed to even consider two prongs of the test. Furthermore, the court noted that the purpose of a temporary restraining order, such as Judge Boyle issued, is to preserve the status quo while the court considers the case. However, for newspapers, the court said, the status quo "is to publish news promptly that editors decide to publish. A restraining order disturbs the status quo and impinges on the exercise of editorial discretion."[49]

A few months later, the First Circuit reheard the case *en banc*, affirmed the three-judge panel's ruling but added a modification. The full court said that in the future a publisher had to "make a good faith effort to seek emergency relief from the appellate courts" before violating a patently invalid gag order. "If timely access to the appellate court is not available or if [a] timely decision is not forthcoming," the publisher may go ahead and publish in violation of the order, subsequently challenging the constitutionality of the gag order as a defense to a contempt citation. The requirement to seek appellate review before violating a court order was not applied to the *Providence Journal* case, the court said, because that would be unfair. Besides, the court indicated it was not clear whether timely appellate relief was available in this case.[50]

---

[46] *Id.* at 509 (quoting *Southern Railway Co. v. Lanham,* 408 F.2d 348, 350 (5th Cir. 1969) (Brown, C.J., dissenting)).

[47] *Id.* at 512 (citation omitted).

[48] *In re Providence Journal,* 820 F.2d 1342 (1st Cir. 1986), *modified,* 820 F.2d 1354 (1st Cir. 1987), *cert. dismissed,* 485 U.S. 693 (1988).

[49] *Id.* at 1346-53.

[50] *Id.* at 1354, 1355.

The Supreme Court failed to reconcile the apparent conflict between the Fifth Circuit and the First Circuit when it dismissed the appeal from the government in the *Providence Journal* case on procedural grounds.[51]

In attempting to understand these two cases, it's important to keep in mind that *Dickinson* is binding precedent only in the Fifth Circuit, and *Providence Journal* is binding precedent only in the First Circuit. In addition, both cases are federal cases, and individual states are free to devise their own rules regarding application of the collateral bar rule when state court judges issue gag orders on the press.[52] A few courts have chosen to follow the First Circuit's lead, ruling that journalists who disobey patently void court orders can escape contempt of court convictions. For example, in 1994 the Kansas Supreme Court reversed the contempt conviction of the *Atchison Daily Globe* and its publisher, who had violated a trial court's order not to report a felony defendant's prior criminal record. The state supreme court ruled that the gag order failed to meet the *Nebraska Press Association* test and, because it was transparently invalid, was not subject to the collateral bar rule. Following the requirement added by the *en banc* decision in *Providence Journal*, the Kansas Supreme Court noted that the newspaper had tried to obtain appellate review but such relief was not available "in time to meet the 12 noon deadline."[53]

Despite some successes in challenging contempt convictions resulting from disobedience of gag orders, many attorneys still advise journalists to obey such orders until they are reversed on appeal or, at the very least, to make a sincere effort to obtain appellate court review of the order before disobeying it.

Restrictions on Trial Participants

While the *Nebraska Press Association* test has made it very difficult for judges to gag the media, it is easier for judges to restrict the flow of information to the media by issuing gag orders aimed at trial participants, especially attorneys. In *Sheppard v. Maxwell*, the Court specifically said the judge "might well have proscribed extrajudicial statements by any lawyer, party, witness, or court of-

ficial which divulged prejudicial matters."[54] Generally, courts view gag orders on trial participants as less distasteful under the First Amendment because they do not prevent the media from disseminating information they possess but simply make it more difficult for journalists to obtain information. In addition, courts have greater power over trial participants, especially lawyers, than they do over non-participant journalists. Newsgathering, however, receives some First Amendment protection, and trial participants have their own First Amendment rights to speak. Thus, there are limits on judges' gag powers. Before considering how those limits apply to the typical gag orders aimed at attorneys, witnesses, defendants and jurors, a somewhat unusual situation — a gag order aimed at newspapers that were themselves participants in the case — will be addressed.

In *Seattle Times Co. v. Rhinehart*, the Supreme Court said that the strict *Nebraska Press Association* test did not apply when the media themselves were parties to the litigation and had obtained information through the pretrial discovery process.[55] The *Seattle Times* and *Walla Walla Union-Bulletin* were defendants in a libel and invasion of privacy lawsuit brought by Keith Rhinehart, head of a religious group called the Aquarian Foundation. The newspapers wanted information about the foundation's members and donors, but the foundation refused, arguing that publication of such information would violate members' and donors' First Amendment rights. A Washington state trial judge ordered the group to release the information but issued a protective order prohibiting the newspapers from publishing the records.

The Supreme Court unanimously upheld the trial judge's order, saying it was not a classic prior restraint requiring exacting First Amendment scrutiny. Nonetheless, the Court said the state needed to demonstrate that a substantial government interest justified restricting the newspapers' right to publish the information. Preventing abuse of the discovery process constituted a substantial governmental interest, the Court concluded, and, therefore, the protective order was not a violation of the First Amendment. However, the Court noted that the newspapers could publish the same information if they obtained it some other way.

Seattle Times v. Rhinehart is an unusual case. Usually restrictive orders prohibit attorneys or witnesses from making extrajudicial, public statements that might prejudice the outcome of a trial. While such orders limit the flow of information to the media, they do not ban the media from disseminating information they pos-

---

[51] 485 U.S. 693 (1988). The special prosecutor who was handling the government's case had failed to obtain the U.S. solicitor general's authorization to petition the Supreme Court for *certiorari*.

[52] For example, in 1984, two years before the First Circuit ruled in *Providence Journal*, the Washington Supreme Court, relying on both the state and U.S. constitutions, struck down a contempt citation against a television and radio station that had violated a "patently invalid" gag order. *Washington v. Coe*, 679 P.2d 353 (Wash. 1984).

[53] *Kansas v. Alston*, 887 P.2d 681, 692 (Kan. 1994).

[54] 384 U.S. at 361.

[55] 467 U.S. 20 (1984).

sess; the orders are aimed at the parties, not the media.

The American Bar Association's Model Rules of Professional Conduct provide that attorneys should not make extrajudicial, public statements that "have a substantial likelihood of prejudicing" a pending case. While not expressly prohibiting any particular types of comments, the rules list certain subjects "more likely than not to have a material prejudicial effect on a proceeding." These include statements about the character, credibility, reputation or criminal record of a party, suspect or witness; the existence or contents of a confession or a suspect's refusal to make a statement; the results of examinations or tests or the refusal of a suspect to take a test; opinions as to a defendant's guilt or innocence; or even that "a defendant has been charged with a crime, unless there is included therein a statement explaining that the defendant is presumed innocent until and unless proven guilty."

In August 1994, amidst the massive publicity surrounding the O.J. Simpson case, the ABA amended its rules to add a right-of-reply for defense lawyers. The new provision says that an attorney "may make a statement that a reasonable lawyer would believe is required to protect a client from the substantial undue prejudicial effect of recent publicity not initiated by the lawyer or the lawyer's client." At the same time, the ABA added language directing criminal prosecutors to "refrain from making extrajudicial comments that have a substantial likelihood of heightening public condemnation of the accused."[56]

About forty states have adopted rules, most following the ABA's model, allowing an attorney to be disciplined for public statements that could prejudice a trial even if the judge hasn't issued an order specifically limiting extrajudicial statements. Attorneys have challenged such rules, arguing that they are prior restraints on speech and, therefore, should be subject to the *Nebraska Press Association* test. In 1991, however, the Supreme Court ruled that the "substantial likelihood of material prejudice" standard, used in most states' attorney rules, does not violate the First Amendment. Chief Justice Rehnquist, noting that lawyers are "officers of the Court," justified applying a different standard to attorneys than to the media and general public. "Because lawyers have special access to information through discovery and client communications, their extrajudicial statements pose a threat to the fairness of a pending proceeding since lawyers' statements are likely to be received as especially authoritative," he said.[57]

The case, *Gentile v. State Bar of Nevada*, involved a challenge

to Nevada's disciplinary rules by a lawyer who had held a press conference in which he declared that his client, charged with felony theft, was innocent and questioned the integrity of the grand jury witnesses. The attorney was subsequently disciplined by the state bar for violating a Nevada Supreme Court rule, which was virtually identical to the ABA's model rule. While the Supreme Court sanctioned use of the substantial likelihood standard for lawyers, it declared Nevada's rule unconstitutionally vague because it did not provide clear notice of exactly what types of statements were permitted. A portion of the rule, which listed acceptable public statements by attorneys, had "misled [Gentile] into thinking that he could give his press conference without fear of discipline," the Court wrote.[58]

Whether a state has adopted specific rules limiting attorneys' extrajudicial statements or not, a trial judge has the inherent power to issue gag orders aimed at attorneys. One of the key criticisms of Judge Lance Ito's conduct of the O.J. Simpson trial was his failure to regulate the out-of-court comments of the attorneys. Ito justified his failure to gag the lawyers by noting that California had not adopted a rule limiting attorney speech, but most commentators agreed that Ito, as the trial judge, did not need a bar association or state supreme court rule to provide him with the power to prohibit prejudicial statements by the lawyers. In fact, during the subsequent civil lawsuit brought against Simpson by the families of the victims, Judge Hiroshi Fujisaki imposed a wide-ranging gag order on all trial participants, including the lawyers.

If an attorney violates a gag order, the result can be a contempt of court conviction, just as when a journalist violates a court order. For example, in 1995 the Second Circuit Court of Appeals upheld the criminal contempt conviction of Bruce Cutler, attorney for alleged organized crime boss John Gotti, because he had violated a trial court order prohibiting extrajudicial statements by attorneys if there was a "reasonable likelihood" that such statements would interfere with a fair trial. The trial court had found that Cutler willfully violated the court order by repeatedly speaking to journalists. Cutler was sentenced to ninety days of house arrest, three years of probation and 180 days suspension from the practice of law in the Eastern District of New York.[59]

Gag orders on lawyers, however, have been struck down when

---

[56] *Model Rules of Professional Conduct*, Rule 3.6 & cmt., Rule 3.8(g) (1994).

[57] *Gentile v. State Bar of Nevada*, 501 U.S. 1030, 1074 (1991).

[58] *Id.* at 1048.

[59] *United States v. Cutler*, 58 F.3d 825, 828 (2d Cir. 1995). This case provides an excellent example of the collateral bar rule at work. The appeals court upheld Cutler's contempt conviction but refused to consider the constitutionality of the gag order since Cutler had violated it without first seeking appellate review.

they were found to be overbroad or when the trial judge has failed to consider alternative measures for protecting the defendant's right to a fair trial. In a case resulting from the trial of the people accused of bombing the World Trade Center, the Second U.S. Circuit Court of Appeals vacated a gag order prohibiting the attorneys from publicly discussing any aspect of the case. The trial judge had issued the blanket order without ever considering whether less restrictive means were available to protect defendants' fair trial rights, the appeals court said.[60] In 1986, a sweeping order prohibiting attorneys from "any discussion of this case with the news media," including telling reporters what time court was to convene, was overturned as "vague and overbroad" by a New York appeals court.[61] The following year, a trial judge's order banning "any public statement" to the media during a sensational murder trial was declared unconstitutional because, first, it prohibited all statements, not just prejudicial ones, and second, the judge had failed to consider whether there were other measures that might have ensured the defendant's fair trial rights.[62]

Occasionally judges issue gag orders aimed at witnesses. Just as with restrictions on attorney speech, such orders will be upheld if they are necessary to protect the defendant's right to a fair trial and alternative measures are not available. In 1984, a U.S. district judge in North Carolina issued an order prohibiting all potential witnesses in a murder trial from making "any extrajudicial statement relating to the testimony in this case that such potential witnesses may give, or relating to any of the parties or issues such potential witnesses expect or should reasonably expect to be involved in this case, or relating to the events leading up to and culminating" in the crime. The order specifically forbade potential witnesses from giving interviews to the press relating to those same topics. The case involved the trial of Ku Klux Klan and Nazi party members for the shooting deaths of five people in Greensboro. In upholding the gag order the U.S. Court of Appeals for the Fourth Circuit noted that there had already been "tremendous publicity" and that many of the potential witnesses were relatives of the victims. The appellate court also agreed with the trial judge that alternative remedies, such as change of venue, jury admonitions or sequestration, would be ineffective or impractical.[63]

In 1990 the Supreme Court upheld the right of a grand jury witness to publish his own testimony after the grand jury term had ended. A grand jury is an investigative body that does not decide a person's guilt or innocence but, instead, determines if there is sufficient evidence to indict, or formally charge, someone with a crime. Grand juries meet in secret, and the grand jurors themselves are prohibited from revealing what goes on during the proceedings. Florida law took the traditional grand jury secrecy even further, however, by prohibiting witnesses from disclosing their own testimony.

Because of articles he had written, Michael Smith, a reporter for the *Charlotte Herald-News,* was called to testify before a grand jury investigating alleged wrongdoing in the State Attorney's Office and Sheriff's Department in Charlotte County. The prosecutor warned Smith that Florida law prohibited him from revealing his own testimony. After the grand jury term ended, Smith wanted to use his testimony in his writing and claimed he had a First Amendment right to do so. Noting that the information Smith wanted to publish related to government misconduct and thus constituted "speech which has traditionally been recognized as lying at the core of the First Amendment," the Supreme Court unanimously held the Florida law unconstitutional.[64] The Court's opinion was narrow, however, restricted solely to a witness publishing his *own* testimony *after* the grand jury term ended.

Occasionally judges also try to gag defendants, but such orders are seldom upheld on appeal. In *United States v. Ford,* a trial judge prohibited a congressman, on trial for mail and bank fraud, from commenting publicly on his own case outside of Congress. The Sixth Circuit overturned the gag order, using the same standard applied to the media in *Nebraska Press Association.* The court wrote:

> We see no legitimate reasons for a lower threshold standard for individuals, including defendants, seeking to express themselves outside of court than for the press.... A criminal defendant awaiting trial in a controversial case has the full power of

---

[60] *United States v. Salameh,* 992 F.2d 445 (2d Cir. 1993).

[61] *NBC v. Cooperman,* 501 N.Y.S.2d 405 (App. Div. 1986).

[62] *Connecticut Magazine v. Moraghan,* 676 F. Supp. 38 (D. Conn. 1987). See also *In re New York Times Co.,* 878 F.2d 67 (2d Cir. 1989); *Levine v. U.S. Dist. Court,* 764 F.2d 590 (9th Cir. 1985); *cert. denied,* 476 U.S. 1158 (1986); *United States v. Marcana Garcia,* 456 F. Supp. 1354 (D.P.R. 1978); *Breiner v. Takao,* 835 P.2d 637 (Haw. 1992).

[63] *In re Russell,* 726 F.2d 1007 (4th Cir. 1984), *cert. denied,* 469 U.S.

---

837 (1984).

[64] *Butterworth v. Smith,* 494 U.S. 624, 632 (1990). In a similar case, the Third U.S. Circuit Court of Appeals ruled that reporters who testified about the alleged misconduct of a Pennsylvania Supreme Court justice before a state Judicial Review Board could not be prohibited from revealing their own testimony. They could, however, be barred from revealing the testimony of other witnesses or information they overheard during their appearances before the board. *First Amendment Coalition v. Judicial Inquiry & Review Bd.,* 784 F.2d 467 (3d Cir. 1986).

government arrayed against him and the full spotlight of media attention focused upon him. The defendant's interest in replying to the charges and to the associated adverse publicity, thus, is at a peak.... The "accused has a First Amendment right to reply publicly to the prosecutor's charges, and the public has a right to hear that reply...."[65]

The following year, the Sixth Circuit struck down another restraint on a criminal defendant as a violation of his First Amendment rights. In that case, the trial judge had agreed to allow a defendant to remain free on bail pending an appeal of his tax evasion conviction on the condition he promise "to refrain from communicating with anyone other than his attorney regarding his beliefs about income taxes during the appeal."[66]

In the wake of the O.J. Simpson trial, media attempts to interview jurors and post-trial statements by jurors have generated considerable controversy. Jurors, of course, are always prohibited from discussing the trial in which they are involved while it is going on, just as they are prohibited from reading, viewing or listening to news reports about the trial. Such during-trial restrictions on jurors are considered essential to preserving the integrity of the jury process. Questions arise, however, when judges impose restrictions on post-verdict juror speech. The two most common reasons for post-verdict restrictions are to protect jurors' privacy and to ensure the secrecy of jury deliberations. Judges have expressed special concern about jurors being asked to reveal the votes and comments of their fellow jurors who may refuse to be interviewed by the press.

The Supreme Court has never ruled on the constitutionality of restrictions on post-verdict juror interviews, but a number of lower courts have upheld narrowly tailored restrictions. If the ban on juror interviews is overly broad, however, it is not likely to survive constitutional scrutiny. In 1991, for example, the Ohio Supreme Court struck down an order prohibiting anyone, including journalists, from discussing a highly publicized murder case with jurors. The court said the order was unconstitutionally over-

broad.[67] More than a decade earlier, a similar order requiring everyone, including the media, to "stay away from the jurors" had been struck down by the U.S. Court of Appeals for the Ninth Circuit.[68]

In 1982, the Fifth U.S. Circuit Court of Appeals struck down a trial judge's restriction on post-verdict interviews with jurors who had convicted two men of transporting illegal aliens. The order prohibited interviews without the permission of the court, and permission would be granted only on a showing of "good cause." When a newspaper and its reporter were denied permission to conduct interviews, they appealed to the Fifth Circuit, which declared the order unconstitutional, saying, "The first amendment right to gather news is 'good cause' enough."[69] But a year later the same court upheld a more limited order prohibiting journalists from asking jurors about the votes of their colleagues and from repeatedly attempting to interview jurors who had said they did not want to be interviewed.[70] Sometimes restrictions on juror interviews will be modified or upheld in part by appellate courts in an attempt to balance the interests at stake. For example, in 1994 the Third U.S. Circuit Court of Appeals upheld a trial judge's order informing jurors that they were under no obligation to speak to journalists and banning journalists from asking a juror about the votes or statements of other jurors. The appellate court, however, struck down two other limitations the trial court had tried to impose on journalists: a ban on repeated requests for an interview from any one juror and a requirement that if a juror asks to end an interview the reporter must immediately stop asking questions.[71]

In 1995 two federal district courts in California declared unconstitutional state laws designed to prevent jurors and witnesses from selling their stories to the media. The laws were enacted by the California legislature in response to the publicity surrounding the O.J. Simpson trial. One made it a misdemeanor for a juror or ex-juror to accept a benefit of more than $50 to talk or write about jury service until ninety days after the conclusion of the trial. It also prohibited anyone from paying a juror or ex-juror more than $50 for the juror's story. The other law prohibited crime witnesses from accepting payment for their stories until one year after the crime had occurred or, if a criminal prosecution had begun, until a final verdict was reached.

[65] 830 F.2d 596, 598-99 (6th Cir. 1987)(quoting Freedman and Starwood, "Prior Restraints on Freedom of Expression by Defendants and Defense Attorneys: *Ratio Decidendi v. Obiter Dictum,*" *Stanford Law Review* 29 (1977): 618.

[66] *United States v. Krzyske,* 836 F.2d 1013 (6th Cir.), *cert. denied,* 488 U.S. 832 (1988). See also *Ohio ex rel. Dispatch Printing Co. v. Golden,* 442 N.E.2d 121 (Ohio App. 1982) (striking down a municipal judge's gag order on the defendant as well as members of the defendant's immediate family and counsel).

[67] *Ohio ex rel. Cincinnati Post v. Court of Common Pleas,* 570 N.E.2d 1101 (Ohio 1991).

[68] *United States v. Sherman,* 581 F.2d 1358 (9th Cir. 1978).

[69] *In re Express-News Corp.,* 695 F.2d 807, 810 (5th Cir. 1982).

[70] *United States v. Harrelson,* 713 F.2d 1114 (5th Cir. 1983), *cert. denied,* 465 U.S. 1041 (1984).

[71] *United States v. Antar,* 38 F.3d 1348 (3d Cir. 1994).

Michael Knox, one of the original jurors in the Simpson case who was dismissed part way through the trial, challenged the gag law. Knox wanted to write a book about his experiences as a juror, and the Los Angeles district attorney informed him and his publisher they would be prosecuted if they entered into a publishing agreement in violation of the new California statute. The federal court ruled that the law was a content-based prior restraint and was not narrowly tailored to serve a compelling government interest. Furthermore, the court said the law was unconstitutionally overbroad and vague.[72] In the other case, a coalition of media organizations challenged the witness gag law as unconstitutional. The court agreed, holding the law violated both the U.S. and California constitutions.[73]

Post-Publication Sanctions

Just as the Supreme Court has established constitutional limitations on judges' powers to gag the media, so too has the Court set up First Amendment barriers to post-publication punishment of the press for reporting about and commenting on the operation of the judicial system. Post-publication sanctions can be divided into two categories: contempt of court citations issued by judges and criminal penalties imposed by statutes for the publication of certain types of information.

Contempt of Court. Judges have the power to find people in contempt if they disobey court orders, show disrespect for the court or otherwise engage in conduct that interferes with the administration of justice. A contempt of court citation can result in a fine, imprisonment or both. Generally there are two types of contempt of court: civil and criminal.

A civil contempt citation is intended to be coercive, to force an individual to obey a court order. For example, if a judge orders a reporter to reveal a confidential source and the journalist refuses, the judge might cite the journalist for civil contempt and order the reporter jailed until the source is named. It is also possible that the judge might impose a fine, say $500 per day for as long as the refusal to testify continues. Civil contempt, since it is designed to be coercive not punitive, is not at issue here but is of concern in Chapter 15, which discusses confidential sources.

Criminal contempt, on the other hand, is intended to punish disobedience of a court order or disrespect for or obstruction of the judicial process. If a reporter tries to interview potential jurors during jury selection, for example, the reporter could be held in criminal contempt of court. Or, if a judge issues a gag order prohibiting the media from publishing certain information and a newspaper disobeys that order, the newspaper, the journalists involved or both could be held in criminal contempt and punished. Some judges have used their criminal contempt powers to punish criticism of and commentary about their own actions and the judicial process. But in the 1940s the Supreme Court imposed strict limitations on judges' ability to use contempt to punish critics. The Court ruled that out-of-court commentary could not be punished as contempt of court unless it presented a "clear and present danger" of interfering with the fair administration of justice.

The first such case to reach the Supreme Court was a joinder of two appeals, *Bridges v. California* and *Times Mirror Co. v. Superior Court*.[74] In the first case, labor leader Harry Bridges was held in contempt after he publicly called a judge's ruling in a labor dispute "outrageous" and threatened to tie up the docks on the Pacific coast if the judicial order against him and his union was enforced. In the second case, the *Los Angeles Times* was held in contempt for a series of anti-union editorials, which, the trial court contended, were aimed at influencing judicial decisions in pending labor disputes. Ironically, the Supreme Court used the same opinion to strike down the contempt convictions of both militant labor leader Bridges and the anti-union *Los Angeles Times*.

Writing for a five-member majority, Justice Hugo Black summarily dismissed the argument that judges' contempt powers were an appropriate tool for preserving public respect for the courts. "The assumption that respect for the judiciary can be won by shielding judges from published criticism wrongly appraises the character of American public opinion.... [A]n enforced silence ... would probably engender resentment, suspicion, and contempt more than it would enhance respect." Resurrecting the old "clear and present danger test," which had first been used by the Court in World War I sedition cases,[75] Justice Black said judges could punish commentary on pending cases only if such publications presented an imminent and extremely serious threat to justice.[76]

Just what a formidable obstacle the clear and present danger test presented to judges attempting to punish their critics was demonstrated in 1946 and 1947 when the Supreme Court heard

[72] *Dove Audio v. Lungren,* No. CV 95-2570 RG (JRX), 1995 WL 432631 (C.D. Cal. June 14, 1995).

[73] *California First Amendment Coalition v. Lungren,* No. C 95-0440-FMS, 1995 U.S. Dist. LEXIS 11655 (N.D. Cal. Aug. 9, 1995).

[74] 314 U.S. 252 (1941).

[75] See *Schenck v. United States,* 249 U.S. 47 (1919); *Abrams v. United States,* 250 U.S. 616 (1919).

[76] 314 U.S. at 270-71.

two more contempt cases. In the first, *Pennekamp v. Florida*, the *Miami Herald* and its editor, John D. Pennekamp, were held in contempt and fined for editorials that accused the courts of working harder to protect criminals than to protect law-abiding citizens. This time the Court unanimously struck down the contempt citations, declaring, "Free discussion of the problems of society is a cardinal principle of Americanism — a principle which all are zealous to preserve."[77]

The second case, *Craig v. Harney*, resulted from a contempt citation against the *Corpus Christi Caller-Times* for criticizing a judge who had issued a directed verdict in a civil case. Admitting that the offending articles were unfair and contained significant errors, the Supreme Court said: "But inaccuracies in reporting are commonplace. Certainly a reporter could not be laid by the heels for contempt because he missed the essential point in a trial or failed to summarize the issues to accord with the views of the judge who sat on the case."[78]

Bridges, *Pennekamp* and *Craig* have virtually eliminated the ability of judges to punish criticism of themselves or general commentary on the judicial system. It's important to remember, however, that none of those cases involved efforts to influence jury decisions, disobedience of court orders or in-courtroom disruptions of judicial proceedings. Judges can and do continue to use their contempt powers to punish such conduct, whether the perpetrator is a journalist or not.

State Statutes. It is not unusual for state laws to declare certain information relating to the justice system — such as juvenile offender, adoption and involuntary commitment records — confidential. Such laws generally prohibit government officials from releasing the information to unauthorized individuals, including journalists. Some states, however, have tried to go even further in protecting confidentiality by enacting laws that penalize the media for publishing certain information relating to the courts. In two cases in the 1970s, the Supreme Court ruled such state laws unconstitutional, holding that government could not punish the publication of truthful information that had been lawfully obtained unless there was a compelling need to do so.

In the first case the *Virginia Pilot* was fined $500 for violating a state statute that made it a crime to publish information about the confidential proceedings of the Virginia Judicial Inquiry and Review Commission. The commission, established to hear complaints about judges' misconduct or disabilities, conducted its proceed-

ings in secret to encourage the public to file complaints and to protect judges from the reputational harm that could result from unwarranted complaints. The *Virginia Pilot* identified a judge who was being investigated and accurately reported that the commission had not filed a formal complaint against the judge. Acknowledging that the commission could meet in secret and keep its records confidential, a unanimous Supreme Court said in *Landmark Communications v. Virginia* that imposing criminal sanctions on the publication of such information, which "lies near the core of the First Amendment," was unconstitutional.[79]

The following year the Court struck down a West Virginia statute that made it a crime for newspapers to publish the names of youths charged as juvenile offenders unless they first obtained written approval from the juvenile court. Two Charleston newspapers were indicted for identifying a 16-year-old who had shot and killed a 15-year-old classmate. The name of the youth was obtained through interviews with witnesses, the police and an assistant prosecuting attorney. Once again the Supreme Court unanimously ruled in favor of the press. The newspapers had argued that the statute imposed a prior restraint on publication since it required a judge's permission to publish a juvenile's name. In *Smith v. Daily Mail Publishing Co.* the Supreme Court said it didn't matter whether the law was labeled a prior restraint or not since "First Amendment protection reaches beyond prior restraints."[80]

Relying on its decision the previous year in *Landmark Communications*, the Court said that publication of lawfully obtained, truthful information could be punished only "to further a state interest of the highest order." While protecting the anonymity of juvenile offenders to enhance their chances of rehabilitation was an important interest, the Court said it was not sufficient to justify the infringement of First Amendment rights caused by imposing criminal sanctions for the publication of true information. The Court noted that while every state had a law providing for the confidentiality of juvenile proceedings, only five states "impose criminal penalties on nonparties for publication of the identity of the juvenile." Finally, the Court said the statute didn't even accomplish its goal since it only punished newspaper publication of juveniles' names. Radio stations in the area had broadcast the youth's name but were not indicted because the statute did not prohibit broadcasts.[81]

---

[77] 328 U.S. 331, 346 (1946).
[78] 331 U.S. 367, 374-75 (1947).

---

[79] 435 U.S. 829, 839 (1978).
[80] 443 U.S. 97, 101 (1979).
[81] *Id.* at 103-05. Since *Smith v. Daily Mail*, at least two other state laws prohibiting the publication of juvenile offenders' names have

Court Closures

As noted, the Supreme Court in *Sheppard v. Maxwell* did not suggest that gag orders on the press be used as a remedy for prejudicial publicity. Nor did the Court suggest closing the courtroom door to the press and public. In fact, in *Sheppard* the Court specifically reiterated its antipathy toward judicial secrecy:

> The principle that justice cannot survive behind walls of silence has long been reflected in the "Anglo-American distrust for secret trials." ... The press does not simply publish information about trials but guards against the miscarriage of justice by subjecting the police, prosecutors, and judicial processes to extensive public scrutiny and criticism. This Court has, therefore, been unwilling to place any direct limitations on the freedom traditionally exercised by the news media for "[w]hat transpires in the court room is public property."[82]

But, like gag orders, court closures became popular tools with some judges seeking to avoid the problems they believed were caused by media coverage of trials. A study by the Reporters Committee for Freedom of the Press identified sixty-one instances of closures of court proceedings or records between 1967 and 1975. As with gag orders in that same period, the number of recorded closures steadily climbed, reaching a peak of twenty-five in 1975.[83] The 1976 report of the Twentieth Century Fund's Task Force on Justice, Publicity and the First Amendment lamented judges' "excessive reliance on secrecy" in the years following *Sheppard*.[84]

Criminal Trials. In 1980, however, the Supreme Court began limiting the ability of judges to shut off access to their courtrooms by ruling in *Richmond Newspapers v. Virginia* that the press and public had a First Amendment right to attend criminal trials.[85] It may seem odd that the Court used the First Amendment's guarantee of freedom of the press as a source of access rights, especially since the Sixth Amendment specifically provides for public

trials. However, the Court had earlier ruled that the Sixth Amendment's guarantee of a public trial, like its other guarantees of a speedy trial by an impartial jury in the district in which the crime was committed, was a right that was personal to the defendant.[86] If the defendant agreed to give up his constitutional right to a public trial, then the press or members of the public could not claim a Sixth Amendment violation.

In 1978 John Paul Stevenson, charged with murdering a hotel manager, waived his right to a public trial. The prosecutor said he had no objections to closure; so Hanover County, Virginia, Circuit Court Judge Richard Taylor agreed to conduct the trial behind closed doors. It's easy to understand why Stevenson's attorney moved to close the trial and why Judge Taylor and the prosecution agreed. This was to be Stevenson's fourth trial on the same charge. The Virginia Supreme Court had overturned his 1976 conviction because of the use of inadmissible evidence. A second trial ended in a mistrial when one of the jurors had to be excused for illness and no alternate was available. A third trial, which Judge Taylor also agreed to close, ended in a mistrial when one prospective juror told others about Stevenson's previous trials.

After Judge Taylor ordered the fourth trial closed, Richmond Newspapers protested and asked for a hearing, which Judge Taylor conducted in secret. At the conclusion of the hearing, Taylor stuck by his decision that the extraordinary circumstances justified a closed trial. The next day Judge Taylor dismissed the jury, ruled the state had not presented sufficient evidence to justify a guilty verdict and declared Stevenson not guilty. The decision was reported in a two-sentence order, and, since the trial had been conducted behind closed doors, there was no way for the public to determine if Judge Taylor's conclusion was justified.

Richmond Newspapers appealed the trial closure to the Virginia Supreme Court, which refused to overturn Judge Taylor's decision. The U.S. Supreme Court, however, ruled 7-1 that the closure was unconstitutional. (Justice Lewis Powell, a Virginian, did not participate in the decision because he was acquainted with some of the people involved in the case.) As in *Nebraska Press Association*, the justices in *Richmond Newspapers* were divided over their reasoning. The majority of seven produced six different opinions, with no opinion garnering the endorsement of more than three justices.

Chief Justice Burger, joined by Justices White and Stevens, rested his opinion on the history and tradition of open trials in the Anglo-American justice system. Contending that trials had been open "to all who care to observe" since before the Norman

---

been declared unconstitutional. *Florida Publishing Co. v. Morgan,* 322 S.E.2d 233 (Ga. 1984); *In re Johnson,* 5 Media L. Rep. (BNA) 2512 (S.C. Fam. Ct. 1980).

[82] 384 U.S. at 349-50 (citations omitted) (quoting *In re Oliver,* 333 U.S. 257, 268 (1948) and *Craig v. Harney,* 331 U.S. 367, 374 (1947)).

[83] Landau, *supra* note 24, at 57.

[84] *Twentieth Century Fund Task Force on Justice, Publicity, and the First Amendment, supra* note 26, at 5.

[85] 448 U.S. 555 (1980).

[86] *Gannett Co., Inc. v. DePasquale,* 443 U.S. 368 (1979).

Conquest, Burger said open trials discourage perjury and official misconduct, inspire public confidence in the justice system, and have "significant community therapeutic value," helping to defuse community outrage over crime. Although the First Amendment contains no express language regarding access to criminal proceedings, Burger wrote that the guarantees of freedom of speech and press and the rights to assemble and petition the government all "share a common core purpose of assuring freedom of communication on matters relating to the functioning of government. Plainly it would be difficult to single out any aspect of government of higher concern and importance to the people than the manner in which criminal trials are conducted." The public right of access to a criminal trial could be overcome only by "an overriding interest," Burger concluded, and only if the trial judge finds that "alternative solutions" are inadequate to ensure fairness. The Chief Justice expressly declined to provide examples of overriding interests that might justify closure, saying Judge Taylor had "made no findings to support closure [and] no inquiry ... as to whether alternative solutions would have met the need to ensure fairness."[87]

In a concurring opinion, which later became very influential in the development of a test for determining when courtrooms could be closed, Justice Brennan, joined by Justice Marshall, stressed the structural value of open courts, that is, the role openness plays in self-government. "[P]ublic access to trials acts as an important check, akin in purpose to the other checks and balances that infuse our system of government," Brennan wrote. Open trials, he said, "play a fundamental role" in ensuring defendants receive fair trials and in assuring the public that "procedural rights are respected, and that justice is afforded equally. Closed trials breed suspicion of prejudice and arbitrariness, which in turn spawns disrespect for law."[88]

Two years after *Richmond Newspapers*, the Supreme Court ruled 6-3 that a blanket rule requiring courtroom closure during the testimony of minor victims in sex crime cases violated the First Amendment.[89] The case began in 1979 when a trial judge in Norfolk County, Massachusetts, closed the trial of a man charged with raping three girls, two sixteen-year-olds and one seventeen-year-old. The judge relied on a state statute, which he interpreted as mandating closure of the entire trial. On appeal, the Supreme Judicial Court of Massachusetts interpreted the statute more narrowly than the trial judge, holding that it only required closure during the testimony of minor sex crime victims. The *Boston Globe* appealed to the Supreme Court.

Writing for the majority in *Globe Newspaper Co. v. Superior Court*, Justice Brennan said that closure of criminal trials had to be determined case by case on the basis of a "compelling governmental interest" and had to be "narrowly tailored to serve that interest." While Brennan conceded that protecting "minor victims of sex crimes from further trauma and embarrassment" was a compelling interest, it did not justify a *mandatory* closure law since such a measure was not narrowly tailored. Case-by-case determinations were needed to consider such factors as "the minor victim's age, psychological maturity and understanding, the nature of the crime, the desires of the victim, and the interests of parents and relatives." Brennan questioned the state's second justification for the law — that closure encouraged minor victims to come forward and testify — because there was no empirical evidence to support the claim that mandatory closure accomplished that goal. Furthermore, since trial transcripts were open to the public, there was no way to guarantee a victim's testimony would remain secret.[90]

In a dissenting opinion, Chief Justice Burger focused again on history, contending, "There is clearly a long history of exclusion of the public from trials involving sexual assaults, particularly those against minors." Because a transcript of the trial was publicly available, Burger argued, the Massachusetts law did not deny the press or public access to information. Therefore, the Chief Justice contended that the only questions were "whether the restrictions imposed are reasonable and whether the interests of the Commonwealth override the very limited incidental effects of the law on First Amendment rights." Closing a trial during a child victim's testimony rationally served the state's interest, Burger concluded.[91]

Continuing the trend of opening up the nation's courtrooms to the press and public, the Supreme Court ruled in 1984 that jury selection is an integral part of a criminal trial and, therefore, is subject to the First Amendment presumption of access. *Press-Enterprise Co. v. Riverside County Superior Court* (which is known as *Press-Enterprise I* to distinguish it from a later case of the same name) began when a California trial judge closed almost six weeks of the *voir dire* — jury selection proceedings — in a rape and murder trial involving a teenage victim. After the defendant was convicted and sentenced to death, the judge still refused to release the transcript of the *voir dire*, saying that "some of the jurors had some special experiences in sensitive areas that do not appear to be appropriate for public discussion."[92] After failing to

[87] 448 U.S. at 564-81.
[88] *Id.* at 595-96 (Brennan, J., concurring).
[89] *Globe Newspaper Co. v. Superior Court,* 457 U.S. 596 (1982).
[90] *Id.* at 607-10.
[91] *Id.* at 614-16 (Burger, C.J., dissenting).
[92] 464 U.S. 501, 504 (1984).

obtain relief from the California appellate courts, the *Press-Enterprise* petitioned the Supreme Court to grant *certiorari*, which it did.

The Court unanimously ruled that closure of the *voir dire* violated the First Amendment. Chief Justice Burger, who wrote the opinion of the Court, used both the historical arguments he had articulated in *Richmond Newspapers* and the structural/functional arguments of Justice Brennan. The "historical evidence," wrote Burger, indicates that "since the development of trial by jury, the process of selection of jurors has presumptively been a public process with exceptions only for good cause shown." As for the functional argument, Burger said: "The open trial thus plays as important a role in the administration of justice today as it did for centuries before our separation from England.... Openness ... enhances both the basic fairness of the criminal trial and the appearance of fairness so essential to public confidence in the system."[93]

Just as Justice Brennan had held in *Globe Newspaper Co.*, the Chief Justice in *Press-Enterprise I* wrote that the presumption of open *voir dire* proceedings "may be overcome only by an overriding interest based on findings that closure is essential to preserve higher values and is narrowly tailored to serve that interest." Furthermore, the trial judge must present specific, written findings to justify closure and demonstrate that alternatives to closure are not available to protect the interests at stake. In this case, the trial judge failed to present findings supporting his conclusion that closure was necessary to protect the defendant's fair trial rights and the jurors' privacy rights. Furthermore, the judge "failed to consider whether alternatives were available to protect the interests of the prospective jurors."[94]

Other Criminal Proceedings. In its latest courtroom access case, the Supreme Court extended the First Amendment presumption of openness to a criminal pretrial proceeding, specifically a preliminary hearing. In some states a preliminary hearing is known as a show-cause hearing; it is designed to determine if the government has sufficient evidence to bind a defendant over for trial. The 1986 case *Press-Enterprise v. Riverside County Superior Court*, generally known as *Press-Enterprise II*, resulted from the closure of a forty-one-day preliminary hearing in the case of Robert Diaz, a nurse accused of murdering twelve patients by administering massive doses of a heart drug.[95] The case required the Court to determine whether the constitutional right of access to criminal

trials extended to other types of judicial proceedings as well.

As he had in *Press-Enterprise I*, Chief Justice Burger, writing for the majority, combined the historical justifications he relied upon in *Richmond Newspapers* with Justice Brennan's concern for the structural value of openness to establish a two-pronged test for deciding when a constitutional right of access attaches to a particular type of judicial proceeding.

The preliminary hearing at issue in *Press-Enterprise II* passed the so-called test "of experience and logic." First, the Court said, "there has been a tradition of accessibility to preliminary hearings of the type conducted in California," and second, "preliminary hearings are sufficiently like a trial" to justify the conclusion that openness was necessary for the proper functioning of the process. Burger noted that the preliminary hearing was often the "final and most important" criminal proceeding since so few cases proceed to trial and, therefore, often presented the only opportunity for the public to observe the criminal justice system. Furthermore, the absence of a jury at a preliminary hearing made public and press attendance even more important to protect "against the corrupt or overzealous prosecutor and against the compliant, biased, or eccentric judge."[96]

Deciding that a First Amendment right of access attached to the preliminary hearing was only the first step in the analysis, however, since, as the Court had noted in all of its previous cases, that right was a qualified one and could be overcome by an overriding or compelling interest. A trial judge, therefore, before closing such a proceeding must provide "specific, on the record findings" that "closure is essential to preserve higher values and is narrowly tailored to serve that interest." Furthermore, the Court said that if the overriding interest to be served by closure was the defendant's right to a fair trial, a judge had to find that there was "a substantial probability" of prejudice resulting from an open proceeding, closure would prevent the harm and reasonable alternatives to closure would not protect the defendant's rights.[97]

The closure test articulated by the Court in *Press-Enterprise II* is similar to the gag order test the Court used in *Nebraska Press Association*, both emphasizing the judge's responsibility to evaluate the effectiveness of the order and to try all other alternatives before infringing on the First Amendment rights of the press and public. A few recent court closure cases demonstrate how the *Press-Enterprise II* test has been applied.

In 1989 a federal magistrate in Charlotte, North Carolina, agreed

---

[93] *Id*. at 505, 508.
[94] *Id*. at 510-11.
[95] 478 U.S. 1 (1986).

[96] *Id*. at 10-13 (quoting *Duncan v. Louisiana*, 391 U.S. 145, 156 (1968)).
[97] *Id*. at 13-14 (quoting *Press-Enterprise I*, 464 U.S. at 510).

When Can a Judicial Proceeding Be Closed?

A judge must apply a specific path to determine whether a judicial proceeding may be closed.

First, the judge must determine whether a First Amendment right of access attaches to the proceeding. The Supreme Court has held that there is a right of access to criminal trials and preliminary hearings, but if a judge is evaluating a closure motion for a different type of proceeding, the judge must consider

1. whether the proceeding has been open to the public historically (the experience test); and,

2. whether public access plays a significant positive role in the functioning of the particular proceeding in question (the logic test).

Second, if the judge decides, as a result of the experience and logic tests, that a right of access exists, the judge must determine whether that right can be overcome by a compelling interest. To close the courtroom, the judge must issue specific, written findings that

1. closure is essential to preserve higher values, such as the defendant's fair trial rights or jurors' or victims' privacy rights; and

2. the closure is narrowly tailored, that is, as brief as possible to serve the interest.

Third, if the overriding interest justifying closure is the defendant's right to a fair trial, the judge must find that

1. there is a substantial probability that an open proceeding will interfere with that right;

2. closure will be effective in protecting the right; and

3. there are no reasonable alternatives to closure.

---

to close a pretrial change of venue hearing in the well-publicized fraud case involving televangelist Jim Bakker and his partner in the PTL religious organization, Richard Dortch. Attorneys for Bakker and Dortch had sought the change of venue claiming adverse pretrial publicity in the Charlotte area. The magistrate closed the hearing, stating that "permitting the public and press to attend this hearing would pose the risk that the alleged prejudicial publicity of which the Defendants complain would be republished and re-aired in the print and electronic media."[98] Such republication would impair the defendants' right to a fair trial, the magistrate concluded. The chief federal judge for the Western District of North Carolina affirmed the magistrate's order.

A number of media organizations appealed to the Fourth Circuit, which declared the closure unconstitutional. As for the first part of the closure test — determining if a right of access attaches to the particular type of proceeding at issue — the appeals court, citing *Press Enterprise II*, simply assumed that there was a presumptive right of access to all criminal trial and pretrial proceedings, including change of venue hearings. Since the compelling interest to be served by closure was the defendants' fair trial rights, the Fourth Circuit jumped to the last portion of the *Press-Enterprise II* test and evaluated, first, whether there was a substantial probability that an open hearing would prejudice the defendants' rights and, second, whether closure would prevent the harm. The court said it was "highly dubious" that "republication of portions of publicity earlier put in the public domain" would cause the defendants' rights to be "decisively prejudiced" beyond the harm already done by the initial publications. More importantly, the court said the magistrate "was simply wrong in thinking that, as a practical matter, closure would prevent that result.... [A]ny press barrage and frenzy occasioned by an open hearing would be as nothing to the firestorms of purely speculative 'republications' that would occur if press access to the hearing is denied." Finally, the court said the magistrate gave "too short shrift" to alternatives to closure, especially *voir dire*. Several highly publicized cases, such as the Watergate, ABSCAM and John DeLorean trials, had demonstrated that juries were "unaffected (indeed, in some instances, blissfully unaware of or untouched) by that publicity," the court wrote.[99]

In another highly publicized case, the Ninth U.S. Circuit Court of Appeals ruled in 1988 that closure of a pretrial detention hearing violated the First Amendment.[100] Stella Nickell was charged with murdering her husband and a woman whom she did not know by placing poison in Excedrin capsules on store shelves to make her husband's death look like a random product-tampering murder. The detention hearing was to determine whether Nickell would be released pending her trial.

Applying the first portion of the *Press-Enterprise II* test, the Ninth Circuit acknowledged that pretrial detention hearings were relatively new proceedings, and, thus, there was no history of public access. However, the court said the structural arguments in favor of openness were sufficient to support a constitutional right of access to the proceeding. The court then concluded that there was inadequate evidence that an open detention hearing would

---

[98] *In re Charlotte Observer*, 882 F.2d 850, 851 (4th Cir. 1989).

[99] *Id.* at 852-55.

[100] *Seattle Times v. U.S. Dist. Court*, 845 F.2d 1513 (9th Cir. 1988).

prejudice Nickell's right to a fair trial and that the trial judge had not sufficiently considered alternatives to closure.

Based on both the First Amendment right of access and a state constitutional provision guaranteeing open courts, a North Carolina trial court in 1994 refused to close pretrial evidence suppression hearings in the case resulting from the murder of Michael Jordan's father, James Jordan.[101] Evidence-suppression hearings present special problems since their sole purpose is to determine whether certain evidence will ever be presented to a jury. If evidence, say an allegedly coerced confession or the results of an allegedly illegal wiretap, is declared inadmissible during a public hearing, the media are still free to report on its existence. The fear, then, is that potential jurors will learn about the evidence, remember it and perhaps be influenced by it even though it was never used in court.

On the other hand, evidentiary hearings are often crucial to the outcome of a criminal case because they can determine the strength of the prosecution's case. If, for example, a judge refuses to suppress a particularly damaging piece of evidence, such as a confession or the results of certain laboratory tests, the case against the defendant may be so strong that he or she decides to plead guilty and no trial is ever held. Furthermore, evidentiary hearings often deal with allegations of police and prosecutorial misconduct, which are important to bring to public attention.

In 1979 the Supreme Court held that the Sixth Amendment did not provide the press and public with a right to attend pretrial evidence suppression hearings.[102] That case, however, preceded *Richmond Newspapers* and was based not on the First Amendment but on the Sixth Amendment. Since the Supreme Court began articulating a broad First Amendment right of access to judicial proceedings, many lower courts have reached the same conclusion as the North Carolina trial court in the James Jordan murder case and have recognized a constitutional right of access to pretrial evidentiary hearings.[103]

Courts have also held that a constitutional right of access attaches to numerous other types of criminal proceedings, including plea and sentencing hearings,[104] bail hearings,[105] a post-trial examination of jurors about potential misconduct,[106] a hearing on a motion to compel a defendant to give a blood sample for an HIV test[107] and a hearing on a criminal defendant's recusal motion (asking the judge to remove himself from the case).[108] However, some types of criminal proceedings, most notably grand jury proceedings, have historically been conducted behind closed doors, and the First Amendment presumption of openness has never applied.

Juvenile Proceedings. Juvenile proceedings have also traditionally been closed to the public. The primary goal of the juvenile justice system is rehabilitation rather than punishment, and, therefore, state laws often provide for closed hearings and confidential records to avoid stigmatizing minors by making their identities and crimes known to the public. Sometimes reporters are allowed to cover juvenile proceedings on the condition that they not identify the youths involved.

The Supreme Court has not ruled on whether the First Amendment right of access applies to juvenile proceedings. However, because there is a history of secrecy associated with juvenile proceedings and because many people who work with juvenile offenders believe that confidentiality plays an important role in rehabilitation, several courts have held that the First Amendment right of access does not apply to such proceedings. For example, in 1981 the Vermont Supreme Court flatly declared, "[A] juvenile proceeding is so unlike a criminal prosecution that the limited right of access described in *Richmond Newspapers* does not govern."[109]

On the other hand, several courts have found a constitutional right of public and press access to juvenile proceedings — either

---

[101] *North Carolina v. Demery*, 22 Media L. Rep. (BNA) 2383 (N.C. Super. Ct. 1994).

[102] *Gannett Co. v. DePasquale*, 443 U.S. 368 (1979).

[103] See, e.g., *United States v. Klepfer*, 734 F.2d 93 (2d Cir. 1984); *Gannett Westchester Rockland Newspapers v. Lacava*, 18 Media L. Rep. (BNA) 1397 (N.Y. App. Div. 1990); *New York v. Franklin*, 22 Media L. Rep. (BNA) 1255 (N.Y. Crim. Ct. 1993); *Ohio v. Nobles*, 21 Media L. Rep. (BNA) 1500 (Ohio Ct. Cm. Pls. 1993).

[104] *United States v. Eppinger*, 49 F.3d 1244 (7th Cir. 1995); *United States v. Soussoudis*, 807 F.2d 383 (4th Cir. 1986); *United States v. Byrd*, 812 F. Supp. 76 (D.C.S.C. 1992); *Baltimore Sun Co. v. Colbert*, 593 A.2d 224 (Md. 1991); *New York Times v. Demakos*, 529 N.Y.S.2d 97 (App. Div. 1988); *Washington v. Campbell*, 21 Media L. Rep. (BNA) 1895 (Wash. Super. Ct. 1993).

[105] *In re Globe Newspaper Co.*, 729 F.2d 47 (1st Cir. 1984); *United States v. Chagra*, 701 F.2d 354 (5th Cir. 1983).

[106] *United States v. Simone*, 14 F.3d 833 (3d Cir. 1994). But see *United States v. Edwards*, 823 F.2d 111 (5th Cir. 1987).

[107] *Florida v. Jenkins*, 21 Media L. Rep. (BNA) 2159 (Fla. Cir. Ct. 1993).

[108] *Glen Falls Newspapers, Inc. v. Berke*, 614 N.Y.S.2d 628 (App. Div. 1994).

[109] *In re J.S.*, 438 A.2d 1125, 1128 (Vt. 1981). See also *In re T.R.*, 556 N.E.2d 439 (Ohio), *cert. denied*, 498 U.S. 958 (1990); *Sherman Publishing Co. v. Goldberg*, 443 A.2d 1252 (R.I. 1982); *In re N.H.B.*, 769 P.2d 844 (Utah App. 1989).

based on the First Amendment or on state constitutional provisions. In 1995, for example, the Tennessee Supreme Court ruled that the public has a qualified First Amendment right to attend the hearings at which juvenile court judges determine whether youths charged with crimes will be transferred to adult court for trial.[110] And both the Oregon and South Carolina supreme courts have interpreted their state constitutions to provide a qualified right of access to juvenile proceedings.[111]

State statutes are also becoming an increasingly important source of access rights. A 1996 study found that during the preceding decade, thirteen state legislatures had amended their statutes to allow greater public access to juvenile proceedings.[112] The study also reported that in seven states all juvenile hearings are presumptively open to the public;[113] in one state, Kansas, all adjudicatory (but not pretrial) hearings for juveniles sixteen and older are open; in twelve states hearings are open when juveniles are charged with certain serious or violent crimes;[114] and in seven states statutes provide that a judge "may" admit the public at his or her discretion.[115] Statutes in twenty-one states still declare juvenile proceedings presumptively closed.[116] However, in two of those states, Virginia and Wisconsin, a juvenile may request a public hearing, and in all the others except New Hampshire judges can grant public access at their discretion.

While state courts hear the vast majority of juvenile cases, under certain circumstances specified in the Federal Juvenile Delinquency Act, federal courts can conduct juvenile proceedings.[117] In recent years, judges have disagreed over whether juvenile proceedings in U.S. district courts should be open to the news media and the public. In April 1994, a U.S. district judge in Wisconsin ruled that the Act did not prohibit the media from attending juvenile hearings as long as the juvenile's confidentiality was protected.[118] In July 1994, the Third U.S. Circuit Court of Appeals reached a similar conclusion, stating that juvenile proceedings "are closely analogous to criminal proceedings, and all the public interests in criminal proceedings ... seem present and equally cogent here."[119] Then, on September 8, 1994, two federal district courts issued contradictory rulings in two separate cases. The U.S. District Court for the Eastern District of New York ruled that the proceeding must be open absent a specific need for closure[120] while the U.S. District Court for Massachusetts held that the Federal Juvenile Delinquency Act required a closed proceeding.[121] The latter decision was upheld by the First Circuit Court of Appeals, which said it was "highly dubious" that a First Amendment right of access existed, "particularly in light of the long, entrenched, and well-founded tradition of confidentiality regarding juvenile proceedings, and the compelling rehabilitative purposes behind this tradition."[122] The Supreme Court denied *certiorari*, there-by leaving standing the contradictory rulings of the lower federal courts.

Civil Proceedings. Although the Supreme Court has not expressly ruled that civil trials are subject to the same First Amendment right of access as criminal proceedings, numerous lower courts, both state and federal, have held that the press and public enjoy a right of access to civil judicial proceedings. Some courts have based this right of access on the First Amendment, following the reasoning articulated by the Supreme Court in *Richmond Newspapers* and its progeny; others have found a common law basis for access; and still others have used a combination of constitutional and common law.

One of the most frequently cited cases involving access to civil proceedings is *Publicker Industries v. Cohen*, decided by the U.S. Court of Appeals for the Third Circuit in 1984. Reporters for the *Philadelphia Inquirer* and *Wall Street Journal* appealed when

---

[110] *Tennessee v. James,* 905 S.W.2d 911 (Tenn. 1995). See also *Florida Publishing Co. v. Morgan,* 322 S.E.2d 233 (Ga. 1984).

[111] *Oregonian Publishing v. Deiz,* 613 P.2d 23 (Ore. 1980); *Ex parte Columbia Newspapers, Inc.,* 333 S.E.2d 337 (S.C. 1985).

[112] Thomas A. Hughes, "Opening the Door of Juvenile Court: Is There an Emerging Right of Public Access?" at 20 (Aug. 10, 1996) (a paper presented to the AEJMC Law Division, Anaheim, Calif.). The thirteen states were Arizona, California, Georgia, Indiana, Louisiana, Massachusetts, Michigan, Minnesota, Missouri, Nevada, North Dakota, Texas and Utah.

[113] Colorado, Florida, Michigan, Montana, Nevada, New Mexico and Texas.

[114] Arizona, California, Delaware, Georgia, Indiana, Louisiana, Maine, Massachusetts, Minnesota, Missouri, North Dakota and Utah.

[115] Arkansas, Iowa, Maryland, New York, North Carolina, Ohio and Tennessee.

[116] Alabama, Alaska, Connecticut, Hawaii, Idaho, Illinois, Kentucky, Mississippi, New Hampshire, New Jersey, Oklahoma, Pennsylvania, Rhode Island, South Carolina, South Dakota, Vermont, Virginia, Washington, West Virginia, Wisconsin and Wyoming. According to the study, two states, Nebraska and Oregon, do not have juvenile court statutes.

[117] 18 U.S.C. § 5032 (1994).

[118] *United States v. Doe,* 22 Media L. Rep. (BNA) 1693 (E.D. Wis. 1994).

[119] *United States v. A.D.,* 28 F.3d 1353, 1358 (3d Cir. 1994).

[120] *United States v. Nelson,* 22 Media L. Rep. 2320 (E.D.N.Y. 1994).

[121] *United States v. Three Juveniles,* 862 F. Supp. 651 (D. Mass. 1994).

[122] *United States v. Three Juveniles,* 61 F.3d 86, 90 (1st Cir. 1995).

they were denied access to hearings in a lawsuit resulting from a corporate proxy fight. The Third Circuit recognized both a constitutional and a common law right of access to civil proceedings, saying that "the public's right of access to civil trials and records is as well established as that of criminal proceedings and records."[123] Other courts have followed the Third Circuit's lead, finding a right of access to an array of civil proceedings.[124]

Not every type of civil proceeding, however, is open to the press and public. Like grand jury and juvenile proceedings, some types of civil hearings traditionally have been closed and remain closed under state statutes. Involuntary commitment and adoption proceedings are two of the most commonly closed types of civil proceedings. And, just as with criminal proceedings, judges sometimes find that even when a right of access exists for a particular type of civil proceeding, that right can be overcome by a compelling interest as long as the closure is narrowly tailored to serve that interest. Two of the most common interests used to justify closing civil proceedings are preventing the disclosure of trade secrets and protecting individual privacy, especially if the litigation involves a child.[125]

Civil discovery proceedings have also generated several access lawsuits in recent years. Discovery is the pretrial phase of a lawsuit during which the litigants attempt to collect the information they need from one another and from third party witnesses. Traditionally, discovery in civil litigation has not been open to the press and public. In fact, it is usually conducted in attorneys' offices rather than in public courthouses. Because there is no history of public access and because so much of the information gathered during discovery never becomes part of the official court record, judges often rule that there is no right of access to the discovery sessions during which depositions are taken. There have been exceptions, however. In one case a federal district judge held that representa-

tives of the media should be allowed to attend sessions when depositions from the mayor of New York and a former police commissioner were being taken in connection with a lawsuit against the city. Because of the great public interest in the case, the court ruled that four journalists be admitted to serve as pool representatives for the rest of the press.[126]

If You're Denied Access. As the above discussion demonstrates, the test developed in *Press-Enterprise I* and *II* presents a formidable obstacle to justifying courtroom closures. Nonetheless, parties involved in both criminal and civil cases continue to ask for closed proceedings, and, occasionally, trial judges acquiesce. Therefore, it is important that journalists be familiar with their First Amendment rights of access and be prepared and willing to protest closure motions. When faced with a motion to close a judicial proceeding, a reporter should raise his or her hand, stand, identify himself or herself to the court, formally object to the closure motion and request a hearing at which the news operation's attorney can appear. Many news media and state press associations have prepared cards containing the statement journalists should make if they are faced with a threatened court closure. Here's the statement the North Carolina Press Association recommends journalists use:

> Your honor, I respectfully request the opportunity to register on the record an objection to the motion to close this proceeding to the public, including the press. Our legal counsel has advised us that standards set forth in recent U.S. Supreme Court decisions regarding the constitutional right of access to judicial proceedings recognize the right to a hearing before the courtroom is closed. Therefore, I respectfully request such a hearing and a brief continuance so I can call our counsel to come to explain our position.

Of course, the reporter should immediately call an editor so the editor can contact the company's attorney.

Denials of Access to Court Records

In the wake of *Richmond Newspapers v. Virginia*, many lower courts have presumed that the First Amendment right of access to

---

123 733 F.2d 1059, 1066 (3d Cir. 1984).

124 See, e.g., *Newman v. Graddick*, 696 F.2d 796 (11th Cir. 1983)(pretrial and post-trial hearings in a class action suit charging overcrowding in a state prison); *Barron v. Florida Freedom Newspapers, Inc.*, 531 So. 2d 113 (Fla. 1988)(divorce proceeding); *In re Brown*, 18 Media L. Rep. (BNA)1460 (Fla. Cir. Ct. 1990)(child custody hearing); *Bingham v. Struve*, 20 Media L. Rep. (BNA) 2226 (N.Y. App. Div. 1992) (libel trial); *Hutchinson v. Luddy*, 18 Media L. Rep. (BNA) 1071 (Pa. Super. Ct. 1990) (pretrial proceedings in a civil suit against a Catholic priest charged with sexual misconduct).

125 See, e.g., *Woven Electronic Corp. v. Advance Group Inc.*, 19 Media L. Rep. (BNA) 1019 (4th Cir. 1991); *In re Iowa Freedom of Information Council*, 724 F.2d 658 (8th Cir. 1983); *Morgan v. Foretich*, 528 A.2d 425 (D.C. 1987); and *Milo v. Milo*, 6 Media L. Rep. (BNA) 2524 (Ohio Ct. C.P. 1981).

126 *Estate of Rosenbaum v. New York City*, 21 Media L. Rep. (BNA) 1987 (E.D.N.Y. 1993). See also *United States v. Didrichsons*, 15 Media L. Rep. (BNA) 1869 (W.D. Wash. 1988); *Avirgan v. Hull*, 14 Media L. Rep. (BNA) 2136 (D.C.D.C. 1987).

court proceedings extends to the documents filed in connection with those proceedings. Indeed, the Supreme Court in deciding *Press Enterprise I* and *II* didn't distinguish between access to a judicial proceeding itself and access to at least one type of court record — the transcript of the proceeding. In *Press Enterprise II*, Chief Justice Burger wrote, "Denying the transcript of a 41-day preliminary hearing would frustrate what we have characterized as the 'community therapeutic value' of openness."[127]

The Constitution, however, is not the only source of a right of access to court records. Many states have statutes providing for public access to judicial documents.[128] In addition, a common law right of access to judicial records has long been recognized by both state and federal courts. Two years before it decided *Richmond Newspapers*, the Supreme Court, in *Nixon v. Warner Communications, Inc.*, acknowledged that the common law created a "presumption ... of access to judicial records."[129]

Courts have ruled that this general right of access applies to a wide array of both criminal and civil court records. For example, in 1988 the Ninth Circuit Court of Appeals held that the pretrial motions and documents filed in the John DeLorean drug prosecution had to be available to the press and public. "There is no reason to distinguish between pretrial proceedings and the documents filed in regard to them," the court declared in finding a constitutional right of access.[130] The same court also ruled that there is a right of access to post-conviction records, including presentencing reports and post-sentencing documents filed in connection with a motion to reduce a sentence.[131] In civil cases, courts have found a right of access to pleadings, documents filed in connection with pretrial motions, summary judgment papers and settlement agreements.[132]

Some types of court records, however, are not generally available to the press and public. For example, grand jury proceedings are closed, as are most grand jury records, including transcripts and evidence. However, when a grand jury hands down an indictment, that becomes a public record although sometimes a court is allowed to seal an indictment until an arrest has been made. Adoption and involuntary commitment records are other types of documents that are often declared confidential by state law and, therefore, not available to the press and public.

Juvenile Records. Just as access to juvenile proceedings is in a state of flux, so, too, is access to juvenile court records. State laws often provide for the sealing of juvenile records. However, during the past decade several courts have recognized at least a qualified right of access to juvenile records.[133] Sometimes judges allow the press access to redacted versions of juveniles records in which the names have been omitted. For example, in one of the cases involving the Federal Juvenile Delinquency Act discussed above, the judge prohibited access to proceedings but did permit release of records that had been edited to hide the identities of the juvenile defendants.[134]

Discovery Documents. As previously indicated, access to civil discovery has become an area of controversy in recent years. Journalists and members of the public not only have sought to be present during the actual taking of depositions but also have tried to obtain access to deposition transcripts and documents obtained as part of discovery. They have enjoyed the most success when seeking access to discovery documents that have been filed with a court but are less likely to be granted access to unfiled materials.

A 1988 D.C. Court of Appeals case, *Mokhiber v. Davis*, illustrates the distinction well. Russell Mokhiber, an investigative reporter, sought access to a variety of discovery documents from a civil lawsuit that had been settled four years earlier. The court held that Mokhiber had no right to see discovery materials that had never been submitted to the court but did have a right of access to "papers submitted to the court for decision," including papers

---

[127] 478 U.S. at 13.

[128] See "Judicial Records: A Guide to Access in State & Federal Courts," *News Media & the Law,* Summer 1995.

[129] 435 U.S. 589, 602 (1978).

[130] *Associated Press v. U.S. Dist. Court,* 705 F.2d 1143, 1145 (9th Cir. 1983).

[131] *United States v. Schlette,* 842 F.2d 1574 (9th Cir. 1988); *CBS v. U.S. Dist. Court,* 765 F.2d 823 (9th Cir. 1985).

[132] *Leucadia, Inc. v. Applied Extrusion Technologies, Inc.,* 998 F.2d 157 (3d Cir. 1993); *Rushford v. New Yorker Magazine, Inc.,* 846 F.2d 249 (4th Cir. 1988); *Bank of Am. Nat'l Trust & Sav. Ass'n v. Hotel Rittenhouse Assocs.,* 800 F.2d 339 (3d Cir. 1986); *Resolution Trust Corp. v. Dean,* 854 F. Supp. 626 (D. Ariz. 1994); *Soc'y of Professional Journalists v. Briggs,* 675 F. Supp. 1308 (D. Utah 1987); *Willie Nelson Music Co. v. Commissioner,* 85 T.C. 914 (1985); *Shenandoah Publishing House, Inc. v. Fanning,* 368 S.E.2d 253 (Va. 1988); *Goldberg v. Johnson,* 485 So. 2d 1386 (Fla. Dist. Ct. App. 1986).

[133] See, e.g., *In re K.F.,* 559 A.2d 663 (Vt. 1989); *Orange County Publications v. Sawyer,* 14 Media L. Rep. (BNA) 1766 (N.Y. Sup. Ct. 1987); *In re Richmond Newspapers, Inc.,* 16 Media L. Rep. (BNA) 1049 (Va. Cir. Ct. 1988).

[134] *United States v. Three Juveniles,* 862 F. Supp. 651 (D. Mass. 1994), *aff'd,* 61 F.3d 86 (1st Cir. 1995), *cert. denied sub nom. Globe Newspaper Co. v. United States,* 116 S. Ct. 1564 (1996).

obtained *via* discovery.[135] Likewise, in an antitrust case, a federal district court in California held that a common law right of access attached to documents as soon as they were filed with the court in either civil or criminal cases.[136] In a few instances, courts have ruled that there is no right of access to discovery materials until the trial has begun or the documents have been introduced at the trial.[137]

While most courts have refused to recognize a right of access to unfiled discovery documents, a few judges have ruled in favor of openness and declined to seal discovery materials except upon a showing of "good cause."[138] For example, a Minnesota trial court in 1992 denied a motion from a St. Paul City Council member who was a defendant in a civil lawsuit to seal all discovery materials on the grounds that disclosure would cause her public humiliation and reputational harm. The court said there was a common law and statutory presumption of openness and, therefore, rejected the closure request as overbroad. However, it did agree to temporarily seal unfiled materials relating to medical, financial and psychological records.[139]

Other courts have also agreed to seal certain discovery documents to protect personal privacy. The Sixth Circuit Court of Appeals in 1987 ruled that protecting the associational privacy rights of non-parties was sufficient cause to justify sealing a list of Ku Klux Klan members that had been obtained as part of discovery in a civil lawsuit resulting from the fire-bombing of a black couple's home.[140] Other reasons frequently given for denying access to discovery materials are to protect trade secrets and to ensure the efficient functioning of the judicial process. A good example of the latter is a 1991 decision of the U.S. District Court for Arizona, which denied access to unfiled discovery materials in a class action suit resulting from savings and loan association failures. The court said that access would impede the progress of the case and create ad-

ministrative burdens for both the court and parties.[141]

Audio-Visual Records. As the use of audio-visual materials in the courtroom has increased, so have efforts by journalists, especially broadcasters, to obtain copies of such materials. Sometimes the parties to litigation and judges are reluctant to allow broadcasters to copy audio-visual records because they fear the airing of such tapes will invade privacy, interfere with fair trial rights, implicate innocent third parties and/or sensationalize and distort the judicial process. Some judges have argued that the right of access to court records is met by simply allowing journalists to see or hear audio-visual evidence when it is used in the courtroom or by providing reporters written transcripts of tapes. Broadcasters who want to air portions of tapes are seldom satisfied with such limited access and claim a right to copy as well as to see and hear audio-visual records.

The Supreme Court addressed the issue in 1978 when it denied media requests to copy former President Richard M. Nixon's Watergate audio tapes. As noted above, in *Nixon v. Warner Communications* the Court recognized a common law presumption of access. However, Justice Powell, writing for the Court, noted that "the right to inspect and copy judicial records is not absolute."[142] In this case, the common law presumption of access was superseded by the Presidential Recordings and Materials Preservation Act, passed by Congress within weeks of President Ford's pardon of Nixon for his involvement in the Watergate scandal. That Act gave the Administrator of General Services the responsibility for processing and arranging public access to the Nixon tapes.[143]

Since *Richmond Newspapers* in 1980, lower courts have generally recognized either a constitutional or common law right to inspect and copy audio-visual records. That right, however, like all of the other access rights discussed thus far, is not absolute and can be outweighed by other interests. Several good examples of how courts balance the interests for and against access came in the early 1980s, when two FBI sting operations, known as ABSCAM and BRILAB, resulted in four different access-to-tapes lawsuits. During ABSCAM the FBI videotaped government officials allegedly accepting bribes from undercover agents. In BRILAB, the tapes were of Texas officials allegedly accepting bribes in the awarding of state employee insurance contracts. Understandably, broadcasters wanted to obtain copies of those tapes to show on the air.

[135] 14 Media L. Rep. (BNA) 2313, 2327 (D.C. 1988).

[136] *In re Coordinated Pretrial Proceedings in Petroleum Prod. Antitrust Litig.,* 101 F.R.D. 34 (C.D. Cal. 1984).

[137] See *In re Reporters Committee for Freedom of the Press,* 773 F.2d 1325 (D.C. Cir. 1985); *Tavoulareas v. Washington Post,* 724 F.2d 1010 (D.C. Cir. 1984); *Booth Newspapers, Inc. v. Midland Cir. Judge,* 377 N.W.2d 868 (Mich. App. 1985); *appeal denied,* 425 Mich. 854 (1986), *cert. denied,* 479 U.S. 1031 (1987).

[138] The "good cause" standard is based on Rule 26(c) of the Federal Rules of Civil Procedure and similar provisions in state rules of civil procedure.

[139] *Baloga v. Maccabee,* 20 Media L. Rep. (BNA) 2201 (Minn. Dist. Ct. 1992). See also *Glenmede Trust Co. v. Thompson,* 56 F.3d 426 (3d Cir. 1995).

[140] *Courier-Journal v. Marshall,* 828 F.2d 361 (6th Cir. 1987).

[141] *In re American Continental Corp./Lincoln Savings & Loan Securities Litig.,* 18 Media L. Rep. (BNA) 2303 (D. Ariz. 1991).

[142] 435 U.S. at 598.

[143] Pub. L. No. 93-526, 88 Stat. 1695 (1974).

In the first ABSCAM tape case, resulting from the trial of former Congressman Michael Myers, the Second U.S. Circuit Court of Appeals allowed the media to copy the tapes, saying that once such evidence was introduced in court, "it would take the most extraordinary circumstances to justify restrictions on the opportunity of those not physically in attendance at the courtroom to see and hear the evidence, when it is in a form that readily permits sight and sound reproduction." The court considered the impact that broadcasting the tapes might have on the fair trial rights of Myers and future ABSCAM defendants but concluded that the risks were not sufficient to justify "curtailing the public's right of access to courtroom evidence." The court added, "Defendants, as well as the news media, frequently overestimate the extent of the public's awareness of news."[144]

In the other two ABSCAM cases, the Third Circuit and D.C. Circuit also granted broadcasters the right to copy the tapes despite claims that airing the tapes would interfere with the defendants' fair trial rights and invade the privacy of unindicted third parties.[145] The D.C. court, however, told the trial judge that he could edit the tapes before releasing them to eliminate portions that might harm innocent third parties.

In the BRILAB case, *Belo Broadcasting Corp. v. Clark*, the Fifth Circuit upheld the trial court's refusal to allow copying of the FBI sting tapes.[146] First, the court said that the media's First Amendment right of access was satisfied when journalists were allowed to view the tapes as they were played in open court and were provided transcripts of the contents. While the court acknowledged that there was a common law right of access to the tapes, it said the fair trial rights of a defendant who had not yet been tried outweighed the access right.

Since ABSCAM and BRILAB, media have continued to try to obtain copies of audio-visual materials used in the courtroom with mixed results. While sometimes journalists are allowed to copy tapes, in other instances courts find that the potential harm to defendants' or third parties' rights justifies denying a right to copy audio-visual records.

Cameras in the Courtrooms

In 1976, only two states — Texas and Colorado — allowed cameras in their courtrooms. Twenty years later, only three states — Indiana, Mississippi and South Dakota — the District of Columbia and most federal courts continued to ban camera coverage. A key reason for this change was the technological advances that eliminated the need for obtrusive flashes, bulky cameras and electrical cords snaking across courtroom floors. Also important, however, were changing public and judicial attitudes. At the same time courts were recognizing the importance of allowing public and press access to the judicial process, video cameras were becoming part of everyday life for most Americans. People became accustomed to being videotaped as they did their shopping and banking, rode on elevators and attended weddings and parties.

This was not the case earlier in the Twentieth Century when cameras were obvious and intrusive, and their presence in the courtroom was viewed as inconsistent with judicial dignity and decorum. The first official bans on cameras in the courtroom followed the 1935 trial of Bruno Hauptmann for the kidnapping of the Lindbergh baby. In 1937 the American Bar Association adopted Canon 35 as part of its Canons of Professional and Judicial Ethics. Canon 35, which declared that cameras "detract from the essential dignity of the proceedings, degrade the court and create misconceptions with respect thereto in the mind of the public," recommended that cameras be banned in all courtrooms. That recommendation, which was amended in 1952 to specifically include television cameras, was followed by most states for more than four decades.

When the Supreme Court heard its first cameras-in-the-courtroom case, *Estes v. Texas*, it agreed with the ABA that television cameras intruded upon "the solemn decorum of court procedure." Justice Clark wrote for the Court that jurors could be distracted by the equipment and by the mere knowledge that the trial was being televised. "Not only will the juror's eyes be fixed on the camera, but also his mind will be preoccupied with the telecasting rather than with the testimony." The judge, Clark continued, had enough to do supervising the trial without also worrying about supervising television crews. Witnesses, Clark wrote, "may be demoralized and frightened, some cocky and given to overstatement; memories may falter, as with anyone speaking publicly, and accuracy of statement may be severely undermined. Embarrassment may impede the search for truth, as may a natural tendency toward overdramatization." Finally, for the defendant, the presence of TV cameras "is a form of mental — if not physical — harassment, resembling a police line-up or the third degree," Clark wrote.[147]

Chief Justice Warren, in a concurring opinion, referred to the noise and disorder of TV equipment but was most concerned

---

[144] *United States v. Myers,* 635 F.2d 945, 952-53 (2d Cir. 1981).

[145] *In re Application of NBC (Criden),* 648 F.2d 814 (3d Cir. 1981); *In re Application of NBC (Jenrette),* 653 F.2d 609 (D.C. Cir. 1981).

[146] 654 F.2d 423 (5th Cir. 1981).

[147] 381 U.S. 532, 546-49 (1965).

about the psychological effects, concluding that the real evil was "the trial participants' awareness that they are being televised."[148] Justice Harlan also wrote a concurring opinion. He shared his colleagues' fears about television's potential for disrupting the judicial process, or, as he put it, causing "serious mischief," but also seemed to recognize that effect was the result of the novelty of the medium. Harlan speculated that someday television might become "so commonplace ... in the daily life of the average person" that its disruptive influence would disappear.[149]

By the 1980s, Justice Harlan's prediction had very nearly come true. In its second cameras-in-the-courtroom case, *Chandler v. Florida*, the Supreme Court in 1981 concluded that "no one has been able to present empirical data sufficient to establish that the mere presence of the broadcast media inherently has an adverse effect on that process."[150] Florida was one of several states that had begun experimenting with allowing cameras in its courtrooms in the 1970s. In *Chandler*, which involved two Miami Beach police officers charged with burglarizing a restaurant, the judge allowed a television camera in the court over the defendants' objections. Although only about three minutes of the trial were ultimately broadcast, the officers appealed their convictions, claiming that the televising of trials was "inherently a denial of due process."

Writing for a unanimous Court, Chief Justice Burger — who, throughout his tenure, steadfastly opposed the introduction of cameras into federal courts — declared that the mere presence of cameras in the courtroom did not automatically deprive a defendant of a fair trial. Burger said broadcast coverage might, in some cases, violate a defendant's constitutional rights, but the mere possibility of prejudice did not justify a ban on televising trials. Instead, an individual defendant would have to prove that "the presence of cameras impaired the ability of the jurors to decide" the case. "To demonstrate prejudice in a specific case a defendant must show something more than juror awareness that the trial is such as to attract the attention of broadcasters," Burger wrote.[151]

While *Chandler v. Florida* permits states to open their courtrooms to cameras, it does not require them to do so. The Supreme Court did *not* say that photographers have a First Amendment right to take their equipment into courtrooms. Instead it simply said that states were free to experiment with television coverage of trials. This point was underscored just two years later in another case out of Miami. U.S. District Judge Alcee Hastings, who

was charged with accepting a bribe, asked to have his trial televised and was joined by news media organizations in challenging the ban on cameras in federal courts. After the trial court denied the motion, the media appealed to the Eleventh U.S. Circuit Court of Appeals, which upheld the lower court ruling, saying there was no constitutional right, under either the First or Sixth Amendment, to bring cameras into courtrooms.[152]

As of 1998, cameras were still banned in most federal courtrooms. The Federal Rules of Criminal Procedure have prohibited the televising of federal criminal trials for nearly fifty years. In the early 1990s, limited television coverage of civil proceedings was tried under an experimental program authorized by the Judicial Conference of the United States, which sets policy for the federal courts. An evaluation of the program by the Federal Judicial Center found that judges became more favorable toward cameras in the courts after the experiment began; judges and court personnel felt the guidelines governing the program were workable and that journalists were generally cooperative; and judges and attorneys reported minimal or no effects of cameras in the courtrooms. Despite such favorable reactions, the Judicial Conference in September 1994 voted 19-6 to terminate the program.

In March 1996 the Judicial Conference revisited the camera question and voted to allow each of the thirteen U.S. Courts of Appeals to "decide for itself whether to permit the taking of photographs and radio and television coverage." The conference continued to voice its opposition to television coverage of federal trial court proceedings, however. Despite that opposition, fourteen of the eighty-nine federal district courts have adopted local rules giving trial judges the discretion to allow televising of civil proceedings. One study reported, however, that only four proceedings in two federal district courts had ever been televised under those local rules.[153]

While the federal courts have been loath to allow cameras, the same has not been true of state courts. As of 1996 only Indiana, Mississippi, South Dakota and the District of Columbia refused to allow some degree of camera coverage of court proceedings. The extent to which coverage is permitted varies:

- Two states — Maine and Oregon — permit coverage of trial courts only.

[148] *Id.* at 570 (Warren, C.J., concurring).
[149] *Id.* at 597 (Harlan, J., concurring).
[150] 449 U.S. 560, 578-79 (1981).
[151] *Id.* at 581.

[152] *United States v. Hastings*, 695 F.2d 1278 (11th Cir.), *cert. denied sub nom. Post-Newsweek Stations v. United States*, 461 U.S. 931 (1983). See also *Conway v. United States*, 852 F.2d 187 (6th Cir.), *cert. denied*, 488 U.S. 943 (1988).
[153] Jeffrey Ballabon and Jonathan Sherman, "Lifting the Veil: TV Cameras in Federal Courts," *Legal Backgrounder*, Nov. 1, 1996.

- Five states — Illinois, Louisiana, Minnesota, Nebraska and New York—allow only appellate court coverage.
- Three states — Idaho, North Dakota and Utah — permit TV cameras only in their supreme courts.
- Two states — Maine and Maryland — only allow civil trials to be televised.
- Two states — Alabama and Oklahoma — require the consent of the defendant for coverage to be allowed in criminal trials.

A few states are still experimenting with camera coverage of proceedings, but most have adopted permanent rules governing cameras.

The extent of coverage permitted, as well as the specific rules journalists must follow, differ from state to state, and journalists are well advised to study their individual state's rules carefully before taking a camera or tape recorder into a courtroom. For example, almost all states require the consent of the presiding judge, and a few also require the consent of some participants. Most states place restrictions on the photographing of jurors and certain types of trial participants, such as juveniles, victims of sex crimes and undercover officers. Most states also limit the number of cameras allowed in the courtroom and specify where cameras may be placed. State rules often require pooling agreements among the various media.

Journalists who violate the rules governing electronic coverage can be found in contempt of court. For example, during a 1991 murder trial in North Carolina, Asheville station WLOS-TV inadvertently broadcast approximately three seconds of film showing some jurors. The trial judge, who had specifically warned station employees not to photograph jurors, found the station in contempt, imposed a $500 fine and prohibited WLOS from bringing cameras or recording equipment into the courthouse for the next sixty days.

BENCH-BAR-PRESS GUIDELINES

The 1964 report by the Warren Commission, established to investigate the assassination of President John F. Kennedy, suggested that accused assassin Lee Harvey Oswald could not have received a fair trial anywhere in the United States had he not been murdered by Jack Ruby. The commission criticized press coverage of the assassination and its aftermath and urged the news media to develop voluntary codes of conduct to prevent free press-fair trial conflicts.

The Warren Commission's call for self-restraint was echoed by a special committee of the American Bar Association, which, in 1969,

issued a report urging journalists and attorneys to work together to develop standards for the reporting of crimes and court proceedings.[154] In response to these reports, as well as the cases discussed at the start of this chapter in which convictions were overturned on the basis of prejudicial publicity, groups of journalists, lawyers, judges and law enforcement officials in about half the states developed free press-fair trial guidelines; those guidelines still exist in many states.

The guidelines are purely voluntary sets of standards designed to head off problems and promote greater understanding and cooperation among the media, the bar and criminal justice officials. In most states, no mechanism for enforcing the guidelines exists. The guidelines generally declare that the public has a right to know and the press has a right to publish certain information about crimes and the persons accused of committing crimes.

They list information that should be made available to the press and public: the accused's name, age, address, employment and similar background information; the substance of the charge; the amount of bail; the name of the complainant and/or victim; the circumstances surrounding the arrest; and the identity of the investigating and arresting agency.

The guidelines also list types of information that may prejudice potential jurors: alleged confessions or admissions by the accused; opinions as to the character, reputation, guilt or innocence of the accused; references to the performance or results of fingerprint, ballistics, polygraph or other types of tests; and the defendant's prior arrests and convictions.

While in the late 1960s and early 1970s many people concerned about clashes between the press and the judiciary saw voluntary cooperation as the best solution, today it appears the guidelines are often ignored or forgotten.[155] In addition, many journalists became suspicious of guidelines when a few judges began transforming them from voluntary to mandatory. In *Nebraska Press Association v. Stuart*, for example, Judge Ruff made the Nebraska guidelines part of his gag order. The Supreme Court found the gag order to be unconstitutional, but a few years later a Washington trial judge made a promise to abide by that state's guidelines a prerequisite for media access to his courtroom.

---

[154] ABA Legal Advisory Committee on Fair Trial and Free Press, *The Rights of Fair Trial and Free Press* (1969).

[155] See James W. Tankard *et al.*, "Compliance with the American Bar Association Voluntary Free Press-Fair Trial Guidelines," *Journalism Quarterly* 56 (1979): 464; Kimberly Thigpen, *Voluntary Press-Bar Guidelines in North Carolina: Ideals and Realities*, Senior Honors Thesis, University of North Carolina-Chapel Hill (1989).

Judge Byron Swedburg told journalists they would not be admitted to a pretrial hearing in an attempted murder case unless they agreed, in writing, to follow the guidelines. Swedburg was concerned about prejudicial pretrial publicity because the defendant in the case was the girlfriend of a notorious murderer known as the Hillside Strangler. When journalists appealed Swedburg's order, the Washington Supreme Court upheld its constitutionality, saying it did not constitute a prior restraint since the judge announced no penalty for journalists who violated the written agreement. The Supreme Court denied *certiorari*.[156]

SUMMARY

While concern about press coverage of crimes and trials dates back at least two centuries, debate over the so-called free press-fair trial issue escalated during the 1960s when the Supreme Court overturned several murder convictions on the grounds that prejudicial publicity had deprived the defendants of their Sixth Amendment right to a fair trial. Televised and often sensationalized coverage of the O.J. Simpson trial in 1995 again brought the controversy to the forefront of public attention. The perceived conflict between the First and Sixth Amendments can occur in three ways: Pretrial publicity can make it difficult to find impartial jurors; during-trial publicity can influence a sitting jury; and the presence of journalists and/or their equipment in the courtroom can cause physical or psychological disruption.

Two broad categories of remedies are available to judges. First are the traditional remedies designed to compensate for—but not eliminate—publicity. The most commonly used of these compensatory remedies are change of venue, continuance, *voir dire* and admonitions to the jury. The second category of remedies consists of those aimed at reducing or eliminating publicity. These remedies are much more problematic since they directly impact on the media's ability to obtain and report information related to the judicial system, and, beginning in the mid-1970s, the Supreme Court began placing First Amendment restrictions on their use.

In 1976 in *Nebraska Press Association v. Stuart*, the Supreme Court said that gag orders on the press constituted prior restraints and could be used only if there was pervasive publicity likely to interfere with a fair trial, no other remedies were available and a gag order would be effective in preventing prejudicial publicity. This test made it extremely difficult for a trial judge to justify gagging the media and significantly reduced the number of gag or-

ders issued and upheld on appeal. Journalists must keep in mind, however, that if a judge issues a gag order, violating it can result in a contempt of court citation even if subsequently the order is struck down on appeal. While some appellate courts have ruled that journalists can violate a patently invalid gag order if timely relief is not available from an appeals court, others have enforced the so-called collateral bar rule, which says that a person cannot disobey a judicial order and then challenge its constitutionality as a defense to contempt of court.

Gag orders aimed at trial participants generally are not subject to the same rigorous test of constitutionality as gag orders aimed directly at the media. In *Gentile v. State Bar of Nevada*, the Supreme Court said it was permissible to punish an attorney who made extrajudicial statements that posed a "substantial likelihood" of interfering with a fair trial. While trial judges have greater leeway in restricting the speech of lawyers and other trial participants, there are First Amendment limits. A gag order cannot be overbroad and cannot be issued unless necessary to protect a defendant's right to a fair trial and no other alternative measures are available.

In addition to restricting the use of prior restraints on media coverage of the courts, the Supreme Court has also applied the First Amendment to limit the use of post-publication sanctions. In the 1940s, the Court ruled that judges could not use their contempt of court powers to punish coverage of and commentary on the judicial process unless such publications presented a "clear and present danger" of interfering with the fair administration of justice. This stringent standard has virtually eliminated the practice of judges citing for contempt journalists and others who criticize the courts. Three decades later the Court strengthened the media's protection against post-publication punishments when it ruled that the media could not be punished for publishing lawfully obtained, truthful information unless necessary to serve a compelling governmental interest.

In a series of cases in the 1980s, the Supreme Court also put a halt to the widespread use of court closures as a means of controlling publicity when it ruled that the press and public enjoyed a First Amendment right of access to criminal proceedings. The Court established a multi-part test for determining when a judicial hearing could be closed, which requires a judge to issue written findings that, among other things, closure is essential to serve higher values and is as narrowly tailored as possible. While the Supreme Court has not ruled directly on whether a constitutional right of access exists to civil proceedings, most lower courts that have considered the issue have found a qualified First Amendment

---

156 *Federated Publications, Inc. v. Swedburg*, 633 P.2d 74 (Wash. 1981), *cert. denied*, 456 U.S. 984 (1982).

right of access and have used the same test the Court mandated for closing criminal proceedings.

Many lower courts have also presumed that the First Amendment right of access extends to judicial records. Whether they recognize a constitutional right of access, however, courts are unanimous that the common law provides both the press and public the right to inspect certain judicial records. Media attempts to gain access to some types of judicial records, especially juvenile records, discovery materials and audio-visual records, have caused numerous conflicts in recent years, and courts have often disagreed about the extent of access rights.

One of the major free press-fair trial battles has involved cameras in the courtroom. In 1965 the Supreme Court overturned a criminal conviction on the grounds that television cameras in the courtroom caused both physical and psychological disruptions inconsistent with the Sixth Amendment's guarantee of a fair trial. In the decades that followed, as cameras became less obtrusive and television became more ubiquitous, some states began to allow video coverage of judicial proceedings, ultimately leading the Supreme Court to revise its position. In *Chandler v. Florida* in 1981, the Court ruled that the mere presence of cameras did not automatically deny a defendant a fair trial. While there is no constitutional right to bring cameras into courts, states are free to experiment with camera coverage, and as of 1997, forty-seven states allowed some form of camera coverage of courts. Most federal courts, however, continued to ban cameras despite generally favorable responses to a limited experiment with camera coverage during the 1990s.

Finally, in response to criticism of press performance and calls for the media to voluntarily adopt ethical standards to protect defendants' rights to fair trials, groups of journalists, lawyers, judges and law enforcement officials in about two dozen states devised free press-fair trial guidelines. Such guidelines generally outline the types of information that could prejudice potential jurors, and, therefore, journalists should be careful about publishing as well as the types of information that should be made available to the press and public.

Every day the news is filled with stories related to the judicial system. Whether it's a celebrity charged with murder, a movie star's messy divorce, a cancer victim suing a tobacco company or a young woman trying to get into an all-male military academy, the courts generate news that affects the public and in which the public is interested. Conflicts between the press and the judiciary are inevitable since each is committed to advancing a different interest and those interests often appear to be at odds with one another. Judges and attorneys see their primary responsibility as ensuring fair trials and the proper functioning of the judicial process. Their key concern is protecting the rights of litigants, witnesses and jurors. Journalists, on the other hand, see their primary responsibility as informing the public and serving as a watchdog over government, including the judicial branch. Their key concern is protecting freedom of the press and the public's right to know.

Certainly sometimes less lofty goals motivate both sides, adding problems. During the last few decades, however, the Supreme Court has made it clear that both the First and Sixth Amendments are of equal importance in our constitutional scheme. Neither takes precedence over the other, nor can one be used as the justification for infringement of the other. The press has broad First Amendment rights to observe and report on the judicial process, and the judiciary must find ways to respect those rights while at the same time ensuring that trials are fair, jurors are unbiased and the judicial process operates smoothly, effectively and openly.

FOR ADDITIONAL READING

Buddenbaum, Judith M., *et al. Pretrial Publicity and Juries: A Review of Research*, Research Report No. 11, School of Journalism, Indiana University (1981).

Bunker, Matthew D. *Justice and the Media: Reconciling Fair Trials and a Free Press*. Mahwah, N.J.: Lawrence Erlbaum Associates, 1997.

Campbell, Douglas S. *Free Press v. Fair Trial: Supreme Court Decisions Since 1807*. Westport, Conn.: Praeger, 1994.

Connors, Mary M. "Prejudicial Publicity: An Assessment." *Journalism Monographs* 41 (1975).

Minow, Newton and Fred Cate. "Who Is an Impartial Juror in an Age of Mass Media?" *American University Law Review* 40 (1991): 631.

Sandys, Marla and Steven M. Chermak. "A Journey into the Unknown: Pretrial Publicity and Capital Cases." *Communication Law & Policy* 1 (1996): 533.

16

Access to Public Documents and Meetings

By Sandra F. Chance

From the earliest days of the United States, jurists, journalists, scholars and other citizens have recognized that speech about government is meaningful only if based on factual information. That information must come, in large part, from the government's own meetings and records. James Madison, for example, observed:

Nothing could be more irrational than to give people power, and to withhold from them information with which power is abused. A people who mean to be their own governors must arm themselves with power which knowledge gives. A popular government without popular information or the means of acquiring it is but a prologue to a farce or a tragedy, or perhaps both.[1]

Despite the logic of such observations, governments at all levels — national, state and local — have a lengthy tradition of closing their records and meetings to public scrutiny. Madison himself

---

The author would like to thank Robert L. Hughes, who wrote the chapter on access for the 1998 edition of *Communication and the Law* and who allowed that chapter to become the framework for this revision.

[1] "Letter to W.T. Barry, Aug. 4, 1822," *The Writings of James Madison,* vol. 1, ed. Gaillard Hunt (New York: G.P. Putnam's Sons, 1910), p. 103.

opted to exclude the press and public from the deliberations on the same First Amendment used today to argue for open meetings and records.

Tension between government secrecy and public access to government information runs through U.S. history. Scandals during the administrations of Presidents Ulysses S. Grant and Warren G. Harding, for example, brought demands for specific information about government. But only in comparatively recent times has access become an issue of continuing and widespread interest.

Before the Great Depression of the 1930s, people understood their government by watching the activities in the Oval Office, the legislative bodies — from Congress to town councils — and a few administrative agencies. With the New Deal that followed in the wake of the Depression, however, government surged in size and complexity. New agencies were established to perform specialized functions once handled, if at all, by elected representatives. Congress, for example, delegated much of its authority over advertising regulation to the Federal Trade Commission.

For all its Byzantine structure and process, Congress is a much easier organization to follow and evaluate than the FTC. Multiply this remote agency by the hundreds of others that were created on the local, state and federal levels and the sense of frustration felt by many citizens is understandable. Government couldn't be understood, and that loss of understanding was accompanied by a sense of loss of control.

The secrecy precipitated by World War II compounded the problem. Shortly after the armistice, a movement emerged to make government more accessible. At first spearheaded by journalists who demanded a legally enforceable "right to know," the movement gradually broadened to include public interest groups and business interests. Over time it was enormously successful in mobilizing the passage of federal and state access statutes. Today these freedom-of-information or right-to-know laws are the primary legal means by which citizens have access to government meetings and records. But they are not the only tools. Federal and state constitutions and the common law also play important roles.

A study of access law — or any law — requires an attempt to pinpoint the policy or objective behind the law. Nor infrequently, the purpose of those behind the law — whether judges, legislators or the Founding Fathers — is considerably different from those who use it.

Some laws, like many state right-to-know laws, often enunciate their rationales, as in a preamble. But many others don't, including the common law and the federal Freedom of Information Act. Courts are left to grope for clues in legislative histories and other sources to discover what to guide the interpretation of ambiguous language.

The importance of this search shouldn't be underestimated. If a statute's purpose is, for example, the discovery of truth or self-fulfillment, there just isn't much government information that would qualify for disclosure in order to foster that policy. If, on the other hand, the objective of a law is to prevent secret rules and regulations, only final decisions need be made public — a narrow right-to-know policy, indeed. Most often, the policy is to permit citizens to participate effectively in government, a standard of openness that comes somewhere in the middle. The benefits of guaranteeing access to government information generally parallel those associated with protecting speech. That is, access to information promotes the discovery of turth, self-government, orderly change and self-fulfillment. Access also enables the press to perform its watchdog function.

In contrast, a government's instinctive preference for secrecy has several specific roots. First, finding and copying public records requires time and labor, and providing facilities for public meetings is inconvenient and expensive. Limited resources can best be directed at whatever a particular government agency regards as its primary function, perhaps issuing drivers' licenses or collecting garbage.

Second, officials argue that opening meetings and records chills creativity and effectiveness in government. If the casual suggestions and give-and-take of frank, brainstorming discussions are open to public examination, and perhaps ridicule, innovators and risk-takers in government won't make bold or daring proposals. The quality of decision-making will suffer.

Third, they point out, some interests such as national security and personal privacy are more important than the public interest in access to government information.

And, finally — though seldom, if ever, stated explicitly — secrecy prevents disclosure of government waste, incompetence, unfairness and criminal activity.

To these specific objections, advocates of public access respond that providing information is not just an annoying appendage to the duties of government and its officials; rather, it is a primary function of government. The public has a need to know what its government is doing if democracy is to work. They also argue that the public has good ideas. By excluding the public from the early stages of decision-making, government is deprived of a fertile source of imaginative suggestions. And by denying the public access during the formative stages of a proposal, it is being excluded at the very time its input can be most effective. Moreover, access to ideas that are rejected can sometimes be as telling about the governmental processes as those that are accepted.

While most right-to-know advocates concede that there are times when a specific interest, such as the movement of troops, will trump a generalized interest in disclosure, they argue that any exceptions must be specific. Officials may attempt to use a narrow, reasonable exception to a general policy of disclosure as a catchall to hide information that ought to be available.

Keep these policies and attitutdes in mind as you go through the survey of constitutional, common law and statutory access issues.

CONSTITUTIONAL ACCESS

In *New York Times Co. v. Sullivan,*[2] the U.S. Supreme Court declared that the "central meaning" of the First Amendment was that it protects discussion about government and its officials. Without guarantees of free speech, self-governance is an unobtainable goal. But the Court has been reluctant to extend that guarantee to access to the government information necessary to give content to that speech.

Only in the context of criminal trials has the Court fully considered the access issue. First in *Richmond Newspapers v. Vir-*

---

[2] 376 U.S. 254 (1964).

ginia,[3] then in *Press-Enterprise Co. v. Superior Court (II)*,[4] the Court held that the acquisition of newsworthy information was entitled to First Amendment protection. The Court took pains, however, to limit its holding to a particular kind of access — that of criminal trials. Indeed, at least two justices emphasized this narrow focus in concurring opinions.

But the logic of the case simply can't be confined to criminal-justice proceedings. The Court based its decision, first, on the premise that access to criminal trials contributes to the self-governing function and promotes the democratic process. It added that criminal trials are historically open. Whether this latter observation is an independent test or merely evidence of the truth of the first part is unclear. But several lower federal courts have seized on this language to allow access based on the First Amendment.

A federal District Court in Ohio, for example, found that the public had a qualified right to access to a city council meeting since such meetings were historically open to the public and the subject matter contributes to the functioning of government.[5] And a district court in Puerto Rico used the same First Amendment analysis to order the governor of Puerto Rico to disclose a record.[6] Both decisions were reversed on other grounds, and not without the appellate courts expressing skepticism that a broadly based constitutional right of access existed.

On the state level, the New York Court of Appeals adopted the Supreme Court's test but used it to deny access to a dentist's disciplinary hearing since there was no evidence that public access plays a significant role in the functioning of that proceeding.[7]

The Supreme Court's own reluctance to take the logical next step after the courtroom cases may be a slippery slope problem: Once a court requires some records and proceedings to be open, can a principled, constitutional line be drawn between matters that must be open and those where secrecy is appropriate? Even Justice William Brennan, one of the Court's staunchest free expression advocates, was wary of runaway access: "Analysis is not advanced by rhetorical statements that all information bears upon public issues [and therefore must be disclosed]; what is crucial in individual cases is whether access to a particular government process is important in terms of that very process."[8]

State constitutions may also provide access rights to government information. The Montana Constitution, for example, provides that "No person shall be deprived of the right to examine documents or to observe the deliberations of all public bodies or agencies ... except in cases in which the demand of individual privacy clearly exceed the merits of public disclosure."[9] Montana's is unusually explicit, but most state constitutions have provisions paralleling the First Amendment that can be employed in the right circumstances.

Claims based on either federal or state constitutions face uncertain prospects. The law is emerging at best. Courts of last resort often move with great caution. Edicts based on the constitution have no appeal short of the unwieldly task of amending the constitution itself. When courts err in interpreting statutes, on the other hand, Congress or state legislatures can easily make adjustments, at least in theory. Without finding a workable rule that can be applied to each of the millions of records and meetings whose openness they would otherwise have to resolve on a case-by-case basis, courts won't rush into this complex area.

Constitutional change may thus seem to move with the speed of glaciers. But the law will never be developed on that level if those seeking access don't make and pursue claims based on First Amendment theories. It was more than three decades after Justice William O. Douglas declared in 1947 that "A trial is a public event" before the Court declared that the Constitution requires courtrooms to be open.[10]

COMMON LAW ACCESS

Under the common law of England — the traditional, judge-made law passed from generation to generation — access to public information was limited. The doors of legislative bodies were usually closed to the public, and citizens were allowed to inspect or copy public records only if they could show what was called a "proper interest." Just what formed a proper interest was uncertain for citizens then and historians now.

Virtually all reported judicial decisions describe controversies over records, not meetings. (Evidently there was no right of access to meetings. After the American Revolution, meetings of legislative bodies on both sides of the Atlantic became more open, without judicial prodding.) The outcomes in the great majority of these

---

[3] 448 U.S. 555 (1980).

[4] 478 U.S. 1 (1986).

[5] *WJW-TV v. Cleveland*, 686 F. Supp. 177 (N.D. Ohio 1988), *rev'd on other grounds*, 878 F.2d 906 (6th Cir. 1989).

[6] *El Dia, Inc. v. Colon*, 783 F. Supp. 15 (D.P.R. 1991), *rev'd on other grounds*, 963 F.2d 488 (1st Cir. 1992).

[7] *Johnson Newspaper Corp. v. Melino*, 77 N.Y.2d 1, 563 N.Y.S.2d 380, 564 N.E.2d 1046 (1990).

[8] *Richmond Newspapers*, 448 U.S. at 589.

[9] Mont. Const. Art. II sec. 9 (1972).

[10] *Craig v. Harney*, 331 U.S. 367, 373 (1947).

older common law cases turned on whether an interest — a need to see the record — was so important that the record would be available in a lawsuit. If a citizen, say, wanted to see all the town's utility bills out of personal curiosity, his interest wasn't proper. If, on the other hand, access to the record was essential to proving he had paid his own bill, then the interest was proper and access was granted.

These cases have long captured the attention of scholars and litigants. But largely forgotten are those cases in which citizens sought access, not to serve some personal or private interest, but to serve the general or public welfare. Given the common law's bad reputation, it may be surprising to learn that those who claimed to represent the public interest were often successful.

By the middle of the Nineteenth Century, for example, English courts were regularly opening the financial records of municipalities for taxpayer inspections. They often reasoned that citizens were like shareholders in a corporation; they had a right, limited though it was, to review the records of their enterprise, in these cases, their government. In the leading case, *Rex v. Guardians of Great Farrington*,[11] an English court held flatly that municipal financial records could no longer be withheld because a taxpayer failed to prove a special interest.

In the United States, as in England, most of the reported decisions concerned the demands of individuals seeking to serve private purposes. Sometimes the interest was merely curiosity; sometimes it was financial. For example, about 100 years ago, title companies — companies that insured the ownership of land — found they could abstract information from deeds and other land records, repackage and resell it at a profit. Officials, fearful of losing both income and control of what they perceived as their property, frequently resisted these incursions. Often requests for these purposes were unsuccessful. There are similar conflicts today between government and resellers of government information, online services, for example.

There were only a few reported cases where plaintiffs, usually newspapers, claimed their business was to represent the public interest. It's not clear why there weren't more. It may be that media seldom requested records or that they got them whenever they did. On the other hand, it is also possible that when access was denied, cases were not contested in court.

The media almost invariably won those cases that were contested, however. Courts typically recited the common law's narrow, historical "proper interest" restrictions and then declared that the "public interest" was a "proper interest." In a leading case,

the Michigan Supreme Court concluded in 1928: "If there is any rule of English common law that denied the public the right of access to public records, it is repugnant to the spirit of our democratic institutions. Ours is a government of the people."[12]

A 1994 decision illustrates how the common law of access functions today. In *Washington Legal Foundation v. United Sentencing Commission*,[13] a public interest group sought access to records the commission used in formulating recommendations. The threshold question was whether the records were "public records" under the common law. Not every document contained in a government file qualifies. Common law records are generally only those that record official actions or are vital to the functioning of government. Even if a record is a "public record," it may still be withheld if, the court said, its "specific interests favoring secrecy outweigh the general and specific interests favoring disclosure." This means the broad public interest in knowing about government may be insufficient to force disclosure; a particular public might also be necessary. It wasn't necessary to do the balancing in this case, however, for the threshold test wasn't met. The records sought were held to be "predecisional" and thus public records under the common law.

Despite its limitations, the common law can be a highly effective access tool. In one case, for example, a common law-based suit forced a government official to create a record that didn't exist, something a statute never does. A sheriff had negotiated a settlement with a discharged deputy but kept no documents relating to the settlement. He said the law didn't require any. A newspaper filed suit under the state freedom of information act and under the common law. The state supreme court ruled that no statute obligated the sheriff to create or maintain records of the settlement agreement. Thus, there was no record to be demanded under the state's right-to-know law.

But the common law claim fared better. The court held that the common law required a record to be made: "Whenever a written record of the transaction of a public officer, in his office, is a convenient and appropriate mode of discharging the duties of his office, it is not only his right but his duty to keep that memorial, whether expressly required to do so or not; and when it is kept it becomes a public document...." The common law required the sheriff first to create a record which he then was ordered to disclose.[14]

---

[11] 109 Eng. Reprint 202 (1829).

[12] *Nowack v. Fuller*, 243 Mich. 200, 219 N.W. 749, 750 (Mich. 1928).
[13] 17 F.3d 1446 (D.C.Cir. 1994).
[14] *Daily Gazette Co. v. Withrow*, 177 W.Va. 110, 350 S.E.2d 738, 747 (1986).

In another case, a newspaper that had been excluded from a meeting of the Atlantic City Convention Center Authority demanded access to audio tapes recorded at the meeting. The newspaper's claim was based on the New Jersey right-to-know law and the common law. The statutory claim was dismissed since the meeting was taped only to make the drafting of minutes easier and more accurate, and therefore the tapes weren't public records under the state's narrow right-to-know law. On the common law claim, however, the New Jersey Supreme Court held that the records were indeed public records since recording was a "convenient, appropriate or customary method" of documenting official action.[15]

Access to records not available otherwise may be possible through requests based on a common-law theory. Legislative bodies, for example, typically exclude themselves from the reach of right-to-know statues. In *Schwartz v. Dept. of Justice,*[16] however, a U.S. District Court noted that all three branches of government are subject to the common law right of access, and it ordered records of Peter A. Rodino Jr., then chairman of the House Judiciary Committee, released. These decisions, of course, are binding only in jurisdictions where the rulings were made, but they represent some creative or last-resort uses to which the common law can be put.

The use of common law is limited, however. Its answer to the question of what is a public record is narrow — generally confined to documents that memorialize some official transaction such as a deed or minutes of a meeting. Even when a document is clearly a public record and the requester's purpose proper, a custodian may withhold it if disclosure is outweighed by some other interest, such as personal privacy.

The discretionary aspect of the common law can frustrate the usual judicial remedy: a writ of mandamus. A writ of mandamus is a court order for an official to comply with the law. Since the common law permits discretion, some courts are reluctant to overrule a custodian who has exercised that discretion in good faith, however wrong the custodian may have been on the primary issue.

In the everyday world, a demand based on the common law is so unusual it is likely to be met by an official with a puzzled or blank look. It will probably only be pursued to a conclusion when more conventional means, such as access statutes, are unavailing, and it will almost certainly entail a time-consuming and expensive suit with an uncertain outcome. Still, given the right circumstances, the common law can be exploited to fill the cracks left by constitutions and statutes.

THE FEDERAL FREEDOM OF INFORMATION ACT

The federal Freedom of Information Act[17] is, in several respects, the most important access tool today. It is certainly the most visible and most analyzed right-to-know law, governing access to the country's largest group of records. A study of the policies and issues of the federal act will also provide insights into comparable state laws, since it provides a framework for analyzing in detail each of the fifty state right-to-know laws, an individual analysis that is beyond the scope of this book.

The FOIA is the outgrowth of the Administrative Procedure Act of 1946. That act was, in turn, a response to the explosive growth of government that began during the 1930s. The emergence of highly specialized, independent regulatory agencies like the Federal Trade Commission, and the agencies of the executive branch, like the Department of Education, triggered fears not just about secrecy but about incomprehensibility. Each of the new agencies had its own rules and procedures, causing many to feel out of touch with government.

The Administrative Procedure Act attempted to restore a sense of order to government by standardizing the procedures used to adopt and enforce rules and by making sure those procedures were accessible to the public. Though this was a considerable improvement, particularly for those regularly doing business with an agency, in another sense it failed because of its focus on how things were done, rather than on what was being done and why. And agencies remained largely their own judges of how well they complied with the act.

In response to these problems and the swelling interest in the public's right to know, the Administrataive Procedure Act was amended in 1966 by the Freedom of Information Act. For the first time, the public had a clear right of access to records of the executive and administrative agencies of government. In contrast to the common law, the legal burden was on the government to justify withholding, not on the requester to justify release.

Some agencies adopted tactics to undermine the law: The exemptions were given sweeping interpretations; fees for finding, copying and segregating exempt from non-exempt material were exorbitant; long delays became routine, and agencies claimed they

---

[15] *Atlantic City Convention Center Authority v. South Jersey Publishing Co.,* 135 N.J. 53, 637 A.2d 1261, 1267 (1993).

[16] 435 F. Supp. 1203 (D.D.C. 1977), *aff'd* 595 F.2d 889 (D.C. Cir. 1979).

[17] 5 U.S.C. sec. 552.

couldn't find the requested information. As a result, the act was extensively amended in 1974. The changes sought to ensure compliance, for example, by limiting the fees agencies could charge to actual costs, expediting the scheduling of FOIA cases and allowing a wrongly denied requester to recover attorney's fees from the agency. The act was again amended in 1976 and in 1986.

How well it works, of course, isn't measured strictly by what it says or how courts interpret it. The attitude of government leadership can be a powerful influence on the practical, day-to-day functioning of the FOIA. In contrast to its predecessors, the Clinton Administration has done a lot, at least on paper, to encourage agencies to comply with the spirit, as well as the letter, of the FOIA.

In 1993, for example, the attorney general reversed the previous administration's policy and ordered agencies to presume that a requested document should be disclosed, rather than search for an exemption under which to hide it. The Office of Management and Budget now assists agencies in making their information available, particularly with electronic access. And in 1995 the president issued a long-awaited executive order that sharply reduced the number of documents that may be classified for national security. Clinton said his order would "lift the veil" on millions of documents and keep others from ever becoming classified. The *New York Times* characterized it as the least secretive policy on government records since the beginning of the Cold War.[18]

But while the administration is taking a broader view of its obligations under the FOIA, the Supreme Court is narrowing its perception of what the act is meant to do and, thus, the kinds of records it makes available. In a key FOIA case, Justice John Paul Stevens, for the majority, wrote:

> [T]he basic purpose of the Freedom of Information Act [is] to open agency action to the light of public scrutiny.... Official information that sheds light on an agency's performance of its statutory duties fall squarely within that statutory purpose. That purpose, however, is not fostered by disclosure of information about private citizens that is accumulated in various government files but that reveals little or nothing about an agency's own conduct.[19]

For many, this view is unsupported by the language of the statute. Justice Ruth Bader Ginsburg observed in another leading case that the "'core purpose' limitation is not found in FOIA's language. A FOIA requester need not show that ... disclosure would serve any public purpose, let alone a 'core purpose' of 'opening agency action to the light of public scrutiny' or advancing 'public understanding of the operations of activities of the government.'"[20]

Some might argue for a more expansive interpretation of the FOIA by arguing its purpose is the discovery of truth, while others might limit its scope by proposing its goal is only to disclose the final actions of government. The law itself contains no statement of purpose, leaving plenty of room for interpretation.

Overview of the FOIA

In general, the FOIA requires federal government agencies to make their records available for inspection and copying unless the records fall into one of nine categories where the public interest might outweigh disclosure. The act does not apply to Congress, the courts or the president's staff.

Some information must be published by an agency — statements of its organization, functions, procedures and rules, for example, and steps one must take to obtain information, including copies of decisions. Many agencies, including all those of special interest to communications law, have public reading rooms where this and other information is available.

Other agency records must be specifically requested. The FOIA does not define "agency record," but judicial interpretations are so broad as to include almost anything containing information, so long as it was created by and is under control of the agency. Audio tapes and computer disks, as well as written materials, are agency records. Some records — appointment books, calendars and telephone longs, for example — may exist only for the convenience of individual employees. These aren't agency records. And the FOIA does not require an agency to create a document that does not exist.

The FOIA requires that a record be "reasonably described" by a requester so it can be located. An agency can charge reasonable search and copying fees. There are standard fee schedules, but individual requirements vary, so a requester should ask for an estimate of costs. The law authorizes waivers for educational and noncommercial scientific institutions and for the news media when the requested information will "contribute significantly to public

---

[18] Douglas Jehl, "Clinton Revamps Policy on Secrecy of U.S. Documents," *New York Times*, 18 April 1995, p. A1.

[19] *Department of Justice v. Reporters Committee for Freedom of the Press*, 489 U.S. 749, 772 (1989).

[20] *Department of Defense v. Federal Labor Relations Authority*, 510 U.S. 487, 507 (1994).

understanding of the operation or activities of Government." To qualify for consideration, a requester will have to explain the purpose of the request, something not otherwise required.

Though the FOIA requires a quick response to a request, substantive compliance — the production of the record or specific grounds for denial — can take months or even years. Some federal agencies are overwhelmed by requests.

If a request is ultimately refused, the FOIA provides for an administrative appeal to the head of the agency and then to U.S. District Court. There are now hundreds of judicial decisions resolving FOIA disputes. The legal burden of justifying secrecy is on the agency. A court can — but is not required to — order the government to pay attorneys' fees if a requester "substantially prevails."

An agency may withold a record under the FOIA only if it is covered by at least one of the act's nine exemptions. Even in those cases, it is never required to withold the record. The exemptions are discretionary; although other laws may require secrecy, the FOIA never does. Moreover, if part of a document is legitimately exempt from required disclosure and the remainder is not, the custodian must release the non-exempt portion if, in the words of the law, it is "reasonably segregable."

FOIA Exemptions

As indicated, records that fall into one of nine categories are exempt from disclosure under the act.

Exemption 1: National Security. This exemption authorizes the president to make and enforce rules to keep information secret in the interest of national defense or foreign policy. These rules are established by an executive order without congressional involvement. While the president has leeway to decide what documents should be protected, the order must make plain both the procedures for classifying and declassifying and the underlying criteria for determining whether any specific document should be classified.

In 1995, President Clinton signed an executive order, keeping a 1993 promise to reverse the policy of the Reagan and Bush administrations which, critics argued, encouraged excessive secrecy. The order includes a requirement that, with certain exceptions, even the most highly classified government document be made public after twenty-five years.

Whether this signals a new era in openness remains to be seen. The Clinton Administration fought public access to the National Health Care Task Force and records of White House aide Vince Foster, who killed himself. This is not unexpected; administra-

tions since that of George Washington have withheld information claiming national security concerns. Even the most outspoken advocates of public access concede that the release of certain information would be devastating for the country. But national security has also been used to shield misconduct or incompetence from public view.

As originally enacted, the exemption gave the executive branch virtually blanket authority to classify information in the interest of national security or foreign policy. In 1973, for example, the Supreme Court held that the mere fact that the administration had classified a document was enough to justify withholding the document.[21] The FOIA, the Court ruled, just didn't allow a national security classification to be challenged. Partly in response to that decision, Exemption 1 was amended in 1974 to permit a court to examine a document in private to determine whether it should be released. The amendment also allowed courts to order the release of non-classified portions of otherwise properly classified documents, that is, segregating portions of a document.

Courts today scrutinize agency actions closely to see whether the government follows its own procedures to classify documents. But they remain reluctant to overrule government experts as to whether the release of a particular document would threaten national security. Given the potential consequences of a mistake, the line between information that is safe and that which is harmful may be too fine for courts to draw with confidence. The Clinton Administration, for example, refused to disclose details of a $25 million telephone system at the White House. Would disclosure expose national secrets? Or extravagance? Or both.

Exemption 2: Administrative Documents. This exempts from required disclosure routine and insignificant matters that are "related solely to the internal personnel rules and practices of an agency." And, though the decisions of lower courts are not uniform, the exemption also protects agency manuals and rules — such as law enforcement manuals — if their release would help people dodge the law. (Materials like these are often also exempt under Exemption 7, Law Enforcement Records.)

The exemption protects routine administrative documents, such as rules about lunch hours or sick leave, because it would be burdensome for an agency to assemble and maintain the material for public inspection, and the public wouldn't reasonably be expected to have an interest. On the other hand, the mere fact that an FOIA request has been made is evidence that information is not of interest solely to an agency.

Some agencies attempt to use Exemption 2 to conceal signifi-

---

[21] *Environmental Protection Agency v. Mink,* 410 U.S. 73 (1973).

cant information. The leading case is *Air Force v. Rose*,[22] in which the Supreme Court rejected the contention that summaries of hearings concerning violations of the Air Force Academy Honor and Ethics Code were merely internal personnel matters. The Court found there was enough legitimate public interest in the integrity of its military academies to remove the records from the shield of this exemption.

Exemption 3: Other Laws. This exempts from required disclosure records that are "specifically exempted from disclosure by statute ... provided that such statute (a) requires that matter be withheld from the public in such a manner as to leave no discretion on the issue, or (b) establishes particular criteria for withholding or refers to particular types of matters to be withheld." An example is 50 U.S.C. sec. 403(g), under which the Central Intelligence Agency is not required to disclose its organization, functions, names, official titles, salaries or number of personnel employed. There are probably hundreds of statutes that authorize withholding. A complete list isn't available.

This exemption applies only to statutes and not to agency rules and regulations. Thus, an agency can't exempt itself; only Congress can do that. Similarly, an agency cannot invoke the exemption because a state law may protect certain records. A U.S. Court of Appeals has held that state juvenile records in possession of federal authorities could not be withheld under this exemption because the federal law protected only federal juvenile delinquency proceedings from disclosure.[23] A record exempt from disclosure under state law may be available under the FOIA. The opposite may also be true.

Exemption 4: Trade Secrets. This exemption protects "trade secrets and commercial or financial information" that individuals and businesses supply to government. For Exemption 4 to apply, the information must be commercially valuable, actually used in a trade or business and maintained in secret.

The idea is to protect the competitive positions of those who submit confidential information to the government. If companies that voluntarily submit information cannot depend upon it being held in confidence, they may refuse to cooperate and government's ability to get information will be impaired. When the government compels production of the information, the rationale becomes strained, and this exemption would seem not to apply.

This distinction was muddied, however, by a 1992 case in which the Court of Appeals for the District of Columbia held that when a company submits information voluntarily, even if the government could have compelled disclosure, the information enjoys exempt status.[24] This decision has been criticized, for it seems to invite collusion between an agency and a business when neither wants the information to be made public. An agency and a business simply agree to voluntary submission, undermining a line of cases that refused to recognize an agency's pledge of confidentiality as a substitute for meeting the standards of Exemption 4. Whether the other circuits will follow this court's lead is unknown. But because of the number of FOIA cases it decides due to its location in the District of Columbia, and the expertise it has developed in this area, the FOIA decisions of the D.C. Circuit merit special attention. They are highly influential.

Businesses themselves sometimes try to protect their interests in secrecy through "reverse FOIA" suits. In these, a business that has provided information to the government sues the government to stop it from making the information public. Reverse FOIA suits only involve information that falls into an exempt category, usually Exemption 4, and that the government has the discretion to release. These suits challenge the release as an abuse of discretion.

Exemption 5: Inter- and Intra-Agency Memoranda. The exemption protects agency memoranda or letters and reflects several common law privileges. Under the common law, some communications are privileged, that is, protected from forced disclosure by a court. These privileges seek to protect some larger purpose. The attorney-client privilege, for example, is said to make the criminal-justice system function better, even though it may create injustices in a particular case by denying access to some evidence.

Because of the privileges, Exemption 5 is probably the most complex and most important exemption: More than 95 percent of all documents are inter- or intra-agency memoranda.

The exemption protects the deliberative process of government that leads to a decision — candid advice and recommendations or the open exchange of ideas — in what is called "executive privilege." The exemption doesn't apply to the final decisions and opinions themselves, and it doesn't apply to statements of policy and instructions to staff that affect the public.

In deciding whether the privilege is applicable, courts examine whether a particular "predecisional" document is "so candid and personal in nature that public disclosure is likely in the future to stifle honest and frank communication within the agency," whether it is in the form of a recommendation or a draft and whether it considers the "pros and cons ... of one view-point or another."[25]

---

[22] 425 U.S. 352 (1976).

[23] *McDonnell v. United States*, 4 F.3d 1227 (3rd Cir. 1994).

[24] *Energy Project v. NRC*, 975 F.2d 871 (D.C.Cir. 1992)(en banc) *cert. denied* 507 U.S. 984 (1993).

[25] *Coastal States Gas Corp. v. Department of Energy*, 644 F.2d 854,

The privilege doesn't protect factual information, only opinions. The distinction between fact and opinion, however, isn't always self-evident and can't be made mechanically. Sometimes the factual component of a document is so merged with the deliberative component that it cannot be segregated. The D.C. Court of Appeals, for example, held that factual material about former United Nations Secretary General Kurt Waldheim was not required to be disclosed under Exemption 5.[26] The department was considering whether to exclude Waldheim as an undesirable alien in light of his alleged activities in World War II. The discretionary selection of material from a large number of primary documents, the court said, revealed significant insights into the Department of Justice's deliberations. In contrast, a complete chronological account of Walheim's military service was not exempt since it didn't suggest the thinking of the decision-makers.

In addition to executive privilege, Exemption 5 incorporates several other common law privileges, including attorney-client confidences and a lawyer's work product — documents prepared in anticipation of actual or foreseeable litigation. But courts also have cited lesser-known privileges, including, for example, one that protects commercial information created by government itself if its disclosure would put the government at a competitive disadvantage in, say, contract negotiations.

Exemption 6: Personal Privacy. This exemption protects "personnel and medical files and similar files the disclosure of which would constitute a clearly unwarranted invasion of personal privacy." Congress enacted the exemption to protect intimate and personal details in government files. No specific kinds of files are categorically exempt, though some are more likely to contain the sort of highly intimate, personal information the exemption is designed to protect. The term "similar files" has been interpreted broadly. One appellate court, for example, held that the voice recordings of the crew in the Challenger rocket was a "similar file" since the tape revealed personal information about particular individuals.[27] The tapes contained the final radio transmissions before the rocket exploded, killing everyone on board.

Some recent decisions, however, have hardly concerned the sort of records usually associated with medical and personnel records. In *U.S. Department of Defense v. FLRA,*[28] for example, two unions sought the home addresses of certain federal employees.

The privacy interest at stake was that of individuals not wanting to be bothered at home with work-related matters.

The Supreme Court reversed a lower court that had ordered release of those addresses. It balanced the competing interests and found that if the privacy interest of the employees was slight, the weight on the public interest side of the judicial balance beam was even slighter. Disclosure of home addresses would not shed appreciable light on government operations or activities. With this case, the Court has instructed lower courts to consider only the broad purpose of the FOIA in striking a balance — to what extent does disclosure enlighten the public about the operations of government? The particular purpose of the requester is irrelevant. Compare this categorical kind of balancing with that of the common law, which may consider the particular use to which the information will be put.

Exemption 7: Law Enforcement Records. The purpose of this exemption is to protect law enforcement records and other information whose disclosure would jeopardize present and future investigations. This could happen because the details of a specific investigation were released, or because of the release of general investigative techniques or policies. The exemption also protects the physical safety of officials, informants and others in the criminal justice system.

As originally enacted, the exemption applied to "investigatory files compiled for law enforcement purposes." Courts interpreted that phrase to give a blanket exemption to any file that met the threshhold test of being "investigatory." In one case, a court ruled that, even though there was no on-going or contemplated law enforcement proceeding, an analysis of the bullet that killed President John F. Kennedy was exempt because it remained part of an "investigatory" file.[29]

Congress narrowed the exemption in 1976 to avoid such interpretations. First, it limited withholding only to situations where release would cause any of several specific kinds of harm, disclosure of the identity of a confidential source, for example. Second, it allowed only the withholding of records, not entire files. Authorities had often withheld an entire file even if only one record in the file contained exempt material. One result of this amendment was to give historians and other access to a wealth of important material — such as that related to executed spies Julius and Ethel Rosenberg — that had remained sealed for decades as an "investigatory file." Agencies complained that the amendment went too far in the other direction and no longer gave adequate protection to some

---

866 (D.C.Cir. 1980).

[26] *Mapother v. Department of Justice,* 3 F.3d 1533 (D.C.Cir. 1993).

[27] *New York Times Co. v. NASA,* 920 F.2d 1002 (D.C.Cir. 1990)(*en banc*).

[28] 510 U.S. 487 (1994).

---

[29] *Wiesberg v. Department of Justice,* 489 F.2d 1195 (D.C. Cir. 1973), *cert. denied,* 416 U.S. 993 (1974).

sensitive law enforcement information, particularly training manuals and other non-investigatory materials. So the exemption was again amended in 1986.

For a record to be exempt from required disclosure, a two-part test must be met. First, it must be determined that the records or information were compiled for "law enforcement purposes." This includes more than investigatory records; training manuals, for example, are exempt.

The Supreme Court answered one crucial question in 1989: Could an agency invoke Exemption 7 to deny access to information that was originally compiled for a purpose other than law enforcement but was later assembled for a criminal investigation? A majority of the Court said it could; the language of the statute didn't require the original purpose of the information to be considered.[30] Justice Antonin Scalia dissented, arguing that the majority focused too tightly on the words of the law. He complained that the decision allows the policy behind the exemption to be "readily evaded (or [made] illusory) if it requires nothing more than gathering up documents the government does not wish to disclose, with a plausible law-enforcement purpose in mind. This is a hole one can drive a truck through."[31]

Whether the information is compiled for law enforcement purposes is only the first part of the test. For the exemption to apply, it must also be shown that release of the information "could reasonably be expected to cause" one of six specific kinds of harm. Four are uncontroversial and have received little judicial attention:

- the withholding of records when disclosure would deny a person a right to a fair trial or impartial adjudication;
- withholding of information that would "endanger the life or physical safety of any individual";
- withholding of records that would disclose law enforcement techniques, guidelines and procedures "if such disclosure could reasonably be expected to risk circumvention of law";
- withholding records that protect the identities of confidential sources so long as there is a mutual expectation of a confidential relationship.

The remaining categories produce much litigation and confusion. One allows withholding if disclosure could "interfere with enforcement proceedings." If enforcement proceedings are over, however, or if none are on the horizon, this exemption shouldn't apply. Nonetheless some agencies claim the exemption on the basis that a case may arise or be reopened.

Records or information may also be withheld if their release could "reasonably be expected to constitute an unwarranted invasion of personal privacy." This exemption is similar to Exemption 6 in that a balancing of the privacy interest and the public interest is required. A comparison of the wording of the two exemptions suggests that privacy interests should receive greater weight here. Before the privacy interest prevails in Exemption 6, the intrusion must be "clearly unwarranted." Here it must only be "unwarranted." In *Department of Justice v. Reporters Committee for Freedom of the Press*, the Court held that a request for information about a person's criminal history was unwarranted since it shed little light on "public understanding of the operations or activities of government."[32]

The case is important, not just for an explanation of the substantive test to be used here, but for the insights it provides about the Court's attitude toward electronic data. Most of the records the Reporters Committee sought were available in one place or another in the form of accessible, traditional, paper records. Getting them would require a lot of leg work. The federal government had them all in one place — a computer. But the Court said the records, in electronic form, were qualitively different; the power of the computer to assemble and manipulate the data held vastly greater potential to violate personal privacy.

Exemption 8: Records of Financial Institutions. This applies to records related to government supervision of financial institutions such as banks and savings and loans. The purpose is to protect the security and integrity of financial institutions.

Exemption 9 applies to "geological and geophysical information and data, including maps, concerning wells." This exemption protects oil well data.

THE ELECTRONIC FOIA AMENDMENTS OF 1996

When President Lyndon Johnson signed the FOIA 30 years ago, the federal government had fewer than 3,000 computers.[33] According to one source, the government owns more than two million computers and seventy-five percent of the government's business will be done electronically by the year 2000.[34]

However, the access guaranteed by the FOIA has not kept pace with this electronic revolution. Some government agencies used their conversion to computerized record-keeping as an excuse not to release information to the public and the press. These bureau-

---

[30] *John Doe Agency v. John Doe Corp.*, 492 U.S. 146 (1989).
[31] *Id.* at 163 (Scalia, J., dissenting).

[32] 489 U.S. 749, 775 (1989).
[33] Tony Mauro, "FOIA: A Good Idea Changing With the Times," *The First Amendment News*, Sept. 1996, p. 1.
[34] *Id.*

crats argued that the new formats make reproducing information too expensive or unwieldy, or that releasing electronic data was not required by the FOIA. In addition, agencies under pressure to raise revenues, began charging fees for data that would have been free in paper form.

To solve some of these problems, Congress passed the Electronic Freedom of Information Act Amendments in 1996, thirty years after the FOIA was passed.

The Electronic Freedom of Information Act Amendments of 1996 (EFOIA),[35] guaranteed that records maintained in computer form are as accessible as paper records. Among other things, the law required agencies make regulations, opinions, policy statements and similar information available on-line, on CD-ROM, or computer disc. It also required agencies to provide information in the format requested whenever possible.[36]

In addition to making electronic records accessible, the 1996 law amended other portions of the FOIA. For example, an important section of the new law allows reporters expedited access if they can demonstrate a "compelling need" for the federal records they request under FOIA.[37]

Agencies are now required to respond faster in two situations. First, when failure to obtain records can pose an imminent threat to an individual's life or physical safety. Second, and of particular interest to reporters, when "a request made by a person primarily engaged in disseminating information, urgency to inform the public concerning actual or alleged federal government activity."[38] According to the new law, expedited access requests must be processed within ten days. In addition, the new law changes the time limit for other requests from ten to twenty days.

Ultimately, the EFOIA should also improve access to database searches. Agencies must make reasonable efforts to search for requested records in electronic form, except when a search would significantly interfere with agency information. Programming created to facilitate a database search does not amount to the creation of records.[39]

Commentators believe that the legislative history surrounding the new law may provide broader access to governmental informa-

tion and limit the Supreme Court's problematic ruling in *Department of Justice v. Reporters Committee.*[40] In *Reporters Committee*, the Supreme Court limited access to governmental records which revealed information relevant to the agency's "core purpose." Access advocates, including those in Congress, disagreed with the Court's decision. Congressional leaders indicated they crafted this FOIA amendment to address this restrictive view of access to public records.

"The purpose of the FOIA is to require agencies of the federal government to make records available to the public through public inspection and upon the request of any person for any public or private use," according to the findings of the Senate.[41] With this finding, Congress challenges the Supreme Court's narrow interpretation of the purpose of FOIA in its landmark *Reporters Committee* decision.

In language intended to clarify the FOIA's purpose, one of the bill's sponsors, Sen. Patrick Leahy (D-VT) said:

The purpose of the FOIA is not limited to making agency records and information available to the public only in cases where such material would shed light on the activities and operations of government. Efforts by the courts to articulate a 'core purpose' for which information should be released imposes a limitation on the FOIA which Congress did not intend and which cannot be found in its language, and distorts the broader import of the Act in effectuating government openness.[42]

Many access advocates have been disappointed with the government's response to the new amendments. Even with the new provisions, it is not unusual to wait for months or even years for a response.[43] According to Jane Kirtley, executive director of the Reporter's Committee for Freedom of the Press, "...for the most part, federal agencies have missed their deadlines for compliance with the Act in the same way they have been missing FOI deadlines for decades."[44]

---

[35] 5 U.S.C. sec. 552.

[36] This provision was intended to overrule a 1984 federal district court decision, *Dismukes v. Department of the Interior*, 603 F. Supp. 760 (D.D.C. 1984), which held that agencies had no obligation to accommodate a requester's preference for computer access as long as the information was available in a reasonably accessible form.

[37] 5 U.S.C. sec. 552 (a)(6)(vi).

[38] 5 U.S.C. sec. 552 (a)(6)(E)(v)(II).

[39] 5 U.S.C. sec. 552(a)(3)(C)

[40] 489 U.S. 749 (1989).

[41] 5 U.S.C. sec. 522 (a)(2)(a).

[42] S. Rep. No. 104-272 (additional views of Sen. Patrick Leahy, p. 23).

[43] FOIA requests answered by the FBI in 1995 had been pending an average of 923 days. Mike Feinsilber, "Government Information Now Computer-Accessible," *The Chattanooga Times,* 19 September 1996, pg. A11.

[44] *Government Reform and Oversight on the Implementation of the Electronic Freedom of Information Act Amendments of 1996: Hearing*

Agencies say they do the best they can with their resources. For example, the FBI spends $21 million a year and employs 300 people to process FOIA requests, which it receives at the rate of one per minute.[45] Contrary to a popular belief, journalists use the FOIA relatively infrequently. In reality, the FOIA is a toll for companies to snoop on each other, with an estimated 75 percent of all FOIA requests coming from corporations.[46] The FBI reported that requests from the news media made up less than three percent of the total requests.[47]

Some agencies meet the time limits to respond to requests. Most do not. According to one estimate, the government receives about 600,000 requests a year and spends an average of $500 to respond to each request.[48]

While the EFOIA has triggered major reforms in electronic information processing, including the development of numerous government-agency Web pages filled with useful information, the courts and executive branch have ignored the amendment's findings intended to broaden FOIA's use to serve "any public or private purpose."[49]

While using the FOIA and EFOIA takes patience and many of its promises have yet to be fulfilled, many of the nation's most important stories, including numerous Pulitzer Prize winners, have come from government documents accessed through the FOIA. Important stories have focused on human rights violations, corruption by public officials, workplace and aircraft accidents, bridge safety, cocaine trafficking, unsafe products, serious health hazards, and questionable research programs on humans.[50]

FEDERAL OPEN MEETINGS LAWS

To supplement the Freedom of Information Act, Congress enacted the Sunshine Act in 1976 to open meetings as well as records.[51] The law requires the meetings of high-level decision-makers in about fifty executive-branch agencies to be open. Information available under the FOIA often represents only what was done, sometimes in a general or cursory way. The Sunshine Act lets the public observe how and why an agency makes the decisions it does.

The act has limited impact. Only agencies that are subject to the FOIA are affected. Thus, groups as important as the President's Council of Economic Advisors or the Board of Governors of the Federal Reserve aren't covered. Moreover, for the law to apply, the agency must be headed by a body of two or more members. Others are exempt on the premise that where an agency is headed by an individual, the need to observe give-and-take discussion among equals is absent.

The law is evaded regularly. Staff members, who aren't subject to the act, represent the views of their bosses to staffers of other agency heads, who then pass the information on to their bosses. In agencies where a quorum for a meeting is larger than two, agency heads can meet two at a time and discuss public matters. Some acknowledge that this isn't an efficient way to work and may not lead to good decision-making, but many agency heads argue that complying is just as inefficient. In April 1995, fifteen current and former agency heads asked Congress to amend the Sunshine Act to allow "broad outlines of policy" to be discussed in closed meetings.[52]

As it stands, the law requires that meetings be announced at least one week in advance and that the announcement include the time, place and subject of the meeting. It prohibits informal discussions and decision-making. The meetings opened by the Sunshine Act "are not intended to be merely reruns staged for the public after agency members have discussed the issue in private and predetermined their views," one Senate report concluded. "The whole decision-making process, not merely the results, must be exposed to public scrutiny."[53]

The act does not give the public a right to participate in the meetings.

The act allows, but does not require, portions of meetings to be closed when the subject matter falls into one or more of ten exemptions. If an exemption applies, the agency must balance the public interest in openness against the particular interest the exemption is designed to protect before closing a meeting.

before the Subcommittee on Government Management, Information and Technology of the House Committee on Government Reform and Oversight, 105th Cong., June 9, 1998, (statement by Jane Kirtley).

[45] Nancy Ferris, "Virtual Records," *Government Executive,* August 1997, p. 43.

[46] Tony Mauro, "FOIA: A Good Idea Changing With the Times, *The First Amendment News,* Sept. 1996, p. 6.

[47] *Id.*

[48] Ferris, "Virtual Records," *supra* note 45, at 43.

[49] See *Government Reform, supra* note 11.

[50] "FOI-Based Journalism," *Quill,* September 1997, pp. 34-36.

[51] 5 U.S.C. sec. 522(b).

[52] Cindy Skrycki, "Getting a Little Burned Up About the Sunshine Act," *Washington Post,* 28 April 1995, p. F1.

[53] Allan Robert Adler, *Litigation under the Federal Open Government Laws* (Washington: American Civil Liberties Union Foundation, 1993): 316-17, quoting Senate Report No. 354, 94th Congress, 1st Session.

Seven of the Sunshine Act's ten exemptions parallel those of the FOIA. The act has nothing like FOIA Exemption 5 (inter- and intra-agency memoranda) or Exemption 9 (geological or geophysical data). Instead, the act's Exemption 5 protects agency discussions that "involve accusing any person of a crime, or formally censuring any person." A general discussion doesn't qualify. It must focus on a specific person and, if it concerns a crime, a specific charge.

Exemption 9 of the act shields two kinds of discussions: those that might jeopardize the stability of a financial institution or might trigger significant speculation in financial instruments, and those that might "significantly frustrate implementation of a proposed agency action." One court has limited the exemption to matters whose disclosure would allow someone to profit at government expense or allow an agency regulation to be evaded.[54] Exemption 10 of the Sunshine Act permits closure when discussions concern a subpoena or participation in a civil action or proceeding, such as arbitration or adjudication.

The Sunshine Act governs the conduct of government agencies; the Federal Advisory Committee Act, enacted in 1972, governs the advisory committee process and opens "to public scrutiny the manner in which government agencies obtain [information] from private individuals."[55] Whether called a "council," "task force," "commission," or something else, an advisory committee is a private group that is either established or utilized by the executive branch to obtain advice. One can also be created by statute.

FACA was passed to expose any waste of government funds on committee meetings that serve no useful function and to allow the public to observe any undue influence of lobbyists and special interest groups on federal decision-makers. In addition to opening deliberations, the act requires that the public have access to all committee records, reports, transcripts, appendices, working papers, drafts, studies, agenda or other documents that were prepared by or made available to the advisory committee. FACA is complex and riddled with qualifications, but it can be useful at times.

STATE RIGHT-TO-KNOW LAWS

All states have laws requiring government records and meetings to be open to the public. In addition to these broad laws, states have specific statutes applicable to particular kinds of records — land deeds or voter registration records, for example — or to particular kinds of meetings — like rezoning hearings.

Citizens are more likely to use these state laws than the federal laws; there are more state and local records, and there are more state and local issues. It's important, therefore, to have some knowledge of both the general and the specific laws where one works and lives. For reporters, this is never more true than with meetings. If access to a record is denied, a requester will almost always have plenty of time to find help and consider the next step. No law requires that a record be handed over immediately; officials are given time to find and deliver the record.

Meetings, however, are timely, and decisions have to be made on the spot. When the city council orders the public to leave the room so that "financial matters" can be discussed, for example, an observer must quickly answer several questions. Does the open meetings law allow secrecy when "financial matters" are discussed? Has the city council taken the required procedural steps, like taking a vote to close them meeting? If there are violations of the law, should the observer object immediately or file some kind of complaint? Or do nothing?

Answers to these questions require a working knowledge of the law, a feel for the workings of the particular governmental body and, sometimes, an understanding of what the observer's boss will authorize — like paying a lawyer to file an action.

Each state right-to-know law is unique. Each differs, not only in its language, but in its political setting and judicial arena. There is no substitute for becoming acquainted with state law. In most states, there are several sources of help, and some suggestions for finding help will be offered later in this chapter. Still, some general observations can be made.

As with any law, a good starting point is the policy behind the law. Precisely what did a legislature attempt to accomplish when it enacted the statute? Many state freedom of information statutes begin with a statement of policy. Some may not be particularly helpful. Kansas, for example, says only that "It is declared to be the public policy of this state that public records shall be open for inspection by any person...."[56] Others have a richer texture. Michigan, for example, declares:

It is the public policy of this state that all persons are entitled to full and complete information regarding the affairs of government and the official acts of those who represent them as public officials and public employees.... The people shall be informed

---

[54] *Common Cause v. NRC*, 674 F.2d 921 (D.C.Cir. 1982).

[55] *National Anti-Hunger Coalition v. Executive Committee of the President's Privacy Sctor Survey on Cost Control*, 711 F.2d 1971 (D.C.Cir. 1983).

[56] Kentucky Rev. Stat sec. 61.870 (1994).

so that they may fully participate in the democratic process.[57]

When a custodian or court must decide whether to release information or open a meeting whose subject matter falls into a gray area, a statute like Michigan's is immensely more helpful to the analysis and may prove persuasive.

The nuts and bolts of the state right-to-know laws share similarities. They generally declare that all records and meetings are open to the public unless exemptions apply. Some states follow the federal lead and exempt only a few broad categories. This broad approach makes for a tidy-looking statute but probably causes more litigation because of the case-by-case balancing that inevitably goes with it.

Other states opt for specific, narrow exemptions, and, over the years, many have built a rather lengthy list. Virginia, for example, exempts more than fifty types of records. Because of its length and apparent complexity, this narrow, specific approach results in an ugly looking law, but one that often works surprisingly well day-to-day because of its precision in describing what is accessible and what is not.

Many policy and legal issues are common to the federal FOIA and state right-to-know statutes. The decisions of the federal court in interpreting the FOIA, of course, are in no way binding on state courts interpreting their own laws. But the experience of federal courts in freedom of information issues may provide persuasive reasoning for states. So a careful review of the federal FOIA is not a bad place to acquire a background to understand local law.

Electronic records raise special issues that courts and legislatures are only beginning to address. Right-to-know laws were passed in an era of paper, folders and filing cabinets. Today many records are kept in electronic databases, accessibly only through computers. Many states have amended their laws to accommodate this fundamental change, broadening the definition of "record" to include information on computer disks and tapes. But the results have been unsatisfactory, and in no jurisdiction has law kept pace with technology.

First, there are physical complications. In earlier days, a request for a record required a custodian to locate and retrieve a specific piece of paper from a filing cabinet. The law, not unreasonably because of the labor needed, didn't require a custodian to create a record that didn't already exist or to abstract or manipulate data from those that did.

Today, however, a custodian can use this reasoning in ways never intended when the laws were passed. In one sense, an electronic record does not exist until someone does something to create it. Thus, every request, in a narrow, literal sense, requires the creation of a record. And the law, based on an era of paper records, never requires the creation of a record.

Custodians rarely, if ever, go to that extreme with routine requests. Requesters tend to get the same information they received when records were on paper. But there is a serious problem with the borderline requests — those that require more than minimal personnel intervention with the computer. At what point does programming, because of the quantity or quality of the data manipulation required or because of the novelty of the finished product, cross the line between the routine (which is required) and the extraordinary (which isn't)? No legislative body has developed a satisfactory answer. Finding and describing that point, at the federal and state levels, is a pressing legal challenge.

Closely related are paper-era prohibitions against abstracting or manipulating data. A right-to-know request to manually abstract data from a particular paper document and then manually correlate it with that taken from other paper records was at one time a practical impossibility. But the development of modern relational databases, accurate scanners and the promise of further advances can make filling these requests no more trouble than a trip to the filing cabinet. Indeed, developments in software and expanded opportunities for direct public access through on-line gateways or public-use terminals promise to eliminate, fairly soon, the physical issues with record access and manipulation. If they are being resolved, other computer-related issues are being worsened.

As a matter of public policy, many state and local governments are selling computer-generated data to pay for computer systems and to provide a regular stream of additional revenue. Commercial interests, direct-mail firms and utilities, for example, are willing to pay well for this data. But if state law requires an agency to provide information virtually free to all comers, it can hardly expect to profit from the data. So many states have either amended or are trying to amend their right-to-know laws to allow them to enter the business of selling government information. The inevitable result is that less data in less powerful forms is available to the public.

The same power that makes electronic information so attractive to many private and commercial interests raises grave privacy concerns to others. One recalls that the Supreme Court found a computer database to be much more than the sum of its parts. It was not the release of the individual rap sheet that the Court found to be an invasion of privacy, it was the vast power of the computer to acquire and manipulate the data. Privacy advocates are raising

---

[57] Michigan Com. Laws Ann. sec. 15.231 (1993).

these issues in many states today.

ACCESS TO PRISONS

The ability to get information about government activities and policies from records and meetings comes from the federal and state right-to-know statutes. Federal and state laws also govern access to particular places and people, including prisons and prisoners.

With more than one million people incarcerated in the United States, and prison systems accounting for the largest budget expenditure in most states, information about what happens behind prison walls is essential in ensuring public accountability. However, as the number of inmates and the amount of money being spent on prisons has increased over the past twenty years, many correctional systems have curtailed the rights of the news media to report on prisons and potential government abuse of prisoners by imposing unprecedented restrictions on inmates contacts with the outside world.

These restrictions flow from a trio of Supreme Court cases in which the court ruled that the First Amendment does not guarantee the press access to correctional facilities or particular prisoners. In *Pell v. Procunier,* the Supreme Court upheld California state correction rules which restricted the media's ability to interview specific prisoners.[58] The Court explained that while the First Amendment prohibited the government from interfering with a free press, the Constitution did not guarantee the press more access than the average citizen.[59] In subsequent rulings, the Court recognized the responsibility of prison officials to maintain order and provide a secure environment, and granted prison systems great latitude in setting up rules restricting interviews.[60]

However, horrible things can and do happen behind prison walls. Unless the media can gain access to prisons, these abuses go unreported and the abusers go unchecked.

According to a new study sponsored by the Society of Professional Journalists, many state correctional systems have seized upon the Supreme Court's rulings to curtail the rights of the news media by imposing unprecedented restrictions on inmates access to the outside world. According to the study, some regulations include outright bans on face-to-face interviews, others contain policies which discriminate between "legitimate" and "entertainment

media." Still others ban the use of electronic equipment within the prison.[61]

California officials, complaining of an overwhelming number of request from reporters to interview "celebrity" prisoners like Charles Manson and the Mendendez brothers, was the first state to embrace new, more restrictive policies designed to prevent high-profile criminals from becoming celebrities. The restrictions also prohibit reporters from covering allegations of beatings, rapes and administrative abuses inside prisons.

While the Supreme Court gave correctional authorities broad discretion to limit news-gathering activities in jails in the 1970s prison access cases, critics of these harsh new policies argue that the Supreme Court did not envision such draconian measures. For example, some policies allow administrators to grant or deny an interview based on the proposed content of the news story. In Connecticut, for instance, journalists are required to prepare written requests for interviews, including a "statement of any perceived benefit to law enforcement agencies." Another criterion requires access requests be based on "whether a print or electronic report results in a significant benefit to law enforcement agencies."[62]

Critics of these regulations believe they conflict with the Supreme Court's prohibition on government regulation of the content of expression. The First Amendment guarantee of freedom of expression means that the "government has no power to restrict expression because of its message, its ideas, its subject matter, or its content" without a compelling interest.[63]

Although a few states have established rules that balance legitimate penological concerns with the public's right to know, the trend is toward broader restrictions, greater secrecy and less accountability to the public.[64]

SUMMARY

Access to government records and meetings is essential to meaningful participation in government. As vital and as obvious as that axiom is, only recently has there been a widespread and sustained effort to guarantee citizen access to governmental information. The federal and some state constitutions provide limited ac-

---

[58] 417 U.S. 817 (1974).
[59] See *Id.*
[60] *Saxbe v. Washington Post Co.,* 417 U.S. 843 (1974); *Houchins v. KQED,* 438 U.S. 1 (1978).

[61] See Charles N. Davis, "Access to Prisons," *Quill,* May 1998, pp. 19-28.
[62] *Id.* at 24; Conn. Dept. of Corrections, Directive No. 1.5 (1995) at 3.
[63] *Police Dept. v. Mosely,* 408 U.S. 92 (1972).
[64] See Davis, *supra* note 5.

cess, particularly in the criminal justice system. Viewed optimistically, the decisions hint at a broader, emerging right of access, but only after a workable rule can be crafted that will draw a sharp, easily applied line between those things which need to be public and those that don't. This can take years.

The common law can supplement other access tools, mainly statutes. The elastic qualities of the common law, one of its historic weaknesses, is an asset to exploit when a tool must be found to reach information inaccessible by other means.

Federal and state statutes — freedom of information or right-to-know laws — are the front-line means of access. There is a federal records law, the Freedom of Information Act, and a federal meetings law, the Sunshine Act. Access to federal electronic records is covered in the Electronic Freedom of Information Act. Each state has its own counterpart to the federal laws and many states are including access to electronic records, as well.

As a group, these laws give each citizen the right to inspect and copy government documents or attend government meetings. Some agencies and, in fact, entire branches of government, typically the judicial branch, are exempt. Each statute also identifies kinds of records or subjects of meetings that are exempt from required disclosure. In most, but not all of these exempt categories, secrecy is not required. The government may open the record or meeting if the public interest in access outweighs the competing interest of the exception.

Federal and state statutes also govern access to prisons and prisoners. New restrictions, which essentially limit meaningful access by reporters to prisoners, have been adopted recently. The right to keep the prison system accountable to the public, in whose name the press carries out its work, continues to be an important fight for the nation's news media.

FOR ADDITIONAL READING

There are many sources of practical help for gaining access to meetings and records, but a few stand out:

Federal Access Law. "How to Use the Federal FOI Act" is a booklet published by The Reporters Committee for Freedom of the Press, Suite 504, 1735 Eye St., N.W., Washington, D.C. 20006. "Step-by-Step Guide to Using the Freedom of Information Act" is published by the American Civil Liberties Union, 122 Maryland Ave., N.E., Washington, D.C. 20002. The price of each is modest. Both are direct, no-nonsense guides that take readers through the process of getting access to federal records. Neither addresses access to meetings.

State Access Law. The Reporters Committee publishes a series of booklets on open government under the general heading "Tapping Officials' Secrets." One is published for each state, and purchasers should ask for the open government book for a specific state. Written for and by lawyers, these are not as readable as some publications but can still be helpful. In addition, most state press associations are willing, even eager, to help with understanding local right-to-know laws.

Access to Prisons. The Society of Professional Journalists produced a special report, "Access to Prisons," in May of 1998. The report appeared in the May 1998 issue of *Quill* magazine. Copies are also available from SPJ by calling 765-653-3333 or through SPJ's web site: http://spj.org/foia/prisons/spjreport/.

The Authors

Dorothy Bowles, a professor at the University of Tennessee, has taught communications law at the graduate and undergraduate levels for twenty years. She is the author of *Kansas Media Law Guide* and *Media Law in Tennessee,* as well as numerous journal articles. She is on the board of directors of the Student Press Law Center and has held several offices in the Association for Education in Journalism and Mass Communications. She has worked as a newspaper reporter and editor and is co-author of one of the leading editing textbooks. Her bachelor's degree is from Texas Tech University, her master's from the University of Kansas, and her Ph.D. from the University of Wisconsin.

Sandra F. Chance is assistant professor and assistant director of the Brechner Center for Freedom of Information at the University of Florida, where she teaches mass communication law. She practiced media law before joining the faculty at Florida and has published articles in numerous academic and professional journals, including *Communication Law and Policy, Journal of Broadcasting & Electronic Media, Journalism & Mass Communication Quarterly, Seton Hall Legislative Journal, Journal of Law and Public Policy, Quill* and *Editor & Publisher.* She is on the board of directors of the First Amendment Foundation and is Sunshine Chair for the Society of Professional Journalists. She is an active member of the Florida Bar's media and communications law committee and is a frequent speaker and workshop leader on media law and freedom of information issues. She was named an Outstanding Teacher for 1988 at the University of Florida. She

holds B.A., M.A. and J.D. degrees from the University of Florida.

Thomas Eveslage is professor of jounalism and associate dean for academic affairs at Temple University's School of Communications and Theater in Philadelphia. He is past director of the master of journalism program and past chair of the Department of Journalism. He holds an M.A. degree in journalism from the University of Minnesota and a Ph.D. in journalism from Southern Illinois University at Carbondale. Dr. Eveslage is on the board of directors of the Student Press Law Center and the Pennsylvania School Press Association. He is a former copy editor and university news director.

F. Dennis Hale is professor and former director of the School of Mass Communication at Bowling Green State University in Bowling Green, Ohio. He has published more than eighty book chapters, convention papers and journal articles, many about mass media law. He is a former head of the Law Division of the Association for Education in Journalism in Mass Communication and has received research grants from the U.S. Justice Department and the Newspaper Research Council.

Steven Helle is a professor and former head of the Department of Journalism at the University of Illinois in Urbana-Champaign. He is co-author of *Last Rights: Revisiting Four Theories of the Press* and has published numerous articles on communication law in, among others, *Duke Law Journal, Journalism and Mass Com-*

munication Quarterly, Villanova Law Review, University of Illinois Law Review, Iowa Law Review, Illinois Bar Journal, Journalism and Mass Communication Educator and Depaul Law Review. A former head of the Law Division of the Association for Education in Journalism and Mass Communication, Dr. Helle has been named to the editorial boards of the Illinois Bar Journal, Journalism Monographs and Communication Law and Policy. He is past chair of the Media Law Committee of the Illinois State Bar Association. Twice he has been named one of the outstanding undergraduate teachers at the University of Illinois, most recently in 1996, when he received the Luckman Undergraduate Distinguished Teaching Award. He was also selected Freedom Forum teacher of the Year in 1998. His J.D. and M.A. degrees are from the University of Iowa.

Louise Williams Hermanson is a professor in the Department of Communication at the University of South Alabama, where she teaches communication law, ethics, print journalism and media history. She has been at South Alabama since 1990. Her research interests focus on alternative dispute resolution in conflicts between media and the public. She has published articles in Journalism & Mass Communication Monographs, Journalism & Mass Communication Quarterly, Journalism & Mass Communication Educator and Oral History Review and chapters in several books. Her bachelor's and master's degrees are from the University of South Carolina, and her Ph.D. is from the University of Minnesota. She is formerly the head of the mass communication program at Fort Valley State College in Georgia and worked as a professional journalist in South Carolina.

W. Wat Hopkins is associate professor of communication studies at Virginia Tech, where he teaches journalism and communication law courses. He has published three books and a number of articles on First Amendment topics, including articles in Journalism Monographs, Journalism & Mass Communication Quarterly and Communication Law and Policy. He is a past head of the Law Division of the Association for Education in Journalism and Mass Communication and is on the editorial board of Journalism & Mass Communcation Quarterly. He received his bachelor's degree from Western Carolina University and his master's and Ph.D. degrees from the University of North Carolina at Chapel Hill.

Paul E. Kostyu is associate professor and department chair of journalism at Ohio Wesleyan University, where he teaches journalism, communication law and communication history courses. His

bachelor's degree is from Heidelberg College, and his master's and Ph.D. degrees are from Bowling Green State University. In addition, he studied for a year in Bangor, Wales, on a Rotary International Foundation Journalism Award. He is a former newspaper reporter, and has published research in Communications and the Law, American Journalism and the Journal of Mass Media Ethics. He is also a co-author of the sixth edition of Reporting for the Media. He recently worked on projects involving computer-assisted reporting for U.S. News & World Report, the Ann Arbor (Michigan) News and the Mansfield (Ohio) News Journal.

Greg Lisby is associate professor of communication at Georgia State University, where he teaches mass communication law and communication ethics. In addition to serving as a member of the editorial board of American Journalism, he has had articles published in Journalism Monographs, Communication and the Law, Journalism Quarterly, Journal of Communication Inquiry, Newspaper Research Journal and Georgia Historical Quarterly. The second edition of his book Mass Communication Law in Georgia was published in 1996. He was also recipient of the 1990 Henry W. Grady Prize for Research in Journalism History.

Cathy Packer is an associate professor in the School of Journalism and Mass Communication at the University of North Carolina at Chapel Hill. She teaches media law and reporting and is the author of Freedom of Expression in the American Military: A Communication Modeling Analysis and is co-editor of The North Carolina Media Law Handbook. She received her master's and doctorate degrees from the University of Minnesota and her bachelor's degree from UNC.

Milagros (Millie) Rivera-Sanchez is associate professor in the Department of Telecommunication, College of Journalism and Communications at the University of Florida. She teaches courses in telecommunication regulation and media law. She has published articles in Journalism and Mass Communication Monographs, Journalism and Mass Communication Quarterly, Journalism History, The Federal Communications Law Journal, Communications and the Law and other journals. Her research interests include regulation of the electronic media in the United States and in Latin America. She holds a bachelor's degree from the University of Puerto Rico and master's and doctorate degrees from the University of Florida.

Susan Dente Ross is an assistant professor and head of the journalism program in the Edward R. Murrow School of Communication at Washington State University. She teaches media law, First Amendment theory, access to public records and journalism skills courses. In addition to conducting research on the regulation of emerging communication technologies, Dr. Ross examines the application of the First Amendment to speech at the margins and studies how marginalized groups use advertising to frame media coverage of social movements.

Joseph Russomanno is an assistant professor in the Walter Cronkite School of Journalism and Telecommunication at Arizona State University. His articles have appeared in *Communication Law and Policy, Communications and the Law, Hamline Law Review,* the *Journal of Broadcasting and Electronic Media* and the *Journal of Communication Inquiry.* He worked as a television news journalist — primarily as a producer and executive producer — for ten years. He received his master's degree from the University of Missouri and his doctorate from the University of Colorado.

Sigman Splichal is assistant professor in the School of Communication at the University of Miami, where he teaches media law and ethics and is director of the Journalism/Photography Program. He began his journalism career in 1971 and was a newspaper writer and editor in Georgia, Florida and Virginia. He received his bachelor's, master's and Ph.D. degrees from the University of Florida. He is the author of numerous law and academic journal articles on legal and ethical topics.

Ruth Walden is a professor in the School of Journalism and Mass Communication at the University of North Carolina at Chapel Hill. Before joining the UNC faculty in 1985, she taught at the University of Utah and University of Wisconsin-Madison. She also was a reporter for newspapers in Wisconsin and Illinois and assistant director of judicial education for the Wisconsin Supreme Court. She is the author of *Mass Communication Law in North Carolina* and has published articles on media law and First Amendment theory in law and communication journals. The former head of the Law Division of the Association for Education in Journalism and Mass Communication, Dr. Walden serves on the editorial boards of *Journalism & Mass Communication Quarterly* and *Communication Law & Policy.* She holds B.A, M.A. and Ph.D. degrees from the University of Wisconsin-Madison.

Kyu Ho Youm is a professor in the Walter Cronkite School of Journalism and Telecommunication at Arizona State University. He has published scholarly articles on communication law subjects in major U.S. and foreign academic journals, including *Journalism & Mass Communication Quarterly, Hastings Communication/Entertainment (COMM/ENT) Law Journal* and the *International and Comparative Law Quarterly* of London. A former head of the AEJMC Law Division and a former chair of the Communication Law and Policy Group of the International Communication Association, he serves on editorial boards of thirteen communication law journals in the United States and England. He received his bachelor's degree in South Korea and his master's and doctorate degrees from Southern Illinois University. He holds a Master of Studies in Law degree from the Yale Law School.

AUTHORS EMERETI

Robert L. Hughes is an attorney in Richmond. He taught communication law for nineteen years at the Virginia Commonwealth University School of Mass Communications. Before that, he was a reporter and editorial writer for newspapers in Charlotte and West Palm Beach. He has a B.A. degree from Davidson College, an M.J. degree from the University of Missouri and a J.D. degree from the University of Florida. He wrote Chapter 16, Access to Documents and Meetings, for the 1998 edition of *Communication and the Law.*

Robert Trager is a professor and associate dean for graduate studies in the School of Journalism and Mass Communication at the University of Colorado at Boulder. He holds a Ph.D. in journalism and mass communication from the University of Minnesota and a J.D. from the Stanford Law School. He has practiced media law in Washington, D.C., and with Time Warner Cable. He is also the founding editor of *Communication Law and Policy,* the law journal of the Law Division of the Association for Education in Journalism and Mass Communication. He wrote Chapter 10, Broadcast Regulation, and Chapter 11, Regulating New Communication Technologies, for the 1998 edition of *Communication and the Law.*

Case Index

Subject Index